THE JOHNS HOPKINS UNIVERSITY PRESS
DIRECTOR'S CIRCLE BOOK FOR 2009

The Johns Hopkins University Press gratefully acknowledges members
of the 2009 Director's Circle for supporting the publication of works such as
British Women Poets of the Long Eighteenth Century.

The Alvord Foundation
Darlene T. Anderson
Anonymous
Alfred and Muriel Berkeley
John and Bonnie Boland
Darlene Bookoff
Sylvia Bookoff
The Melvin and Betty Fine Foundation
Jack Goellner and Barbara Lamb
The Hodson Trust
Charles and Elizabeth Hughes
J. M. Kaplan Fund
John and Kathleen Keane
The Kiplinger Foundation
Anders Richter
David E. Ryer
B. F. Saul Company
R. Champlin and Debbie Sheridan
Albert H. Small, Sr.
Winston and Marilyn Tabb
Daun and Patricia Van Ee
Robert L. Warren and Family

British Women Poets of the Long Eighteenth Century

AN ANTHOLOGY

Edited by

Paula R. Backscheider & Catherine E. Ingrassia

THE JOHNS HOPKINS UNIVERSITY PRESS   BALTIMORE

© 2009 The Johns Hopkins University Press
All rights reserved. Published 2009
Printed in the United States of America on acid-free paper
2 4 6 8 9 7 5 3 1

The Johns Hopkins University Press
2715 North Charles Street
Baltimore, Maryland 21218-4363
www.press.jhu.edu

Library of Congress Cataloging-in-Publication Data

British women poets of the long eighteenth century : an anthology /
[edited by] Paula R. Backscheider, Catherine E. Ingrassia.
p. cm.
Includes bibliographical references.
ISBN-13: 978-0-8018-9277-6 (alk. paper)
ISBN-10: 0-8018-9277-5 (alk. paper)
ISBN-13: 978-0-8018-9278-3 (pbk. : alk. paper)
ISBN-10: 0-8018-9278-3 (pbk. : alk. paper)
1. English poetry—Women authors. 2. English poetry—18th century.
I. Backscheider, Paula R. II. Ingrassia, Catherine.
PR1177.B756 2009
821'.50809287—dc22   2008042171

A catalog record for this book is available from the British Library.

*Special discounts are available for bulk purchases of this book. For more
information, please contact Special Sales at 410-516-6936 or
specialsales@press.jhu.edu.*

For our future poets
Sophia Vita McCrimmon
Jocelyn Valerie Burridge

CONTENTS

C. Poems of Common Life

D. The Ode

E. The Ballad

F. Satire

G. The Hymn

H. The Fable

I. The Elegy

J. The Verse Narrative

K. Pastoral Poetry

L. The Verse Epistle

PART TWO. POETRY AS LIFE WRITING

A. Friendship Poems

B. Poems of Retirement and Retreat

C. Love Poems

D. Religious Poetry

E. The Poetry of War

F. Poems on the Public Sphere

G. Poems on Pain and Illness

H. Poems on Nature

I. Poems on Ecology

J. Poems on Seeking Personal Happiness

K. Poems on Marriage

L. Poems on Motherhood

M. Poems on the New Year, Birthdays, and Aging

N. Poems on Death

PART THREE. WRITING ON WRITING

A. Alternative Traditions

B. The Muses

C. The Experience of Writing

D. The Experience of Reception

E. The Determination to Write

F. The Nightingale in Poetry

ACKNOWLEDGMENTS

This volume would not have been possible without the generous support of two people: Robert D. Holsworth, dean of the College of Humanities and Sciences at Virginia Commonwealth University from 2004 to 2008, and Bonnie MacEwan, dean of the Auburn University Libraries. Their assistance fostered the conditions for collaboration and helped ensure the timely completion of this project. Additionally, Fred Hawkridge, interim dean of the College of Humanities and Sciences at Virginia Commonwealth University, facilitated the last stages of the project.

The following librarians aided in the securing of copy-texts for poems in the volume: Tricia Boyd, Special Collections, Edinburgh University Library; Milissa Burkart and I. Marc Carlson, Special Collections, McFarlin Library, University of Tulsa; Jill Gage, Roger and Julie Baskes Department of Special Collections, The Newberry Library; Mary Haegert, Houghton Library, Harvard University; Will Hansen, The Newberry Library; Richard High, Special Collections, University of Leeds; Thomas P. Jabine, Library of Congress; Adrian James, Society of Antiquaries Library Collection; Rebecca Jewett, Rare Books and Manuscripts, Ohio State University Library; Jeffrey Makala, Rare Books and Special Collections, Thomas Cooper Library, University of South Carolina; John Matthews, Richard J. Daley Library, University of Illinois at Chicago; Nancy Noe, Ralph Brown Draughon Library, Auburn University; Meg Sherry Rich, Department of Rare Books and Special Collections, Princeton University Library; Molly Schwartzburg, Harry Ransom Center, University of Texas at Austin; Jane Segal, Fondren Library, Rice University; Vaughan Stanley, Special Collections, Washington and Lee University; Diane Steinhaus, Music Library, University of North Carolina; and Sandra Stelts, Rare Books and Manuscripts, Paterno Library, Pennsylvania State University. The Eighteenth-Century Collections Online were an invaluable resource, and we thank Matt MisKelly for his advice.

The following scholars gave their knowledge and assistance generously: Anna Battigelli, State University of New York, Plattsburgh; Adam Budd, University of Edinburgh; John Burke, University of Alabama; Simon Chaplin, director of Museums and Special Collections, Royal College of Surgeons of England;

Patricia Hoffmann, State University of New York, Plattsburgh; Claudia Thomas Kairoff, Wake Forest University; Jennifer Keith, University of North Carolina, Greensboro; Kathryn King, Montevallo University; Gerald LaLonde, Grinnell College; Devoney Looser, University of Missouri, Columbia; Paula MacDowell, New York University; Peter L. D. Reid, Tufts University; Betty Rizzo, City University of New York; Judith Slagle, East Tennessee State University; and James A. Winn, Boston University. Additionally, the Virginia Commonwealth University graduate and undergraduate students in English 491, spring 2007, and English 611, spring 2008, provided original insights into the poems.

Lynn Cowles provided excellent work as a research assistant at Virginia Commonwealth University, as did Micaela Ellson and Lacy Marschalk at Auburn University. Cowles, Lacey Williams, LeaAnne Eaton, and Blake Wyatt helped transcribe and check copy-texts. Elizabeth Cater Childs, an instructor in the Department of Technical and Professional Communication, Auburn University, formatted the manuscript for submission to the press, and Micaela Ellson assumed responsibility for final collation of poems and manuscript preparation. Finally, we owe debts of a more personal nature to those family members who became silent partners in this collaboration. With love, respect, and gratitude, we acknowledge the patience and good will of Nick Backscheider, Miles McCrimmon, Pablo McCrimmon, and Sophia McCrimmon. This project would not have been possible without them.

INTRODUCTION

During the time period that this anthology covers, people read poetry for entertainment, news, and self-improvement. Relevant, accessible, and topical, it was appreciated and regarded as "a natural vehicle of expression."[1] People of all classes memorized poetry, read it aloud at gatherings, discussed it, and spontaneously composed verse in response to requests and for special occasions. Poetry performed the same work as periodicals. It taught the middle classes how to dress, how to participate in au courant activities, how to age gracefully, and how to judge current fashions (in dress, politics, plays, and more). Moralists and social arbiters recommended it. Giles Jacob's *Essays Relating to the Conduct of Life* offers advice about choosing a spouse and raising children and has a chapter entitled "On Poetry and Poets." The text preaches the importance of poetry to life: "It occasions the most charming Emotions, and raises the Soul to Rapture and Extasy."[2] Poetry was news, and it provided news; people paid to hear orators and actors read it and traveled miles to hear the aging Anna Seward read her verse novel. The kinds of poetry an individual read functioned as a marker of political allegiance, degree of sensibility, and intellect; poetic taste became another cultural code.

Yet this public function of reading and writing poetry should not suggest that poets failed to aspire to the highest aesthetic achievements or that the poetry of the period lacks emotion and fails to draw on personal experience. Quite the contrary. Some women poets worked over a lifetime to master their art and experimented richly and successfully. Many women offered carefully observed, often deeply personal reflections on all aspects of human experience. To be a poet in eighteenth-century Britain was a very specific choice, but it was also seen as a desirable, available one. Hundreds of women wrote and published poetry during the long eighteenth century, a historical practice ignored by most literary historians and modern poetry anthologies. Between 1660 and 1800, 243

1. Bonamy Dobrée, *English Literature in the Early Eighteenth Century, 1700–1740* (New York: Oxford University Press, 1959), 123.
2. Giles Jacob, *Essays Relating to the Conduct of Life,* 3rd ed. (London, 1730), 113.

women published books of poetry, 28.8 percent of all books of poetry published in the period.[3] More than 800 women poets in England and America published 1,402 first editions in the years 1770–1835.[4] Their presence indicates the powerful demand for poetry as a literary form and the cultural acceptability of women writing poetry. As early as 1685, people noted a "fashion" for poetry by women. Women's rate of publication of poetry escalated, and by the last decades of the century women were the most prolific producers of poetry in Britain. John Duncombe's *Feminiad: A Poem* (1754) and later writers treated women poets as one of the glories of the British nation, and twentieth-century critics pointed out that women poets "impel the history of poetry in the last quarter of Britain's eighteenth century."[5]

During the Restoration, women associated with the court and the theater were the most frequent publishers of poetry, and the wives and daughters of clergymen, perhaps because they had access to libraries, were consistently represented. As the decades passed, women poets became increasingly diverse in their socioeconomic, regional, and educational backgrounds, as well as in their gender ideology and their religious and political opinions. Aristocrats, middle-class teachers, professional writers, tradesmen's wives, and provincial servants all published. Some women wrote dozens of poems, and some hundreds. Some wrote a little throughout their lives, some wrote intensely at intervals, and some wrote from girlhood to the end of their lives, coming to think of themselves as career poets working to master an age-old craft. We emphasize that we do not treat "women poets" as a homogeneous category, although there is no avoiding the use of the term as shorthand; in fact, our anthology brings to the fore the deep differences among women and the verse they wrote.

By the mid-eighteenth century, periodicals and anthologies were major popularizers of poetry and poets. Publication became increasingly easy, and women contributors were treated with respect, even courted, as Elizabeth Singer Rowe had been by the *Athenian Mercury* fifty years earlier. Provincial subscription publishing made access to print even easier, and women's friends and relatives and self-proclaimed lovers of literature paid the subscription price and made available the work of poets such as Jane Brereton, Mary Whateley Darwall, and Eliza-

3. Judith Phillips Stanton, "Statistical Profile of Women Writing in English from 1660–1800," in *Eighteenth-Century Women and the Arts,* ed. Frederick M. Keener and Susan B. Lorsch (Westport, CT: Greenwood, 1988), 250–51.

4. James Robert de J. Jackson, *Annals of English Verse, 1770–1835: A Preliminary Survey of the Volumes Published* (New York: Garland, 1985). These statistics and a wider discussion of the eighteenth-century publishing industry and reading practices can be found in Paula R. Backscheider, *Eighteenth-Century Women Poets and Their Poetry: Inventing Agency, Inventing Genre* (Baltimore: Johns Hopkins University Press, 2005), xvii, 2–14.

5. This representative statement is from Stuart Curran, "The I Altered," in *Romanticism and Feminism,* ed. Anne K. Mellor (Bloomington: Indiana University Press, 1988), 187–88.

beth Hands. Miscellanies, collections, and anthologies were nothing like today's educational tomes. They were news and compiled for adults who wanted to keep up with the literary scene. They were profitable, as were periodicals that printed poetry; by 1745 there were thirty periodical journals, some of which devoted several pages to original poetry. Collections of poems and substantial individual poems by women came to be reviewed consistently, and these reviews, unlike today's literary criticism, were intended for cultivated general readers. The reviews, like poetry, were followed by men and women and discussed in mixed company.[6] Later reviews sometimes mentioned the benefits of reading poetry by women, and critics have pointed out that "women's writing seems to be given especially rapid advancement in the third quarter of the eighteenth century."[7]

A watershed was the 1755 publication of a two-volume anthology of poetry entitled *Poems by Eminent Ladies,* which featured the work of eighteen prominent women poets. The collection, so popular that it was pirated in 1757 and revised in a 1773 edition and again in the 1780s, captures the dominant cultural attitude toward women poets.[8] The very presence of the volume, with a title page that advertises the apparently recognizable names of the poets, demonstrates the serious regard for women's poetry. The preface naturalizes the excellence and skill with which women write, lauding them as "not only an honour to their sex, but to their native-country."[9] Indeed the preface assures readers that they "will here meet with many pieces on a great variety of subjects excellent in their way; . . . this collection is not inferior to any miscellany compiled from the works of men."[10] Although certainly designed to promote the collection, the preface's discussion of women's poetry and of the women themselves treats them as comparable to their male contemporaries and their poetry. "Great abilities are not confined to the men," it states, and these poems have been "particularly distinguished by the most lavish encomiums" from recognizable male poets with

6. Although she is speaking of France, Joan de Jean's point that these discussions were an important way that women contributed to commentary on literary texts is valid for Great Britain. See "Rooms of Their Own: Literary Salons in Seventeenth-Century France," in *The Cambridge History of Literary Criticism,* vol. 3, ed. Glyn P. Norton (Cambridge: Cambridge University Press, 1999), 378–83.

7. Kathryn King, *Jane Barker, Exile: A Literary Career, 1675–1725* (Oxford: Oxford University Press, 2000), 36; Richard Terry, *Poetry and the Making of the English Literary Past, 1660–1781* (Oxford: Oxford University Press, 2001), 265–76, quotation from 265.

8. The poets included in the anthology were Mary Barber, Aphra Behn, Elizabeth Carter, Mary Chudleigh, Catharine Trotter Cockburn, Constantia Grierson, Mary Jones, Anne Killigrew, Mary Leapor, Judith Madan, Delarivière Manley, Mary Masters, Mary Monck, Lady Mary Wortley Montagu, Katherine Philips, Laetitia Pilkington, Elizabeth Singer Rowe, and Anne Finch.

9. George Colman and Bonnell Thornton, eds., *Poems by Eminent Ladies. Particularly, Mrs. Barber, Mrs. Behn, Miss Carter,* . . . *To which is prefixed, a short account of each writer,* 2 vols. (London, 1755), 1:iii.

10. Colman and Thornton, *Poems by Eminent Ladies,* 1:iii–iv.

whom the women circulate: John Dryden, Alexander Pope, and Jonathan Swift. The positive reception of the volume is assured, "unless it can be demonstrated that fancy and judgment are wholly confined to one half of our species; a notion, to which the readers of these volumes will not readily assent."[11] Thus, women's poetry was the best argument for the excellence of women poets.

Women poets became literary and social arbiters, influential voices, and public intellectuals. As Paula Feldman writes, they were "major players and serious competitors in the literary marketplace" and "active participants in, and sometimes instigators of, important literary debates."[12] This period of female poetic dominance was brief. Women poets were largely omitted from the great collections of poems published at the beginning of the nineteenth century, and their coverage in twentieth-century anthologies and courses was sporadic and, for decades at a time, negligent. Scholarship on women's poetry owes a substantial debt to Germaine Greer and her collaborators for *Kissing the Rod* (1988), which took the unusual step of selecting poems that emphasized how women who were "trying to develop their creativity supported each other" and women's diversity (as opposed to what Margaret Ezell has called "the search for sameness");[13] to Roger Lonsdale, whose anthology *Eighteenth-Century Women Poets* (1989) compiled representative work by nearly one hundred poets; and to Joyce Fullard, whose *British Women Poets, 1660–1800* (1990) included eighty-two women and a group of anonymous poems. Greer's and Lonsdale's meticulous biographical and bibliographic research marked a serious consideration of these poets and, because of their wide circulation, introduced many poets to scholars and students for the first time, while Fullard's thematic arrangement called attention to the variety of subjects women addressed, including "Writing and Writers" and "Patriotism and War."[14] Several excellent anthologies published after these include some of the poets that we do. In overlapping and adjacent periods, *Early Modern Women Poets (1520–1700)* (2001), edited by Jane Stevenson and Peter Davidson, includes, among others, Elizabeth Thomas, Anne Wharton, Jane Barker, and Aphra Behn, and Paula R. Feldman's *British Women Poets of the*

---

11. Colman and Thornton, *Poems by Eminent Ladies*, 1:iii.

12. Paula R. Feldman, *British Women Poets of the Romantic Era* (Baltimore: Johns Hopkins University Press, 1997), xxv. Among the poets she names that are anthologized here are Anna Seward, Mary Robinson, Charlotte Smith, Joanna Baillie, Hannah More, and Anna Laetitia Barbauld.

13. Germaine Greer, Susan Hastings, Jeslyn Medoff, and Melinda Sansone, eds., *Kissing the Rod: An Anthology of Seventeenth-Century Women's Poetry* (London: Virago, 1988), xvi; Margaret J. M. Ezell, "Re-visioning the Restoration: Or, How to Stop Obscuring Early Women Writers," in *The New Historical Literary Study*, ed. Jeffrey N. Cox and Larry J. Reynolds (Princeton, NJ: Princeton University Press, 1993), 138.

14. Joyce Fullard, ed., *British Women Poets, 1660–1800: An Anthology* (Troy, NY: Whitston, 1990); Greer et al., *Kissing the Rod*; Roger Lonsdale, ed., *Eighteenth-Century Women Poets: An Oxford Anthology* (Oxford: Oxford University Press, 1990), xxi. Some critics have noted that Lonsdale's practice of excerpting poems, especially omitting opening stanzas, misrepresents the contributions of some authors.

Romantic Era (1997) covers Anna Seward, Jane West, Charlotte Smith, Carolina Nairne, and eight more. These books and other even more specialized anthologies such as James Basker's *Amazing Grace* (2002) and Marcus Wood's *The Poetry of Slavery* (2003) have expanded our understanding of the number and variety of female poets between 1660 and 1830.[15] A number of projects with microfilm, databases, and Web availability, such as the Brown University Women Writers' Project, the English Poetry Database, Early English Books, and, especially notable, the Eighteenth-Century Short Title Catalogue (ESTC) and, based on it, Eighteenth-Century Collections Online (ECCO), to name only a few, provide significantly wider access to scholars and students.

High-quality editions of individual women's poetry are beginning to appear. Isobel Grundy and Robert Halsband's recovery of Lady Mary Wortley Montagu's poems set standards of biographical, textual, and critical attention, as did series editions of poetry by Mary Chudleigh (Margaret Ezell), Charlotte Smith (Stuart Curran), and Mary Robinson (Judith Pascoe), to name a few. Foundational work, including biographies, on individual women poets is also expanding, although slowly, and developing our understanding of the diversity and quality of women's verse. There are now excellent biographies of Jane Barker (Kathryn King), Anne Finch (Barbara McGovern), Lady Mary Wortley Montagu (Isobel Grundy), and Joanna Baillie (Judith Slagle).[16] Expansive studies explore women's poetry within the individual periods or poetic movements. Charles Haskell Hin-

15. Jane Stevenson and Peter Davidson, *Early Modern Women Poets (1520–1700): An Anthology* (Oxford: Oxford University Press, 2001); Feldman, *British Women Poets of the Romantic Era;* James Basker, *Amazing Grace: An Anthology of Poems about Slavery, 1660–1810* (New Haven, CT: Yale University Press, 2002); Marcus Wood, *The Poetry of Slavery* (Oxford: Oxford University Press, 2003). Basker excerpts heavily, but he includes more than forty women poets and discusses their importance in his introduction; Wood includes Mary Robinson, Hannah More, Anna Laetitia Barbauld, Amelia Opie, and others. Other notable anthologies include Isobel Armstrong and Joseph Bristow, with Cath Sharrock, *Nineteenth-Century Women Poets: An Oxford Anthology* (Oxford: Clarendon, 1996); and Duncan Wu, *Romantic Women Poets: An Anthology* (Oxford: Blackwell, 1997).

16. The recovery of, and scholarship on, women poets is considerable and still growing. The texts mentioned include *The Poems and Prose of Mary, Lady Chudleigh,* ed. Margaret J. M. Ezell (New York: Oxford University Press, 1993); *The Poems of Charlotte Smith,* ed. Stuart Curran (New York: Oxford University Press, 1993); *Mary Robinson: Selected Poems,* ed. Judith Pascoe (Peterborough, ON: Broadview, 2000); Barbara McGovern, *Anne Finch and Her Poetry: A Critical Biography* (Athens: University of Georgia Press, 1992); *The Anne Finch Wellesley Manuscript Poems: A Critical Edition,* ed. Barbara McGovern and Charles H. Hinnant (Athens: University of Georgia Press, 1998); and *Lady Mary Wortley Montagu: Essays and Poems and "Simplicity, A Comedy,"* ed. Robert Halsband and Isobel Grundy (Oxford: Clarendon, 1993). Other representative work of recovery and scholarship would include, but by no means be limited to, Richard Greene, *Mary Leapor: A Study in Eighteenth-Century Women's Poetry* (Oxford: Clarendon, 1993); *Elizabeth Carter, 1717–1806: An Edition of Some Unpublished Letters,* ed. Gwen Hampshire (Newark: University of Delaware Press, 2005); *Anna Letitia Barbauld: Selected Poetry and Prose,* ed. William McCarthy and Elizabeth Kraft (Peterborough, ON: Broadview, 2002); *The Poems of Anna Letitia Barbauld,* ed. William McCarthy and Elizabeth Kraft (Athens: University of Georgia Press, 1994); Ann Messenger, *Woman and Poet in the Eighteenth Century: The Life of Mary Whateley Darwall (1738–1825)* (New York: AMS, 1999); and *The Poetry of Mary Barber,* ed. Bernard Tucker (Lewiston, ON: Edwin Mellen, 1992).

nant's *Poetry of Anne Finch* (1994), Carol Barash's *English Women's Poetry, 1649–1714* (1996), and Donna Landry's *Muses of Resistance* (1990) have been followed by a few equally revisionary books, such as William Christmas's *Lab'ring Muses* (2001) and Jacqueline Labbe's *Charlotte Smith* (2003).[17] Except for Paula Backscheider's *Eighteenth-Century Women Poets and Their Poetry* (2005), there have been no attempts to reconceptualize a sizeable body of the women's work within the eighteenth century. It has, however, become fairly common for major books on poetry to devote a chapter to women's work, as, for instance, Richard Terry does in *Poetry and the Making of the English Literary Past, 1660–1781* (2001). A steady stream of high-quality journal and collection articles on individual women or specific configurations of women provides the largest body of criticism. Most of this scholarship evaluates women's work within a fully realized context that avoids the generalizing mistakes of the past.

Principles of Selection

The first anthology of long-eighteenth-century women's poetry since 1990, ours is a response to what we see as a persistent need to document the history of women's poetic expression during the long eighteenth century and to rewrite the literary history of that period, a history from which women have been largely excluded or, in effect, ghettoized. It includes 368 complete poems by 80 women. A handful of poets, including Elizabeth Boyd, Harriet Falconar, Jane Wiseman Holt, Elizabeth Tollet, and Anne Wharton, are represented by only one or two poems; many, including Anne Killigrew, Jane Barker, Mary Jones, and Anne Bannerman, have about a half a dozen; and a few, long recognized as major poetic figures (Anne Finch, Charlotte Smith, Anna Laetitia Barbauld), are represented by more than a dozen poems. The anthology is divided into three parts. Each part has its own introduction, as does each individual group of poems. To support today's scholarly efforts and to generate further work on women poets, it is essential now to have an anthology that places unabridged primary texts in front of students, scholars, and readers.

We began by reading the complete works of as many women poets as we could, and we decided to print as copy-texts of poems the first printed version that the poets controlled in order to set the poems in the context in which they first appeared. In some cases, that meant those first printed or corrected in pe-

---

17. Charles H. Hinnant, *The Poetry of Anne Finch: An Essay in Interpretation* (Newark: University of Delaware Press, 1994); Carol Barash, *English Women's Poetry, 1649–1714: Politics, Community, and Linguistic Authority* (Oxford: Clarendon, 1996); Donna Landry, *The Muses of Resistance: Labouring-Class Women's Poetry in Britain, 1739–1796* (Cambridge: Cambridge University Press, 1990); William J. Christmas, *The Lab'ring Muses: Work, Writing, and the Social Order in English Plebian Poetry, 1730–1830* (Newark: University of Delaware Press, 2001); Jacqueline M. Labbe, *Charlotte Smith: Romanticism, Poetry, and the Culture of Gender* (Manchester: Manchester University Press, 2003).

riodicals; in one case, when no version seemed to have been under the author's control, it was a manuscript copy. Some of the poems come from letters, plays, novels, and memoirs. In short, our anthology draws upon all forms of publication: single-author poems and collections; miscellanies and mixed collections except street libels, charms, and broadsheets; periodicals; and manuscripts. Our searches foregrounded the multiple ways that poetry was published and, perhaps more importantly, how accidental and fortunate the survival of some poetry is.

A number of principles guided our selections as we contemplated the vast amount of poetry by women and came to terms with the difficulties in selection and representation. We did some limited surveys of specialists' desires, and we reluctantly acknowledged that inevitably someone's favorite poet or poem was going to be omitted. As the preface to Robert Dodsley's *Collection of Poems in Four Volumes. By Several Hands* states, "The Reader must not expect to be pleased with every particular poem which is here presented to him. It is impossible to furnish out an entertainment of this nature, where every part shall be relished by every guest."[18] Even though our anthology of women poets from the long eighteenth century is the largest ever published, we are painfully conscious of the poets and poems we have not been able to include.

Our first priority was to give a fair survey of what women wrote—the forms, the styles, the themes, and the topics. For individual groups of poems, we searched for a variety of tones, presentation strategies, and poetic forms, and the complexity, subtlety, and diversity of women and their poetic voices emerge in section after section. For as many poets as possible, we provided representative samples of their work. For Anne Finch, there are songs, satires, a dramatic epilogue, fables, odes, extempore verse, a biblical paraphrase, a cavalier-style invitation, and the influential *Nocturnal Rêverie;* for Sarah Dixon, there are comic and satiric poems, a serious poem on retirement, one on 30 January (the anniversary of the execution of King Charles I), and two poems on writing.

Our process of selection addresses some of the stereotypes that are barriers to reading and studying women's poetry. The reality of this poetry is the best counter to crippling expectations about it. Often dismissed as sentimental, about trivial subjects, and imitative rather than original, the poetry is allegedly by nameless women whose oblivion is deserved. As Stevenson and Davidson write, "It has . . . been assumed . . . that women wrote primarily about their personal emotions, their religion, perhaps, their husbands and children."[19] Stuart Curran describes his difficulties in moving away from the familiar presentation of "a gendered dialogue begun by Wordsworth and Coleridge rather than the one, *as an*

---

18. Robert Dodsley, ed., *A Collection of Poems in Four Volumes. By Several Hands,* 4 vols. (London, 1755), 1:1–2.

19. Stevenson and Davidson, *Early Modern Women Poets,* xxxvii.

accurate history would render it, that was initiated by Smith and Robinson."[20] The same half-dozen women poets appear in present-day anthologies, often represented by the same poems, leading readers to believe that Anne Finch, Aphra Behn, and Lady Mary Wortley Montagu were the only women writing poetry at this time (but apparently not much of it, and that in "signature" rather than varied tones).[21] Even when the selections are excellent and representative poems, as Finch's ubiquitously printed *The Introduction* and *Nocturnal Rêverie* are, the low number of poems and their lack of variety contribute to institutionalizing preexisting stereotypes about the amount, variety, quality, and subjects of women's verse. Among the most deleterious principles of selection in other anthologies is the desire to present women as influenced by or in relationship to men. For example, Lady Mary Wortley Montagu's poem *The Reasons That Induced Dr. Swift to write a Poem called The Lady's Dressing Room* is inevitably paired with Jonathan Swift's *The Lady's Dressing Room*.[22] While this pairing provides instructors with an opportunity for easy lesson planning, it reduces Montagu's poetic voice to one of bitterness, satire, and derivative creativity; clearly, her poetic powers are much more complex, diverse, and generative. The selection of poems that express anger or aggression toward men, such as Behn's *The Disappointment* and Mary Chudleigh's *Wife and Servant*, turns the poetry against women and, again, reduces them to one-note poets. In contrast, we attempt to illustrate the many moods and opinions women express toward, for instance, the patriarchy. In many cases we were able not only to contrast the work of several women but also to demonstrate that individual women expressed a range of responses, as Finch did about writing and Mary Jones did about print culture. Sometimes we selected poems that express highly similar opinions, for attention to their differing forms and small details yields new understandings.

Second, for a number of reasons, we decided to arrange the anthology in groups of poems. We recognize that readers have strong opinions about the organization

20. Stuart Curran, "Romantic Women Poets: Inscribing the Self," in *Women's Poetry in the Enlightenment: The Making of the Canon, 1730–1820*, ed. Isobel Armstrong and Virginia Blain (New York: St. Martin's, 1999), 147, emphasis ours.

21. For example, *The Norton Anthology of English Literature, Volume C: The Restoration and Eighteenth Century*, ed. Lawrence Lipking and James Noggle (New York: Norton, 2005), includes three poems by Anne Finch, three poems by Lady Mary Wortley Montagu, one poem by Aphra Behn, and, in a section entitled "Debating Women: Arguments in Verse" (pp. 2589–2610), poems by Mary Leapor and Anne Irwin. *The Longman Anthology of British Literature, Volume 1C: The Restoration and the Eighteenth Century*, ed. David Damrosch and Stuart Sherman (New York: Longman, 2006), includes an only slightly larger collection: in addition to works by Behn and Montagu, it includes poems by Margaret Cavendish and Mary Chudleigh. In both anthologies, the poems by women make up a very small portion.

22. Both the *Longman Anthology* and the *Norton Anthology* pair these two poems. Between them, these two anthologies command the majority of the anthology market for undergraduate survey courses at American colleges and universities.

of anthologies, and our decision, arrived at only after many reorganizations, will not appeal to everyone. In our opinion, a topical arrangement has four important advantages. First, the very real stylistic and ideological differences among women are highlighted. For example, Anna Seward's skeptical critique of fasts proclaimed during wartime contrasts markedly with Jane Cave Winscom's pious response, and the poems are in quite different forms. Second, the topics that engage women emerge, and they range from the well known (marriage, religion) to the hardly recognized (public-sphere issues). Third, such groupings occasionally provide arresting histories of a poetic kind. For instance, the development of hymns from odes and meditations to texts for congregational singing adds interest to the section on hymns (1.G), while the perception of "tyrant custom" evolving to include the periodical press as a disciplining force provides an additional dimension to the "Poems on Seeking Personal Happiness" section (2.J). Finally, and somewhat ironically, arranging the book chronologically by poet actually decreases the ability to observe an individual's responses to the specific literary, political, and cultural milieu of her poems. Reference to a single poet, one who fits in a pattern Stevenson and Davidson identify as "virginity/widowhood,"[23] illustrates this fact: Mary Whateley Darwall published books of poetry in 1764 and 1794, and each is strongly marked by the events and artistic tastes of its specific time. To facilitate study of individual poets, we have included an alternate table of contents that lists the poets alphabetically and their poems in the order that they appear in the volume.

The third principle of selection is based on the vexed question, Is it a good poem? Certainly, to make selections on the basis of what might be construed as "aesthetics" opens us to charges of relativism and personal judgments. Yet, having read widely and deeply in the poetry of women from this period, we believe that we, as literary scholars and critics, can distinguish between the mundane and the moving, the trite and the subtle. The unforgettable image, the incisive comment, the innovative metrical scheme, or the trenchant representation of a key historical event distinguishes poem after poem, and these are the sinews of the anthology. We share the feminist critic's skepticism about the standards of the long eighteenth century and our own time, however, and ask our readers to do the same. We recognize that aesthetic judgments are historically constructed and culturally specific and suggest, after Toni Bowers, that "rather than denigrate (or praise) [eighteenth-century women's poetry] wholesale, critics might better ask why we define 'good' literature as we do, how our assumptions about literary value still work to valorize some voices and exclude others, and how our capaci-

---

23. Stevenson and Davidson, *Early Modern Women Poets,* xxxii–iii. They note that "it is almost impossible to extrapolate general rules from the way in which any one woman managed the relationship between her life and her writing," a point Backscheider makes in the conclusion to *Eighteenth-Century Women Poets and Their Poetry.*

ties for pleasure [and appreciation] might be augmented by respectful engagement with works we have been trained to resist or dismiss."[24] We asked as open-mindedly as we could, "Do we find 'the sense of the beautiful'—gentle, funny, terrible, in images, in construction, in sentiments—in this poem?" "Does it speak to us, move us, excite us in some way?" "Does it represent the best work of a skilled poet working with technical sophistication within her craft?" Stuart Curran has argued that the question whether a poem is "good" is usually ideological rather than aesthetic and is "predicated on a gendered aesthetic code whose integers are arbitrarily restricted to a nostalgic reification of male experience."[25] His observation not only critiques current practices and prejudices but also points to a need for new aesthetic codes, codes that the poems in our anthology may help generate. In privileging the principle of "good poem," we recognize the urgent need to give poetry by women serious treatment as poetry. Barbara Lewalski summarizes a growing feeling among feminist critics when she writes that "these texts urgently need to be read with the full scholarly apparatus of textual analysis, historical synthesis, and literary interpretation in play, since they come before us bare and unaccommodated, without the accretion of scholarly and critical opinion through the ages that so largely determines how we understand and value literary works."[26]

This criterion for selection is balanced by the recognition that women's poetry is an important source of biographical and sociohistorical information. Barbara Lewalski continues by noting that: "another consequence [of the narrow treatment of poetry by women] is that early modern women's voices, perspectives, and texts are seldom brought to bear upon questions that have become central for literary scholars of the period: the power of social and cultural institutions, the ideology of absolutism and patriarchy, the formation of subjectivity, the forms of authorial 'self-fashioning,' the possibility and manifestations of resistance and subversion."[27] She gives literary study and social history their due, and the way the two strands are interwoven in her statement testifies to the inseparability of form and content. Although women's poetry has long been studied more often as a source of information about women's lives than as artistic expression, it is still relatively neglected and underused and underinterpreted as biographical, historical, and social evidence. Linda Colley wrote that "we know extraordinarily little about how the majority of British civilians responded to this succession of wars, and to the innovations, conquests and dangers that accompa-

24. Adapted from Toni Bowers's statement in "Sex, Lies, and Invisibility," in *The Columbia History of the British Novel*, ed. John Richetti (New York: Columbia University Press, 1994), 71.

25. Curran, "Romantic Women Poets," 147.

26. Barbara Lewalski, *Writing Women in Jacobean England* (Cambridge, MA: Harvard University Press, 1993), 1–2.

27. Lewalski, *Writing Women in Jacobean England*, 2.

nied them."[28] The poems included here contradict her statement, as they do the apprehension of lack of evidence about many other subjects. We include, then, poems rich in women's history and opinions and, again, have attempted to assure inclusion of the opinions, ideologies, and technical strategies of diverse women. Foregrounded are points within cultural environments that women felt impelled to address, some century-long concerns and others brief pressure points. Again, individual women sometimes held different opinions at different times, and their opinions may have changed over time. Benefiting from the gamut of social classes, locales, and educational experiences represented by these women poets, we bring together diverse shades of opinion on religion, political events, gender, class, and cultural mores. Some of these poems open up the questions of competing aesthetic systems even as they reintroduce women's voices and opinions into major debates and social movements.

Plan of the Book

Part 1, "Poetic Kinds and Genres," is designed to be true to the women poets of the long eighteenth century and to encourage more vigorous twenty-first-century engagement with form and technique. Not only does it represent what women wrote but it also challenges a common opinion that women seldom wanted or seldom were able to use or invent sophisticated literary forms. Here, as in the rest of the book, we use the more inclusive term *poetic kinds* rather than *genre*. The term *kinds* unites families of poems and sees topic, content, and mode as more often unifying factors than structure, which strongly defines traditional genres, such as the sonnet.[29] The poems included in part 1 demonstrate how skillfully women worked within existing forms and experimented with different poetic kinds, both the traditionally respected and the vernacular and even faddish. As the introduction to part 1 explains, most of the women poets obviously had read carefully Renaissance and Augustan poetry, represented to them by Edmund Spenser, Richard Crashaw, George Herbert, John Milton, Abraham Cowley, Aphra Behn, John Dryden, Joseph Addison, and Matthew Prior, among others. The poetic kinds inherited from their English predecessors and the classical Greeks and Romans were important to them, and whether they imitated, adapted, or used them as counterpoint, women willingly wrote in relation to them. As Pamela Plimpton has observed, "Most . . . realized . . . that in order for their poetry to be recognized as poetry and enter into the aesthetic standard of the day, it needed to conform to certain expected conventions—to the poetics

28. Linda Colley, *Britons: Forging the Nation, 1707–1837* (New Haven, CT: Yale University Press, 1992), 3.

29. See Rosalie Colie, *The Resources of Kind,* ed. Barbara Lewalski (Berkeley: University of California Press, 1973), 1–31. The term *kinds* is commonly used by Renaissance scholars; it is also central to James Sutherland's *Preface to Eighteenth-Century Poetry* (Oxford: Clarendon, 1948).

practiced by society's eminent poets. A woman poet may in fact want very much to prove her command of craft within the masculinist tradition she sees herself writing in."[30]

Little of the poetry in this anthology has been addressed with the full arsenal of textual and literary methodologies. Even the work on Anne Finch and Charlotte Smith, the most studied, cannot yet match the scholarly and critical commentary on even relatively minor male poets such as Christopher Smart. Alice Eardley's comparison of the treatment of sonnets by Mary Wroth, John Donne, and John Milton could be replicated with eighteenth-century writers and highlights the need for the kinds of close formal analysis now being published about the work of a few of the long-eighteenth-century women poets in scholarly journals.[31] Part 1 of our anthology illustrates that writing women were more often like writing men than different from them. Their poetry testifies not only to their understanding of respected classical forms but also to their understanding and mastery of adapted, new, and fashionable forms. Sometimes women were leaders in popularizing a form, as Anne Finch did the fable and Charlotte Smith the sonnet. Elizabeth Thomas and Mary Chudleigh contributed to the renewed power of the ode; Elizabeth Carter reenvisioned the retirement poem, and Mary Whateley Darwall, Anna Barbauld, and Anna Seward helped reinvigorate the elegy. Sometimes women's poetry contributed greatly to the establishment of a specifically English form of a classical or Continental Renaissance form, and many poems are masterfully constructed, gracefully written, and distinctively marked by the original perspectives and expressions of their authors.

Part 2, "Poetry as Life Writing," puts poems on fourteen subjects in dynamic relationship with one another. This part is designed to be a springboard launching inquiries into women's shared and differing experiences, opinions, and modes of expression. National, local, and personal contexts give these poems unusual interest and significance even as they encourage attention to the formal elements that carry and reinforce meaning and call attention to working poets. The first group, for instance, friendship poems, illustrates the advantages of this organization. Recognized as the only important form of poetry that women inherited from women, it is also commonly conceived of as sentimental, static, and effete, locked into the Matchless Orinda's archaic platonic language. The group does testify to Katherine Philips's long-lived influence but it also shows that in many poets' hands the form changes with the times and demonstrates flexibility and usefulness extending to our own time. That women are comic, descriptive, confiding, grief stricken, and contented and chose to write about friendship in lyrics,

30. Pamela Plimpton, "Inconstant Constancy: A Poetics of Seventeenth- and Eighteenth-Century British Women Poets, 1620–1825" (PhD diss., University of Oregon, 1998), 17–18.
31. Alice Eardley, "Recreating the Canon: Women Writers and Anthologies of Early Modern Verse," *Women's Writing* 14 (2007): 280–82.

odes, epistles, sonnets, satires, elegies, and more makes our point. On all of the subjects in part 2, women write vividly, passionately, and at times erotically, and they complicate and often defy commonly held beliefs about women and topics such as maternal love, solitude, spirituality, nature, and war.

The subjects of the next three groups—retirement, love, and religion—were also contexts within which the poets found meaning for their lives, actions, and experiences and developed subjectivity. The sections flow from one to another. For instance, unlike retirement poems by men, women's seldom depict a solitary, disaffected or melancholy outsider; instead they describe a pleasant retreat with a friend who is present, imagined, or addressed. And so "Poems on Retirement and Retreat" is organically placed between "Friendship Poems" and "Love Poems." As Kathryn King pointed out, religion, the last of these four groups, was more than "faith, spirituality, doctrine, or devotional experience"; it was women's "most basic sense of identity."[32] The middle groups of poems in part 2 demonstrate women's engagement with the public sphere and the degree to which poetry was used to comment on central issues and concerns of the day. These poems—in sections on war, the public sphere, pain and illness, nature, and ecology—are remarkable for their detailed and impassioned accounts of all manner of social action and public policy. Poems about military battles, riots, divorce, slavery, vaccination, and the treatment of animals, among other subjects, belie the notion that women existed primarily in the domestic sphere or had a limited range of interests.

Many of these poems reflect on the nature of the relationships that define the authors' subject position, and the group entitled "Poems on Seeking Personal Happiness" is strategically placed between the poems about large forces that influenced and constructed them and those about social conceptions of "woman." In the poems in the last five groups in part 2, women write about the various stages of their own lives and the lives of other women or of womankind. Their poems on marriage, motherhood, birthdays, age, and death are filled with independent and unconventional thoughts and written with careful, reinforcing selections of metrics and imagery.

The poems in part 3, "Writing on Writing," give intriguing insight into another human interest, the origins of writers' inspiration. The introduction details the development of the literary marketplace and women's central role in it and thereby provides a context for the ways women write about writing. Women writers have been largely described, even essentialized, by others; in these poems women represent themselves as poets and participants in the literary world. They reflect on the process of writing, and they capture the voices of supportive friends, fellow poets, mocking women, and caviling critics. One of the most active areas of feminist research encompasses how women composed, worked within their

32. King, *Jane Barker*, 20–21.

literary environment, gained access to publication, were received by the public, and maneuvered in the print culture of their time. Perhaps one of the most significant contributions these poems make to literary and social history is the revelation of the degree to which women simultaneously negotiate the commercial literary marketplace, including the print trade, and the alternate economies they establish for themselves in the special place poetry-writing held in British history and in the worlds of female friendship and family. The poems contradict yet another myth about women, that they were too "modest" to publish.

Women belonged to various communities—female, mixed sex, coterie, even periodical. They worked alongside male poets, challenging them, imitating them, engaging with them, and influencing them. Many of them were, and felt that they were, the peers of the male poets. They wrote skillfully and prolifically and operated effectively in the print trade, publishing by every available means and putting their poems in play in the literary marketplace with considerable savvy and determination. They developed new poetic forms, experimented with existing ones, and, by any measure, significantly advanced the variety and quality of poetry during this period. Many of them were encouraged and as respected as male poets. We cannot bring that time back, but we can invite you to enjoy their artistry and think about their contributions.

Editorial Principles

Among this anthology's many goals are to make these poems accessible to the student, the scholar, and the general reader, while retaining as far as possible the historical specificity of these texts so that specialists in the field can quote them with confidence. To that end, we have silently corrected the few obvious errors; eliminated the long *s*; and modernized the use of quotation marks, which during the period would appear at the beginning of every line within a quotation. Beyond that, however, we have preserved the characteristics of the text as it originally appeared. Punctuation has been retained, as it was often especially self-conscious in a time when poets imagined their work read aloud. To that end, we preserved long dashes and spaces on either side of dashes. Archaic or variant spelling has largely been retained, as have poem titles (some of which are sentences) and original italics and capitalization when not an ornamental opening convention. The poets' notes to texts have been retained, for they are integral to the poems and interesting in their own right. We have glossed those words, names, allusions, or topical events that might not be immediately apparent to the twenty-first-century reader. Many of these women had extensive knowledge of British and classical traditions, natural sciences, and history, as well as a fierce engagement with the social and political issues of their times. It is difficult to capture fully the knowledge and diverse range of subjects over which many of these poets had mastery. These poems reflect this deep knowledge and engagement and thus require appropriate annotation.

To demonstrate movement and changes in poetry through the long eighteenth century, within each section we have almost invariably arranged poems chronologically by date of first publication. Among the exceptions are the sonnets from Mary Robinson's *Sappho and Phaon* and the sample of Charlotte Smith's sonnet sequence (1.B); the fable adapted by both Anne Finch and Hannah More (1.H); the ekphrasis poems at the end of the section "Poems on Nature"(2.H); and Frances Greville's *Ode to Indifference* and responses to it in the section "Poems on Seeking Personal Happiness" (2.J). The date of first publication appears at the end of the poem. If the date of first publication and the date of composition differ widely, however, the poem is ordered by its date of composition; in those instances both dates are noted at the end of the poem, with the date of composition given first (example: 1711; 1998). The copy-text used was the first published version of the poem over which the poet had control, because it clearly illustrates the woman poet responding to her context and captures her deep engagement with the political, social, and poetic milieu in which she first wrote the poem. In rare cases the copy-text was a modern scholarly edition of that version. In these cases the date for the copy-text in the source list does not match the date of first publication. Some women had collections of poems published later in their lives or posthumous collections edited by others. We question the editorial control some women had over these later editions;[33] additionally, some poets made subsequent changes that diminished the poem's connection with its original context. Sources of the copy-text for all poems appear at the end of each section. For easy reference, we also provide the part and section number for each poem mentioned in the text or notes.

Many of the women poets included here will be unfamiliar, in some cases perhaps unknown, even to specialists in the fields of women's studies and eighteenth-century poetry. In order to reduce confusion, we consistently use the name of the poet at the time of her death and spell names as they are given in Janet Todd's *Dictionary of British and American Women Writers, 1660–1800*. We recognize uncertainties about, for instance, whether Mary is best styled *Monk* or *Monck*[34] and awkwardnesses in the cases of some poets, such as Sarah Fyge Field Egerton and Mary Whateley Darwall, who published significant work under both their maiden and married names. An especially vexed case is that of

33. In addition to the distance that some women, including Charlotte Smith, lived from their publishers (and therefore the inability to check page proofs), evidence of editing of some women's poetry survives. Notable examples are editorial interventions in Elizabeth Singer Rowe's books of poetry and Robert Dodsley's "improvements" to many of the poems submitted to him.

34. Roger Lonsdale, *New Oxford Book of Eighteenth-Century Verse* (Oxford: Clarendon, 1989), 70.

Priscilla Poynton. The title page of her only book of poems, *Poems on Several Occasions* (1770), identifies her as "Miss Priscilla Pointon," but advertisements for subscribers in the Birmingham *Gazette* (1768) identify her as "Poynton," and five subscribers to the volume, one for ten copies, spelled their name "Poynton." Evidence awkwardly suggests that "Poynton" is correct. And because Lady Mary Wortley Montagu is so well known as "Lady Mary," often without her surnames, we have retained her title.

The number of poets and poems in this anthology is significant, but we also seek to rethink the anthology as a genre. The word *anthology* comes from the Greek term *anthologia,* for a collection of flowers, and has come to mean a collection of literary pieces such as poems, plays, or short stories. But we hope that this volume is more than simply a collection of poems by women. We have tried to offer ways to think critically, historically, and aesthetically about these texts. We attempt both to provide primary texts and to offer some preliminary critical and theoretical tools for reading, analyzing, and contextualizing the poems. Thus, the specific annotations to individual poems, the introductions to sections of poetry, and the overall organization of the book are designed to prompt the reader to consider both the poem and the movement of women's poetry during the long eighteenth century. Finally, these poets were masters of their craft and had a thorough command of the intricacies of poetics. To appreciate fully the work of these women poets, the reader will benefit from some knowledge of the various meters, rhyme schemes, and poetic devices the poets used with such ease. Thus, the following section, "How to Read Eighteenth-Century Poetry," offers a succinct guide to reading poetry.

Ultimately, we hope this anthology will be suggestive rather than exhaustive. Although it signals the continued efforts to recover the poetry of women of the long eighteenth century, it only begins to represent the published and unpublished poems women wrote during the period. As Isobel Grundy notes, "Rediscovery is not an event; it is a process."[35] We hope this volume is a catalyst for future work, an inspiring rather than a prescriptive text.

35. Isobel Grundy, "(Re)discovering Women's Texts," in *Women and Literature in Britain, 1700–1800,* ed. Vivien Jones (Cambridge: Cambridge University Press, 2000), 181.

HOW TO READ
EIGHTEENTH-CENTURY POETRY

Eighteenth-century poetry is full of voices and dramatic scenes. Poets imagine what people say, ventriloquize, parody, mock, and dramatize others' speech and thoughts, and they try on different identities, reveal different aspects of their personalities, celebrate and confess different moods and responses to experiences. A good way to begin enjoying a poem is to ask who is speaking and how many voices can be identified. If there is only one voice, to whom is that character speaking? Is it a dear friend (as it is in many poems by women)? Is it a carping critic who does not think that women should write or who holds limiting opinions about women's abilities and what they can be allowed to do?

Enjoying the poetry begins with a general grasp of the voices, the sounds of the voices, and the narrative of the poem. That narrative can be a story, a conversation or debate, the progress of feelings, or the movement of an active, fascinating mind. Women wrote original stories and fables, retold familiar tales, and transformed biblical and classical stories into gripping adaptations. Few will forget the horror of Salome describing the head of John the Baptist as gazing at her with a lover's faithfulness as she cradles it in Anne Killigrew's *Herodias Daughter Presenting to Her Mother St. John's Head* or the majesty of Jephthah's daughter, condemned to death by her father's rash vow, announcing that she will spend two months with her women friends before she submits to death in Ann Yearsley's *On Jephthah's Vow* (both in 2.D). In some poems, the poets' thoughts move over a subject, such as love, mortality, liberty, or happiness, as sun does over water, sometimes penetrating its depths, sometimes making ripples sparkle, always moving and changing. In some dialogue poems, women debate the advantages of playing hard to get versus showing their love. Mary Chudleigh's *On the Death of my dear Daughter Eliza Maria Chudleigh* moves through the moods of grief (2.N), and even so short a poem as Helen Maria Williams's *Sonnet: To the Strawberry* is a vivid portrayal of the flow of a mind in exile recalling the "Plant of my native soil" (1.B).

If there are multiple voices, what do they represent? Are they sharing an experience, their hearts and souls touching? Are they competing, exploring, debating, playing? Is the poet writing about a controversy of the time—political, philosophical, scientific? Is the poet representing some of the many debates about the nature and place of women? What is at stake? What do the voices *sound* like? How does that contribute to understanding the poet's position and art? The theater was the prestige genre of the time, and many poets wrote plays or at least prologues and epilogues. They saw and read plays, and many of the poets were as highly visual as twenty-first-century readers allegedly are. Sets—or as poets would say, setting—matter. Is it a fussily furnished London sitting room? A fashionable wilderness garden in the country? Sappho's island? A deserted village street at dawn as a war veteran returns home? Which war?

Their poetry is filled with dramatic episodes and scenes and with gripping visual images. Many of the poems might be hilarious or moving theatrical moments; imagining the two men bragging about their conquests with women in Lady Mary Wortley Montagu's *Tuesday: St. James's Coffee-House* is a good example (1.F). Equally dramatic are the catty card party in which women discuss the outrage of a servant girl turning poet in Elizabeth Hands's *A Poem, On the Supposition of the Book having been published and read* (3.D) and the nearly speechless wild boy's mourning his mother's murder in Mary Robinson's *The Savage of Aveyron* (1.J).

Although we identify poets with the voice of their poetry far more than we do novelists with their texts, it is a mistake to do so without thoughtful consideration. Does the poet signal to you that she wants you to take the voice as hers? Does she deliberately insert autobiographical experiences, as both Mary Barber and Elizabeth Hands do in their poems about publishing by subscription (both in 3.D)? Has she left statements outside the poems identifying it as her voice? Elizabeth Singer Rowe, for instance, circulated some of her most adventurous religious poems among a few friends, identified them as her personal meditations, and left them, with her comments, to be published for others. Even if the voice is hers, what does that mean? All of us have different voices, different performative selves, and different states of mind. We can act a part on a stage, and we can caricature the culture's gendered behaviors and its common social types. Consider a few of Anne Finch's lines on the experience of writing:

> To *Fable* I descend with soft Delight,
>
> . . . .
>
> To fill my Page, and rid my Thoughts of Care,
> As they to Birds and Beasts new Gifts impart,
> And Teach, as Poets shou'd, whilst they Divert.
>
> *The Critick and the Writer of Fables* (3.D)

> Did I, my lines intend for publick view,
> How many censures, wou'd their faults persue,

. . . .

And all might say, they're by a Woman writt.
Alas! a woman that attempts the pen,
Such an intruder on the rights of men.

The Introduction (3.D)

Ardelia [Finch's pen name] came last as expecting least praise

. . . .

Not seeking for Fame, which so little does last,
That e're we can taste itt, the Pleasure is Past.

. . . .

Yett the Bays [the prize], if her share, wou'd be highly esteem'd.

The Circuit of Appollo (3.A)

'Tis true I write and tell me by what Rule
I am alone forbid to play the fool
To follow through the Groves a wand'ring Muse

The Appology (3.E)

For this the gift by Heaven assign'd
With verse to sooth my active mind

. . . .

Be Allelujah join'd.

An Hymn of Thanksgiving after a Dangerous fit of sickness (2.G)

These selections are playful, serious, reflective, outraged, among other moods, and they state contradictory attitudes toward, for instance, fame. Some, such as *The Circuit of Apollo*, the "progress poem" with its canon-making ambitions, are in poetic genres with very strong conventions, and others are in deeply personal forms. Should we take what seems to be heartfelt thanks for her poetic gift in *A Hymn of Thanksgiving* as more revelatory than her likening it to "playing the fool" and, in a line not quoted, to getting drunk in *The Appology*?

Reading poetry is and is not like reading prose. The surest way to reduce a poem to an incomprehensible mess is to ignore punctuation and stop at the end of each line. Try reading this passage from Jane West's *Independence: Ode III* (note the subject) first by stopping at the end of each line and then by paying careful attention to the punctuation:

Who on the labours of the Muse
    Impassion'd energy bestows?
Whose inspiration can diffuse

> The warmth with which the patriot glows?
> Oh, thou; the theme of many a bard,
> By sages woo'd with fond regard,
>   In every vein a good supreme!
> Without thee, weak is Virtue's arm;
> Feeble is Wisdom's hope to charm;
> Nor yet must timid Truth display her radiant beam.

(1.D)

Not only is the meaning communicated but the emotions that the poet is attempting to convey are brought to the surface. While a story or a novel can be summarized in many fewer words than composed the original text, good synopses of poems are almost always longer than the poems. The difference is the way words are used. Individual words in poetry bear much more weight and are heavily connotative and often intertextual. In Mary Robinson's *Sonnet XLIII* (1.B), spoken by Sappho as she prepares to throw herself off the Leucadian promontory into the sea, she waits "Till the last stream of living lustre dies." This line captures both the last light before nightfall and Sappho's last breath of life and light of soul. By its very nature, poetry resists literal interpretation, and the text is what we call *figurative* (ideas are transmuted into images, often through such figures of speech as metaphors). Seward's carefully selected mythological references in her Colebrooke Dale poems (2.1) and Carter's constellations and planets in *While Clear the Night* (2.H) bear unusual weight and speak to an attention to detail and to precise selection of word and image that contrasts with ordinary prose. The word order in sentences may be unusual. Not only do poets work with rhyme and fixed numbers of syllables per line but they reorder words for emphasis and to create special sound effects. One of the most interesting sections of Charlotte Smith's *Conversations Introducing Poetry* is the dialogue in which she answers the charge that poetry is sometimes obscure by explaining poets' need to invert words and phrases and make other adjustments from the most common syntaxes for the sake of rhyme and meter.[1] Sometimes it is necessary to pause and identify the subjects and verbs of sentences, letting other words and phrases drop out of consciousness for a moment. Note, for instance, how far apart the subject and verb are in Anna Seward's sonnet *To Mr. Henry Cary:*

> Prais'd be the Poet, who the Sonnet's claim,
>   Severest of the orders that belong
>   Distinct and separate to the Delphic Song,
>   Shall venerate, ...   (1.B)

---

1. Charlotte Smith, *Conversations Introducing Poetry*, 2 vols. (1804; London, 1819), 2:119–20. *Syntax* is the technical term for the way words are put together to form phrases and sentences.

Transposed, the sentence says that the poet venerates the sonnet's claim to being the preeminent poetic form. When we read poetry, we experience and can bring to attention such characteristics as placement of words, texture, force, compression, and sounds that are seldom crucial to the meaning of prose.

The Details

Although some of the poets in this anthology seemed to write for a mere fraction of their lives, many were serious, lifelong students of their art. Some read widely; they studied the great classical and Renaissance poets, they knew the English "tradition," and they paid careful attention to the poetry being written all around them. Even the less privileged made great efforts to read poetry, and their work often shows serious engagement with style and ambitious experimentation. Mary Whateley Darwall published her two books of poetry thirty years apart. Reading through them makes clear both how independent a poet she was and how aware she was of forms that had become popular in the interval. Sometimes women led trends, sometimes they joined them, and sometimes they slanted them in new directions anticipating what would become the dominant form. Many poems are glossed with tags, such as "In the manner of Spencer," "After Milton," "Sonnetto from Marini," and "Five Pieces out of the *Aminta* of Tasso." Other verses deliberately echo the most famous lines written by Shakespeare, Waller, Pope, Gray, and almost any English poet of the seventeenth and eighteenth centuries that can be named. Some have interpreted this as women's insecurity or even plagiarism. The great Charlotte Smith was accused of borrowing so often that each edition of her *Elegiac Sonnets* was more heavily annotated than the last.[2] It cannot be forgotten, however, that to echo a line as famous as "What tho' while yet an infant young, / The numbers trembled on my tongue" (Clara Reeve, *To My Friend,* 3.D) or to name a poem *Abelard to Eloisa* (Judith Madan, I.L) invites comparison to, in this case, Pope. Individual women deliberately stepped onto the stage with another great poet, daring to have their poems read in relation to the recognized master poems of their time.

Serious artists and craftspeople master and experiment with the tools available for their work. It is possible, then, to find a woman writing the same "poem" in several different poetic genres or kinds. An ode, a sonnet, a Horatian epistle, and even a fable may explore the same point, experience, or emotion. Just as Pope deliberately set out to master every classical genre and to demonstrate that

---

2. Charlotte Smith, like many eighteenth-century writers, was accused of plagiarism, and such charges against women were especially disabling. A nuanced study that demonstrates that men as well as women were singled out and that class as well as gender was a major factor is Paulina Kewes, *Authorship and Appropriation: Writing for the Stage in England, 1660–1710* (Oxford: Clarendon, 2004). For a summary of scholarship and interpretation of Smith's quotations, see Paula R. Backscheider, *Eighteenth-Century Women Poets and Their Poetry* (Baltimore: Johns Hopkins University Press, 2005), 335–38 and the accompanying notes.

mastery by the forms in which he wrote for his 1717 *Works,* so women practiced and experimented with energy, delight, and skill. Many kinds of poetry make special demands on the poet, as we know the sonnet does with its constriction into fourteen lines of iambic pentameter. Some of the poetic kinds in part 1 had strong formal requirements inherited from classical times or the Renaissance. In the long eighteenth century, poets institutionalized strong conventions and expectations for other kinds of poetry, such as the philosophical verse essay. Poetic fashions and fads also influenced what was written and how each kind of poetry was written. The introductions to the sections in part 1 describe the history and special demands of each form.

Meter, Scansion, Rhyme, and Figurative Language

Considering the technical aspects of a poem is an important way to observe and describe a poet's skill and mastery of the art. The tools of any art are highly technical, and poetry is no exception. Knowing the terms that poets and specialists use gives us a vocabulary for talking about poetry in more sophisticated, clear, and concise ways.[3]

To appreciate and understand poetry more fully, knowledge of *meter* helps. Every line of poetry can be divided into *feet,* groups of stressed and unstressed syllables arranged in a fixed pattern.[4] This pattern helps convey meaning and tone (feeling or mood) and establishes the rhythm and musicality of poems. The most common meter in the Restoration and eighteenth century was

• *Iambic,* an unstressed syllable followed by a stressed one (da-DA, da-DA).

Other common feet include the following:

• *Trochee,* a stressed syllable followed by an unstressed syllable (DA-da, DA-da).
• *Anapest,* two unstressed syllables followed by a stressed syllable (da-da-DA, da-da-DA).
• *Dactyl,* the opposite of anapest (DA-da-da, DA-da, da).
• *Amphibrach,* an unstressed syllable followed by a stressed syllable and then an unstressed syllable (da-DA-da, da-DA-da).
• *Spondee,* two equally stressed syllables, often used for emphasis and required by some words, such as *heartbreak.*

---

3. This section of the introduction draws upon J. A. Cuddon, *A Dictionary of Literary Terms* (Garden City, NY: Doubleday, 1977); Alastair Fowler, *Kinds of Literature: An Introduction to the Theory of Genres and Modes* (Cambridge, MA: Harvard University Press, 1982); George B. Woods, *Versification in English Poetry* (Chicago: Scott, Foresman, 1958); H. W. Fowler, *A Dictionary of Modern English Usage* (Oxford: Clarendon, 1927); Alex Preminger and T. V. F. Brogan, *The New Princeton Encyclopedia of Poetry and Poetics* (Princeton, NJ: Princeton University Press, 1993); and Terry Eagleton, *How to Read a Poem* (Oxford: Blackwell, 2007).

4. Here and throughout, we are speaking of English poetry. Classical poetry is scanned, for instance, by the length of time it takes to pronounce the syllables.

Poets have tried to find ways to help remember the feet. One of the best is Samuel Taylor Coleridge's *Metrical Feet: Lesson for a Boy*[5] (stresses are marked throughout, but feet are indicated where they are illustrated rather than in every line; Coleridge carries trochaic feet over into the second line, for instance):

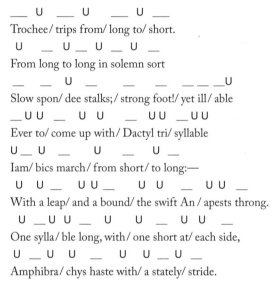

Memorizing a few phrases and hearing them with overstressed syllables will help. Examples might be "Iambics march," "Slow spondee stalks," and " 'With a leap and a bound' = anapests."

Poetry is described partly by *scansion*, determining how many feet, of what kind, there are per line. A line of verse of one foot is *monometer*; of two feet, *dimeter*; of three, *trimeter*; of four, *tetrameter*; of five, *pentameter*; of six, *hexameter*; of seven, *heptameter*; of eight, *octameter*. The most common line in eighteenth-century poetry is iambic pentameter, five feet (ten syllables) in iambics, as in the following line by Finch: "Did *I,/* my *lines/* in*tend/* for *pub/* lic *view.*" In another place Finch uses anapestic tetrameter: "In com*pos/* ing a *song,/* or a *Scene/* of a *Play.*" Poets vary feet within lines and within the poem itself. For instance, the insertion of a spondee or anapestic line can change the emphasis, the mood, and the sound of a poem dramatically. Critics have derived general effects from various meters. Margaret Doody writes that hexameter is "a measure less official, more comic, more pungent, than iambic pentameter with its history of *gravitas* and public responsibility."[6] Some variations have names, which specialists learn

5. Quoted in Woods, *Versification in English Poetry*, 2. This pamphlet has been an invaluable source.

6. Margaret Doody, "Women Poets of the Eighteenth Century," in *Women and Literature in Britain, 1700–1800*, ed. Vivien Jones (Cambridge: Cambridge University Press, 2000) 222–23. See also Doody's illuminating discussion of iambic tetrameter, the second most popular verse form, in *The Daring Muse: Augustan Poetry Reconsidered* (Cambridge: Cambridge University Press, 1985), 239–44.

and use. An example is *anacrusis,* dactylic dimeter with trochaic variation. At this point, readers should be able to translate that into a poem with poetic lines having two feet, primarily accented DA-da-da/ DA-da-da but with an occasional trochaic foot, perhaps a line with DA-da-da/ DA-da.

Poetry is also described by its *rhyme scheme.* A new letter is assigned to the last syllable of each line until a rhyme is repeated. That syllable is assigned the letter of the syllable with which it rhymes. Thus, the Coleridge poem above rhymes *aabbccdd.* Some lines of poetry do not precisely rhyme or do not rhyme at all. It is useful to remember that pronunciation today differs from that of the eighteenth century and that one dialect can produce a rhyme that another dialect does not. Poets also use near rhymes, para-rhyme, half-rhymes, slant rhymes, and a variety of other rhymes that do not conform to the canonical definition but are within the bounds of acceptable rhymes. Many of these are approximate rhymes, such as *justice* and *hostess,* which Swift uses, but others, such as *bless* and *bliss* and *pair* and *peer,* are not.[7] Some poets deliberately use sight rhymes, words that appear to rhyme but when spoken do not. Restoration and eighteenth-century poets and dramatists often used what is called blank verse, unrhymed iambic pentameter. It was widely believed to be the natural rhythm of dignified English speech. Iambic pentameter that rhymes *aabbcc,* and so on, is called *heroic couplets,* and poets and critics believed that this pattern raised the nobility of the language even as it necessarily made it more difficult to write. Some kinds of poetry, such as the sonnet and the English elegy, have rhyme schemes that many critics and poets consider required, and at various times debates arise over the "legitimacy" of variants. Rhyme schemes contribute to the enjoyment of reading poetry, just as music does to song, and they are important guiding signals for the reader, as they unify and divide parts of the poem. For example, they mark the divisions in a sonnet and also provide a repetitive pattern that helps unify ballads and the heroic quatrain.

In order to increase the beauty, power, and meaning of a poem, the poets included in this volume use a variety of rhetorical and poetic devices. Among the most common in the poetry of the period are the following:

- *Enjambment,* in couplet meters, continuation of a sentence or phrase beyond the end of one line into the first line of the next. This technique was used to great effect by Milton in his sonnets and is extremely common in the period's poetry in heroic couplets. Anna Seward used enjambment often, as in *To Colebrooke Dale* (2.1): "And the swart Cyclops ever-clanging forge / Din in thy dells;—permits the dark-red gleams, / From umber'd fires on all thy hills. . . ."

7. See Preminger and Brogan, *New Princeton Encyclopedia of Poetry and Poetics,* s.v. "near rhyme."

- *Anastrophe,* upsetting for effect the normal order, such as a reversal of noun and verb or other elements in a sentence, for example, "Me he restored, and him her hanged."
- *Apostrophe,* words addressed to a present or absent person or thing that breaks the thread of discourse. In Anne Finch's *The Poor Man's Lamb* (1.J), in the middle of the story of David's seduction of Bathsheba, the narrator exclaims, "Where art thou *Nathan* [the prophet and moralist]?"
- *Caesura,* the point at which a line breaks into two parts. Both Latin hexameters and Old English poetry required such breaks, and it was a frequent strategy employed by John Milton. Judith Madan writes in her *Abelard to Eloisa* (1.L), "O bless'd Insensibles! that knew not Love!"
- *Ejaculation,* a sudden, emphatic utterance or exclamation, usually at the beginning of a line, such as the frequently used "O!"
- *Syncope,* the shortening of a word by omission of a syllable or sound in the middle of it.

Sometimes poems of one type are colored or tinted by modes. Modes are created with the language, tones, motifs, and imagery of a recognizable genre, such as the pastoral. By the mid-eighteenth century a large number of poems or parts of poems of all kinds were in elegiac mode, and many georgic poems had epic features; both are experienced as modes. Poetry also relies on repetition for many effects; words or phrases may be repeated, as *in vain* is in many elegies. To communicate ideas, control effect, and shape sound, poets use other technical tactics, such as various classes of consonants and masculine and feminine rhymes. *B,* hard *g, d, p, k,* and *t* are *explosives;* other categories of consonants are *fricatives* and *sibilants.* A *masculine rhyme* is a single-syllable rhyme, such as *Dawn* and *Lawn* in the first two lines of Laetitia Pilkington's *The Happy Pair* (1.E); a *feminine rhyme* is a rhyme of words of two or more syllables, such as *divine* and *refine,* which appear later in the same poem. Ballads, songs, and hymns, of course, repeat refrains or choruses. The following sound techniques are among the most common:

- *Onomatopoeia,* the sound of the word echoes the sense of the word, for example, *puff, puff* and *boom.*
- *Alliteration,* the repetition of initial consonant sounds or of vowel sounds in close proximity, for example, "living lustre" in Robinson's poem about Sappho (1.B).
- *Assonance,* the repetition of vowel sounds.
- *Consonance,* the recurrence of specific consonants in combination with various vowels and other consonants.

Finch enjoys using alliteration and consonance in combination, as in "I am alone forbid to play the fool" and "As they to Birds and Beasts new gifts impart," in the poems quoted above. Such patterns increase the musicality of her lines and, as with *forbid* and *fool,* contribute to the tone and performative potential of the poem.

The compression and power of poetry comes in part from its *figurative language.* Among the most frequent kinds of figurative language (also called *tropes*) are the following:

- *Image,* representation of a sensory experience or an invitation to imagine something through one or more of the five senses. An example from Helen Maria Williams's *To Twilight* (1.B) is her allusion to the sound of a bird: "rich in melody her accents rise."
- *Symbol,* object standing for something else. The meaning of a symbol may be determined by tradition, as that for the phoenix is, or it may emerge out of the context of the individual poem, as the strawberry does in Helen Maria Williams's *Sonnet: To the Strawberry* (1.B).
- *Allegory,* a narrative in which the underlying meaning is different from the literal one. Helen Maria Williams's *Elegy: On finding a young Thrush in the Street* is an example (1.1).
- *Personification,* giving an inanimate object or abstract idea the attributes of a human being, as Charlotte Smith does when she has Spring weave garlands of flowers in *Written at the Close of Spring* (1.B).
- *Metaphor,* the description of one thing in terms of another, such as in "She is as beautiful as a rose and just as thorny."
- *Metonymy,* the replacement of the name of an object or concept with an attribute of it or a word or phrase closely related to it or suggested by it. In the opening line of Finch's poem *To Death,* for example, for death she uses "O King of Terrors" (2.N). A well-known example is "The pen is mightier than the sword."
- *Synecdoche,* a kind of metonymy in which a part is substituted for the whole, or vice versa, as *waves* might be for *ocean* or, as in Elizabeth Carter's *To [Dr. Walwyn],* the river Isis stands for Oxford University: "train'd / Where learned *Isis* flows" (2.1).
- *Hyperbole,* exaggeration, as in Mary Leapor's *Damon and Strephon* (1.K): "Is *Sylvius* dead? . . . / . . . / Thou Sun, forbear to gild this fatal Day; / Nor you my Lambkins dare to think of Play."
- *Litotes,* understatement.
- *Oxymoron,* combination of contradictory or incongruous words, such as *terrible beauty* or *cheerful pessimist.*
- *Zeugma,* linking elements in a contiguous way and creating an equivalence between things known to be disparate, as in Alexander Pope's famous lines, "Not louder Shrieks to pitying Heav'n are cast, / When Husbands, or when Lap-dogs breathe their last" (*Rape of the Lock,* canto 5, lines 157-58).

Reading poetry for the fullest enjoyment is a process. It begins with experiencing the poem as a whole and trying to hear it, then moves to studying its blocks of meaning—sentences, verses, transitions, and unified segments. Finally comes appreciation of the technical skill of the woman who once sat with her pen and wrote and rewrote the poem. What is the pace of the poem? Is it rapid and angry? Rapid and happy? Slow and sad? Slow and solemn? How intense is feeling in the poem? What meter did she choose? How did she make the poem sound the way it does, part by part and line by line? What images and figures of speech give the effect? What do they tell you about the woman's knowledge, mind, and craft? What is the relationship between this sound and the meaning of the poem? Sometimes everything in a poem works together to reinforce meaning and mood, but sometimes there is a contradiction between what the words and sentences literally mean and the message that the technical elements give. When a poem has such a contradiction, the poet is signaling that she is being, for instance, ironic or satiric. A good example is Mary Leapor's pastoral *Damon and Strephon* (i.k). Lingering over a poem is infinitely rewarding, as new depths of meaning and multiple writing strategies emerge before your eyes.

PART ONE

Poetic Kinds and Genres

Introduction

"In the English Versification there are Two Things chiefly to be consider'd," begins Edward Bysshe in *The Art of English Poetry* (1702). "1. The Verses. 2. The several Sorts of Poems or Compositions in Verse."[1] On the first page of his chapter entitled "Rules for Making English Verse" Bysshe discusses the central importance of "verses" (meter and rhyme), hierarchy, and poetic kind—what he terms "the several Sorts of Poems and Compositions." The popular volume, which had gone through seven editions by 1724, offers the eighteenth-century reader (and nascent poet) a primer on writing poetry. With section titles such as "Of the Structure of English Verses" and "Some other Instructions Concerning the Rhyme," Bysshe's text captures the degree to which poetry was read, written, and discussed, as well as the high regard in which it was held. His book was not an anomaly but one of a growing number of publications devoted to discussing poetic form and the role poetry could play in one's life.

Poets writing during the period covered by this volume engaged a series of established forms (Bysshe's "several Sorts") that were located within an understood and widely recognized hierarchy of literary value. As James Sutherland has discussed in detail, "the eighteenth-century poet set out to write not only a poem rather than poetry, but a poem which belonged to one of the recognized Kinds."[2] Critics, poets, and readers understood the expectations and limitations of various poetic kinds and their relative value within a poetic hierarchy. While to the modern literary critic the concept of a literary hierarchy seems to be clearly a discursive construct, Bonamy Dobrée reminds us that it "was very real to the poets."[3] The form of a poem was of "special significance at a period in which writers were highly conscious of tradition and convention—whether they chose to comply with the norms or transgress them."[4] Such an awareness of

1. Edward Bysshe, *The Art of English Poetry* (London, 1702), 1.
2. James Sutherland, *The Preface to Eighteenth-Century Poetry* (Oxford: Clarendon, 1948), 23.
3. Bonamy Dobrée, *English Literature in the Early Eighteenth Century, 1700–1740* (New York: Oxford University Press, 1959), 127.
4. Bill Overton, "The Verse Epistle," in *A Companion to Eighteenth-Century Poetry*, ed. Christine Gerrard (Oxford: Blackwell, 2006), 421.

poetic kind stands in stark contrast to the "organic form" privileged by the later poets of the Romantic period.

The poetic hierarchy evolved primarily from the classical literary traditions, which is one reason why the period has been fashioned as the "Augustan" age. As the period of peace during the reign of Augustus Caesar, the first Roman emperor, ushered in a period of literary production and cultural advancement, so too the years following the English Civil War in England were seen as a time of new-found stability and refinement. Joseph Addison's demand for England's superiority in "arts and arms" expresses the belief that both were essential to a great nation and reinforces poetry as an important and elevated literary form. The revered Roman poets Virgil and Horace (whom most poets would have read, usually in the original text) emerged as powerful influences on the poetic forms and, to some extent, the content of the period's verse. A poet like Alexander Pope could self-consciously fashion his career on Virgil's. Beginning with the pastorals and culminating with the *Dunciad*, his "epic" for the age, he worked through the different poetic forms in which Virgil had written to demonstrate his poetic mettle and his development as a professional poet. Readers and fellow poets would have recognized this deliberate progression through carefully selected forms.

The women poets in this volume wrote with an equal understanding of the hierarchy of form and the shape of their career, "in which such things as their 'progress' in mastering forms, metrics, and other elements of the craft and their ambitions are clearly visible."[5] Anne Finch, Mary Barber, Charlotte Smith, and Anna Laetitia Barbauld are but a few of the poets in this volume who paid keen attention to the poetic kinds and hierarchies, recognizing the challenge and the opportunities they presented. Finch simultaneously acknowledges the hierarchy's dominance, while deflating its importance in *The Critick and the Writer of Fables* (3.D). Satirically commenting on five dominant poetic forms, Finch highlights the often conflicting demands between a poet's interest, her critical reception, and the tastes of the town. The "easily persuaded Poet" listens while the interrupting "Critick" pronounces epic "old Bombast" and the pastoral "insipid Dreams" that lull "both the Writers, and the Readers" to sleep. He advises the poet to write satire, "To shew us private, or the publick Faults," while the poet, "weary . . . of the *Pindarick* way" or the ode, seeks to "descend with soft Delight" to the fable. The misguided Critick values only satire, "that single Stream," while

---

5. Paula R. Backscheider, *Eighteenth-Century Women Poets and Their Poetry* (Baltimore: Johns Hopkins University Press, 2005), 15. Backscheider goes on to note that "while we may not agree with the sense of the 'hierarchy' of their subjects or even of their poetic forms, we can discern the conception of these hierarchies and their striving toward excellence in them" (15).

the poet reminds him that "so many choice Productions swarm," that is, so many other forms exist. Finch's clever poem suggests that the perceived value of the different forms and their clearly marked expectations is an inescapable context for any poet and represents the vital discourse surrounding the composition of poetry. Finch's poem explicitly comments *on* form, but every poem in the volume represents a deliberate choice *of* form. Negotiating established poetic kinds and hierarchies required great skill, craft, and ability. Working within forms primarily created by men, women faced the dual challenge of demonstrating a mastery of those poetic conventions while simultaneously using them to serve often very different poetic purposes; they worked to move the forms forward and make them their own. Throughout the century, women made significant contributions to classical and English forms, advancing the popularity and development of enduring forms such as the sonnet, the ode, and the elegy. They took pains to manipulate, appropriate, and revise existing models. Controlled, deliberate experimentation by these poets enriched their use of the form and intensified their choices of specific poetic kinds.

An understanding of the history of each poetic kind is essential to understanding the tradition in which a poet was writing and how she adapted that form to her own poetic purpose. A detailed discussion of form can be found in the introductions to the individual sections in part 1. To provide a clear sense of the range, versatility, and experimentation of the poets, these sections alternate between formal poetic kinds and those that might be considered popular and or informal. This arrangement also provides an understanding of the liveliness of eighteenth-century verse and, in a sense, imitates the order of individual poems in an eighteenth-century anthology. Beginning in 1755, the title page of Robert Dodsley's *Collection of Poems*, a highly popular anthology of the period, illustrates how a variety of poetic kinds were juxtaposed within one reading space to satisfy the reader's desire for variety and novelty, while simultaneously alluding to prior literary traditions. Verse of this time, continues Barbara Benedict, "refers to literary history, but . . . this history is balanced by the conscious topicality of the contents."[6] An eighteenth-century reader would find an ode followed by a ballad, then perhaps an epigram and a verse epistle. A range of poetic kinds could appear in that order because the reader, and before her the poet, had a clear sense of how those poetic kinds related to one another within a literary tradition. We cannot, in the confines of this introduction, exhaustively discuss the origins of the dominant literary hierarchy of eighteenth-century England, the ordering of poems that would have been relatively transparent to a reader of Dodsley's col-

6. Barbara M. Benedict, "The Paradox of the Anthology: Collecting and *Différence* in Eighteenth-Century Britain," *New Literary History* 34 (2003): 244.

lection. What we can do, however, is briefly provide some guiding principles to explain the hierarchy and offer an approximate ordering of those forms. Not all forms are included in this volume: our commitment to reproducing all poems in full makes it impossible to include, for example, a complete epic. But nearly every poetic kind is mentioned below to provide the reader with an understanding of their relative relationships within a range of poetic forms.

Poetic kinds that originated in a previous classical form retained the prestige, historical weight, and high cultural value of that form, while kinds that either emerged in a vernacular or were significantly adapted to a vernacular form, though no less vital and important, were perceived as less elevated forms. The epic was the highest poetic form, comparable only to tragedy in the classical ordering of genres; it was a "literary summit which could be approached only humbly ... after a candidate had surmounted the foothills of pastoral and georgic."[7] A long narrative poem recounting the deeds of a national hero (and often serving specifically nationalist purposes), the epic was a major poem about a significant public persona or event. At the same level as the epic and other kinds of heroic poetry, the philosophical verse essay was an established didactic form that privileged meaning over poetic beauty and sought to explore the fundamental nature of things. Of nearly equal prestige are the ode and the elegy, among the great classical forms embraced by women writers during the period. An ode, originally a Greek form, is a long, lyric poem in stanzas of varied metrical patterns; its subjects are usually intense or exalted, often very abstract. Another lyrical form, the elegy is not simply a poem lamenting an individual's death; it is, more expansively, a poem of reflection and meditation, often focusing on love, war, or loss. Among the most elevated of the poetic kinds, the elegy shares the epic's complexity of form and its role in constructing a nation's history.

The fable, the pastoral, and the georgic, each with classical origins, were vital, often reinvented poetic forms. During the long eighteenth century, fables were complex, prestigious, and popular texts designed to convey a moral lesson, often using animals or mythical and marvelous creatures. Anne Finch's fables illustrate the possibilities of that form. Pastoral or bucolic poetry is, in the broadest sense, poetry concerned with the idealized lives, loves, and songs of the shepherds (*pastor* in Latin). The third-century Greek poet Theocritus developed the form in his *Idylls,* which presents song competitions or dialogues between the shepherds, recounts unrequited love, and offers songs of grief. Closely allied with the pastoral is the georgic, an ancient form modeled on Virgil's *Georgics.* A georgic focuses on providing didactic information about agriculture and the work of farming, an element of which is evident in the opening stanzas of Frances Seymour's

7. Richard Terry, "Epic and Mock Heroic," in *A Companion to Eighteenth-Century Poetry,* ed. Christine Gerrard (Oxford: Blackwell, 2006), 356.

Life at Richkings (1.c) or Elizabeth Tollet's *To My Brother at St. John's College in Cambridge* (not included).

While satire owes something to the Greek comedies of Aristophanes, it is a thoroughly Roman classical form. The word itself comes from the Latin *satura* or *satura lanx*, meaning a dish of mixed ingredients or a kind of medley; in a literary context, that refers to the multiple forms—dialogue, fable, verse, prose—satire could take. Quite simply, a satire is a text that comments on the foibles, evils, or vices of contemporary society. The great satires of the Roman poet Horace, designed for instruction, as well as those by Juvenal, designed more for punishment, had a profound effect on the satirists of the Restoration and the eighteenth century, who read them (in Latin) and used them as models. The verse epistle is, at its most basic level, a letter written in poetic form. The form's important classical antecedents were notably Ovid's *Heroides* and Horace's verse epistles. During the long eighteenth century, the verse epistle was a vehicle for poems that often engaged in contemporary political or social events, and it was, according to recent scholarship, one of the four most popular forms of the period, exceeded only by the hymn, the ode, and the song.[8]

These classical forms, all of which retain their elevated poetic status, were widely read and written during the eighteenth century, with its growing social and commercial market for poetry. At the same time, women writers also advanced the renewal or revitalization of a number of vernacular and less formal poetic kinds. For example, the sonnet, a fourteen-line poem usually in iambic pentameter, was a dominant poetic form during the early modern period but had fallen somewhat out of fashion after the death of Milton. Women were responsible for the continued experimentation with the sonnet form, as Jane Barker did by writing a sixteen-line sonnet. Leading the sonnet revival of the last two decades of the eighteenth century, Anna Seward, Charlotte Smith, and Mary Robinson were committed to making the sonnet a vital and relevant form. Hymns are an ancient form of poetry that contemporary readers might associate primarily with songs sung in church. Yet, in the long eighteenth century hymns were a respected, important poetic gesture, one traced to Hebrew, Greek, and Roman poetry.

Verse narrative, ballads, social verse, and poems of common life are also vernacular forms important and relevant to the eighteenth-century poet. A verse narrative is a poem that has a linear story with a focus on narrative rather than exclusively lyrical or expressive elements. Accessible, compelling, and consistently popular, verse narrative developed as a rich form in the eighteenth cen-

---

8. Overton, "Verse Epistle," 418. Overton's book-length study of the verse epistle, *The Eighteenth-Century British Verse Epistle* (Basingstoke: Palgrave Macmillan, 2007), also suggests that it was a form in which women wrote more extensively than men.

tury and anticipated some of the longer verse narratives of the nineteenth century. Technically, epics, ballads, and fables qualify as verse narrative, and elements of these closely related poetic kinds inform verse narrative, which is marked by blended genres.

The ballad, which originated in an oral and popular tradition, had two forms in the eighteenth century, literary and popular. Literary ballads are complex narrative poems that imitated the conventions of the traditional, more simplistic, anonymous folk ballad. Popular ballads, like the "broadside" ballads, tell simple stories of love, valor, or a relevant cultural event. "Ballads," notes Paula McDowell "were among the most 'speedy' and mobile discursive forms, for they were rapidly composed and disseminated by voice, manuscript, and print."[9] Ballads, accessible and often accompanied by a graphic illustration of the narrative, can be a means to retain historical knowledge and thus are often used to create or bolster a sense of national identity and cultural memory. In the preface to his 1765 collection of ballads, *Reliques of Ancient English Poetry*, Thomas Percy describes the form as possessing "a pleasing simplicity, and many artless graces, which in the opinion of no mean critics have been thought to compensate for the want of higher beauties, and if they do not dazzle the imagination, are frequently found to interest the heart."[10] Closely allied with ballads are songs, a form that appears throughout the volume, though not in a dedicated section. "The importance of songs of all types to early eighteenth-century Britain," writes Dianne Dugaw, "is obvious to anyone familiar with publishing of the time."[11] A tremendously popular form, a song may be read or set to music. For example, Eliza Tuite's *Song. In the Year 1794* (2.E), with its refrain "Britons, Strike Home," was clearly meant to be sung, while others, such as Anne Yearsley's *Song* (2.c), could not only be set to music but also stand as a poem.

The first section of part 1, "Social Verse," includes a variety of different kinds of light verse. Social verse, which came to be known as *vers de société* in the nineteenth century, is a form of witty, often ironic poetry written to amuse a polite or sophisticated audience. Although considered "light verse," *vers de société* was not insignificant and retained a literary dignity; it was challenging to do well, and it was often insightful about social mores and cultural details. The form retains its association with a certain spontaneous or extemporaneous composition. Poems of common life, in section 1.c, also an important and recognizable form during the

9. Paula McDowell, "'The Manufacture and Lingua-facture of Ballad-Making': Broadside Ballads in Long Eighteenth-Century Ballad Discourse," *Eighteenth Century: Theory and Interpretation* 47 (2006): 160.

10. Thomas Percy, *Reliques of Ancient English Poetry: Consisting of old heroic ballads, songs, and other pieces of our earlier poets, (chiefly of the lyric kind.)*, 3 vols. (London, 1765), 1:x.

11. Dianne Dugaw, "On the 'Darling Songs' of Poets, Scholars, and Singers: An Introduction," *Eighteenth Century: Theory and Interpretation* 47 (2006): 108.

eighteenth century, make readers conscious of previously unrecognized details in the daily life of ordinary people. Largely shorn of poetic diction and ornamentation, these poems seem to be informal, straightforward, and in some way removed from the formal expectations of the literary hierarchy. They use plain diction, often tetrameter, and finely wrought cultural detail to capture and comment upon the world. However, poems of common life, like *vers de société,* were still read and composed within this hierarchical environment of poetic kinds, some drawing on traditional classical forms.

These poetic kinds, which created a structured environment in which to write poetry, did not limit the experimentation and innovation of the female poets represented. Indeed, many of these women revived otherwise moribund forms or significantly expanded the uses of popular ones, as Charlotte Smith did the sonnet and Anne Finch the fable. Joanna Baillie, whose *A Winter Day* appears with the poems of common life (1.c), reflects on her earlier poetry in the preface to *Fugitive Verses* (1840), in which that poem was republished. She describes her poems as verse with "more homely subjects, in simple diction," a description that captures the simplicity and profundity of poems of common life. She suggests that the reader, diverted by the attractions of the day, "may be very well pleased after all to seat himself on a bench by his neighbour's door, and look at the meadows around him, or country people passing along the common from their daily work." [12] Her self-reflective comment reveals her freedom, shared by other women in this volume, to escape the aesthetic standards that we now recognize as constructed, while simultaneously meeting the challenge to write good poetry. The poems in part 1 demonstrate a deep engagement with a range of poetic kinds and illustrate women's innovative approach to the hierarchical and generic possibilities they encountered in the period. Collectively, the poems enrich our understanding of this period's vital and varied poetic production.

12. Joanna Baillie, *Fugitive Verses* (London, 1840), vi, v.

⊹A⊱

Social Verse

During the eighteenth century, poetry was an inherently social and sociable form whether it was read, recited, or, as illustrated in this section, composed extemporaneously. The popularity and pervasiveness of poetry as text and social act suggest the important cultural function it served. It was an evening's entertainment and a fashionable pursuit, a mark of refinement and a social barometer. "Gay's Pastorals sometimes delight us," writes Frances Seymour of aristocratic country life (*Life at Richkings*, 1.c). Wordplay and demonstrations of wit took many forms—dinner invitations, anagrams, and riddles. A collection entitled *The Masquerade. A Collection of new Enigmas, Logogriphs, Charades, Rebusses, Queries and Transpositions*, like the contemporaneous *Poetical Delights*, offers a wealth of word games "as entertainment . . . for a winter's evening."[1] Similarly, *Christmas Amusement*, written by "Mr. Puzzlebrains," details a winter house party at which the young people present agreed that "each should exercise his or her ingenuity, in the composition of a *Riddle, Charade, Rebus*, or *Enigma*; all of which were to be deposited in an elegant VASE . . . to be opened the succeeding Christmas, at which festive season they were to re-assemble" and solve the puzzles.[2] These were what one volume termed "amusing recreations." Fashionable women purchased *The Ladies' Diary*, which included "enigmas, rebuses, charades."[3] Verbal dexterity and a nimble wit were hallmarks of an educated, refined individual (which is perhaps why Edward Bysshe included a rhyming dictionary in his highly popular *Art of English Poetry*). Jane Austen's Emma demands that Mr. Elton write his own poetic charade, "the only security for its freshness; and nothing could be easier to you."[4] His poetic ability becomes a measure of his social worth. Similarly, cultured women were expected to be able to write a polished verse just as they were expected to be able to dance and sketch. The upper classes' way of dashing off poetry to comply with a friend's request, to celebrate a private occasion, or to display an ability to write sophisticated, polished verse gradually spread, and the ability to compose extemporaneously became an important part of the process of gentrification. Models for such poetry existed in popular anthologies such as Robert Dodsley's *Collections*, which contained the kind of light verse popularized by Matthew Prior (1664–1721), an influential poet in *vers de société* (society verse).

The cultural value assigned to social verse established an alternative economy for poetry, an economy to which Finch pointedly refers in *To a Lady who having desired me to compose somthing upon the foregoing Subject*. The title of the poem playfully captures the cultural expectations for this kind of social—and ultimately competitive—poetic production. "Prevail'd" upon "to speak the four first lines extempore," Finch illustrates the social economy in which poetic currency circulates; one can potentially be "rifled" or robbed when asked to spontaneously compose (or "stand and deliver"). This social commerce, which risks revealing Finch's "indigence," implicitly contrasts with the commercial literary economy. Extemporaneous composition is literally inscribed in the title of Lady Mary Wortley Montagu's *On the Death of Mrs. Bowes*. Written "in a great deal of Company," on the day of Mrs. Bowes's death, the poem was matched by one that Mary Astell wrote in response "on the opposite side of the same sheet of paper," suggesting the simultaneously competitive and collaborative nature of social verse. Indeed, versions of the poem not transcribed by Lady Mary contain four additional lines that were "possibly the contribution of one of the 'Company.'"[5] One can similarly imagine Mary Barber's *Epigram on the "Battle of the Books"* being composed or recited in company. Such cleverness also characterizes Barber's ironic refusal of an invitation, *To a Lady, Who Invited the Author into the Country*, or Mary Jones's *To Miss Clayton* (2.A). Both, like Laetitia Pilkington's *An Invitation to a Gentleman*, use the occasion of a spontaneous letter to demonstrate satiric wit, observe social mores, and illustrate metrical ease with the iambic tetrameter common to this poetic kind.

While Finch's capable poem suggests her ability to meet her host's challenge, it subtly alludes to the potential transience of literary power, something Elizabeth Carter addresses in *Written Extempore on the Sea-Shore*. Carter's solitude in nature prompts a meditation on the ephemerality of life and the immediacy of her emotions and poetic expressions of the same: "Blest Emblem of that equal State, / Which I this Moment feel within." Gazing at the sea prompts an almost Arnoldian musing on the "restless fluctuating Deep": "Expressive of the human Mind, / In thy for ever varying Form, / My own inconstant Self I find." Explorations of literary power similarly resonate in Anna Seward's *Elegy Written at the Sea-Side* (2.C) or Mary Whateley Darwall's *Impromptu. On Being Requested to Write Some Verses*. Darwall maintains a metrical levity while exploring a question that underlies many of these poems: how is poetic power sustained? The shared elements of the light, polished, social verse in this section appear throughout the volume, thereby underscoring poetry's central role in the cultural interactions of eighteenth-century women.

Notes

1. *The Masquerade. A Collection of new Enigmas, Logogriphs, Charades, Rebusses, Queries and Transpositions,* vol. 1 (London, 1797), iii–iv; Thomas Whiting, *The Poetical Delights. Containing enigmas, charades, rebuses, &c. with their answers; selected from an extensive correspondence* (London, 1797).

2. "Peregrine Puzzlebrains," in *The Christmas Amusement; or, the Happy Association of Mirth and Ingenuity: Being an Elegant Collection of Original Riddles, Charades, &c.* (London, 1799), iv.

3. Charles Hutton, *The Diary Companion, being a supplement to The Ladies' Diary* (London, 1792). The term *amusing recreations* is the title of Mary Pilkington's text of the same name, *Amusing Recreations; or a collection of charades and riddles on political characters, and various subjects* (London, 1798).

4. Jane Austen, *Emma,* ed. Stephen M. Parrish (New York: Norton, 1999), 45.

5. Isobel Grundy, *Lady Mary Wortley Montagu: Comet of the Enlightenment* (Oxford: Oxford University Press, 1999), 240.

To a Lady who having desired me to compose somthing upon the foregoing Subject[1] prevail'd with me to speak the four first lines extempore and wou'd have had me so proceed in the rest which I sent to her at more leasure, with the following verses

Anne Finch

Of this small tribute of my wit
   Now freely I'm the giver
Yet Celia was it not unfit
   To cry stand and deliver?[2]

Since what was rifled[3] on the spot
   So trivial did appear
'Twere better to be gag'd or shot
   Then Men that sum shou'd here

For were such indigence but known
   To traders with the Muses   10
ARDELIA's[4] commerce none wou'd own
   Which now no wit refuses

For ready talents shou'd you try
   From Pall-mall to the City[5]
The stock of all the passers by
   All wou'd not be found witty.

Even Prior,[6] who that day I met
   (Tho' none prepar'd can doubt him)
Perhaps like me had he been set
   Had not much more about him   20

---

1. "Foregoing Subject" refers to the topic of the preceding poem in the Wellesley manuscript, *To the Lord March on the Death of His Sparrow.*

2. Highwaymen's well-known confrontation to those they would rob, meaning "Stop and hand over your valuables."

3. Plundered.

4. Finch's poetic name for herself.

5. Pall Mall, in Westminster, runs parallel with the Mall; the City is the financial and mercantile part of London, originally referring to the area within the original Roman walls of London.

6. Matthew Prior (1664–1721), a famous British diplomatist, was arguably the most important poet writing in English between the death of John Dryden in 1700 and the poetic arrival of Pope in 1712.

Extempore cannot be good
   My head with little leasure
(If 'tis not lost in a blue hood)
   Shall serve you thus with pleasure.

(1711; 1998)

On the Death of Mrs. *Bowes.*
Lady Mary Wortley Montagu

Written extempore upon a Card, in a great deal of Company,
Monday Dec. 14, 1724. by the Rt. Hon. Lady M. W. M.[7]

Hail happy Bride![8] for thou art truly blest!
Three Months of Rapture crown'd with endless Rest!
Merit, like yours, was Heav'ns peculiar Care,
You lov'd,——yet trusted Happiness sincere:
To you the Sweets of Love were only shewn,
The sure succeeding bitter Dregs unknown:
You had not yet the fatal Change deplor'd,
The tender Lover, for the imperious Lord;
Nor felt the Pains that jealous Fondness brings,
10   Nor wept that Coldness from Possession springs.
Above your Sex distinguish'd in your Fate,
You trusted,——yet experienced no Deceit.
Soft were the Hours, and wing'd with Pleasure flew,
No vain Repentance gave a Sigh to you:
And if superior Bliss, Heav'n can bestow,
With Fellow Angels you enjoy it now.

(1724)

---

7. Isobel Grundy notes that versions of the poem not copied by Lady Mary, including this one, published in the *Weekly Journal*, contain four additional lines, which she suggests were "possibly the contribution of one of the 'Company.'" *Lady Mary Wortley Montagu: Essays and Poems and "Simplicity, A Comedy,"* ed. Robert Halsband and Isobel Grundy (Oxford: Clarendon, 1993), 233. Lines 3–6 do not appear in the manuscript version of the poem.

8. Mrs. Bowes was Eleanor Verney (1710–24), daughter of the Honorable Thomas Verney. She died on 14 December 1724, at the age of fourteen, having married George Bowes (1701–60) on 1 October 1724. Mrs. Bowes's mother was Lady Mary's neighbor at Twickenham; George Bowes was Edward Wortley Montagu's principal partner in the coal trade. Adrian Green, "'A Clumsey Countery Girl': The Material and Print Culture of Betty Bowes," in *Creating and Consuming Culture in North-East England, 1660–1830,* ed. Helen Berry and Jeremy Gregory (Aldershot: Ashgate, 2004), 76.

To a Lady, who Invited the Author into the Country
Mary Barber

How gladly, Madam, would I go,
To see your Gardens, and *Chateau;*[9]
From thence the fine Improvements view,
Or walk your verdant Avenue;[10]
Delighted, hear the Thrushes sing,
Or listen to some bubbling Spring;
If Fate had giv'n me Leave to roam!
But Citizens[11] must stay at Home.

WE're lonesome since you went away,
And should be dead — but for our Tea;   10
That *Helicon*[12] of female Wits,
Which fills their Heads with rhyming Fits!
This Liquor seldom heats the Brain,
But turns it oft, and makes us vain;
With Fumes supplies Imagination,
Which we mistake for Inspiration.
This makes us cramp our Sense in Fetters,
And teaze our Friends with chiming Letters.

I GRIEVE your Brother has the Gout;[13]
Tho' he's so *stoically* stout,   20
I've heard him mourn his Loss of Pain,
And wish it in his Feet again.
What Woe poor Mortals must endure,
When Anguish is their only Cure!

STREPHON is ill; and I perceive,
His lov'd *Elvira* grows so grave,

---

9. Large country home.
10. The chief approach to a country house, usually bordered by trees.
11. In this case, city-dwellers.
12. Mountain in Boeotia, Greece, that was the home of the poets Hesiod and Pindar and one of the original places of worship of the Muses; subsequently used allusively in reference to poetic inspiration.
13. For more than twenty years Barber herself suffered from gout, a disease caused by high uric acids and characterized by painful inflammation of the smaller joints, especially that of the big toe.

I fear, like *Niobe*,[14] her Moan
Will turn herself and me to Stone.
Have I not Cause to dread this Fate,
30   Who scarce so much as smile of late?

    WHILST lovely Landscapes you survey,
And peaceful pass your Hours away,
Refresh'd with various blooming Sweets;
I'm sick of Smells, and dirty Streets,
Stifled with Smoke, and stunn'd with Noise
Of ev'ry thing — but my own Boys;[15]
Thro' Rounds of *plodding*[16] doom'd to run,
And very seldom see the Sun:
Yet sometimes pow'rful Fancy reigns,
40   And glads my Eyes with sylvan[17] Scenes;
Where Time, enamour'd, slacks his Pace,
Enchanted by the warbling Race;
And, in Atonement for his Stay,
Thro' Cities hurries on the Day.

    O! WOULD kind Heav'n reverse my Fate,
Give me to quit a Life I hate,
To flow'ry Fields I soon would fly:
Let others stay—to *cheat* and *lye*.
There, in some blissful Solitude,
50   Where eating Care should ne'er intrude,
The Muse should do the Country Right,
And paint the glorious Scenes *you* slight.

Dublin, 1728   (1734)

    14. According to Greek mythology, after Apollo and Artemis killed all fourteen of her children, Niobe fled to Mount Siplyon, where she turned to stone, although she continued to weep.
    15. Barber's sons, often a source of poetic material for her.
    16. Drudgery.
    17. Wooded.

An Epigram on the "Battle of the Books"[18]
Mary Barber

Swift for the *Antients* has argu'd so well,
'Tis apparent from thence, that the *Moderns* excel.

(1734)

An Invitation to a Gentleman
Laetitia Pilkington

A Female moderately Fair,
Pleas'd with your Spirit, Wit and Air,
To me assigns the pleasing Task,
Your Company to Night to ask:
She has prepar'd a Feast refin'd,
A sacred Banquet for the Mind;
And you shall sup in solemn State,
Whilst round the tuneful Sisters[19] wait;
Who, if you wish for Drink, shall bring
You Water from *Pieria*'s Spring,[20]   10
More elevating than Champaigne,
And far more apt to heat the Brain.
Pindar,[21] who wrote in antient Days,
Has celebrated Water's Praise;
But if, with *Flaccus,*[22] you encline
To like the Product of the Vine,
And chuse a more substantial Feast,
She'll do her best, to hit your Taste.

(1748)

18. A short satire written by Jonathan Swift and published as part of the prolegomena to his *Tale of a Tub* in 1704, it depicts a literal battle between books in the St. James Library between the Ancient and the Modern authors.

19. Muses.

20. Pieria, a region Macedonia, was one of the original sites of worship of the Muses. "Pierian's Spring" is used figuratively to represent the source of poetic inspiration.

21. The greatest lyric poet of ancient Greece, known for his odes.

22. Roman poet, author of the epic *Argonautica.*

Written Extempore on the Sea-Shore
Elizabeth Carter

Thou restless fluctuating Deep,
    Expressive of the human Mind,
In thy for ever varying Form,
    My own inconstant Self I find.

How soft now flow thy peaceful Waves,
    In just Gradations to the Shore:
While on thy Brow, unclouded shines
    The Regent of the midnight Hour.

Blest Emblem of that equal State,
10   Which I this Moment feel within:
Where Thought to Thought succeeding rolls,
    And all is placid and serene.

As o'er thy smoothly flowing Tide,
    Their Light the trembling Moon-Beams dart,
My lov'd *Eudocia's*[23] Image smiles,
    And gayly brightens all my Heart.

But ah! this flatt'ring Scene of Peace,
    By neither can be long possest,
When *Eurus*[24] breaks thy transient Calm,
20   And rising Sorrows shake my Breast.

Obscur'd thy *Cynthia's*[25] Silver Ray
    When Clouds opposing intervene:
And ev'ry Joy that Friendship gives
    Shall fade beneath the Gloom of Spleen.

(1762)

23. Eudocia (c. 400–460), wife of Theodosius II, emperor of the Eastern Roman Empire, wrote religious poetry.
24. The east wind.
25. The moon's.

Impromptu: On Being Requested to Write Some Verses
Mary Whateley Darwall

By the softly-murm'ring stream,
Where I fondly us'd to dream,
O'er the daisy-painted lawn,
Where I met the meek-ey'd dawn;
Thro' the grove or up the mountain,
Or beside some mossy fountain,
Where I wander'd, oft befriended
By the muse, who then attended
Ev'ry rural haunt I sought,
Sooth'd each care, improv'd each thought;—   10
Now alas! in vain I rove:—
Nor fountain, lawn, nor dale nor grove
Can inspire the tuneful strain.
Youth is fled, and fancy's train,
Ever flitting on the wing,
Follow HEBE[26] and the spring.

(1794)

Sources

Finch: *The Anne Finch Wellesley Manuscript Poems: A Critical Edition*, ed. Barbara McGovern and Charles H. Hinnant (Athens: University of Georgia Press, 1998), 78–79; Montagu: *The Weekly Journal, or Saturday's Post*, 8 (26 December 1724), 2004; Barber: *Poems on Several Occasions* (London, 1734), 132–35, 164; Pilkington: *The Memoirs of Mrs. Lætitia Pilkington*, 2 vols. (Dublin, 1748), 1:119; Carter: *Poems on Several Occasions* (London, 1762), 38–39; Darwall: *Poems on Several Occasions. By Mrs. Darwall (Formerly Miss Whateley) in Two Volumes*, 2 vols. (Walsall, 1794), 1:81–82.

26. Goddess of youth; she had the power to make the old young again.

❧B❧

The Sonnet

In *To Mr. Henry Cary* Anna Seward describes the sonnet form as "arduous," composed of "strict energic measures," and conveying "A grandeur, grace, and spirit, all their own."[1] Since the Renaissance, the sonnet has been considered the epitome of poetic achievement and a test of a poet's technical skill and seriousness. From the time of the sonnet revival that began in the early 1780s, poets have written an unbroken stream of tributes to the form and its challenges. In one of a series of revealing sonnets of this kind, William Wordsworth wrote, "Scorn not the Sonnet, critic, you have frowned, / Mindless of its just honors; — with this key / Shakespeare unlocked his heart. . . ." One hundred years later, Olive Schreiner observed, "The poet, when his heart is weighted, writes a sonnet."[2] Wordsworth's lines inscribe the newness of the sonnet revival, and both writers remark on the appeal and the power the women poets in this section found in the sonnet. In this compressed, heady form they "unlocked the heart."

Sonnet comes from *sonnetto*, the Italian word for a little poem with instrumental accompaniment. Petrarch imposed a subject (the moods of love) and established the form, which was fourteen lines of iambic pentameter with an octave (eight lines) and a sestet (six lines) with one of two rhyme schemes; no more than five rhymes were allowed. The rhyme scheme is *abba, abba* and then either *cde, cde* or *cd, cd, cd*. The octave often introduces an image, an emotion, a question, or a problem and reflects on it; the sestet responds to it, and the volta[3] between the parts is quite marked. The Italian, or Petrarchan, sonnet has remained one of the two major forms. The English, or Shakespearean, sonnet is the form that the Earl of Surry and Thomas Wyatt adapted from the Italian. It has three quatrains, each of which presents an aspect of an idea, and a concluding couplet, which ties the quatrains together. The rhyme scheme is often *abab, cdcd, efef, gg*. Edmund Spenser, Sir Philip Sidney, Samuel Daniel, and William Shakespeare made it a major English form. In Shakespeare's and Spenser's hands, it became more meditative, intellectual, and dynamic, and the form with three quatrains and a couplet gained ascendancy. Spenser introduced influential variants on the sonnet form, and one of Anna Williams's sonnets in Spenser's style is included in this section.

In the seventeenth century, John Donne's *Holy Sonnets* transformed the Petrarchan idealized love object into the Christian God, while radically retaining much of the erotic language and imagery. Milton brought other sonnet forms and subjects into English literary history and erased the volta with rhetorical devices, syntax, and content to unify his sonnets into powerful, intellectually and emotionally charged statements or meditations. He acknowledged his debt to Giovanni della Casa, who was known for privileging formal beauty and dignity and did not use the metrical and rhetorical divisions of Petrarch. As Milton would do, he used inversions, enjambment, interpolations, duplex structures, and especially the caesura to break down the formal limits of quatrains and tercets so that the idea would flow powerfully through the octave-sestet boundary.[4] Mary Monck's sonnet on sleep is an example of a woman's use of della Casa's innovations, and we have paired it with her sonnet on the same subject that imitates Giambattista Marino's style.

By the eighteenth century, the sonnet, this difficult form with its depths of personal emotion, intellectual rigor, dignity, and sensuousness, had fallen into disfavor in spite of its rich legacy. Although Milton's great sonnets and his writing of occasional ones expanded the appeal of the form and suggested further technical experiments, they attracted little notice and no serious imitators for decades. That he expanded the subject matter to the highly personal *(When I consider how my light is spent)*, the occasional *(Lawrence of virtuous Father)*, and the political *(On the late massacre in Piedmont)* was a part of literary history waiting for its greatest moment. Anna Seward, represented by three sonnets in this anthology, was one of Milton's most important followers and a tireless proponent of what she believed to be the "legitimate" sonnet. In fact, her greatest contribution to the sonnet revival was her championship of the Miltonic sonnet, which she appreciated for its structure and "its grave, dignified, occasional nature."[5] She praised his sonnets for combining "elevated sentiments with majestic simplicity, and domestic feelings with energetic tenderness."[6] Drawing on his precedent, she stretched the subject matter of sonnets considerably, including unusual topics for her time, such as environmental issues, subjects common to occasional poetry, public and family individuals, and critical controversies. Appropriately, the sonnet that represents her in this section, like *Sonnet XVI: Translated from Boileau* (not included), forcefully and clearly states her opinion and invokes the authority of Apollo, Petrarch, and Milton.

Most of the sonnets in this section are from the sonnet revival that began in the 1770s and 1780s. It has been called as important a literary movement and as "genuine [an] artistic movement" as the experimentation with the sonnet in Renaissance England.[7] By 1802 the opinion of the *Critical Review* that "the sonnet has been revived by Charlotte Smith" was accepted.[8] Women were among the earliest eighteenth-century experimenters and scholars of the form, and by the end of the century the contributions and achievements of women, including Anna Seward, Mary Robinson, and Helen Maria Williams, were of equal if not greater significance than those of the male writers of sonnets (Thomas Warton and William Lisle Bowles, for instance).

In fact, women wrote sonnets throughout the Restoration and the eighteenth century, and this section includes a representative sample of them. Aware that the greatest writers of sonnets experimented boldly, a few women may have explored the possibilities of a sixteen-line sonnet. Jane Barker's *On the Death of My Brother* represents this expansion of the English sonnet; it has three quatrains answered by a final quatrain rather than a couplet. Given the importance of quatrains to the form, such an extension seems logical. Thomas Edwards published the first significant group of sonnets (thirteen) since the seventeenth century in Dodsley's 1748 *Miscellany* and fifty more in *Canons of Criticism* (1748), his attack on Warburton's edition of Shakespeare. A quiet movement was under way, and women were an important part of it. In 1755 *Poems by Eminent Ladies* included three sonnets by Mary Monck. About the same time, Catherine Talbot wrote a series of sonnets to express her grief over the end of her engagement to George Berkeley. Most of the women wrote sonnets in all of the variants of the form and invented new ones. As an example of their mastery of both, we provide both an Italian and an English sonnet by Helen Maria Williams.

Among the most impressive poetic feats is the construction of a sonnet sequence. Shakespeare, Sidney, and Spenser all wrote them, and this section of our anthology concludes with two poems from Mary Robinson's sonnet sequence *Sappho and Phaon* and eight sonnets from Charlotte Smith's. A sonnet sequence explores all of the moods of a human feeling, as Robinson's—and Spenser's, Sidney's, and Shakespeare's—did of love. In fact, *Sappho and Phaon* revived the amatory sonnet sequence, which grew to considerable prominence in the poetry of the Rossettis, Elizabeth Browning, George Meredith, and other nineteenth-century poets. Smith's sonnets explore all of the moods of melancholy, the great poetic mood of her generation, and, in fact, she was writing the most difficult kind of sequence, the chain. In a chain sequence, each sonnet is linked to the next and to the series through allusions, images, and repetitions. For example, the fourth sonnet, *To the Moon,* provides a link to the opening of the third sonnet ("Tell'st to the moon thy tale . . ."), and concludes with the delayed naming of the perspective, "Poor wearied pilgrim."[9] The next sonnet opens with the image of a happy child weaving bluebells into garlands, and the images and mood shifts replicate that of the opening sonnet. Like most poets writing sonnet sequences, Smith continued to add poems throughout her career. In the third edition, she extended the chain, and we provide *To Spring,* the sonnet with which she replaced *To Sleep* in the second edition.

Notes

1. *To Mr. Henry Cary* is partly devoted to furthering Seward's claim that the Miltonic form of the sonnet was the "true" or "legitimate" form. Robinson takes a stand in the controversy by subtitling *Sappho and Phaon* "in a Series of Legitimate Sonnets, with Thoughts on Poetical Subjects."

2. Wordsworth's *Scorn not the Sonnet* is in *A Century of Sonnets,* ed. Paula R. Feldman and Daniel Robinson (Oxford: Oxford University Press, 1999), 131; and Olive Schreiner's observation is from *From Man to Man; or, Perhaps Only* (New York: Harper & Brothers, 1927), 301.

3. Literally, "turn," the transition point between octave and sestet in a sonnet.

4. John Milton, *Complete Shorter Poems,* ed. John Carey (London: Longman, 1968), 89. For an explanation of the technical terms, see "How to Read Eighteenth-Century Poetry."

5. Claudia Thomas Kairoff, e-mail message to editors, 12 August 2007; this paragraph has benefited from both her conversation and her e-mail messages.

6. Anna Seward, quoted in John Brewer, *The Pleasures of the Imagination: English Culture in the Eighteenth Century* (Chicago: University of Chicago Press, 1997), 579.

7. Stuart Curran, *Poetic Form and British Romanticism* (New York: Oxford University Press, 1986), 30–31.

8. *Critical Review* 34 (January 1802): 393. For a good overview of the sonnet revival, see Feldman and Robinson, *Century of Sonnets,* 3–19.

9. Smith may have remembered the pilgrim sonnet in William Shakespeare's *Romeo and Juliet,* spoken at the lovers' first meeting (2.1.95–108). She was also drawing on Petrarch's first sonnet, an address to the reader: "O gracious and loving souls, / . . . / Ah! stay to see what my suffering is!"

On the Death of my Brother
A Sonnet

Jane Barker

I.

Ask me not why the *Rose* doth fade,
   Lillies look pale, and *Flowers* dye;
Question not why the *Myrtle shade*
   Her wonted shadows doth deny.

II.

Seek not to know from whence begun
   The sadness of the *Nightingale:*[1]
Nor why the *Heliotrope*[2] and *Sun,*
   Their constant *Amity* do fail.

III.

The *Turtle's*[3] grief look not upon,
10   Nor reason why the *Palm-trees*[4] mourn;
When, Widow-like, they're left alone,
   Nor *Phœnix*[5] why her self doth burn.

IV.

For since *He*'s dead, which Life did give
   To all these things, which here I name;
They fade, change, wither, cease to live,
   Pine and consume into a Flame.

(1688)

---

1. See 3.F, "The Nightingale in Poetry." This reference is to the poetic tradition in which the nightingale keeps herself awake by pressing against a thorn rather than to the classical story of Philomel.

2. Apollo jilted Clytie for her sister Leucothoe. When Clytie died of love, Apollo, the sun god, changed her into a flower, the heliotrope, which always turns toward the sun.

3. Small brown mourning doves, commonly called turtledoves.

4. In Roman, Egyptian, and Israelite processions, palm branches were waved for sacrificed and resurrected deities.

5. In classical mythology, the phoenix is a bird resembling an eagle but with sumptuous red and gold plumage. Said to live for five or six hundred years in the deserts of Arabia, it makes a nest of spices, sings a beautiful dirge, and burns itself to ashes on a funeral pyre ignited by the sun and fanned by its own wings, only to rise from its ashes with renewed youth and repeat the cycle.

To My Young Lover
Jane Barker

Incautious *Youth*, why do'st thou so mis-place
Thy fine *Encomiums*[6] on an o'er-blown Face;
Which after all the Varnish of thy Quill,
Its *Pristine* wrinkles shew apparent still:
Nor is it in the power of *Youth* to move
An *Age-chill'd* heart to any strokes of Love.
Then chuse some budding *Beauty*, which in time
May crown thy Wishes in thy blooming prime:
For nought can make a more preposterous show,
Than *April* Flowers stuck on St. *Michael*'s Bow.[7]   10
To consecrate thy first-born Sighs to me,
A *superannuated*[8] Deity;
Makes that Idolatry and deadly Sin,
Which otherwise had only *Venial*[9] been.

(1688)

Sonetto from Monsignor Della Casa[10]
Mary Monck

O Sleep, thou gentle Off-spring of still Night's
Soft humid Shades; sick Mortals sweet repose,
Pleasing Forgetfulness of all the Ills
That human Life imbitter and perplex.

Aid now my Soul, that languishes, and finds
No Rest; and ease my weak and weary Limbs:
Bend hitherwards, O Sleep, thy aery flight,
And o'er me drop thy dark extended Wing.

---

6. A formal expression of praise; eulogy.

7. Bough. St. Michael's Day, or Michaelmas, is 29 September; St. Michael's pears ripen around Michaelmas.

8. Obsolete, useless because antiquated.

9. Minor sin, one that can be pardoned, as opposed to a mortal sin.

10. Giovanni della Casa (1503–56) was archbishop of Benevento. This sonnet exhibits Monck's understanding of Casa's influential form, with his use of enjambment, caesura, and placement of alliterative words.

Where is that Silence, shy of Day, and Sun,
10   And those light Dreams that with uncertain steps
Wav'ring attend on the nocturnal Walks?
Alas! in vain I thee invoke, in vain
Court the cool Sable Shades: O restless Bed
Fill'd full with Thorns; O racking dreadful Nights.

(1716)

Sonetto from Marini[11]
Mary Monck

Soft Sleep, thou Son of Silence and of Night,
Parent of wild imaginary Forms,
Thro' whose dark quiet Paths the Lover oft
Straying does haply find his wish'd-for Bliss.

Now ev'ry Heart, but mine, in sweet Repose
Slumbers amidst these light and aery Shades;
Forsake thy closer Caverns, gentle Sleep,
Thy Grots[12] *Cim̄erian*,[13] gloomy as my Thoughts.

Approach me with thy lov'd Forgetfulness,
10   Bring that bright Form, whereon I joy to gaze,
Let it speak Comfort to my lone Desires.

But if to see the Semblance of the Fair
In thee's deny'd me, I at least shall find
The Image of that Death I long to meet.

(1716)

---

11. Giambattista Marino (often spelled Marini) (1569–1625) was known for flamboyant imagery and style. His influential style was termed *marinismo*.

12. Grottos, or small caves or caverns, or artificial structures made to resemble them.

13. A mythical people described by Homer as inhabiting a land of perpetual darkness. The macron doubles the letter *m*.

La Disperata[14]
Catherine Talbot

I yeild, I yeild, I every prize resign,
Each hope of every joy that once was mine;
I have no right, I have alas no claim,
To pleasure, Honor, Love, esteem or Fame;
Mean[15] is my path of life, chimæras[16] all
That once, Vain Fancy, *Hopes & joys* could call;
despised, Neglected, thro' the World I stray,
To me a Wild, deserted joyless way;
Shut out from every Scene of gay delight,
The Sun, the Stars grow painful to my Sight;   10
No heart partakes my grief, I weep alone,
Or to the Silent groves repeat my Moan:
Weep on Sad eyes, till creeping age has brought
A dull Lethargic truce from Anxious Thought.

(c. 1758–61)

A Sonnet
To a Lady of Indiscreet Virtue
In Imitation of Spencer[17]
Anna Williams

While you, fair ANNA, innocently gay,
    And free and open, all reserve disdain,
Wherever fancy leads securely stray,
    And conscious of no ill, can fear no stain,
Let calm discretion guide with steady rein,
    Let early caution twitch your gentle ear;
She'll tell you Censure lays her wily train
    To blast those beauties which too bright appear.

---

14. The desperate woman; the lament. Talbot wrote this sonnet after renouncing George Berkeley, the younger man she loved.

15. Impoverished, greatly inferior in quality.

16. In Greek mythology, a chimæra was a monster with the head of a lion, the body of a goat, and the tail of a dragon; synonym for a wild, unrealistic fantasy.

17. Edmund Spenser (1552–99), Elizabethan poet best known for *The Faerie Queene* and his sonnet cycle.

Ah me! I see the monster lurking near,
10   I know her haggard eye and pois'nous tongue,
She scans your actions with malicious leer,
   Eager to wrest and represent them wrong:
Yet shall your conduct, circumspect and clear,
Nor baleful touch, nor fangs envenom'd fear.

(1766)

Sonnet
To Twilight
Helen Maria Williams

Meek Twilight! soften the declining day,
   And bring the hour my pensive spirit loves;
When, o'er the mountain slow descends the ray
   That gives to silence the deserted groves.
Ah, let the happy court the morning still,
   When, in her blooming loveliness array'd,
She bids fresh beauty light the vale, or hill,
   And rapture warble in the vocal shade.
Sweet is the odour of the morning's flower,
10   And rich in melody her accents rise;
Yet dearer to my soul the shadowy hour,
   At which her blossoms close, her music dies—
For then, while languid nature droops her head,
She wakes the tear 'tis luxury to shed.

(1786)

Sonnet
To the Strawberry[18]
Helen Maria Williams

The Strawberry blooms upon its lowly bed,
Plant of my native soil!—the Lime may fling
More potent fragrance on the zephyr's wing;

18. This sonnet was to be included in Williams's 1795 translation of Jacques-Henri Bernardin de Saint Pierre's *Paul et Virginie* (1789).

The milky Cocoa richer juices shed;
The white Guava lovelier blossoms spread—
But not like thee to fond remembrance bring
The vanish'd hours of life's enchanting spring,
Short calendar of joys for ever fled!—
Thou bidst the scenes of childhood rise to view,
The wild-wood path which fancy loves to trace;   10
Where veil'd in leaves, thy fruit of rosy hue
Lurk'd on its pliant stem with modest grace—
But ah! when thought would later years renew,
Alas, successive sorrows croud the space!

(1795)

Sonnet LXIV
To Mr. Henry Cary,
On the Publication of His Sonnets[19]
Anna Seward

Prais'd be the Poet, who the Sonnet's claim,
   Severest of the orders that belong
   Distinct and separate to the Delphic Song,[20]
   Shall venerate, nor its appropriate name
Lawless assume. Peculiar is its frame,
   From him deriv'd, who shunn'd the City Throng,
   And warbled sweet thy rocks and streams among,
   Lonely Valclusa![21]—and that Heir of Fame,
Our greater MILTON,[22] hath, by many a lay
   Form'd on that arduous model, fully shown   10
   That English Verse may happily display
   Those strict energic[23] measures, which alone

---

19. *Sonnets and Odes by Henry Francis Cary, Author of an Irregular Ode to General Eliott* was published in 1788, when Cary was sixteen years old. He met Anna Seward in 1790, and they corresponded until her death in 1809.

20. The Delphic Oracle was the most important shrine to Apollo. The oracular messages were spoken in a frenzied trance by a priestess seated on a golden tripod and then interpreted by a priest who usually spoke in verse.

21. Home of Petrarch and Laura. Seward's is an Italian, or Petrarchan, sonnet.

22. John Milton, author of *Paradise Lost;* one of the most influential sonnet writers in English litererature.

23. Powerful, energetic.

Deserve the name of SONNET, and convey
A grandeur, grace and spirit, all their own.

(1799)

Sonnet V
To the Owl
Anne Bannerman

I love thee, cheerless, melancholy bird!
  Soothing to me is thy funereal cry;[24]
  Here build thy lonely nest, and ever nigh
My dwelling, be thy sullen wailings heard.

Amid the howlings of the northern blast,
  Thou lov'st to mingle thy discordant scream,
  Which to the visionary mind may seem
To call the sufferer to eternal rest.

And sometimes, with the Spirit of the deep,
  Thou swell'st the roarings of the stormy waves;
  While, rising shroudless from their wat'ry graves,
Aerial forms along the billows sweep.
  Hark! loud, and louder still, the tempest raves;—
And still I hear thee from the dizzy steep.

10

(1800)

Sonnet Introductory from *Sappho and Phaon*[25]
Mary Robinson

Favour'd by Heav'n are those, ordain'd to taste
The bliss supreme that kindles fancy's fire;

24. The owl's hoot is an ancient omen of death or disaster; to see or hear an owl during the day was especially ominous.

25. This sonnet opens Robinson's *Sappho and Phaon*, the remarkable sonnet sequence that tells Sappho's thoughts and emotions had she the detachment to describe her own experiences. In the next sonnet, the forty-third in the sequence, Sappho stands on the Leucadian promontory before throwing herself into the sea.

Whose magic fingers sweep the muses' lyre,
In varying cadence, eloquently chaste!
Well may the mind, with tuneful numbers grac'd,
  To Fame's immortal attributes aspire,
  Above the treach'rous spells of low desire,
That wound the sense, by vulgar joys debas'd.
  For thou, blest POESY! with godlike pow'rs
To calm the miseries of man wert[26] giv'n;   10
  When passion rends, and hopeless love devours,
By mem'ry goaded, and by frenzy driv'n,
  'Tis thine to guide him 'midst Elysian[27] bow'rs,
And shew his fainting soul, — a glimpse of Heav'n.

                  (1796)

Sonnet XLIII

Mary Robinson

While from the dizzy precipice I gaze,
  The world receding from my pensive eyes,
  High o'er my head the tyrant eagle flies,
Cloth'd in the sinking sun's transcendent blaze!
The meek-ey'd moon, 'midst clouds of amber plays
  As o'er the purpling plains of light she hies,[28]
  Till the last stream of living lustre dies,
And the cool concave owns her temper'd rays!
  So shall this glowing, palpitating soul,
Welcome returning Reason's placid beam,   10
  While o'er my breast the waves Lethean[29] roll,
To calm rebellious Fancy's fev'rish dream;
  Then shall my Lyre disdain love's dread control,
And loftier passions, prompt the loftier theme!

                  (1796)

26. Were.
27. In Greek mythology, Elysium was the paradise of poets and the home of the blessed.
28. Hurries.
29. In Greek mythology, those who taste the water of the Lethe forget; thus *Lethean* means something that causes forgetfulness or oblivion.

Sonnet I
Charlotte Smith

The partial Muse has, from my earliest hours,
   Smil'd on the rugged path I'm doomed to tread,
And still with sportive hand has snatch'd wild flowers,
   To weave fantastic garlands for my head:[30]
But far, far happier is the lot of those
   Who never learn'd her dear delusive art,
Which, while it decks the head with many a rose,
   Reserves the thorn—to fester in the heart.[31]
For still she bids soft Pity's melting eye
10   Stream o'er the ills she knows not to remove,
Points every pang, and deepens every sigh
   Of mourning friendship, or unhappy love.
Ah! then, how dear the Muse's favours cost,
If those paint sorrow best who feel it most![32]

                           (1784)

Sonnet II
Written at the Close of Spring
Charlotte Smith

The garlands fade that Spring so lately wove,
   Each simple flower which she had nurs'd in dew,
Anemonies,[33] that spangled every grove,
   The primrose wan, and hare-bell mildly blue.
No more shall violets linger in the dell,

---

30. Allusion to King Lear "fantastically garlanded with wild flowers" when he is destitute and mad in William Shakespeare's play (4.6.80). Loraine Fletcher, *Charlotte Smith: A Critical Biography* (New York: St. Martin's, 1998), 47.

31. See 3.F, "The Nightingale in Poetry." This reference is to the poetic tradition in which the nightingale keeps herself awake by pressing against a thorn rather than to the classical story of Philomel. Stuart Curran glosses *Toujours Roussignols, toujours des canson tristes,* in the preface to the sixth edition of Smith's *Elegiac Sonnets,* as follows: "'Always nightingales, always sad songs.' The nightingale, in one legend, having been deserted in love, pressed her heart against a thorn and lamented her fate in song." Curran, ed., *The Poems of Charlotte Smith* (New York: Oxford University Press, 1993), 5.

32. In later editions, Smith italicized this line, the standard way the century marked quotations, and added lines 365–66 from Pope's *Eloisa to Abelard:* "The well-sung woes shall soothe my pensive ghost; / He best can paint them who shall feel them most."

33. *Anemony Nemeroso,* the wood anemony. *Smith.*

Or purple orchis[34] variegate the plain,
Till spring again shall call forth every bell,
   And dress with humid hands her wreaths again.
      Ah! poor humanity! so frail, so fair,[35]
        Are the fond visions of thy early day,   10
      Till tyrant passions, and corrosive care,
        Bid all thy fairy colours fade away!
Another May new buds and flowers shall bring;
Ah! why has happiness no second spring?

                (1784)

Sonnet III
To a Nightingale
Charlotte Smith

Poor melancholy bird, that all night long
   Tell'st to the moon thy tale of tender woe;
    From what sad cause can such sweet sorrow flow,
And whence this mournful melody of song?

Thy poet's musing fancy would translate
   What mean the sounds that swell thy little breast,
    When still at dewy eve thou leav'st thy nest,
Thus to the listening night to sing thy fate.

Pale Sorrow's victims wert thou once among,
   Tho' now releas'd in woodlands wild to rove,   10
    Or hast thou felt from friends some cruel wrong,
Or diedst thou martyr of disastrous love?
Ah! songstress sad! that such my lot might be,
To sigh and sing at liberty—like thee![36]

                (1784)

---

34. Orchids.

35. The irregularity of the lines in this quatrain seems to be part of Smith's experimentation with the sonnet form. She regularized them in the third edition of her poems, returned to this form in the fourth, and then restored the traditional form for good in the 1789 fifth edition. By that time attacks on "irregular" sonnets were appearing in literary periodicals.

36. The earliest surviving poems by Smith date from the late 1770s, shortly after the death of her beloved first child. She published her poems in June 1784 in the hope of making enough money to

Sonnet IV
To the Moon
Charlotte Smith

Queen of the silver bow,[37] by thy pale beam,
 Alone and pensive, I delight to stray,
And watch thy shadow trembling in the stream,
 Or mark the floating clouds that cross thy way.
And, while I gaze, thy mild and placid light
 Sheds a soft calm upon my troubled breast;
And oft I think, fair planet[38] of the night,
 That in thy orb the wretched may have rest:
The sufferers of the earth perhaps may go,
10 Releas'd by death, to thy benignant sphere,
And the sad children of despair and woe
 Forget, in thee, their cup of sorrow here.
Oh! that I soon may reach thy world serene,
Poor wearied pilgrim—in this toiling scene!

          (1784)

Sonnet V
To the South Downs[39]
Charlotte Smith

Ah, hills belov'd! where once, an happy child,
 Your beechen shades, 'your turf, your flowers among,'[40]
I wove your blue-bells into garlands wild,
 And woke your echoes with my artless song.
Ah, hills belov'd! your turf, your flowers remain;

---

rescue her husband from debtors' prison, where she had spent considerable time with him since December 1783. At that time families often accompanied debtors to prison.

37. Diana, goddess of the moon and of hunting; she was often depicted with a bow and a quiver of arrows.

38. Because of Galileo's 1609 discoveries, people in 1784 knew that the moon was not a planet, but it continued to be designated as such in poetry.

39. One of two fertile hill ranges in southern England. The South Downs are in Sussex, separated from the North Downs by the Weald district and cut by the Arun, Adur, Ouse, and Cuckmere rivers.

40. In later editions of her poems, Smith identified this phrase as a quotation from Thomas Gray's *Ode on a Distant Prospect of Eton College:* "Whose turf, whose shades, whose flowers among" (line 8).

But can they peace to this sad breast restore,
   For one poor moment soothe the sense of pain,
      And teach a breaking heart to throb no more?
And you, Aruna![41] in the vale below,
      As to the sea your limpid waves ye bear,   10
Can you one kind Lethean[42] cup bestow,
      To drink a long oblivion to my care?
Ah, no!—when all, e'en hope's last ray is gone,
There's no oblivion—but in death alone!

                  (1784)

Sonnet VI
To Hope
Charlotte Smith

Oh, Hope! thou soother sweet of human woe!
   How shall I lure thee to my haunts forlorn?
For me wilt thou renew the wither'd rose,
   And clear my painful path of pointed thorn?
Ah, come, sweet nymph! in smiles and softness drest,
   Like the young hours that lead the tender year;
Enchantress, come! and charm my cares to rest;—
   Alas! the flatterer flies, and will not hear!—
A prey to fear, anxiety, and pain,
   Must I a sad existence still deplore;   10
Lo! the flowers fade, but all the thorns remain,
   'For me the vernal garland blooms no more.'[43]
Come then, 'pale Misery's love,'[44] be thou my cure,
And I will bless thee, who, tho' slow, art sure.

                  (1784)

41. The River Arun. *Smith.*

42. In Greek mythology, those who taste the water of the Lethe forget; thus *Lethean* means something that causes forgetfulness or oblivion.

43. In later editions of her poems, Smith identifies this quotation as line 32 from Pope's *Imitation of the first Ode of the fourth Book of Horace.*

44. Shakespeare's *King John. Smith.*[*King John* 3.4.35. *Eds.*]

Sonnet VII
On the Departure of the Nightingale
Charlotte Smith

Sweet poet of the woods, a long adieu!
   Farewel, soft minstrel of the early year!
Ah! 'twill be long ere thou shalt sing anew,
   And pour thy music on the 'night's dull ear.'[45]
Whether on spring thy wandering flights await,[46]
   Or whether silent in our groves ye dwell,
The pensive Muse shall 'own thee for her mate,'[47]
   And still protect the song she loves so well.
With cautious steps the love-lorn youth shall glide
   Thro' the lone brake that hides thy mossy nest;
And shepherd girls from eyes profane shall hide
   The gentle bird, who sings of pity best.[48]
For still thy voice shall soft affections move,
And still be dear to sorrow and to love.

                               (1784)

10

Sonnet VIII
To Sleep
Charlotte Smith

Come, balmy Sleep, tir'd nature's soft resort,
   On these sad temples all thy poppies shed;
And bid gay dreams, from Morpheus'[49] airy court,
   Float in light vision round my aching head! —
Secure of all thy blessings, partial Power,
   On his hard bed the peasant throws him down;

45. In later editions of her poems, Smith identifies this quotation from the prologue of Shakespeare's *Henry V*, line 11.
46. Alludes to the supposed migration of the nightingale. *Smith.*
47. In later editions of her poems, Smith identifies this quotation from lines 13–14 of Milton's sonnet *O Nightingale that on yon bloomy Spray:* "Whether the Muse or Love call thee his mate, / Both them I serve, and of their train am I."
48. An echo of Pope's line quoted in Smith's *Sonnet I,* above.
49. Ovid's name for the son of Sleep and the god of dreams.

And the poor sea boy, 'in the rudest hour,'[50]
   Enjoys thee more than he who wears a crown.
Clasp'd in her faithful shepherd's guardian arms,
   Well may the village girl sweet slumbers prove;   10
And they, oh gentle Sleep! still taste thy charms,
   Who wake to labour, liberty,[51] and love.
But still thy opiate aid dost thou deny,
To calm the anxious breast, to close the streaming eye.

(1784)

Sonnet VIII
To Spring[52]
Charlotte Smith

Again the wood, and long with-drawing vale,
   In many a tint of tender green are drest,
Where the young leaves unfolding scarce conceal
   Beneath their early shade the half-form'd nest
Of finch or wood-lark; and the primrose pale,
   And lavish cowslip, wildly scatter'd round,
Give their sweet spirits to the sighing gale.
   Ah! season of delight!—could aught be found
     To soothe awhile the tortur'd bosom's pain,
Of sorrow's rankling shaft to cure the wound,[53]   10
     And bring life's first delusions once again,
'Twere surely met in thee!—Thy prospect fair,
Thy sounds of harmony, thy balmy air,
Have power to cure all sadness—but despair.[54]

(1786)

---

50. Shakespeare's *Henry IV. Smith.* [Reference to lines from Shakespeare's *Henry IV, Part 2* 3.1.18–20: "Wilt thou upon the high and giddy mast / Seal up the ship boy's eyes, and rock his brains / In cradle of the rude impetuous surge?" *Eds.*]

51. In the first edition of Smith's poems, the theme of liberty is stronger than in the lightly revised and expanded third edition.

52. In the second edition of her poems, Smith moved *To Sleep* to a later place in the sequence and substituted this sonnet, *To Spring*, thereby extending and enhancing the chain of sonnets.

53. Allusion to the nightingale, a central theme in the sequence.

54. "To the heart inspires / Vernal delight and joy, able to drive / All sadness but despair." *Paradise Lost,* Fourth Book. *Smith.* [From Milton's *Paradise Lost*, bk. 4, lines 154–56. *Eds.*]

Sources

Barker: *Poetical Recreations* (London, 1688), 107, 61. Monck: *Marinda. Poems and Translations upon Several Occasions* (London, 1716), 87, 91. Talbot: Rhoda Zuk, ed., *Catherine Talbot and Hester Chapone, Bluestocking Feminism: Writings of the Bluestocking Circle, 1738–1785,* vol. 3 (London: Pickering & Chatto, 1999), 159. A. Williams: *Miscellanies in Prose and Verse* (London, 1766), 3. H. Williams: *Poems,* 2 vols. (London, 1786), 1:17–18; H. Williams: Jacques-Henri Bernardin de Saint Pierre, *Paul et Virginie,* trans. Helen Maria Williams (London, 1795), 91. Seward: *Original Sonnets on Various Subjects; and Odes Paraphrased from Horace,* 2nd ed. (London, 1799), 66. Bannerman: *Poems by Anne Bannerman* (Edinburgh, 1800), 81. Robinson: *Sappho and Phaon: In a Series of Legitimate Sonnets* (London, 1796), 39, 81. Smith: *Elegiac Sonnets, and Other Essays* (London, 1784), 1–8, and *Elegiac Sonnets. With Twenty Additional Sonnets* (3rd edition; London, 1786), 9.

⨉C⨉

Poems of Common Life

"Come, then, domestic Muse," urges Anna Laetitia Barbauld "loosely prattling on / Of farm or orchard, pleasant curds and cream, / Or drowning flies, . . . / . . . / Come, Muse, and sing . . ." *(Washing-Day)*. When Barbauld invokes her domestic muse, she marks a turn to the poetry of common life, an important poetic kind in the eighteenth century. A reader limited to widely antholo-gized poems such as *Washing-Day,* Mary Collier's *The Woman's Labour,* or Mary Leapor's *Crumble Hall* (the latter two not included in this anthology) would think that the poetry of common life explored only female domestic responsibil-ities or, based on Leapor and Collier, was produced primarily by working-class poets. Indeed, in discussing these poems, when they have been discussed at all, many critics classify them merely as "domestic verse" concentrating on the quo-tidian and ultimately insignificant. However, as the poems in this section dem-onstrate, such reading flattens their subtlety and ignores the wider tradition from which they emerge. Written by poets of all social backgrounds, this vibrant form confounds the notion that eighteenth-century poetry was defined only by formal verse in heroic couplets or that specific domestic details were found exclusively in prose fiction. Carefully observed, the often personal poems offer as much cul-tural detail as contemporaneous novels and form a distinct, if underdiscussed, poetic kind revealing the new self-confidence of the middling classes in the sig-nificance of their own lives.

Readers today are perhaps most familiar with the poetry of Jonathan Swift, which possesses domestic detail and "the vigorous presence of the mundane, the unliterary"[1] of common-life poetry. His contemporaries John Gay, John Dyer, and Matthew Prior, all widely read, wrote poems with characteristics they share with poems in this section. Prior, one of the most important poets before Al-exander Pope, wrote domestic verse that reveals his "talent for depicting . . . the intimate . . . but central concerns of ordinary people";[2] he "eschews pretentious-ness"[3] and represents "the ordinary ways of ordinary men."[4] He uses familiar, col-loquial language and displays the anti-pastoral impulse that propels Gay's *Shep-herd's Week* (to which Frances Seymour refers in *Life at Richkings*) or *Trivia.* Gay translates classical modes into modern, urban settings, subverting pastoral names (one nymph is named Buxoma) and romantic elements ("Her breath by far excell'd the breathing cow's"). In *The Slattern*, Sarah Dixon parodies extemporaneous poetic composition (explored in section 1.A), as well as the pastoral, with her portrait of the serving maid Salina; her muse is "dampened" when she is unable to decide "which Name to use, / Of *Damon, Pythias*, or *Endymion*"; and she abandons her poetic enterprise when her "Petticoat broke a string." John Dyer's *The Fleece* complicates the pastoral mode when he invokes a muse that can help him tell "The care of Sheep, the Labors of the Loom, / And arts of Trade."[5]

Emerging at the same time—and occasionally from the same literary milieu—as Prior and his colleagues, the poems in this section detail the "actualities of common life,"[6] consistent with the form's ability to sound "realistic and resilient at the same time it describes gritty reality and resilient people."[7] In *To the Countess of Pomfret: Life at Richkings*, Frances Seymour, Countess of Hertford, a patron of Dyer's, demonstrates the attention to agricultural labor so notable in *The Fleece*. Previously anthologized without the first two stanzas, which change the tone of the poem, *Life at Richkings* offers a trenchant look at the inherent economic disparities of the period. "Scenes of ruin fright the country round" as the laboring poor seek a subsistence living. The poem moves from iambic pentameter to the tetrameter more common to this poetic kind, from social observation to satiric description, as Hertford writes of the leisured classes striving to fill their time with Shakespeare (who "an hour diverts"), cards, and bountiful, fashionable meals ("Eggs, cream, fresh butter, or calves'-feet; / And cooling fruits, or sav'ry greens,— / 'Sparagus, peas, or kidney-beans"). Similarly, Mary Jones's *Epistle, from Fern-Hill* explores the humorous consequences of "Complaisance" for houseguests who are oppressed by the relentless "Good Manners" of their hosts. While echoing the description of Timon's Villa in Pope's *Epistle to Burlington* (where the speaker is exhausted by a rapidly served meal and his host's "civil pride"), by mentioning Swift specifically ("I reading *Swift*, and spilling tea"), Jones signals her poems' shared sensibility with Swift, especially his Market Hill poems. For example, Swift's poem *Dean Swift at Sir Arthur Acheson's* laments the presence of the "insulting tyrant Dean" whose stay "doth swell the bills: / ... it is surprising, / How much he eats, how much he swills"; like Jones, Swift presents the costs (domestic and psychological) of such a guest: "His brace of puppies how they stuff! / ... / His horses too eat all our hay."[8] Like Swift's *Description of a City Shower* (1710), Elizabeth Hands's *On seeing a Mad Heifer run through the Village* captures a cultural cross section of life revealed in a moment when social divisions dissolve. Mary Robinson's *London's Summer Morning* actively engages the rhetorical structure, mock pastoral, and urban pastoral of Swift's *City Shower* or *A Description of the Morning* (1709), creating a visual and aural portrait of the commercial world.

While many poems of common life are comic or satiric in their tone, an equal number focus on serious social issues such as homelessness, child labor, and poverty. Joanna Baillie's less frequently anthologized *A Winter Day* emerged from her desire to emulate the work of her aunt, the poet Anne Hunter. "One dark morning of a dull winter day," writes Baillie, "standing on the hearth in Windmill Street and looking at the mean dirty houses on the opposite side of the street, the contrast of my situation from the winter scenes of my own country came powerfully to my mind. . . . and with little further deliberation I forthwith set myself to write the 'Winter day' in blank verse."[9] The evocative image of the homeless veteran and the "contrast of . . . situation" between him and the barely surviving family is among the most haunting in this section. The scarred and hungry chimney sweep, seeking to be heard by any who will listen—"'twould draw a tear, / Knew you my helpless state"—seeks the same end ("could I hide me under ground") as William Blake's *Chimney Sweeper* (1789, 1794). The poetry of common life represented here belies the need for William Wordsworth's injunction in his preface to *The Lyrical Ballads* "to chuse incidents and situations from common life . . . whereby ordinary things should be presented to the mind in an unusual way."[10] It complicates our understanding of domestic life and, in turn, the poetic diversity and richness of the period.

Notes

1. Margaret Anne Doody, "Swift among the Women," *Yearbook of English Studies* 18 (1988): 83.

2. Ronald Rower, "Pastoral Wars: Matthew Prior's Poems to Cloe," *Ball State University Forum* 19 (1978): 39, quoted in Faith Gildenhuys, "Convention and Consciousness in Prior's Love Lyrics," *Studies in English Literature* 35, no. 3 (1995): 451.

3. Maynard Mack, "Matthew Prior: Et Multa Prior Arte . . . ," *Sewanee Review* 68 (Winter 1960): 173.

4. Frances Mayhew Rippy, *Matthew Prior* (Boston: Twayne, 1986), 82.

5. John Dyer, *Poems* (London, 1770), pt. 1, *The Fleece*, bk. 1, p. 53.

6. Paula R. Backscheider, "Inverting the Image of Swift's 'Triumfeminate,'" *Journal for Early Modern Cultural Studies* 4 (2004): 61.

7. Karina Williamson, "The Tenth Muse: Women Writers and the Poetry of Common Life," in *Early Romantics: Perspectives in British Poetry from Pope to Wordsworth*, ed. Thomas Woodman (New York: St. Martin's, 1998), 196.

8. *The Poems of Jonathan Swift*, ed. Harold Williams, 2nd ed., 3 vols. (Oxford: Clarendon, 1958), 3:859.

9. Quoted in Judy Slagle, *Joanna Baillie: A Literary Life* (Madison, NJ: Fairleigh Dickinson University Press, 2002), 55–56. We are grateful to Dr. Slagle for drawing this quotation to our attention.

10. William Wordsworth, preface to *The Lyrical Ballads, with Pastoral and Other Poems*, 3rd ed. (London, 1802), vii.

Written for my Son, and spoken by him in School, upon his Master's first bringing in a Rod

Mary Barber

Our Master, in a fatal Hour,
Brought in this Rod, to shew his Pow'r.
O dreadful Birch! O baleful Tree!
Thou Instrument of Tyranny!
Thou deadly Damp to youthful Joys;
The Sight of thee our Peace destroys.
Not DAMOCLES,[1] with greater Dread,
Beheld the Weapon o'er his Head.

10

THAT Sage[2] was surely more discerning,
Who taught to play us into Learning,
By 'graving Letters on the Dice:
May Heav'n reward the kind Device,
And crown him with immortal Fame,
Who taught at once to read and game!

TAKE my Advice;[3] pursue that Rule:
You'll make a Fortune by your School.
You'll soon have all the Elder Brothers,
And be the Darling of their Mothers.

20

O may I live to hail the Day,
When Boys shall go to School to play!
To Grammar Rules we'll bid Defiance,
For Play will then become a Science.

(1734)

---

1. Damocles, a flatterer, having extolled the happiness of Dionysius, tyrant of Syracuse, was placed by him at a banquet with a sword suspended over his head by a hair, to impress upon him the perilous nature of that happiness.

2. *See* Lock *upon* Education. *Barber.* [John Locke, in *Some Thoughts Concerning Education* (1692), imagines educational toys, such as "Dice and Play-things, with the Letters on them, to teach Children the *Alphabet* by playing" or an ivory ball with letters pasted upon it or games based upon vowels and consonants (148.256). *Eds.*]

3. Bowing to his Master. *Barber.*

The Slattern[4]

Sarah Dixon

1.

Salina saunt'ring in a Shade,
    Her Shoes were slipt,[5] her Gown unty'd;
A single Pinner[6] on her Head,
    And thus the easie *Trollop*[7] cry'd;

2.

Thus disengag'd from all the Crew,
    Which on a *Lady's Rising*[8] wait,
I can without Constraint pursue,
    The Pleasure of this soft Retreat.

3.

She oft had heard, that *Poets* chose
    To be retir'd from Noise and Rout;[9]   10
And fancy'd she could now compose,
    If she could find a Subject out.

4.

By Chance she had one Pocket on;
    Therein a Pencil neatly made:
She pull'd it out, and sat her down,
    And thought she'd more than half her Trade.

5.

The back-side of a *Billet deux*[10]
    Was ready to receive her Notions;
The first Thing she resolv'd to do,
    To put in Rhime her Morn Devotions.   20

---

4. An untidy and slovenly woman whose appearance is sometimes taken to suggest sexual availability.

5. Loose or untidy shoes, slippers.

6. A close-fitting cap.

7. Another term for an untidy or slovenly woman, also with the connotation of sexual availability.

8. Salina and her fellow servants are waiting for their mistress to wake up.

9. A disorderly, tumultuous, or disreputable crowd.

10. Love letter.

6.

She then began with the *Sublime;*[11]
   But found the Theme so much above her,
She past it till another Time,
   And chose to Poetize[12] her Lover.

7.

The great Dispute, which Name to use,
   Of *Damon, Pythias,* or *Endymion;*[13]
Did, by the Way, so damp her Muse,
   That soon she alter'd her Opinion.

8.

Aid me, *Melpomene!*[14] she cries,
30   The Weakness of my Sex to sing;
While I lament their Vanities,
   Do thou thy choicest Numbers[15] bring.

9.

Bless me! how trifling is the Lass,
   Spends ever half the Day in Dressing;
It makes me hate a Looking-Glass,
   And loathe a *Toilet*[16] past expressing.

10.

No farther had the Nymph the Power;
   Abrupt she threw the Paper by;
Quo' she, 'tis an unlucky Hour,
40   Walk one Turn more, and then I'll try.

11.

Help, *Thalia!*[17] comic Strains to sing;
   Apollo,[18] pray attend it;

11. In poetry, a discourse affecting the mind with a sense of overwhelming grandeur, calculated to inspire awe, deep reverence, or lofty emotion by reason of its beauty.

12. To write poetically about.

13. Common male names in pastoral poetry. In Greek mythology, Damon and Pythias symbolize friendship and trust; Endymion was an Aeolian shepherd.

14. One of the nine Muses, Melpomene was the Muse of tragedy.

15. Poetics; shorthand for rhyme, meter, and other poetic features.

16. Dressing table.

17. The Muse of comedy.

18. God of music and poetry and leader of the Muses.

Just then, her Petticoat broke a String,
And forced her Home to mend it.

(1740)

To the Countess of Pomfret: Life at Richkings[19]
Frances Seymour

After the groves, the portico,[20] and lawn,
Describ'd, have had their gen'ral picture drawn,
What can (that's new) remain for me to say—
Unless I talk of poultry, farms, and hay?
Hay (woeful thought!) sells for three pound each load,
Growing upon the land, before 'tis mow'd.
Three furlongs[21] only hence, a field is seen
Well sown with corn, where you scarce spy the green,
So many flow'rs o'errun th' ungrateful soil—
The hind[22] will reap a nosegay[23] for his toil.   10
While Wiltshire[24] swains[25] a harder fate sustain:
The downs[26] burnt up, for want of genial rain;
The thirsty flocks expire upon the ground;
And scenes of ruin fright the country round.
The dreadful doom which God in wrath foretold
To Israel's disobedience of old,
In these unhappy suff'rers comes to pass;—
Their earth seems iron, and their heavens brass.
   But, not to dwell on prospects sad as these,
Which eyes like yours can ne'er behold with ease,   20
I'll try if, in a gayer style,
Our life describ'd can make you smile;
To see what we accept as joys,

19. Also known as Richings (and later changed to Percy Lodge, as it is referred to by William Shenstone), Richkings was the estate in Colnbrook, Buckinghamshire, acquired by the Duke and Duchess of Hertford in 1739.
   20. Pergola.
   21. One furlong is ten acres.
   22. Farm servant.
   23. Small bouquet.
   24. County in southern England known for its chalky plains, or "downs."
   25. Country men, rustic laborers.
   26. Treeless undulating chalk uplands of the south and southeast of England, serving chiefly for pasturage.

And what pursuits our time employs.
    We sometimes ride, and sometimes walk;
We play at chess, or laugh, or talk:
Sometimes, beside the crystal stream,
We meditate some serious theme;
Or in the grot,[27] beside the spring,

30
We hear the feather'd warblers sing.
Shakspeare (perhaps) an hour diverts,
Or Scot[28] directs to mend our hearts.
With Clark,[29] God's attributes we explore;
And, taught by him, admire them more.
Gay's Pastorals[30] sometimes delight us,
Or Tasso's[31] grisly spectres fright us:
Sometimes we trace Armida's bowers,
And view Rinaldo[32] chain'd with flowers.
Often, from thoughts sublime as these

40
I sink at once—and make a cheese;[33]
Or see my various poultry fed,
And treat my swans with scraps of bread.
Sometimes upon the smooth canal
We row the boat, or spread the sail;
Till the bright evening-star[34] is seen,
And dewy spangles[35] deck the green.[36]
Then tolls the bell, and all unite
In pray'r that God would bless the night.
From this (tho' I confess the change

50
From pray'r to cards is somewhat strange)
To cards we go, till ten has struck:
And then, however bad our luck,

27. Grotto.

28. Alexander Scott (1520–15$\frac{82}{83}$), poet who wrote twenty-five short lyrics about love.

29. Samuel Clarke (1675–1729), one of the Church of England's leading theologians. He gave the prestigious Boyle lecture two years in a row (1704 and 1705), the second one entitled *A Demonstration of the Being and Attributes of God.*

30. Reference to *The Shepherd's Week* (1714), a burlesque pastoral by John Gay (1685–1732).

31. Torquato Tasso (1544–95), a sixteenth-century Italian poet.

32. Armida is a beautiful enchantress in Tasso's *Jerusalem Delivered* (1580) who bewitches Rinaldo, one of the Crusaders, with her charms.

33. A fruit conserve having the consistency of cheese.

34. The evening star was called Hesperus, but it was usually the planet Venus, which sometimes shines vividly in the west about sunset.

35. Reflecting spots of light.

36. Grassy area; Seymour is describing the reflections of stars on the dewy grass.

Our stomachs ne'er refuse to eat
Eggs, cream, fresh butter, or calves'-feet;
And cooling fruits, or sav'ry greens,—
'Sparagus, peas, or kidney-beans.
Our supper past, an hour we sit,
And talk of hist'ry, Spain, or wit:
But Scandal far is banish'd hence,
Nor dares intrude with false pretence   60
Of pitying looks, or holy rage
Against the vices of the age:
We know we all were born in sin,
And find enough to blame *within*.

(1740; 1805)

Epistle, from Fern-Hill[37]
Mary Jones

Charlot,[38] who my controller is chief,
And dearly loves a little mischief,
Whene'er I talk of packing up,
To all my measures puts a stop:
And tho' I plunge from bad to worse,
Grown duller than her own dull horse;
Yet out of Complaisance[39] exceeding,
Or pure Perverseness,[40] call'd *Good-breeding,*
Will never let me have my way
In any thing I do, or say.   10

    At table, if I ask for Veal,
In complaisance, she gives me Quail.
I like your Beer; 'tis brisk, and fine—
"O no; *John,* give Miss —— some Wine."
And tho' from two to four you stuff,
She never thinks you're sick enough:

37. Fern Hill, located in Windsor Forest, is the home of the Clayton family.
38. Charlotte Clayton (c. 1679–1742), daughter of John Dyve, was Jones's longtime friend and the subject of many of her poems.
39. Habit of making oneself agreeable; deference to the wishes of others.
40. Contrariness.

In vain your Hunger's cur'd, and Thirst;
If you'd oblige her, you must burst.

Whether in pity, or in ire,
20   Sometimes I'm seated next the fire;
So very close, I pant for breath,
In pure *Good-manners* scorch'd to death.
Content I feel her kindness kill,
I only beg to make my Will;
But still in all I do, or say,
This nusance *Breeding*'s in the way;
O'er which to step I'm much too lazy,
And too obliging to be easy.

Oft I do cry, I'm almost undone
30   To see our Friends in *Brooke-street, London.*[41]
As seriously the Nymph invites
Her slave to stay till moon-shine nights.
Lo! from her lips what Language breaks!
What sweet perswasion, when she speaks!
Her Words so soft! her Sense so strong!
I only wish—to slit her Tongue.

But this, you'll say's to make a clutter,
Forsooth! about one's bread and butter.
Why, be it so; yet I'll aver,[42]
40   That I'm as great a plague to Her;
For well-bred folks are ne'er so civil,
As when they wish you at the D——l.
So, *Charlot,* for our mutual ease,
Let's e'en shake hands, and part in peace;
To keep me here, is but to teaze ye,
To let me go, would be to ease ye.

As when (to speak in phrase more humble)
The Gen'ral's guts begin to grumble,

41. Brook Street runs off Grosvenor Square, an area developed in the early eighteenth century. Roger Lonsdale suggests that the Lovelaces, close family friends of Jones's, lived on Brook Street. Lonsdale, ed., *Eighteenth-Century Women Poets: An Oxford Anthology* (Oxford: Clarendon, 1989), 524.
42. Assert; declare true.

Whate'er the cause that inward stirs,
Or pork, or pease, or wind, or worse;   50
He wisely thinks the more 'tis pent,
The more 'twill struggle for a vent:
So only begs you'll hold your nose,
And gently lifting up his clothes,
Away th' imprison'd vapour flies,
And mounts a zephyr[43] to the skies.[44]

    So I (with rev'rence be it spoken)
Of such a Guest am no bad token;
In *Charlot*'s chamber ever rumbling,
Her Pamphlets, and her Papers tumbling,   60
Displacing all the things she places, ⎫
And, as is usual in such cases,   ⎬
Making her cut most sad wry faces. ⎭
Yet, spite of all this rebel rout,
She's too well bred to let me out,
For fear you squeamish Nymphs at Court[45]
(Virgins of not the best report)
Should on the tale malicious dwell,
When me you see, or of me tell.

    O *Charlot!* when alone we sit,   70
Laughing at all our own (no) wit,
You wisely with your Cat at play,
I reading *Swift,* and spilling tea;
How would it please my ravish'd[46] ear,
To hear you, from your easy chair,
With look serene, and brow uncurl'd,
Cry out, A —— for all the world!
But You, a slave to too much breeding,
And I, a fool, with too much reading,
Follow the hive, as bees their drone,[47]   80
Without one purpose of our own:

43. A breeze or wind.
44. The language is allusive of the so-called excremental verse of Jonathan Swift (1667–1745), which repeatedly uses the scatological connotations of zephyr and vapor.
45. Charlotte became a member of Queen Caroline's household in 1714.
46. Entranced, delighted.
47. Male honey bee who impregnates the queen bee and then dies immediately.

Till tir'd with blund'ring and mistaking,
We die sad fools of others making.

Stand it recorded on yon post,
That both are fools then, to our cost! }
The question's only, which is most?
I, that I never yet have shewn
One steady purpose of my own;
Or You, with both your blue eyes waking,
90 Run blund'ring on, by *Choice* mistaking?—
Alas! we both might sleep contented,
Our errors purg'd, our faults repented;
Could you, unmov'd, a squeamish look meet,
Or I forget our Friend in *Brooke-Street*.

(1750)

Reflections On a Grave digging in Westminster Abbey
Anna Williams

Fatigu'd with noisy crouds and pompous show,
To gloomy isles, and scenes of death I go,
Where mouldering trophies[48] hang, while falling dust
Confutes[49] the warrior's hope, the proud man's trust.
Where marble statues bending seem to mourn,
And point to flattery on the sculptur'd urn;
Detain with useless praise the wand'ring eye,
To tell where learning, greatness, beauty lye.
These all the hapless[50] state of mortals show,
10 The sad vicissitude[51] of things below.

REFLECTION dwells on images like these,
And sober thought creeps on by slow degrees;
A solemn stillness purifies my breast,
Calms all my thought, and bids my passions rest;
In contemplation deep, I seem to see
What now I am, what shortly I shall be;

48. Decaying or crumbling memorials.
49. Confounds or disproves.
50. Unfortunate.
51. Mutability.

Till by the noise of the descending spade
From studious thought recall'd, I turn my head.
Behold the gaping earth, and view beneath
Thy boasted victories, resistless death.   20
The table chest that holds the mouldering dust,
No longer able to retain its trust,
To pieces fall'n, displays the dismal scene,
And shews the loathsome sceleton within.
Behold that eyeless scull, with ghastly stare,
And learn to estimate your charms, ye Fair.
Here once the curious palate;[52] here a tongue,
On which perhaps persuasive language hung;
Here once was plac'd the sound-discerning ear;
The seat of mem'ry and of judgment here;   30
Here low'r'd the scornful look, the haughty brow,
Alas! how alter'd, how neglected now?
Now on the naked bones is left no trace,
Where every feature shew'd its proper grace;
Fragments of limbs disjointed strew the floor,
Scarce can the eye discern the form they wore;
These once with ligaments were firmly strung,
Their veins and arteries in order hung,
Each part adapted well, complete the whole,
A dwelling suited to th' ethereal[53] soul.   40

    THIS monitory[54] vault awhile survey,
Ye great, ye rich, ye giddy, proud, or gay;
Not flatter'd beauty, nor commanding state,
Can shun the general lot, or baffle fate:
The shatter'd body's ruin to survive
Is sacred virtue's great prerogative,
A life well spent dispels the dreadful gloom,
And cheers the terrors of the dreary tomb;
The marble dome, the sculptur'd bust shall fail,
And virtue only over time prevail.   50

(1766)

---

52. Refined taste for food and drink; the palate is, literally, the roof of the mouth.
53. Born beyond the earth's atmosphere; heavenly or celestial.
54. Warning.

Written, originally extempore, on seeing a Mad Heifer run through the Village where the Author lives

Elizabeth Hands

When summer smil'd, and birds on ev'ry spray,[55]
In joyous warblings tun'd their vocal lay,
Nature on all sides shew'd a lovely scene,
And people's minds were, like the air, serene;
Sudden from th' herd we saw an heifer[56] stray,
And to our peaceful village bend her way.
She spurns the ground with madness as she flies,
And clouds of dust, like autumn mists, arise;
Then bellows loud: the villagers alarm'd,
10   Come rushing forth, with various weapons arm'd:
Some run with pieces of old broken rakes,
And some from hedges pluck the rotten stakes;
Here one in haste, with hand-staff[57] of his flail,[58]
And there another comes with half a rail:
Whips, without lashes, sturdy plough-boys bring,
While clods of dirt and pebbles others fling:
Voices tumultuous rend the listening ear;
Stop her—one cries; another—turn her there:
But furiously she rushes by them all,
20   And some huzza,[59] and some to cursing fall:
A mother snatch'd her infant off the road,
Close to the spot of ground where next she trod;
Camilla walking, trembled and turn'd pale;
See o'er her gentle heart what fears prevail!
At last the beast, unable to withstand
Such force united, leapt into a pond:
The water quickly cool'd her madden'd rage;
No more she'll fright our village, I presage.

(1789)

55. Twigs or shrubs.
56. A young female cow.
57. Wooden handle.
58. Tool for threshing corn by hand.
59. Shout "huzza."

A Winter Day
Joanna Baillie

The cock, warm roosting 'midst his feather'd dames,
Now lifts his beak and snuffs the morning air,
Stretches his neck and claps his heavy wings,
Gives three hoarse crows, and glad his task is done;
Low, chuckling, turns himself upon the roost,
Then nestles down again amongst his mates.
The lab'ring hind,[60] who on his bed of straw,
Beneath his home-made coverings, coarse, but warm,
Lock'd in the kindly arms of her who spun them,
Dreams of the gain that next year's crop should bring;   10
Or at some fair disposing of his wool,
Or by some lucky and unlook'd-for bargain,
Fills his skin purse with heaps of tempting gold,
Now wakes from sleep at the unwelcome call,
And finds himself but just the same poor man
As when he went to rest.——
He hears the blast against his window beat,
And wishes to himself he were a lord,
That he might lie a-bed.——
He rubs his eyes, and stretches out his arms;   20
Heigh ho! heigh ho! he drawls with gaping mouth,
Then most unwillingly creeps out of bed,
And without looking-glass puts on his clothes.
With rueful face he blows the smother'd fire,
And lights his candle at the red'ning coal;
First sees that all be right amongst his cattle,
Then hies[61] him to the barn with heavy tread,
Printing his footsteps on the new fall'n snow.
From out the heap of corn he pulls his sheaves,[62]
Dislodging the poor red-breast from his shelter,   30
Where all the live-long night he slept secure;
But now afrighted, with uncertain flight
He flutters round the walls, to seek some hole,
At which he may escape out to the frost.

60. Farm servant.
61. Goes quickly.
62. Bundles of reaped grain.

And now the flail, high whirling o'er his head,
Descends with force upon the jumping sheave,
Whilst every rugged wall, and neighb'ring cot[63]
Re-echoes back the noise of his strokes.

    The fam'ly cares call next upon the wife
40   To quit her mean[64] but comfortable bed.
And first she stirs the fire, and blows the flame,
Then from her heap of sticks, for winter stor'd,
An armful brings; loud crackling as they burn,
Thick fly the red sparks upward to the roof,
While slowly mounts the smoke in wreathy clouds.
On goes the seething pot with morning cheer,
For which some little wishful hearts await,
Who, peeping from the bed-clothes, spy, well pleas'd,
The cheery light that blazes on the wall,
50   And bawl for leave to rise.——
Their busy mother knows not where to turn,
Her morning work comes now so thick upon her.
One she must help to tye his little coat,
Unpin his cap, and seek another's shoe.
When all is o'er, out to the door they run,
With new comb'd sleeky hair, and glist'ning cheeks,
Each with some little project in his head.
One on the ice must try his new sol'd shoes:
To view his well-set trap another hies,
60   In hopes to find some poor unwary bird
(No worthless prize) entangled in his snare;
Whilst one, less active, with round rosy face,
Spreads out his purple fingers to the fire,
And peeps, most wishfully, into the pot.

    But let us leave the warm and cheerful house,
To view the bleak and dreary scene without,
And mark the dawning of a winter day.
For now the morning vapour, red and grumly,[65]
Rests heavy on the hills; and o'er the heav'ns

63. Cottage.
64. Humble.
65. Dismal; a dialect word catching the sense of grim and glum (gloomy).

Wide spreading forth in lighter gradual shades,   70
Just faintly colours the pale muddy sky.
Then slowly from behind the southern hills,
Inlarg'd and ruddy looks the rising sun,
Shooting his beams askance[66] the hoary[67] waste,
Which gild the brow of ev'ry swelling height,
And deepen every valley with a shade.
The crusted window of each scatter'd cot,
The icicles that fringe the thatched roof,
The new swept slide upon the frozen pool,
All lightly glance, new kindled with his rays;   80
And e'en the rugged face of scowling Winter
Looks somewhat gay. But for a little while
He lifts his glory o'er the bright'ning earth,
Then hides his head behind a misty cloud.

   The birds now quit their holes and lurking sheds,
Most mute and melancholy, where thro' night
All nestling close to keep each other warm,
In downy sleep they had forgot their hardships;
But not to chant and carol in the air,
Or lightly swing upon some waving bough,   90
And merrily return each other's notes;
No; silently they hop from bush to bush,
Yet find no seeds to stop their craving want,
Then bend their flight to the low smoking cot,
Chirp on the roof, or at the window peck,
To tell their wants to those who lodge within.
The poor lank hare flies homeward to his den,
But little burthen'd with his nightly meal
Of wither'd greens grubb'd[68] from the farmer's garden;
A poor and scanty portion snatch'd in fear;   100
And fearful creatures, forc'd abroad by want,
Are now to ev'ry enemy a prey.

   The husbandman lays bye his heavy flail,
And to the house returns, where on him wait

66. Sideways.
67. Gray.
68. Dug up.

His smoking breakfast and impatient children;
Who, spoon in hand, and longing to begin,
Towards the door cast many a weary look
To see their dad come in.——
Then round they sit, a chearful company,
110   All eagerly begin, and with heap'd spoons
Besmear from ear to ear their rosy cheeks.
The faithful dog stands by his master's side
Wagging his tail, and looking in his face;
While humble puss pays court to all around,
And purs and rubs them with her furry sides;
Nor goes this little flattery unrewarded.
But the laborious sit not long at table;
The grateful father lifts his eyes to heav'n
To bless his God, whose ever bounteous hand
120   Him and his little ones doth daily feed;
Then rises satisfied to work again.

The chearful rousing noise of industry
Is heard, with varied sounds, thro' all the village.
The humming wheel,[69] the thrifty housewife's tongue,
Who scolds to keep her maidens at their work,
Rough grating cards,[70] and voice of squaling children
Issue from every house.——
But, hark!—the sportsman from the neighb'ring hedge
His thunder sends![71]—loud bark each village cur;
130   Up from her wheel each curious maiden starts,
And hastens to the door, whilst matrons chide,
Yet run to look themselves, in spite of thrift,
And all the little town is in a stir.

Strutting before, the cock leads forth his train,
And, chuckling near the barn among the straw,
Reminds the farmer of his morning's service;
His grateful master throws a lib'ral handful;
They flock about it, whilst the hungry sparrows
Perch'd on the roof, look down with envious eye,

69. Spinning wheel.
70. Rough instruments with iron teeth, used in pairs to comb out the fibers of wool or hemp.
71. The sportsman has shot his rifle.

Then, aiming well, amidst the feeders light,   140
And seize upon the feast with greedy bill,
Till angry partlets[72] peck them off the field.
But at a distance, on the leafless tree,
All woe be gone, the lonely blackbird sits;
The cold north wind ruffles his glossy feathers;
Full oft' he looks, but dare not make approach;
Then turns his yellow bill to peck his side,
And claps his wings close to his sharpen'd breast.
The wand'ring fowler,[73] from behind the hedge,
Fastens his eye upon him, points his gun,   150
And firing wantonly[74] as at a mark,
E'en lays him low in that same cheerful spot
Which oft' hath echo'd with his ev'ning's song.

    The day now at its height, the pent-up kine[75]
Are driven from their stalls to take the air.
How stupidly they stare! and feel how strange!
They open wide their smoking mouths to low,
But scarcely can their feeble sound be heard;
Then turn and lick themselves, and step by step
Move dull and heavy to their stalls again.   160
In scatter'd groups the little idle boys
With purple fingers, moulding in the snow
Their icy ammunition, pant for war;
And, drawing up in opposite array,
Send forth a mighty shower of well aim'd balls,
Whilst little hero's try their growing strength,
And burn to beat the en'my off the field.
Or on the well worn ice in eager throngs,
Aiming their race, shoot rapidly along,
Trip up each other's heels, and on the surface   170
With knotted shoes, draw many a chalky line.
Untir'd of play, they never cease their sport
Till the faint sun has almost run his course,
And threat'ning clouds, slow rising from the north,
Spread grumly darkness o'er the face of heav'n;

72. Hens.
73. Hunter of birds.
74. Recklessly.
75. Archaic plural of *cow.*

Then, by degrees, they scatter to their homes,
With many a broken head and bloody nose,
To claim their mothers' pity, who, most skilful,
Cures all their troubles with a bit of bread.

180   The night comes on a pace——
Chill blows the blast, and drives the snow in wreaths.
Now ev'ry creature looks around for shelter,
And, whether man or beast, all move alike
Towards their several homes; and happy they
Who have a house to screen them from the cold!
Lo, o'er the frost a rev'rend[76] form advances!
His hair white as the snow on which he treads,
His forehead mark'd with many a care-worn furrow,
Whose feeble body, bending o'er a staff,
190   Still shew that once it was the seat of strength,
Tho' now it shakes like some old ruin'd tow'r.
Cloth'd indeed, but not disgrac'd with rags,
He still maintains that decent dignity
Which well becomes those who have serv'd their country.
With tott'ring steps he to the cottage moves:
The wife within, who hears his hollow cough,
And patt'ring of his stick upon the threshold,
Sends out her little boy to see who's there.
The child looks up to view the stranger's face,
200   And seeing it enlighten'd with a smile,
Holds out his little hand to lead him in.
Rous'd from her work, the mother turns her head,
And sees them, not ill-pleas'd.——
The stranger whines not with a piteous tale,
But only asks a little, to relieve
A poor old soldier's wants.——
The gentle matron brings the ready chair,
And bids him sit, to rest his wearied limbs,
And warm himself before her blazing fire.
210   The children, full of curiosity,
Flock round, and with their fingers in their mouths,
Stand staring at him; whilst the stranger, pleas'd,

---

76. Worthy of great respect.

Takes up the youngest boy upon his knee.
Proud of its seat, it wags its little feet,
And prates, and laughs, and plays with his white locks.
But soon the soldier's face lays off its smiles;
His thoughtful mind is turn'd on other days,
When his own boys were wont to play around him,
Who now lie distant from their native land
In honourable, but untimely graves.   220
He feels how helpless and forlorn he is,
And bitter tears gush from his dim-worn eyes.
His toilsome daily labour at an end,
In comes the wearied master of the house,
And marks with satisfaction his old guest,
With all his children round.——
His honest heart is fill'd with manly kindness;
He bids him stay, and share their homely meal,
And take with them his quarters for the night.
The weary wanderer thankfully accepts,   230
And, seated with the cheerful family,
Around the plain but hospitable board,[77]
Forgets the many hardships he has pass'd.

    When all are satisfied, about the fire
They draw their seats, and form a cheerful ring.
The thrifty housewife turns her spinning wheel;
The husband, useful even in his rest,
A little basket weaves of willow twigs,
To bear her eggs to town on market days;
And work but serves t'enliven conversation.   240
Some idle neighbours now come straggling in,
Draw round their chairs, and widen out the circle.
Without a glass the tale and jest go round;
And every one, in his own native way,
Does what he can to cheer the merry group.
Each tells some little story of himself,
That constant subject upon which mankind,
Whether in court or country, love to dwell.
How at a fair he sav'd a simple clown[78]

77. Table.
78. Rustic person.

250   From being trick'd in buying of a cow;
      Or laid a bet upon his horse's head
      Against his neighbour's, bought for twice his price,
      Which fail'd not to repay his better skill:
      Or on a harvest day, bound in an hour
      More sheaves of corn than any of his fellows,
      Tho' ne'er so keen, could do in twice the time.
      But chief the landlord, at his own fire-side,
      Doth claim the right of being listen'd to;
      Nor dares a little bawling tongue be heard,
260   Tho' but in play, to break upon his story.
      The children sit and listen with the rest;
      And should the youngest raise its little voice,
      The careful mother, ever on the watch,
      And always pleas'd with what her husband says,
      Gives it a gentle tap upon the fingers,
      Or stops its ill tim'd prattle[79] with a kiss.
      The soldier next, but not unask'd, begins,
      And tells in better speech what he has seen;
      Making his simple audience to shrink
270   With tales of war and blood. They gaze upon him,
      And almost weep to see the man so poor,
      So bent and feeble, helpless and forlorn,
      That oft' has stood undaunted in the battle
      Whilst thund'ring cannons shook the quaking earth,
      And showering bullets hiss'd around his head.
      With little care they pass away the night,
      Till time draws on when they should go to bed;
      Then all break up, and each retires to rest
      With peaceful mind, nor torn with vexing cares,
280   Nor dancing with the unequal beat of pleasure.

         But long accustom'd to observe the weather,
      The labourer cannot lay him down in peace
      Till he has look'd to mark what bodes the night.
      He turns the heavy door, thrusts out his head,
      Sees wreathes of snow heap'd up on ev'ry side,
      And black and grumly all above his head,

---

79. Childish chatter.

Save when a red gleam shoots along the waste[80]
To make the gloomy night more terrible.
Loud blows the northern blast——
He hears it hollow grumbling from afar,   290
Then, gath'ring strength, roll on with doubl'd might,
And break in dreadful bellowings o'er his head;
Like pithless saplings[81] bend the vexed trees,
And their wide branches crack. He shuts the door,
And, thankful for the roof that covers him,
Hies him to bed.

                                        (1790)

On Halloween
Janet Little

Some folk in courts for pleasure sue,
    An' some ransack the theatre:
The airy nymph is won by few;
    She's of so coy a nature.
She shuns the great bedaub'd with lace,
    Intent on rural jokin
An' spite o' breeding, deigns to grace
    A merry Airshire rockin,[82]
                    Sometimes at night.

At Halloween,[83] when fairy sprites   10
    Perform their mystic gambols,[84]
When ilka[85] witch her neebour greets,
    On their nocturnal rambles;
When elves at midnight-hour are seen,
    Near hollow caverns sportin,

---

80. In this instance, an empty space of sky.
81. Young trees without a strong center core.
82. A party in Ayr (Ayrshire), a county in southwest Scotland. Ayr is a port city on the Firth of Clyde.
83. Like Robert Burns' poem *Halloween* (1786), this poem captures the folk rituals related to prophecy and courtship surrounding Halloween.
84. Leaps or springs in dancing; frolicsome movements.
85. Each.

> Then lads an' lasses aft convene,
>   In hopes to ken[86] their fortune,
>   By freets[87] that night.

20

> At Jennet Reid's not long ago,
>   Was held an annual meeting,
> Of lasses fair an' fine also,
>   With charms the most inviting:
> Though it was wat,[88] an' wondrous mirk,[89]
>   It stopp'd nae kind intention;
> Some sprightly youths, frae Loudoun-kirk,[90]
>   Did haste to the convention,
>   Wi' glee that night.

30

> The nuts upon a clean hearthstane
>   Were plac'd by ane anither,
> An' some gat lads,[91] an' some gat nane,[92]
>   Just as they bleez'd the gither.[93]
> Some sullen cooffs[94] refuse to burn;
>   Bad luck can ne'er be mended;
> But or they a' had got a turn,
>   The pokefu'[95] nits was ended
>   Owre soon that night.

40

> A candle on a stick was hung,
>   An' ti'd up to the kipple:[96]
> Ilk lad an' lass, baith auld an' young,
>   Did try to catch the apple;

86. Know.

87. Superstitious formulas or charms, omens, or anything to which superstition attaches.

88. Wet.

89. Dark.

90. From Loudoun church. Loudoun Valley is in northern East Ayrshire. Loudoun Kirk was the parish church until the seventeenth century; after that it became a burial place.

91. Lots.

92. None.

93. "Burned the nuts." Burns represents this practice in his poem and describes it thus in his note: "They name the lad and lass to each particular nut, as they lay them in the fire; and according as they burn quietly together, or start from beside one another, the course and issue of the courtship will be."

94. Rogues.

95. Sackful.

96. Rafter.

Which aft, in spite o' a' their care,
    Their furious jaws escaped;
They touch'd it ay, but did nae mair,
    Though greedily they gaped,
                Fu' wide that night.

The dishes then, by joint advice,
    Were plac'd upon the floor;
Some stammer'd[97] on the toom[98] ane thrice,
    In that unlucky hour.[99]
Poor Mall maun to the garret go,   50
    Nae rays o' comfort meeting;
Because sae aft she's answer'd no,
    She'll spend her days in greeting,
                An' ilka night.

Poor James sat trembling for his fate;
    He lang had dree'd the worst o't;
Though they had tugg'd and rugg'd till yet,
    To touch the dish he durst not.
The empty bowl, before his eyes,
    Replete with ills appeared;   60
No man nor maid could make him rise,
    The consequence he feared
                Sae much that night.

Wi' heartsome glee the minutes past,
    Each act to mirth conspired:
The cushion game[100] perform'd at last,
    Was most of all admired.

97. Staggered.

98. Occasion.

99. Burns describes the ritual in a footnote to *Halloween:* "Take three dishes, put clean water in one, foul water in another, and leave the third empty; blindfold a person, and lead him to the hearth where the dishes are ranged; he (or she) dips the left hand: if by chance in the clean water, the future husband or wife will come to the bar of Matrimony, a Maid; if in the foul, a widow; if in the empty dish, it foretells, with equal certainty, no marriage at all. It is repeated three times; and every time the arrangement of the dishes is altered."

100. A dance game in which the men chose a partner by laying a cushion on the floor before the woman, upon which she would kneel and receive a kiss. She would then arise, take up the cushion, and the couple would dance while singing.

From Janet's bed a bolster[101] came,
   Nor lad nor lass was missing;
70   But ilka ane wha caught the same,
     Was pleas'd wi' routh[102] o' kissing,
            Fu' sweet that night.

Soon as they heard the forward clock
   Proclaim 'twas nine, they started,
An' ilka lass took up her rock;[103]
   Reluctantly they parted,
In hopes to meet some other time,
   Exempt from false aspersion;
Nor will they count it any crime,
80   To hae sic like diversion
            Some future night.

(1792)

Washing-Day

Anna Laetitia Barbauld

————*and their voice,*
Turning again towards childish treble, pipes
And whistles in its sound.————[104]

THE Muses are turned gossips; they have lost
The buskin'd[105] step, and clear high-sounding phrase,
Language of gods. Come, then, domestic Muse,
In slip-shod[106] measure loosely prattling on
Of farm or orchard, pleasant curds and cream,
Or drowning flies, or shoe lost in the mire
By little whimpering boy, with rueful face;
Come, Muse, and sing the dreaded *Washing-Day*.

101. Pillow.
102. Abundance.
103. Distaff, a staff that holds unspun flax, wool, or tow from which thread is drawn.
104. A reference to William Shakespeare's *As You Like It* 2.7.160–62, which reads, "and his bigge manly voice, / Turning againe toward childish treble pipes, / And whistles in his sound."
105. A reference to the boots worn by actors in Athenian tragedy; "to put on the buskins" is to write in the tragic style.
106. Careless, poorly done; originally it meant wearing loose or untidy shoes that were down at the heel.

—Ye who beneath the yoke of wedlock bend,
With bowed soul, full well ye ken[107] the day   10
Which week, smooth sliding after week, brings on
Too soon; for to that day nor peace belongs
Nor comfort; e're the first grey streak of dawn,
The red arm'd washers come and chase repose.
Nor pleasant smile, nor quaint device of mirth,
E'er visited that day; the very cat,
From the wet kitchen scared, and reeking hearth,
Visits the parlour, an unwonted guest.
The silent breakfast-meal is soon dispatch'd
Uninterrupted, save by anxious looks   20
Cast at the lowering sky, if sky should lower.
From that last evil, oh preserve us, heavens!
For should the skies pour down, adieu to all
Remains of quiet; then expect to hear
Of sad disasters—dirt and gravel stains
Hard to efface, and loaded lines at once
Snapped short—and linen-horse[108] by dog thrown down,
And all the petty miseries of life.
Saints have been calm while stretched upon the rack,
And Montezuma[109] smil'd on burning coals;   30
But never yet did housewife notable
Greet with a smile a rainy washing-day.
—But grant the welkin[110] fair, require not thou
Who call'st thyself perchance the master there,
Or study swept, or nicely dusted coat,
Or usual 'tendance; ask not, indiscreet,
Thy stockings mended, tho' the yawning rents
Gape wide as Erebus,[111] nor hope to find
Some snug recess impervious; should'st thou try
The customed garden walks, thine eye shall rue   40

---

107. Know.

108. A frame on which linen is dried.

109. Ninth emperor during the Aztec reign over Mexico. Subsequent editions of the poem more accurately use the European name of Montezuma's nephew, Guatimozin, who led the resistance against Cortez. William Burke describes how the Spanish tortured Guatimozin by laying him "upon burning coals, to extort a discovery of his wealth," but "his countenance did not betray the least yielding or weakness under the torture." *An Account of the European Settlements in America,* 2 vols. (London, 1757), 1:121.

110. Sky.

111. In Greek mythology, the god of primordial darkness and son of Chaos. Also the region of Hades through which souls must pass soon after death.

The budding fragrance of thy tender shrubs,
Myrtle or rose, all crushed beneath the weight
Of coarse check'd apron, with impatient hand
Twitch'd off when showers impend: or crossing lines
Shall mar thy musings, as the wet cold sheet
Flaps in thy face abrupt. Woe to the friend
Whose evil stars have urged him forth to claim
On such a day the hospitable rites;
Looks, blank at best, and stinted courtesy,
50   Shall he receive; vainly he feeds his hopes
With dinner of roast chicken, savoury pie,
Or tart or pudding:—pudding he nor tart
That day shall eat; nor, tho' the husband try,
Mending what can't be help'd, to kindle mirth
From cheer deficient, shall his consort's brow
Clear up propitious;[112] the unlucky guest
In silence dines, and early slinks away.
      I well remember, when a child, the awe
This day struck into me; for then the maids,
60   I scarce knew why, looked cross, and drove me from them;
Nor soft caress could I obtain, nor hope
Usual indulgencies; jelly or creams,
Relique of costly suppers, and set by
For me their petted one; or butter'd toast,
When butter was forbid; or thrilling tale
Of ghost, or witch, or murder—so I went
And shelter'd me beside the parlour fire,
There my dear grandmother, eldest of forms,
Tended the little ones, and watched from harm,
70   Anxiously fond, tho' oft her spectacles
With elfin cunning hid, and oft the pins
Drawn from her ravell'd stocking, might have sour'd
One less indulgent.——
At intervals my mother's voice was heard,
Urging dispatch; briskly the work went on,
All hands employed to wash, to rinse, to wring,
To fold, and starch, and clap,[113] and iron, and plait.[114]
Then would I sit me down, and ponder much

112. Gracious, cheerful.
113. To smooth or flatten.
114. To fold.

Why washings were. Sometimes thro' hollow bole[115]
Of pipe amused we blew, and sent aloft   80
The floating bubbles, little dreaming then
To see, Mongolfier,[116] thy silken ball
Ride buoyant thro' the clouds—so near approach
The sports of children and the toils of men.
Earth, air, and sky, and ocean, hath its bubbles,
And verse is one of them——this most of all.

(1797)

The Chimney-Sweeper's Complaint
Mary Alcock

A chimney sweeper's[117] boy am I;
    Pity my wretched fate!
Ah, turn your eyes; 'twould draw a tear,
    Knew you my helpless state.

Far from my home, no parents I
    Am ever doom'd to see;
My master, should I sue to him,
    He'd flog the skin from me.

Ah, dearest Madam, dearest Sir,
    Have pity on my youth;   10
Tho' black, and cover'd o'er with rags,
    I tell you nought but truth.

My feeble limbs, benumb'd with cold,
    Totter beneath the sack,
Which ere the morning dawn appears
    Is loaded on my back.

---

115. Cylinder.

116. Joseph-Michel and Jacques-Étienne Montgolfier were French brothers who developed the hot-air balloon and conducted the first untethered balloon flights in 1783.

117. Children as young as six were used as chimney sweeps, or "climbing boys," because of their ability to climb the small chimney openings. The conditions of their employment were notoriously bad. Legislation prohibiting the use of children as chimney sweeps was not introduced until 1864, with Lord Shaftesbury's Act for the Regulation of Chimney Sweepers.

My legs you see are burnt and bruis'd,
　　My feet are gall'd[118] by stones,
My flesh for lack of food is gone,
20　　　I'm little else but bones.

Yet still my master makes me work,
　　Nor spares me day or night;
His 'prentice boy he says I am,
　　And he will have his right.

"Up to the highest top," he cries,
　　"There call out chimney-sweep!"
With panting heart and weeping eyes
　　Trembling I upwards creep.

But stop! no more—I see him come;
30　　　Kind Sir, remember me!
Oh, could I hide me under ground,
　　How thankful should I be!

　　　　　　　　　　　(1799)

Sonnet I: The Watch-Man
Anne Bannerman

From some rude rock, that overhangs the deep,
　　When the low winds proclaim the autumnal storm,
And murm'ring sounds along the waters sweep;
　　Where the lone light-house lifts its spiral form;

I mark, between the blast's infuriate[119] fits,
　　The gleaming taper's solitary ray,
And fancy wanders, where the watch-man sits,
　　With fearful heart, to view the lightnings play

Upon the surface of the gloomy waves;
10　　　As burst the thunders on his rocking tower,

118. Chaffed or cracked.
119. Raging.

And at its foot the mining ocean raves;
   Appall'd, he listens thro' the midnight hour,
And calls on Heaven:—The billows urge their way,
Upheave the rooted base, and all is swept away.

                         (1800)

London's Summer Morning
Mary Robinson

Who has not wak'd to list[120] the busy sounds
Of summer's morning, in the sultry smoke
Of noisy London? On the pavement hot
The sooty chimney-boy, with dingy face
And tatter'd covering, shrilly bawls his trade,
Rousing the sleepy housemaid. At the door
The milk-pail rattles, and the tinkling bell
Proclaims the dustman's[121] office; while the street
Is lost in clouds impervious. Now begins
The din of hackney-coaches,[122] waggons, carts;   10
While tinmen's[123] shops, and noisy trunk-makers,
Knife-grinders, coopers,[124] squeaking cork-cutters,
Fruit-barrows, and the hunger-giving cries
Of vegetable venders, fill the air.
Now ev'ry shop displays its varied trade,
And the fresh-sprinkled pavement cools the feet
Of early walkers. At the private door
The ruddy housemaid twirls the busy mop,
Annoying the smart 'prentice, or neat girl,
Tripping with band-box[125] lightly. Now the sun   20
Darts burning splendour on the glitt'ring pane,
Save where the canvas awning throws a shade
On the gay merchandize. Now, spruce and trim,
In shops (where beauty smiles with industry,)

---

120. Listen to.
121. A man who carts away dust and refuse.
122. Coaches for hire.
123. A man who works in or sells tin.
124. One who makes casks, buckets, or tubs.
125. A flimsy cardboard box for a wig, a hat, or millinery.

Sits the smart damsel; while the passenger
Peeps thro' the window, watching ev'ry charm.
Now pastry dainties catch the eye minute
Of humming insects, while the limy snare
Waits to enthral them. Now the lamp-lighter
30   Mounts the tall ladder, nimbly vent'rous,
To trim the half-fill'd lamp; while at his feet
The pot-boy[126] yells discordant! All along
The sultry pavement, the old-clothes-man[127] cries
In tone monotonous, and side-long views
The area for his traffic: now the bag
Is slily open'd, and the half-worn suit
(Sometimes the pilfer'd treasure of the base
Domestic spoiler), for one half its worth,
Sinks in the green abyss.[128] The porter[129] now
40   Bears his huge load along the burning way;
And the poor poet wakes from busy dreams,
To paint the summer morning.

(1806)

My Ain Fire-Side
Elizabeth Hamilton

O, I hae seen great anes,[130] and been in great ha's,[131]
'Mang[132] Lords and 'mang Ladies a' cover'd wi' braws;[133]
At feasts made for Princes, wi' Princes I've been,
Whar the great shine o' splendour has dazzled my een.[134]
But a sight sae[135] delightfu' I trow[136] I ne'er 'spied,

---

126. A boy employed in a pub to serve drinks or collect glasses.
127. A dealer in old or secondhand clothes.
128. He is buying stolen clothes. *Green bag* was slang for "attorney," one of those gentlemen who, according to Francis Grose, "it is said, when they have no deeds to carry, frequently fill them with an old pair of breeches or any other trumpery, to give themselves the appearance of business." *A Classical Dictionary of the Vulgar Tongue* (London, 1785), s.v. "Green Bag."
129. A person employed to carry luggage or goods.
130. Ones.
131. Halls.
132. Among, mingling with.
133. Fine clothes.
134. Eyes.
135. So.
136. Swear.

As the bonnie blythe[137] blink o' my ain[138] fire-side.
  My ain fire-side, my ain fire-side,
  Oh, cheering's the blink o' my ain fire-side!

Ance mair, Guid be thankit! by my ain heartsome[139] ingle,[140]
Wi' the friends o' my youth I cordially mingle: 10
Nae form to compel me to seem wae[141] or glad,
I may laugh when I'm merry—and sigh when I'm sad;
Nae fausehood to dreed, and nae malice to fear,
But truth to delight me—and friendship to chear.—
Of a' roads to happiness ever was tried,
There's nane half sae sure as ane's ain fire-side,
  Ane's ain fire-side, ane's ain fire-side,
  Oh! happiness sits by ane's ain fire-side!

When I draw in my stool on my cozie hearth-stane,
My heart loups[142] sae light, I scarce ken't[143] for my ain;   20
Care's flown on the winds—it's clean out o' sight,
Past sorrows they seem but as dreams o' the night;
I hear but kent[144] voices;—kent faces I see,
And mark fond affection glint saft frae ilk ee.[145]
Nae fleechings[146] o' flattery—nae boastings o' pride,
'Tis heart speaks to heart, at ane's ain fire-side;
  My ain fire-side, my ain fire-side,
  Oh! there's nought to compare to my ain fire-side!

(1810)

Sources

Barber: *Poems on Several Occasions* (London, 1734), 36–37; Dixon: *Poems on Several Occasions* (Canterbury, 1740), 68–70; Seymour: *Correspondence between Frances, Countess of Hartford (afterwards Duchess of Somerset,) and Henrietta Louisa, Countess of Pomfret, between the*

137. Beautiful, cheerful.
138. Own.
139. Encouraging.
140. Hearth.
141. Woe.
142. Leaps.
143. Know it.
144. Familiar.
145. From each eye.
146. Coaxing or wheedling.

Years 1738 and 1741, 3 vols. (London, 1805), 2:37–39; Jones: *Miscellanies in Prose and Verse* (Oxford, 1750), 133–38; Williams: *Miscellanies in Prose and Verse* (London, 1766), 68–70; Hands: *The Death of Amnon. A Poem. With an Appendix: Containing Pastorals, and other Poetical Pieces* (Coventry, 1789), 115–16; Baillie: *Poems; Wherein It Is Attempted to Describe Certain Views of Nature and of Rustic Manners* (London, 1790), 1–16; Little: *The Poetical Works of Janet Little, the Scotch Milkmaid* (Air [Ayr], 1792), 167–70; Barbauld: *Monthly Magazine* 4 (December 1797): 452; Alcock: *Poems, &c. &c. By the Late Mrs. Mary Alcock* (London, 1799), 22–24; Bannerman: *Poems by Anne Bannerman* (Edinburgh, 1800), 77; Robinson: *The Poetical Works of the Late Mrs. Mary Robinson,* 3 vols. (London, 1806), 3:223–24; Hamilton: *Remains of Nithsdale and Galloway Song,* ed. R. H. Cromek (London, 1810), 53–54.

✦D✦

The Ode

Intense, lyrical, compelling, and at times deeply personal, the odes in this section demonstrate the powerful potential of the form in the hands of a capable poet. Traditionally dignified, even stately in tone and style, with complex stanza patterns, odes continue to be composed for ceremonial state occasions. As a form, the ode allows for gripping expression of complex thoughts on modest or elevated subjects and has come to be chosen as well for private moments of crisis or joy. Characterized by almost unrivaled flexibility in terms of meter, rhyme, and stanza, the ode provided a potent vehicle for women to develop emergent meaning incrementally, at times recursively, creating poems whose complexity of form matched their complexity of thought. As J. Paul Hunter writes, odes often include high claims about philosophical abstractions, states of mind, and human ponderings.[1] The odes included here have, both discretely and in aggregate, a powerful cumulative effect.

The ode is among the oldest poetic forms, tracing its roots to Hebraic psalms and poetry, Homeric hymns, and fragments of odes by Alcaeus and Sappho (notably *Ode to Aphrodite*, c. 600 BC). According to legend, Stesichorus (640–555 BC) introduced the tripartite model derived from the choric songs of Greek drama to heroic hymns. Pindar, writing in both Alcaics and Sapphics, developed it for public occasions. At the ode's most formal, the strophe and antistrophe are identical in verse form, while the epode is different in length and structure. Pindar's odes, written to be performed, are characterized by vivid imagery, complex metrical patterns, and apparently shifting subjects actually united by emotional relationships. Some three-part odes, such as William Collins's *Ode on the Poetical Character*, employ a strophe, a mesode, and an antistrophe, and many English odes have only a strophe and an antistrophe. Each allows presentation of different moods, sides of questions, and interpretations, sometimes with a resolution.

In Latin literature the ode is identified with Horace, whose odes are contemplative, polished, and largely private. Although he wrote public odes in the Pindaric style, he came to be admired for employing simpler Alcaics and Sapphics and writing in disciplined stanzas with regular meters. Dignified, temperate, and musical in different ways from Pindaric odes, Horatian odes ranged from familiar to stately to urbane in tone. Like Horace, later poets wrote "greater" and "lesser" odes (determined by subject and style) and often composed both as dramatic monologues.

Abraham Cowley's *Pindarique Odes, Written in Imitation of the Stile & Manner of the Odes of Pindar* (1656) may have been the most important influence on the Restoration and eighteenth-century ode. It emphasized thematic discursiveness and personal revelation and freed the form from its elaborate, rigid structure. Cowley defined the distinguishing feature of the ode as consisting "more in *Digressions,* than in the main *subject.*" He also recognized that Pindar had written about his art and the poet, and he made that more prominent and appealing. Poets embraced this form, which Cowley described as now in "English habit,"[2] to the extent that Samuel Johnson complained that it "immediately overspread our books of poetry; all the boys and girls caught the pleasing fashion, and they that could do nothing else could write like Pindar."[3] As Margaret Doody wittily observed, it had given the Augustans a "formless form."[4]

In fact, Cowley's odes began a rich period of experimentation, one to which the best women poets contributed. Mary Chudleigh's *On the Vanities of this Life* explores the pleasures, temptations, and end of life, and Elizabeth Thomas employs the same form in *On the Death of the Lady Chudleigh,* which she styles as a fragment, a sign that words are inadequate for the occasion. The ode praises Chudleigh as a poet, a philosopher, and a Christian, a poet who "Could charm the Mind, exalt the Sense." As Thomas recounts the forms in which Chudleigh composed—pastorals, satire, love poems—she underscores them all by writing in the form most associated with women at this time. Cowley, who "a host of women poets in the period from roughly 1660–1730 found . . . a model, a stimulus, even a kindred spirit,"[5] similarly stands as a literary precursor for Mary Savage as she describes him in her tribute. She weaves Cowley's own words into her appraisal of his value to her and her female contemporaries. The intertextuality of these poems creates a kind of lyric palimpsest.

The two most familiar odes in this section are Anne Finch's *The Spleen* and Elizabeth Carter's *To Wisdom,* each deeply personal in its own way. Finch's powerful meditation on her own affliction, the spleen, remains a touchstone poem both for women writers of this period and as an incisive description of that state of mind.[6] Finch demonstrates that no class, sex, or person can be certain of immunity from the spleen. The questions of whom and how spleen strikes lead into a vivid description of its effect on her as a writer and wife and then to a reflective view of the human condition. The ode shows a deep understanding of the Pindaric form, and its elevation of a modest, personal subject into relationships with national and eternal themes was one of the aspirations of poets who wrote in the form.

Carter, arguably the most learned woman of the eighteenth century, celebrates wisdom as an "eternal Source / Of intellectual light!" This quality centrally informed her personal and professional life. *To Wisdom* was published during the second wave of great English odes, and along with the collections of odes by Collins, Mark Akenside, and Joseph Warton, it, her perfect Horatian "To ——" (2.c), and other odes became highly influential. Many later odes used personified abstractions as Carter's did, and allegories and amusing encounters, such as Harriet Falconar's in *On Ambition*, added a dimension to the ode's serious subjects. Odes from the latter part of the century, including Maria Falconar's *Ode to Freedom* and Jane West's *Independence*, are challenging poems that explore concepts increasingly perceived as under assault in a changing empire in which British citizens and indigenous peoples were at risk under "oppression's proud decree" *(Independence)*. In the same vein is Anne Bannerman's *Spirit of the Air*, which details the horrors of "Afric's bleeding shore" and imagines an avenging power that can put "the spoilers of their kind, / Inglorious, in untimely graves." The ode, which may be compared to Percy Bysshe Shelley's *Ode to the West Wind* (1820), illustrates women's contributions to revitalizing the form.

As a form the ode, suggests Ralph Cohen, is poetry that deals "with the association of ideas and feelings" but nevertheless possesses a "unity . . . includ[ing] innumerable connections among incidents and subjects."[7] That complexity, the range of connections, and sophisticated poetics distinguish this section's poems and amply demonstrate the heights to which these women took the form and why the ode was one of the dominant modes of the eighteenth century.

Notes

1. J. Paul Hunter, "Couplets and Conversation," in *The Cambridge Companion to Eighteenth-Century Poetry*, ed. John Sitter (Cambridge: Cambridge University Press, 2001), 24.

2. Abraham Cowley, preface to *Pindarique Odes* (London, 1656).

3. Samuel Johnson, "Cowley," in *The Lives of the English Poets*, ed. George Birkbeck Hill, 3 vols. (Oxford: Clarendon, 1905), 1:48.

4. Margaret Doody, quoted in Margaret M. Koehler, "The Ode," in *A Companion to Eighteenth-Century Poetry*, ed. Christine Gerrard (Oxford: Blackwell, 2006), 393. Koehler's essay is a brief history of the ode in the century.

5. Kathryn King, "Cowley among the Women: or, Poetry in the Contact Zone," in *Women and Literary History: "For There She Was,"* ed. Katherine Binhammer and Jeanne Wood (Newark: University of Delaware Press, 2003), 45.

6. By the early eighteenth century, *spleen* had become something of a catchall term

for a state of mind (most often moodiness, melancholy, lassitude, peevishness, depression, irritation, or some combination of these) with physical symptoms. See the discussion of this condition and Finch's poem in Paula R. Backscheider, *Eighteenth-Century Women Poets and Their Poetry* (Baltimore: Johns Hopkins University Press, 2005), 73–79.

7. Ralph Cohen, "The Return to the Ode," in Sitter, ed., *Cambridge Companion to Eighteenth-Century Poetry*, 206.

-+>->->->->•-<-<-<-<-<-

On the Vanities of this Life: A Pindarick Ode
Mary Chudleigh

1.

What makes fond[1] Man the trifle Life desire,
 And with such Ardor court his Pain?
'Tis Madness, worse than Madness, to admire
What brings Ten thousand Miseries in its Train:
To each soft moment, Hours of Care succeed,
 And for the Pleasures of a Day,
  With Years of Grief we pay;
So much our lasting Sorrows, our fleeting Joys exceed.
In vain, in vain, we Happiness pursue,
 That mighty Blessing is not here;   10
 That, like the false misguiding Fire,[2]
Is farthest off, when we believe it near:
 Yet still we follow till we tire,
 And in the fatal Chase Expire:
 Each gaudy nothing which we view,
 We fancy is the wish'd for Prize,
Its painted Glories captivate our Eyes;
Blinded by Pride, we hug our own Mistake,
And foolishly adore that Idol which we make.

2.

Some hope to find it on the Coasts of Fame,[3]   20
And hazard all to gain a glorious Name;
 Proud of Deformity and Scars,
They seek for Honour in the bloodiest Wars;
 On Dangers, unconcern'd, they run,
 And Death it self disdain to shun:
This, the Rich with Wonder see,
 And fancy they are happier far
 Than those deluded Heroes are:
But this, alas! is their Mistake;
 They only dream that they are blest,   30

1. Foolish, silly.

2. Like *ignis fatuus*, the phosphorescent light that hovers over swampy ground at night, therefore something that deludes.

3. Coasts of foreign lands; an allusion to the chivalric code, which called for knights to prove themselves on distant battlefields.

For when they from their pleasing Slumbers wake,
They'll find their Minds with Swarms of Cares opprest,
   So crouded, that no part is free
     To entertain Felicity:
   The Pain to get, and Fear to lose,
   Like Harpies,[4] all their Joys devour:
   Who such a wretched Life wou'd chuse?
Or think those happy who must Fortune trust?
That fickle Goddess[5] is but seldom just.
40   Exterior things can ne'er be truly good,
     Because within her Pow'r;
   This the wise Ancients understood,
And only wish'd for what wou'd Life sustain;
Esteeming all beyond superfluous and vain.

3.
   Some think the Great are only blest,
Those God-like Men who shine above the rest:
   In whom united Glories meet,
And all the lower World pay Homage at their Feet:
On their exalted Heights they sit in State,
50   And their Commands bind like the Laws of Fate:
Their Regal Scepters,[6] and their glitt'ring Crowns,
   Imprint an awful[7] Fear in ev'ry Breast:
Death shoots his killing Arrows thro' their Frowns;
Their Smiles are welcom, as the Beams of Light
Were to the infant World, when first it rose from Night.
Thus, in the Firmament[8] of Pow'r above,
   Each in his radiant Sphere does move,
     Remote from common View;
   Th' admiring Croud with Wonder gaze,
60   The distant Glories their weak Eyes amaze:
But cou'd they search into the Truth of Things,
Cou'd they but look into the Thoughts of Kings;

4. Monsters with a woman's face and body and a bird's wings and claws who act as ministers of divine vengeance.

5. Fortuna, who during this period was traditionally represented with a wheel (suggesting its unpredictable spin), holding a cornucopia and scattering coins.

6. Ornamental staffs, the mark of regal authority.

7. Awe-inspiring.

8. In the Ptolemaic astronomical system, the arch or vault of the sky, where the clouds and the stars appear.

If all their hidden Cares they knew,
Their Jealousies, their Fears, their Pain,
   And all the Troubles of their Reign,
They then wou'd pity those they now admire;
And with their humble State content, wou'd nothing more desire.

4.
If any thing like Happiness is here,
   If any thing deserves our Care,
      'Tis only by the Good possest;   70
      By those who Virtue's Laws obey,
And cheerfully proceed in her unerring Way;
Whose Souls are cleans'd from all the Dregs[9] of Sin,
From all the base Alloys[10] of their inferior Part,
And fit to harbour that Celestial Guest,
     Who ne'r will be confin'd
     But to a holy Breast.
     The pure and spotless Mind,
       Has all within
That the most boundless Wish can crave;   80
The most aspiring Temper hope to have:
     Nor needs the Helps of Art,
     Nor vain Supplies of Sense,
Assur'd of all in only Innocence.

5.
Malice and Envy, Discontent, and Pride,
Those fatal Inmates of the Vicious Mind,
Which into dang'rous Paths th' unthinking Guide,
Ne'er to the pious Breast admittance find.
As th' upper Region is Serene and clear,
   No Winds, no Clouds are there,   90
So with perpetual Calms the virtuous Soul is blest,
   Those Antepasts[11] of everlasting Rest:
Like some firm Rock amidst the raging Waves
She[12] stands, and their united Force outbraves;

---

9. Residue.

10. Mixtures of metals of varying values; the image suggests eliminating those base parts, or metals, that diminish the overall value.

11. Something taken before a meal to whet the appetite; in this case, a kind of preview.

12. Here and below, the pronoun refers to the virtuous soul.

Contends, till from her Earthly Shackles free,
    She takes her flight
   Into immense Eternity,
And in those Realms of unexhausted Light,
Forgets the Pressures of her former State.
100   O'er-joy'd to find her self beyond the reach of Fate.

6.

O happy Place! where ev'ry thing will please,
  Where neither Sickness, Fear, nor Strife,
Nor any of the painful Cares of Life,
    Will interrupt her Ease:
  Where ev'ry Object charms the Sight,
  And yields fresh Wonder and Delight,
  Where nothing's heard but Songs of Joy,
    Full of Extasie[13] Divine,
Seraphick[14] Hymns! which Love inspire,
110   And fill the Breast with sacred Fire:
    Love refin'd from drossy[15] Heat,
  Rais'd to a Flame sublime and great,
  In ev'ry Heav'nly Face do's shine,
  And each Celestial Tongue employ:
  What e'er we can of Friendship know,
  What e'er we Passion call below,
  Does but a weak Resemblance bear,
To that blest Union which is ever there,
Where Love, like Life, do's animate the whole,
120   As if it were but one blest individual Soul.

7.

Such as a lasting Happiness would have,
  Must seek it in the peaceful Grave,
Where free from Wrongs the Dead remain.
    Life is a long continu'd Pain,
      A lingring slow Disease.

---

13. The state of rapture in which the body was supposed to become incapable of sensation, while the soul was engaged in the contemplation of divine things.

14. Songs like those angels sing; the seraphs were one of the nine orders of angels and had three pairs of wings.

15. Impure.

Which Remedies a while may ease,
But cannot work a perfect Cure:
Musick with its inchanting Lays,[16]
May for a while our Spirits raise,
Honour and Wealth may charm the Sense,   130
And by their pow'rful Influence
May gently lull our Cares asleep;
But when we think our selves secure,
And fondly hope we shall no future Ills endure,
    Our Griefs awake again,
And with redoubl'd Rage augment our Pain:
    In vain we stand on our Defence,
    In vain a constant Watch we keep,
        In vain each Path we guard;
    Unseen into our Souls they creep,   140
And when they once are there, 'tis very hard
    With all our Strength to force them thence;
Like bold Intruders on the whole they seize,
A Part will not th' insatiate[17] Victors please.

8.
        In vain, alas! in vain,
        We Reason's Aid implore,
That will but add a quicker Sense of Pain,
    But not our former Joys restore:
Those few who by strict Rules their Lives have led,
Who Reason's Laws attentively have read;   150
Who to its Dictates glad Submission pay,
And by their Passions never led astray,
Go resolutely on in its severest Way,
Could never solid Satisfaction find:
The most that Reason can, is to persuade the Mind,
    Its Troubles decently to bear,
And not permit a Murmur, or a Tear,
To tell th' inquiring World that any such are there:
But while we strive our Suff'rings to disown,
And blush to have our Frailties known;   160
While from the publick View our Griefs we hide,

16. Songs.
17. Insatiable.

And keep them Pris'ners in our Breast,
We seem to be, but are not truly blest;
What like Contentment looks, is but th' Effect of Pride:
    From it we no advantage win,
    But are the same we were before,
The smarting Pains corrode us still within;
Confinement do's but make them rage the more:
    Upon the vital Stock[18] they prey,
170   And by insensible degrees they wast our Life away.

9.
In vain from Books we hope to gain Relief,
    Knowledge does but increase our Grief:
    The more we read, the more we find
Of th' unexhausted Store still left behind:
    To dig the wealthy Mine we try,
        No Pain, no Labour spare;
But the lov'd Treasure too profound does lie,
    And mocks our utmost Industry:
Like some inchanted Isle it does appear;
180   The pleas'd Spectator thinks it near;
But when with wide spread Sails he makes to shore,
His Hopes are lost, the Phantom's seen no more:
Asham'd, and tir'd, we of Success despair,
    Our fruitless Studies we repent,
And blush to see, that after all our Care,
After whole Years on tedious Volumes spent,
    We only darkly understand
    That which we thought we fully knew;
Thro' Labyrinths we go without a Clue,
190   Till in the dang'rous Maze our selves we lose,
And neither know which Path t'avoid, or which to chuse.
From Thought to Thought, our restless Minds are tost,
Like Ship-wreck'd Mariners we seek the Land,
And in a Sea of Doubts are almost lost.
The *Phœnix* Truth[19] wrapt up in Mists does lie,

---

18. Source of line of descent.

19. The mythical bird that rises from the ashes of its own funeral pyre with renewed youth. Abraham Cowley (1618–67) used the same phrase (subsequently quoted by Samuel Johnson in his treatment of Cowley in *The Lives of the English Poets*, ed. George Birkbeck Hill, 3 vols. [Oxford: Clarendon, 1905]) in *The Tree of Knowledge* (1656).

Not to be clearly seen before we die;
Not till our Souls free from confining Clay,
Open their Eyes in everlasting Day.

(1703)

The Spleen: A Pindarique Ode, &c.
Anne Finch

What art thou, *Spleen*,[20] which every thing dost ape?[21]
   Thou *Proteus*[22] to abuse Mankind,
     Who never yet thy hidden Cause cou'd find;
Or fix thee to remain in one continu'd Shape;
    Still varying thy perplexing Form,
    Now a dead Sea thoul't represent
      A Calm of stupid Discontent,
The dashing on the Rocks wilt rage into a Storm:
Trembling sometimes thou dost appear,
    Dissolv'd into a panick Fear.   10
On Sleep intruding do'st thy Shadows spread,
    Thy gloomy Terrors round the silent Bed,
And crowd with boding Dreams the melancholy Head.
Or when the mid-night Hour is told,
And drooping Lids thou still do'st waking hold,
    Thy fond Delusions cheat the Eyes;
    Before 'em antick Spectres dance,
Unusual Fires their pointed Heads advance,
    And aiery Phantoms rise.[23]
    Such was the monstrous Vision seen,   20
When *Brutus* (now beneath his Cares opprest,
And all *Rome's* Fortunes rolling in his Breast,
    Before *Philippi's* latest Field

---

20. A complicated term originating in the ancient theory of humors of the body, *spleen* by this time had become a general term for a psychological state (melancholy, depression, moodiness) with physical symptoms.

21. Imitate.

22. A Greek sea god able to change shape at will. George Cheyne describes spleen as a "Proteus-like Distemper." *The English Malady* (London, 1733), 196.

23. Among the symptoms associated with spleen were "Night Sweats, a fix'd *Melancholy, Terror,* and *Dread,* a violent *Headach,* and a want of Natural Sleep." Cheyne, *English Malady,* 279.

Before his Fate did to *Octavius* yield)[24]
  Was vanquish'd by the *Spleen*.

II.

  Falsly the mortal part[25] we blame
  Of our depress'd and pond'rous Frame,
  Which till the first degrading Sin
  Let thee its dull attendant, in;[26]
30   Still with the other did comply;
Nor clogg'd the active Soul, dispos'd to fly,
And range the Mansions of its native Sky:
  Nor whilst in his own Heaven he dwelt,
  Whilst Man his Paradise possest,
  His fertile Garden in the fragrant East,
    And all united Odours smelt.
  No pointed Sweets[27] until thy Reign
  Cou'd shock the Sense, or in the face
  A Flush, Unhandsome Colour place:
40 Now the *Jonquil*[28] o'recomes the feeble Brain,
  We faint beneath the Aromatick pain,
  Till some offensive scent thy Powers appease,
And Pleasure we resign for short and nauseous Ease.

III.

  New are thy Motions and thy Dress,
  In every one thou dost possess:
  Here some attentive secret Friend
Thy false Suggestions must attend,
Thy whisper'd Griefs, thy fancy'd Sorrows hear,
Breath'd in a Sigh, and witness'd by a Tear:
50   Whilst in the light and vulgar Crowd
  Thy Slaves more clamorous and loud,
By laughter unprovok'd thy Influence too confess.
  In the imperious *Wife* thou Vapours art,

---

24. In William Shakespeare's *Julius Caesar* (4.3) Brutus, prior to meeting Octavius at the battle of Philippi, the final battle in the Wars of the Second Triumvirate, sees the ghost of Caesar in the flicker of a candle as he lies awake on the eve of battle.
25. The physical human body.
26. Finch figures spleen as a postlapsarian concept.
27. Piercing or pungently sweet fragrance.
28. The narcissus, a spring-flowering bulbous plant.

Which from o'er-heated Passions rise
In clouds to the attractive Brain,
Until descending thence again
Thro' the o'er-cast and showring Eyes,
    Upon the Husband's softned Heart,
He the disputed Point must yield,
Something resign of the contested Field;   60
'Till Lordly Man, born to Imperial Sway,
Compounds for Peace, to make his Right away
And Woman arm'd with *Spleen* do's servilely obey.

IV.

The Fool, to imitate the Wits,
    Complains of thy pretended Fits;[29]
And Dulness, born with him would lay
    Upon thy accidental Sway;
Because thou do'st sometimes presume
    Into the ablest Heads to come,
That often Men of Thoughts refin'd,   70
    Impatient of unequal Sense,
Such slow returns, where they so much dispense,
Retiring from the Crowd, are to thy Shades confin'd,
In me alas! thou dost too much prevail,
I feel thy force, while I against thee rail?
I feel my Verse decay, and my crampt Numbers fail.
Through thy black Jaundies[30] I all Objects see,
    As dark and terrible as thee;
My Lines decry'd, and my Imployment thought
An useless Folly, or presumptuous Fault;   80
    While in the Muses Paths I stray,
While in their Groves, and by their Springs,
My Hand delights to trace unusual things,
And deviates from the known and common way:
    Nor will in fading Silks compose,
    Faintly th' inimitable Rose:
Fill up an ill drawn Bird, or paint on Glass[31]

29. Spleen was increasingly associated with literary composition and writing and with extreme sensibility or melancholy genius.

30. Jaundice, the disordered, or "black," vision caused by the spleen.

31. Rather than to embroidery, sketching, or china-painting, Finch turns her creative energy to poetry and the Muses.

The Sovereigns blur'd and undistinguish'd Face,
The threatning Angel, and the speaking Ass.[32]

V.

90   Patron thou art of every gross abuse,
        The sullen *Husband's* feign'd excuse,
        When the ill humour with his Wife he spends,
And bears recruited Wit and Spirits to his Friends.
        The Son of *Bacchus*[33] pleads thy Power,
        As to the Glass he still[34] repairs,
        Pretends but to remove thy Cares;
Snatcht from thy Shades one gay and smiling hour,
And drown thy Kingdom with a Purple Show'r.[35]
        When the Coquet[36] whom every Fool admires,
100   Wou'd in variety be fair,
        And shifting hastily the Scene,
        From light impertinent and vain,
        Assumes a soft and melancholy Air,
        And of her Eyes rebates the wand'ring Fires,
        The careless Posture, and the Head reclin'd;
        The thoughtful and composed Face
        Proclaiming the withdrawn and absent Mind,
            Allows the Fop[37] more liberty to gaze;
        Who gently for the tender Cause enquires:
110   The Cause indeed is a defect in Sense;
But still the *Spleen's* alledg'd, and still the dull Pretence.

VI.

        But these are thy fantastick[38] Harms,
        The tricks of thy pernicious Rage,
        Which do the weaker sort engage;
Worse are the dire effects of thy more powerful Charms.
        By thee Religion all we know

---

32. In Numbers 22:21–35, three times Balaam's ass sees the angel standing in their path, and three times the ass moves away from the angel, only to be beaten by Balaam. After the third beating, the ass speaks to Balaam.

33. A tippler; someone who drinks. Bacchus is the Roman god of wine.

34. Continues to.

35. Shower of wine.

36. Flirt.

37. A pretender to wit who is foolishly attentive to his appearance and affected in his manner.

38. Beyond expectation and description, various, arbitrary.

That should enlighten here below,
   Is veil'd in darkness, and perplext
With anxious Doubts, with endless Scruples vext,
And some restraint imply'd from each perverted Text.   120
   Whilst tast not, touch not what is freely given,
Is but the Niggard's[39] Voice, disgracing bounteous Heaven.
   From Speech restrain'd, by thy deceits abus'd,
     To Desarts banish'd, and in Cells reclus'd;
     Mistaken Votaries to the Powers Divine,
     While they a purer Sacrifice design
Do but the *Spleen* adore, and worship at thy Shrine.

VII.

   In vain to chase thee,[40] every Art we try;
     In vain all Remedies apply;
     In vain the *Indian* Leaf[41] infuse,   130
     Or the pearch'd Eastern Berry[42] bruise;
Some pass in vain those bounds, and nobler Liquors use.
   Now Harmony in vain we bring,
     Inspire the Flute, and touch the String;
     From Harmony no help is had:
Musick but sooths thee, if too sweetly sad;
And if too light, but turns thee gladly mad.
     Not skilful *Lower*[43] thy Source cou'd find,
     Or through the well-dissected Body trace
     The secret and mysterious ways,   140
By which thou dost destroy and prey upon the Mind;
   Tho' in the Search, too deep for Humane Thought,
     With unsuccessful Toil he wrought,
    'Till in pursuit of thee himself was by thee caught;
   Retain'd thy Prisoner, thy acknowledg'd Slave,
And sunk beneath thy Weight to a lamented Grave.

(1709)

---

39. Miser's.
40. To get rid of thee.
41. Tea.
42. Roasted coffee beans.
43. Richard Lower (1631–91), a distinguished physician and member of the Royal Society, was a leading expert on the spleen. Finch and her contemporaries would have known that he had succumbed to melancholy and ultimately committed suicide.

On the Death of the Lady Chudleigh. An Ode
Elizabeth Thomas

As on my *Bed,* in Dead of Night,
　With anxious *Thoughts* distrest,
I restless lay, and wish'd for Light,
But *sigh,* and *turn,* in vain I might,
　Alas, I found no Rest!
An *Icy* Chilness shudder'd thro' each Vein, ⎫
And past, and present Ills, a num'rous Train, ⎬
With all their *dark Idea's* revell'd in my *Brain.* ⎭
　　At length the ruddy *Morn* appear'd,
10　　Diffusive *Beams* my Spirits chear'd;
And I no more with racking *Thoughts* opprest,
Grew gently calm, and sunk to pleasing Rest.

II.
　　When Lo!
Indulgent *Sleep* before me brought
The much lov'd Object of my waking *Thought;*
　A *Moses* Brightness[44] o'er her *Face* did shine,
　And ev'ry Feature spoke a *Joy divine:*
Serene her *Look,* and *heav'nly* was her *Air,*
More *tall* than *Life* she seem'd, and more than *Mortal fair.*
20　　I'm come, she cried, to bid a *long Adieu!*
　　And had a Mind to let you know,
　　　I must a *wond'rous Journey* go,
　And could not part without another View:
　　Excuse me, *Friend,* I can no longer stay,
I must prepare——*To morrow is the Day.*
　Struck with Surprize! and ravish'd with the Grace! ⎫
I sought to hold her in a dear Embrace, ⎬
But light as *Air,* she vanish'd from the Place. ⎭
　　Waking, I cried! *unhappy Maid,*
30　　　With Tears thy Loss deplore!
Marissa's[45] venerable Shade[46]

---

44. When Moses returned from meeting God on Mt. Sinai with the second set of stone tablets, his face shone so brightly with a reflection of God's "glory" that he had to veil it. Exod. 34:29–30; 2 Cor. 3:12–13.

45. Mary Chudleigh's; the poem is about her.

46. Ghost.

Has now its last kind Office paid,
 And dwells on Earth no more.
Too sure, alas, the *Vision* does foretel!
Ah me! I hear it now confirm'd——*Illustrious Friend farewel.*

III.

Ill fated *Wretch!* oh whither wilt thou fly! ⎫
 To shun impending Destiny?   ⎬
Where wilt thou *centre next?* on what new *Friend* rely? ⎭
 Once did I think, *O foolish and prophane!*
 A solid Good on Earth to find;   40
And *Friendship!* sacred *Friendship* was my Aim!
 Joy of my *Heart,* and *Blessing* of my *Mind.*
 Beyond Desert I soon was blest,
 And great *Sulpitia*[47] warm'd my *Breast:*
 Her sweet *Address,* the *Muse* inspir'd, ⎫
 Her *pious Life* by all admir'd,   ⎬
My *Heart* with constant *Emulation* fir'd. ⎭
 Bright *Musidora!*[48] Soul of *Harmony,*
 What grateful *Songs* are due to thee,
 Who gen'rously didst condescend,   50
 To be both *Patroness* and *Friend?*
Divine *Marissa!* last in *Time,* not *Place,*
 But first in ev'ry God-like *Grace.*
 With kind *Affection* did me bless, ⎫
 Ah *Gracious Heav'n!* what Happiness ⎬
 Did I in *Three* such *Friends*[49] possess! ⎭
 Proud of my *Joys,* I grew secure,
  Nor fear'd a Turn of *Fate;*
 For oh! what could I not endure,
  When by *Experience* I was sure,   60
  My *Friends* would ease the Weight?
Such *Love,* such *Tenderness,* in each was shewn,
As ev'ry *Joy,* or *Grief* of mine, pertain'd to them alone.

---

47. Sulpitia, a Roman poet, was the poetic name given to Anne, Lady Dowager De La Warr, whose daughter-in-law paid for Thomas's funeral.

48. Musidora, Greek for "gift of the muses," is Mrs. Diana Bridgeman. Richard Gwinnett, *Pylades and Corinna: or, Memoirs of the Lives, Amours, and Writings of Richard Gwinnett Esq; . . . and Mrs. Elizabeth Thomas,* 2 vols. (London, 1731–32), 2:75.

49. Chudleigh, De La Warr, and Bridgeman.

IV.

Ah *Bliss!* too great to last,
    An Age of Wo,
    I undergo
For happy *Minutes* past.
Pious *Sulpitia* yielded up her *Breath,*
And charming *Musidora* snatch'd by *Death,*
70   My *Sorrows* knew no Bounds:
Ev'n yet they live within my *Heart,*
Nor Length of Years can cure the Smart,
    Or heal the fatal Wounds.
But good *Marissa* still remain'd,
    And with an *Eloquence* divine,
My *Loss* condol'd, my *Grief* restrain'd,
    And taught me to *resign.*
Blest with her *Love,* I could not wretched be,
Nor while she *liv'd,* feel perfect *Misery.*
80   But now——
    In vain I *sigh!* in vain I *mourn!*
        And my sad *State* deplore;
        Marissa from her Marble *Urn,*
            Can ne'er to *Life* return,
            Never! never more!
        My list'ning *Ear,*
    No more her *pious Words* must hear,
No more her Form shall bless my longing *Eyes,*
In *Death's* cold Arms, alas, *Marissa* lies!
90   Here, rest my *Muse*—Yet 'ere thy *Labours* cease,
        In grateful Lays,
        Resound her Praise;
Then consecrate thy *Harp* to everlasting Peace.
    With *mortal Friendships* grieve no more thy Mind,
Henceforth *celestial be thy Joys,* thy *future Love refin'd.*

V.

    And fond deluded *Maid!*
No more address the *fictious Nine*[50] for Aid;
    Or invocate *Apollo's* Shrine,[51]

---

50. The Muses.

51. The Greek god Apollo was patron of music and poetry. The shrine of Apollo is located on the side of Mount Parnassus, a location regarded as the source of literary, especially poetic, inspiration and home to the Muses.

For Influence Divine:
A better *Genii*[52] shall thy *Notes* inspire,
   Her *matchless Virtues!* her *immortal Lyre!*[53]
Alone, shall animate thy *Pen*, shall crown thy just *Desire.*

   Unpolish'd *Verse* bewail'd this Turn of *Fate*,
   Unpolish'd *Truth* shall now her Worth relate,
     Nor need there *Art* or *Eloquence*
     To raise *Belief,* and charm the *Sense:*
Her *deathless Works,* and *sacred Memory,*
   All borrow'd *Helps* defy,
Secure, within themselves, of *Immortality.*
Succeeding *Ages,* and impartial *Fame,*
   Shall celebrate *Marissa's* Name!
And her the *Tenth,* and *latest Muse* proclaim.

VI.

   Whether in soft *Idalian*[54] Strains,
   She deign'd to sing of *Flocks* and *Plains,*
     Of *Hills* and *Groves,*
     And rural *Loves,*
   Of beauteous *Nymphs* and *Swains.*
   Or in swift trilling *Lyricks*[55] wrote,
   Or to keen *Satyr*[56] turn'd her Thought,
   And by a sharp, tho' pleasing Wound,
The secret Springs of *Vice* and *Irreligion* found.
   Such *Graces* did in each appear,
     Such *Strength* in ev'ry Line;
Horace[57] himself must yield to her,
   And old *Theocritus*[58] prefer
   Her Justness of Design.
(Rich in superior *Excellence,*
Her *chaster Muse* by nobler Ways,

100

110

120

52. Genius or spirit.
53. Stringed instrument like a harp, now a symbol of lyric poetry.
54. Belonging to the ancient town of Idalium in Cyprus, where Aphrodite was worshipped.
55. Lyric poetry.
56. Satire.
57. Roman poet (65–8 BC) known for his satiric and lyrical poetry, particularly odes, as well as for *Ars Poetica,* a verse epistle to the Pisos, a father and two sons, in which he gives influential critical opinions.
58. Greek bucolic poet (308–240 BC) who established the formal characteristics of the pastoral. In 1684 Thomas Creech published his works in an English translation. In this passage, Thomas is identifying the various kinds of poetry Chudleigh produced.

Could charm the *Mind,* exalt the *Sense,*
130   And bright *Idea's* raise.)
True to their *Worth,* impartial to their *Crimes,*
    She good did chuse,
    And bad refuse,
A *bright Example* to succeeding Times.
    So the *judicious Bee,*
Tastes ev'ry *Flow'r,* and ev'ry *Tree,*
And bitter Turns to sweet, by native *Chymistry,* }

    The Remainder lost.[59]

(1722)

To Wisdom. A nocturnal Ode[60]

Elizabeth Carter

The solitary bird of night
Thro' the pale shades now wings his flight,
    And quits the time shook tow'r,
Where shelter'd from the blaze of day
In philosophic gloom he lay
    Beneath his ivy bow'r.

With joy, I hear the solemn sound,
Which midnight echoes waft around,
    And sighing gales repeat;
10 Fav'rite of *Pallas!*[61] I attend,
And, faithful to thy summons, bend
    At Wisdom's awful[62] seat.

59. With this line Thomas marks her poem as a poetic fragment, a popular convention.

60. After reading this poem in manuscript, Samuel Richardson originally published it in *Clarissa* (letter 54) in 1747 without Carter's permission. She gave it to the *Gentleman's Magazine* in corrected form, and it was published with the following note: "We have had the following beautiful ODE above a year, under an injunction, which was general on all the copies given out, not to print it; but as it has appeared in *Clarissa* with several faults, we think ourselves at liberty to give our readers so agreeable an entertainment, from a correcter copy." Richardson's piracy caused Carter some distress, which was alleviated by the authorized publication of the corrected poem and by a public apology from Richardson and a private reconciliation with her.

61. Pallas Athena, goddess of wisdom and knowledge and the daughter of Zeus, was usually attended by an owl.

62. Awe-inspiring.

She loves the cool, the silent eve,
Where no false shows of life deceive,
   Beneath the lunar ray.
Here *Folly* quits each vain disguise,
Nor sport her gayly-colour'd dyes,
   As in the beam of day.

O *Pallas!* queen of ev'ry art
'That glads the sense, or mends the heart,   20
   Blest source of purer joys,
In ev'ry form of beauty, bright,
That captivates the mental sight
   With pleasure, and surprise,

To thy unspotted shrine I bow,
Attend thy modest suppliant's vow
   That breathes no wild desires,
But taught by thy unerring rules
To shun the fruitless wish of fools,
   To nobler views aspires!   30

Not Fortune's gem, Ambition's plume,
Nor *Cytherea's*[63] short liv'd bloom,
   Be objects of my pray'r,
Let Av'rice, Vanity, and Pride
These glitt'ring envy'd toys divide
   The dull rewards of Care.

To me thy better gifts impart,
Each moral beauty of the heart,
   By studious thought refin'd;
For wealth, the smiles of glad content,   40
For pow'r, its amplest best extent,
   An empire o'er my mind.

When Fortune drops her gay parade,
When Pleasure's transient roses fade,
   And wither on the tomb,
Unchang'd is thy immortal prize,

63. Aphrodite, the Greek goddess of love, renowned for her beauty.

Thy ever verdant lawrels[64] rise
    In undecaying bloom.

By thee protected I defy
50   The Coxcomb's[65] sneer, the stupid lye
        Of Ignorance and Spite,
    Alike contemn the leaden Fool,
    And all the pointed ridicule
        Of undiscerning Wit.

From envy, hurry, noise and strife,
    The dull impertinence of life,
        In thy retreat I rest,
    Persue thee to the peaceful groves,
    Where *Plato*'s[66] sacred spirit roves
60   In all thy beauties drest.

He bade *Ilyssus* tuneful stream[67]
    Convey thy philosophic theme
        Of PERFECT, FAIR, and GOOD.
    Attentive *Athens* caught the sound,
    And all her list'ning sons around
        In awful silence stood.

Reclaim'd, her wild licentious youth
    Confest the potent voice of truth,
        And felt its just controul;
70   The passions ceas'd their loud alarms,
    And *Virtue's* soft persuasive charms,
        O'er all their senses stole.

Thy breath inspires the Poet's song,
    The Patriot's free unbias'd tongue,
        The Hero's gen'rous strife.
    Thine are Retirement's silent joys,

---

64. The laurel wreath is a mark of poetic distinction.
65. A fop or fool.
66. Plato (c. 429–c. 347 BC) was a philosopher who, along with Socrates and Aristotle, belonged to the great trio of ancient Greeks who laid the philosophical foundations of Western culture.
67. River flowing south of Athens where Plato's *Phaedrus* is set.

And all the sweet, engaging tyes
   Of still, domestic life.

No more to fabled names confin'd,
To THEE! supreme, all perfect Mind,   80
   My thoughts direct their flight.
Wisdom's thy gift, and all her force
From thee deriv'd, eternal Source
   Of intellectual light!

O send her sure, her steady ray
To regulate my doubtful way
   Thro' life's perplexing road,
The mists of Error to controul,
And thro' its gloom direct my soul
   To happiness and good.   90

Beneath her clear discerning eye,
The visionary shadows fly
   Of *Folly's* painted show,
She sees thro' ev'ry fair disguise,
That all but *Virtue's* solid joys
   Is vanity, and woe.

(1747)

The following Consolatary[68] ODE was the first Poetical Composition of the AUTHOR's

Priscilla Poynton

Should'st thou, my Reader, lend a pitying sigh,
Ne'er ask for whom thy bosom heaves so high;
Though great my loss, just Heaven decreed it so,
Nor sighs, nor tears, can mitigate my woe.

Full twice six shining summers pass'd away,[69]
The dread thirteenth, in darkness wrapp'd my day;

68. Comforting.
69. Poynton became blind at the age of twelve.

When on a rapid wing my dear sight fled,
And left me here, with drooping, mournful head;
In dolorous pain,[70] who can forbear to say,
10   How dull the hours! how slow they move away!
My ripening joys, by stern misfortune cross'd,
All blasted seem'd, and I to pleasure lost;
For with my sight each pleasing object flew;
Grant joys, kind Heav'n! more lasting and more true;
Grant that my sufferings, blessings may become,
And fix my care upon a heavenly home.
Let but my soul in those bright mansions shine,
I'll bless the day which made misfortune mine;
With choir angelic there my voice I'll raise,
20   In hallelujahs to my Maker's praise;
Rivers of pleasure there will round me flow,
And bliss too great for mortals here to know.
Oh! should my sight no more return again,
Be still my heart, nor of thy fate complain;
For resignation best can sooth our woe,
However dire appears the fatal blow.
Then let me not at earthly loss repine, ⎫
Since he decreed it, who is all divine,   ⎬
But chearful to his will myself resign.   ⎭

(1770)

Ode to the Manes[71] of Cowley
Mary Savage

To Mr. R——d C——k,[72] on his purchasing the house at
CHERTSEY,[73] where COWLEY died.

Oh! come sweet muse, with me retire,
To where thy COWLEY did expire;
   To the grove, and to the field,
   Which to him did pleasure yield;
   Where he pass'd his latter days,

---

70. The Author's loss of sight was occasioned by a violent head-ach. *Poynton.*
71. Spirit or ghost of a dead person, considered an object of homage or reverence.
72. Richard Clark, Esq., chamberlain of London, who purchased Porch House, Cowley's final home.
73. Town in Surrey on the River Thames.

Shunning courts, and shunning praise,
Thither come and touch thy lyre,
And to me, thy humble slave, inspire
With purest thoughts, sublime, refin'd,
Such as possess'd his favour'd mind.   10

II.

There beg his aid, sweet muse,
The raptures faithful love can bring;
Request again, he'll tell thee true,
What pangs ill fated love persue;
He'll name the shaft that wounds each heart,
With thrilling, joy, or poignant smart:[74]
For sure he knew—he could not feign,
All love's pleasure—all love's pain;
"That panting, trembling, sighing, dying,"[75]
That jealous anguish hope denying,   20
Which a lover's breast must feel,
Disclose with fear, with pain conceal;
He can teach thee how to dress,
All that fancy would express;
Riding triumphant on love's flutt'ring wing,
He view'd each heart, and mov'd each secret string.

III.

Or passing o'er the fire of youth,
Wou'd thy soul seek for sacred truth,
Intreat him to impart the lay,
Prophetic of that heav'nly ray,   30
Which inspir'd him when he sung,
Of David, Jesse's much lov'd son;[76]
Of his valour, rais'd to fame,

74. Sharp pain.

75. This unattributed line appeared in a longer poetic passage on the final page of *Spectator* 208 (29 October 1711).

76. A reference to *Davideis*, Cowley's four-book, unfinished epic based on the life of the young David before he became king of Judah, which explores the friendship between David and Jonathan, the eldest son of Saul. The intense relationship between David and Jonathan, detailed in the books of Samuel, is captured by David's well-known words to Jonathan, "Very pleasant hast thou been unto me: / Thy love to me was wonderful, / Passing the love of women." 2 Sam. 1:26. *Davideis* is unfinished because its opinions about monarchy, including a comparison of the establishment of the Jewish monarchy to the fall of Adam and Eve, were politically dangerous.

By the proud Goliath's shame;[77]
Of that friendship, far above
"All that e'er was called love"[78]
Which join'd, in sacred bands, his honest heart
With Jonathan's, its faithful counter-part.

IV.

Perhaps too much I did thee ask,
40   If so——decline the arduous task;
Living, to thee, he well might spare,
Of genius, a sufficient share;
For half that he possest, would spread thy fame,
To praise give birth, and gain an endless name:
Yet sure with gentle smile, he'll deign to hear,
And lend one pious sigh to waft my pray'r,
That, tho' unblest with his poetic fire,
My heart, like his, to virtue may aspire,
That peace and competence may be my lot,
50   By fame unmar'd—but not by friends forgot,
"For ne'er ambition did my fancy cheat,
With any wish so mean as to be great;"[79]
That chearful ease, to act the allotted part,
May lift to Heaven, with thanks a grateful heart,
And give a seeming length to life's short line,
Passing unmark'd, the trace of its decline;
"Pleas'd with the present hour, and thoughtful for the past,
Neither to fear, or wish, th' approaches of the last."[80]

(1777)

---

77. The story of David's slaying Goliath, the Philistine giant, is recounted in 1 Sam. 17. When the Philistines came to make war against Saul, David was the only Israelite to answer Goliath's challenge for individual combat. Armed with nothing but a sling and pebbles, he killed Goliath, causing the Philistines to flee. David first met Jonathan after slaying Goliath.

78. Cowley's *Septimnius and Acme,* a translation of Catullus's *Ode XLV,* line 8.

79. This quotation from Cowley's essay "Of Greatness" was widely quoted throughout the eighteenth century, appearing, for example, as the final statement in Steele's *Spectator* 114 (11 July 1711).

80. This is an excerpt of lines 28–31 from Cowley's translation of Martial, Marcus Valerius Martialis (40?–104?), bk. 10, epigram 42. The complete lines read, "Be satisfi'd, and pleas'd with what thou art, / Act chearfully and well th' allotted part; / Enjoy the present Hour, be thankful for the Past, / And neither fear, nor wish, th' approaches of the last." Abraham Cowley, *The Works of Abraham Cowley,* ed. Thomas Sprat (London, 1668), 147.

Ode to the Moon
Ann Murry

To thee, fair regent of the Night,
   I dedicate my lays;
Thy silver beams, reflected light,
   Excite our love and praise!

Sequester'd from the beams of Day,
   The midnight awful scene
Converts the mind, by nature gay,
   To prospects more serene.

Above each vain terrestrial art
   Of Life's perplexing care,   10
Thy genuine graces strike the heart,
   Free from delusive glare.

This useful lesson they instil,
   That modest Virtues shine;
Like thee the constant course fulfil,
   With majesty divine.

(1779)

On Ambition
Harriet Falconar

The feeble glimmering of the setting sun
   Threw o'er the Western sky a partial light,
When, ere the sable reign of night began,
   A form celestial stood before my sight;
And thus she spoke, Ambition is my name,
I bring a message from the courts of fame.

   This said, she pointed to a glittering spire,
      That, elevated, rose in air, sublime;
   To this (she said) direct thy fond desire,
      This pile of glory scorns the hand of time;   10

For, there the trumpet of triumphant fame
Shall to the world thy glorious deeds proclaim.

Mistaken mortal, leave this humble vale,
　　Forsake these bow'rs of indolence and ease,
For those, whose sweetness scents th' ambrosial gale,
　　Where fancy forms ten thousand scenes to please;
Then mount my car,[81] (th' exulting goddess cries,)
With me explore the regions of the skies!

The pleasing accents charm'd my list'ning ear,
　　My raptur'd eyes the blissful scenes survey;
I listen'd; for, 'twas harmony to hear,
　　Nor knew the perils of the dang'rous way.
Scarce had she spoke, when, from the op'ning sky,
A brighter nymph salutes my wandering eye.

At her sublime approach, the fair disguise,
　　That flutt'ring, fond, Ambition long had wore,
Fell from her form; away th' enchantress flies;
　　And, in an instant, was beheld no more:
Astonishment and terror fill'd my breast,
When thus my better guide these words addrest.

My name is Virtue, and the child of heav'n,
　　I came to save thee from Ambition's snare,
To teach poor, erring, mortals I was giv'n
　　To guide their steps with diligence and care.
This said, the radiant goddess took her flight,
Her beauties vanish'd in the shades of night.

(1788)

---

81. Chariot.

Ode to Freedom
Maria Falconar

Tell me what bold, what enterprising, hand
   For thee, O nymph, shall wake the golden lyre;[82]
Hail, guardian genius of Britannia's land!
   Spirit of Milton, thou my verse inspire![83]

Ah! what avails the wealth that India yields,
   Where summer suns perpetual warmth bestow?
Her mines of glitt'ring gems and spicy fields,
   While her sad sons expire in servile woe!

For thee, sweet nymph, the tenants of the grove
   Endure the perils of the wintry sky;   10
O'er the bleak hills, they, solitary, rove,
   They live for Freedom, and with Freedom die.

                            (1788)

Independence. Ode III
Jane West

I.

   Sweet Muse, to whose protecting shrine,
      Driv'n by the spectre Care, I flee,
   When oft, at busy days decline,
      I sigh for leisure and for thee;
   Say, in earth's habitable round,
   Can perfect happiness be found,
      Proportion'd to the craving soul?
   If still beneath the solar road
   Bright Independence makes abode,
Her's is this perfect bliss, this joy without controul.   10

82. Stringed instrument like a harp, now a symbol of lyric poetry.

83. John Milton (1608–74) wrote powerful political poems, including the sonnet *On the late massacre in Piemont*, which Falconar may have in mind. Although most modern anthologies change the place name to *Piedmont*, it is *Piemont* in the 1673 unique printing in Milton's lifetime, and standard editions preserve the original spelling.

II.

Nymph, 'tis thy animating voice
   That wakes the springs of latent worth;
In thee the savage tribes rejoice;
   The polish'd nations of the earth
Caught, at thy shrine, the sacred flame,
Which led to liberty and fame
   The Grecian and the Roman arms,
When Kings, with unenlighten'd pride,
The native rights of man defied,
20   When rapine[84] stalk'd on earth, and fill'd it with alarms.

III.

Who on the labours of the Muse
   Impassion'd energy bestows?
Whose inspiration can diffuse
   The warmth with which the patriot glows?
Oh, thou; the theme of many a bard,
By sages woo'd with fond regard,
   In every vein a good supreme!
Without thee, weak is Virtue's arm;
Feeble is Wisdom's hope to charm;
30   Nor yet must timid Truth display her radiant beam.

IV.

Thy favour'd vot'ries do not fear
   The scorns which wealth will oft bestow;
Nor need they hide th' indignant tear,
   Stern obligation forc'd to flow.
Degrading flattery does not soil
The lip o'er which thy chearful smile
   Diffuses a becoming pride.
Nor will their hearts pretend to feel
The hurry of officious zeal,
40   Nor the cold civil wish, that hopes to be denied.

V.

These still with manly ease avow
   The genuine impulse of the soul;

---

84. Robbery or plunder.

To Nature's shrine alone they bow,
  Obedient but to her controul.
Fastidious tastes, capricious laws,
The cant of censure and applause,
  Claim'd by the fashion of the day,
Their minds with noble freedom spurn;
For merit, and for truth they burn,
And in their search employ unclouded Reason's ray.   50

VI.
  Such are the characters, who prove
    To what our nature can aspire,
  Who feel the dignity of love,
    And friendship's never failing fire,
  Who in each state, to duty just,
  Perform the delegated trust,
    Guided by honour's radiant star.
  Regardless tho' the vulgar blame;
  Proof to the dangerous charms of fame,
Their hopes and fears revère a doom more awful far.   60

VII.
  O Goddess of the brave and wise!
    Where'er thy radiant seat is plac'd
  Beneath mild Britain's temper'd skies,
    Or in the cold Sarmatian waste,[85]
  There still, as in their native air,
  The nobler virtues flourish fair.
    Firm constancy, unwearied zeal,
  Courage that spurns degrading fear,
  Faith unprofessing, yet sincere;
All that can greatly act, all that can finely feel.   70

VIII.
  Bright object of my ardent prayer!
    When will thy soul-enliv'ning beam
  Dispel the wintry clouds of care,

85. Area north of the Black Sea in what is now Russia.

And gild the cot[86] by Welland's stream?[87]
There oft thy harbinger[88] I see:
The ruddy[89] sylvan,[90] Industry:
   He still directs our daily toil.
Nor yet does adverse Fate deny
Each humbler hope to gratify,
80   But when, ah when will tardy Independence smile?

    IX.
Away, Complaint! Thy chilling spleen
   With langour[91] numbs the active powers:
For as I view the passing scene,
   My path seems strew'd with festal[92] flowers.
Millions, who bear the human form,
Assail'd by Fortune's ruthless storm,
   To heaven of hated life complain.
Adversity's sharp stings they feel,
They cringe beneath oppression's wheel,
90   They pine with hopeless woe, or faint with cureless pain.

    X.
Ye sons of affluence and fame,
   To noble independence born,
Remov'd from want's imputed[93] shame,
   And mis'ry's undeserved scorn,
Preserve the birth-right ye possess:
Oh! trifle not with happiness;
   From lavish dissipation fly.
Force not your noble souls to bear
An irksome round of anxious care,
100   Nor let the sordid bribe your mean subservience buy.

86. Cottage, here a small and humble structure.
87. River in Lincolnshire.
88. Forerunner.
89. Having a healthy, fresh complexion.
90. Anyone or anything living in the woods; a being of the woods. The rustic forester, flush from his industrious efforts, represents the possibilities of independence wrought through hard work.
91. Lassitude, apathy, or fatigue.
92. Festive.
93. Ascribed or charged (as a fault).

XI.

   Preserve the birth-right ye possess,
     The banquet of the lib'ral mind,
   The pow'r to succour, and to bless,
     To speed the int'rests of mankind.
   Ev'n, like the glorious orb of day,
   Your salutary[94] beams convey
     To all within your ample sphere.
   Oppressive opulence subdue,
   Lead slighted merit forth to view,
Dispel the orphan's grief, and wipe the widow's tear.   110

XII.

   Yet while with condescension[95] sweet
     Ye lay the pride of birth aside,
   The injur'd sufferer to meet,
     The blush of modesty to hide;
   Still, when occasion calls it forth,
   Assume the dignity of worth,
     To check oppression's proud decree.
   Admiring nations shall perceive,
   What minds unbiass'd can atchieve,
And bless benignant[96] heav'n, which made you great and free.   120

(1791)

Ode I. The Spirit of the Air
Anne Bannerman

I.

   Be hush'd, ye angry winds, that sweep,
     Resistless, o'er the polar coast:
   Thou swell'st no more, tremendous deep!
     I lock thee in eternal frost.
   My will supreme, mine awful sway,
   The earth, the air, the sea obey;

94. Wholesome or conducive to well-being.
95. Courteous disregard of rank.
96. Gracious or benevolent.

My glance pervades the realms of space;
Each hidden spring, this arm can trace;
O'er all the prostrate world my power extends,
10   Alike on Zembla's[97] ice, on Zaara's[98] burning sands.

II.

Amid the lightning's forky[99] flame,
    While, driven on high, the billows[100] roll;
'Tis mine to loose the struggling frame,
    And mine to soothe the parting soul:
I come, on viewless winds reclin'd,
To cheer the wretch, whom fetters bind,
To crush the oppressor's giant crest,
To hurl destruction on his breast,
Amid the spoils his abject soul adores;
20   And trembling earth recoils along her utmost shores.

III.

What form is that, half-hid in air,
    Round whose pale brow the torrents roar?
'Tis Freedom! mark her deep despair;
    She points to Afric's[101] bleeding shore.
Hark! what a groan!—with horror wild,
I see the mother clasp her child;
"My son, my son!" she madly cries;—
Spare, monsters, spare her agonies.—
Too late, for, rapid, to the vessel's side
30   She flies, and, plunging, sinks beneath the billowy tide.

IV.

Proceed unmov'd, ye men of blood!
    Your course along the waters urge;
No winds shall vex the unruffled flood,
    Nor toss on high the deaf'ning surge.
Now, for your happy homes prepare;
But, curb your joy, I meet you there.

97. Arctic. Nova Zembla is a group of islands in the Arctic Ocean north of Archangel in Russia.
98. Variation of *Sahara,* the desert of North Africa.
99. Forked.
100. Swell on the ocean produced by wind.
101. Africa's. At the time, 50 percent of the slave trade was conducted by the British.

Then, as your friends, your infant race,
   Rush wildly to your fond embrace,
Before your eyes a ghastly form shall stand,
And o'er her infant weep, and wave her beck'ning hand.   40

V.

Fierce thro' the desert's frightful sand,
   When Cancer[102] rules the burning day,
The Arab leads his daring band,
   Exulting on their perilous way.
"Prepare," he cries, "prepare for war:
Mark yonder sandy cloud afar;
We share the blood, we share the toil,
And we shall share the glorious spoil;
Collect your courage, now the foe is nigh;
Victorious, we return;—subdued, revenge and die."   50

VI.

But, vengeful, on the rushing wind,
   I come to toss the sandy waves;
To whelm[103] the spoilers of their kind,
   Inglorious, in untimely graves.
Yon livid flame, that flings on high
Its terrors thro' the redd'ning sky;
Glares on your van,[104] in awful state,
The herald of impending fate.
I speak—the suffocating blast descends
In clouds of fluid fire; and nature's conflict ends.   60

VII.

Where the wild ocean's heaving waves
   Boil round Magellan's stormy coast;[105]
When long and loud the tempest raves,
   I mark the straining vessel tost,

102. Cancer, a constellation, is also the fourth sign in the Zodiac and rules at the beginning of summer, from 22 June to 22 July.
103. Overwhelm.
104. Vanguard or advancing military force.
105. Coastal South American territories around the Straits of Magellan, such as Chile and Tierra del Fuego.

By night along unfathom'd[106] seas,
I see the living current freeze;
As horror grasps each fainting form,
High mid the fury of the storm;
Till the tall masts in scatter'd fragments lie,
70   And, plung'd amid the surge, the sufferers sink, and die.

VIII.

Soft be your bed, and sweet your rest,
   Ye luckless tenants of the deep!
And, o'er each cold and shroudless breast,
   May spirits of the waters weep!
And still, when awful midnight reigns,
My harp shall join in solemn strains;
My voice shall echo to the waves,
That dash above your coral graves;
Blest be the gloom, that wraps each sacred head,
80   And blest th' unbroken sleep, and silence of the dead!

IX.

High on yon cloud's cerulean[107] seat,
   I ride sublime thro' æther blue,
To fling, while reigns the power of heat,
   On fainting earth the summer dew:
I bid the rose in crimson glow,
And spread the lily's robe of snow;
I waft from heaven the balmy breeze,
That sighs along the sleeping seas;
What time the spirit of the rock is nigh,
90   To pour upon the night his heaven-taught melody.

X.

But, far beyond the solar blaze,
   Again I wing my rapid flight;
Again I cleave the liquid maze,
   Exulting in immortal might.
O'er me nor cold, nor heat, prevails,

106. Unexplored or of unknown depths.
107. Deep blue, color of the sky.

Nor poison from malignant gales;
I glide along the trackless coast,
That binds the magazines[108] of frost;
Encompass'd by the raging storm,
I smile at danger's threat'ning form;   100
I mock destruction on his tow'ring seat,
And leave the roaring winds, contending at my feet.

(1800)

Life

Anna Laetitia Barbauld

Animula, vagula, blandula.[109]

Life! I know not what thou art,
But know that thou and I must part;
And when, or how, or where we met,
I own to me's a secret yet.
But this I know, when thou art fled,
Where'er they lay these limbs, this head,
No clod so valueless shall be,
As all that then remains of me.
O whither, whither dost thou fly,
Where bend unseen thy trackless course,   10
    And in this strange divorce,
Ah tell where I must seek this compound I?

To the vast ocean of empyreal[110] flame,
    From whence thy essence came,
Dost thou thy flight pursue, when freed
From matter's base encumbering weed?
    Or dost thou, hid from sight,
    Wait, like some spell-bound knight,
Through blank oblivious years th' appointed hour,

---

108. Storehouses.

109. "Little soul, wandering, pleasant." This quotation comes from a longer poem allegedly uttered by the Roman emperor Hadrian (AD 76–138) on his deathbed; it was a familiar colloquial phrase during the period.

110. Celestial.

20   To break thy trance and reassume thy power?
          Yet canst thou without thought or feeling be?
          O say what art thou, when no more thou'rt thee?

          Life! we've been long together,
          Through pleasant and through cloudy weather;
              'Tis hard to part when friends are dear;
              Perhaps 'twill cost a sigh, a tear;
              Then steal away, give little warning,
                  Choose thine own time;
          Say not Good night, but in some brighter clime
30   Bid me Good morning.

                                        (1812; 1825)

Sources

Chudleigh: *Poems on Several Occasions. Together with the Song of the Three Children Para-phras'd* (London, 1703), 14–20; Finch: *The Spleen, A Pindarique Ode* (London, 1709), 3–8; Thomas: *Miscellany Poems on Several Subjects* (London, 1722), 273–80; Carter: *Gentleman's Magazine* 17 (December 1747): 585; Poynton: *Poems on Several Occasions* (Birmingham, 1770), 11–12; Savage: *Poems on Various Subjects and Occasions*, 2 vols. (London, 1777), 2:31–36; Murry: *Poems on Various Subjects* (London, 1779), 102–3; H. Falconar: *Poems, by Maria and Harriet Falconar* (London, 1788), 73–75; M. Falconar: *Poems, by Maria and Harriet Falconar* (London, 1788), 93; West: *Miscellaneous Poems, and a Tragedy* (York, 1791), 18–24; Banner-man: *Poems by Anne Bannerman* (Edinburgh, 1800), 55–60; Barbauld: *The Works of Anna Lætitia Barbauld. With a Memoir by Lucy Aikin,* 2 vols. (London, 1825), 1:261–62.

⊀E⊁

The Ballad

The ballad is an ancient, beloved form of poetry. Scholars believe that ballads provided the main materials for Homer's epics, and nations all over the world make efforts to collect folk ballads. Composed to be sung or recited, they tell a story, often a tale of love and physical courage. They may immortalize the history of a people; in the time before written literature was highly developed, they served first as news and then as a way to preserve and convey history. The eighteenth century was such a key moment in the literary history of ballads that influential scholars argue that it is an eighteenth-century poetic form; recently, in its seventh edition, the *Norton Anthology of English Literature* has moved them from immediately before "The Sixteenth Century" to the end of the eighteenth century.[1] In the century, major collections, such as Allan Ramsay's *The Tea-Table Miscellany* (1724–27) and Thomas Percy's *Reliques of Ancient English Poetry* (1765), were published; hundreds of political, news, and street ballads were written,[2] and the literary ballad became a major poetic form. At that time *ballad* connoted "almost anything sung in the streets or gathered into lower-class miscellanies; and even in the minds of the literary antiquaries, ballads were intimately connected, or confused, with all manner of song and old poetry."[3] Today, however, scholars limit ballads to strophic narrative popular songs and recognize that the ballad revival that followed the publication of important collections "was a complex movement that knit together diverse influences—traditional and oral, commercial and written, political, ethnic, scholarly, educational, and literary."[4] They fit the description of literary kind well, for they are a recognizable family rather than a genre with strict formal demands.

Most of the ballads in this section are part of the great ballad revival of the late eighteenth century, but there are two representatives of the earlier period. *Disconsolate Judy's Lamentation,* the only anonymous poem included in the anthology, is an essential addition because it represents the popular, timely broadside ballads and underscores that many are unattributable to any author.[5] Written from the point of view of a woman whose love has been impressed into the British navy and who knows that his ship is missing but does not yet know that it has been lost,[6] the ballad shows the writer's awareness of the dangers of the sea and her unusual knowledge of specific details. Because of the names of places and the ship's commander, the ballad testifies to the wide dissemination of news and the imbrication of broadside ballads and news. In *The Happy Pair*, a ballad somewhat reminiscent of Restoration erotic pastorals, Laetitia Pilkington adapts the form to concerns and fads of her generation by depicting the love of a lower-class couple as happier than the materialistic alliances of the rich. In their day, ballads were timely, and this section reflects that fact. Susanna Blamire uses the traveler-returning motif, this time for the story of a man coming home from Britain's modern East Indian Empire. Carolina Oliphant Nairne's *Jeanie Deans* takes as its subject the heroine of Sir Walter Scott's 1818 novel, *The Heart of Midlothian*. It mentions common, beloved landmarks around Edinburgh and pays a tribute to Deans and to a Scottish statesman.

By the beginning of the nineteenth century, collectors such as Walter Scott called ballads that could be linked to the Middle Ages and were preserved in oral or manuscript forms "traditional." Like those ballads, the literary ballads that followed them were set in feudal times, as is Amelia Opie's *The Warrior's Return*. In a story that combines love and war, it recalls history by looking back to the English participation in the Crusades. Literary ballads, like Opie's and others printed here, are written by individual poets but preserve such distinguishing features of ballads as the refrain and other incremental repetitions, abrupt beginnings, and tragic conclusions. Opie chooses to use the traditional ballad stanza, the quatrain, and the most common rhyme scheme, *abcb*. Many ballads tell the same story or, like *The Warrior's Return*, use the same plots with countless other ballads. Writing during a threatening time of war in Great Britain, Opie uses a familiar, horrible fear as her tale's subject, but the skill with which she creates dialogue and lingers over details at key moments gives the poem originality. From the opening verse, whose awful foreboding cannot be appreciated until the poem is reread, the tension builds.

Many versions of popular ballads survive, and poets rework them for their own amusement and adapt them to new singers and times. Nairne is described in the *Dictionary of National Biography* as standing "first and alone" as a writer of Jacobite songs. Reared in a culture that preserved and enjoyed popular songs, some traditional, she wrote ballads throughout her life. Her *Auld Langsyne* is a reworking of the great Scottish New Year's Eve song. The setting is a party attended by almost everyone. When midnight strikes, the hot-pint, a mixture of strong beer, whiskey, eggs, and more, is brought out. The company kisses and sings *Weel may we a'be* and, later, *Auld Lang Syne*. Everyone pours out of the house to visit neighbors, and some describe the streets as being more filled with people between twelve and one than at midday. Robert Burns had repeated the opening of the 1776 version, printed in *Ancient and Modern Scottish Songs, Heroic Ballads, etc.*, "Shoul'd auld acquaintance be forgot," but Nairne, as was typical of her, created a simple, highly lyrical version that differs markedly from Burns's drinking song. Deeply aware of the part ballads play in a culture, she wrote for special occasions and also to preserve modern history and literature. We provide two examples, *Jeanie Deans* and *The Pleughman,* the latter an early piece written for her brother to sing to his tenants at an annual dinner.

All of these poems show that the poets understood the traditional functions of ballads in a culture. Ballads both shape and affirm nationhood and preserve minority cultures and opinions. Like satire, they create and reinforce the in-group and the Others.[7] The ballads contrast the British to other nations—the French, the Turks, the non-Christians, and more—and, as Nairne's ballads do, reaffirm the distinctive character and culture of Scotland, a culture undergoing many changes because of the 1707 Union with England, which meant the loss of the Scottish parliament, and adjusting to the aftermath of the Jacobite Rebellion of 1745. They pass along superstitions, folklore, and timeless tales of war, love, and endurance; bring together those who believed in long-lost causes such as Bonnie Prince Charlie's invasion (Nairne's ballads in 2.F); and sometimes unexpectedly respond to an immediate situation. Although ballads seem simple, the form is demanding. The very simplicity of the language and narrative, the kinds of purity and incremental repetition, and especially the musicality resulting from rhyme, meter, and imagery make the ballad one of the most challenging kinds of poetry to write.

Notes

1. Mary Ellen Brown, "Placed, Replaced, or Misplaced? The Ballads' Progress," *Eighteenth Century: Theory and Interpretation* 47 (2006): 116–18.

2. See Paula MacDowell's revisionary essay "'The Manufacture and Lingua-facture of *Ballad-Making*': Broadside Ballads in Long Eighteenth-Century Ballad Discourse," *Eighteenth Century: Theory and Interpretation* 47 (2006): 151–52, 155–56, 158–61, 171–73.

3. Quoted from Albert Friedman's book *The Ballad Revival* in Diane Dugaw, "On the 'Darling Songs' of Poets, Scholars, and Singers: An Introduction," *Eighteenth Century: Theory and Interpretation* 47 (2006): 100. This introduction has benefited from Dugaw's essay and the special edition in which it appears.

4. Dugaw, "On the 'Darling Songs,'" 110.

5. On the timely eighteenth-century broadside ballad, see MacDowell, "Manufacture and Lingua-facture of *Ballad-Making*," 151–78.

6. Daniel J. Ennis discusses other women's protest ballads in *Enter the Press-Gang: Naval Impressment in Eighteenth-Century British Literature* (Newark: University of Delaware Press, 2002), 156–60, 202nn. 52, 56; see also his discussions of impressment and its prevalence.

7. Popular-culture theorists have proven that people avoid satires that contradict their ideologies while reading those in agreement, and that doing so strengthens their opinions. The comic strip *Doonesbury* is an example of satire either followed or shunned.

Disconsolate Judy's Lamentation
for the Absence of her True Love, Johnny on board the *Victory*[1]
with Admiral Balchen,[2] now missing
Anonymous

Tune of "Down by a crystal river side"

Come pity me, young maidens all,
Who am brought into wretched thrall.[3]
My love was pressed[4] away to sea,
And is on board the *Victory*.

When of him I did take my leave
He said, 'Dear Judy, do not grieve;
Although I absent from you be,
Stout is our ship, the *Victory*.

10   'Brave Balchen is a gallant man,
And will conduct us safe to land;
Then my dear Judy I shall see
When safe returns the *Victory*.'

Ah, John, indeed my heart did fail
When you to Lisbon was to sail,
For dangers they are great at sea.
Oh, now where is the *Victory*?

O John, my lovely sailor dear,
My heart is sore oppressed with fear.

---

1. The *Victory* was a relatively new ship, one the Royal Navy considered "the finest ship afloat." She encountered a violent storm in the English Channel on 3 October 1744. Other ships saw distress flares and heard salvos of guns, but no trace of the ship was found until wreckage drifted onto the French coast days later. It is assumed that the ship was forced onto a reef called the Caskets. This ballad was written before Judy knew the ship was lost. *The Oxford Book of Sea Songs* (Oxford: Oxford University Press, 1986), 97n.

2. Admiral John Balchen (1670–1744) began his career in the navy at age fifteen and was a lieutenant by age twenty-two. He retired in August 1743 but was called back to command the 100-gun flagship *Victory* for a combined fleet of seventeen British and eight Dutch warships against the French in the War of the Austrian Succession.

3. Captive of misery or distress; enslaved by her suspenseful waiting.

4. Common shortening of *impressed*, meaning forced into service. Press gangs often kidnapped, coerced, or tricked young men.

A letter, true love, send to me
From on board the *Victory*.   20

No cruel balls[5] has hurt my dear,
No fatal rocks you have come near;
Nor taken by an enemy,
You nor the gallant *Victory*.

Nine hundred men[6] on board you have,
A jolly crew both stout and brave
As ever did go out to sea.
God send safe home the *Victory*.

Dear Johnny, I at Portsmouth[7] wait
And watch for you early and late,   30
Wishing each moment for to see
Come sailing in the *Victory*.

(1744)

The Happy Pair
A Ballad

Laetitia Pilkington

At dewy Dawn
As o'er the Lawn,
Young *Roger* early stray'd,
He chanc'd to meet
With *Jenny* sweet,
That blooming Country Maid;
Her Cheeks so red
With Blushes spread,
Shew'd like the breaking Day,
Her modest Look   10
The Shepherd took;
She stole his Heart away.

---

5. Cannon balls.
6. In fact, eleven hundred men were lost.
7. Major British seaport on the English Channel.

With tender Air,
He woo'd the Fair,
And movingly addrest;
For Love divine,
Can Clowns[8] refine,
And warm the coldest Breast;
Her Eyes he prais'd,
20   And fondly gaz'd,
On her inchanting Face,
Where Innocence,
And Health dispence,
Each winning rosy Grace.

Young *Jenny*'s Breast,
Love's Pow'r confest,
And felt an equal Fire;
Nor had she Art,
To hide her Smart,
30   Or check the soft Desire.
Hymen[9] unites
In blissful Rites,
The fair, the matchless two;
And Wedlock ne'er
Could boast a Pair
More lovely or more true.

Ye Rich and Great,
How seldom Fate
Gives you so mild a Doom;
40   Whose wand'ring Flames,
And wanton[10] Dames,
A mutual Plague become;
While Coach and Six
Your Passions fix,
You buy your State too dearly:
Ah, courtly Folks!

8. Country men, peasants, uncouth men.
9. Greek god of marriage, usually represented carrying a veil and a torch.
10. Frolicsome, undisciplined, even unchaste.

You're but the Jokes
Of those who love sincerely.

(1748)

The Warrior's Return
Amelia Opie

Sir Walter returned from the far Holy Land,[11]
    And a blood-tinctured[12] falchion[13] he bore;
But such precious blood as now darkened his sword
    Had never distained it before.

Fast fluttered his heart as his own castle towers
    He saw on the mountain's green height;
"My wife, and my son!" he exclaimed, while his tears
    Obscured for some moments his sight.

For terror now whispered, the wife he had left
    Full fifteen long twelvemonths before,   10
The child he had claspt in his farewel embrace,
    Might both, *then,* alas! be no more.

Then, sighing, he thought of his Editha's tears
    As his steed bore him far from her sight,
And her accents of love, while she fervently cried,
    "Great God! guard his life in the fight!"

And then he remembered, in language half formed
    How his child strove to bid him adieu;
While scarcely he now can believe, as a man,
    That infant may soon meet his view.   20

But should he not live! . . . . To escape from that fear,
    He eagerly spurred his bold steed:

---

11. From the eleventh to the fourteenth century European Christians fought a series of wars to take the Holy Land, Palestine, from the Muslims.

12. Dyed or tinted with blood.

13. Broad sword.

Nor stopped he again, till his own castle moat
  Forbade on the way to proceed.

'Twas day-break: yet still past the windows he saw
  Busy forms lightly trip to and fro:
"Blest sight! that she lives," he exclaimed with a smile,
  "Those symptoms of housewifery show:

"For, stranger to sloth, and on business intent,
30   The dawn calls her forth from her bed;
And see, through the castle, all busy appear,
  By her to their duty still led."

That instant the knight by the warder[14] was seen,
  For far flamed the cross on his breast;
And while loud blew the horn, now a smile, now a tear,
  Sir Walter's mixt feelings expressed.

"'Tis I, my loved vassals!" the warrior exclaimed, ...
  The voice reached his Editha's ears;
Who, breathless and speechless, soon rushed to his arms,
40   Her transport betraying by tears.

"And dost thou still love me?" he uttered, when first
  A silence so rapturous he broke;
She tried to reply, but in vain . . . . while her sobs
  A volume of tenderness spoke.

"Behold how I'm changed! how I'm scarred!" he exclaimed,
  "Each charm that I boasted is o'er:" . . . .
"Thou hast bled for THY GOD," she replied, "and each scar
  Endears thee, my warrior, the more."

"But where is my child?" he cried, pale with alarm,
50   "Thou namest not my Alfred . . . . my boy!" . . . . . .
"And comes he not with you?" she said; . . . . "then some woe
  Embitters our beverage of joy."

"What meanest thou, my love?" . . . . "When to manhood he grew,
  And heard of his father's great name,

14. Watchman.

'O let me', he cried, 'to the Holy Land go,
   To share my sire's dangers, and fame.

"'Perchance my young arm, by the cause nerved with strength,
   May lower the Pagan's proud crest:
And the brave Christian knights, in reward of my zeal,
   May bind the red cross on my breast.'   60

"'And think'st thou,' I said, 'with the son I can part,
   Till the father be safe in my arms?
No . . . . hope not I'll add to the fears of the wife
   The mother's as poignant alarms.'

"I ceased . . . . and his head on my bosom reclined,
   While his golden hair shaded his cheek;
When, parting his ringlets, I saw the big tears
   His heart's disappointment bespeak.

"The sight overcame me: 'Most loved,' I exclaimed,
   'Go, share in thy father's renown!   70
Thy mother will gladly, to dry up *thy* tears,
   Endure an increase of *her own.*'

"He kissed me . . . he thanked me. . . . I armed him myself,
   And girt his pure sword on his side;
So lovely he looked, that the mother's fond fears
   Were lost in the mother's fond pride."

"He went then? . . . . How long has my warrior been gone?"
   "A twelvemonth, my Walter, and more."
"Indeed! . . . . then he scarcely could reach the far land
   Until the last battle was o'er."   80

"I told him, my Walter, what armour was yours,
   And what the device on your shield,
In hopes of your meeting." . . . . "Alas!" he returned,
   "My armour I changed on the field!

"A friend whom I loved from the dawning of youth,
   For conquest and courage renowned,
Fell, fighting beside me, and thus he exclaimed,
   While life issued fast from the wound:

"'And must I then die ere the flag of the Cross
90   Waves proudly o'er Saracen[15] towers?
But grant me, loved Walter, this dying request,
      For victory must surely be ours:

"'My armour well tried, and my falchion, my shield,
      In memory of me deign to wear!
'T would sooth me to know, when the victory comes on,
      That something of mine will be there!'

"I granted his wish, and his arms I assumed,
      While yet he the action could see,
And marked with delight that his last closing look
100   Was fixt with fond pleasure on me.

"Yet now, this remembrance so dear to my heart
      Is clouded by anxious regret;
Since, but for this change on the field of the fight,
      The father and son would have met!"

"But if he has fought, and has fallen, my love!" . . . .
      "Suppress," cried the knight with a frown,
"A fear so ill-founded; . . . . if Alfred had died,
      He'd have fallen a *child of renown.*"

Yet vainly he strove by the father's proud hopes
110   To conquer the father's fond fears;
He feared for the life of his boy, though with smiles
      He answered his Editha's tears.

And more and more forced grew the smile on his lip,
      His brow more o'erclouded with thought;
At length he exclaimed, "From the field of renown
      One mournful memorial I've brought.

"I grieve that I won it! . . . . A Saracen chief
      Fell bleeding before me in fight,

15. Common term for Arabs and Muslims.

When lo! as I claimed him my prisoner and prize,
    A warrior disputed my right.   120

"'I'm new to the battle,' he cried, 'and this prize
    Will wreathe my young brow with renown,
Now will I the conquest resign but with life: . . . .
    That chief by *this* arm was o'erthrown.'

"His daring enraged me, ... for mine seemed the stroke
    Which laid the proud Saracen low; . . . .
Besides, from his bosom depended no cross,
    His right to such daring to show."

"But surely, my Walter, the daring bespoke
    A soul nobly eager for fame: 130
So many *your* laurels, that one you could spare, ...
    O tell me you granted his claim!"

"No, Editha, no! . . . . martial pride steeled my heart,
    The youth I to combat defied;
He fought like a hero! But *vainly* he fought, ...
    Beneath my strong falchion he died."

"O ill-fated youth! how I bleed for his fate!
    Perhaps that *his* mother, like me,
Had armed him, and blest him, and prays for his life,
    As *I* pray, my Alfred, for thee!   140

"But never again shall he gladden her eyes,
    And haste her fond blessing to crave!
O Walter! I tremble lest you in return
    Be doomed to the sorrow you gave!

"Say, did not the cross, when your victim he fell,
    Lie heavy and cold on your breast; . . . .
That symbol of him full of meekness and love,
    Whose deeds *mercy* only expressed?"

"Yes . . . . pity, shame, penitence seized on my soul;
    So sweet too his voice was in tone!   150
Methought as he lay, and in agony groaned,
    His accents resembled thine own.

"His casque[16] I unlaced, and I chafed his cold brow,
　　And fain every wound would have healed;
So young, and so lovely he seemed, that I wept
　　As by him I tenderly kneeled.

"He saw my distress, and his last dying grasp
　　Forgiveness and kindness expressed;
And then, with a look I shall never forget,
160　　He breathed his last sigh on my breast."

"But what's this memorial?" with cheek deadly pale
　　His Editha falteringly cried: ....
"This scarf from his bosom!" .... he uttered no more.
　　For Editha sunk by his side.

Ah then in her danger, her pale look of death,
　　He forgot all the laurels he'd won.
"O father accurst!" she exclaimed, "in that youth
　　You slaughtered your Alfred .... your son!"[17]

　　　　　　　　　　　　　　　　　(1808)

The Nabob[18]

Susanna Blamire

Air: Traveller's Return

When silent time, wi' lightly foot,
　　Had trod on thirty years,
I sought again my native land
　　Wi' mony hopes and fears:
Wha kens[19] gin[20] the dear friends I left

16. Part of the helmet of a suit of armor.

17. The fateful exchange of armor is an old and familiar theme. The *Iliad* has two examples, and Arthurian legends include the exchange between Sir Balin and Sir Balan. These and examples from other cultures, such as that between Sohrab and Rustum from Persia, were known in Britain. See C18-L archive, 11 July 2007, http://lists.psu.edu/cgi-bin/wa?S1=C18-L.

18. Term derived from the title of governors of a town or district in the Mogul Empire; in England after 1750 it was a sometimes derogatory name for men who returned from India with great wealth. Blamire presents her nabob in a sympathetic light.

19. Knows.

20. If.

May still continue mine?
Or gin I e'er again shall taste
The joys I left langsyne?[21]

As I drew near my ancient pile,[22]
   My heart beat a' the way;   10
Ilk[23] place I pass'd seem'd yet to speak
   O' some dear former day;
Those days that follow'd me afar,
   Those happy days o' mine,
Whilk made me think the present joys
   A' naething to langsyne!

The ivy'd tower now met my eye,
   Where minstrels used to blaw;[24]
Nae friend stepp'd forth wi' open hand,
   Nae weel-kenn'd[25] face I saw;   20
Till Donald totter'd to the door,
   Wham[26] I left in his prime,
And grat to see the lad return
   He bore about langsyne.

I ran to ilka dear friend's room,
   As if to find them there,
I knew where ilk ane used to sit,
   And hang o'er mony a chair;
Till soft remembrance threw a veil
   Across these een o' mine,   30
I clos'd the door, and sobb'd aloud,
   To think on auld langsyne!

Some pensy[27] chiels,[28] a new sprung race,
   Wad next their welcome pay,

21. Long ago.
22. Lofty mass of buildings.
23. Each.
24. Blow. Scottish minstrels blew horns.
25. Well known, familiar.
26. Whom.
27. Self-important, conceited.
28. Children; literally, "childs."

Wha shudder'd at my Gothic wa's,[29]
   And wish'd my groves away:
"Cut, cut," they cried, "those aged elms,
   Lay low yon mournfu' pine:"
Na! na! our fathers' names grow there,
40   Memorials o' langsyne.

To wean me frae these waefu' thoughts,
   They took me to the town;
But sair[30] on ilka weel-kenn'd face
   I miss'd the youthfu' bloom.
At balls they pointed to a nymph
   Wham a' declar'd divine;
But sure her mother's blushing cheeks
   Were fairer far langsyne!

In vain I sought in music's sound
50   To find that magic art,
Which oft in Scotland's ancient lays[31]
   Has thrill'd through a' my heart:
The sang had mony an artfu' turn;
   My ear confess'd 'twas fine;
But miss'd the simple melody
   I listen'd to langsyne.

Ye sons to comrades o' my youth,
   Forgie[32] an auld man's spleen,
Wha 'midst your gayest scenes still mourns
60   The days he ance[33] has seen:
When time has past, and seasons fled,
   Your hearts will feel like mine;
And aye[34] the sang will maist[35] delight
   That minds ye o' langsyne!

(1842)

29. Ways.
30. Sorrow.
31. Ballads.
32. Forgive.
33. Once.
34. Always.
35. Most.

Auld Langsyne[36]

Carolina Oliphant Nairne

What gude the present day can gie,
　　May that be yours an' mine;
But beams o' fancy sweetest rest
　　On auld langsyne.
　　　　On auld langsyne, my dear,
　　　　　On auld langsyne;
　　　　The bluid is cauld that winna[37] warm
　　　　　At thoughts o' langsyne,

We twa hae seen the simmer sun,
　　And thought it aye would shine;　　　　　　　　10
But mony a cloud has come between
　　Sin' auld langsyne.
　　　　　　Sin' auld langsyne, &c.

But still my heart beats warm to thee,
　　And sae to me does thine;
Blest be the pow'r that still has left
　　The frien's o' langsyne.
　　　　O' auld langsyne, my dear,
　　　　　O' auld langsyne;
　　　　The bluid is cauld that winna warm　　　　20
　　　　　At thoughts o' langsyne.

(1869)

36. Old times past; literally, "old long since." Although Robert Burns's "Auld Lang Syne" is better known than Nairne's, they may be contemporaneous, and both are reworkings of the ancient song. Burns's first line, for instance, is the same as that of an anonymous 1776 version, and he claimed he had written his down as an elderly man sang it.
37. Will not.

Jeanie Deans[38]
Carolina Oliphant Nairne

ST. LEONARDS' hill was lightsome land,
  Where gowan'd grass[39] was growin',
For man and beast were food and rest,
  And milk and honey flowin'.
A father's blessing followed close,
  Where'er her foot was treading,
And Jeanie's humble, harmless joys,
  On every side were spreading wide,
  On every side were spreading.

10   The mossy turf on Arthur Seat,
      St. Anthon's well aye springing,
    The lammies playing at her feet,
      The birdies round her singing,
    The solemn haunts o' Holyrood,[40]
      Wi' bats and houlits[41] eerie,
    The tow'ring craigs o' Salisbury,
      The lowly wells o' Weary,
      O, the lowly wells o' Weary.

      But evil days and evil men
20   Came owre their sunny dwelling,
    Like thunder storms on sunny skies,
      Or wastefu' waters swelling.
    What ance[42] was sweet is bitter now;
      The sun of joy is setting;
    In eyes that wont to glance wi' glee,—
      The briny tear is wetting fast,
      The briny tear is wetting.

---

38. One of the main characters in Sir Walter Scott's novel *The Heart of Midlothian,* Jeanie Deans walked to London from Edinburgh, gained an audience with Queen Caroline, and secured a pardon for her sister, who had been condemned to death.

39. Yellow and white flowers growing in a grassy field.

40. The ancient residence and abbey of Scottish royalty. At various times the English destroyed it or parts of it.

41. Owlets.

42. Once.

Her inmost thought to heaven is sent,
   In faithful supplication;
Her earthly stay's Macallummore,[43]   30
   The guardian o' the nation.
A hero's heart—a sister's love—
   A martyr's truth unbending;
They're a' in Jeanie's tartan plaid,—
   And she is gane, her liefu' lane,[44]
To Lunnon[45] toun she's wending.

(1869)

The Pleughman[46]
Carolina Oliphant Nairne

There's high and low, there's rich and poor,
   There's trades and crafts eneuch, man;
But east and west his trade's the best,
   That kens to guide pleugh, man.

Then come, weel speed my pleughman lad,
   And hey my merry pleughman;
Of a' the trades that I do ken,
   Commend me to the pleughman.

His dreams are sweet upon his bed,
   His cares are light and few, man;   10
His mother's blessin's on his head,
   That tents[47] her weel, the pleughman.
      Then come, weel speed, &c.

43. John, Duke of Argyle and Greenwich, is here identified by his title, that of the head of the Clan Campbell. In Scott's *Heart of Midlothian* Jeanie Deans manages to have an audience with him. He treats her kindly and helps her gain the pardon for her sister. He was known in his time as a courteous, intelligent, honorable statesman and soldier. Jenny calls him her "country's friend" and the "poor man's friend." *The Heart of Midlothian* ed. David Hewitt and Alison Lumsden (Edinburgh: Edinburgh University Press, 2004), chap. 36.

44. Solitary path; literally "lonely lane."

45. London.

46. Plowman.

47. Attends, tends to.

The lark sae sweet, that starts to meet
    The morning fresh and new, man;
Blithe tho' she be, as blithe is he
    That sings as sweet, the pleughman.
        Then come, weel speed, &c.

All fresh and gay, at dawn of day,
20   Their labours they renew, man;
Heaven bless the seed and bless the soil,
    And Heaven bless the pleughman.
        Then come, weel speed, &c.

(1869)

Sources

Anonymous: Roy Palmer, ed., *The Oxford Book of Sea Songs* (Oxford: Oxford University Press, 1986), 96–97; Pilkington: *The Memoirs of Mrs. Lætitia Pilkington,* 2 vols. (Dublin, 1748), 1:221–23; Opie: *The Warrior's Return, and Other Poems,* 2nd ed. (London, 1808), 3–17; Blamire: *The Poetical Works of Miss Susanna Blamire* (London, 1842), 198–202; Nairne: *Life and Songs of the Baroness Nairne with a Memoir and Poems of Carolina Oliphant the Younger,* ed. Charles Rogers, 2nd ed. (London: Griffin, 1869), 155, 75–76, 53.

⊁{F}⊁

Satire

The Restoration and eighteenth century is sometimes called the Age of Satire. The status and reputation of satire is explained by Anne Finch in *The Critick and the Writer of Fables* (3.D). The critic tells the poet to turn away from all other poetic genres: "But urge thy Pen, if thou wouldst move our Thoughts, / To shew us private, or the publick Faults." Alexander Pope called it "sacred Weapon! left for Truth's defence, / Sole Dread of Folly, Vice, and Insolence!"[1] Samuel Johnson defined satire in his *Dictionary* as "A poem in which wickedness or folly is censured."[2] This umbrella definition stretches to cover good-natured satire, confident of its power to reform, as well as outraged, vitriolic satire, whose goal is stigmatizing and punishing. Satirists believe themselves responsible for exposés and set themselves up as guardians of standards—moral, aesthetic, social, even architectural and scientific. Yet most of them have a realistic, even wry understanding of themselves and the likely effect of their art. Jonathan Swift, for instance, wrote, "Satyr is a sort of Glass, wherein Beholders do generally discover every body's Face but their Own."[3]

The common opinion has been that women poets wrote little satire and that when they did, they found it an uncomfortable form.[4] Women known to favor satire and to have devastating skill in it have had their femininity and personality questioned. The greatest satirists in the history of English literature—Pope, Swift, John Gay, and Henry Fielding—wrote in this period, and the woman poet most known as a satirist, Lady Mary Wortley Montagu, knew them all well. Superior to them in class and willing to match wits with the most aggressive, Pope and Swift, she has usually been represented in anthologies with one of her poems that are in direct dialogue with them. Most common are *Verses Address'd to the Imitator of Horace* (Pope), a poem on which Montagu in fact collaborated with Lord Hervey, and *The Reasons that Induced Dr. S[wift] to write a Poem call'd the Lady's Dressing Room* (neither included). This section of the anthology begins with a typical example of Montagu's satiric skill, *Epistle [to Lord Bathurst]*, which is also representative of the challenges of this devilishly difficult genre. The rapid fire lashes her heroic couplets deliver and the power with which she uses details about Lord Bathurst to pronounce a judgment on the unifying explanation of his actions illustrate her intelligence and craftsmanship. Her opening line parodies the "Happy the Man" poems in the tradition of Horace's Ode 29, Book 3, and Virgil's *Georgics*, Book 2, and thereby raises the poem from an attack on an individual to a general satire of people like Bathurst. As Johnson's definition of satire continues, "Proper *satire* is distinguished, by the generality of the reflections, from a *lampoon*, which is aimed against a particular person." Also in this section is her *Tuesday: St. James's Coffee-House;* although the two men indulging in a bragging contest have been identified, they are her delightful imagining of how some men sometimes talk about women. By adapting the eclogue form, the Virgilian pastoral poem's singing match, for these dateless men, she created one of the town eclogues that made her famous and offered a model for other poets. We include here *City Splendor,* a town eclogue by Ann Murry, also known as a formidable satirist. Like *Tuesday,* it displays the poet's skill in characterizing a common human type and also gives modern readers an intimate look into eighteenth-century lives and attitudes.

Mary Barber, Mary Robinson, and Anna Laetitia Barbauld were also recognized and appreciated as satirists in their own time, and Charlotte Lennox's *The Female Quixote* (1752) is a near-canonical satiric novel. Some of the women were colorful characters whose experiences gave them material for satire. Ann Thicknesse, for instance, made her name as a singer and player of musical water glasses. She also performed on the viola da gamba and wrote a guide to performing on water glasses, then a novel instrument. Her father attempted to stop her concerts by confining her and later by blocking roads to the houses where she was performing. We have selected one of the songs she sang, a satire of a rakish husband set to a famous hunting tune. Lennox spent her childhood in New York, then lived with a "deranged" aunt, and later had an unsuccessful try at becoming an actress. Her *Art of Coquettry* is very much about performances, specifically those that young society women learn. Robinson was the Prince of Wales's scandalous "Perdita" and later the lover of Bloody Tarleton, but she also succeeded Robert Southey as poetry editor of the *Morning Post.* In the first of the two satires by her included here, she laughs at parochial attitudes, and in the second, published under one of her pen names, Portia, she uses caesuras within tetrameter quatrains to expose the contradictions and injustices all around her.

Other satires in this section represent women's frequent targets. Barber, for instance, imagines the outraged diatribe of a conservative clergyman whose views of marriage and the place of wives disagree with hers. Carolina Oliphant Nairne also writes her satire from the point of view of the man, but in contrast to Barber's portrayal of an oppressed wife, hers is of a comically abused husband. The final poem, *West End Fair,* by Barbauld, describes Dame Charity's lighthearted trip to a spring fair with Dame Fashion. Barbauld, who did so much good in her life, depicts Charity as quite exhausted and needing a "play-day." She uses satiric touches within a poem that exemplifies just how amiable satire can be.

Notes

1. Alexander Pope, *Epilogue to the Satires: Dialogue II* (London, 1738), lines 212–13.

2. Samuel Johnson, *A Dictionary of the English Language,* 2nd ed., 2 vols. (London, 1756), s.v. "Satire."

3. Jonathan Swift, *A Full and True Account of the Battel . . . Between the Antient and the Modern Books,* ed. A. C. Guthkelch and D. Nichol Smith (1920; Oxford: Clarendon, 1958), 215.

4. This opinion can be found in common handbooks even today. "Female satirists are *very* rare," writes J. A. Cuddon in *A Dictionary of Literary Terms* (Garden City, NY: Doubleday, 1977), s.v. "satire."

Epistle [to Lord Bathurst][1]

Lady Mary Wortley Montagu

How happy you who vary'd Joys persue,
And every Hour presents you something new!
Plans, Schemes, and Models, all Palladio's Art[2]
For six long Months has gain'd upon your Heart,
Of Colonades, and Corridores you talk,
The winding Stair case, and the cover'd Walk,
Proportion'd Colums strikes before your Eye,
Corinthian[3] Beauty, Ionian[4] Majesty,
You blend the Orders with Vitruvian[5] Toil
10   And raise with wondrous Joy the fancy'd Pile.
    But the dull Workman's slow-performing Hand
But coldly executes his Lord's command,
With Dirt and Mortar soon you grow displeas'd,
Planting Succeeds, and Avenues are rais'd,
Canals are cut, and Mountains Level made,
Bowers of retreat, and Gallerys of shade.
The shaven Turf presents a living Green,
The bordering Flowers in Mystic knots are seen.
With study'd Art on Nature you refine—
20   The Spring beheld you warm in this Design,
But scarce the cold attacks your favourite Trees,
Your Inclinations fail, and wishes freeze,
You quit the Grove, so lately so admir'd,
With other views your eager Hopes are fir'd,
Post to the City you direct your way,
Not blooming Paradice would bribe your stay,
Ambition shows you Power's brightest Side,

1. Allen, first Baron Bathurst, was a generous, gregarious man well known as a womanizer and a social drinker; his extravagant plans for his huge estates in Gloucestershire even included a fanciful design for uniting the Thames and Severn rivers. Maynard Mack, *Alexander Pope: A Life* (New Haven, CT: Yale University Press, 1985). This poem can be compared to Pope's *Epistle III. To Allen Lord Bathurst*.

2. The arch-and-column style of the Renaissance architect Andrea Palladio, born Andrea di Pietro (1508–80), was very popular in England and America in the seventeenth and eighteenth centuries.

3. Slender, fluted column with an ornate bell-shaped crown decorated with acanthus leaves.

4. Slender column with a scroll-shaped crown.

5. Marcus Vitruvius Pollio wrote the encyclopedic ten-volume *De Architectura* (c. 25 BC), which was an important source of information about architecture, building materials, and interior and exterior decorations during the classical revival in England.

'Tis meanly poor in Solitude to hide,
Tho certain Pain attends the Cares of State,
A Good Man owes his Country to be great,   30
Should act abroad the high distinguish'd Part,
Or shew at least the purpose of his Heart;
With Thoughts like these, the shining Court you seek
Full of new projects for—allmost a Week.
You then Despise the Tinsel glittering Snare;
Think vile Mankind below a serious Care:
Life is too short for any distant Aim,
And cold the dull reward of Future Fame.
Be happy then; while yet you have to live:
And Love is all the Blessing Heaven can give;   40
Fir'd by new passion you address the fair,
Survey the Opera as a gay Parterre,[6]
Young Cloe's bloom had made you certain Prize
But for a sidelong Glance of Cœlia's[7] Eyes,
Your beating Heart acknowledges her power,
Your eager Eyes her lovely form devour,
You feel the Poison swelling in your Breast
And all your Soul by fond Desire possess'd.
In dying sighs a long three hours is past,
To some Assembly[8] with Impatient haste,   50
With trembling Hope and doubtfull Fear you move,
Resolv'd to tempt your Fate, and own your Love:
But there Bellinda[9] meets you on the Stairs.
Easy, her Shape, attracting all her Airs,
A smile she gives, and with a smile can wound,
Her melting voice has Music in the Sound,
Her every Motion wears resistless Grace,
Wit in her Mien, and Pleasure in her Face;
Here while you vow Eternity of Love,
Cloe and Cœlia unregarded move.   60
      Thus on the Sands of Affric's burning plains
However deeply made no long Impress remains,
The lightest Leaf can leave its figure there,

6. One of those sitting in the pit, the part of the theater immediately in front of the orchestra.

7. Cloe, or Chloe, and Celia are generic names for lady loves in the pastoral and Renaissance traditions.

8. A social gathering of both sexes for conversation, flirtation, news, and cards.

9. Perhaps named after the heroine of Alexander Pope's *Rape of the Lock;* see 1.139–41 and 2.9–15.

The strongest Form is scatter'd by the Air,
So yeilding the Warm temper of your Mind,
So touch'd by every Eye; so toss'd by every Wind, ⎫
O how unlike has Heaven my Soul design'd!   ⎬
⎭
   Unseen, unheard, the Throng around me move,
Not wishing Praise, insensible of Love,
70   No Whispers soften, nor no Beautys Fire,
Careless I see the Dance, and coldly hear the Lyre.
   So numerous Herds are driven o're the Rock,
No print is left of all the passing Flock,
So sings the Wind around the solid stone,
So vainly beats the Waves with fruitless moan,
Tedious the Toil, and great the Workman's care
Who dare attempt to fix Impressions there.
But should some Swain more skillfull than the rest
Engrave his Name on this cold Marble Breast
80   Not rolling ages could deface that Name—
Through all the storms of Life tis still the same,
Tho length of Years with moss may shade the Ground
Deep thô unseen remains the secret wound.

                          (1725; 1748)

The Conclusion of a Letter to the Rev. Mr. C——[10]
Mary Barber

   Tis Time to conclude; for I make it a Rule,
To leave off all Writing, when *Con.*[11] comes from School.
He dislikes what I've written, and says, I had better
To send what he calls a *poetical* Letter.

   To this I reply'd, You are out of your Wits;
A Letter in Verse would put him in Fits:
He thinks it a Crime in a Woman, to read—
Then, what would he say, should your Counsel succeed?

10. Philip Chamberlain, a canon of St. Patrick's Cathedral, Dublin, during the time Jonathan Swift, Barber's close friend, was dean there. Swift's dislike of Chamberlain was the source of many arguments with the Archbishop.

11. Constantine Barber, the poet's oldest son, born in 1714.

I pity poor *Barber,*[12] his Wife's so romantick:
A Letter in Rhyme!—Why, the Woman is frantick!   10
This Reading the Poets has quite turn'd her Head!
On my Life, she should have a dark Room, and Straw Bed.[13]
I often heard say, that St. *Patrick*[14] took care,
No poisonous Creature should live in this Air:
He only regarded the Body, I find;
But *Plato*[15] consider'd who poison'd the Mind.
Would they'd follow his Precepts, who sit at the Helm,
And drive Poetasters[16] from out of the Realm!

Her Husband has surely a terrible Life;
There's nothing I dread, like a verse-writing Wife: 20
Defend me, ye Powers, from that fatal Curse;
Which must heighten the Plagues of, *for better for worse!*

May I have a Wife, that will dust her own Floor;
And not the fine Minx, recommended by *More.*[17]
(That he was a Dotard, is granted, I hope,
Who dy'd for asserting the Rights of the *Pope.*)[18]
If ever I marry, I'll chuse me a Spouse,
That shall *serve* and *obey,* as she's bound by her Vows;
That shall, when I'm dressing, attend like a Valet;
Then go to the kitchen, and study my Palate.   30
She has Wisdom enough, that keeps out of the Dirt,
And can make a good *Pudding,* and cut out a *Shirt.*
What Good's in a Dame, that will pore on a Book?
No!—Give me the Wife, that shall save me a Cook.

12. Jonathan Barber, her husband. English by birth, he was a woolen draper.

13. Standard treatment for the mentally ill.

14. Patron saint of Ireland; according to legend, he banished snakes from the island.

15. Greek philosopher. In the *Republic* he argued that poetry should be driven out of the ideal state.

16. Inferior poets.

17. See Sir Thomas More's *Advice to his Son. Barber.* [This allusion refers to lines from *Ad Candidum, Qualis Uxor deligenda.* The line translates to "May she be *Learned,* if possible, or at least capable of being made so!" and was published in the *Guardian* 163 (17 September 1713) and subsequently printed in collected editions of the periodical. The verses were addressed to a friend, not a son. *Eds.*]

18. More, author of *Utopia,* was a leading humanist and statesman. He became Lord Chancellor in 1529, resigned from that office in 1532, and was imprisoned in the Tower of London and then beheaded when he refused to subscribe to the Act of Supremacy, which made King Henry VIII head of the Church of England and called the pope's authority in question.

THUS far I had written—Then turn'd to my Son,
To give him Advice, ere my Letter was done.
My Son, should you marry, look out for a Wife,
That's fitted to lighten the Labours of Life.
Be sure, wed a Woman you thoroughly know,
40   And shun, above all Things, a *housewifely Shrew;*
That would fly to your Study, with Fire in her Looks,
And ask what you got by your poring on Books;
Think Dressing of Dinner the Height of all Science,
And to Peace, and good Humour bid open Defiance.

AVOID the fine Lady, whose Beauty's her Care;
Who sets a high Price on her Shape, and her Air;
Who in Dress, and in Visits, employs the whole Day;
And longs for the Ev'ning, to sit down to Play.[19]

CHUSE a Woman of Wisdom, as well as good Breeding,
50   With a Turn, at least no Aversion, to Reading:
In the Care of her Person, exact and refin'd;
Yet still, let her principal Care be her Mind:
Who can, when her Family Cares give her Leisure,
Without the dear Cards, pass an Ev'ning with Pleasure;
In forming her Children to Virtue and Knowledge,
Nor trust, for that Care, to a School, or a College:
By Learning made humble, not thence taking Airs,
To despise, or neglect, her domestick Affairs:
Nor think her less fitted for doing her Duty,
60   By knowing its Reasons, its Use, and its Beauty.

WHEN you gain her Affection, take care to preserve it;
Lest others persuade her, you do not deserve it.
Still study to heighten the Joys of her Life;
Nor treat her the worse, for her being your Wife.
If in Judgment she errs, set her right, without Pride:
Tis the Province of insolent Fools, to deride.
A Husband's first Praise, is a *Friend* and *Protector:*
Then change not these Titles, for *Tyrant* and *Hector.*
Let your Person be neat, unaffectedly clean,
70   Tho' alone with your Wife the whole Day you remain.

19. Gambling, especially with cards.

Chuse Books, for her Study, to fashion her Mind,
To emulate those who excell'd of her Kind.
Be Religion the principal Care of your Life,
As you hope to be blest in your Children and Wife:
So you, in your Marriage, shall gain its true End;
And find, in your Wife, a *Companion* and *Friend.*

(1734)

Tuesday
St. James's Coffee-House[20]
Silliander and Patch[21]
Lady Mary Wortley Montagu

Thou so many favours hast receiv'd,
Wondrous to tell, and hard to be believ'd,
Oh! H----D,[22] to my lays[23] attention lend,
Hear how two lovers boastingly contend;
Like thee successful, such their bloomy youth,
Renown'd alike for gallantry and truth.
    St. JAMES's bell[24] had toll'd some wretches in,
(As tatter'd riding-hoods[25] alone could sin)
The happier sinners now their charms put out,
And to their manteaus[26] their complexions suit: 10
The opera queens had finish'd half their faces,
And city-dames already taken places;

20. Many of the *Tatler* essays are addressed from this St. James Street coffeehouse; it was highly fashionable, and David Garrick, Sir Joshua Reynolds, and Oliver Goldsmith were frequent visitors.

21. John Campbell (c. 1693–1770), who later became Duke of Argyll, and Algernon Seymour (1684–1750), who would become the seventh Duke of Somerset in 1748. Although little is known about Seymour's early education, he undertook the Grand Tour in 1703 and returned after narrowly escaping pirates in 1706. Seymour was also a distinguished military man.

22. Probably Charles Howard (1696–1765), a family friend of Montagu's. Identification by Isobel Grundy in *Lady Mary Wortley Montagu: Essays and Poems and "Simplicity, A Comedy,"* ed. Robert Halsband and Grundy (Oxford: Clarendon, 1993), 185n. 3.

23. Ballads; lyric or narrative poems meant to be sung.

24. The bells of St. James Piccadilly, dating from 1684, designed and built by Sir Christopher Wren.

25. A large hood worn when horseback riding that covered the shoulders and was sometimes longer. Intended to protect the hair, face, and neck, it could conceal the wearer's identity.

26. Loose cloak, usually sleeveless.

Fops of all kinds to see the Lion,[27] run;
The beauties stay till the first act's begun,
And beaux step home to put fresh linen[28] on.
No well-dress'd youth in coffee-house remain'd,
But pensive PATCH, who on the window lean'd;
And SILLIANDER, that alert and gay,
First pick'd his teeth, and then began to say.

SILLIANDER

20   Why all these sighs? ah! why so pensive grown?
Some cause there is why thus you sit alone.
Does hapless passion all this sorrow move?
Or dost thou envy where the ladies love?

PATCH

If, whom they love, my envy must pursue,
'Tis sure, at least, I never envy You.

SILLIANDER

No, I'm unhappy, You are in the right,
'Tis You they favour, and 'tis Me they slight.
Yet I cou'd tell, but that I hate to boast,
A club of ladies where 'tis Me they toast.

PATCH

30   Toasting does seldom any favour prove;
Like us, they never toast the thing they love.
A certain Duke one night my health begun;
With chearful pledges round the room it run,
Till the young SYLVIA[29] press'd to drink it too,

27. In a popular scene in the opera *Hydaspes*, by Francesco Mancini, Nicolini, wearing a special suit to make him appear nude, kills a lion. The opera enjoyed forty-six performances between 1710 and 1716. Hydaspes, the hero, is condemned to fight a lion in the amphitheater before his beloved. He sings a long aria to the lion and then kills it with his bare hands. A sensational account of the opera is given in *Spectator* 13 (15 March 1711). In a 1719 burlesque presented at Lincoln's Inn Fields, *Harlequin-Hydaspes: or, The Greshamite. A Mock-Opera*, Harlequin kills the lion.

28. Undergarments.

29. Silvia, alternately spelled Sylvia, loved by Valentine in William Shakespeare's *Two Gentlemen of Verona*, is addressed in the song "Who is Silvia?" Her favorite stag was killed by the Trojan Iulus, which led to war between Aeneas and his hosts in Italy. There are other famous Silvias in literature, and the name was conventional by this time.

Started, and vow'd she knew not what to do:
What, drink a fellow's health! she dy'd with shame:
Yet blush'd whenever she pronounc'd my name.

SILLIANDER

   Ill fates pursue me, may I never find
The dice propitious, or the ladies kind,
If fair Miss FLIPPY's fan I did not tear,   40
And one from me she condescends to wear.

PATCH

   Women are always ready to receive;
'Tis then a favour when the sex will give.
A lady (but she is too great to name)
Beauteous in person, spotless is her fame,
With gentle strugglings let me force this ring;
Another day may give another thing.

SILLIANDER

   I cou'd say something—see this billet-doux—[30]
And as for presents—look upon my shoe—
These buckles[31] were not forc'd, nor half a theft,   50
But a young Countess fondly made the gift.

PATCH

   My Countess is more nice,[32] more artful too,
Affects to fly that I may fierce pursue:
This snuff-box[33] which I begg'd, she still deny'd,
And when I strove to snatch it, seem'd to hide;
She laugh'd and fled, and as I sought to seize,
With affectation cramm'd it down her stays:
Yet hop'd she did not place it there unseen,
I press'd her breasts, and pull'd it from between.

30. Love letter.
  31. Buckles could be ornamental as well as practical and could be decorated with jewels, silver designs, and such.
  32. Coy, affecting to be or genuinely modest or refined.
  33. Both men and women took—that is, inhaled—snuff (pulverized tobacco) in the eighteenth
century. Expensive snuff boxes might be made of gold or silver and have jeweled, carved, or brocade
tops.

SILLIANDER

60   Last night, as I stood ogling of her Grace,
Drinking delicious poison from her face,
The soft enchantress did that face decline,
Nor ever rais'd her eyes to meet with mine;
With sudden art some secret did pretend,
Lean'd cross two chairs to whisper to a friend,
While the stiff whalebone with the motion rose,
And thousand beauties to my sight expose.

PATCH

    Early this morn—(but I was ask'd to come)
I drank bohea[34] in CÆLIA's dressing-room:
70   Warm from her bed, to me alone within,
Her night-gown fasten'd with a single pin;
Her night-cloaths tumbled with resistless grace,
And her bright hair play'd careless round her face;
Reaching the kettle, made her gown unpin,
She wore no waistcoat, and her shift was thin.

SILLIANDER

    See TITIANA driving to the park,
Hark! let us follow, 'tis not yet too dark;
In her all beauties of the spring are seen,
Her cheeks are rosy, and her mantle green.

PATCH

80   See, TINTORETTA[35] to the opera goes!
Haste, or the crowd will not permit our bows;
In her the glory of the heav'ns we view,
Her eyes are star-like, and her mantle blue.

SILLIANDER

    What colour does in CÆLIA's stockings shine?
Reveal the secret, and the prize is thine.

---

34. Black tea from China.
35. The names Titiana and Tintoretta allude to the use of cosmetics. Isobel Grundy, *Lady Mary Wortley Montagu: Comet of the Enlightenment* (Oxford: Oxford University Press, 1999), 188.

PATCH

What are her garters! tell me if you can;
I'll freely own thee for the happier man.

Thus PATCH continued his heroic strain,
While SILLIANDER but contends in vain.
After a conquest so important gain'd,   90
Unrival'd PATCH in ev'ry ruelle[36] reign'd.

(1747)

The Art of Coquettry[37]
Charlotte Lennox

Ye lovely Maids, whose yet unpractis'd Hearts
Ne'er felt the Force of Love's resistless Darts;
Who justly set a Value on your Charms,
Power all your Wish, but Beauty all your Arms:[38]
Who o'er Mankind wou'd fain exert your Sway,
And teach the lordly Tyrant to obey:
Attend my Rules to you alone addrest,
Deep let them sink in every female Breast.
The Queen of Love[39] herself my Bosom fires,
Assists my Numbers,[40] and my Thoughts inspires.   10
Me she instructed in each secret Art,
How to enslave, and keep the vanquish'd Heart;
When the stol'n Sigh to heave, or drop the Tear,
The melting Languish,[41] the obliging Fear;
Half-stifled Wishes, broken, kind Replies,
And all the various Motions of the Eyes.
To teach the Fair by different Ways to move
The soften'd Soul, and bend the Heart to Love.

36. Morning reception held in a lady's bedroom.

37. Flirting; practicing insincere behavior intended to awaken admiration or love in the opposite sex with no intention of reciprocating.

38. A deliberate reminder of Alexander Pope's analysis of women in *To a Lady. Of the Characters of Women:* "In Men, we various Ruling Passions find, / In Women, two almost divide the kind; / Those, only fix'd, they first or last obey, / The Love of Pleasure, and the Love of Sway" (lines 207–10).

39. Venus, Roman goddess of beauty and love, mother of Cupid.

40. Metrical feet and verses.

41. The affectation of lassitude with posed reclining.

Proud of her Charms, and conscious of her Face,
20   The haughty Beauty calls forth every Grace;
With fierce Defiance throws the killing Dart,
By Force she wins, by Force she keeps the Heart.[42]
The witty Fair one nobler Game pursues,
Aims at the Head, but the rapt Soul subdues.
The languid Nymph enslaves with softer Art,
With sweet Neglect she steals into the Heart;
Slowly she moves her swimming Eyes around,
Conceals her Shaft, but meditates the Wound:
Her gentle Languishments the Gazers move,
30   Her Voice is Musick, and her Looks are Love.
Tho' not to all Heaven does these Gifts impart,
What's theirs by Nature may be yours by Art.
But let your Airs be suited to your Face,
Nor to a Languish[43] tack a sprightly Grace.
The short round Face, brisk Eyes, and auburn Hair,
Must smiling Joy in every Motion wear;
Her quick unsettled Glances deal around,
Hide her Design, and seem by Chance to wound.
Dark rolling Eyes a Languish may assume,
40   And tender Looks and melting Airs become:
The pensive Head upon the Hand reclin'd,
As if some sweet Disorder fill'd the Mind.
Let the heav'd Breast a struggling Sigh restrain,
And seem to stop the falling Tear with Pain.
The Youth, who all the soft Distress believes,
Soon wants the kind Compassion which he gives.
But Beauty, Wit, and Youth may sometimes fail,
Nor always o'er the stubborn Soul prevail.
Then let the fair One have recourse to Art,
50   And, if not vanquish, undermine the Heart.
First form your artful Looks with studious Care,
From mild to grave, from tender to severe.
Oft on the careless Youth your Glances dart,
A tender Meaning let each Look impart.
Whene'er he meets your Looks with modest Pride,
And soft Confusion turn your Eyes aside,

42. These lines recall Pope's Belinda as she engages in combat in *The Rape of the Lock*.
43. A tender, melting glance, one of the flirtatious arts women practiced.

Let a soft Sigh steal out, as if by Chance,
Then cautious turn, and steal another Glance.
Caught by these Arts, with Pride and Hope elate,
The destin'd Victim rushes on his Fate: 60
Pleas'd, his imagin'd Victory pursues,
And the kind Maid with soften'd Glances views;
Contemplates now her Shape, her Air, her Face,
And thinks each Feature wears an added Grace:
'Till Gratitude, which first his Bosom proves,
By slow Degrees is ripen'd into Love.
'Tis harder still to fix than gain a Heart;
What's won by Beauty, must be kept by Art.
Too kind a Treatment the blest Lover cloys,
And oft Despair the growing Flame destroys: 70
Sometimes with Smiles receive him, sometimes Tears,
And wisely balance both his Hopes and Fears.
Perhaps he mourns his ill-requited Pains,
Condemns your Sway, and strives to break his Chains;
Behaves as if he now your Scorn defy'd,
And thinks at least he shall alarm your Pride:
But with Indifference view the seeming Change,
And let your Eyes after new Conquests range;
While his torn Breast with jealous Fury burns,
He hopes, despairs, hates, and adores by Turns;   80
With Anguish now repents the weak Deceit,
And powerful Passion bears him to your Feet.
Strive not the jealous Lover to perplex,
Ill suits Suspension with that haughty Sex;
Rashly they judge, and always think the worst,
And Love is often banish'd by Distrust.
To these an open free Behaviour wear,
Avoid Disguise, and seem at least sincere.
Whene'er you meet affect a glad Surprize,
And give unmelting Softness to your Eyes: 90
By some unguarded Word your Love reveal,
And anxiously the rising Blush conceal.
By Arts like these the Jealous you deceive,
Then most deluded when they most believe.
But while in all you seek to raise Desire,
Beware the fatal Passion you inspire:
Each soft intruding Wish in Time reprove,

And guard against the sweet Invader Love.
Not for the tender were these Rules design'd,
100   Who in their Faces show their yielding Mind:
Eyes that a native Languishment can wear,
Whose Smiles are artless, and whose Blush sincere;
But the gay Nymph who Liberty can prize.
And vindicate the Triumph of her Eyes:
Who o'er Mankind a haughty Rule maintains,
Whose Wit can manage what her Beauty gains:
Such by these Arts their Empire may improve,
And what they lost by Nature gain by Love.

(1747)

A New Song to the Tune of *Chevy-Chase*[44]
Ann Thicknesse

I.
'Tis of a noble L[or]d I sing;
An E[ar]l of high renown;
Of whose atchievements fame doth ring,
Throughout this mighty town.

II.
Youthful and handsome once was he,
And am'rous all his life;
And all historians do agree
That once he lov'd his wife.

III.
By Cupid arm'd with all his arts,
10   T'assist the wanton trade;
Among the gentle virgins hearts
He grievous havock made.

44. Revered, popular ballad polished and revised from the ancient "Hunting of the Cheviot." Addison's *Spectator* 70 and 74 (21 and 25 May 1711) gave it a patriotic gloss and compared it to the works of Homer and Virgil. The tune was used for a variety of purposes; in *The Beggar's Opera*, act 3, sc. 13, John Gay has MacHeath sing a drunken song set to it.

IV.

He laughing play'd with Cupid's snares;
It but his Hours amused;
And often has been heard to swear,
He never was refus'd.

V.

Time who destroy'd the walls of Troy,
This Champion did defy;
He kept the post of youth and joy,
Nor from love's field wou'd fly.   20

VI.

In that vile place, the city call'd,
A lovely maiden dwell'd;
Whose charms his mighty heart subdued,
And all his valour quell'd.

VII.

One day as am'rous Phæbus deign'd
This pupil to inspire;
While she to learn her lesson feign'd,
She stole his fav'rite lyre.

VIII.

His stolen prize, in spight of shame,
To all the world is known;   30
Its praises too she boldly claims,
And wears them as her own.

IX.

He saw her smile; he heard her sing;
He felt the raging smart;
The pain so often felt before,
Again possess'd his heart.

X.

Upon his knees the hero fell,
He sigh'd, he wept, he swore;

Offer'd his heart, his life, his soul,
40   And eke[45] his wealthy store.

XI.
He try'd all ways that those who love
Use to express their pain;
From her white hand he took————her glove,
And drew it on again.

XII.
Then to the charmer of his heart,
He made his ardent pray'r,
And vow'd to settle on his part,
Eight hundred pounds a year!

XIII.
The Maid with scorn his suit repell'd;
50   Her virtue stood the field;
Her heart refused to be compell'd
On such base terms to yield.

XIV.
This island L[or]d was sorely griev'd
To find she stood her ground;
His pride was picqu'd, his hope deceiv'd,
Its first repulse had found.

XV.
Dishonest love can never bear
True virtue's pride and scorn;
Repulsed, its refuge is despair,
60   Or to revenge will turn.

XVI.
I scorn my fate, the maiden said;
The world's applause I'll try;
While vice her votaries has paid,
Shall virtue silent die?

45. Also.

XVII.
The p[ee]r[46] inform'd of her design,
Most meanly condescends
To soil her fame, her project spoil's
In whispers to her friends.

XVIII.
With idle tales of this and that,
He female ears amused;   70
To shew his zeal, and his revenge,
Five guineas he refused.

XIX.
Now God reform all noble L[or]ds,
That lead unrighteous lives;
May shame be still their just reward,
That do defraud their wives.

(1761)

City Splendor,
A Town Eclogue[47]
Ann Murry

MR. WEALTHY
Well! now my dear, beloved Wife,
We must extend our plan of life.
How will our country cousins stare,
To see me soon a great Lord-May'r![48]

MRS. WEALTHY
The rich State-Coach you will not grace,
Adorn'd by Chaplain, Sword, and Mace.[49]

---

46. Member of the British peerage, in this case an earl.

47. A poem in the form of a dialogue or soliloquy. The term was used for Virgil's pastorals, and Murry is following Lady Mary Wortley Montagu in writing satiric city eclogues.

48. Mayor of a city with a charter, which at that time included London, York, and Dublin. Charters had been granted by William the Conqueror to guarantee special rights.

49. Signs of the office. The lord mayor's household, like those of many people of rank, had a chaplain. The lord mayor carried the ancient sword and mace of his city at ceremonial events.

As for myself, the golden Chain[50]
I must confess will make me vain;
And then how much shall be delighted,
10   When by his Majesty you're knighted!
Adieu now to my one horse chair,
I'll have a Coach to take the air.
With speed we'll quit vile Wormwood-Street,[51]
And decorate our Country-seat;
The House must be entirely-furnish'd,
And all the Glasses,[52] gilt and burnish'd.

Mr. WEALTHY
Figures I'll buy to grace the nitches,
And make canals of all the ditches;[53]
Which, stor'd with various kinds of fish,
20   On Sundays may afford a dish,
The Sheriffs[54] richly to regale,
With Poultry, Beef, and Yorkshire Ale.
Thus much I promise all my party,
An English welcome, rough and hearty.

Mrs. WEALTHY
Indeed, my dear! you shock my sight;
I fear you'll never grow polite.
I, to be sure, was born a heiress,
And fit to be a Lady-May'ress;
But as for you, with all your riches,
30   You wear such dirty Leather-Breeches;
And such a frightful shabby wig,
It looks like bristles of a Pig.
Your Day-Book and your Ledger seem,
To be your most engaging theme.
What need so often to repeat,

50. The gold chain with heavy seal as ornament is another emblem of the office of lord mayor.

51. A small, dark street in Bishopsgate with an unattractive name. It was near Liverpool Street and London Wall, where the wormwood plant sprung up on waste ground and climbed the wall.

52. Windows.

53. Fashionable "improvement" to a country estate.

54. A high official in cities, the representative of royal authority presided at parliamentary elections and performed other important duties.

Your expectations of the Fleet![55]
And then you talk so much of Trade,
Boasting your debts are punctual paid:
Which is not now at all the fashion.

Mr. WEALTHY
You really put me in a passion.   40
Politeness is an empty name:
On Riches I depend for fame.

Mrs. WEALTHY
With all your mighty boasted wealth,
You neither taste of peace or health.
I hate extravagance and waste,
Yet like things in the modern taste.
Your Father's meanness you inherit,
And have no proper pride or spirit.
When at the Mansion-House[56] I live,
Such Entertainments I will give,   50
And such a Lord-May'rs feast and ball,
As shall delight the crouded hall.
No Barbers,[57] Clowns,[58] or paltry Singers,
Or Pick-Pockets with nimble fingers,
But people of the first degree,
Shall form the brilliant company.

Mr. WEALTHY
We must not break establish'd rules,
To banish Knaves, Poltroons,[59] or Fools;
The Aldermen must hold their place,[60]
And serve the Cavalcade to grace;   60
By help of whom, the Lord-May'rs day,
Will City consequence display;

55. Fleet Prison, where Mr. Wealthy has confined his debtors and from whom he expects at least partial payment.
56. Official residence of the lord mayor of London.
57. Practitioners of surgery and dentistry, with less training and skill than, for instance, surgeons.
58. Country people, rustics.
59. Worthless coward; cowardly rascal.
60. An alderman was the chief officer and magistrate of a city ward, just below the lord mayor in status and authority.

The Common-Council[61] are invited,
And all their families delighted.
Our Barges[62] are extremely fine,
Bless me! what plenty when we dine.
The liquor like a mighty ocean,
Affords an inexhaustless potion,
Of which we quaff like eager fish;

70   Like Cormorants attack each dish;
Transported by our happy fare,
Talk Politics, Eat, Drink, and Swear.

MRS. WEALTHY
I hate these kind of brutal feasts,
Less fit for Men than savage beasts;
Below the brute creation sunk,
When by intemperance they're drunk.

MR. WEALTHY
I must confess 'tis very wrong,
Those faults to Citizens[63] belong;
We glory in our Cent. per Cent,[64]

80   On profit ever found intent;
And laugh at vain ideal schemes,
Fictitious fancies, idle dreams,
Chimeras[65] of the ton, and taste,
And spendthrifts fortunes soon laid waste:
Marking the fall and rise of stocks,
We keep our deeds in iron box.

MRS. WEALTHY
Pray when shall Juliet come from France?
On Easter-Monday how she'll dance!

61. Electoral assembly of all the City Livery Company men. It chose the two sheriffs and the two aldermen who would join the Court of Aldermen.

62. Much travel in London was by barge, and the lord mayor's was luxurious and richly decorated. During processions such as on Lord Mayor's Day, it was decorated with historical symbols and musicians played on it.

63. London dwellers, shopkeepers, merchants, and tradesmen, often ridiculed throughout the century, as Frances Burney does in *Evelina*.

64. Interest equal in amount to the principal; literally, a hundred (cent.) for every hundred.

65. In Greek mythology, a chimera was a monster with the head of a lion, the body of a goat, and dragon's tail; synonym for a wild, unrealistic fantasy.

I think my dear, we'll fetch her over;
Or meet her when she comes to Dover;   90
Her education is complete,
And for her height, 'tis near six feet.

Mr. WEALTHY
How much of all her charms you boast!

Mrs. WEALTHY
I could engage she'll be a toast.
Juliet is quite her mother's daughter,
And will occasion[66] desp'rate slaughter;
For, as you know, when I was young,
My beauty did not pass unsung:
I always made a mighty shew,
And hop'd to gain an Earl or Beau.   100
But after all my care and pains,
My father sought substantial gains;
And threaten'd his severe displeasure,
If I refus'd your worship's treasure.
Thus, in the prime and pride of life,
I was compell'd to be your wife.
Nor should I murmur at my lot,
If you your vulgar ways forgot;
And was for Magistracy fit,
With grace and dignity to sit.   110
I cannot but, my dear, declare,
That now I wish, you wore your Hair.
Your aukward Taylor has no taste;
Your clothes must be superbly lac'd.
Yet, after all, you'll look so rough,
To my rich gems, and silver stuff.[67]
Methinks, I see the servants wait,
To follow us to Court in state.
King of the City! what a sound!
Myself the Queen! my head turns round!   120
My Daughter too, the Princess Royal!
I hope our subjects will be loyal.

66. Cause.
67. Woven material for making clothing.

Inlist in Freedom's glorious cause;
The surest means to gain applause.

MR. WEALTHY
Of Cash I have such wond'rous plenty,
That Earls or Dukes, I'd purchase twenty;
And therefore have no cause to spare,
My riches to exalt my heir:
So that I am resolv'd to spend,
130   My money with a cheerful friend.
At Newington[68] I mean to build
A Drawing-Room, with pictures fill'd;
Then I'll pull down that odious paling,
And have some wooden Chinese railing;[69]
That we may see the road with ease;
Which all our visitors will please.
Upon our spacious rural lawn,
We'll keep some sheep, and feed the fawn;
Some able workman shall repair,
140   The ruins and the root-house chair.
I have my eye on Farmer Craddock,
To buy his fields to make a Paddock.
How very great a paddock sounds,
Well stor'd with deer, and flocks, and hounds!
When I have gain'd sufficient treasure,
I then will be a man of pleasure;
Build and rebuild, plant and lay waste,
Agreeable to the rules of taste;
The country air will make me healthy,
150   And who so great as Sir John Wealthy!

(1779)

---

68. Fashionable suburb of London to which prosperous merchants moved.
69. He imagines replacing his fence made of pales, strips of wood, with the more open, fashionable fencing that would allow passers-by to admire his house, and give those in the house a good view of the road.

Lines on hearing it declared that No Women were so Handsome as the English

Mary Robinson

Beauty, the attribute of Heaven!
In various forms to mortals given,
With magic skill enslaves mankind,
As sportive fancy sways the mind.
Search the wide world, go where you will,
VARIETY pursues you still;
Capricious Nature knows no bound,
Her unexhausted gifts are found
In ev'ry clime, in ev'ry face,
Each has its own peculiar grace.   10

To GALLIA's[70] frolic scenes repair,
There reigns the tyny DEBONAIRE;
The mincing step—the slender waist,
The lip with bright vermilion grac'd:
The short pert nose—the pearly teeth,
With the small dimpled chin beneath,—
The social converse, gay and free,
The smart BON-MOT[71]—and REPARTEE.[72]

ITALIA boasts the melting fair,
The pointed step—the haughty air,   20
Th' empassion'd tone, the languid eye,
The song of thrilling harmony;
Insidious LOVE conceal'd in smiles,
That charms—and as it charms beguiles.

View GRECIAN MAIDS, whose finish'd forms
The wond'ring sculptor's fancy warms!
There let thy ravish'd eye behold
The softest gems of Nature's mould;

70. France.
71. Witty saying.
72. Swift, witty retort or reply.

Each charm, that REYNOLDS[73] learnt to trace,
30   From SHERIDAN's[74] bewitching face.

  Imperious TURKEY's pride is seen
In Beauty's rich luxuriant mien;
The dark and sparkling orbs that glow
Beneath a polish'd front of snow:
The auburn curl that zephyr[75] blows
About the cheek of brightest rose;
The shorten'd zone, the swelling breast,
With costly gems profusely drest;
Reclin'd in softly-waving bow'rs,
40   On painted beds of fragrant flow'rs;
Where od'rous canopies dispense
ARABIA's spices to the sense;
Where listless indolence and ease,
Proclaim the sov'reign wish, to please.
'Tis thus, capricious FANCY shows
How far her frolic empire goes!
On ASIA's sands, on ALPINE snow,
We trace her steps where'er we go;
The BRITISH Maid with timid grace;
50   The tawny INDIAN's varnish'd face;
The jetty AFRICAN; the fair
Nurs'd by EUROPA's softer air;
With various charms delight the mind,
For FANCY governs ALL MANKIND.

                                        (1791)

---

73. Sir Joshua Reynolds (1723–92), one of the foremost portrait painters of the century.

74. Mrs. Sheridan's portrait, by Sir Joshua Reynolds, in the character of St. Cecilia. *Robinson.* [Robinson frequented the National Academy exhibits. In this painting, which Reynolds believed to be the best he had ever done, Elizabeth Sheridan, a talented singer, is depicted as the patron saint of music. *Eds.*]

75. The west wind, lover of Flora, goddess of flowers; any soft, warm wind.

January, 1795
Mary Robinson

I
Pavement slip'ry; People sneezing;
Lords in ermine, beggars freezing;
Nobles, scarce the Wretched heeding;
Gallant Soldiers—fighting!—bleeding!

II
Lofty Mansions, warm and spacious;
Courtiers, cringing and voracious:
Titled Gluttons, dainties carving;
Genius, in a garret, starving!

III
Wives, who laugh at passive Spouses;
Theatres, and Meeting-houses;[76]   10
Balls, where simpring Misses languish;
Hospitals, and groans of anguish.

IV
Arts and Sciences bewailing;
Commerce drooping, Credit failing!
Placemen,[77] mocking subjects loyal;
Separations; Weddings Royal!

V
Authors, who can't earn a dinner;
Many a subtle rogue, a winner!
Fugitives, for shelter seeking;
Misers hoarding, Tradesmen breaking![78]   20

VI
Ladies gambling, night and morning;
Fools, the works of Genius scorning!

76. Nonconformist churches; that is, not Church of England.
77. Undeserving appointees to positions.
78. Going bankrupt.

Ancient Dames for Girls mistaken,
Youthful Damsels—quite forsaken!

VII
Some in luxury delighting;
More in talking than in fighting;
Lovers old, and Beaux decrepid;
Lordlings, empty and insipid.

VIII
Poets, Painters, and Musicians;
Lawyers, Doctors, Politicians;
Pamphlets, Newspapers, and Odes,
Seeking Fame, by diff'rent roads.

IX
Taste and Talents quite deserted;
All the laws of Truth perverted;
Arrogance o'er Merit soaring!
Merit, silently deploring!

X
Gallant Souls with empty purses;
Gen'rals, only fit for Nurses!
Schoolboys, smit with Martial spirit,
Taking place of vet'ran merit!

XI
Honest men, who can't get places;
Knaves, who shew unblushing faces;
Ruin hasten'd, Peace retarded!
Candour spurn'd, and Art rewarded!

(1795)

When First I Got Married
Carolina Oliphant Nairne

When first that I got married,
  A happy man to be;
My wife turn'd out a very cross,

We never could agree;
And what I thought my greatest bliss,
    Was grief without compare;
For all that I can say or do,
    She's mine for evermair.
        And she's aye plaguing me,
            She's aye plaguing me,   10
        And she's aye plaguing me,
            She winna let me be.

For the first week or something mair,
    A bonny thing she was;
But ere the second Sunday came,
    She made me cry alas!
Alas! alas! I often cry,
    It's needless here to tell;
For what's the cause of all my grief,
    Fu' weel she kens[79] hersel'.   20
        For she's aye plaguing me, &c.

I daurna[80] ca' the house my ain,
    Or ony thing that's in't,
For if I chance to speak a word,
    She flies like fire from flint;
An' when her barley ends[81] are on,
    Which often is the case,
The very first thing that she gets,
    She dashes in my face.
        And she's aye dashing me, &c.   30

When I am for merriment,
    She dowie[82] is an' sad;
And when I am for soberness,
    She gangs distracted mad.
When I am in a speaking mood,
    She silent sits and dumb;
And when I wish for silence,

79. Knows, recognizes.
80. Dare not.
81. When she is drunk.
82. Dismal.

She rattles like a drum.
　For she's aye drummin' me, &c.

40　　　　　Oh, marriage is a paradise,
　　As I have heard folk tell,
But it's been to me, from first to last,
　　A purgatory fell;[83]
Yet I hae ae comfort left,
　　Ae comfort, an' nae mair,
The pains o' death will break my bonds,
　　And bury a' my care.
　　　　And she'll sune bury me,
　　　　　She'll sune bury me,
50　　　　　She'll sune bury me,
　　　　　An' then she'll let me be.

　　　　　　　　　　　(1807)

West End Fair[84]

Anna Laetitia Barbauld

Dame Charity[85] one day was tired
With nursing of her children three,—
　　So might you be
If you had nursed and nursed so long
　　A little squalling throng;—
So she, like any earthly lady,
Resolved for once she'd have a play-day.

"I cannot always go about
To hospitals and prisons trudging,
10　　　Or fag[86] from morn to night
　　Teaching to spell and write
　　　A barefoot rout,[87]

---

83. Savage, cruel.
84. One of the many small local fairs, this one was at West End, Hampstead.
85. Charity was the daughter of Zeus.
86. Drudge.
87. A rout was a fashionable evening assembly, a contrast to Barbauld's comic barefoot gathering.

Swept from the streets by poor Lancaster,[88]
    My sub-master.

"That Howard[89] ran me out of breath,
And Thornton[90] and a hundred more
    Will be my death:
The air is sweet, the month is gay,
And I," said she, "must have a holiday."

So said, she doffed her robes of brown   20
In which she commonly is seen,—
    Like French Beguine,—[91]
And sent for ornaments to town:
And Taste in Flavia's form stood by,
Penciled her eyebrows, curled her hair,
Disposed each ornament with care,
And hung her round with trinkets rare,—
She scarely, looking in the glass,
    Knew her own face.

So forth she sallied blithe and gay,   30
And met dame Fashion by the way;
And many a kind and friendly greeting
    Passed on their meeting:
Nor let the fact your wonder move,
    Abroad, and on a gala-day,
Fashion and she are hand and glove.

    So on they walked together,
    Bright was the weather;
Dame Charity was frank and warm;
But being rather apt to tire,   40
    She leant on Fashion's arm.

---

88. Joseph Lancaster (1778–1838), who educated poor children with his innovative system of "sub-masters." McCarthy and Kraft, *The Poems of Anna Letitia Barbauld*, ed. McCarthy and Kraft (Athens: University of Georgia Press, 1994), 303n. 13–14.

89. John Howard (1726–90), prison reformer.

90. Henry Thornton (1760–1850), founder of the British and Foreign Bible Society and a supporter of Hannah More's Sunday school movement. McCarthy and Kraft, *Poems of Anna Letitia Barbauld*, 303n. 16.

91. Lay sisters not bound by permanent vows.

And now away for West End fair,
Where whiskey,[92] chariot, coach, and chair,
   Are all in requisition.
   In neat attire the Graces[93]
Behind the counters take their places,
   And humbly do petition
To dress the booths with flowers and sweets,
   As fine as any May-day,
Where Charity with Fashion meets,
   And keeps her play-day.

(1825)

Sources

Montagu: *Lady Mary Wortley Montagu: Essays and Poems and "Simplicity, A Comedy,"* ed. Robert Halsband and Isobel Grundy (Oxford: Clarendon, 1977), 242–44. Barber: *Poems on Several Occasions* (London, 1734), 58–62. Montagu: *Six Town Eclogues. With some other Poems* (London, 1747), 9–14. Lennox: *Poems on Several Occasions. Written by a Young Lady* (London, 1747), 61–67. Thicknesse: *A Letter from Miss F——d, Addressed to a Person of Distinction* (London, 1761), 41–47. Murry: *Poems on Various Subjects* (London, 1779), 85–94. Robinson: *Poems by Mrs. M. Robinson,* 2 vols. (London, 1791), 1:94–96; "January, 1795," *Morning Post and the Fashionable World* 2 (29 January 1795), n.pag. Nairne: *Life and Songs of the Baroness Nairne with a Memoir and Poems of Carolina Oliphant the Younger,* ed. Charles Rogers, 2nd ed. (London: Griffin, 1869), 63–64. Barbauld: *The Works of Anna Lætitia Barbauld. With a Memoir by Lucy Aikin,* 2 vols. (London, 1825), 1:220–23.

92. Light, one-horse carriage.
93. Sister goddesses who controlled pleasure, charm, and beauty in human life: Aglaia (Brilliance), Euphrosyne (Joy), and Thalia (Bloom).

⋊G⋉

The Hymn

The hymns in this section provide a kind of history of conceptions and uses of the hymn in the long eighteenth century. The hymns written before 1710 tend to be odes or, even if in hymn stanza, were not intended for singing. The later hymns were written for solo or congregational singing, and some survive in hymnbooks into our own time. By the time of Elizabeth Singer Rowe's death in 1737, poets who wrote hymns were writing in an entirely different context from those writing in 1696 or 1715, and those in 1780 in yet another situation. The classical hymn, which celebrated public events and generals and military victories as well as religious occasions, was often in ode form. It was reputed to have been written as early as Homer, and Edmund Spenser's *Fowre Hymnes,* James Thomson's *Hymn on Solitude,* and Sarah Fyge Egerton's *The Extacy* are in this tradition. Spenser, Ben Jonson, and Milton wrote hymns as odes, and according to the *Oxford English Dictionary,* one definition of *hymn* was "religious ode," originally meaning "a song or ode in praise of gods or heroes." The slow acceptance of congregational singing and then its revolutionary growth during the Evangelical movement are subtle threads woven through the history of the hymn as well. Many denominations resisted congregational singing or insisted that only paraphrases of biblical passages, especially the Psalms, were acceptable. They believed that church song should come from the "Word of God" alone, and they sung almost nothing but Psalms. John Calvin had thought carols were frivolous and had distrusted melody. The Presbyterians and Independents embraced hymns first, and the Methodists did so in 1739. The resistance to hymns actually grew; there were sixteen non-Psalms in the 1713 Anglican book of worship but only thirteen in 1737. The Baptists and the Quakers opposed congregational singing, including the metrical Psalms, and the General Baptists did not embrace congregational singing until the 1770s.[1]

Dozens of hymns by Isaac Watts and Charles Wesley remain in hymnbooks, but they are rarely considered poets. Critics refer to them as existing in a "compartment of literature," and a few protest their exclusion, one even going so far as to remark that doing so "impoverishes our understanding of eighteenth-century poetry."[2] Some would say that it impoverishes our literary history. In a major reference book, Bonamy Dobrée praises Watts for "his variety, his metrical experiment, and his imagery" and for his "fusion of image with thought and emotion."[3] These are distinguishing characteristics of all of the hymns in this section.

It has been argued that hymns are the great personal lyrics of the century, and all of the hymns in this section reinforce that claim. They were written for many of the same reasons that people write poetry and often as devotional exercises. A new, broad recognition of the personal benefits of hymn writing came before the acceptance of congregational singing. Mary Chudleigh wrote several of these hymns that bridge the private and public, including *The Elevation,* which opens this section of poems. Other proclaimed benefits included meditation, greater understanding of the scriptures, and cultivation of appropriate religious attitudes toward all the experiences of life. Inseparable from understanding composition this way is conceiving of reading hymns for these purposes, and neither is a common practice today. Even after singing in church became common, people continued to write hymns for meditation that were never intended to be sung. Elizabeth Singer Rowe, in one of her most reprinted books, *Devout Exercises of the Heart, in Meditation and Soliloquy, Prayer and Praise* (1737), writes about the benefits to herself and others that the texts bestowed when circulated in manuscript. Hannah More's *A New Christmas Hymn* was written for the *Cheap Repository Tracts; Entertaining, Moral, and Religious* rather than for performance. These tracts were published weekly to provide a "useful" and entertaining alternative to the "vicious Tracts circulated by hawkers."[4] By the time they were collected in the edition in which this poem appears, nearly 2 million had been sold (many to be given to schools, prisons, workhouses, hospitals, and churches). This particular volume was advertised widely as being an appropriate textbook for boarding schools as well as for family reading. More's poem uses the techniques of the popular biblical paraphrases as well as of hymns to increase its educational and devotional potential.

Important distinctions also exist between the hymns composed by those who stand in pulpits and those who sit in pews. For instance, the concluding verse of one of Rowe's hymns begins in a manner reminiscent of Watts's *O God our help in ages past:* "My God, my hope, my vast reward, / And all I wou'd possess" (not included). In contrast to Watts's hymn, hers uses the first-person singular pronoun, and she usually creates an individual standing before her God rather than a community of believers rehearsing their faith. Although Octavia Walsh's hymn begins with the sense of a group of believers, it quickly becomes personal, "In me his Glory he display'd, / The Creature which his Hand has made." Although some of Helen Maria Williams's hymns still appear in hymnbooks, the one in this section, *A Hymn, Written among the Alps,* was her response to the things she saw during the time she took refuge in the Alps during the French

Revolution and too topical for general worship. She included it in her *Tour in Switzerland* (1798) rather than publishing it with poems or hymns.

Eighteenth-century hymns are also important because they contributed greatly to bringing new imagery and technical strategies to poetry. A lively debate sprung up in which some thinkers asserted that God "taught Poetry first to the Hebrews" and that the Hebrews produced a canon that "creates superior competing forms" to those of the Greeks and Romans.[5] Poets, therefore, drew upon biblical as well as classical poetry. The influence of the Psalms, the songs of prophets and the Virgin Mary, and of Pindaric and Horatian hymns and odes flowed into hymns. Some of the century's best odes were religious. For example, *The Extacy* may be Egerton's best poem. A carefully composed hymn with Miltonic echoes, it shows considerable understanding of the formal demands of both odes and eighteenth-century hymns. The opening address and the use of repetition are conventional in hymns, and Egerton uses them to good effect. J. R. Watson, who has analyzed thousands of hymns, points out that strong first lines call for attention and signal that something meaningful is about to be said. Many use imperatives and the soul as metonymy, as this hymn does.[6] The expansive perspective that surveys the world of God's creations and man's misuse of them is also common. For example, Egerton takes us "Deep in Earths center." Her ode is divided into six marked stanzas reflecting the patterned stanza movement inherited from choral dance and song. The odd-numbered verses are optimistic and use images of rising; the even-numbered ones present scenes of darkness, misery, chaos, and sin. Her expansive poem anticipates themes associated with great mid-century poems, such as Thomas Gray's *Elegy Written in a Country Church-Yard,* and the global and celestial sweep of late-century poems, including Anne Bannerman's epic *The Genii,* both of which imaginatively use travel in a winged chariot.

A sign of the importance of the triumph of congregational singing, Elizabeth Singer Rowe's 1696 *Poems* included religious poetry but no hymns, while the 1739 *Miscellaneous Works* includes thirteen hymns in the first volume alone. In the second half of the century, many hymns by women were performed publicly. Some of them are in twenty-first-century hymnals. For example, three of Mary Masters's are *Be the loving God my friend, O my adored Redeemer! deign to be,* and *'Tis religion that can give Sweetest pleasures while we live* (none included).[7] In this section, the hymns by Judith Madan, Anna Laetitia Barbauld, Susannah Harrison, Helen Maria Williams *(A Hymn),* and Mary Whateley Darwall were all sung by congregations. Madan's, Barbauld's, and Williams's are still included in hymnbooks, and a dozen other hymns by Barbauld continue to be printed and sung. Although most modern readers probably are entering an unfamiliar world in this section, the poems will be, we think, richly rewarding.

Notes

1. The story of this long struggle is recounted in Louis F. Benson, *The English Hymn: Its Development and Use* (1915; Richmond, VA: John Knox Press, 1962); see esp. chaps. 2–4.

2. David Morris, "A Poetry of Absence," in *The Cambridge Companion to Eighteenth-Century Poetry*, ed. John Sitter (Cambridge: Cambridge University Press, 2001), 231. Critics who document the neglect and undervaluing of religious poetry in the eighteenth century include Margaret Doody, in *The Daring Muse: Augustan Poetry Reconsidered* (Cambridge: Cambridge University Press, 1985), esp. 139, and Madeline Marshall and Janet Todd, in *English Congregational Hymns in the Eighteenth Century* (Lexington: University Press of Kentucky, 1982).

3. Bonamy Dobrée, *English Literature in the Early Eighteenth Century, 1700–1740* (Oxford: Clarendon, 1959), 153–58.

4. "Advertisement," in *Cheap Repository Tracts* (London, 1798), v.

5. Paula R. Backscheider, *Eighteenth-Century Women Poets and Their Poetry* (Baltimore: Johns Hopkins University Press, 2005), 138–40.

6. J. R. Watson, *The English Hymn: A Critical and Historical Study* (Oxford: Clarendon, 1997), 146–48.

7. Samuel J. Rogal, *Sisters of Sacred Song* (New York: Garland, 1981), s.v. "Masters."

The Elevation
Mary Chudleigh

1.

O how ambitious is my Soul,
   How high she now aspires!
There's nothing can on Earth controul,
   Or limit her Desires.

2.

Upon the Wings of Thought she flies
   Above the reach of Sight,
And finds a way thro' pathless Skies
   To everlasting Light:

3.

From whence with blameless Scorn she views
   The Follies of Mankind;   10
And smiles to see how each pursues
   Joys fleeting as the Wind.

4.

Yonder's the little Ball of Earth,
   It lessens as I rise;
That Stage of transitory Mirth,
   Of lasting Miseries:

5.

My Scorn does into Pity turn,
   And I lament the Fate
Of Souls, that still in Bodies mourn,
   For Faults which they create: 20

6.

Souls without Spot, till Flesh they wear,
   Which their pure Substance stains:
While thy th'uneasie Burthen bear,
   They're never free from Pains.

(1703)

The Extacy

Sarah Fyge Egerton

I.

Mount, Mount, my Soul on high,
Cut thro' the spacious Sky;
Scale the great Mountainous heaps that be,
Betwixt the upper World, and thee.
Stop not, till thou the utmost Region know,
Leave all the Glittering Worlds below:
   Then take thy Noble flight,
Into the sacred Magazine[1] of Light,
View the bright, the Empyrean Throne[2]

10   Of the great, the Almighty ONE.
All the Miriades[3] of shining Hosts survey,
With the seraphick blazing Throng;
Celebrating their Eternal Day,
   With an Eternal Song.
In vain my dazled Soul would gaze around,
(The beatifick Glorys so confound)
It must be quite disrob'd, e'er tread this Holy Ground. }

II.

   Descend you daring Spirit, think 'tis fair,
If thou may'st traverse the inferior Air,

20   Content with humbler Curiosities,
   View the expanded the Skies,
With radient Worlds, 'tis richly deck'd,
   By the Almighty Architect.
   Mount *Charles*'s Wain,[4]
Drive over all the Ætherial Plain,
   And to augment thy Speed,
With blazing Comets lash the Restive[5] Steeds.
Make them neigh aloud and Foam,
Till all the Sky a Milky way become;

1. Storehouse; military supply warehouse.
2. Of or pertaining to the sphere of fire or highest heaven or the home of God and pure light.
3. Myriads, countless numbers.
4. Charlemagne's wagon or the seven bright stars in Ursa Major forming the constellation sometimes called the Plough and sometimes the Big Dipper.
5. Resisting control, refractory; balking or moving backwards or sideways rather than forward.

What tho' they Fret and Rage,   30
    To pass their wonted Stage.
Make them Praunce o'er all the amazing Place,
    Quite to the empty Space,
And as ye go, see what Inhabitants there are,
In every World, of every Star;
Their Shape, their Manners and their State,
    Write in Journals as ye go,
And to the inquiring Earth relate;
    By dropping it below.
When weary'd with your universal round,   40
    Let the Sphears harmonious[6] sound,
Refresh and Charm your Spirits, till they be
Fit to fly back to their first ventur'd one Immensity.
But oh! the Harmony's too soft, too sweet, ⎫
The Eternal strains too ravishingly great, ⎬
    I cannot bear such Transports yet,   ⎭
Well then, I'll leave these mighty heights and go
And over-look the little Globe below.

III.

    In this Amphibious Ball, is vast variety,
        To entertain my Curiosity: 50
Here the great Waters of the mighty deep,
Their fixt amazing Bounds do keep;
    In vain they Rage and Roar,
But dare not touch on the restraining Shoar.
Here finny Herds[7] of th' smallest sort,
    Safely Play and Sport;
Wanton[8] I'th' Flood, with no more Danger then
    The Pastimes of Leviathan.[9]
    Here does in Triumph ride,
The stately Trophies of *Britania*'s Pride: 60
Her Ships which to the *Indies* Trade,
    Such Noble Fabricks are made;
    And so numerous appear,

6. A legend portrays the universe as created and set and kept in motion by the harmony of heavenly music.
7. Schools of fish.
8. Play.
9. Mythical sea monster; in the Bible a serpent or whale.

The frighted Natives do our Traffick fear,
  And doubt we will invade.
  Securely too in these,
  They visit the Antipodes.[10]
From *Britain* they, the courteous Race begun, ⎫
A piece of complaisance unknown,   ⎬
70 To all but civil *Drake*,[11] and the obliging Sun. ⎭
Neptune[12] with pompous Pride does bear
Those glorious Terrors; Ships of War.
The floating Towr's they in *Battalia*[13] draw;
  Keep all the circling Realms in awe.
Yet these vast Bodies, the soft Waters bear:
So the great Bird of *Jove*,[14] mounts in the trackless Air.
On the smooth Floods, the swelling Billows rise,
As if the liquid Mountains touch'd the Skies:
Then quick they plunged, with an Impetuous hast,
80 And seem'd to speak Destruction as they pass'd,
Yet Arm'd with Avarice and Curiosities,
Men scorn the Dangers, of the threatning Seas.

IV.
  Next on the solid Parts, I cast my Eye,
  Did vast scorcht Desarts spie;
Which untamed Beasts, and Monsters bred,
  By them alone inhabited,
I saw huge Mountains of uncommon Earth,
  Some belcht with Terror forth;
  A sulpherous Smoak,
90 Loud as amazing Thunder spoke,
From the unexhausted Bowels came,
Ashes and Stones, evacuated by Flame;
Remote from these are frigid Mountains too;
  Thick cloth'd in fleecy Snow.
Some by restringent Air congeal'd as hard,
As if with Adamantine[15] barr'd:

---

10. Places on the opposite sides of the earth, usually England and Australia at this time.
11. Sir Francis Drake (1540?–1596), the first English captain to sail around the world.
12. Roman god of the sea.
13. Battalions; tactical fighting units.
14. The eagle, which carried Jove's thunderbolt arrows.
15. Impenetrable, unbreakable stone.

Stupendious Rocks of hideous Stones I found,
Whose dangerous Heads, lean'd o're the threaten'd Ground.
Deep in Earths center, far from human sight,
I search'd with intellectual Light;   100
    (Pierc'd to the gloomy Ray,
Where subterrenean Fires, in silence play,
Like the faint Glimps of an imprison'd Day.)
Where unmolested Streams with gentle force,
    Press, to their Primeveal source;
(And sometimes upward, gush thro' poreous Earth,
Give to the healing Baths, a useful Birth;)
In its more wealthy parts, the Minerals lay,
And ponderous Mettals, shining Nerves display:
In her bright Bowels, radient Gems remains,   110
Till cruel Man dissects, and rends her Saphir vains.
    With Grief and Wonder I behold,
    The Noble, but mischevious Gold;
Oh! with what Toil, and mighty Pain,
Men the inchanting Mettle gain.
This Tyrant Clay Lords it o'er human kind,
Tho' they themselves in dirt, at first the Monarch find;
Lets their Stupidity, no more upbraid,
Who worshipp'd Gods, which their own Hands had made,
Since we're by Gold to greater Crimes betray'd.   120
Our Country, Faith, Friends, Honour for its sold,
Nay, Heaven and Love, is sacrific'd to Gold;
We're worse Idolaters, than they,
Who only Homage gave; since we mischeviously obey.

V.

    Then the habitable World appear'd,
By Art, vast Towns and pompous Temples rear'd.
The pleasing Fields, awhile detain'd my sight
    With a serene delight:
The flowry Meads,[16] with various Colours dy'd,
And smiling Nature, in her verdant Pride;   130
Here ancient Woods, and blooming Groves,
    (Fit recesses, for celestial Loves,)

16. Meadows.

Where purling Streams, glide with delightful hast,
On whose cool Banks, are spreading Willows plac'd:
The chearful Birds sing on the shading Bough,
In such glad Notes, as Nature did bestow.
The bleating Flocks and Herds, o'erspread the Plains,
And recompence the joyful Peasants pains.
   Here the unenvy'd Village stood,
140   Rais'd of native Clay, and neighbouring Wood.
The Inhabitants as void of Pride, or Art,
Blest with plain Diet, and an honest Heart;
They Plow'd the Ground, and Sow'd the pregnant Grain,
Reap'd joyfully; the plentious Crop again:
Innocent Slaves, to whose rude Care we owe,
The chief supports of Life, and utmost needs below.
Remoter helps are Springs to Luxury,   ⎫
Rich Wines and Spices, and the Tyrian die,[17] ⎬
Do not our Wants, but Wantonness supply. ⎭
150   Here in his humble Cott, the Rustick lies,
Knows not the Curse, of being Great or Wise;
Ambition, Treachery, and Fear,
   Are Strangers here.
Secure and quiet they go plodding on,
Happy, because too mean to be undone.

VI.
   Then I espy'd from far,
Troops of shining Men, ingag'd in War,
Their artful Weapons, are with Rage imploy'd,
And Man, by Man, is Savagely destroy'd:
160   Poor mercenary Slaves they die,
   But seldom know for why;
Oh! what Confusions here I cannot bear,   ⎫
These horrid Groans that reach my distant Ear ⎬
From slaugher'd heaps, of dying Accents there. ⎭
Sometimes wast Towns in Flames appear,
Huge Castles mount, and shatter in the Air,
   But ah! what pity 'tis,
Mankind should Glory in such Arts as these;
Then to the populous Cities, I repair'd,

17. The famous royal purple dye of Greece and Rome, perfected in Tyre.

Found they were little less insnar'd;   170
Tho' not Alarm'd with mighty noise of Wars,
Yet curs'd with grating, private Jars,
Envy and Strife, Self-Interest, and Deceits,
Extravagance and Noise, her Fate compleats.
Then I survey'd the splendid Court,
Found pageant Follies, Revelling and Sport,
Base Falshood, Lust, Ambition, Emnity,
    Soft wanton Intervals, and Luxury,
Destructive Flattery, and hateful Pride,
    And all the City Sins beside.   180
    Thinks I, what shall I do,
    If I must live again below,
For I remember'd that I had been there,
    And a return to Earth, did fear.
Grant ye bless'd Powers, said I,
If I must downwards fly;
I may Descend upon the blooming Plain,
Bless'd with the harmless Nymph, and humble Swain,[18] }
There let me ever undisturb'd remain.

                                            (1703)

The Goodness of Providence
Octavia Walsh

I.
O Let our Praise ascend the Skies,
From Heav'n and Earth its Accents rise
    In Glory, to Heav'n's mighty King:
O! let our Praise his Courts ascend,
The vaulted Skies in sunder rend,
    And fall before that never-ceasing Spring.

II.
That Pow'r which BEING did bestow
On Heav'n above and Earth below,
    And what the Ocean hides;

---

18. Country man; lover.

10
Which fix'd the Stars, in yielding Air,
And told the raging Sea, how far
   It might advance its Tides.

III.
Whose Word alone Mankind did frame,
Whose Word alone destroys the same,
   And turns again to Clay;
Whose Word disjoins the trembling Earth,
And gives Mankind a second Birth,
   To endless Night or Day.

IV.
In me his Glory he display'd,
20
The Creature which his Hand has made;
   Yet pleas'd his Might to show;
In making me fierce Terrors taste,
In earthly Happiness first plac'd,
   To make my Fall more low.

V.
When sunk in Anguish and Despair,
He shew'd a tender Father's Care,
   Who does wild Sons correct;
And tho' sometimes he hides his Face,
Denies his never-failing Grace,
30
   He will me not reject.

VI.
He shew'd me plain when Life he lent,
It was not to be idly spent
   In sublunary Joy;
But that tow'rds Heaven I bend my Mind,
And there eternal Pleasures find,
   Which know of no Alloy.

VII.
What Lover us'd such gentle Art,
In gaining of an equal Heart,
   As this great King for mine?

His Rival first he did remove,   40
Then to revive my deaden'd Love,
   He try'd by Ways divine.

VIII.
O sacred LORD, tho' Earth denies
To my poor Life its due Supplies,
   And Heav'n in Anger lours;[19]
Though o'er my Head its Thunders break,
The Ground convulsive Terrors shake,
   And raining Flame devours;

IX.
Though Mountains to high Heav'n aspire
In furious Streams of liquid Fire,   50
   And Hell displays its Woes;
Though the wide Ocean feels its Pow'rs,
And raging Flame its Waves devours,
   And all its Depths disclose;

X.
Yet, in thy Mercy still secure,
These Storms with Patience I'll endure,
   And with their Fury cope;
Their dreadful Force may move my Fear,
But ne'er shall make me once despair,
   Or lose in thee my Hope.   60

XI.
One Look of thine shall strait dispel,
Chain up the Furies that rebel,
   And so the Blessed save;
Or else thou canst their Souls remove
To thine eternal Realms above,
   To triumph o'er the Grave.

(1734)

19. Scowls.

Hymn I
Elizabeth Singer Rowe

I.
The glorious armies of the sky
  To thee, O mighty king!
Triumphant anthems consecrate,
  And hallelujahs sing.

II.
But still their most exalted flights
  Fall vastly short of thee;
How distant then must human praise
  From thy perfections be!

III.
Yet how, my God, shall I refrain,
  When to my ravish'd sense
Each creature in its various ways
  Displays thy excellence?

IV.
The active lights that shine above,
  In their eternal dance,
Reveal their skilful maker's praise
  With silent elegance.

V.
The blushes of the morn confess
  That thou art much more fair:
When in the east its beams revive
  To gild the fields of air;

VI.
The fragrant, the refreshing breath
  Of ev'ry flow'ry bloom,
In balmy whispers owns from thee
  Their pleasing odours come.

VII.
The singing birds, the warbling winds,
   And waters murm'ring fall,
To praise the first almighty cause[20]
   With diff'rent voices call.

VIII.
Thy num'rous works exalt thee thus,
   And shall I silent be?   30
No, rather let me cease to breathe,
   Than cease from praising thee.

                (1739)

A Funeral Hymn
Judith Madan

I
In this World of Sin and Sorrow,
   Compass'd round with many a Care,
From Eternity we borrow
   Hope,[21] that can exclude Despair.
Thee, triumphant GOD and SAVIOUR,
   In the Glass[22] of Faith we see:
O assist each faint Endeavour,
   Raise our earth-born Souls to Thee!

II
Place that awful Scene before us
   Of the last tremendous Day,   10
When to Life thou shalt restore us.
   Ling'ring Ages, haste away!
Then this vile and sinful Nature
   Incorruption[23] shall put on.

---

20. The cause to which every series of causes can be traced; in the Christian tradition, God is the first cause.
21. Romans 8.24, 25. *Madan.*
22. Mirror.
23. I Corinthians 15.53. *Madan.*

Life-renewing, glorious SAVIOUR,
Let Thy gracious Will be done!

(1763)

Hymn II

Anna Laetitia Barbauld

Praise to GOD, immortal praise,[24]
For the love that crowns our days;
Bounteous source of every joy,
Let thy praise our tongues employ;

For the blessings of the field,
For the stores the gardens yield,
For the vine's exalted juice,
For the generous olive's use:

Flocks that whiten all the plain,
10   Yellow sheaves of ripen'd grain;
Clouds that drop their fatt'ning dews,
Suns that temperate warmth diffuse:

All that Spring with bounteous hand
Scatters o'er the smiling land:
All that liberal Autumn pours
From her rich o'erflowing stores:

These to thee, my GOD, we owe;
Source whence all our blessings flow;
And for these, my soul shall raise
20   Grateful vows and solemn praise.

Yet should rising whirlwinds tear
From its stem the ripening ear;[25]

24. ALTHOUGH the fig tree shall not blossom, neither shall fruit be in the vines, the labour of the olive shall fail, and the fields shall yield no meat, the flock shall be cut off from the fold, and there shall be no herd in the stalls: yet I will rejoice in the LORD, I will joy in the GOD of my salvation. HABAKKUK, iii.17, 18. *Barbauld.*
25. Ear of corn.

Should the fig-tree's blasted shoot
Drop her-green untimely fruit;

Should the vine put forth no more,
Nor the olive yield her store;
Though the sick'ning flocks should fall,
And the herds desert the stall;

Should thine alter'd hand restrain
The early and the latter rain;   30
Blast each opening bud of joy,
And the rising year destroy;

Yet to thee my soul should raise
Grateful vows, and solemn praise;
And, when every blessing's flown,
Love thee—for thyself alone.

(1773)

Hymn XXXV
Behold he cometh with Clouds, and every Eye shall see Him. Rev. i.7[26]

Susannah Harrison

Behold, He comes, the Saviour comes,
    Dress'd in his bright Array,
Awake, ye Saints, and burst your Tombs,
    And view the glorious Day.

He comes, attended from on high,
    With Thousands, thro' the Skies,
His Glory shines; and every Eye
    Shall see him with Surprize.

Lo, in the Clouds the Judge descends
    With his illustrious Train,   10

26. "Behold, he cometh with clouds; and every eye shall see him, and they *also* which pierced him: and all kindreds of the earth shall wail because of him. Even so, Amen." Rev. 1:7.

Sinners he severs from his Friends,
    And dooms to endless Pain.

He comes, to make his Justice known,
    To vindicate his Word:
The Guilty view him on his Throne,
    And wail before the Lord.

Till now, they never sought his Face
    Nor wept for Sin before:
O how tremendous is their Case!
20   They weep to laugh no more.

Once they despis'd his glorious Name,
    And set at nought his Worth;
But now they feel with bitter Shame,
    His fierce vindictive Wrath.

They now behold the Saints rejoice,
    And mount above the Skies;
These praise the Lamb with chearful Voice,
    And triumph as they rise.

Yes, and my Soul shall bear her Part,
30   In their melodious Song;
My Saviour's Grace shall tune my Heart
    His Love inspire my Tongue.

                              (1780)

A Hymn

Helen Maria Williams

While thee I seek, protecting Power!
    Be my vain wishes still'd;
And may this consecrated hour
    With better hopes be fill'd.

Thy love the powers of thought bestow'd,
    To thee my thoughts would soar;

Thy mercy o'er my life has flow'd—
    That mercy I adore.

In each event of life, how clear,
    Thy ruling hand I see;   10
Each blessing to my soul more dear,
    Because conferr'd by thee.

In every joy that crowns my days,
    In every pain I bear,
My heart shall find delight in praise,
    Or seek relief in prayer.

When gladness wings my favour'd hour,
    Thy love my thoughts shall fill:
Resign'd, when storms of sorrow lower,
    My soul shall meet thy will.   20

My lifted eye without a tear
    The lowring storm shall see;
My stedfast heart shall know no fear—
    That heart will rest on Thee!

               (1786)

Evening Hymn
Sung by the Congregation of Walsall[27]
Mary Whateley Darwall

I.
O Lord, before thy awful throne,
    Again our souls in duty bend;
To thee our wants and woes are known,
    To us thy pow'rful aid extend.

II.
Direct our hearts to sing thy praise
    In concert with the heav'nly choir:

27. Darwall moved to Walsall, Staffordshire, near the end of 1789.

Let love divine inflame our lays,
　And gratitude the strain inspire!

III.
Thy goodness call'd us forth to light,
10　　Thy bounteous hand our life sustains,
Thou guid'st us thro' the gloom of night,
　Where dangers threat, where terror reigns.

IV.
O! lead us by thy saving grace,
　Through life's deceitful thorny way,
Till we appear before thy face,
　In the bright realms of endless day.

(1794)

A New Christmas Hymn
Hannah More

O how wond'rous is the story
　Of our blest Redeemer's birth!
See the mighty Lord of Glory
　Leaves his heaven to visit earth!

Hear with transport, every creature,
　Hear the Gospel's joyful sound;
Christ appears in human nature,
　In our sinful world is found;

Comes to pardon our transgression,
10　　Like a cloud our sins to blot;
Comes to his own favour'd nation,
　But his own receive him not.

If the angels who attended
　To declare the Saviour's birth,
Who from heaven with songs descended
　To proclaim Good will on earth:

If, in pity to our blindness,
　　They had brought the pardon needed,
Still Jehovah's wond'rous kindness
　　Had our warmest hopes exceeded;　　　　　　　　20

If some Prophet had been sent
　　With Salvation's joyful news,
Who that heard the blest event
　　Could their warmest love refuse?

But 'twas HE to whom in Heaven
　　Hallelujahs never cease;
He, the mighty GOD, was given,
　　Given to us a Prince of Peace.

None but he who did create us
　　Could redeem from sin and hell;　　　　　　　　30
None but he could re-instate us
　　In the rank from which we fell.

Had he come, the glorious stranger,
　　Deck'd with all the world calls great,
Had he liv'd in pomp and grandeur,
　　Crown'd with more than royal state;

Still our tongues with praise o'erflowing,
　　On such boundless love would dwell,
Still our hearts with rapture glowing,
　　Speak what words could never tell.　　　　　　　40

But what wonder should it raise
　　Thus our lowest state to borrow!
O the high mysterious ways,
　　GOD's own Son a child of sorrow!

'Twas to bring us endless pleasure,
　　He our suffering nature bore,
'Twas to give us heavenly treasure
　　He was willing to be poor.

Come ye rich, survey the stable
 Where your infant Saviour lies;
From your full o'erflowing table
 Send the hungry good supplies.

Boast not your ennobled stations,
 Boast not that you're highly fed;
Jesus, hear it all ye nations,
 Had not where to lay his head.

Learn of me, thus cries the Saviour,
 If my kingdom you'd inherit,
Sinner, quit your proud behaviour,
 Learn my meek and lowly spirit.

Come ye servants, see your station,
 Freed from all reproach and shame;
He who purchas'd your salvation,
 Bore a servant's humble name.

Come ye poor, some comfort gather,
 Faint not in the race you run,
Hard the lot your gracious father
 Gave his dear, his only Son.

Think, that if your humbler stations,
 Less of worldly good bestow,
You escape those strong temptations
 Which from wealth and grandeur flow.

See your Saviour is ascended!
 See he looks with pity down!
Trust him all will soon be mended,
 Bear his cross you'll share his crown.

(1798)

A Hymn,
Written among the Alps[28]
Helen Maria Williams

Creation's God! with thought elate,
  Thy hand divine I see;
Impressed on scenes, where all is great,
  Where all is full of thee!

II.
Where stern the Alpine mountains raise
  Their heads of massive snow;
Whence on the rolling storm I gaze,
  That hangs——how far below!

III.
Where, on some bold stupendous height,
  The eagle sits alone;   10
Or soaring wings his sullen flight
  To haunts yet more his own;

IV.
Where the sharp rock the chamois[29] treads,
  Or slippery summit scales;
Or where the whitening snow-bird[30] spreads
  Her plumes to icy gales;

V.
Where the rude cliff's steep column glows
  With morning's tint of blue;
Or evening on the Glacier throws
  The rose's blushing hue;   20

28. Williams was in the Alps, a haven during the worst of the French Revolution, for six months beginning in June 1794. She introduced this hymn in her *Tour in Switzerland* as composed on the "Alpine summits": "conscious how feebly it paints their sublime imagery, and persuaded no pen can define those sensations which are felt by the lover of nature, who wanders amidst those regions of stupendous greatness, and feels, mingled with the thrill of astonishment, the transport of adoration" (15).

29. Agile goat antelope indigenous to the Alps.

30. Snow bunting, a bird indigenous to the Alps.

VI.

Or where by twilight's softer light,
  The mountain shadow bends;
And sudden casts a partial night,
  As black its form descends;

VII.

Where the full ray of noon, alone
  Down the deep valley falls;
Or, where the sun-beam never shone
  Between its rifted walls;

VIII.

Where cloudless regions calm the soul,
  Bid mortal cares be still;
Can passion's wayward wish controul,
  And rectify the will;

IX.

Where midst some vast expanse, the mind
  Which swelling virtue fires,
Forgets that earth it leaves behind,
  And to its heaven aspires;

X.

Where far along the desart-sphere
  Resounds no creature's call;
And undisturbing mortal ear,
  The Avalanches fall;

XI.

Where, rushing from their snowy source,
  The daring torrents urge
Their loud-toned waters headlong course,
  And lift their feathered surge;

XII.

Where swift the lines of light, and shade,
  Flit o'er the lucid lake,
Or the shrill winds its breast invade,
  And its green billows wake;

30

40

XIII.

Where on the slope, with speckled dye,
　　The pigmy herds[31] I scan,　　　　　　　　　　50
Or soothed the scattered *chalets*[32] spy,
　　The last abodes of man;

XIV.

Or, where the flocks refuse to pass,
　　And the lone peasant mows,
Fixed on his knees, the pendant grass,
　　Which down the steep he throws;

XV.

Or where the dangerous pathway leads
　　High o'er the gulph profound;
From whence the shrinking eye recedes,
　　Nor finds repose around;　　　　　　　　　　60

XVI.

Where red the mountain-ash reclines
　　Along the clefted rock;
Where firm, the dark unbending pines
　　The howling tempests mock;

XVII.

Where, level with the ice-ribb'd bound,[33]
　　The yellow harvests glow;
Or vales with purple vines are crown'd
　　Beneath impending snow;

XVIII.

Where the rich minerals catch the ray
　　With varying lustre bright,　　　　　　　　　　70
And glittering fragments strew the way
　　With sparks of liquid light;

31. Goats that do not grow larger than twenty inches at the withers.
32. Small house with a gently sloping, overhanging roof; in the Alps, often that of a herdsman.
33. Boundary made of ridges or lines of ice, like ribs, formed where rocks, boulders, and other debris have accumulated, that appear as the mountains are ascended and, for some space, alternate with vegetation and ground cover.

XIX.
Or, where the moss forbears to creep,
    Where loftier summits rear
Their untrod snows, and frozen sleep
    Locks all th' uncoloured year;

XX.
In every scene, where every hour
    Sheds some terrific grace,
In nature's vast, overwhelming power,
80   THEE, THEE, my GOD, I trace!

(1798)

Sources

Chudleigh: *The Poems and Prose of Mary, Lady Chudleigh,* ed. Margaret J. M. Ezell (New York: Oxford University Press, 1993), 78–79; Egerton: *Poems on Several Occasions, Together with a Pastoral* (London, 1703), 2–11; Walsh: Simon Patrick, *A Collection of Select Original Poems and Translations, Chiefly on Divine Subjects* (London, 1734), 112–15; Rowe: *The Miscellaneous Works in Prose and Verse of Mrs. Elizabeth Rowe,* 2 vols. (London, 1739), 1:29–31; Madan: Falconer Madan, *The Madan Family* (Oxford, 1933), 103; Barbauld: *Poems* (London, 1773), 115–17; Harrison: *Songs in the Night* (London, 1780), 33–34; Williams: *Poems,* 2 vols. (London, 1786), 1:97–99; Darwall: *Poems on Several Occasions. By Mrs. Darwall (Formerly Miss Whateley) in Two Volumes,* 2 vols. (Walsall, 1794), 2:121–22; More: *Cheap Repository Tracts; Entertaining, Moral, and Religious* (London, 1798), 454–56; Williams: *A Tour in Switzerland,* 2 vols. (London, 1798), 2:16–19.

The Fable

Cleverly illustrated editions of Aesop's fables are still regularly published for children, and most readers of this anthology can remember *The Boy Who Cried Wolf* or *The Fox and the Grapes*. What is forgotten is how popular and prestigious reading and writing fables was in the past. Translations of Aesop, LaFontaine, and L'Estrange were enormously popular, and John Ogilby, Aphra Behn, John Dryden, Matthew Prior, Jonathan Swift, John Gay, and others wrote and translated them. Fables make up one-third of Anne Finch's poetry and compose half of the poems in her *Miscellany Poems* (1713). Critics agree that for the earlier period the fable "belongs with the irregular Pindaric ode as one of the master texts through which the writers of the time tested their capacities."[1] French neoclassical criticism awarded the fable "all the dignity of a heroic classical form," a tradition continued through John Dennis and Richard Blackmore to Joseph Addison and other literary critics.[2] Multiple editions of each writer's fables sold; for example, Dryden's were published in 1700, with more editions in 1713, 1721, 1734, and 1745. British fables tended to be succinct, paradoxical, and often subversive, and readers delighted in interpreting them.

The fable is one of the forms in which Finch undertook the sustained, culturally engaged experimentation with content, structure, and prosody that is typical of career poets. Contributing to what Mark Loveridge called the "fevered fable-culture of the late 1720s,"[3] she continued the movement to make fables about English events and structures of feeling. Most significantly, she moved the fable in an entirely new direction by using it to comment on the situation of women. Mary Leapor's *The Fox and the Hen,* in this section, follows her lead. In their fables both women violated almost every conventional expectation about the content and opinions in women's poetry. Finch's *Critick and the Writer of Fables* (3.D) describes the pleasure of writing fables, and we open this section by pairing her *Atheist and the Acorn* with Hannah More's reworking of the same fable for the *Cheap Repository Tracts.* We break with chronological order in this case because the poems are good illustrations of different styles and conceptions of different audiences. More's more conversational fable, which also reinforces the moral message in more direct ways, suits the purposes of the tracts.

These tracts were intended to be instructive but also entertaining reading for the lower classes, and many copies were used in Sunday schools, church groups, and schools.

The fables that follow are representative of the many uses to which women put the form. Some fables are simple, lyrical poems, as is Eliza Tuite's lovely tribute to her friend, *The Tulip and the Rose*. Others are clever, rather acerbic observations on human nature, as are Hester Thrale Piozzi's *The Three Warnings* and Mary Robinson's shocking *Mistress Gurton's Cat*. Some fables are deeply political. Helen Leigh's *The Linnet* is a meditation on freedom and the reciprocity within contract government published in the anniversary year of the Glorious Revolution. Mary Alcock's *The Hive of Bees* is an allegory of the terrible year 1792 in France with a happy ending that would not happen. Both Swift and Gay agreed that poetic fables were exceptionally difficult to compose, and the virtuosity and poetic skill demonstrated by women poets actually surpasses theirs.

Notes

1. Charles H. Hinnant, *The Poetry of Anne Finch: An Essay in Interpretation* (Newark: University of Delaware Press, 1994), 166–67.

2. Mark Loveridge, *A History of the Augustan Fable* (Cambridge: Cambridge University Press, 1998), 41.

3. Loveridge, *History of the Augustan Fable*, 55.

The Atheist and the Acorn
Anne Finch

Methinks this World is oddly made,
    And ev'ry thing's amiss,
A dull presuming Atheist said,
As stretch'd he lay beneath a Shade;
    And instanced in this:

Behold, quoth he, that mighty thing,
    A *Pumpkin,* large and round,
Is held but by a little String,
Which upwards cannot make it spring,
    Or bear it from the Ground.   10

Whilst on this *Oak,* a Fruit so small,
    So disproportion'd, grows;
That, who with Sence surveys this *All,*
This universal Casual Ball,
    Its ill Contrivance knows.

My better Judgment wou'd have hung
    That Weight upon a Tree,
And left this Mast, thus slightly strung,
'Mongst things which on the Surface sprung,
    And small and feeble be.   20

No more the Caviller cou'd say,
    Nor farther Faults descry;
For, as he upwards gazing lay,
An *Acorn,* loosen'd from the Stay,[1]
    Fell down upon his Eye.

Th' offended Part with Tears ran o'er,
    As punish'd for the Sin:

---

1. Finch extends her nautical metaphor from mast in the previous verse to stay, the rope leading from the top of the mast to a spar or some other part of the ship.

Fool! had that Bough a *Pumpkin* bore,
Thy Whimseys must have work'd no more,
30   Nor Scull had kept them in.

(1713)

The Two Gardeners[2]

Hannah More

Two Gardeners once beneath an oak,
Lay down to rest, when Jack thus spoke;
"You must confess, dear Will, that nature
Is but a blundering kind of creature;
And I—nay why that look of terror?
Could teach her how to mend her error."
"Your talk," quoth Will, "is bold and odd,
What you call nature I call God."
"Well, call him by what name you will."
10   Quoth Jack, "he manages but ill;
Nay, from the very tree we're under,
I'll prove that Providence can blunder."
Quoth Will, "through thick and thin you dash,
I shudder, Jack, at words so rash;
I trust to what the Scriptures tell,
He hath done always all things well."
Quoth Jack, "I'm lately grown a wit,
And think all good a lucky hit.
To this vast oak lift up thine eyes,
20   Then view that acorn's paltry size;
How foolish! on a tree so small,
To place that tiny cup and ball.
Now look again, yon pompion[3] see,
It weighs two pounds at least, nay three,
Yet this large fruit where is it found?
Why, meanly trailing on the ground.
Had Providence ask'd my advice,

2. This poem is one of More's contributions to the project Cheap Repository for Moral and Religious Tracts.
3. A Gourd. *More.* [Pumpkin. *Eds.*]

I wou'd have chang'd it in a trice;[4]
I would have said at nature's birth,
Let acorns creep upon the earth;   30
But let the pompion, vast and round,
On the oak's lofty boughs be found."
He said—and as he rashly spoke,
Lo! from the branches of the oak,
A wind, which suddenly arose,
Beat show'rs of acorns on his nose;
"Oh! oh!" quoth Jack, "I'm wrong I see,
And God is wiser far than me.
For did a show'r of pompions large,
Thus on my naked face discharge,   40
I had been bruis'd and blinded quite;
What heav'n appoints I find is right;
Whene'er I'm tempted to rebel,
I'll think how light the acorns fell;
Whereas on oaks had pompions hung,
My broken skull had stopp'd my tongue."

THE END.

(1796)

The Fox and the Hen
A Fable
Mary Leapor

'Twas on a fair and healthy Plain,
There liv'd a poor but honest Swain,[5]
Had to his Lot[6] a little Ground,
Defended by a quick-set Mound:
'Twas there he milk'd his brindled Kine,[7]
And there he fed his harmless Swine:
His Pigeons flutter'd to and fro,

4. Instantly.
5. Country man; lover.
6. What falls to a person by chance or destiny.
7. Cows.

And bask'd[8] his Poultry in a Row:
Much we might say of each of these,   ·
As how his Pigs in Consort wheeze;
How the sweet Hay his Heifers chew,
And how the Pigeons softly coo:
But we shall wave this motley Strain,
And keep to one that's short and plain:
Nor paint the Dunghill's feather'd King,
For of the Hen we mean to sing.

    A Hen there was, a strange one too,
Cou'd sing (believe me, it is true)
Or rather (as you may presume)
Wou'd prate and cackle in a Tune:
This quickly spread the Pullet's Fame,
And Birds and Beasts together came:
All mixt in one promiscuous Throng,
To visit Partlet[9] and her Song.
It chanc'd there came amongst the Crew,
Of witty Foxes not a few:
But one more smart than all the rest,
His serious Neighbour thus addrest:

"What think you of this Partlet here?
'Tis true her Voice is pretty clear:
Yet without pausing I can tell,
In what much more she wou'd excel:
Methinks she'd eat exceeding well."
This heard the list'ning Hen, as she
Sat perch'd upon a Maple-tree.

    The shrewd Proposal gall'd her Pride,
And thus to *Reynard*[10] she reply'd:
"Sir, you're extremely right I vow,
But how will you come at me now?
You dare not mount this lofty Tree,
So there I'm pretty safe, you see.

8. Enjoyed the sunshine.
9. Used as the proper name of any hen, for example, Mrs. Partlet.
10. Used as the proper name of a fox.

From long ago, (or Record lies)
You Foxes have been counted wise:
But sure this Story don't agree
With your Device of eating me.
For you, Dame Fortune still intends
Some coarser Food than singing Hens:
Besides e'er you can reach so high,
Remember you must learn to fly.

"I own 'tis but a scurvy way,   50
You have as yet to seize your Prey,
By sculking from the Beams of Light,
And robbing Hen-roosts in the Night:
Yet you must keep this vulgar Trade
Of thieving till your Wings are made.

"Had I the keeping of you tho',
I'd make your subtle Worship know,
We Chickens are your Betters due,
Not fatted up for such as you:
Shut up in Cub with rusty Chain,   60
I'd make you lick your Lips in vain:
And take a special Care, be sure,
No Pullet[11] shou'd come near your Door:
But try if you cou'd feed or no,
Upon a Kite[12] or Carrion Crow."
Here ceas'd the Hen. The baffl'd Beast
March'd off without his promis'd Feast.

(1748)

The Three Warnings: A Tale
Hester Thrale Piozzi

The tree of deepest root is found
Least willing still to quit the ground;
'Twas therefore said by antient sages,

---

11. Young hen just beginning to lay eggs.
12. Bird of prey.

That love of life increas'd with years
So much, that in our latter stages,
When pains grow sharp, and sickness rages,
The greatest love of life appears.

This great affection to believe,
Which all confess, but few perceive,
If old assertions can't prevail,
Be pleas'd to hear a modern tale.
When sports went round, and all were gay
On neighbour Dobson's wedding-day,
Death call'd aside the jocund groom
With him into another room:
And looking grave, "You must," says he,
"Quit your sweet bride, and come with me."
"With you, and quit my Susan's side!
With you!" the hapless husband cry'd:
"Young as I am! 'tis monstrous hard!
Besides, in truth, I'm not prepar'd:
My thoughts on other matters go,
This is my wedding-night, you know."

What more he urg'd I have not heard,
His reasons could not well be stronger;
So Death the poor delinquent spar'd,
And left to live a little longer.
Yet calling up a serious look,
His hour-glass trembled while he spoke,
"Neighbour," he said, "farewell: No more
Shall Death disturb your mirthful hour;
And further, to avoid all blame
Of cruelty upon my name,
To give you time for preparation,
And fit you for your future station,
Three several Warnings you shall have,
Before you're summon'd to the grave:
Willing for once I'll quit my prey,
And grant a kind reprieve;
In hopes you'll have no more to say,
But when I call again this way,
Well-pleas'd the world will leave."

10

20

30

40

To these conditions both consented,
And parted perfectly contented.

What next the hero of our tale befell,
How long he liv'd, how wise, how well,
How roundly he pursu'd his course,
And smok'd his pipe, and strok'd his horse,
    The willing Muse shall tell:
He chaffer'd[13] then, he bought, he sold,   50
Nor once perceiv'd his growing old,
    Nor thought of Death as near;
His friends not false, his wife no shrew,
Many his gains, his children few,
    He pass'd his hours in peace;
But while he view'd his wealth increase,
While thus along Life's dusty road
The beaten track content he trod,
Old Time, whose haste no mortal spares,
Uncall'd, unheeded, unawares,   60
    Brought on his eightieth year.

And now one night in musing mood,
    As all alone he sate,
Th' unwelcome messenger of Fate
    Once more before him stood.

Half kill'd with anger and surprize,
"So soon return'd!" old Dobson cries.
    "So soon, d'ye call it!" Death replies:
"Surely, my friend, you're but in jest.
    Since I was here before,   70
'Tis six-and-thirty years at least,
    And you are now fourscore."
    "So much the worse," the Clown[14] rejoin'd:
"To spare the aged would be kind:
However, see your search be legal;
And your authority—Is't regal?

13. Haggled, bargained.
14. Country man, peasant, uncouth man.

Else you are come on a fool's errand,
With but a secretary's warrant.
Besides, you promis'd me Three Warnings,
80   Which I have look'd for nights and mornings.
But for that loss of time and ease,
I can recover damages."

   "I know," cries Death, "that at the best,
I seldom am a welcome guest;
But don't be captious,[15] friend, at least;
I little thought you'd still be able
To stump about your farm and stable;
Your years have run to a great length,
I wish you joy tho' of your strength."

90   "Hold," says the Farmer, "not so fast,
I have been lame these four years past."

   "And no great wonder," Death replies,
"However, you still keep your eyes;
And sure to see one's loves and friends,
For legs and arms would make amends."

   "Perhaps," says Dobson, "so it might,
But latterly I've lost my sight."

   "This is a shocking story, faith,
Yet there's some comfort still," says Death;
100   "Each strives your sadness to amuse;
I warrant you hear all the news."

   "There's none," cries he; "and if there were,
I'm grown so deaf I could not hear."

   "Nay then," the spectre stern rejoin'd,
   "These are unjustifiable yearnings;
If you are lame, and deaf, and blind,
You've had your three sufficient Warnings.

   "So come along, no more we'll part:"
He said, and touch'd him with his dart;
110   And now old Dobson turning pale,
Yields to his fate—so ends my tale.

                        (1770)

---

15. Fault-finding, argumentative.

The Linnet; a Fable
Helen Leigh

Young Celia[16] was beauteous, and blithe as the morn,
    On her cheek bloom'd the lilly and rose,
And sweet was her breath as the blossoming thorn,
    When, to hail spring returning it blows.

Her bosom, with love, and with tenderness glow'd,
    But her Linnet was all her delight;
On the sweet little warbler that love she bestow'd,
    And carest him from morning to night.

How oft wou'd she open the door of his cage,
    From which he enraptur'd wou'd fly,   10
And, perch'd on her hand, her attention engage,
    While her lover unheeded stood by!

Yet oft, the ingrate wou'd for Liberty pine,
    As he saw from her window the grove;
And oft wou'd he wish his companions to join,
    Again thro' the woodlands to rove.

Unrestrain'd by his Mistress, one Midsummer morn,
    When Phœbus[17] illumin'd the east,
He flew to some birds, who were perch'd on a thorn,
    And forsook his wont[18] seat on her breast.   20

"Ungrateful deserter!" cry'd Celia, "away,
    And meet the reward of your crime;
For shou'd you escape the keen sportsman's survey,
    You'll die of Repentance in time.

"But ah! his departure I ever shall mourn,
    He was all that was charming and sweet;
And shou'd the dear fugitive once more return,
    He shall still greater tenderness meet:

16. In Renaissance literature, a name for a ladylove.
17. Apollo, the sun god, here the personification of the sun.
18. Accustomed, habitual.

"But vain the suggestion!—for tho' he may fly,
30   More quick from a gun flies the shot;
And, so num'rous the engines, prepar'd to destroy,
        That death is most surely his lot."

Thus, with direful forebodings, was Celia opprest,
        His loss often cost her a tear;
While he, far away from his mistress and rest,
        Silly bird!—found destruction was near.

From a net, which was artfully spread to ensnare,
        He saw a poor bird get away,
And, at some little distance, a kite[19] in the air,
40   Apparently, eager of prey:

In deep consternation, his monstrous beak,
        With wonder a while he survey'd,
Rejoic'd to escape it;—but found his mistake,
        By his former vain notions betray'd.

Said he to himself, in disconsolate strain,
        "How happy, the state I regret!
Cou'd I my fair mistress's fondness regain—
        That fondness I ne'er can forget:

"I again shou'd be fed by her delicate hand,
50   As three times I was yesterday,
When she strok'd my smooth feathers—and now here I stand,
        Neglected—to hunger a prey.

"Ah! Celia, your bosom with kindness replete,
        Has been cruelly stung by my flight,
But I'll haste to return, and abjure at your feet
        My crime, and be blest with your sight."

He spoke—and, like light'ning, flew back to the spot,
        Where his mistress receiv'd him with joy;
He is faithful, she loves him—thus happy his lot,
60   He'll never more venture to fly.

19. Bird of prey.

Like this simple Linnet, how oft may we see,
   The fond youth, and the love-stricken maid,
From their parents embraces imprudently flee,
   By false notions of freedom betray'd!

(1788)

The Hive of Bees:
A Fable, Written in December 1792[20]
Mary Alcock

In antient legends of past time we find,
Birds, beasts, and insects us'd to speak their mind,
And oft by fable serious truths impart
To mend the morals and to strike the heart:
Nay Solomon himself would deign to say,
Go to the Ant,[21] thou sluggard! learn her way.
But now alas! in these degenerate times,
Insects have learn'd from men to ape their crimes;
The fable's turn'd—false morals now are shewn
In place of true—a sad reverse you'll own.   10

   A hive of bees within a certain grove
Had long enjoy'd contentment, peace, and love,
Fed on each source of sweet that earth bestows,
Ev'n from the cowslip to the stately rose;
Each morn had sipp'd of dew from Heav'n, which fell
And lodg'd in silver'd cup or golden bell;
Had drawn the nectar of each fragrant flower
To carry treasures to their native bower,
And there in cells of curious form they stor'd

20. Seventeen ninety-two was the year of the September Massacres in France and the beginning of the trial of King Louis XVI. He and Queen Marie Antoinette would be executed the next year. In England, Tom Paine went on trial, and the advent of organizations for Constitutional "information" or "reform," the Church-and-King riots, and divisions among powerful politicians, some intensified by events in France, alarmed the British. This poem is an allegory of events.

21. "Go to the ant, thou sluggard; / Consider her ways, and be wise." Prov. 6:6. The book of Proverbs, in the Old Testament, is attributed (as a courtesy and to give it more influence) to King Solomon; it was compiled during the fifth and fourth pre-Christian centuries by the masters who taught in the academies for young men. George A. Buttrick, ed., *Interpreter's Dictionary of the Bible*, 4 vols. (New York: Abingdon, 1962), s.v. "Proverbs, Book of."

20   Their several tributes to the general hoard;
          Then safe at night were shelter'd by those bowers,
          Where first they swarm'd, when in their infant hours
          Each morn they sallied with the rising sun,
          Nor e'er returned until their task was done;
          For arts and industry had made them great,
          And seemingly had fix'd their happy state;
          A state, where nature's policy doth trace
          To every bee his station, rank, and place:
          Some form'd to labour for the public good,
30   Others to nurse the young, and chew their food;
          Some on the watch as centinels[22] between
          Whatever danger may assail their queen;
          For every hive is in itself protected,
          Whilst to its sovereign it is well affected.

          But now no further to dilate my story,
          This hive, when at its highest pitch of glory,
          Like other states did subjects still contain
          Of discontented mind and heated brain,
          Prone to adopt and lead some new opinion,
40   Spurning restraint, and grasping at dominion;
          These oft with greedy list'ning ear repair'd
          Close to a neighb'ring hive, from whence they heard
          A murmuring hum, as if from discontent,
          Of liberty, no queen, no government;
          Let all be equal, and these lordly drones
          Be set to work to shape these ugly cones:
          'Tis slavery I swear—no more will I   ⎫
          Lag home with honey in my bag and thigh, ⎬
          Much sooner will I dart my sting and die. ⎭

50   Thus saying, oft their measures they'd debate,
          And in convention plot against the state;
          But here disorder mark'd their wretched way,
          Each claim'd his right, a right to bear the sway,
          And lest the loyal bees their haunts should see,
          They dar'd not light upon a flower or tree,

22. Sentinels.

Where aught[23] of substance, fit for daily food,
Might be extracted for the public good;
But conscious of their base intent, they shun
Whatever spreads its blossoms to the sun,
And to the deadly nightshade darkling flew,   60
Or on the hemlock swarm'd, or pois'nous yew,
And there their mischiefs hatch'd in fell debate,
There plann'd the downfal of their queen and state:
So loud they buzz'd their murmurs thro' the trees
Of liberty, no work—the rights of bees—
That echo swift convey'd the infectious sound,
And Liberty—no work—rebellow'd round.

    Their plot now ripe, they act the fatal scene,
Murder the guards, and then confine their queen;
Rebellion buzzes thro' the straw-built dome—   70
"Seize, seize the honey, and lay waste the comb!
Destroy each cell, for labour now is o'er,
We'll feast and revel on the public store."

    And now how gladly would I draw a veil
O'er the remaining sequel of my tale;
But recent facts require I should relate
How bad example marr'd the happy state.
Tho' most with horror heard the foul disgrace
Brought on the noblest of the insect race,
Yet those who had enlisted in the plan,   80
And long'd like them to copy after man,
Now vend their poisons, and in treasons dire
Against their friends, their queen, their hive conspire,
Whilst swarms from forth the rebel state combine
To prosecute the horrible design,
And, shame to tell, tho' courteously receiv'd,
League against those by whom they are reliev'd.

    Arous'd at length, the loyal bees unite
To save their state, and arm them for the fight,
True to their sovereign, who with gentle sway   90
So mildly rul'd, 'twas freedom to obey;

23. Anything at all.

And now behold them eager and alert
To expel the traitors and their schemes avert;
Taught by examples terrible as these,
That faction blasts the happiness of bees,
Active they keep their vigilance alive
To guard their monarch, property, and hive.

(1792; 1799)

Song
The Tulip and the Rose
Eliza Tuite

See, Laura,[24] how yon faded flow'r
   Lies now neglected and alone;
And yet, within the passing hour,
   The gard'ner's pride, that tulip shone.

For gaudy colours only priz'd,
   It lost its value with its bloom,
Now by its former friends despis'd,
   Its rivals triumph in its doom;

While this sweet rose, tho' now decay'd,
   Has still retain'd her fragrant breath,
And on thy spotless bosom laid,
   Might long be envied e'en in death.

The tulip here the nymph pourtrays,
   Who trusts to outward charms alone;
The rose's lasting sweet conveys
   The lovely emblem of thy own.

(1796)

10

24. In imitation of Petrarch, poets frequently addressed poems, especially about love, to "Laura," and it became a convention. Petrarch said he first saw the woman who inspired his love poetry in 1327. She was, according to him, already married and died in the 1348 plague. He calls her "Laura" in the poems, and her identity is unknown; in fact, some scholars doubt her existence.

Mistress Gurton's Cat
A Domestic Tale
Mary Robinson

Old MISTRESS GURTON[25] had a Cat,
   A Tabby, loveliest of the race,
Sleek as a doe, and tame, and fat
   With velvet paws, and whisker'd face;
The Doves of VENUS[26] not so fair,
   Nor JUNO's Peacocks[27] half so grand
As MISTRESS GURTON's Tabby rare,
   The proudest of the purring band;
So dignified in all her paces—
She seem'd, a pupil of the Graces![28]   10
There never was a finer creature
In all the varying whims of Nature!

All liked Grimalkin,[29] passing well!
Save MISTRESS GURTON, and, 'tis said,
She oft with furious ire would swell,
When, through neglect or hunger keen,
Puss, with a pilfer'd scrap, was seen,
Swearing beneath the pent-house shed:[30]
For, like some fav'rites, she was bent
On all things, yet with none content;   20
And still, whate'er her place or diet,
She could not pick her bone, in quiet.

Sometimes, new milk GRIMALKIN stole,
And sometimes—over-set the bowl!
For over eagerness will prove,

25. *Gammer Gurton's Needle,* one of the earliest comedies in English, was reprinted several times in the eighteenth century.

26. The dove is the symbol of Venus (also known as Aphrodite). The goddess raised them in her temples, and they were carved on her jewels.   .

27. The peacock is sacred to Juno, Queen of Heaven; the eyed feathers of the bird's tail symbolize the goddess's starry heavens and her all-seeing vigilance.

28. Aglaia (Brilliance), Thalia (Bloom), and Euphrosyne (Joy) were the attendants of Aphrodite and are represented as enhancing the enjoyments of life for all they visit.

29. The spirit of a witch; according to legend, any witch could assume the body of a cat nine times. Cats who misbehaved were often called Grimalkin.

30. Small building attached to a larger, original one.

Oft times the bane[31] of what we love;
And sometimes, to her neighbour's home,
GRIMALKIN, like a thief would roam,
Teaching poor Cats, of humbler kind,
30   For high example sways the mind!
Sometimes she paced the garden wall,
Thick guarded by the shatter'd pane,
And lightly treading with disdain,
Fear'd not Ambition's certain fall!
Old China broke, or scratch'd her Dame
And brought domestic friends to shame!
And many a time this Cat was curst,
Of squalling, thieving things, the worst!
Wish'd Dead! and menanc'd with a string,
40   For Cats of such scant Fame, deserv'd to swing!

One day, report,[32] for ever busy,
Resolv'd to make Dame Gurton easy;
A Neighbour came, with solemn look,
And thus, the dismal tidings broke.
"Know you, that poor GRIMALKIN died
Last night, upon the pent-house side?
I heard her for assistance call;
I heard her shrill and dying squall!
I heard her, in reproachful tone,
50   Pour, to the stars, her feeble groan!
Alone, I heard her piercing cries—
'*With not a Friend, to close her Eyes!*'"[33]

"Poor Puss! I vow it grieves me sore,
Never to see thy beauties more!
Never again to hear thee purr,
To stroke thy back, of Zebra fur;
To see thy emral'd eyes—so bright, ⎫
Flashing around their lust'rous light ⎬
Amid the solemn shades of night! ⎭

31. Ruin, poison.
32. Robinson is personifying *report,* which means "rumor" or "gossip."
33. John Dryden's *Alexander's Feast* (1697) includes the often-quoted lament, "With not a Friend, to close his Eyes" (line 83).

"Methinks I see her pretty paws—   60
As gracefully she paced along;
I hear her voice, so shrill, among
The chimney rows! I see her claws,
While, like a Tyger, she pursued
Undauntedly the pilf'ring race;
I see her lovely whisker'd face
When she her nimble prey subdued!
And then, how she would frisk, and play,
And purr the Evening hours away:
Now stretch'd beside the social fire;   70
Now on the sunny lawn, at noon,
Watching the vagrant Birds that flew,
Across the scene of varied hue,
To peck the Fruit. Or when the Moon
Stole o'er the hills, in silv'ry suit,
How would she chaunt her lovelorn Tale
    Soft as the wild Eolian Lyre![34]
'Till ev'ry brute, on hill, in dale,
    Listen'd with wonder mute!"

"O! Cease!" exclaim'd DAME GURTON, straight,[35]   80
"Has my poor Puss been torn away?
Alas! how cruel is my fate,
How shall I pass the tedious day?
Where can her mourning mistress find
So sweet a Cat? so meek! so kind!
So keen a mouser, such a beauty,
So orderly, so fond, so true,
That every gentle task of duty
The dear, domestic creature knew!
Hers, was the mildest tend'rest heart!   90
She knew no little *cattish* art;
Not cross, like *fav'rite Cats,* was she
But seem'd the queen of Cats to be!
I cannot live—since doom'd, alas! to part
From poor GRIMALKIN kind, the darling of my heart!"

34. Aeolus was the Greek god of winds, and his harp sounded with the faintest of breezes. Thus, an Aeolian lyre was a wind-harp, a box about three inches long with catgut strings, made to be set in windows or other places where the wind could produce harmonics from the strings.
35. Suddenly.

And now DAME GURTON, bath'd in tears,
With a black top-knot vast, appears:
Some say that a black gown she wore,
As many oft have done before,
100   For Beings, valued less, I ween,[36]
Than this, of Tabby Cats, the fav'rite Queen!
But lo! soon after, one fair day,
Puss, who had only been a roving—
Across the pent-house took her way,
To see her Dame, so sad, and loving;
Eager to greet the mourning fair
She enter'd by a window, where
A China bowl of luscious cream
Was quiv'ring in the sunny beam.

110   Puss, who was somewhat tired and dry,
And somewhat fond of bev'rage sweet;
Beholding such a tempting treat,
Resolved its depth to try.
She saw the warm and dazzling ray
Upon the spotless surface play:
She purr'd around its circle wide,
And gazed, and long'd, and mew'd and sigh'd!
But Fate, unfriendly, did that hour controul,
She overset the cream, and smash'd the gilded bowl!

120   As MISTRESS GURTON heard the thief,
   She started from her easy chair,
And, quite unmindful of her grief,
   Began aloud to swear!
"Curse that voracious beast!" she cried,
   "Here SUSAN,[37] bring a cord—
I'll hang the vicious, ugly creature—
The veriest plague e'er form'd by nature!"
And MISTRESS GURTON kept her word—
   And Poor GRIMALKIN—DIED!

36. Imagine, think.
37. Generic name for a servant.

Thus, often, we with anguish sore   130
The *dead,* in clam'rous grief deplore;
Who, were they once *alive* again
Would meet the sting of cold disdain!
For FRIENDS, whom trifling faults can sever,
Are *valued most,* WHEN LOST FOR EVER!

(1800)

Sources

Finch: *Miscellany Poems, on Several Occasions* (London, 1713), 202–4; More: *The Two Gardeners* (London, 1796), 3–6; Leapor: *Poems upon Several Occasions* (London, 1748), 97–100; Piozzi: *A Collection of Poems in Four Volumes. By Several Hands,* ed. Robert Dodsley, 2nd ed., 4 vols. (London, 1770), 3:258–62; Leigh: *Miscellaneous Poems* (Manchester, 1788), 41–44; Alcock: *Poems, &c. &c. By the Late Mrs. Mary Alcock* (London, 1799), 25–30; Tuite: *Poems by Lady Tuite* (London, 1796), 169–70; Robinson: *Lyrical Tales* (London, 1800), 22–29.

The Elegy

"Methinks, I see her, — as she late was seen, / Humble and free, obliging and serene." This line from Jane Brereton's *On the Death of a Lady* is what elegy means to most of us: a short, dignified poem of mourning occasioned by a death. Few have the skill or honor to be chosen to commemorate a loved one on a headstone, as Anna Laetitia Barbauld did for her sister-in-law; the epitaph reads in part, "Ill can this stone thy finished virtues tell." The elegy, rather than exclusively a poem lamenting an individual's death, takes several distinctive forms, including the classical, the memorial, the pastoral, and the English contemplative. Most frequently it is a poem of meditation, often on love, war, or death. By the end of the eighteenth century the elegy was one of the three or four most popular forms of poetry. The elegiac mode had penetrated almost every poetic genre, and the elegy was established as one of the most flexible and beloved poetic kinds.

Elegy originally referred not to genre or content but to the verse form called the "elegiac distich." The true elegiac stanza was couplets alternating hexameters and pentameters; the Greeks let them flow from line to line, but the Romans closed the couplet. The difficult pastoral elegy, of which the first poem in this section is an example, is one of the oldest classical forms. As a way to mourn an exemplary public figure it never lost favor, and some of its conventions, such as the dialogue form, expressions of intense mourning followed by consolation, and nature imagery used in stylized ways, are skillfully deployed by Elizabeth Thomas. However, it was new interest in the meditative and contemplative elegy as practiced by the earliest Greek elegists and carried on by the Romans that made the form timely and even gripping. Second in antiquity only to the epic, this kind of elegy "was the vehicle not only for passing emotions but for considered ideas."[1] Both Jane West's *Elegy III. To Laura* and Mary Whateley Darwall's *Elegy on the Ruins of Kenilworth Castle* draw on this tradition and suggest how deeply read women poets were. The ode and the elegy were the great classical forms embraced and renewed by mid-century poets. The elegy's English origins were equally majestic, as they can be traced through a line of British poems that are brooding meditations on the brevity of life, beginning with *The Wanderer* and

The Pearl. One of the best-known poems in the language, Thomas Gray's *Elegy in a Country Church Yard,* is within this tradition.

In the Renaissance, Petrarchan love poetry had been included in the category of elegy. West's peaceful poem is written from Petrarch's point of view and ranges widely over the pair's emotions. Many other excellent poems of this type survive. For example, Mary Leapor's *The Beauties of the Spring* is a formal elegy in this tradition and infinitely appropriate to her own time: "In those still Groves no martial Clamours sound, / No streaming Purple stains the guiltless Ground."[2] The poem moves melodiously between the secluded, romantic "friends" and the hints of war, strife, and poverty beyond their grove. By the seventeenth century English poets had come to prefer and defend quatrains, their "elegiac stanza." The "heroic quatrain," iambic pentameter lines rhyming *abab,* became associated with the English elegy. Samuel Johnson quoted Dryden as identifying the heroic quatrain as "the most magnificent of all the measures which our language affords."[3] The poems in this section by Clara Reeve, Helen Maria Williams, Jane West, and Mary Whateley Darwall are written in this metrical form. Susanna Blamire's thought-provoking *Written in a Churchyard,* a poem in dialogue with Gray's major ideas, experiments with having the quatrains flow without breaks. The ethical standards of Greek culture animated the elegies and gave them lasting historical as well as artistic interest; for example, Solon, an Athenian statesman whom Plato named as one of the Seven Sages, explained his political principles in the form. British poets took up the tradition and used the form to express their opinions and values in a time when constitutional, social, and political issues kept the nation in turmoil. Darwall wrote many elegies, and the carefully structured *Elegy on the Ruins of Kenilworth Castle* begins with allusions to notable moments in the castle's history and ends with an affirmation of timeless British principles.

Funeral and memorial elegies by women are often obviously thoughtful and carefully crafted works of art. Funeral elegies were written to be read or recited at funerals; they were sometimes affixed to the hearse and sometimes dropped in the grave with flowers.[4] The variety of the memorial poems is impressive, as illustrated by Mary Jones's dignified *In Memory of the Rt. Hon. Lord Aubrey Beauclerk* (2.F) and Mary Robinson's *Monody on the Death of Mr. Garrick* (not included), in which she recognizes David Garrick's significance as the person who made Shakespeare the national poet and draws upon her own theatrical experience. In this section, we include three very different poems of lament. Each draws upon a different set of allusions and images, and each is a compressed, gripping reflection on the experience of grief. For instance, Mary Masters's *Upon the Same* is the second of two poems that she wrote on the birth of her sister's twins, one of whom died almost instantly. The craftsmanship of Jane Brereton's and Elizabeth Tollet's poems is more impressive for the simplicity of their recollections and tributes to their friends. Equally diverse are the three contemplative poems. Varied as they are, the poems in this section only hint at the richness of the elegies women wrote. Elegies are always part of individuals' and nations' histories and give readers much to experience and ponder. As Samuel Johnson wrote, "Nature and Reason have dictated to every Nation, that to preserve good Actions from Oblivion, is both the Interest and Duty of Mankind."[5] These largely private elegies go beyond individual, deeply felt friendship to offering us unusual access to what qualities women felt deserved tribute and preservation. As such, they fulfill the elegy's traditional historical and social purposes but add a dimension that has largely been ignored.

Notes

1. C. M. Bowra, *Early Greek Elegists* (Cambridge: W. Heffer and Sons, 1960), 3.

2. Mary Leapor, *The Beauties of the Spring,* in Leapor, *Poems upon Several Occasions* (London, 1748), 17.

3. Quoted in Paula R. Backscheider, *Eighteenth-Century Women Poets and Their Poetry* (Baltimore: Johns Hopkins University Press, 2005), 271–72.

4. See John W. Draper, *The Funeral Elegy and the Rise of English Romanticism* (New York: New York University Press, 1929), 9.

5. Samuel Johnson, "Essay on Epitaphs," *Gentleman's Magazine* 10 (December 1740): 593.

A Pastoral Elegy, on Henry late Duke of Norfolk, begun by Pylades in the Country, and finish'd by the Author in Town[1]

Elizabeth Thomas

PYLADES.[2]
Oh! whence *Eliza* flow those pregnant Tears,
That call for mine, and raise my utmost Fears?
Why sit you drooping in this Shade alone,
And make the Woods lament to hear your Moan?
Tell me why thus excessively you grieve?
I fain[3] wou'd know, because I'd fain relieve.

ELIZA.
My *Grief* is greater than I can express,
Exceeds all Bounds, admits of no Redress.

PYLADES.
Oh therefore tell! that I may bear a Part,
And bring some comfort to thy throbbing Heart, }   10
Companions in *Affliction* ease the Smart.

ELIZA.
I wou'd not, for that Cause, my Woes reveal,
Nor let my *dearest Friend* my Sorrow feel,
And since I am *afflicted, lost, undone,*
Compleatly *wretched,* let me be alone.

PYLADES.
Unless I may with you participate
In all your *Passions,* ev'ry Turn of *Fate;*
Unless I'm suffer'd to condole with you,
How can I think your promis'd *Friendship* true?
In Vain on your Affection I depend,   20

---

1. Thomas's *Miscellany Poems* also included *To the Late Duke of Norfolk. An Ode.* This poem suggests that it was written about the time of his death in 1701, shortly after Thomas's fiancé completed his studies at the Middle Temple and failed to find a position.

2. Richard Gwinnett (1675–1717), to whom Elizabeth Thomas was engaged for sixteen years. The marriage was delayed first, by financial necessity and then by the illness of Thomas's mother. Thomas lived in London, and Gwinnett lived on his father's estate. They carried on a literary correspondence that includes letters, poems, and philosophical essays.

3. Gladly.

If *unsincere;* in Vain you call me *Friend;*
And I conjure you, if you think me so,
No longer thus from me conceal your *Wo.*

ELIZA.
Well! since with such a forcible Constraint:
You press to know the Cause of my Complaint.
Wherein your self an equal Portion bear,
With melting Heart the dismal Tidings hear.
Oh *Pylades!* our mutual Hopes are fled,
How shall I speak those Words? great *Pollio's*[4] dead.

PYLADES.
30   Forbid it Heav'n! our gen'rous *Patron* gone?
Great! Good! and *Just!* all Worth contain'd in one.

ELIZA.
Alas, too true!
Last Night I heard the sad amazing News,
As I was going forth to fold my Ewes;
Unhappy Ewes! which now may bleat in vain,
And with unpitied Cries fill all the Plain:
Once my Delight, but now no more my Care,
Go wander Flocks, while I lye sobbing here.

PYLADES.
If Silence, or if Sighs cou'd ease our Pain,
40   Or our lost *Pollio* bring to Life again;
With silent Tears we'd wash our Griefs away,
And in long Sighs! wear out each tedious Day:
But Lo! I hear the melancholy Sound
Thro' all the Plains goes heavily around,
Pollio's no more! Great *Pollio* is no more!
Rebounds from ev'ry Rock, and distant Shore:
The *Woods,* and *Hills* the dismal News disperse,

4. Henry Howard (1655–1701), seventh Duke of Norfolk. Thomas implies that he had encouraged her as a poet, and he was in John Dryden's circle. For an intimate letter from Dryden to Thomas, see James Winn, *John Dryden and His World* (New Haven, CT: Yale University Press, 1987), 508. The poem alludes to Norfolk's long service in government offices, which included membership in the Privy Council and various military positions.

Lamenting Eccho's the sad Words reherse,
And ev'ry hollow *Cave,* with doleful Tone,
Redoubles *Nature's* universal Groan.   50
Then in pathetick Verse his Death proclaim,
And in sweet Numbers celebrate his Fame.

ELIZA.
That he vouchsaf'd to hear my humble Lays,[5]
Shew'd his unbounded *Goodness,* not my *Praise;*
Nor were his condescending Smiles e'er meant
For *Commendation,* but *Encouragement:*
Judiciously he'd calm the *Muse's* Heat,
And regulate her inharmonious Feet:
Direct her in a new and nobler Way,
Yet call her down, when she had soar'd astray.   60
Thus did he not my humble *Song* despise,
In Hopes I might to higher *Notes* arise:
Then weep sad *Maid,* thy fatal Loss deplore,
Thy great, thy godlike *Censor,* is no more.

PYLADES.
Behold, *Eliza,* where our *Pan*[6] appears,
See what a melancholy Look he wears,
Vast is his Sorrow boundless as his Mind,
But manly *Virtue* hath his Tears confin'd:
What broken Accents from his *Lips* do flow!
Musing he walks, and seems depress'd with Wo.   70
Then with a Sigh, he cries my *Pollio's* gone!
And hark, how all the Swains[7] his Loss bemoan:
These Thoughts, methinks, should give us some Relief,
Pan mourns his Fate, *Pan* shares our mutual Grief.

ELIZA.
The royal Sorrow is to *Pollio* due,
Pan knew his Heart, and *Pan* possess'd it too:
To our great *Pastor,* he was ever dear,
And next to *Pan,* we *Pollio* did revere;

5. Ballads; lyric or narrative poems meant to be sung.
6. Greek god of pastures, herds, flocks, and forests.
7. Country men; lovers.

For *Pollio* strove th' Arcadians[8] still to please,
80   And, by his thoughtful Care, secur'd our Ease.
Justice he lov'd, and *Peace* was his Delight: ⎫
Mild was his *Face,* yet so divinely bright,   ⎬
Wolves, Bears, and *Tygers,* fled his awful Sight. ⎭
Unhappy *Plains!* your dismal State deplore,
Unhappy Flocks! your Guardian is no more.

PYLADES.
Forsaken *Nymphs,* and *Swains,* your Loss proclaim;
Hills, Vales, and *Groves,* reverberate his Name.

ELIZA.
See! see, lamenting *Swain!* with wond'ring Eyes,
What beauteous Streams of Light, adorn the Skies!
90   What wond'rous Harmony is this we hear?
See! Shepherd see! our *Pollio* does appear:
Behold, what dazling Glories round him shine,
The mortal Part cast off, he now is all divine.
Smiling he sits, crown'd with immortal Bays,[9]
And with a gracious Nod accepts our duteous Lays.

PYLADES.
Then let our Sorrows vanish all away,
Like Clouds dispers'd before approaching Day;
Let's Cease untimely, and in vain to mourn;
For *Pollio* gone, who never must return:
100   Benign he sits in his exalted State,
Fix'd in the Skies above the Pow'r of Fate:
Where, like a glorious Star, he shall remain,
To shed auspicious Influence on our Plain:
And while he sits above secure of *Fame,*
Let's here below perpetuate his Name.

(1722)

8. Those who live in the land of pastoral simplicity and happiness in Virgil's *Eclogues.* Renaissance poets continued the tradition of the idealized land.
9. Leaves of the laurel tree were used to make wreaths for poets or conquerors.

Upon the Same: [To my Infant Niece; her little Sister dying the Instant she Was Born]
Mary Masters

How wonderful art Thou, O Lord, most high!
Who dares thy active Providence deny?
Whate'er occurs beneath the rising Sun,
By thy Permission or Command is done.
My Soul adores, and magnifies thy Pow'r,
For precious Mercies, I receive each Hour.
Blessings on me, or on my Friends bestow'd,
Excite perpetual Praises to my God.
Who could the cruel Pangs of Child-birth bear,
If not supported by thy tender Care?   10
Those wond'rous Agonies of Nature shew,
An Act of Justice and of Goodness too:
Thy Justice, which the Suff'ring did ordain,
Thy Goodness, that relieves the mighty Pain.

   My Sister, lately from these Torments freed,
(For so thou hadst indulgently decreed)
Forgets, how great, how vast her Sorrows were,
And in a Mother's Fondness sinks her Care.
By thy preserving Pow'r the Infant lives,
And Pleasure to its joyful Parents gives: 20
Its little Sister dies, by thy Command,
An equal Blessing from thy bounteous Hand.
From *This* recall'd, to *That* thou givest Breath;
Then blessed be the Lord of Life and Death.

(1733)

On the Death of a Lady
Jane Brereton

Must I in silence still the loss lament,
Nor give, o'er-charg'd, my swelling sorrows vent?
Must still the anxious sigh, the melting roar,
Be all the vouchers, that my grief's sincere?
Can I relief in sad reflection find,

While her dear image fills my pensive mind?
Or, can my thoughts, when taught in verse to flow,
Express her worth, or mitigate my woe?
　　My mind presents her, as she did appear
10 When well she pass'd, her short probation here
And warmly practis'd ev'ry heavenly grace
To prove a conqueror in the christian race.
Methinks, I see her,—as she late was seen,
Humble and free, obliging and serene;
Methinks, I hear her,——and with joy attend
To the sweet converse of th' instructive friend
In whose pure soul each hallow'd virtue glow'd
As radiant stars emblaze the milky-road.[10]
　　Whose soft compassion, sympathizing care,
20 Extensive spread, and unconfin'd as air;
Whose manners winning, easy, and refin'd,
The sure result of an accomplish'd mind.
Tho' polish'd, yet not varnish'd with one wile;
An ISRAELITE! *in whom there was no guile.*[11]
　　When I, dear saint! do not thy loss deplore,
And on thy well-spent life, reflect no more;
When thy memorial is no longer dear,
Or thy lov'd name swells not the flowing tear,
When I forget thy virtues; may I be
30 Forgot by those, who most resemble thee.

·(1735)

Adieu my Friend
Elizabeth Tollet

Adieu my Friend! and may thy Woes
　　Be all in long Oblivion lost:
If Innocence can give Repose;
　　Or gentle Verse can please thy Ghost.

10. Milky Way.

11. John 1:47. Jesus said this of Nathaniel. Psalm 32:2 blesses "the man . . . in whose spirit there is no guile." Nathaniel's transparent character earns him the name Israelite. George A. Buttrick, ed., *Interpreter's Bible*, 12 vols. (New York: Abingdon, 1952), 8:448. A surprising number of eighteenth-century people quote this verse.

No pious Rite, no solemn Knell[12]
    Attended thy belov'd Remains:
Nor shall the letter'd Marble tell
    What silent Earth the Charge contains.

Obscure, beneath the nameless Stone,
    With thee shall Truth and Virtue sleep: 10
While, with her Lamp, the Muse alone,
    Shall watch thy sacred Dust and weep.

Blue Violets, and Snow-Drops pale,
    In pearly Dew for thee shall mourn:
And humble Lillies of the Vale[13]
    Shall cover thy neglected Urn.

(1755)

An Elegy. Written at Putney[14] in the Year MDCCLIX
Clara Reeve

Illusive joys the gaudy world holds forth
    To sooth her children in her ways untry'd,
T' entice them with a good of seeming worth,
    Then mock their pains, and all their cares deride.

Imagination warms the youthful heart,
    Prompts it to face the sun's too pow'rful rays;
On Fancy's[15] pinions[16] borne, with treacherous art
    It plays awhile, and wantons[17] in the blaze.

12. Mournful bell.

13. Lilies of the Valley, a popular spring plant with fragrant, white bell-shaped flowers.

14. Part of London along a sweeping curve of the Thames River that had existed since the Iron Age. In the eighteenth century, it grew into a fashionable outer suburb. Since Reeve lived in Ipswich, she was probably visiting a friend.

15. A creative faculty, usually treated as lighter and more whimsical and playful than imagination or as an assistant to it. Imagination, with the power to transform its material, was considered the higher power.

16. Wings.

17. Reeve illustrates the dangerous effects of imagination with a reminder of Icarus, who in Greek mythology flew too close to the sun. First he "wantons," that is, frolics luxuriously in the air. Then the wax attaching his wings to his body melted, causing him to plummet into the sea.

But ah, too soon the waxen pinions melt,
 And Icarus falls hov'ring thro' the air!
The wiles of Folly are not known till felt,
 And Wisdom but assists us to despair.

Not wealth, nor title fill'd my idle brain,
 My soul abhor'd and shunn'd the groveling theme;
I follow'd distant in the Muses' train,
 And sung my artless lays[18] beside the stream.

Did I indulge, in Fancy's soft embrace,
 A wish, but Reason's dictates might approve;
I ask'd but what from Nature I cou'd trace;
 I ask'd the joys of friendship and of love.

Alas no more for me those names survive!
 Yet from my soul they never shall be 'ras'd,[19]
Altho' condemn'd in solitude to live,
 No more of friendship, or of love to taste.

From a too tender heart my sorrow sprung,
 An arrow barb'd with insult enter'd deep;
From infancy with various crosses wrung,
 Too soft to suffer, yet too proud to creep.

I woo'd not Fortune's smiles, I scorn'd her lure,
 Upon her altar not one off'ring lay;
She vow'd my happiness shou'd ne'er endure,
 But every joy fly swifter than the day.

The laurel wreath[20] is blasted on my brow,
 By the cold blight of disappointment chill'd,
Disdain and Fortune have congeal'd to snow
 The ray of Genius, that my bosom fill'd.

Oh let me underneath this gloomy shade,
 My secret woes in soothing strains prolong!

18. Ballads; lyric or narrative poems meant to be sung.
19. Erased, obliterated.
20. In classical times, leaves from this tree were made into wreaths for poets.

The flowing numbers swell along the glade,
   Till Thames re-echo and approve my song.   40

(1759; 1769)

Written in a Churchyard,
On Seeing a Number of Cattle Grazing In It. 1766.
Susanna Blamire

Be still my heart, and let this moving sight
   Whisper a moral to each future lay;[21]
Let this convince how like the lightning's flight
   Is earthly pageantry's precarious stay.
Within this place of consecrated trust
   The neighbouring herds their daily pasture find;
And idly bounding o'er each hallow'd bust,
   Form a sad prospect to the pensive mind.
Whilst o'er the graves thus carelessly they tread,
   Allur'd by hunger to the deed profane,   10
They crop the verdure[22] rising from the bed
   Of some fond parent, or some love-sick swain.[23]
No more does vengeance to revenge the deed
   Lodge in their breasts, or vigour aid the blow;
The power to make the sad offenders bleed
   The prostrate image ne'er again shall know.
Nor can the time-worn epitaph rehearse
   The name or titles which its owner bore;
No more the sorrow lives within the verse,
   For memory paints the moving scene no more.   20
Perhaps 'tis one whose noble deeds attain'd
   Honour and fame in time of hostile war;—
Whose arm the Captive's liberty regain'd,
   And stamp'd his valour with a glorious scar.
Alas! his widow might attend him here,
   And children, too, the slow procession join,
And his fond friends indulge the trickling tear

21. Ballad; lyric or narrative poem meant to be sung.
22. Fresh green grass and plants.
23. Country man; lover.

O'er his last honours at the awful shrine.
Perhaps some orphan here might see inurn'd[24]
30   The only guardian of her orphan years;
And, on the precipice of errors turn'd,
      Become reclaim'd by sweet repentant tears.
The lover, too, might strain an eager look,
      Once more attempting to survey the fair
Who, for his sake, her early friends forsook,
      With him her days of joy or grief to share.
What beauty or what charms adorn'd the frame
      Of this cold image, now to earth consign'd;
Or what just praise the heart's high worth might claim,
40   The time-worn letters now no more remind.
Then what is honour? — what is wealth or fame?
      Since the possessor waits the common doom!
As much rever'd we find the peasant's name
      As the rich lord's, when in the levelling tomb.
To both alike this tribute we may send,
      The heart-swollen sigh, or the lamenting tear;
And without difference o'er their ashes bend,
      For all distinctions find a level here.
For nought avails the marble o'er each head,
50   Nor all the art which sculpture can bestow,
To save the memory of the honour'd dead,
      Or strike the living with their wonted awe.
Then come, ye vain, whom Fortune deigns to bless,
      This scene at once shall all her frauds expose;
And ye who Beauty's loveliest charms possess
      From this may find a moral in the rose.
For soon infirmity shall fix her seat,
      And dissolution lastly close the scene;
No more shall youth your jocund[25] acts repeat,
60   Or age relate what graver years have been.
Yet think not death awaits the course of years,
      He comes whilst youth her shield of health supports;
In every place the potent king appears,
      To youth, to age, to every scene resorts.

24. Ashes preserved in an urn.
25. Joyful, merry.

But why, my heart, that palpitating beat!
　　Can death's idea cause that pensive gloom?
Since in the world such thorny cares we meet,
　　And since 'tis peace within the silent tomb.
Yet still the thought of nature's sad decay,
　　And the reception in the world unknown,　　　　　　　　70
Must cast a cloud o'er hope's celestial ray,
　　If not dispell'd by conscious worth alone:
May this support me in the awful hour
　　When earthly prospects fade before my view;
O! then, my friends, into my bosom pour
　　Some soothing balsam[26] at the last adieu.
Say, in Elysium[27] we shall meet again,
　　Nor there shall error hold th' enchanting rod;
But freed from earth at once we'll break the chain,
　　And thus releas'd shall ne'er offend our God.　　　　　　80
Then hence aversion to the body's doom,
　　Nor let this scene a pensive murmur raise,
Nor let thought grieve when pondering o'er the tomb,
　　Though on my grave the senseless herd should graze.

(1766; 1842)

ELEGY
On finding a young THRUSH in the Street, who escaped from
the Writer's Hand, as she was bringing him home, and, falling
down the Area of a House, could not be found[28]

Helen Maria Williams

Mistaken Bird, ah, whither hast thou stray'd?
My friendly grasp, why eager to elude?
This hand was on thy pinion[29] lightly laid,
And fear'd to hurt thee by a touch too rude.

26. Aromatic healing oil.

27. Home of the blessed in Greek mythology and the paradise of poets.

28. In *Julia, A Novel,* Williams has the heroine find a wounded bird, but it escapes from her hands; unable to find it, Julia "writes" this poem.

29. The distal segment of a bird's wing where the feathers fan out beautifully; it corresponds to the human forearm.

Is there no foresight in a Thrush's breast,
That thou down yonder gulph from me would'st go?
That gloomy area lurking cats infest,
And there the dog may rove, alike thy foe.

I would with lavish crumbs my Bird have fed,
10   And bought a crystal cup to wet thy bill;
I would have made of down and moss thy bed,
Soft, though not fashion'd with a Thrush's skill.

Soon as thy strengthen'd wing could mount the sky,
My willing hand had set my captive free:
Ah, not for her, who loves the muse, to buy
A selfish pleasure, bought with pain to thee!

The vital air, and liberty, and light,
Had all been thine: and love, and rapt'rous song,
And sweet parental joys, in rapid flight,
20   Had led the circle of thy life along.

Securely to my window hadst thou flown,
And ever thy accustom'd morsel found;
Nor should thy trusting breast the wants have known,
Which other Thrushes knew, when winter frown'd.

Fram'd with the wisdom Nature lent to thee,
Thy house of straw had brav'd the tempest's rage;
And thou, thro' many a spring, hadst liv'd to see
The utmost limit of a Thrush's age.

Ill-fated Bird! and does the Thrush's race,
30   Like Man's, mistake the path that leads to bliss;
Or, when his eye that tranquil path can trace,
The good he well discerns, thro' folly miss?

(1790)

Elegy III. To Laura[30]
Jane West

How long, how well, we've lov'd; Oh Laura, say!
  Bid recollection trace the distant hour
When first we met in life's delightful May,
  And our warm hearts confess'd fair Friendship's power.

Recall the portrait of the ingenuous mind,
  Which from experience no stern precepts drew:
When gay, impetuous, innocent, and kind,
  From taste congenial love spontaneous grew.

Deep had we quaff'd the cup of childish joy;
  The simple sweet our nicer taste disdain'd.   10
We thought youth's promis'd feast would never cloy,
  And of the future fairy prospects feign'd.

Time lifts the curtain of expected years;
  Eager we rush the imagin'd good to find.
Say, if the blessing, when possess'd, appears
  Fair, as the phantom that allur'd thy mind.

Doth the stern world those faultless friends disclose,
  Thy guileless candour imag'd to thy soul?
Doth virtue guard thee from insidious blows,
  Or sense the shafts of calumny controul?   20

For me! I thought the golden wreath of fame
  Still in my reach, and like a trifler play'd:
But when I turn'd the glorious prize to claim,
  My hopes had faded in oblivion's shade.

The dear associates, we in youth rever'd,
  The world's rude changes from our arms have drove:

30. In imitation of Petrarch, poets frequently addressed poems, especially about love, to "Laura," and it became a convention. Petrarch said that he first saw the woman who inspired his love poetry in 1327. She was, according to him, already married and died in the 1348 plague. He calls her "Laura" in the poems, and her identity is unknown; in fact, some scholars doubt her existence.

Some in the grave's dark cells, have disappear'd;
 Some lost by distance; some estrang'd in love.

Yet there are views, which never will deceive,
30 In one sure prospect no false colours blend:
Death on our brows will press his cypress wreath,[31]
 And all our wishes in the dust will end.

Perchance, ere yet, yon zenith'd sun shall lave[32]
 In the salt deep, my conflict will be o'er.
Then, Laura, bending o'er my turf-clad grave,
 Shall shed the tear, which I shall feel no more.

Or, if allotted many lengthened years,
 We walk consociate[33] through the tedious gloom,
'Till each lov'd object gradual disappears,
40 And our dim vision but discerns the tomb:

Still our try'd faith shall shame the fickle herd,
 Whose civil forms are cold and unendear'd:
Nor shall a casual flight, or dubious word,
 Efface the kindness we have long rever'd.

Friendship's sweet pleasures bless'd our early hours
 With tender fellowship of hopes and fears:
Our ripen'd age shall feel its nobler powers;
 Its calm endearments sooth our drooping years.

Then, when the levities of mirth offend,
50 When passion ceases its tormenting strife;
How sweet in converse with an aged friend,
 To trace th' eventful history of life.

From present sorrow, lassitude, and pains,
 To lift the soul to glory's promis'd sphere:

31. Cypress is sacred to the god of Death, Dis. The Romans dedicated the cypress tree to Pluto because, once cut, the tree never grows again.
 32. The sun, now at its highest point, shall bathe.
 33. In friendly companionship.

There may we meet, and, where love ever reigns,
    Perfect the union which we cherish'd here.

(1791)

Elegy on the Ruins of Kenilworth Castle.[34] Respectfully inscribed to the Right Honourable the Earl of Clarendon[35]

Mary Whateley Darwall

When Phœbus[36] to old Ocean's oozy bed
    Descending, veil'd his glories from the sight;—
When solemn eve her dewy mantle spread,
    And Cynthia[37] rose, pale regent of the night;—

Revolving in my mind the changeful state
    Of sublunary grandeur, pomp and shew;
How time, inexorable, marks the date
    Of all that's gay, or great, or good below;

Chance led me, as I meditating rov'd,
    Where KENILWORTH its gothic glories rear'd,   10
Which CLINTON[38] built, which great ELIZA[39] lov'd,
    ELIZA, to th' historic Muse endear'd.

Stupendous walls! to ruin's rage consign'd,
    Mould'ring, submissive to the arm of fate;
Thro' your lone arches let me entrance find,
    And, silent, ponder on your pristine state.

34. Darwall visited Kenilworth Castle, which was founded in the twelfth century and was the site where Edward II was forced to relinquish his crown. The ruins of an Augustinian priory are on the grounds.

35. Thomas Villiers (1709–86), first Earl of Clarendon, second creation (the title was revived and granted him in 1776). The castle belonged to the Clarendon family.

36. Apollo, the sun god, here the personification of the sun.

37. Diana, goddess of the moon, here the moon personified.

38. Geoffrey de Clinton (d. c. 1133) founded the castle about 1120.

39. The castle became royal property through its owner John of Gaunt, and Queen Elizabeth presented it to Robert Dudley, Earl of Leicester. Leicester entertained the queen there, and Sir Walter Scott describes one lavish event held in her honor in 1575 in his novel *Kenilworth*.

Where the athletic porter frown'd severe,
  And scowl'd defiance o'er th' embattled plain,
No sound, save echo's dying voice, we hear,
20   Nor form perceive, save fancy's airy train.

Here the gay herald erst proclaim'd the prize,
  And summon'd to the field each noble youth,
That wish'd to win the author of his sighs,
  The beauteous dame he lov'd with zeal and truth.

A glance from her bright eye, or ribband[40] wove
  In mystic knots of love, cou'd well repay
Each danger he in well-fought fields cou'd prove,
  And crown with ecstacy the hard-won day.

When the gay circus[41] glow'd with beauty's beam,
30   And ev'ry knight beheld his sov'reign's face,
Who cou'd be daunted at the faulchion's[42] gleam,
  Or shun his fierce opponent's dire embrace?

No more these dreadful, pompous sports prevail!
  Love, pleas'd, accepts a milder sacrifice,—
The time-try'd faith, the gently-soothing tale
  Now from the coldest heart obtain the prize.

Where (Britain's glory) the bright virgin queen,[43]
  With bevies of the courtly fair ones, stray'd,
Like Dian's[44] buskin'd[45] nymphs, in forests green,
40   To chace the tim'rous roe thro' grove and glade;—

Now the rough plough-share marks its crooked way,
  Or sun-burnt hinds, with ruthless hands, despoil

40. Ribbon.
41. In Roman times, place for chariot racing, athletic and gladiatorial contests, and other exhibitions.
42. Short, broad sword with a convex cutting edge.
43. Queen Elizabeth I.
44. Diana, Roman goddess of the moon, of forests, of animals, and of childbirth.
45. A thick-soled calf-high or knee-high boot. Diana and her nymphs were often represented as huntresses.

The flow'ry meads[46] of all their rich array,
    And rudely glory in their rustic toil.

Where the broad stream in sportive eddies play'd,
    And at due distance kept the hostile throng;
Now the green slope, with blooming flow'rs array'd,
    Invites the rural train to dance and song.

O'er the rude walls the mantling ivy twines,
    And waves luxuriant round the nodding tow'rs;   50
Here skims the bat, the boding screech-owl pines,
    And the hoarse raven wakes the midnight hours.

Imagination crowds the vacant scene
    With glimm'ring ghosts, that haunt the dreary shade;
The mournful maid,—the warrior's dreadful mein,[47]
    Flitting by moon-light thro' the darkling glade.

If chance the village maid shou'd vent'rous stray
    Near these lone piles by vesper's[48] silver light,
What sounds does fancy to her ear convey!
    What forms present to her deluded sight!   60

If the sad bird of night pours forth her moan,
    Or waving shadows dance before the wind,—
She hears some restless spirit's hollow groan,
    And nameless terrors seize her timid mind.

Soon thro' the hamlet spreads the wond'rous tale,
    Enlarg'd by superstition as it flies:
Each rustic hearer stands aghast and pale,
    The taper twinkles and the cricket cries.

But reason's eye in other light surveys
    This mould'ring monument of earthly state,   70

46. Meadows.
47. Obsolete form of *mien;* bearing, manner expressing character.
48. Evening star.

Which, to the soul this warning truth conveys,—
    "Aspire to glories of a longer date."

For when oblivion shrouds the high-arch'd dome,
    And grandeur yields to time's all-conqu'ring sway,
The deathless soul shall find his destin'd home,—
    The cloudless regions of eternal day.

(1794)

Epitaph on [Susannah Barbauld Marissal][49]
Anna Laetitia Barbauld

Farewell, mild saint!—meek child of love, farewell!
Ill can this stone thy finished virtues tell.
Rest, rest in peace! the task of life is o'er;
Sorrows shall sting, and sickness waste no more.
But hard our task from one so loved to part,
While fond remembrance clings round every heart,—
Hard to resign the sister, friend, and wife,
And all that cheers, and all that softens life.
Farewell! for thee the gates of bliss unclose,
10   And endless joy succeeds to transient woes.

(1797)

Sources

Thomas: *Miscellany Poems on Several Subjects* (London, 1722), 221–27; Masters: *Poems on Several Occasions* (London, 1733), 138–39; Brereton: *On the Death of a Lady,* in *Gentleman's Magazine* 5 (March 1735): 155; Tollet: *Poems on Several Occasions* (London, 1755), 154–55; Reeve: *Original Poems on Several Occasions* (London, 1769), 1–3; Blamire: *The Poetical Works of Miss Susanna Blamire* (Edinburgh, 1842), 164–67; Williams: *Julia, A Novel; Interspersed with Some Poetical Pieces,* 2 vols. (London, 1790), 2:27–29; West: *Miscellaneous Poems, and a Tragedy* (York, 1791), 42–45; Darwall: *Poems on Several Occasions. By Mrs. Darwall (Formerly Miss Whateley) in Two Volumes,* 2 vols. (Walsall, 1794), 2:1–7; Barbauld: *The Works of Anna Laetitia Barbauld. With a Memoir by Lucy Aikin,* 2 vols. (London, 1825), 1:103.

49. This poem is engraved on Susannah Marissal's tombstone. Anna Laetitia Barbauld's sister-in-law, who often visited Barbauld and her husband; she died on 7 July 1797 at age fifty-one.

⊰J⊱

The Verse Narrative

One of the most natural forms of human utterance is narrative, and stories are as old as speech. Too often students think that lyric poetry has always been the dominant form, but until the early twentieth century narrative poetry was the most popular. Some of the earliest poetic forms, such as the epic, the ballad, biblical victory songs, fables, and the metrical romance, were narratives and offered powerful, accessible poetry to entire peoples. In a time when recitation and reading aloud were enjoyable activities and the nation experienced a growing desire for personal, polished accomplishments, narrative poetry thrived. Verse narratives such as the ones in this section gave the pleasures of prose fiction and poetry, and some look toward the modern short story. By the mid-eighteenth century, male poets had struggled to write high-quality epics and produced a few superb mock epics, but they and the women poets turned to other narrative forms and richly developed them. For example, Anne Finch's *The Poor Man's Lamb* is a biblical dramatization and includes some of the skillful techniques that enrich her fables. Its full-blown, detailed story is a virtuoso display of her ability to write lively dialogue as well as nature and narrative poetry. Far from an isolated period piece, her poem might be related to Christopher Smart's *Song to David* and T. S. Eliot's *Journey of the Magi*. Some women produced novella-length narrative poetry; examples are Elizabeth Singer Rowe's *History of Joseph* (1736) and Anna Seward's *Louisa: A Poetical Novel* (1784) (neither included). Other sections herein are devoted to the closely related poetic kinds, the ballad and the fable, and because of the regard poets had for narrative poetry of all kinds many examples are found throughout this book. The examples in this section suggest the impressive variety and sources of inspiration in women's poetry.

One of the most significant contributions the eighteenth century made to the Romantic period was the revival of the metrical romance, a popular form of entertainment from the Middle Ages that told stories of adventure, love, chivalry, and daring actions. Women were the leaders and innovators, as they were in the sonnet revival, and many excellent examples of their poetry survive. Both the ballad revival and the writing of gothic and pseudo-ancient verse, such as James Macpherson's Ossianic poems, amplified the renewed interest in a form as old as the Middle Ages. The rise of tourism and interest in remote parts of the British Isles encouraged regionalism, and poems such as Mary Whateley Darwall's *Elegy on the Ruins of Kenilworth Castle* (1.1) led to the blending of narrative with other forms of poetry. These poems laid the foundation for Samuel Taylor Coleridge's *Christabel*, Lord Byron's *The Corsair*, and John Keats's *Eve of St. Agnes*. The form remained appealing to women as important, innovative poems such as Elizabeth Barrett Browning's *Aurora Leigh* (1856) and Christina Rossetti's *Goblin Market* (1862) demonstrate.

In this section, Catherine Rebecca Manners's and Carolina Oliphant Nairne's poems are set in remote times. Manners weaves strikingly pointed political commentary into a very personal love story. For that and its technical excellence, the poem rises firmly above hundreds of mediocre metrical romances. In the threatening and war-torn final decades of the century, many, like this one, are about lovers experiencing separation and fear. They are set all over the globe and in every era. Mary Robinson adapts current news, a "wild boy" brought to Paris for display and study, into an arresting tale of solitary consciousnesses.[1] She imagines his history in *The Savage of Aveyron*, weaving his story with that of a lonely traveler like his mother. Jane West's *Alleyne and Ella, A Legendary Tale* (1799, not included) was based, she wrote, on a magazine story. Ella is in love with Alleyne, who is fighting in Spain, but Ella's father gives him only one month to return and claim her, or she will be forced to marry Earl Edgar. Helen Maria Williams's *American Tale* (1786, not included) is a well-composed story of a daughter finding her father in an American prison, learning that he has been aided by an American ("fierce against Britannia's band / His erring sword he draws"), and finding her own lost lover. Other tales are set in the Far East, tiny coastal Scottish villages, and the Caribbean. Some of the most familiar in the last group are representations of slaves' experiences, such as Mary Stockdale's *Fidelle; or, the Negro Child*, Amelia Opie's *The Black Man's Lament; or, How to Make Sugar* (both in 2.F), and Mary Robinson's *The Negro Girl* (1800, not included).

Most narrative poems blend genres, and the final poem in this section is by the great ballad writer Carolina Nairne. Her poem is unusual in the way the baron's hall and the mother's body are the tropes that carry the story, and her work is an excellent example of the way the oral tradition, the literary ballad, and the Romantic metrical tale flowed together. Seven years younger than Robert Burns, whose narrative tales like *Tam O'Shanter* are an important part of this evolution, she self-consciously worked with the inherited history, stories, and ballads, even as poems such as *O Stately Stood the Baron's Ha'* share the specific war themes and perspectives of her contemporaries and point forward to the exoticism and moods of the Romantics. A highly trained musician, Nairne blends art and folk song, Scots dialect and standard English, reasserts female propriety within Scottish songs, and makes ballads appropriate for fashionable drawing-room entertainments.[2] Robinson's poem also blends forms, including ballad and ode, in ways that point back to the oldest forms of poetry and forward to Romanticism. She continues the eighteenth-century practice of drawing upon and disseminating news. Because of hers and the wild boy's notoriety, *The Savage of Aveyron* becomes news about news.

Dramatic readings of narrative poems were popular afternoon and evening entertainment both within families and in social gatherings. People traveled miles to hear Anna Seward read, and neighbors enjoyed the skill of long-forgotten local people. The full story of how these poems were experienced, the details of the rise in interest in the verse narrative,[3] and the eighteenth century's legacies to the Romantic era remains to be written.

Notes

1. The boy, who was between twelve and fifteen years old, was living in the forest in Lacaune, France, when he was captured on 25 July 1799. Judith Pascoe, editor of Robinson's poems, notes that newspaper accounts about the boy were frequently published; see her note to the poem in *Mary Robinson: Selected Poems,* ed. Judith Pascoe (Peterborough, ON: Broadview, 2000), 332–33.

2. See Susan Steward, *Crimes of Writing: Problems in the Containment of Representation* (Durham, NC: Duke University Press, 1994), 102–31; Carol McGuirk, "Jacobite History to National Song: Robert Burns and Carolina Oliphant (Baroness Nairne)," *Eighteenth Century: Theory and Interpretation* 47 (2006): 253–87; Leith Davis, "Gender, Genre and the Imagining of the Scottish Nation: The Songs of Lady Nairne," in *Scottish Women Poets of the Romantic Period,* ed. Nancy Kushigian and Stephen Behrendt, www.alexanderstreet2.com/SWRPLive/bios/S7038-D001.html (accessed 13 July 2007).

3. See Stephen C. Behrendt. *British Women Poets and the Romantic Writing Community,* on the long verse, narrative tale (Baltimore: Johns Hopkins University Press, 2009), 172–83, 235–38.

The Poor Man's Lamb:
Or, Nathan's Parable to David after the Murder of Uriah, and his Marriage with Bathsheba.[1]
Turn'd into Verse and Paraphras'd.

Anne Finch

Now spent the alter'd King,[2] in am'rous Cares,
The Hours of sacred Hymns and solemn Pray'rs:
In vain the Altar waits his slow returns,
Where unattended Incense faintly burns:
In vain the whisp'ring Priests their Fears express,
And of the Change a thousand Causes guess.
Heedless of all their Censures He retires,
And in his Palace feeds his secret Fires;
Impatient, till from *Rabbah*[3] Tydings tell,
10   That near those Walls the poor *Uriah* fell,
Led to the Onset by a Chosen Few,
Who at the treacherous Signal, soon withdrew;
Nor to his Rescue e'er return'd again,
Till by fierce *Ammon*'s Sword[4] they saw the Victim slain.
'Tis pass'd, 'tis done! the holy Marriage-Knot,
Too strong to be unty'd, at last is cut.
And now to *Bathsheba* the King declares,
That with his Heart, the Kingdom too is hers;
That *Israel*'s Throne, and longing Monarch's Arms
20   Are to be fill'd but with her widow'd Charms.
Nor must the Days of formal Tears exceed,
To cross the Living, and abuse the Dead.
This she denies; and signs of Grief are worn;
But mourns no more than may her Face adorn,
Give to those Eyes, which Love and Empire fir'd,

1. Uriah was one of the Mighty Men in King David's select order of the Thirty. While Uriah was away fighting, David saw his wife, Bathsheba, bathing and seduced her, then schemed to have Uriah killed in battle. After Uriah's death, Bathsheba mourned for her husband. Later David married Bathsheba, and she is named as the mother of Solomon and in the genealogy of Jesus. The prophet Nathan came to David and told him the fictional legal case that Finch paraphrases, 2 Samuel 12. The story is in 2 Sam. 10–12.

2. David allegedly wrote many of the Psalms. As a shepherd boy, David killed Goliath, and later he was anointed king by the prophet Samuel.

3. Capital city of Ammon, which David's troops were besieging.

4. Personification of the Ammonites, the tribe from the edge of the Syrian desert. Exactly which of them killed Uriah is not recorded.

A melting Softness more to be desir'd;
Till the fixt Time, tho' hard to be endur'd,
Was pass'd, and a sad Consort's Name[5] procur'd:
When, with the Pomp that suits a Prince's Thought,
By Passion sway'd, and glorious Woman taught,   30
A *Queen* she's made, than *Michal*[6] seated higher,
Whilst light unusual Airs prophane the hallow'd *Lyre*.[7]

Where art thou *Nathan*? where's that Spirit now,
Giv'n to brave Vice, tho' on a Prince's Brow?
In what low Cave, or on what Desert Coast,
Now Virtue wants it, is thy Presence lost?

But lo! he comes, the Rev'rend *Bard*[8] appears, ⎫
Defil'd with Dust his awful silver Hairs,   ⎬
And his rough Garment, wet with falling Tears. ⎭
The King this mark'd, and conscious wou'd have fled,   40
The healing Balm which for his Wounds was shed:
Till the more wary Priest the Serpents Art,   ⎫
Join'd to the Dove-like Temper of his Heart,   ⎬
And thus retards the Prince just ready now to part. ⎭
Hear me, the Cause betwixt two Neighbours hear,
Thou, who for Justice dost the Sceptre bear:
Help the Opprest, nor let me weep alone
For him, that calls for Succour from the Throne.
Good Princes for Protection are Ador'd,
And Greater by the *Shield*, than by the *Sword*.   50
This clears the Doubt, and now no more he fears
The Cause his Own, and therefore stays and hears:
When thus the *Prophet:*—
———In a flow'ry Plain
A King-like Man does in full Plenty reign;
Casts round his Eyes, in vain, to reach the Bound,

5. Spouse or consort of a monarch.

6. Daughter of Saul, who set her bride-price for David at one hundred dead Philistines, hoping that David would be killed. David met the price, yet Saul gave her to Paltiel. David later demanded and got her as part of a treaty.

7. David was a renowned musician who played the lyre.

8. In addition to being a prophet, Nathan is also known as the writer of chronicles and developer of temple music. George A. Buttrick, ed., *Interpreter's Dictionary of the Bible*, 4 vols. (New York: Abingdon, 1962), s.v. "Nathan."

Which *Jordan*'s Flood[9] sets to his fertile Ground:
Countless his Flocks, whilst *Lebanon*[10] contains
A Herd as large, kept by his numerous Swains,

60 That fill with morning Bellowings the cool Air,
And to the Cedar's shade at scorching Noon repair.
Near to this Wood a lowly *Cottage* stands,
Built by the humble Owner's painful Hands;
Fenc'd by a Stubble-roof, from Rain and Heat,
Secur'd without, within all Plain and Neat.
A Field of small Extent surrounds the Place,
In which One single *Ewe* did sport and graze:
This his whole Stock, till in full time there came,
To bless his utmost Hopes, a snowy *Lamb;*

70 Which, lest the Season yet too Cold might prove,
And Northern Blasts annoy it from the Grove,
Or tow'ring Fowl on the weak Prey might sieze,
(For with his Store his *Fears* must too increase)
He brings it Home, and lays it by his Side,
At once his Wealth, his Pleasure and his Pride;
Still bars the Door, by Labour call'd away,
And, when returning at the Close of Day,
With One small Mess himself, and that sustains,
And half his Dish it shares, and half his slender Gains.

80 When to the Great Man's table now there comes
A *Lord* as great, follow'd by hungry Grooms:
For these must be provided sundry Meats,
The Best for Some, for Others coarser Cates.[11]
One Servant, diligent above the rest
To help his Master to contrive the Feast,
Extols the Lamb was nourished with such Care, ⎫
So fed, so lodg'd, it must be Princely Fare;   ⎬
And having this, my Lord his own may spare.   ⎭
In haste he sends, led by no Law, but Will,

90 Not to entreat, or purchase, but to Kill.
The Messenger's arriv'd: the harmless Spoil,
Unus'd to fly, runs Bleating to the Toil:
Whilst for the Innocent the Owner fear'd,

9. The Jordan is the longest and most important river in Palestine.
10. Mountain range in Syria.
11. Provisions.

And, sure wou'd move, cou'd Poverty be heard.
Oh spare (he cries) *the Product of my Cares,*
My Stock's Encrease, the Blessing on my Pray'rs;
My growing Hope, and Treasure of my Life!
More was he speaking, when the murd'ring Knife
Shew'd him, his Suit, tho' just, must be deny'd,
And the white Fleece in its own Scarlet dy'd;   100
Whilst the poor helpless Wretch stands weeping by,
And lifts his Hands for Justice to the Sky.

   Which he shall find, th' incensed *King* replies,
When for the proud Offence th' Oppressor dies.
O *Nathan*! by the *Holy* Name I swear,⎫
Our Land such Wrongs unpunished shall not bear⎬
If, with the Fault, th' Offender thou declare.⎭

   To whom the *Prophet,* closing with the Time,
Thou art the Man replies, and thine th' ill-natur'd Crime.
Nor think, against thy Place, or State, I err;   110
A Pow'r above thee does this Charge prefer;
Urg'd by whose *Spirit,* hither am I brought
T' expostulate his *Goodness,* and thy *Fault;*
To lead thee back to those forgotten Years,
In Labour spent, and lowly Rustick Cares,
When in the Wilderness thy Flocks but few,⎫
Thou didst the Shepherd's simple Art pursue⎬
Thro' crusting Frosts, and penetrating Dew:⎭
Till wondring *Jesse*[12] saw six Brothers past,
And Thou Elected, Thou the Least and Last;   120
A Sceptre to thy Rural Hand convey'd,
And in thy Bosom Royal Beauties laid;
A lovely Princess made thy Prize that Day,
When on the shaken Ground the *Giant* lay[13]
Stupid in Death, beyond the Reach of Cries
That bore thy shouted Fame to list'ning Skies,
And drove the flying Foe as fast away,
As Winds, of old, *Locusts* to *Egypt*'s Sea.[14]

---

12. Father of David.

13. David killed the giant Goliath, the Philistine, with a slingshot. 1 Sam. 17.

14. Reference to one of the plagues brought down on Egypt by Moses to free the Israelites from slavery.

Thy Heart with Love, thy Temples with Renown, ⎫
130   Th' All-giving Hand of Heav'n did largely crown, ⎬
Whilst yet thy Cheek was spread with youthful Down. ⎭
What more cou'd craving Man of God implore?
Or what for favour'd Man cou'd God do more?
Yet cou'd not these, nor *Israel*'s Throne, suffice
Intemp'rate Wishes, drawn thro' wand'ring Eyes.
One Beauty (not thy own) and seen by chance,
Melts down the Work of Grace with an alluring Glance;
Chafes the Spirit, fed by sacred Art,
And blots the Title AFTER GOD'S OWN HEART;[15]
140   Black Murder breeds to level at *his* Head,
Who boasts so fair a Part'ner of his Bed,
Nor longer must possess those envy'd Charms,
The single Treasure of his House, and Arms:
Giving, by this thy Fall, cause to Blaspheme
To all the Heathen the *Almighty* Name.
For which the *Sword* shall still thy Race pursue,
And, in revolted *Israel*'s scornful View,
Thy captiv'd Wives shall be in Triumph led
Unto a bold Usurper's shameful Bed;
150   Who from thy Bowels sprung shall seize thy Throne,
And scourge thee by a Sin beyond thy own.
Thou hast thy Fault in secret Darkness done;
But this the World shall see before the Noonday's Sun.

Enough! the King, enough! the *Saint* replies,
And pours his swift Repentance from his Eyes;
Falls on the Ground, and tears the Nuptial Vest,
By which his Crime's Completion was exprest:
Then with a Sigh blasting to Carnal Love,
Drawn deep as Hell, and piercing Heaven, above
160   Let *Me* (he cries) let *Me* attend his Rod,
For *I* have sinn'd, for *I* have lost my God.

Hold! (says the *Prophet*) of that Speech beware,
God ne'er was lost, unless by Man's Despair.
The Wound that is thus willingly reveal'd,
Th' Almighty is as willing should be heal'd.

15. Phrase used to describe what the prophet Samuel said was desired in a new leader for Israel: "the Lord hath sought him a man after his own heart." 1 Sam. 13:4. That man was David.

Thus wash'd in Tears, thy Soul as fair does show }
As the first Fleece, which on the Lamb does grow,
Or on the Mountain's top the lately fallen Snow.
Yet to the World that Justice may appear
Acting her Part impartial, and severe,   170
The *Offspring* of thy Sin shall soon resign
That Life,[16] for which thou must not once repine;
But with submissive Grief his Fate deplore,
And bless the Hand, that does inflict no more.

   Shall I then pay but Part, and owe the Whole?
My Body's Fruit, for my offending Soul?
Shall I no more endure (the King demands)
And 'scape thus lightly his offended Hands?
Oh! let him All resume, my Crown, my Fame;
Reduce me to the Nothing, whence I came;   180
Call back his Favours, faster than he gave;
And, if but Pardon'd, strip me to my Grave:

   Since (tho' he seems to *Lose*) He surely *Wins*,
Who gives but earthly Comforts for his Sins.

                  (1713)

Eugenio and Eliza
A Tale
Founded on Fact
Catherine Rebecca Manners

The rising Sun had ting'd the east with gold,
   And scarce a cloud obscur'd his azure reign——
(That Sun, whose fatal beams did first unfold
   The dreadful scene of Naseby's[17] sanguine plain;

---

16. The death of the child of David and Bathsheba is recounted in 2 Sam. 12:14–23. Their next child was Solomon.

17. Decisive battle of the English Civil War in which the Royalists, led by King Charles I (1600–1649) and Prince Rupert (1619–1682), were defeated by the Parliamentarians, under Oliver Cromwell and Sir Thomas Fairfax (1612–1671), on 14 June 1645.

Where Charles, misguided monarch, wise too late,
    Saw the last efforts of his party fail;
Saw Rupert's luckless triumph[18] urge his fate,
    And Cromwell's[19] rising destiny prevail)——

When young Eliza left her lonely shed,
10   And wander'd pensive amid heaps of slain,
Not by a base desire of plunder led,
    But hope to sooth some dying Warrior's pain.

Though mean her parents, and obscure her lot,
    Each nobler feeling to her heart was known;
And, though the humble inmate of a cot,[20]
    Her form and mind had grac'd the proudest throne.

But hopeless passion o'er each opening grace
    Had cast a tender, melancholy air;
Eliza lov'd a youth of noble race,
20   And from the first she languish'd in despair.

Twelve months had pass'd since o'er Eugenio's form
    With fond surprise her wondering eyes had stray'd;
But, while his charms her artless bosom warm,
    By him unnoted pass'd the blooming maid.

From that sad hour a stranger to repose,
    She shunn'd the wake, she shunn'd the festive green;
And still where'er Affliction calls she goes,
    A pale attendant at each mournful scene.

At every step with horror she recoil'd,
30   While her moist eyes the dreadful carnage view'd

---

18. Prince Rupert lost this battle by pursuing the enemy too far. *Manners.* [Prince Rupert, nephew of Charles I and son of Frederick V, Elector of the Palatine, was the most talented commander of the Royalist forces. He was a daring cavalry officer, and it was at the battle of Edgehill, not Naseby, where he pursued the enemy too far from the battlefield. After Naseby, Rupert counseled a treaty with Parliament; Charles withdrew his commission. *Eds.*]

19. Oliver Cromwell (1599–1658) rapidly rose to leadership of the parliamentary leaders who opposed the king, and his military genius led to his promotion to second in command to Fairfax. He became Lord Protector of England during the Interregnum.

20. Cottage.

Of hostile kindred upon kindred pil'd,
    And British fields with British blood imbu'd.

But as, advancing o'er the dismal field
    Where devastation sadden'd all around,
She view'd those lids in endless darkness seal'd,
    And heard of dying groans the plaintive sound——

A form of grace superior drew her eyes,
    Bending to view the Warrior's face she stood;
O fatal sight! her lov'd Eugenio lies
    On earth extended, and deform'd with blood.   40

Struck at the view, awhile in silent grief
    She stood, nor yet a sigh confess'd her pain;
Nor yet her bursting tears could bring relief,
    While her chill blood ran cold through ev'ry vein.

At length, adown her cheek and snowy breast
    The pearly tears in quick succession ran;
And with a voice by sorrow half supress'd,
    In broken accents, thus the fair began:

"O thou, whom lovely and belov'd in vain,
    Unpitying Fate has snatch'd in early bloom,   50
Is this the meed[21] thy patriot virtues gain?
    Dearer than life, is this thy hapless doom?

"When last I saw thee, o'er thy manly cheek
    Health's orient glow a mantling lustre cast;
Enamour'd Glory seem'd thy paths to seek,
    Fortune in thee her favourite child embrac'd.

"Now cold on earth thou liest——no weeping friend
    With pious tears receiv'd thy parting breath;
No kindred round thy bleeding corse[22] attend,
    With grief like mine to mourn thy early death.   60

21. Reward, recompense.
22. Corpse, dead body.

"Ah! what avail'd the virtues of thy youth,
  The mind that dar'd Rebellion's fury brave,
Thy constant loyalty, thy matchless truth?
  Those very virtues sunk thee to the grave."

Kneeling as thus she spoke, his hand she press'd,
  And view'd his form with ev'ry charm replete;
But what emotions fill'd her raptur'd breast
  When still she found his languid pulses beat!

70   Some neighbouring peasants led by chance that way,
  Touch'd by the sorrows of the weeping fair,
With pitying eyes the fainting youth survey,
  And to Eliza's well-known cottage bear.

There, with a Leech's[23] care, her hands applied
  Some lenient herbs to every rankling wound;
Herbs, by the test of long experience tried,
  Of sovereign virtue in each trial found.

While anxious Love its lavish care supplies,
  Eugenio's face resumes a fresher hue;
And on the maid he fix'd his opening eyes,
80   While tears of joy her polish'd cheeks bedew.

The dawn of gratitude and wonder join'd,
  With varying thoughts distract his labouring breast;
And, anxious to relieve his dubious mind,
  In faltering words he thus the fair address'd:

"O say, what friend, solicitous to save,
  Procur'd for me your hospitable care?
For, when at Naseby the last sigh I gave,
  Nor Friendship nor Humanity was there."

Blushing, the maid with down-cast looks replied,
90   "To Heaven alone thy gratitude is due:

23. Healer's.

That God, whose angels round the good preside,
    To thy relief my feeble succour drew.

"I found thee senseless 'mid a heap of slain;
    I bore thee here, and Heaven thy life has spar'd:
That life restor'd, I ask nor thanks nor gain;
    A virtuous action is its own reward."

With mute surprise th' attentive youth admir'd,
    'Mid scenes so rude, a form so passing fair;
But more he wonder'd, when, by Heaven inspir'd,
    Her words bespoke a guardian angel's care.   100

And every day new beauties caught his view,
    And every hour new virtues charm'd his mind,
Till admiration into passion grew,
    By pure esteem and gratitude refin'd.

In vain, to change the purpose of his heart,
    Ambition frown'd contemptuous on the maid,
Pride urg'd him from her humble cot to part,
    And martial ardor call'd him from the shade.

He saw his country, in subjection led,
    Pay servile homage to a zealot's nod,   110
Who sternly claim'd his captive Sovereign's head,[24]
    And thought by anarchy to serve his God.

He knew his single efforts would be vain,
    His Prince from factious thousands to support,
And scorn'd to mingle with the abject train
    Who, led by interest, swell'd a guilty Court.

Since Virtue's cause no more his arms could claim,
    And hope of conquest could no longer move,
Fix'd, he resolves to wed the beauteous dame,
    And consecrate his future life to love.   120

24. Charles I was beheaded on 30 January 1649 after being tried by a special high court of justice.

Fast by the cot a spreading linden grew,
   Whose boughs o'ershadow'd a fantastic seat,
Where the pale primrose and the violet blue
   Breath'd from the verdant[25] turf a mingled sweet.

There, with Eliza often by his side,
   Eugenio shunn'd the scorching heats of noon;
Amid night's stillness there he often hied,[26]
   And solitary watch'd the silver moon.

Perusing there the philosophic page,
130   Untir'd the livelong day he would remain,
Or for the Poet quit the graver Sage,
   And raptur'd glance through Fancy's airy reign.[27]

Beneath the branches of this silent shade,
   By hours of past tranquillity endear'd,
He vow'd his passion to the blushing maid,
   Whose timid love his loss each moment fear'd.

Untaught in the pernicious schools of Art,
   Which curb the genuine feelings as they rise,
She own'd the sentiments that fill'd a heart
140   Whose conscious purity contemn'd disguise.

The sacred rites perform'd, with festive state
   To his high dome Eugenio led the fair:
'Mid lofty woods arose the ancient seat,
   Whose solid grandeur time could not impair.

There unperceiv'd life's current flow'd away,
   Nor could old age their constant love destroy;
And often they deplor'd, yet bless'd that day,
   To others source of grief, to them of joy.

They liv'd to see the artful Cromwell die,
150   And from their transient power his offspring driven,

25. Rich green grass and vegetation.
26. Hurried.
27. Daydream; indulge in fancy, a creative faculty, usually treated as lighter and more whimsical and playful than imagination or as an assistant to it.

And then beheld th' imperial dignity
    Once more to the inglorious Stuarts given.[28]

Charles they survey'd, in luxury, and ease,
    And sensual pleasures, pass life's ill-spent day;[29]
And bigot James an injur'd nation raise,
    Then coward shun the battle's dread array.[30]

Next Nassau, crown'd by policy and arms,
    In early youth for matchless prudence known,
Unmov'd in dangers, fearless in alarms,
    With royal Mary[31] shar'd the British throne.   160

Last Anna's prosperous reign in age they view'd,[32]
    And Marlborough glorious from Germania's war——
Marlborough, for councils as for fight endued,
    Who with his own spread England's fame afar:[33]

Then, pleas'd their country's triumphs to behold,
    In youthful verdure while her laurels bloom,
Their aged lids in Death's soft sleep they fold,
    And not unwilling sink into the tomb.

                    (1793)

---

28. After Cromwell died, his son Richard became Lord Protector but was unable to govern effectively. Charles II was invited to return in 1660 and restored the Stuart monarchy.

29. The hedonism of Charles II's court and his many mistresses were common knowledge.

30. Charles II (1630–85) had no legitimate children, and his brother, a Catholic, became James II (1633–1701). James's religion and his autocratic ways made him unpopular, and he was driven into exile in France in 1688. Rather than fight for his throne, he rather ignominiously left England.

31. William and Mary had been invited to replace James, motivating his escape. Mary, considered by most of the English as a legitimate heir to the throne, was the daughter of James II. William of Orange was the son of King Charles I's oldest daughter and was known as Nassau from a family line. He was a fine administrator and a good military leader.

32. Queen Anne (1665–1714) reigned from 1702 to 1714 and saw the Union of England and Scotland and the increase of British power all over the world.

33. John Churchill, Duke of Marlborough (1650–1722), was one of the greatest generals in British history. Among the victories he won over the French in the War of the Spanish Succession were Blenheim and Rameilles. The stately home given him by Queen Anne is named Blenheim.

The Savage of Aveyron
Mary Robinson

'Twas in the mazes of a wood,
The lonely wood of AVEYRON,[34]
I heard a melancholy tone:—
   It seem'd to freeze my blood!
A torrent near was flowing fast,
And hollow was the midnight blast
As o'er the leafless woods it past,
   While terror-fraught I stood!
O! mazy woods of AVEYRON!
    O! wilds of dreary solitude!
    Amid thy thorny alleys rude[35]
I thought myself alone!
   I thought no living thing could be
   So weary of the world as me, —
While on my winding path the pale moon shone.

Sometimes the tone was loud and sad,
And sometimes dulcet, faint, and slow;
And then a tone of frantic woe:
   It almost made me mad.
The burthen was "Alone! alone!"
And then the heart did feebly groan; —
Then suddenly a cheerful tone
   Proclaim'd a spirit glad!
O! mazy woods of AVEYRON!
    O! wilds of dreary solitude!
    Amid your thorny alleys rude
I wish'd myself—a traveller alone.

   "Alone!" I heard the wild boy say, —
And swift he climb'd a blasted oak;

10

20

---

34. Mountainous region of south-central France. "The Savage of Aveyron" was found there in July 1799 and brought to Paris, where he was a spectacle and fascinated the public. Under the care of a physician at the French National Institution for the Deaf and Dumb, he learned quickly. Robinson could have read many accounts of him; see, for instance, "The Savage of Aveyron," *Britannic Magazine* 9 (1801): 109–11, originally published in 1800.

35. Wild, rugged.

And there, while morning's herald woke,   30
   He watch'd the opening day.
Yet dark and sunken was his eye,
Like a lorn[36] maniac's, wild and shy,
And scowling like a winter sky,
   Without one beaming ray!
Then, mazy woods of AVEYRON!
   Then, wilds of dreary solitude!
   Amid thy thorny alleys rude
I sigh'd to be—a traveller alone.

   "Alone, alone!" I heard him shriek,   40
'Twas like the shriek of dying man!
And then to mutter he began,—
   But, O! *he could not speak!*
I saw him point to Heav'n, and sigh,
The big drop trembl'd in his eye;
And slowly from the yellow sky,
   I saw the pale morn break.
I saw the woods of AVEYRON,
   Their wilds of dreary solitude:
   I mark'd their thorny alleys rude,   50
And wish'd to be—a traveler alone!

   His hair was long and black, and he
From infancy *alone* had been:
For since his fifth year he had seen,
   None mark'd his destiny!
No mortal ear had heard his groan,
For him no beam of Hope had shone:
While said he sigh'd—*"alone, alone!"*
   Beneath the blasted tree.
And then, O! woods of AVEYRON,   60
   O! wilds of dreary solitude,
   Amid your thorny alleys rude
I thought myself a traveller—alone.

36. Lost, doomed.

And now upon the blasted tree
He carv'd *three* notches, broad and long,
And all the while he sang a song—
   Of nature's melody!
And though of words he nothing knew,
And, though his dulcet tones were few,
70   Across the yielding bark he drew,
   Deep sighing, notches THREE.
O! mazy woods of AVEYRON,
   O! wilds of dreary solitude,
   Amid your thorny alleys rude
Upon this BLASTED OAK no sun beam shone!

   And now he pointed one, two, three;
Again he shriek'd with wild dismay;
And now he paced the thorny way,
   Quitting the blasted tree.
80   It was a dark December morn,
The dew was frozen on the thorn:
But to a wretch so sad, so lorn,
   All days alike would be!
Yet, mazy woods of AVEYRON,
   Yet, wilds of dreary solitude,
   Amid your frosty alleys rude
I wish'd to be—a traveller alone.

   He follow'd me along the wood
To a small grot[37] his hands had made,
90   Deep in a black rock's sullen shade,
   Beside a tumbling flood.
Upon the earth I saw him spread
Of wither'd leaves a narrow bed,
Yellow as gold, and streak'd with red,
   They look'd like streaks of blood!
Pull'd from the woods of AVEYRON,
   And scatter'd o'er the solitude
   By midnight whirlwinds strong and rude,
To pillow the scorch'd brain that throbb'd alone.

37. Cave.

Wild berries were his winter food,   100
With them his sallow lip was dy'd;
On chesnuts wild he fed beside,
    Steep'd in the foamy flood.
Chequer'd with scars his breast was seen,
Wounds streaming fresh with anguish keen,
And marks where other wounds had been
    Torn by the brambles rude.
Such was the boy of AVEYRON,
    The tenant of that solitude,
    Where still, by misery unsubdued,   110
He wander'd *nine long winters,* all alone.

    Before the step of his rude throne,
The *squirrel* sported, tame and gay;
The *dormouse* slept its life away,
    Nor heard his midnight groan.
About his form a garb he wore,
Ragged it was, and mark'd with gore,
And yet, where'er 'twas folded o'er,
    Full many a spangle shone!
Like little stars, O! AVEYRON,   120
    They gleam'd amid thy solitude;
    Or like, along thy alleys rude,
The summer dew-drops sparkling in the sun.

    It once had been a lady's vest,
White as the whitest mountain's snow,
Till ruffian hands had taught to flow
    The fountain of her breast!
Remembrance bade the WILD BOY trace
Her beauteous form, her angel face,
Her eye that beam'd with Heavenly grace,   130
    Her fainting voice that blest, —
When in the woods of AVEYRON,
    Deep in their deepest solitude,
    Three barb'rous ruffians shed her blood,
And mock'd, with cruel taunts, her dying groan.

    Remembrance trac'd the summer bright,
When all the trees were fresh and green,

When lost, the alleys long between,
   The lady past the night:
140   She past the night, bewilder'd wild,
She past it with her fearless child,
Who raised his little arms, and smil'd
   To see the morning light.
While in the woods of AVEYRON,
   Beneath the broad oak's canopy,
   She mark'd aghast the RUFFIANS THREE,
Waiting to seize the traveller alone!

   Beneath the broad oak's canopy
The lovely lady's bones were laid;
150   But since that hour no breeze has play'd
   About the blasted tree!
The leaves all wither'd ere the sun
His next day's rapid course had run,
And ere the summer day was done
   It winter seem'd to be:
And still, O! woods of AVEYRON,
   Amid thy dreary solitude
   The oak a sapless trunk has stood,
To mark the spot where MURDER foul was done!

160   From HER the WILD BOY learn'd "ALONE,"
She tried to say, *my babe will die!*
But angels caught her parting sigh,
   The BABE her *dying tone.*
And from that hour the BOY has been
Lord of the solitary scene,
Wand'ring the dreary shades between,
   Making his dismal moan!
Till, mazy woods of AVEYRON,
   Dark wilds of dreary solitude,
170   Amid your thorny alleys rude
I thought myself alone.
   And could a wretch more wretched be,
   More wild, or fancy-fraught than he,
Whose melancholy tale would pierce AN HEART
      OF STONE.

          (1801)

O Stately Stood the Baron's Ha'[38]

Carolina Oliphant Nairne

Air—"Widow, are ye waukin'"

O stately stood the Baron's ha',
    His lady fair as ony;[39]
Her gracefu' mien was like a queen,
    Her smile it dimpled bonnie.
The heir of a' the Baron's wealth,
    A manly bairn was he,
O, and aye he'd rin, and play his lane,[40]
    Aneath the greenwood tree, O.

But wae, wae[41] was the heavy maen,[42]
    Gaed[43] thro' that castle ha', O,   10
When gloamin' cam', ae simmer's e'en,[44]
    Young Ronald was awa', O,
They sought him east, they sought him west,
    Baith[45] north and south they sought him,—
And noble was the offered boon[46]
    To them that wad ha'e brought him.

The lady pined, her cheek grew wan,
    The wound was past a' curin',
The bowers whaur first she fostered him
    Were past her heart's endurin'.   20
Her lovin' lord, wi' tender care,
    Took her to wander far, O,
And the only thought e'er dried her e'e,
    Flew aboon the mornin' star, O.

38. Hall.
39. Any.
40. Alone: "his lane" is colloquial Scottish for "by himself," "by his lone self."
41. Woe.
42. Moan.
43. Went; literally *goed.*
44. When twilight came, one summer's evening.
45. Both.
46. Reward.

Her feckless[47] frame could little bide,
    Slow turned the tardy wheels, O,—
They saw a nut-brown bonny boy,
    Fast rinnin' at their heels, O.
"Stay, faither, mither, stay for me!
30   I'll never, never leave ye!
It wasna me that gaed awa,—
    'Twas the gipsies took me frae ye."

Now, tell wha may, their joy that day,
    Wha ne'er thought joy to meet, O,
Fresh roses budded on her cheek,
    And her smile it dimpled sweet, O.
Frae greenwood bowers and stately towers,
    Nae mair[48] they wandered far, O,
And their gratefu' lays,[49] o' love and praise,
40   Flew aboon[50] the mornin' star, O!

(1869)

Sources

Finch: *Miscellany Poems, on Several Occasions* (London, 1713), 73–83; Manners: *Poems by Lady Manners* (London, 1793), 25–33; Robinson: *Mary Robinson: Selected Poems*, ed. Judith Pascoe (Peterborough, ON: Broadview, 2000), 332–38; Nairne: *Life and Songs of the Baroness Nairne with a Memoir and Poems of Carolina Oliphant the Younger*, ed. Charles Rogers, 2nd ed. (London: Griffin, 1869), 192–93.

47. Feeble.
48. More.
49. Ballad; lyric or narrative poem meant to be sung.
50. Above.

⊰K⊱

Pastoral Poetry

The pastoral is a fictional, usually idealized representation of rural life; its name comes from the Latin word *pastor*, meaning "shepherd." Poems are commonly set in a golden age of peace, plenty, and contentment; characters are innocent, and the simple life is glorified. Its origins are traced to Theocritus's *Idylls* (third century BC) and Virgil's *Eclogues*. The major poetic types are the dialogue, or singing match; the monologue, usually a poem of praise or complaint regarding a lover; and the elegy, or lament for a dead person. The pastoral's popularity peaked between 1550 and 1750, a period when Edmund Spenser's *Shepheardes Calender*, John Milton's *Lycidas*, and Christopher Marlowe's *Passionate Shepherd to his Love*, with Sir Walter Raleigh's reply, appeared. It is more accurate to speak of a European literary culture than an English one in the early modern period, and pastoral dramas such as Torquato Tasso's *Aminta* and romances such as Honoré d'Urfé's *L'Astrée* and Sir Philip Sidney's *Arcadia* increased the admiration for the mode. William Shakespeare's pastoral plays are still beloved and among his most frequently performed today.

In the eighteenth century, vigorous critical attention and experimental adaptations of the form gave it new respect and interest. Alexander Pope captures a source of its prestige in his *Discourse on Pastoral Poetry* (1704): "The original of Poetry is ascribed to that age which succeeded the creation of the world: And as the keeping of flocks seems to have been the first employment of mankind, the most ancient sort of poetry was probably pastoral." He imagines the shepherds leading a "solitary and sedentary life" of singing, celebrating "their own felicity." "From hence a Poem was invented, and afterwards improv'd to a perfect image of that happy time."[1] The pastoral genre has survived, waxing and waning in popularity for more than two thousand years and attracting a rich attendant set of adaptations (such as town rather than rural eclogues like Lady Mary Wortley Montagu's and Ann Murry's in 1.F) and parodies (such as John Gay's *A Shepherd's Week* and, in this section, Mary Leapor's *Damon and Strephon: A Pastoral Complaint*). Traditional uses of the pastoral, such as Elizabeth Thomas's *A Pastoral Elegy, on Henry late Duke of Norfolk* (1.1), abound.

The pastoral, even when employed as an episode or motif rather than as an entire poem, became highly conventional, if not predictable, in subject matter and details. Ann Messenger begins an important book on Restoration and eighteenth-century women's pastoral poetry as follows: "Most canonical pastoral poetry of the Restoration and eighteenth century is dull stuff. Strephon moons about in flowery meadows bewailing Silvia's cold-heartedness.... Meanwhile, nightingales warble, rills purl...."[2] Indeed, subject matter and details such as names, language, and imagery became predictable. Notably, however, Messenger writes, "*canonical* poetry," and of course almost none of the poems in this anthology are canonical. As with other forms, women did strikingly original things with a very traditional poetic kind. And, in fact, adhering carefully to convention was not as detrimental in a time that saw poets and their poems in competitive relationships and valued "What oft was Thought, but ne'er so well *Exprest*."[3] The abundance of pastoral literature surrounding women poets to some extent complicates interpretation of their poems. For example, the names—Phillis, Chloe, Aminta, Daphne, Strephon, Damon, Silvander, and Corydon—come from Aesop's fables, from classical literature, and from all of English and European literature and the sister arts. Some writers use the names to amuse readers when they recognize them, as Rowe does in *A Pastoral;* some to give a quick insight into the nature of a character, as Hands does with Thirsis; while others seem to employ the names to invoke the general tradition.

One of the most frequently written pastoral poems in this period was the dialogue, and this section opens with two quite different uses of the form by Elizabeth Singer Rowe. *A Pastoral: Henry and Lucy,* like many poems by women, first appeared in a prose fiction, her *Letters Moral and Entertaining.* Although the poem is a dialogue between lovers, it does not represent contrasting perspectives but is a unified, original, didactic poem praising God. Both Dante and Chaucer had used the idealized pastoral world as a metaphor for the Garden of Eden, and Rowe has Lucy and Henry compare themselves to "the first Pair." In the second poem by Rowe, *A Pastoral,* Phillis and Aminta are secular young ladies engaged in the classic pastoral dialogue. The two have very different opinions, and Rowe's knowledge of the conventions and ability to manipulate them for the delight of her readers is evident in such small touches as the brief singing contest in the conclusion.

The dialogues by Jane Brereton, Mary Leapor, and Esther Lewis Clark are comic adaptations. Brereton follows Horace's Ode 9, Book 3, closely. She writes the same number of verses and retains the sparring and prevarications that lead to the somewhat insulting reconciliation. Genteel poet that she is, she calls her lover "rough" rather than Horace's more colorful "less stable than the tossing cork," but the avowal of love carefully imitates Horace's language.[4] Leapor exaggerates every speech; rather than finding the pastoral denigrated, readers read on to experience the next turn her ingenious mind will give frisking lambs, gentle winds, and unfading flowers. In *A Song,* Clark's shepherdess responds to Strephon, "But Chloris and Daphne, and Phillis beside, / By turns you've pretended to court for a bride." Sounding more like the clear-eyed heroines of Restoration drama than like the softly singing shepherdesses of pastorals, this Stella is a modern, smart young woman.

Jane West's *Pastoral I* is a monologue of the forlorn-lover type going back to classical times. She demonstrates that the tradition was far from exhausted, and the poem weaves the most ancient conventions with elements from the sentimental verse narratives popular in her own day. The singing contest likewise took on new life. A common subject for women's pastoral dialogues was a competition between heterosexual love and friendship, and Elizabeth Hands's *Love and Friendship* also demonstrates what well-read, imaginative poets continued to do with the form. Hands's poem is one of the best in the love-versus-friendship line and also shows the tastes of her time, as it is somewhat sentimentally resolved by the unusual appearance of a third speaker. The wealth of energetic, creative poems in this section and scattered throughout this anthology indicates the uses and appeal of pastoral and introduces a fresh subject for exploration.

Notes

1. Alexander Pope, *A Discourse on Pastoral Poetry,* in *The Poems of Alexander Pope,* ed. John Butt (1963; New Haven, CT: Yale University Press, 1969), 119. This essay is an excellent introduction to the opinion of the form and what Pope believed its beauties to be; see 119–23.

2. Ann Messenger, *Pastoral Tradition and the Female Talent: Studies in Augustan Poetry* (New York: AMS, 2001), 1.

3. Alexander Pope, *An Essay on Criticism* (London, 1711), line 298.

4. See the translation in *Horace: The Odes and Epodes,* trans. C. E. Bennett (London: Heinemann, 1914), 213.

A Pastoral
Henry and Lucy[1]
Elizabeth Singer Rowe

HENRY.
Lucy, while resting in this verdant Shade,
By pow'r divine thus elegantly made,
Say, can'st thou envy Pomp and regal Rooms,
Gay with the Luxury of *Persian* Looms;
Or painted Roofs, whose Beauty would entice
The Thoughts thro' all the fabled Joys of Vice?
Fabled indeed! true Joys it cannot boast,
Since Pleasure flies when Innocence is lost;
Remorse, Despair, and every cruel Guest,
10   Become the Inmates of the guilty Breast.

LUCY.
How spotless, *Henry,* is thy well-turn'd Mind,
Averse to Ill, to follow Good inclin'd:
With the conversing, ev'ry Day I learn
New Charms in sacred Virtue to discern;
And emulous[2] of thee, with Joy pursue
That Goodness I admire and love in you.

HENRY.
Thou need'st not learn of me in Nature's Book,[3]
Thou may'st on thy Creator's Wisdom look:
And as the Planets run their constant Race,
20   His glorious Footsteps in their Order trace;
He bids the Sun in all its Beauty rise,
To bless our Soil and guild the vaulted Skies;
And by the Word of his Almighty Pow'r,
Ordains the Moon to cheer the Midnight Hour;
While sparkling Stars in solemn Order wait
Upon her silent Course, to grace her State.

---

1. This pastoral dialogue appears in the final volume of *Letters Moral and Entertaining,* "written" and "sent" by Rosalinda to her friend Lady Sophia "without any apology, or giving myself the airs of being an author." Pt. 3, p. 137.

2. Desirous of rivaling or imitating.

3. People believed that God had given them two books for instruction, the Bible and the Book of Nature, the natural world God had created.

LUCY.

Nor in the Skies alone his Pow'r is seen,
We view it in the Grove and flow'ry Green,
To imitate whose Charms all Art is faint;
The Rose's glowing Blush what Hand can paint?   30
Or equal the pale Lilly's snowy Hue,
Or emulate the Corn-flow'rs glossy Blue?

HENRY.

Sure, *Lucy,* we like the first Pair[4] are blest,
While here secure with Innocence and Rest
Our Happy Hours on downy Pinions[5] fly;
When thus assisted by Faith's steadfast Eye,
Upon our Maker's Works we humbly gaze,
And for their Goodness render him the Praise.
Thus in the Patriarch's Days, the *Jewish* Swains[6]
Who fed their Flocks on *Mamre*'s[7] Fruitful Plains   40
Worship'd *Jehovah* in the Woods and Field,
And prais'd his Name for all the Fruit they yield;
Implor'd his Mercy to direct their Ways,
To guard their Nights, and sanctify their Days.
But see! the Ev'ning o'er the dewy Lawn
Already has her sable Curtain drawn,
Homeward we'll go, and as we slowly walk
Beguile the tedious Way with farther Talk.

(1733)

A Pastoral
Elizabeth Singer Rowe

In vain my muse would imitate the strains
Which charm'd the nymphs on *Windsor*'s[8] verdant plains;

---

4. Adam and Eve.
5. Wings.
6. Country men; lovers.
7. A site about two miles from what became Hebron, Mamre is historically important. Abraham erected an altar there and later pled for the sparing of Sodom and Gomorrah there. He purchased a cave as a tomb for his burial and that of his wife, Sarah, and the other patriarchs and their wives.
8. Site of Windsor Castle, the residence of English monarchs since William I; it is surrounded by beautiful parks.

Where *Pope,* with wond'rous art, in tuneful lays,
Won from *Apollo*'s[9] hand immortal bays.[10]

THE morning scarce appear'd, when *Phillis*[11] rose,
And call'd *Aminta*[12] from a short repose;
With cautious steps they left the peaceful bow'r,
Both, by appointment, chose the silent hour.
To tell, in rural strains, their mutual care,
10   And the soft secret of their breasts to share:
Securely seated near a purling stream,
By turns they sing, while love supplies the theme.

PHILLIS.
THE starry lights above are scarce expir'd,
And scarce the shades from open plains retir'd;
The tuneful lark has hardly stretch'd her wing,
And warbling linnets just begin to sing;
Nor yet industrious bees their hives forsake,
Nor skim the fish the surface of the lake.

AMINTA.
NOR yet the flow'rs disclose their various hue,
20   But fold their leaves, opprest with hoary dew;
Blue mists around conceal the neighb'ring hills,
And dusky fogs hang o'er the murm'ring rills;
While *Zephyr*[13] faintly sighs among the trees,
And moves the branches with a lazy breeze:
No jovial pipe resounds along the plains,
Safe in their hamlets sleep the drouzy swains.[14]

PHILLIS.
FOR me *Mirtillo*[15] sighs; the charming youth
Persuades with so much eloquence and truth,

9. God of music and poetry.
10. Alexander Pope's *Windsor Forest,* a topographical poem published in 1713, is here presented as earning Pope "immortal bays," the wreath of bay leaves traditionally presented to a hero or poet.
11. Conventional name for a rustic maiden, from a character in Virgil's third and fifth *Eclogues.*
12. The name is from Torquato Tasso's pastoral play *Aminta* (1573), which Rowe much admired.
13. The west wind, lover of Flora, goddess of flowers; any soft, warm wind.
14. Country men; lovers.
15. A character in George Frideric Handel's opera *Il Pastor Fido* (*The Faithful Shepherd,* 1712), which was very popular in 1734. The opera is set in Arcadia, where the Arcadians are oppressed by the goddess Diana, who can only be appeased by the marriage of "two of a heavenly race." The Arcadians

Whene'er he talks my flocks unheeded stray;
To hear him I could linger out the day,   30
Untir'd till night, 'till all the stars were gone,
Till o'er the eastern hills the morn came on.

AMINTA.

For me *Silvander*[16] pines, as full of truth,
In secret too, perhaps, I love the youth;
Yet treat him ill, while with dissembled pride
I mock his vows, his soft complaints deride;
And fly him swifter than a sportive fawn
Skips thro' the woods, and dances o'er the lawn.

PHILLIS.

Unpractis'd in the turns of female art,
My looks declare the meaning of my heart;   40
To own so just and innocent a flame,
Can fix no blemish on a virgin's name:
When first my lips the tender truth express'd,
A thousand joys *Mirtillo*'s eyes confess'd.

AMINTA.

No boasting swain such truths from me shall hear,
Such words shall never reach *Silvander*'s ear.
With *Thisbe*[17] once, his favour'd dog, I play'd,
Which from his master thro' the woods had stray'd;
Still on the path my watchful eyes I kept,
When from the thicket the pleas'd owner stept;   50
His smiling looks an inward joy confess'd
To find, by me, the darling dog caress'd:
Surpriz'd, from off my lap his dog I threw,
And swift as lightning thro' the forest flew.

---

believe that the shepherdess Amarilli and the huntsman Silvio are the two who can appease Diana. Amarilli, however, declares her love for Mirtillo and is condemned to death for breaking her vow to Silvio. Mirtillo demands to die in Amarilli's place, the two lovers are pardoned and allowed to marry, and peace is restored to Arcadia.

16. Eponymous hero of a romance by Gautier de Costes La Calprenède (1609?–1663); Katherine Philips's poem *To Sir Edward Deering* styles Deering as "Silvander," and the name was frequently used.

17. The dog is named after Thisbe, the woman who was to meet her lover Pyramus in Ovid's *Metamorphoses* but was frightened away by a lion. She fled, the lion smeared her veil with blood, and, sequentially and mistakenly, both lovers committed suicide.

PHILLIS.

Whene'er *Mirtillo*'s sportive kid I find,
With wreathing flow'rs his twisted horns I bind,
And fondly stroke him in his master's sight,⎫
Nor e'er abuse the harmless thing in spight,⎬
Or think the guiltless favour worth my flight.⎭

AMINTA.

60   The nymphs and swains *Apollo*'s[18] revels grac'd,
In sprightly dances the smooth green they trac'd;
Silvander begg'd I would his partner stand,
I turn'd, and gave to *Corilas* my hand.

PHILLIS.

I to *Mirtillo* did my hand refuse;
But after that no other swain would chuse:
At *Cynthia*'s revels[19] *Hylas*[20] strove in vain,
And *Lycidas*[21] the favour to obtain.

AMINTA.

A basket of the finest rushes wrought,⎫
With jess'min, pinks, and purple vi'lets fraught,⎬
70   With modest zeal, to me *Silvander* brought:⎭
His present I rejected with disdain,
And threw the fragrant treasures on the plain.
Soon as the youth retir'd, with wond'rous care
I search'd them round, nor would one blossom spare;
With some, in wreaths, my curling locks I grac'd,
And others nicely in my bosom plac'd.

PHILLIS.

Fresh sprigs of myrtle[22] oft my breast adorn,
And roses gather'd in a dewy morn:

---

18. God of music and poetry.

19. *Cynthia's Revels* is a pastoral play by Ben Jonson, performed in 1600. Its characters included Mercury, Echo, and Cupid.

20. In mythology, a youth detained by nymphs of the spring to which he went for water.

21. Name of the shepherd in Virgil's third *Eclogue* that Milton used to eulogize Edward King in his *Lycidas* (1638).

22. Myrtle was sacred to Aphrodite, goddess of love and beauty.

Of all the garden's flow'ry riches, these
Mirtillo loves, and I his fancy please.   80

AMINTA.

SILVANDER told a secret in my ear,
Which twice I made pretences not to hear;
He nearer drew, invited to the bliss,
And in the am'rous whisper stole a kiss.
My rising blushes the bold theft reveal'd,
Dorinda scarce from laughing out with-held:
I left the shepherd, feign'd myself enrag'd,
And with his rival in discourse engag'd.

PHILLIS.

IN yonder bow'r I sate, when tow'rds the place
Mirtillo hasten'd with a lover's pace;   90
I feign'd myself to careless sleep resign'd,
My head against a mossy bank reclin'd;
Approaching near, sweet may thy slumbers be,
He softly cry'd, and all thy dreams of me!
I laugh'd, nor longer could conceal the cheat,
But told the am'rous youth the fond deceit.

AMINTA.

WHEN in the echoing vale *Silvander* plays,
And on his reed performs the rural lays,
Behind the shading trees I oft' retire,
And undiscover'd, the sweet notes admire: 100
But when in public I his numbers heard,
To his unskilful *Egon*'s[23] I prefer'd;
Tho' with the swan's expiring melody,
The cuckow's tiresome note as well may vye.

PHILLIS

WHATE'ER *Mirtillo* dictates meets applause,
His voice attention still as midnight draws;
His voice more gentle than the summer's breeze,
That mildly whispers thro' the trembling trees;

---

23. The name of a shepherd in Virgil's third *Eclogue.*

Soft as the nightingale's complaining song,
110   Or murm'ring currents as they roll along;
Without disguise the skilful youth I praise,
Admire his numbers, and repeat his lays.

(1739)

The 9ᵗʰ Ode of the 3d Book of Horace: Imitated
Jane Brereton

HE.
While I alone possess'd your Love,
    And reign'd unrival'd in your Breast,
No Mortal greater Joy could prove,
    Nor *Jove*[24] himself could be more Blest.

SHE.
While to my Eyes alone you bow'd,
    And own'd me Queen of your Desires;
The Queen of Heav'n[25] was ne'er so proud,
    Tho' she with Love great *Jove* inspires.

HE.
To *Cloe*'s[26] pow'rful Voice and Wit,
10   My Heart is now a willing Slave;
For whom to die I would submit,
    If that her dearer Life could save.

SHE.
Young *Damon*[27] now's my only Care,
    Who meets my Flame with tend'rest Truth;
For whom a double Death I'd bear,
    If Fate would spare the lovely Youth.

24. Supreme Roman god, the great father god and protector of the state; also Jupiter, the Greek god Zeus.
25. Juno, wife of Jupiter and protectress of marriage and of women.
26. Generic name for a rustic maiden; the shepherdess in *Daphnis and Chloe,* a pastoral romance by Longus.
27. Conventional name for rustic swains; the goatherd in Virgil's *Eclogues* was named Damon.

HE.
What if my former Flame renews,
    And I renounce fair *Cloe*'s Charms;
Would you young *Damon* then refuse,
    And me receive in those dear Arms?   20

SHE.
Tho' thou so rough, so pettish art,
    Tho' he so gentle, gay and trim;
So firm thou'rt fix'd in this fond Heart,
    I'd die with thee, ere live with him.

(1744)

Damon and Strephon
A Pastoral Complaint

Mary Leapor

Damon.[28]
Say, why these Sighs that in thy Bosom rise?
Why from thy Cheek the wonted Crimson flies?
Why on the Ground are fix'd thy streaming Eyes?

Strephon.[29]
Still let this Bosom swell with aking Woe,
And from my Eyes the streaming Sorrows flow.
But Oh! the Cause--- (See Clouds are gath'ring round;
And Zephyrs[30] wait to catch the mournful Sound;
The sick'ning Trees all shed their blooming Store)
Why wouldst thou hear it?---- *Sylvius*[31] is no more.

Damon.
Is *Sylvius* dead? ---- then *Phillis*[32] rend thy Hair,   10
And blot those Features that were late so fair.

28. Conventional name for rustic swains; the goatherd in Virgil's *Eclogues* was named Damon.

29. Conventional name for a rustic lover from Philip Sidney's prose romance *Arcadia,* which opens with his lament for Urania.

30. West winds, lovers of Flora, goddess of flowers; any soft, warm winds.

31. Conventional pastoral name for a shepherd from the grandson of Aeneas, who was accidentally killed in the chase by his son Brutus.

32. Conventional pastoral name for a maiden.

Thou Sun, forbear to gild this fatal Day;
Nor you my Lambkins dare to think of Play.[33]

Strephon.
No more alas! --- no more the tuneful Swain
Shall with soft Numbers charm the list'ning Plain.
No more his Flute shall greet the dawning Spring;
Nor to his Hand rebound the trembling String.

Damon.
Ah cruel Death! wou'd none but *Sylvius* do?
No meaner Swain amongst the worthy few?
20   Why didst thou take (and leave the baser Tribe)
The Flow'r of Shepherds and the Muses Pride?

Strephon.
None knew like him the heav'nly Notes to swell,
And moral Tales in pleasing Numbers tell.
While *Sylvius* sung, none thought the Day too long;
But all repin'd at the too hasty Song.

Damon.
Ye solemn Winds that whistle through the Glade,
Or rudely bluster in the darker Shade,
Go bear our Sorrows to the distant Shore,
And tell them *Sylvius* chears our Plains no more.

Strephon.
30   Vain are our Sighs, our Tears as vainly flow,
And each sad Bosom swells with fruitless Woe!
As northern Blasts destroy the Autumn Store,
So *Sylvius* fell and shall return no more.

Damon.
Enough of Sorrow---- now your Garlands bring;
Crop all the Beauties of the early Spring;
Around his Tomb these willing Hands shall twine
The choicest Briers of sweet Eglantine.[34]

---

33. Perhaps a parody of lines in Henry Fielding's *Tragedy of Tragedies* (1731).

34. The sweetbrier, a species of rose with delicate pink flowers, small aromatic leaves, and long thorns; it was a popular garden plant.

Strephon.

On his cold Grave a Laurel[35] I bestow,
Which late did in my Father's Garden grow:
This Wreath *Amyntas*[36] ask'd to shade her Brow,   40
But to my *Sylvius* I resign it now.

Damon.

The pensive Swains shall strike their Bosoms there,
And soft-ey'd Virgins drop a gentle Tear:
May some good Angel guard the sacred Ground,
And Flow'rs unfading shed their Sweets around.

(1748)

A Song
Esther Lewis Clark

I.

   Thus Strephon[37] one day in a warbling grove,
To prudent young Stella[38] began to make love,
Of ev'ry fair nymph that trips o'er the gay green,
Sure thou art the fairest my eyes have e'er seen.

II.

   I swear by thy beauties, I love thee much more,
Than ever a swain lov'd a virgin before,
And prize thee far more than a kingdom or crown,
Then why dost thou dress that fair face in a frown.

III.

   Strephon, had you before ne'er courted a maid,
I might merit pity if I were betray'd;   10

35. In classical times, leaves from this tree were made into wreaths for poets and conquerors.

36. Character in Edmund Spenser's *Colin Clouts come home againe,* an allegorical pastoral about Queen Elizabeth I and her court.

37. Conventional name for rustic lover from Philip Sidney's prose romance *Arcadia,* which opens with his lament for Urania.

38. "Star" in Latin; here conventional name for virtuous, beautiful maiden, derived from Philip Sidney's chaste Stella loved by Astrophel in the sonnet sequence *Astrophel and Stella.*

But Chloris[39] and Daphne,[40] and Phillis[41] beside,
By turns you've pretended to court for a bride.

IV.

    One yielded, was ruin'd, and the others still pine
The loss of their hearts, and the falshood of thine;
Such love I disdain, and such lover's despise,
And scorn to accept of so worthless a prize.

V.

    Beware of, ye fair-ones, the dangerous pride
Of wounding a heart which before has been try'd;
Been try'd and found wanting in honour and truth,
Nor weep in old-age for the errors of youth.

VI.

    By vanity prompted attempt not to prove
The force of your charms in this field of false love,
The man who a passion unfeeling will feign,
Shou'd by ev'ry female be shun'd with disdain.

VII.

    The heart yet untry'd may prove faithful and just,
But false to the second, if false to the first;
Then warn'd by example be wise e'er too late,
She merits her ruin, who dares to tempt fate.

(1789)

Love and Friendship.
A Pastoral
Elizabeth Hands

Two nymphs to whom the pow'rs of verse belong,
Alike ambitious to excel in song,

---

39. Conventional name for a shepherdess.
    40. Conventional pastoral name from the daughter of a river god who escaped Apollo's amorous advances by being changed into a laurel tree.
    41. Conventional name for a rustic maiden, from a character in Virgil's third and fifth *Eclogues.*

With equal sweetness sang alternate strains,
And courteous echo told the list'ning plains;
That of her lover sung, this of her friend;
Ye rural nymphs and village swains[42] attend.

CELIA.[43]

  O Love, soft sov'reign, ruler of the heart!
Deep are thy wounds, and pleasing is the smart;
When Strephon[44] smiles the wint'ry fields look gay,
Cold hearts are warm'd, and hard ones melt away.   10

SYLVIA.[45]

Through ev'ry scene of temp'ral bliss is there
A greater blessing than a friend sincere?
'Tis Corydon[46] that bears that tender name,
And Sylvia's breast returns the gen'rous flame.

CELIA.

  When happy I survey my Strephon's charms,
His beauty holds me faster than his arms,
My heart is in a flood of pleasures toss'd,
I faint, I die, and am in raptures lost.

SYLVIA.

  And what are all these tumults of the heart,
But certain omens of a future smart?   20
In friendship we more solid comforts find,
It cheers the heart, nor leaves a sting behind.

CELIA.

  Surely no lark in spring was e'er so glad
To see the morn, as I to see my lad;

42. Country men; lovers.

43. In Renaissance literature, a name for a ladylove.

44. Conventional name for rustic lover from Philip Sidney's prose romance *Arcadia,* which opens with his lament for Urania.

45. Silvia, loved by Valentine in William Shakespeare's *Two Gentlemen of Verona,* is addressed in the song, "Who is Silvia?" There are other famous Silvias in literature, and the name was conventional by this time.

46. Conventional name for a shepherd from Theocritus's *Idylls* and Virgil's *Eclogues,* also used by Shakespeare and other English poets and playwrights.

At his approach all anxious griefs remove,
And ev'ry other joy gives place to love.

SYLVIA.

   O happy I! with such a friend to live!
Our joys united double pleasure give;
Our inmost thoughts with freedom we unfold,
30   And grief's no longer grief, when once 'tis told.

CELIA.

   All that is lovely in my swain I find,
But am to all his imperfections blind;
What have I said? I surely do him wrong,
No imperfections can to him belong.

SYLVIA.

   The faithful friend sees with impartial eyes,
Nor scorns reproof, but speaks without disguise;
Blind to all faults, the eager lover sues,
Friends see aright, and ev'ry fault excuse.

   Then Daphne[47] from beneath a hawthorn sprung,
40   Where she attentive sat to hear the song;
Her breast was conscious of the tender glow,
That faithful friends, in mutual friendship know;
Her tender heart, by love's impulses mov'd,
With ardour beat to sing the swain she lov'd;
With emulation fir'd, the conscious maid
Thus to the fair contending virgins said.

DAPHNE.

   Blest Celia, happy in a lover dear;
Blest Sylvia, happy in a friend sincere;
But surely I am doubly blest to find,
50   At once a friend sincere, and lover kind;
My Thirsis[48] is my friend, my friend I say
And who in love can bear a greater sway

47. Conventional pastoral name from the daughter of a river god who escaped Apollo's amorous advances by being changed into a laurel tree.
48. Companion to Amintas in Torquato Tasso's pastoral play *Aminta* (1573). Anne Finch and other women poets versified his part (see, for instance, Finch's *Some Pieces out of the First Act of the Aminta of Tasso*). Henry Purcell's *Thirsis and Daphne* (1691) had popularized the story of Thirsis. Andrew

Strephon must his superior power own,
Nor is he less sincere than Corydon.

(1789)

Pastoral I.
Celadon.
Jane West

Oh! Celadon,[49] did not the hours
    Appear to glide rapid away,
When with me 'mid fresh blossoming flowers
    You carold the beauties of May.
When spring, with its infantine[50] green,
    Lightly ting'd the tall elms of the grove;
Ah! Celadon, sweet was the scene,
    Its beauty was heighten'd by love.

Of all you then sang, not a strain
    But I still can distinctly repeat;   10
Ah! youth, but reproaches are vain,
    Can you say your behaviour is meet?
Is it just to abandon with scorn
    The heart you so hardly subdu'd,
And to leave the poor virgin forlorn,
    Whom late you so fervently woo'd?

When you gave me the eglantine wreath,[51]
    You embellished the gift with your praise;
You only design'd to deceive,
    Yet you spake to the heart in your lays.[52]   20
My beauty was then all your theme,
    In beauty I never took pride;

Marvell's *Dialogue between Thyrsis and Dorinda* (1659) and Milton's *Comus* (1634) also featured this "attendant Spirit." Probably also a reference to Carl Philip Emanuel Bach's *Phillis und Thirsis* (1765).

49. A faithful shepherd lover, from the devoted suitor of Astrée in Honoré D'Urfé's *L'Astrée*.

50. Infantile; new.

51. Wreath woven from the sweetbrier, a species of rose with delicate pink flowers, small aromatic leaves, and long thorns; it was a popular garden plant.

52. Ballad; lyric or narrative poem meant to be sung.

I thought it procur'd your esteem,
   I knew not its value beside.

You promis'd your passion should last
   Till by death's icy rigour represt,
Yet now all your ardour is past,
   And you live at that passion to jest.
Was the fetter that bound you too weak;
30   Oh! why is my Celadon strange?[53]
'Till sorrow had faded my cheek,
   I saw in the fountain no change.

Can you say my behaviour was light,
   Was it easy my favour to gain,
When I promis'd your love to requite,
   Could others attention obtain?
To a test all my words may be brought,
   Let my life by suspicion be try'd;
You, Celadon, knew every thought,
40   I had none that I studied to hide.

You sure must remember the day
   You wounded your hand with the hook;
Again how I fainted away
   When you rescu'd my lamb from the brook.
Oh! how my heart flutters; e'en yet
   I think of your danger with tears,
Yet Celadon strives to forget,
   At once, both my love and my fears.

Fond fool! do I utter my grief
50   To the man from whose falsehood it sprung;
Shall the nest plunder'd dove seek relief
   From the stripling that ravished her young?
Yet shepherds are free from deceit,
   Their manners are simple and plain;
From all kind compassion I meet,
   And all thy injustice disdain.

---

53. Cold, apparently estranged.

My mother has often times read,
   While I reel'd off my spindle[54] at night,
That lions and tygers have bled;
   All vanquish'd by shepherds in fight.   60
'Tis right for such deeds to exult,
   For virtue and courage they prove;
But, oh! it is base to insult
   The girl you have injur'd in love.

Your bride she is lovely, I fear,
   I've heard she is richer than me;
The lot of the poor is severe,
   Ev'n lovers from poverty flee.
Yet my father, I've often been told,
   Had once a large portion of sheep,   70
But the winter flood broke down his fold,
   And buried them all in the deep.

My mother, alas! she is dead;
   My sorrow she now cannot feel;
To earn her a morsel of bread
   I work'd very hard at my wheel.
She said, for my duty and love,
   A blessing I surely should know;
I trust I shall find it above,
   For grief is my portion below.   80

I have heard our good curate[55] oft tell
   Many things about Angels of light,
That in virtue and truth they excel;
   Such Celadon seem'd in my sight.
Oh! break thou too credulous heart,
   I am sick of thy passionate strife;
The victim of Celadon's art
   Is weary of him and of life.

54. A simple instrument for spinning by hand.

55. A clergyman employed to assist a rector or vicar; any ecclesiastic entrusted with the cure of souls, such as a parish priest.

Yet the curses of vengeance to frame
90   Is a sin that I dare not commit;
This heart, which still throbs at his name,
    Will never the outrage permit.
My wrongs, oh! they all are forgiven,
    And my last dying wish it shall be;
May he never be question'd by heaven,
    For vows he has broken to me.

Go fetch home thy new wedded fair,
    Thy joys I will never molest;
I have found out a cure for despair;
100   My heart shall be quickly at rest.
No more shall the night's peaceful air
    Be vex'd by my clamorous breath
I have found out a cure for despair,
    'Tis silence—the silence of death.

(1791)

Sources

Rowe: *Friendship in Death: in Twenty Letters from the Dead to the Living. To which are added, Letters Moral and Entertaining* (London, 1733), pt. 3, pp. 13–15; *The Miscellaneous Works in Prose and Verse of Mrs. Elizabeth Rowe*, 2 vols. (London, 1739), 1:107–11. Brereton: *Poems on Several Occasions* (London, 1744), 18–19. Leapor: *Poems upon Several Occasions* (London, 1748), 18–21. Clark: *Poems Moral and Entertaining* (Bath, 1789), 177–78. Hands: *The Death of Amnon: A Poem with an Appendix: Containing Pastorals, and other Poetical Pieces* (Coventry, 1789), 66–68. West: *Miscellaneous Poems, and a Tragedy* (York, 1791), 57–62.

The Verse Epistle

A respected, popular, and flexible form, the verse epistle is a poem addressed to a specific person, most often a friend, lover, or patron. In the Blackwell *Companion to Eighteenth-Century Poetry,* Bill Overton remarks that the form "has received less than its due of critical attention" because it is so difficult to define.[1] Yet as the poems in this section demonstrate, the verse epistle was a vibrant form with classical roots and great capacity for adaptation. Many can be identified with one of the two great classical sources, Horace's verse epistles and Ovid's *Heroides,* but many others cannot.

Ovid's *Heroides* is a set of fictional poetic letters from legendary women to husbands or lovers. In the first fifteen letters, tragic or sentimental letters from betrayed, neglected, deserted, and unhappy women (Dido, Medea, Ariadne) outnumber those from, for instance, women like Penelope, who worried about their husbands' well-being. Women throughout the century contested the lugubrious, mourning women of the *Heroides* and the many poems British men wrote in imitation of them. For example, Lady Mary Wortley Montagu's *Epistle from Mrs. Y—— to Her Husband* adapts the Ovidian complaint of the abandoned lover into a condemnation of the unjust legal system. Staging a letter from Mary Yonge to the libertine husband who divorced her, Montagu explores the double standard that governs cultural mores and anticipates the insults to which Mrs. Yonge will now be subject. She rewrites a number of Ovidian conventions, such as that of contrasting "rational" behavior with the understanding of the situation and especially of the feelings that lovers, who have "felt them most," will have.[2] The verse epistle, like many eighteenth-century forms, often begins specifically but drives toward wide application and significance. Montagu replaces the line of deserted, lovesick women in the *Heroides* with the image of a line of outraged, wronged women, including those bartered or tricked into marriage as well as the divorced.

Letters 16–21 of the *Heroides* are in pairs, and the fictional women answered the men. Both kinds of Ovidian epistles were popular, and the same subjects were replicated and new ones introduced. Judith Madan's *Abelard to Eloisa* can be read beside Aphra Behn's *Ovid to Julia. A Letter* and *Oenone to Paris,* Elizabeth

Singer Rowe's *Lord Guilford Dudley to Lady Jane Gray,* and Montagu's *Epistle from Arthur G[ra]y* (not included). Madan's *Abelard to Eloisa* is in dialogue with Alexander Pope's *Eloisa to Abelard.*[3] In contrast to Pope's, her poem draws more heavily on the biographical facts of the lovers' lives after they were separated and foregrounds the part the Monastery of the Paraclete played in their history. Like Montagu, Madan turns the *Heroides* on its head, in this case by creating a disconsolate, highly emotional man. Many of her lines echo and subtly comment on Pope's.

Even greater than Ovid's influence was that of Horace, the great writer of philosophical and moral verse epistles. He transformed the form, which dates at least to 146 BC, by employing plain, accessible language and style. He included personal details, and his address was often easy and familiar, yet he, like other poets, framed the epistles as springing from deep feelings about the most profound of all human questions and uncertainties—about reality and about the nature, soul, happiness, destiny, and end of individuals and humankind. Poems in this tradition by Ben Jonson, John Dryden, and Alexander Pope are well known, but contemporaneous poems by women are their equals. They range from sophisticated, philosophical meditations like Lady Mary Wortley Montagu's *Constantinople* to serious critiques of public morality like Anna Laetitia Barbauld's *Epistle to William Wilberforce* (2.F) to lighthearted, familiar letters with serious undertones like Ann Thomas's *To Laura, on the French Fleet Parading before Plymouth in August 1779* (2.E). As might be expected from her classical education, Elizabeth Carter's verse epistles, many included in this anthology, are largely Horatian. Montagu's *Constantinople* is a beautiful illustration of the structure and movement typical of the best Horatian verse epistles. By its conclusion, she has compared Britain and Turkey, swept through human history, and constructed a contrast between this expansive, reflective state of mind and that of knaves, coxcombs, the mob, and party zealots—all characteristic of the London of her time. As was conventional in such a serious poem, she writes in heroic couplets, the metrics traditionally used in serious poetry and tragedies, including Shakespeare's.

The final example in this section illustrates another original use poets made of the verse epistle. Anna Seward's *Verses, Inviting Stella to Tea on the Public Fast-Day, February, MDCCLXXXI* is notable because of the amount of acerbic political commentary it contains, some of which might be styled seditious and perhaps blasphemous. She chose iambic tetrameter, a very common device in verse epistles and appropriate for the tone of her observations. As it was for Montagu in *Epistle from Mrs. Y——,* the epistle form here is a pretext and a strategy, and it enabled daring commentary on current events. The first part of Seward's poem is an invitation to a repast, a common theme for verse epistles, and the second is in the voice of "a Patriot" who lectures her on tea. Gender is a strong, underlying theme, for tea is "chaste, fragrant, Indian weed" for the women, while for men it is a "drug," "Indian shrub," and compared to the laurel water that Captain John Donnellan, master of ceremonies at the Pantheon, used to murder Sir Theodosius Boughton, his brother-in-law. Comparison of this poem with Montagu's *Constantinople* shows the direction that the Horatian epistle had taken toward more informal, familiar language. As such, the verse epistle had become one of women's favorite forms, and this anthology includes many of them. Many are occasional, as are those addressed to friends on their birthdays. They may be warm and personal, as Jane Brereton's to her women friends are, or as pointed and acerbic as Mary Masters's *To a Gentleman who Questioned my being the Author* (3.D). This flexible form was used for numerous, familiar subjects in original ways. For instance, Mary Jones's *Epistle, from Fern-Hill* (1.C.), Mary Barber's *To a Lady, Who Invited the Author into the Country* (1.A.), and Charlotte Lennox's *To Mira. Inviting her to a Retreat in the Country* (2.B) have a satiric edge, sharp self-awareness, and are variants on the country-versus-city poems of the period.

Notes

1. Bill Overton, "The Verse Epistle," in *A Companion to Eighteenth-Century Poetry,* ed. Christine Gerrard (Oxford: Blackwell, 2006), 417. In the first seven volumes of his *Classical Arrangement of Fugitive Poetry* (1789), the prolific anthologizer John Bell included 180 verse epistles, which he divided into seven categories, including "Familiar and Humorous," "Descriptive and Narrative," and "Heroic and Amatory." Overton, "Verse Epistle," 419–21.

2. Alexander Pope includes this convention at the conclusion of his *Eloisa to Abelard.*

3. Pope may be the poet women invoke most frequently. See Donna Landry, *The Muses of Resistance: Labouring-Class Women's Poetry in Britain, 1739–1796* (Cambridge: Cambridge University Press, 1990); Valerie Rumbold, *Women's Place in Pope's World* (Cambridge: Cambridge University Press, 1989); Claudia N. Thomas, *Alexander Pope and His Eighteenth-Century Women Readers* (Carbondale: Southern Illinois University Press, 1994); and Donald Mell, ed., *Pope, Swift, and Women Writers* (Newark: University of Delaware Press, 1996).

Constantinople
To [William Feilding][1]
Lady Mary Wortley Montagu

Give me, Great God (said I) a Little Farm[2]
In Summer shady and in Winter warm,
Where a clear Spring gives birth to a cool brook
By nature sliding down a Mossy rock,
Not artfully in Leaden Pipes convey'd
Nor greatly falling in a forc'd Cascade,
Pure and unsulli'd winding through the Shade.
All-Bounteous Heaven has added to my Prayer
A softer Climat and a Purer air.

10   Our frozen Isle[3] now chiling winter binds,
Deform'd with rains and rough with blasting winds,
The wither'd woods grown white with hoary froast
By driving Storms their verdent Beauty's lost,
The trembling Birds their leafless coverts shun
And seek in Distant Climes a warmer Sun,
The water Nimphs their Silenc'd urns deplore,
Even Thames benum'd, a river now no more;
The barren meadows give no more delight,
By Glistening Snow made painfull to the Sight.

20   Here Summer reigns with one Eternal Smile,
And Double Harvests bless the happy Soil.
Fair, fertile, fields! to whom indulgent Heaven
Has every charm of every Season given,
No killing Cold deforms the beauteous year,
The Springing flowers no comeing winter fear,
But as the Parent rose decayes and dyes
The infant buds with brighter collours rise
And with fresh Sweets the Mother's-Scent Supplies.

---

1. This verse letter was written in the poet's garden kiosk (summer house) in Constantinople to her uncle William Feilding. Montagu: *Lady Mary Wortley Montagu: Essays and Poems and "Simplicity, A Comedy,"* ed. Robert Halsband and Isobel Grundy (Oxford: Clarendon, 1993), 206n. 1.

2. A paraphrase of the opening of Horace's *Satire* 2.6: "Hoc erat in votis: modus agri non ita magnus, / hortus ubi et tecto vicinus iugis aquae fons ..." (This is what I prayed for!—a piece of land not so very large, where there would be a garden, and near the house a spring of ever-flowing water ...). *Horace: Satires, Epistles and Ars Poetica,* trans. H. Rushton Fairclough (London: Heinemann, 1926), 210–11.

3. Great Britain.

Near them the Vi'let glows with odours blest
And blooms in more than Tyrian Purple[4] drest,   30
The rich Jonquills[5] their golden gleem display
And shine in glory emulating day.
These chearfull groves their Living Leaves retain,⎫
The streams still murmur undefil'd by rain,   ⎬
And rising green adorns the fruitfull plain.   ⎭
The warbling Kind uninterrupted Sing,
Warm'd with enjoyment of perpetual Spring.
    Here from my Window I at once survey
The crouded City, and Resounding Sea,
In Distant views see Asian Mountains rise   40
And lose their Snowy Summits in the Skies.
Above those Mountains high Olympus tow'rs
(The Parliamental seat of heavenly Pow'rs).[6]
New to the sight, my ravish'd Eyes admire
Each gilded Crescent and each antique Spire,
The Marble Mosques beneath whose ample Domes
Fierce Warlike Sultans sleep in peacefull Tombs.
Those lofty Structures, once the Christian boast,
Their Names, their Glorys, and their Beautys lost,
Those Altars bright with Gold, with Sculpture grac'd,   50
By Barbarous Zeal of Savage Foes defac'd:
Sophia[7] alone her Ancient Sound retains
Thô unbeleiving Vows her shrine prophanes.
Where Holy Saints have dy'd, in Sacred Cells
Where Monarchs pray'd, the Frantic Derviche[8] dwells.
How art thou falln, Imperial City, low!
Where are thy Hopes of Roman Glory now?

4. The color of the famous royal purple dye of Greece and Rome perfected in Tyre.

5. A species of narcissus; often called a daffodil.

6. The home of the ancient Greek gods where Zeus held his court; mountain range in northern Greece on the border between Macedonia and Thessaly.

7. Emperor Justinian I commissioned Hagia Sophia as a Christian cathedral in Istanbul in the sixth century. Its beautiful mosaics were covered up and partly destroyed when it was converted into a mosque in 1453, but it remains a monument to architectural inspiration. Early writers described its Christian and ornamental features at length, and this section of the poem suggests that Lady Mary had read or heard of them.

8. English attempt at the Persian word *dārvīsh,* for Islam ascetics in a Sufi order, each of which traces its origins to a mystic teacher and then to the Prophet, Muhammad. Their dhikr, or prayer, services sometimes involve heightened religious exaltation and whirling by the Mawlawiyah, the "masters." European tourists called these religious leaders "whirling dervishes."

Where are thy Palaces by Prelates rais'd;
Where preistly Pomp in Purple Lustre blaz'd?
60   Where Grecian Artists all their Skill display'd
Before the Happy Sciences decay'd,
So vast, that youthfull Kings might there reside,
So splendid, to content a Patriarch's pride,
Convents where Emperours profess'd of Old,
The Labour'd Pillars that their Triumphs told
(Vain Monuments of Men that once were great!)
Sunk undistinguish'd in one common Fate!
    One Little Spot the small Fenar[9] contains,
Of Greek Nobillity, the poor remains,
70   Where other Helens show like powerfull Charms
As once engag'd the Warring World in Arms,[10]
Those Names which Royal Auncestry can boast
In mean Mechanic arts obscurely lost,
Those Eyes a second Homer[11] might inspire,
Fix'd at the loom, destroy their useless Fire.
    Greiv'd at a view which strikes upon my Mind
The short-liv'd Vanity of Humankind,
In Gaudy Objects I indulge my Sight
And turn where Eastern Pomp gives Gay Delight.
80   See; the vast Train in Various Habits drest, ⎫
By the bright Scimetar[12] and sable vest,   ⎬
The Vizier[13] proud, distinguish'd o're the rest. ⎭
Six slaves in gay Attire his Bridle hold,
His Bridle rich with Gems, his stirrups Gold,
His snowy Steed adorn'd with Lavish Pride,   ⎫
Whole troops of Soldiers mounted by his Side,   ⎬
These toss the Plumy Crest, Arabian Coursers[14] guide. ⎭
With awfull Duty, all decline their Eyes,
No Bellowing Shouts of noisie crouds arise,
90   Silence, in solemn state the March attends

9. Greek section of Constantinople.

10. Allusion to Helen of Troy, in Greek mythology the daughter of Zeus and Leda and reputed to be the most beautiful woman in history. Paris, son of King Priam, was to choose the most beautiful woman in a contest among the goddesses Hera, Athena, and Aphrodite. Each offered him a bribe; he accepted Aphrodite's: to wed the most beautiful woman in the world. That was Helen, who was already married to Menelaus, king of Sparta. Paris took her to Troy, resulting in the Trojan War.

11. The *Iliad* and the *Odyssey* are attributed to this Greek poet.

12. Scimitar, a curved Oriental sword.

13. High officer in the Turkish empire.

14. Swift horses.

Till at the Dread Divan[15] the slow Procession ends.
  Yet not these prospects, all profusely Gay,
The gilded Navy that adorns the Sea,
The rising City in Confusion fair,
Magnificently form'd irregular,
Where Woods and Palaces at once surprise, ⎫
Gardens, on Gardens, Domes on Domes arise, ⎬
And endless Beauties tire the wandring Eyes, ⎭
So sooths my wishes or so charms my Mind
As this retreat, secure from Human kind,   100
No Knave's successfull craft does Spleen excite,
No Coxcomb's Tawdry Splendour shocks my Sight,
No Mob Alarm awakes my Female Fears,
No unrewarded Merit asks my Tears,
Nor Praise my Mind, nor Envy hurts my Ear,
Even Fame it selfe can hardly reach me here,
Impertinence with all her tattling train,
Fair sounding Flattery's delicious bane,
Censorious Folly, noisy Party rage,   ⎫
The thousand Tongues with which she must engage⎬   100
Who dare have Virtue in a vicious Age.   ⎭

(1717; 1720)

Epistle from Mrs. Y[onge] to Her Husband. 1724[16]
Lady Mary Wortley Montagu

Think not this Paper comes with vain pretence
To move your Pity, or to mourn th'offence.
Too well I know that hard Obdurate Heart;
No soft'ning mercy there will take my part,
Nor can a Woman's Arguments prevail,
When even your Patron's wise Example fails,[17]

15. Tribunal; public audience room.

16. Mary Yonge was married to Sir William Yonge, from whom she had an acrimonious divorce in 1724. Yonge, a libertine, and his wife separated, during which time she began a relationship with Colonel Thomas Norton. Yonge offered evidence of the adultery, presented a case for damages, and was granted a divorce in the consistory court of the bishop of London and by a special act of Parliament, which gave him permission to remarry.

17. Prime Minister Robert Walpole (1676–1745), William Yonge's "mentor," allegedly conducted adulterous relationships and tolerated them in his wife.

But this last privelege I still retain,
Th' Oppress'd and Injur'd allways may complain.
   Too, too severely Laws of Honour bind
10   The Weak Submissive Sex of Woman-kind.
If sighs have gain'd or force compell'd our Hand,
Deceiv'd by Art, or urg'd by stern Command,
What ever Motive binds the fatal Tye,
The Judging World expects our Constancy.
   Just Heaven! (for sure in Heaven does Justice reign
Thô Tricks below that sacred Name prophane)
To you appealing I submit my Cause
Nor fear a Judgment from Impartial Laws.
All Bargains[18] but conditional are made,
20   The Purchase void, the Creditor unpaid,
Defrauded Servants are from Service free,
A wounded Slave regains his Liberty.
For Wives ill us'd no remedy remains,
To daily Racks condemn'd, and to eternal Chains.
   From whence is this unjust Distinction grown?
Are we not form'd with Passions like your own?
Nature with equal Fire our Souls endu'd,
Our Minds as Haughty, and as warm our blood,
O'er the wide World your pleasures you persue,⎫
30   The Change is justify'd by something new;   ⎬
But we must sigh in Silence—and be true.   ⎭
Our Sexes Weakness you expose and blame
(Of every Prattling[19] Fop the common Theme),
Yet from this Weakness you suppose is due
Sublimer Virtu than your Cato[20] knew.
Had Heaven design'd us Tryals so severe,
It would have form'd our Tempers then to bear.
   And I have borne (o what have I not borne!)
The pang of Jealousie, th'Insults of Scorn.
40   Weary'd at length, I from your sight remove,
And place my Future Hopes, in Secret Love.
In the gay Bloom of glowing Youth retir'd,

18. Compact between two people.
19. Chatting in a foolish or inconsequential fashion.
20. Marcus Porcius Cato (95–46 BC), politician known for his virtue; opponent of Caesar. After Caesar's victory, Cato committed suicide.

I quit the Woman's Joy to be admir'd,
With that small Pension your hard Heart allows,
Renounce your Fortune, and release your Vows.
To Custom (thô unjust) so much is due,
I hide my Frailty, from the Public view.
My Conscience clear, yet sensible of Shame,
My Life I hazard, to preserve my Fame.
And I prefer this low inglorious State,   50
To vile dependance on the Thing I hate— }
—But you persue me to this last retreat. }
Dragg'd into Light, my tender Crime is shown
And every Circumstance of Fondness[21] known.
Beneath the Shelter of the Law you stand,
And urge my Ruin with a cruel Hand.
While to my Fault thus rigidly severe,
Tamely Submissive to the Man you fear.[22]

   This wretched Out-cast, this abandonn'd Wife,
Has yet this Joy to sweeten shameful Life,   60
By your mean[23] Conduct, infamously loose,
You are at once m'Accuser, and Excuse.
Let me be damn'd by the Censorious Prude
(Stupidly Dull, or Spiritually Lewd),
My hapless Case will surely Pity find
From every Just and reasonable Mind,
When to the final Sentence I submit,
The Lips condemn me, but their Souls acquit.

   No more my Husband, to your Pleasures go,
The Sweets of your recover'd Freedom know,   70
Go; Court the brittle Freindship of the Great,
Smile at his Board,[24] or at his Levée[25] wait
And when dismiss'd to Madam's Toilet[26] fly,
More than her Chambermaids, or Glasses, Lye,
Tell her how Young she looks, how heavenly fair,
Admire the Lillys, and the Roses, there,
Your high Ambition may be gratify'd,

21. In both senses: foolishness and affection.
22. Walpole.
23. Low rather than mean-spirited.
24. Table.
25. Morning reception of visitors by person of distinction.
26. Reception of visitors by a lady during the concluding stages of her getting dressed.

Some Cousin of her own be made your Bride,
And you the Father of a Glorious Race
80   Endow'd with Ch———l's strength and Low———r's face.[27]

(1724; 1972)

Abelard to Eloisa[28]
Judith Madan

In my dark Cell, low prostrate on the Ground,
Mourning my Crimes, thy Letter Entrance found;
Too soon my Soul the well known Name confest,
My beating Heart sprung fiercely in my Breast;
Thro' my whole Frame a guilty Transport glow'd,
And streaming Torrents from my Eyes fast flow'd.

O *Eloisa*! art thou still the same?
Dost thou still nourish this destructive Flame?
Have not the gentle Rules of Peace, and Heaven
10   From thy soft Soul this fatal Passion driven?
Alas! I thought you disengag'd, and free,
And can you still, still sigh, and weep for me?
What pow'rful Deity, what hallow'd Shrine,
Can save me from a Love, a Faith, like Thine?
Where shall I fly, when not this awful Cave,
Whose rugged Feet the surging Billows lave;
When not these gloomy Cloister's solemn Walls,
O'er whose rough Sides the languid Ivy crawls;

27. Charles Churchill (d. 1745), lieutenant colonel and MP for Castle Rising, alleged to have had an affair with Lady Walpole, and Anthony Lowther (d. 1741), MP for Westmoreland. A poem detailing Lowther's romantic intrigue with Sophia Howe states, "Nanty Lowther was a pretty man." Sir Charles Hanbury Williams, *Isabella; Or, the Morning*, in *The New Foundling Hospital for Wit*, 6 vols. (London, 1784), 3:43.

28. In the twelfth century, Pierre Abélard was an intellectually gifted and popular lecturer at the cathedral school of Notre Dame, Paris, when he became the tutor of the brilliant Héloïse, niece of the canon of the cathedral. They became lovers, and she became pregnant, whereupon she begged him not to sacrifice his career by marrying her. They were secretly married, which, when discovered, enraged her uncle. He forced Héloïse into a nunnery and emasculated Abélard at the altar of the cathedral. Abélard became a monk and an important theologian. He and Héloïse wrote passionate letters to each other and are buried in the same tomb. Alexander Pope's *Eloisa to Abelard* (1717) is one of his best-known poems.

When my dread Vows, in vain, their Force oppose,
Opposed Love, alas! how vain are Vows!   20
In fruitless Penance here I wear away
Each tedious Night, each sad revolving Day:
I fast, I pray; and with deceitful Art
Veil thy dear Image from my tortur'd Heart.
My tortur'd Heart conflicting Passions move,
I hope, despair, repent, but still I love.
A thousand jarring Thoughts my Bosom tear,
For Thou, not God, My *Eloisè* art there.
To the false World's deluding Pleasures dead,
No longer by its wand'ring Fires misled;   30
In learn'd Disputes, harsh Precepts I infuse,[29]
And give that Counsel, I want Pow'r to use.
The rigid Maxims of the Grave, and Wise,
Have quench'd each milder Sparkle in my Eyes;
Each lovely Feature of this well-known Face,
By Grief revers'd, assumes a sterner Grace:
O *Eloisa*! would the Fates once more
(Indulgent to thy Wish) this Form restore,
How wouldst thou from these Arms with Horror start,
To miss those Charms, familiar, to thy Heart!   40
Nought could thy quick, thy piercing Judgment see,
To speak thy *Abelard,* but Love of thee:
Lean Abstinence, pale Grief, and haggard Care,
The dire Attendants of forlorn Despair;
Have *Abelard* the gay, the young, remov'd,
And in the Hermit, sunk the Man you lov'd.

　　Wrapt in the Gloom these holy Mansions shed,
The thorny Paths of Penitence I tread;
Lost to the World, from all its Interest free,
And torn from all my Soul held dear in thee;   50
Ambition, with its Train of Frailties, gone,
All Loves, all Forms forgot, but thine alone.

　　Amidst the Blaze of Day, and Dusk of Night,
My *Eloisa* rises to my Sight;

29. Part of the theological controversy over rationalism, Abélard was attacked as a heretic by Saint Bernard.

Veil'd, as in *Paraclete*'s Sea-bath'd Tow'rs,[30]
The wretched Mourner counts the lagging Hours;
I hear her Sigh, see the swift-falling Tears,
Weep all her Griefs, and pine with all her Cares.
O Vows! O Convents! your stern Force impart,
60   And frown the melting Phantom from my Heart;
Let other Sighs a worthier Sorrow show,
Let other Tears, for Sin, repentant flow;
Low to the Earth, my guilty Eyes I roll,
And humble to the Dust my contrite Soul.
Forgiving Pow'r! your gracious Call I meet,
Who first impower'd this rebel Heart to beat;
Who thro' this trembling, this offending Frame,
For nobler Ends diffus'd Life's active Flame:
O change the Temper of this throbbing Breast,
70   And form a-new each beating Pulse to rest!
Let springing Grace, fair Faith and Hope remove,
The fatal Traces of voluptuous Love;
Voluptuous Love from his soft Mansion tear,
And leave no Tracks of *Eloisa* there.

Are these the Wishes of thy inmost Soul?
Would I its softest tend'rest Peace countroul?
Would I, thus touch'd, this gloomy Heart resign
To the cold Substance of the Marble Shrine?[31]
Transform'd like these pale Saints that round me move,
80   O bless'd Insensibles! that knew not Love!
Ah! rather let me keep this hapless Flame,
Adieu, false Honour, unavailing Fame!
Not your harsh Rules, but tender Love, supplies
The Streams that gush from my despairing Eyes:
I feel the Traytor melt around my Heart,
And thro' my Veins with treach'rous Influence dart!

Inspire me Heav'n! assist me, Grace divine!
Aid me ye Saints! unknown, to Crimes like mine!
You, while on Earth, all Pangs severe could prove,

---

30. Héloise and Abélard would be buried at the Monastery of the Paraclete, which Abélard had established and then given to Héloise, who was appointed an abbess there. Paraclete is the title of the Holy Spirit in the New Testament and is often translated as "Comforter" or "Advocate."
31. Tomb.

All but the tort'ring Pangs of hopeless Love.   90
An holier Rage in your pure Bosoms dwelt,
Nor can you pity what you never felt:[32]
A sympathizing Grief alone can cure,
The Hand that heals, must feel, what I endure.
Thou *Eloisè*! alone, canst give me Ease,
And bid my strugling Soul subside in Peace;
Restore me to my long lost Heav'n of Rest,
And take thy self from my reluctant Breast:
If Crimes, like mine, could an Allay[33] receive,
That bless'd Allay, thy wond'rous Charms must give.   100
Thy Form, which first my Heart to Love inclin'd,
Still wanders in my lost, my guilty Mind:
I saw thee as the new-blown Blossoms fair,
Sprightly as Light, and soft as Summer-Air;
Wit, Youth, and Beauty, in each Feature shone,
Bless'd by my Fate, I gaz'd, and was undone!
There dy'd the gen'rous Fire, whose vig'rous Flame,
Enlarg'd my Soul, and urg'd me on to Fame;
Nor Fame, nor Wealth, my soften'd Heart could move,
My Heart, insensible to all but Love!   110
Snatch'd from myself, my Learning tasteless grew,
And vain, Philosophy, oppos'd to you.

    A Train of Woes we mourn; nor should we mourn,
The Hours that cannot, ought not, to return;
As once to Love, I sway'd thy yielding Mind,
Too fond, alas! too fatally inclin'd!
To Virtue now let me thy Breast inspire,
And fan, with Zeal divine, the holy Fire;
Teach you to injur'd Heav'n, all chang'd to turn,
And bid thy Soul with sacred Raptures burn.   120
O that my own Example could impart
This noble Warmth to thy soft trembling Heart!
That mine, with pious undissembled Care,
Might aid the latent Virtue strugling there!
Alas, I rave! nor Grace, nor Zeal divine,
Burns in a Breast o'erwhelm'd with Crimes like mine:

32. Reworking of line 366 of Pope's poem: "He best can paint 'em, who shall feel 'em most."
33. Abatement, mitigation, softening.

Too sure I find (whilst I the Fortune prove
Of feeble Piety, conflicting Love)
On black Despair, my forc'd Devotion built.
130   Absence, to me, has greater Pangs than Guilt.

Ah! yet, my *Eloisè,* thy Charms I view,
Yet my Sighs break, and my Tears flow for you;
Each weak Resistance stronger knits my Chain,
I sigh, weep, love, despair, repent in vain!
Haste *Eloisa,* haste, thy Lover free,
Amidst thy warmer Pray'rs, O think of me!
Wing with Thy rising Zeal my grov'ling Mind,
And let me Mine, from thy Repentance find:
Ah! labour, strive, thy Love, thy self controul,
140   The Change will sure affect my kindred Soul:
In blest Concert our purer Sighs shall grieve,
And, Heav'n assisting, shall our Crimes forgive.
But if unhappy, wretched, lost in vain,
Faintly th' unequal Combat you sustain:
If not to Heaven you feel your Bosom rise,
Nor Tears, refin'd, fall contrite from your Eyes:
If still thy Heart thy wonted Passions move,
And thy Tongue prompts thy tender Soul to Love;
Deaf to the weak Essays[34] of living Breath,
150   Attend the stronger Eloquence of Death.

When that kind Pow'r this captive Soul shall free,
(Which, only then, can cease to doat on thee)
When gently sunk to my eternal Sleep,
The *Paraclete* my peaceful Urn shall keep;
Then *Eloisa,* then, thy Lover view,
See, these quench'd Eyes, no longer fix'd on you,
From their dead Orbs that tender Uttrance flown,
Which first on Yours my Heart's soft Tales made known.
This Breath no more; at length, to Ease consign'd,
160   Pant, like light Aspines quiv'ring with the Wind;[35]
See, all my wild tumultuous Passions o'er,

34. Attempts.
35. Aspen trees have light leaves that quiver in the slightest breeze and make a soft sound as they touch.

And thou, amazing Scene! belov'd no more:
Behold the destin'd End of human Love,
But let the Sight thy Zeal alone improve;
Let not thy conscious Soul, with Sorrow mov'd,
Recal how much, how tenderly you lov'd!
With pious Care thy fruitless Grief restrain,
Nor let a Tear thy sacred Veil prophane;
Nor e'en a Sigh on my cold Urn bestow,
But let thy Breath with sacred Rapture glow;   170
Let Love divine, frail mortal Love, dethrone,
And to thy Mind immortal Joys make known;
Let Heav'n, relenting, strike thy ravish'd View,
And still the bright, the blest Pursuit, renew:
So, with thy Crimes, shall thy Misfortunes cease,
And thy wreck'd Soul be calmly hush'd to Peace.

(1728)

Verses, Inviting Stella to Tea on the Public Fast-Day, February, MDCCLXXXI

Anna Seward

Dear Stella, 'midst the pious sorrow
Our Monarch bids us feel to-morrow;
The ah's! and oh's! supremely trist,[36]
The abstinence from beef and whist,[37]
Wisely ordain'd to please the Lord,
And force him whet our edgeless sword;
Till, skipping o'er th' Atlantic Rill,[38]
We cut Provincial throats at will:
'Midst all the penitence we feel
For merry sins—'midst all the zeal   10
For vengeance on the saucy Foe,
Who lays our boasted Legions low,
I wish, when sullen evening comes,

36. Sad, sorrowful.

37. A popular card game ordinarily played by four people. Card-playing, a favorite form of recreation, was somewhat morally controversial and frowned upon on holy days and fast days, when people were supposed to focus on their faith.

38. A rill is actually a small stream.

To gild for me its falling glooms,
You would, without cold pause, agree
Beneath these walls to sip your tea.
From the chaste, fragrant, Indian weed,
Our sins no pampering juices feed:
And tho' the Hours, with contrite faces,
20   May banish the ungodly Aces,[39]
And take of food a sparing bit,
They'll gluttonize on Stella's WIT.

"*Tea*," cries a Patriot, "on *that* day!
'Twere good you flung the drug away!
Rememb'ring 'twas the cruel source
Of sad distrust, and long divorce,
'Twixt Nations which, combin'd, had hurl'd
Their conquering jav'lin round the world.

"O Indian shrub! thy fragrant flowers
30   To England's weal[40] had deadly powers,
When Tyranny, with impious hand,
To venom turn'd its essence bland;
To venom subtle, fierce, and fell,
As drench'd the dart of Isdabel.[41]

"Have we forgot that curs'd libation,
That cost the lives of half the nation?
When Boston, with indignant thought,
Saw poison in the perfum'd draught,
And caus'd her troubled Bay to be,
40   But one vast bowl of bitter tea:[42]

39. Card playing.

40. A sense of material wealth; used more generally to convey a sense of well-being, happiness, or prosperity.

41. Joseph Warton (c. 1722–1800) mentions "Izdabel" in his poem *The Dying Indian:* "The dart of Izdabel prevails! 'twas dipt / In double poison." *A Collection of Poems in Four Volumes. By Several Hands,* ed. Robert Dodsley, 4 vols. (London, 1755), 4:209. The poem details the last moments of the life of an American Indian, during which he laments the Spanish corruption of his culture.

42. Alluding to the ships' cargoes of tea which the Colonists, on finding it taxed, threw into the Bay of Boston; upon which hostilities between them and the Mother Country commenced. *Seward.* [The Boston Tea Party, 16 December 1773, an incident in which 342 chests of tea belonging to the British East India Company were thrown from ships into Boston Harbor by American patriots disguised as Mohawk Indians. The colonists were protesting both a tax on tea (taxation without representation) and the perceived monopoly of the East India Company. *Eds.*]

While Até,[43] chiefly-bidden guest,
Come sternly to the fatal feast,
And mingled with th' envenom'd flood,
Brothers', Parents', Children's blood:
Dire as the Banquet Atreus serv'd,
When his own Sons Thyestes carv'd,
And Phœbus, shrinking from the sight,[44]
Drew o'er his orb the pall of night.

"To-morrow then, at least, refrain,
Nor quaff thy gasping Country's Bane!   50
For, O! reflect, poetic Daughter,
'Twas vanquish'd Britain's Laurel-water."[45]

(1781; 1791)

Sources

Montagu: *Lady Mary Wortley Montagu: Essays and Poems and "Simplicity, A Comedy,"* ed. Robert Halsband and Isobel Grundy (Oxford: Clarendon, 1993), 206–10; Isobel Grundy, "Ovid and Eighteenth-Century Divorce: An Unpublished Poem by Lady Mary Wortley Montagu," *Review of English Studies,* n.s., 23 (1972): 424–26. Madan: William Pattison, *The Poetical Works of Mr. William Pattison* (London, 1728), 67–77. Seward: *Gentleman's Magazine* 61 (December 1791): 1140.

43. Infatuation, mad impulse; personified by the Greeks as the goddess of mischief and authoress of rash destructive deeds.

44. When Atreus's wife, Aerope, had an affair with his brother Thyestes, Atreus feigned forgiveness and held a banquet of reconciliation in Thyestes' honor. Before the banquet, he killed Thyestes' sons, cut them up, and cooked everything except their hands and feet. He served this meat to Thyestes, taunted him with the hands and feet, and then banished him.

45. Alluding to the then recent murder of Sir Theodosius Boughton, by laurel-water. *Seward.* [Boughton was poisoned by his brother-in-law, John Donnellan, master of ceremonies at the Pantheon on Oxford Street in London, in 1780. *Eds.*]

PART TWO

Poetry as Life Writing

Introduction

The recovery of women's writing and of information about women's lives remains an important, ongoing endeavor of feminist literary critics and historians. Margaret Ezell wrote, "How excellent it would be if one discovered some new source to provide access to the literary culture of early modern Britain ... one ... without the intervening layers of commentary from generations of editors and scholars explaining its lack of significance."[1] Poetry by almost all eighteenth-century women fits this description. This anthology is to a considerable extent a work of recuperation, and grouping a large number of poems under the rubric "life writing" is a recognition of the evidence they offer about women's poetic practices, their lives and feelings, and the times in which they lived. Considering poetry as life writing concentrates attention on poetry writing as process and practice, a contextualizing, horizontal look at writing that shifts emphasis away from canon, a vertical construct. Significantly, thinking about these women's texts as both poetry and life writing demands attention to the inseparability of form, content, and contexts. The poems in part 2 represent only a small percentage of what women's poetry could add to the archive, and we have sought out poems about public and private experiences and included poems that underscore the diversity of the times and the women.

Part 1, "Poetic Kinds and Genres," provides a foundation for recognition of women's serious commitment to the highest standards of artistry, of their technical experiments, and of many women poets' deep knowledge of poetic traditions and the inherited and invented genres available to them. Because part 2 emphasizes poetry writing as practice and process, it leads naturally into part 3, "Writing on Writing." The differences among women in terms of time period, class, locale, personality, gender, education, and experiences become increasingly clear here in part 2. Although most women never forget that they share a collective

1. Margaret J. M. Ezell, "The Posthumous Publication of Women's Manuscripts and the History of Authorship," in *Women's Writing and the Circulation of Ideas: Manuscript Publication in England, 1550–1800*, ed. George L. Justice and Nathan Tinker (Cambridge: Cambridge University Press, 2002), 121.

identity with other women, their individuality is especially developed in part 3, in which their poems about writing and reception are brought together.

Life writing is a comfortable, somewhat baggy term that describes all kinds of biographical and autobiographical discourses. Nancy K. Miller, who recently labeled "autobiography studies" "a new and rapidly expanding field," observes that the rubric of life writing "remains open to new departures as critics and scholars respond to the proliferation of self-narration and self-portraiture in both popular and high culture modes."[2] *Life writing* was a popular term in the seventeenth and eighteenth centuries and referred to all kinds of autologous texts, some *belles lettres,* such as travel narratives, and others unstructured and highly experimental, such as Charlotte Charke's *Narrative of the Life of Mrs. Charlotte Charke.*[3] In the last twenty years, theorists have often described life writing as documents of many kinds written out of a life or lives. It may cover a considerable part of a person's life or coherent segments of it, or it may be about ways of living and material culture. In fact, *life writing* creates a category protected from the inherited genre demands of *autobiography* and *biography,* and it is especially useful for feminists because the boundaries are permeable and may include *both* autobiography and biography. We may learn as much about a subject's life as about the writer's, as much about women in a particular situation or locale as about an individual.

Now a major source of social history, women's life writing has come to be recognized as rich in information about everyday practices and domestic detail *and* deeply engaged with national events and social issues. The mother of the Muses is the Titan Mnemosyne (Memory), and at the heart of both poetry and life writing are memory and imagination. "Both consist in thinking of things in their absence," observes Mary Warnock, speaking of life writing. Like most biographers and autobiographers, she realizes that they "overlap and cannot be wholly distinguished."[4] In many poems, as in life writing, memory and imagination are often both means and content, trope and substance. The two genres complement each other in myriad ways. Life writing is, of course, a space for processes of the self, such as identity formation and recognition of subject positions, and it is increasingly recognized as giving excellent access to the ideologies

2. Nancy K. Miller, "The Entangled Self: Genre Bondage in the Age of the Memoir," *PMLA* 122 (2007): 545. Thomas Mayer and Daniel Woolf agree that the term *life writing* allows consideration of "a much broader range of forms than even an elastic meaning of *biography* can easily stretch around," *The Rhetorics of Life-Writing* (Ann Arbor: University of Michigan Press, 1995), 26n1. Carolyn Barros and Johanna Smith note that the term "draws in and validates variant forms of first-person narratives," *Life-Writings by British Women* (Boston: Northeastern University Press, 2000), 21.

3. Discomfort with autobiography and distrust of their authors was prevalent in the Restoration and for much of the eighteenth century. See J. Paul Hunter, *Before Novels* (New York: Norton, 1990), 313–23; and esp. Hunter's "The Insistant 'I,'" *Novel* 13 (1979): 19–37. On the late emergence of the term *autobiography,* see Felicity Nussbaum, *The Autobiographical Subject* (Baltimore: Johns Hopkins University Press, 1989), xi–xii, which documents the proliferation of narratives of "self" in the same time period.

4. Mary Warnock, *Memory* (London: Faber and Faber, 1987), 12.

that surround individuals, who at various times and in various ways conform to, compromise with, or resist them.

That much poetry conforms to this conception of life writing is clear. Poetry has always been considered to be more personally revelatory than fiction or drama and to be the genre in which the artist comes to know her- or himself and, sometimes, to reveal the soul. In the poems, women reflect on their situations as individuals and as women, challenge or resign themselves, and, in dozens of modes from fantasy to satire, imagine alternatives to "the way things are." Poetry offers a place where we can see social, ideological, and genre forces constructing a woman and revealing various group identities and also, because of the very nature of poetry, a place revealing the writer's individuality, autonomy, and agency. Feminists and postcolonial critics have demonstrated repeatedly that women and minorities share, and recognize that they share, a culturally imposed collective identity. As Susan Stanford Friedman says, "Not recognizing themselves in the reflections of cultural representation, women develop a dual consciousness—the self as culturally defined and the self as different from cultural prescription."[5] Theorists note that oppressed or dominated peoples "often particularize a dialectic between these two generalized subject-positions, between the subject as acted upon and produced by social discourse and the subject as acting to change social discourse and, therefore, its own subject position."[6] Poems by some writers, such as Sarah Fyge Egerton and Mary Jones, are obvious examples. A fascinating aspect of the poems in part 2 is the various positions women take in relation to the ideologies and technologies of gender alive in their culture. These poems engage a wide spectrum, as do Anna Seward's *Verses, Inviting Stella to Tea* (1.L), Sarah Fyge Egerton's *The Emulation* (2.J), Hannah More's *Bishop Bonner's Ghost* (2.D), and many of the poems in sections 2.M, "Poems on the New Year, Birthdays, and Aging," and 1.F, "Satire."

Treating imaginative literature of any kind as life writing is fraught with difficulties, and reading women's poetry as life writing carries special risks. Too often accused of being incapable of writing anything but autobiography, and that prone to the sentimental or confessional, women poets have been charged with writing on a narrow range of subjects, concentrating on trivial themes, and "hiding from the real agonies of the spirit; refusing to face up to what existence is."[7]

5. Susan Stanford Friedman, "Women's Autobiographical Selves: *Theory and Practice*," in *The Private Self*, ed. Shari Benstock (Chapel Hill: University of North Carolina Press, 1988), 39.

6. See Shirley Neuman, "Autobiography: From Different Poetics to a Poetics of Difference," in *Essays in Life Writing*, ed. Marlene Kadar (Toronto: University of Toronto Press, 1992), 223.

7. See Celeste Schenck, "All of a Piece: Women's Poetry and Autobiography," in *Life/Lines: Theorizing Women's Autobiography*, ed. Bella Brodzki and Celeste Schenck (Ithaca, NY: Cornell University Press, 1988), 289; and Paula R. Backscheider, *Eighteenth-Century Women Poets and Their Poetry* (Baltimore: Johns Hopkins University Press, 2005), 399. See also Sidonie Smith and Julia Watson, "Introduction: Situating Subjectivity in Women's Autobiographical Practices," in *Women, Autobiography, Theory*, ed. Smith and Watson (Madison: University of Wisconsin Press, 1998), 3–52.

Identifying women's poetry with life writing can reinforce stereotypes that their writing about the self is "personal" and informal, even accidental, rather than "artistic" and "literary." A focus on life writing can also work against seeing the poetry as poetry and recognizing the need for sophisticated analysis of form and technique. The challenge, then, is to treat the poems in part 2 as life writing and as poetry. A few useful models exist. For example, Bonnie Costello explores a model of lyric subjectivity that separates voice from identity and is seen as "taking shape in relation to the contradictory and unarticulated aspirations of the culture." She freely acknowledges "our perennial uncertainty about the nature of lyric voice and the relations between the poet, the poem, and society."[8]

The pathbreaking Adrienne Rich describes Eleanor Ross Taylor's poetry as "fierce, rich, and difficult" and as giving access to the "underground life of women," "the woman in the family, coping, hoarding, preserving, observing, keeping up appearances, seeing through the myths and hypocrisies, nursing the sick, conspiring with sister-women, possessed of a will to survive and to see others survive."[9] This description could have been written about the poems in this section. The poems on war, for instance, are sometimes fierce, and they observe, preserve, and pierce through "myths and hypocrisies." The friendship poems often "conspire with sister-women" and are exquisite glimpses of the "underground life of women." The various kinds of love among women and the sustenance of women's enduring friendships with women are not so much stated as they are the very fabric of many poems. The secret lives of women are revealed in portraits of them gossiping about handsome soldiers, slipping away to a secluded garden where they can be completely free, encouraging each other toward unconventional female destinies, composing prophetic poems about the most significant public events of the time, and saying at the death of a child or mother, "I understand. I know." In their very different ways, the poems on pain and illness, death, marriage, and motherhood show women coping, surviving, and encouraging others to do so. Many of the poems are "fierce, rich, and difficult," as are Anne Bannerman's *Verses on an Illumination for a Naval Victory* (2.E), Anna Laetitia Barbauld's *Eighteen Hundred and Eleven* (2.F), Anne Finch's *To Death* (2.N), and Elizabeth Tollet's *Imitation of Horace, Lib. II Ode 3* (2.N). Their literariness and consummate skill are undeniable. Other poems seem utterly simple

8. Bonnie Costello, "Elizabeth Bishop's Impersonal Personal," *American Literary History* 15 (2003): 334–66, quotations from 340 and 335; Costello's essay has influenced this introduction in many ways. See also Terry Threadgold, *Feminist Poetics: Poiesis, Performance, Histories* (London: Routledge, 1997).

9. Adrienne Rich, "Woman Observing, Preserving, Conspiring, Surviving: The Poems of Eleanor Ross Taylor (1972)," in Rich, *On Lies, Secrets, and Silence: Selected Prose, 1966–1978* (New York: Norton, 1979), 84. Her essay on Emily Dickinson in the same collection, "Vesuvius at Home: The Power of Emily Dickinson" (157–83), is a classic.

and transparent, as do Mehetabel Wright's *To an Infant expiring the second day of its Birth* (2.L), Mary Masters's *I shall keep your Correspondence as Misers do their Gold* (2.A), and Laetitia Pilkington's *Verses wrote in a Library* (2.J). As Alexander Pope observed, however, making verse seem "simple" or "easy" is exceptionally difficult: "Then polish all with so much life and ease, / You think 'tis Nature, and a knack to please; / 'But Ease in writing flows from Art, not Chance, / As those move easiest who have learn'd to dance.'"[10] The poems in this anthology treat subjects also documented in diaries, letters, and novels, but they expand our knowledge, perhaps especially because of the variety of their representations of human responses to a wide range of experiences and even to what has been called "the ages of man."

Literary criticism of women's life writing has consistently found obstacles, such as the shape and genre conventions of the canon of autobiography[11] and social conditioning that leads women to mask or disguise the private. In contrast, poetry seems empowering, a source of strategies and examples authorizing and even authenticating women's representations and, therefore, their lives and individual styles and choices. Sidonie Smith has said that the "history of an autobiographical subject is the history of recitations of the [performative] self."[12] In poems, women can try on identities and personalities; they can create voices very unlike their own and, comfortably disguised, voices that express their most hidden longings and also opinions that would be socially unacceptable in other forms. From within a preexisting poetic stance women can join the culture's literary, social, and intellectual debates, assuming equal authority to speak and enabled to escape gender restrictions.[13] Some of these stances are traditional and old, many adapted from familiar forms, and others are revisionary and new. Because some of these poems were written to share thoughts and feelings with close friends with no thought of print publication, they seem transparently honest, and their tone is often unmistakably intimate. Many are marked by self-conscious artistry and genre awareness. Some poems are written in traditional genres that authorize self-reflection and personal responses to experience. In some cases, the form gives additional dignity to the ordinary lives, activities, and thoughts of women. Sonnets, elegies, and even satire and fable, all found in part 2, are examples. Although Rich later criticized formalism for forcing her into male-

10. Alexander Pope, *The Second Epistle of the Second Book of Horace Imitated*, lines 176–79.

11. The canon of autobiography is well known: Augustine's *Confessions*, Benvenuto Cellini's *Autobiography*, Rousseau's *Confessions*, and John Bunyan's *Grace Abounding to the Chief of Sinners*, and so it continues.

12. See Sidonie Smith and Julia Watson, "Fifty-two Genres of Life Narrative," in *Reading Autobiography: A Guide for Interpreting Life Narratives* (Minneapolis: University of Minnesota Press, 2001), 197; Sidonie Smith, "Performativity, Autobiographical Practice, Resistance," *a/b: Auto/Biography Studies* 10 (1995): 21.

13. See Susan Lanser, *Fictions of Authority* (Ithaca, NY: Cornell University Press, 1992), esp. 15, 17.

defined models, she noted that for a while formalism, "like asbestos gloves . . . allowed me to handle materials I couldn't pick up bare-handed."[14] These poets are deeply knowledgeable about genre conventions, and in order to express different experiences and responses from those men describe, they blend, mix, and juxtapose poetic kinds. In fascinating ways, the male tradition and the masterpieces of a genre provide a subtext or contrapuntal force in some poems and actually bring women's point of view more forcefully to the surface.

Women poets invite autobiographical scrutiny in different ways and to different degrees. Mary Barber uses the real names of her family and friends, and she and Jane Brereton supply many details that allow us to identify people, places, and events. Many of Elizabeth Carter's poems are addressed to specific, identifiable people, and the poems are sometimes usefully glossed by her correspondence—as are some of Mary Masters's poems. Many of Laetitia Pilkington's poems are embedded in her *Memoirs.* Some of the women give prominence to themselves as women, as Sarah Fyge Egerton and Mary Chudleigh do. Others call attention to themselves as poets, as Anne Finch and Mary Whateley Darwall do. With them, we hear explicitly what was true for many of the poets: the necessity of poetic expression. These poems give rise to questions such as "What events, encounters, and forces seem to call up affective responses?"[15] Where does the Subject locate itself? When do we experience the Subject experiencing itself as Object? Shari Benstock argues that some forms of autobiography "posit a self called to witness (as an authority) to 'his' own being, that propose a double referent for the first-person narrative (the present 'I' and the past 'I'), . . . the Subject is made an Object of investigation."[16] This observation leads back to the compositional significance of memory and imagination and the ways they are interwoven in both genres and especially in identity formation.

Yet another question is how we identify which gestures in poems are autobiographical. The compression, metrics, and rhetorical strategies, as well as the strength of the conventions of poetic genres, set poetry apart from other autobiographical forms and complicate their use as life writing, yet poetry is the genre in which the artist is most authorized to interweave compositional practices and self-exploration and self-statement. Some poets' work, such as that of Mary Barber, Mehetabel Wright, and Jane Cave Winscom, follows their life trajectories, and the gestures and identifying references are often specific. Life-writing specialists have much to say about the value of fragmentary evidence. For instance, Celeste Schenck, in an essay on women's poetry and autobiography, concludes, "The serial effort at sketching a self in time and over time is the poetic equivalent

14. Rich, *On Lies, Secrets, and Silence,* 40.

15. Charles Altieri's work on the theory of affects offers intriguing possibilities. See, for example, "Autobiography and the Limits of Moral Criticism," *a/b: Auto/Biography Studies* 19 (2004): 156–75, quotation, 168.

16. Shari Benstock, "Authoring the Autobiographical" in Benstock, ed., *The Private Self,* 19.

of snapshots recording a process of personal becoming during a period of historical change."[17] "It is obvious that individuals use life-story narration and autobiographical accounting to construct their *individuality*, a continuity over time. That is how a sense of self is discursively accomplished," writes Pertti Alasuutari. "It allows us to adopt a view of life and self that better adapts to changed conditions or which, because the conception of oneself is changed, changes the conditions by viewing them in a new light."[18] This flexible, nonproscriptive view of life writing works well for women, whose story lines are often "multiple, intermingled, ambivalent as to valence, and recursive." In contrast to men's stories, which "concentrate on the pursuit of single goals," the stories of women "usually weave together themes of achievement, along with themes of family obligations, personal development, love lives, children's welfare, and friends."[19]

For identifying autobiographical gestures in the work of other women poets, the best guide may be James Olney's hypothesis that the autobiographical gesture is not content but "the formal device of recapitulation and recall" and the extended engagement with the uses of memory, "the web of reverie," and internal states of consciousness.[20] Some of the poems in part 2 seem steeped in memory, and the portrayals of experiences and states of mind are as varied as the women themselves. In many, the past, the present, and the imagined future come dynamically together, as they do in Susannah Harrison's *LXXXIII: Longing for Public Worship* (2.D), Susanna Blamire's *When the Sunbeams of Joy* (2.M), and Charlotte Smith's *Thirty-eight* (2.M). The middle lines, for instance, in Jane Barker's simple, dignified *On the Death of My Dear Friend and Play-fellow* (2.N) read, "Where we indulg'd our easie Appetites, / With Pocket-Apples, Plumbs, and such delights." From this specific recollection Barker lets her imagination take flight not only into the present and future but also into space: "We can teach Clouds to weep, and Winds to sigh at Sea."

The poems in part 2 overthrow almost every commonplace and stereotype about women and women's poetry. Complexity and simplicity, contradiction and reconciliation, juxtapositions and balances—the fabric of every aspect of women's lives and writing practices—are reproduced in these poems. As important as

---

17. Schenck, "All of a Piece," 290. Charlotte Linde considers a life story as "all the stories told by an individual during his or her lifetime that (a) make a point about the [speaker's character] . . . and (b) have extended reportability (meaning that some events can be verified)." "Explanatory Systems in Oral Life Stories," in *Cultural Models in Language and Thought*, ed. Dorothy Holland and Naomi Quinn (Cambridge: Cambridge University Press, 1987), 344.

18. Pertti Alasuutari, "The Discursive Construction of Personality," in *The Narrative Study of Lives*, ed. Amia Lieblich and Ruthellen Josselson, vol. 5 (London: Sage, 1997), 7, 16, emphasis ours.

19. Mary M. Gergen and Kenneth J. Gergen, "Narratives of the Gendered Body in Popular Autobiography," in Lieblich and Josselson, *Narrative Study of Lives*, vol. 1 (London: Sage, 1993), 195–96.

20. James Olney, "Some Versions of Memory," in *Autobiography: Essays Theoretical and Critical*, ed. Olney (Princeton, NJ: Princeton University Press, 1980), 251–52. See also Sidonie Smith and Julia Watson's summary of his argument in *Reading Autobiography*, 200.

the subjects of family obligations, love, religion, and friends were to these poets, so were coming to terms with war, participating in public-sphere debates, spreading environmental awareness, and joining others in celebrating or condemning major events. Their individuality and their different experiences emerge forcefully. The poems in sections 2.E, "The Poetry of War," and 2.F, "Poems on the Public Sphere," for instance, reveal bloodthirsty passions for winning battles and heartache over the poverty of veterans and widows and the mutilation and deaths of family and friends. The battle of Culloden and the Duke of Cumberland look very different to different women. Anna Seward's and Jane Cave Winscom's reactions to the fast days ordered in wartime could not be more different. Many of their themes anticipate major concerns of today. For example, Kathleen Woodward points out that "aging—how we define ourselves as women as our social roles, our bodies, and our subjectivities change over time—is one of the great autobiographical themes."[21] Women's diverse responses to the same events, opinions, and life stages reinforce the fact that what we say about each poet should be grounded in material circumstances and in particular and local instances of personal, family, and social history. This has, of course, seldom been done.

To see these poems simultaneously as poetry and as life writing beneficially brings details and the significance of space to the fore, and both contribute to re-creating the texture of everyday life. In poems, women toss sleepless or ill in their beds, sit by their children's bedsides, read the news, peel apples, and enjoy church anthems, the beauty of a friend's embroidery, or having a pet bird. Felicity Nussbaum notes that "women writers have been seeking their own spaces, metaphorical rooms of their own, for centuries." Although her statement has yielded somewhat to the twenty years of feminist work done since she wrote it, women's spaces are still "largely unspoken, unwritten, and unrepresented ones that have not yet been fully articulated or explained."[22] Her words obviously invoke Virginia Woolf,[23] but for the women poets of the eighteenth century secluded outdoor spaces were as important as the indoor places women marked out as their own for sewing, cooking, reading, instructing children, and entertaining a woman friend. These spaces may be a no-man's land, as Elizabeth Carter's gardens often are, or they may be contested, as, for instance, in Mary Barber's poems where they always seem to be populated and invaded. Poets sometimes peeled the facade away from the myths of civility, order, and beauty associated with spaces, as do Ann Murry in *City Splendor* (1.F) and Mary Leapor

21. Kathleen Woodward, "Simone de Beauvoir: *Aging and its Discontents*," in Benstock, *Private Self*, 90.

22. Felicity Nussbaum, "Eighteenth-Century Women's Autobiographical Commonplaces," in Benstock, *Private Self*, 147, 148.

23. Woolf's *A Room of One's Own* is one of the most important feminist texts in history. Famously, she wrote that "a woman must have money and a room of her own" if she is to be a writer (1929; New York: Harcourt, Brace, Jovanovich, 1959), 4.

in *Crumble Hall* (not included). Sometimes, as in Anne Bannerman's *Verses on an Illumination for a Naval Victory,* the most crowded spaces could be isolating and alienating. In other poems, such as Rebecca Manners's about Lehena, Ireland, and Anne Hunter's about Blackheath, the places seem to welcome the poet and fill a special place in her heart. The poetry in this anthology makes these spaces newly and more fully accessible.

We can turn to the poems in this part to learn women's sources of happiness, their sense of alienation or belonging, and the causes of struggle that they apprehended and engaged (or lamented) decade by decade. Above all, the poetry in this section testifies to how deeply and completely writing and reading poetry was interwoven into the lives of these women. It gives access to the great questions and to the everyday practices. As Lord Byron wrote, "'Tis to create, and in creating live / A being more intense, that we endow / With form our fancy, gaining as we give / The life we image...."[24] Women perform the voices, selves, ideologies, identities, and personalities around them; in doing so they create both a being more intense and the imagined life. Sometimes they create a strong dialectic between self-definition and a historical, sociopolitically prescribed role. Separate selfhood, relational selfhood, shared identities, collective identity—the tensions these generate in the performative roles and voices women create within their poetry can never be entirely separated out; nor can, perhaps, self-definitions and autobiographical statements. In section 2.B, "Poems of Retirement and Retreat," for instance, we confront especially strong genre expectations and speaker positions, yet the twilight setting chosen for so many of them creates a liminal space especially fortuitous for the expression of a self. Between day and night, past and future, and the performative roles of the day's work and the night's putting-to-bed, the liminal time encourages a sense of a deeper self. Fortunately, life writing, unlike biography and autobiography, is open-ended, in process, documentary and descriptive rather than "going somewhere" (often somewhere defined by either the success or the confession/redemption trajectory). Likewise, many poets' work stretches over a lifetime, exploring, experimenting, changing.

The first four groups of poems in this part ("Friendship Poems," "Poems of Retirement and Retreat," "Love Poems," and "Religious Poetry") are about subjects of deep, personal significance to women and weave together emotional states, identity construction, representations of lifestyles, and explorations of gender, among other things. The next five groups ("The Poetry of War," "Poems on the Public Sphere," "Poems on Pain and Illness," "Poems on Nature," and "Poems on Ecology") are intensely engaged with the public sphere and issues of diplomacy, public policy, and crucial personal and national values. The final group of poems begins with poems about the quest for personal happiness; they

24. George Noel Gordon, Lord Byron, *Childe Harold's Pilgrimage* (London, 1816), canto 3, lines 47–50.

searchingly consider lifestyles, those forced on women but primarily those they choose and construct. After this somewhat introductory section, the categories represent milestones, beginning with marriage and motherhood and concluding with death. These poems reveal women's fears and dreams about marriage and often raise with riveting power familiar questions: "How will I die and how will I face the manner of my death?" The poems brought together in section 2.M, "Poems on the New Year, Birthdays, and Aging," are little-known, and their meditations on the passage of time, a subject that holds the group together, often come to decidedly unexpected conclusions.

The content of literary works usually attracts the greatest attention, and even when the form is remarked upon, how it functions and how it or its deployment is revisionary are almost never discussed in any detail. That is especially true regarding women's poetry, as reading analyses of John Milton's sonnets beside those of Smith make glaringly obvious.[25] The poems in part 2 call out for close study of their formal and technical characteristics. Jane Brereton's *To Mrs Roberts on Her Spinning* (2.M), Elizabeth Carter's *While Clear the Night* (2.H), and Maria Cowper's *Where Has My Ambition Led Me?* (2.D) are among the many apparently transparent poems that such study rewards, while other poems, such as Mary Chudleigh's *On the Death of my dear Daughter Eliza Maria Chudleigh* (2.N), Charlotte Smith's *Sonnet XLVI: Written at Penshurst, in Autumn 1788* (2.F), and Anna Laetitia Barbauld's *Eighteen Hundred and Eleven* (2.F) in their very different ways demand it.

As we create ways to bring form and content together and to balance privileging poetry and privileging life writing, we will advance literary, social, and women's history and biography. Poetry is often seen as a privileged site of individual expression, and it and life writing provide an effective medium of self-determination. They become complementary vehicles for "critical discourse about relations of power in social formations and the possibility of change."[26] We look to both poetry and life writing for rich accounts of how lives are led and experienced and for depictions of the possibilities for alternate ways of life and selves. These poems, more than two hundred years after they were written, continue to offer these things in abundance.

---

25. In addition to drawing attention to the contrast in treatment of Milton's poetry, Alice Eardley makes a number of strong statements in "Recreating the Canon: Women Writers and Anthologies of Early Modern Verse," *Women's Writing* 14 (2007): 270–89. Among them are that scholars and anthologizers "privilege poetry reflecting 'the experience of being a woman'" (and we would add "especially domestic and private" experience); "the general assumption that women were not consciously engaging in a sophisticated use of literary form"; and that "political reservations rather than the nature of the material" contribute to the neglect of form (277, 280, 281).

26. Ann Vickery, "Poetic Fields and the 'Painted Birds' of Language Writing," in *Leaving Lines of Gender: A Feminist Genealogy of Language Writing* (Hanover, NH: Wesleyan University Press, 2000), 37.

Friendship Poems

"To Friendship nobler Strains belong," writes Charlotte Lennox in *To Mira. Inviting her to a Retreat in the Country* (2.B), asserting the necessity of an appropriate poetic form for this important subject: female friendship. It is now perhaps difficult to apprehend fully the complicated web of intimacies—emotional, physical, intellectual, poetic—that characterized women's friendships. As cultural historians have noted, women's same-sex relationships—with sisters, friends, or lovers—were often the most intense and sustained in their lives. Arranged marriages, shared domestic responsibilities, and close physical proximity often meant that women formed "emotional ties" that were "deep and binding and provided one of the fundamental existential realities of women's lives."[1] The complex poems that depict those relationships form a distinct and uniquely female form. These poems negotiate a delicate balance between imagining female relationships as ethereal, almost transcendent—"The next to Angels Love, if not the same" (Katherine Philips, *A Friend*)—and, for some, simultaneously filled with erotic intensity, as in Aphra Behn's *To the fair Clarinda, who made Love to me, imagin'd more than Woman* (2.C). And, of course, the categories are not mutually exclusive. From the hundreds of friendship poems written during this period, we carefully selected many in different forms to illustrate the poetic flexibility as well as women's artistry, and we have deliberately grouped those with shared themes or subjects. The poems in this section are important for understanding female poets' sense of agency and their growing literary authority. Women were simultaneously uninhibited about the depths of their emotion and highly self-aware of their poetic expression of that emotion.

Katherine Philips, represented here by three poems, was the most influential female writer of friendship poems and established important elements that continued into the eighteenth century. While, as Carol Barash reminds us, some of these friendship poems had specific political resonances, as did the friendships themselves,[2] Philips used the form to explore emotional intimacy, erotic intensity, and the harmony of souls between friends. Friendship, writes Katherine Philips, "'Tis Love refine'd and purg'd from all its dross" (*A Friend*). The refinement Philips ascribes to friendships is reiterated by later poets who applaud friendship as "Passion in abstract, void of all designs" (Sarah Fyge Eger-ton, *On Friendship*) and "Pleasures from grosser Sense refin'd" (Mary Chan-dler, *On Friendship*). It is, Elizabeth Hands notes, "more to me than love" (*An Epistle*). That idealization may account for the encomiastic quality of poems depicting women's performances; Jane Brereton likens Sybil Egerton's singing to a "Taste of Heav'n, below" in *On Mrs Sybil Egerton's Singing an Anthem in Wrex-ham Church, June 21, 1730*.

Yet that ethereal, transcendent quality does not preclude the erotic, and a substantial body of scholarship has explored the role of homoerotic desire in these poems. The lesbian tone of Philips's poems and letters has been amply documented,[3] and the intensity of the emotion is clear: "I have no thought but what's to thee reveal'd, / Nor thou desire that is from me conceal'd" *(L'Amitie. To Mrs. Mary Awbrey)*. The line separating female friendship from same-sex love is narrow, perhaps complicated by the fact that the most passionate feelings could be expressed about women to whom the poet was a friend and not a lover. As is evident from poems in this section, as well as those in sections 2.B, on retirement and retreat, and 2.C, on love, this intensity infuses poems that explore different dimensions of women's relationships. These poems also allude, however, to the ways in which female relationships can be vindictive and competitive in a cul-ture defined by compulsory heterosexuality. In *To Miss Clayton. Occasion'd by her breaking an appointment to visit the Author* Mary Jones gently chides her friend while also tapping playfully into the cultural stereotypes of women as unreliable and untrustworthy: "But what are women's oaths, and vows, / . . . ? / Ah, trust us not, ye faithful swains! / Who cannot trust each other."

These poems also celebrate the centrality of female friendship in the for-mation of poetic communities, female spheres in which women can applaud one another's accomplishments. These relationships are intimately tied to poetic production: "sacred Friendship . . . our Muse inspires" (Mary Leapor, *Essay on Friendship*). Poets discuss the importance of imagination in female friendship as both a substitute for the friend—"Imagination brings you to my sight; / Fatigu'd I sink into my painted chair, / And your ideal form attends me there" (Elizabeth Hands, *An Epistle*)—and a spur to further literary production, something the poems in section 3.B, "The Muses," explore in detail. "Friendship inspires; / The sacred lay / My bosom fires," writes Elizabeth Hands in *Friendship. An Ode* (3.B). The established friendships on which the poems were predicated enable women to represent themselves and their relationships with flexibility, power, and in-sight. The same intimacies, shared frames of reference, and familiarity suffuse poems throughout the volume, not just in this section. For example, poems in part 3, recounting female literary production, depict the importance of a sup-portive coterie of female colleagues; poems in sections 1.A, "Social Verse," and 1.C, "Poems of Common Life," convey the intricate web of public and private female relationships; and many of the poems in section 2.b, "Poems of Retirement and Retreat," are an extension of the friendship poem and describe a woman seeking a contemplative space to share with a female intimate. To understand women's social interaction, literary bonds, and, ultimately, poetic production requires an understanding of the role of female friendship: women's intimacies with other women profoundly shaped their conception of a personal and poetic self.

Notes

1. Carroll Smith-Rosenberg, "The Female World of Love and Ritual: Relations between Women in Nineteenth-Century America," *Signs* 1 (1975): 11. Smith-Rosenberg, though describing women in eighteenth- and nineteenth-century America, uses terms highly relevant to the structural relationships in England during the eighteenth century. For a fuller discussion, see also her *Disorderly Conduct: Visions of Gender in Victorian America* (New York: Oxford University Press, 1985). Following Smith-Rosenberg's germinative work, other studies, such as Sharon Marcus's *Between Women: Friendship, Desire, and Marriage in Victorian England* (Princeton, NJ: Princeton University Press, 2007), have further illuminated our understandings of these relationships.

2. Carol Barash, *English Women's Poetry, 1649–1714: Politics, Community, and Linguistic Authority* (Oxford: Clarendon, 1996), esp. chap. 2.

3. Same-sex desire in Philips's poetry has been widely and persuasively discussed, as has the Sapphic dimension to poetry of this period. Representative discussions of Philips include, but are not limited to, Kamille Stone Stanton, "Painting Sentinels: Erotics, Politics, and Redemption in the Friendship Poetry of Katherine Philips (1631–1664)," *Comitatus* 38 (2007): 155–72; Harriette Andreadis, "Re-Configuring Early Modern Friendship: Katherine Philips and Homoerotic Desire," *Studies in English Literature* 46 (2006): 523–42; Paula Loscocco, "Inventing the English Sappho: Katherine Philips's Donnean Poetry," *Journal of English and Germanic Philology* 102 (2003): 59–87; and Elaine Hobby, "Orinda and Female Intimacy," in *Early Women Writers: 1600–1720,* ed. Anita Pacheco (London: Longman, 1998), 73–88.

A retir'd Friendship, to Ardelia[1]

Katherine Philips

Come, my *Ardelia,* to this Bower,
   Where kindly mingling Souls awhile
Let's innocently spend an hour,
   And at all serious follies smile.

2.
Here is no quarrelling for Crowns,[2]
   Nor fear of changes in our Fate;
No trembling at the great ones frowns,
   Nor any slavery of State.

3.
Here's no disguise nor treachery,
   Nor any deep conceal'd design;
From Bloud and Plots this place is free,
   And calm as are those looks of thine.

4.
Here let us sit and bless our Stars,
   Who did such happy quiet give,
As that remov'd from noise of Wars
   In one anothers hearts we live.

5.
Why should we entertain a fear?
   Love cares not how the World is turn'd:
If crouds of dangers should appear,
   Yet Friendship can be unconcern'd.

6.
We wear about us such a charm,
   No horrour can be our offence;

10

20

1. In manuscript, this poem is dated 23 August 1651, which would place it squarely during the Interregnum and shortly after a royalist rebellion in Wales that Philips's husband helped suppress. *The Collected Works of Katherine Philips, "The Matchless Orinda,"* ed. Patrick Thomas, 3 vols. (Stump Cross, UK: Stump Cross Books, 1990–93), 1:339. For a discussion of the importance of retirement to women's friendships, see the introduction to section 2.B.

2. The battle of Worcester, which occurred about the time this poem was written, ended Charles II's attempts to regain the English throne.

For mischief's self can doe no harm
   To Friendship or to Innocence.

7.
Let's mark how soon *Apollo's* beams[3]
   Command the flocks to quit their meat,[4]
And not entreat the neighbouring Springs
   To quench their thirst, but cool their heat.

8.
In such a scorching Age as this
   Who would not ever seek a shade,   30
Deserve their Happiness to miss,
   As having their own peace betray'd.

9.
But we (of one anothers mind
   Assur'd) the boisterous World disdain;
With quiet Souls and unconfin'd
   Enjoy what Princes wish in vain.

                    (1651; 1664)

L'Amitie.[5] To Mrs. Mary Awbrey[6]
Katherine Philips

Soul of my Soul, my joy, my crown, my Friend,
A name which all the rest doth comprehend;
How happy are we now, whose Souls are grown
By an incomparable mixture one:
Whose well-acquainted Minds are now as near
As Love, or Vows, or Friendship can endear?
I have no thought but what's to thee reveal'd,
Nor thou desire that is from me conceal'd.
Thy Heart locks up my Secrets richly set,
And my Breast is thy private Cabinet.   10

---

3. Apollo, the god of light and music, is often identified with the sun.
4. Any kind of solid food, as opposed to liquid.
5. *L'amitié* is the French word for "friendship."
6. Mary Aubrey was a friend of Philips's at Mrs. Salmon's boarding school in Hackney. She subsequently was known as "Rosania" in Philips's poetry and in their circle.

Thou shed'st no tear but what my moisture lent,
And if I sigh, it is thy breath is spent.
United thus, what Horrour can appear
Worthy our Sorrow, Anger, or our Fear?
Let the dull World alone to talk and fight,
And with their vast Ambitions Nature fright;
Let them despise so Innocent a flame,
While Envy, Pride and Faction play their game:
But we by Love sublim'd[7] so high shall rise,
20   To pity Kings, and Conquerours despise;
Since we that Sacred Union have engrost
Which they and all the sullen World have lost.

(1664)

A Friend
Katherine Philips

1.

Love, Nature's Plot, this great Creation's Soul,
   The Being and the Harmony of things,
Doth still preserve and propagate the whole,
   From whence Mans Happiness & Safety springs:
The earliest, whitest,[8] blessedst Times did draw
From her alone their universal Law.

2.

Friendship's an Abstract of this noble Flame,
   'Tis Love refin'd and purg'd from all its dross,
The next to Angels Love,[9] if not the same,
10   As strong in passion is, though not so gross:
It antedates a glad Eternity,
And is an Heaven in Epitome.[10]

7. Refined, elevated.
8. Most auspicious, happiest.
9. In *The Collected Works of Katherine Philips*, 1:366, Patrick Thomas suggests that Philips is alluding to the idea of angelic love introduced in Thomas Stanley's 1651 translation of Pico della Mirandola's *Platonick Discourse upon Love:* "Vulgar love is onely in Souls immerst in Matter, and overcome by it, or at least hindred by perturbations and passions. Angelick Love is in the Intellect, eternal as it is."
10. In a diminutive form.

3.

Nobler then Kindred or then Marriage-band,
   Because more free; Wedlock-felicity
It self doth onely by this Union stand,
   And turns to Friendship or to Misery.
Force or Design Matches to pass may bring,
But Friendship doth from Love and Honour spring.

4.

If Souls no Sexes have,[11] for Men t' exclude
   Women from Friendship's vast capacity,   20
Is a Design injurious or rude,
   Onely maintain'd by partial tyranny.
Love is allow'd to us and Innocence,
And noblest Friendships do proceed from thence.

5.

The chiefest thing in Friends is Sympathy:
   There is a Secret that doth Friendship guide,
Which makes two Souls before they know agree,
   Who by a thousand mixtures are ally'd,
And chang'd and lost, so that it is not known
Within which breast doth now reside their own.   30

6.

Essential Honour must be in a Friend,
   Not such as every breath fans to and fro;
But born within, is its own judge and end,
   And dares not sin though sure that none should know.
Where Friendship's spoke, Honesty's understood;
For none can be a Friend that is not Good.

7.

Friendship doth carry more then common trust,
   And Treachery is here the greatest sin.
Secrets deposed then none ever must
   Presume to open, but who put them in.   40
They that in one Chest lay up all their stock,
Had need be sure that none can pick the Lock.

11. Contemporary theological and scholastic thinking held that souls had no gender.

8.

A breast too open Friendship does not love,
  For that the others Trust will not conceal;
Nor one too much reserv'd can it approve,
  Its own Condition this will not reveal.
We empty Passions for a double end,
To be refresh'd and guarded by a Friend.

9.

Wisdom and Knowledge Friendship does require,
50   The first for Counsel, this for Company;
And though not mainly, yet we may desire
  For complaisance and Ingenuity.
Though ev'ry thing may love, yet 'tis a Rule,
He cannot be a Friend that is a Fool.

10.

Discretion uses Parts, and best knows how;
  And Patience will all Qualities commend:
That serves a need best, but this doth allow
  The Weaknesses and Passions of a Friend.
We are not yet come to the Quire[12] above:
60 Who cannot Pardon here, can never Love.

11.

Thick Waters shew no Images of things;
  Friends are each others Mirrours, and should be
Clearer then Crystal or the Mountain Springs,
  And free from Clouds, Design or Flattery.
For vulgar Souls no part of Friendship share:
Poets and Friends are born to what they are.

12.

Friends should observe & chide each others Faults,
  To be severe then is most just and kind;
Nothing can 'scape their search who know the thoughts:
70   This they should give and take with equal Mind.
For Friendship, when this Freedom is deny'd,
Is like a Painter when his hands are ty'd.

12. The nine orders of angels in the heavenly hierarchy, choir.

13.

A Friend should find out each Necessity,
    And then unask'd reliev't at any rate:
It is not Friendship, but Formality,
    To be desir'd; for Kindness keeps no state.
Of Friends he doth the Benefactour prove,
That gives his Friend a means t' express his Love.

14.

Absence doth not from Friendship's right excuse:
    They who preserve each others heart and fame   80
Parting can ne're divide, it may diffuse;
    As Liquors which asunder are the same.
Though Presence help'd them at the first to greet,
Their Souls know now without those aids to meet.

15.

Constant and Solid, whom no storms can shake,
    Nor death unfix, a right Friend ought to be;
And if condemned to survive, doth make
    No second choice, but Grief and Memory.
But Friendship's best Fate is, when it can spend
A Life, a Fortune, all to serve a Friend.   90

(1664)

On Friendship
Sarah Fyge Egerton

Friendship (the great pursuit of noble Minds)
Passion in abstract, void of all designs;
Each generous Pen, doth celebrate thy Fame,
And yet I doubt, thou'rt nothing but a Name.
Some pregnant Fancy, in a raptur'd height,
Produc'd this mighty notional[13] Delight.
The Muses virtuosal[14] Chymistry,[15]

13. Imaginary.
14. Of a female virtuoso or learned person.
15. Chemistry, which is both a science and an art, is the branch of physical science that deals with forms of matter. The imagery throughout the poem draws from the discourse of chemistry.

To turn all Fortunes to Felicity;
'Tis fancy'd well, and this I dare ingage,
10   Were all Men Friends, 'twould be the golden Age;
But tell me where, this Extract may be found,
And what Ingredients make the Rich Compound;
Or in what Soul, is true kindly heat,
That can this great Experiment compleat.
Sometimes a fond good Nature lights upon
A soft and civil Temper like its own;
Strait they resolve to be those happy things,
Which when combin'd, pity contending Kings:
Yet e'er they reach these sublimated[16] Joys,
20   They'r poorly lost, in Treachery or Toys.[17]
The mighty Notions of the exalted State,
Sink to a vulgar Commerce, or Debate:
Sure, like the Chymick Stone,[18] it was design'd, ⎫
But to imploy the curious searching Mind,   ⎬
In the pursuit of what, none e'er shall find;   ⎭
Their Quality's I'm sure do prove all one,
Who trusts too much to either is undone.

(1703)

Friendship between Ephelia and Ardelia[19]
Anne Finch

Eph. What *Friendship* is, ARDELIA shew.
Ard. 'Tis to love, as I love You.
Eph. This Account, so short (tho' kind)
      Suits not my enquiring Mind.

---

16. Rarified, pure. *Sublimation* was a commonly used term in chemistry at the time; it signified a type of chemical operation in which dry solids were heated such that vapors emitted by the solids could be collected.

17. Tricks.

18. Also known as the philosopher's stone, which was a central part of alchemy. During this period, chemistry and alchemy were closely allied.

19. Ardelia was Finch's poetic name for herself. The identity of Ephelia is the subject of some critical debate. On her website Ellen Moody suggests that Ephelia is probably Finch's sister-in-law Francis Finch Thynne, Lady Weymouth (www.jimandellen.org/finch/poemIII.html). Myra Reynolds asserts that Ephelia is Lady Worseley, Finch's niece by marriage and the subject of several of her letters and other poems. *The Poems of Anne Countess of Winchilsea* (Chicago: University of Chicago Press, 1903), ed. Reynolds, xxxviii.

Therefore farther now repeat;
What is *Friendship* when compleat?
Ard. 'Tis to share all Joy and Grief;
'Tis to lend all due Relief
From the Tongue, the Heart, the Hand;
'Tis to mortgage House and Land;   10
For a Friend be sold a Slave;
'Tis to die upon a Grave,
If a Friend therein do lie.
Eph. This indeed, tho' carry'd high,
This, tho' more than e'er was done
Underneath the rolling Sun,
This has all been said before.
Can ARDELIA say no more?
Ard. Words indeed no more can shew:
But 'tis to love, as I love you.   20

(1713)

On Friendship
Mary Chandler

FRIENDSHIP, the heav'nly Theme, I sing,
    Thou Source of sweetest Joy!
Pleasures from grosser Sense refin'd,
    Still new, that never cloy.

'Tis sacred Friendship softens Life,
    And smooth's the rugged Stream;
Uniting Joys, will Joys create,
    And sharing lessen Pain.

'Tis pure as the etherial Flame,
    That lights the Lamps above,   10
Or, as the new-born Infant's Thought,
    Or, as his Mother's Love.

The sordid Soul ne'er knows thy Charms,
    Nor such divine Delight;
He whom thy gen'rous Passion warms,
    Soars to an Angel's Height.

Friendship, is founded on Esteem,
  'Tis Elegance of Choice,
Acquaintance pick'd from Crouds of Men,
  By heav'nly Reason's Voice.

20

Distinguish'd by superiour Worth,
  And Virtue all divine,
Behavior elegant, whose Taste,
  Learning, and Wit, refine.

When such discourse, Instruction flows,
  Not idle empty Sound,
No Breath envenom'd Flatt'ry knows,
  Or Envy's ruthless Wound.

Reason and Truth, inspire each Tongue,
  The Soul, bright Knowledge gains,
Such, ADAM ask'd, and GABRIEL sung,
  In heav'nly MILTON's Strains.[20]

30

Such, the Companions of my Hours,
  And such, my lov'd Employ,
I wou'd indulge my nobler Pow'rs,
  But know no guilty Joy.

And thus, as swift-wing'd Time brings on
  Death nearer to our View,
Tun'd to sweet Harmony, our Souls
  Will take a short Adieu.

40

'Till the last Trump's delightful Sound
  Shall wake our sleeping Clay,[21]

20. In Milton's *Paradise Lost* Gabriel is one of the four archangels and the one assigned to guard Eden, where he observes Adam and Eve and compels Satan (temporarily) to leave. Although in the Bible Gabriel is a messenger of God (see, for example, Luke 1 and Daniel 8), he does not actually "sing" or have an extended exchange with Adam in *Paradise Lost*. Thus, the line refers not to a conversation between Adam and Gabriel but rather to their discrete queries and proclamations on reason, truth, and knowledge.

21. An allusion to the Rapture, detailed in Corinthians 15:52: "the trumpet shall sound, and the dead shall be raised incorruptible, and we shall be changed."

Then swift, to find our Fellow-Souls,
    As light we haste away.

(1729)

To the Memory of Mrs Mary Whitelamb
Daughter of the late Rev. Mr Wesley Rector
of Epworth and Wroot[22]
Mehetabel Wright

If blissful spirits condescend to know
And hover round what once they lov'd below,
Maria! gentlest excellence! attend
To one who glories to have call'd thee friend!
Remote in merit, tho' allied in blood,
Tho' worthless I, and thou divinely good.
    Accept, dear shade! from me these artless lays,
Who never durst unjustly blame or praise.
    How thy œconomy and sense outweigh'd
The finest wit, in utmost pomp display'd,   10
Let others sing, while I attempt to paint
The godlike virtues of the friend and saint.
    From earliest dawn of life thro' thee alone
The faint sublime, the finish'd christian shone;
Yet wou'd not grace one grain of pride allow,
Or cry, stand off, I'm holier than thou!
With business or devotion never cloy'd,
No moment of thy time pass'd unemploy'd:
Well-natur'd mirth mature discretion join'd,
Most sure attendants on the virtuous mind!   20
A worth so singular, since time began,
But one surpass'd, and he was more than man.
Ah me that heav'n had from this bosom tore
The best, the firmest friend to meet no more,
Ere *Stella* cou'd discharge the smallest part
Of what she ow'd to such immense desert,
Or cou'd reward with aught but empty praise

22. Mary Whitelamb (1696–1734) was Mehetabel Wesley Wright's older sister who died 1 November 1734, shortly after the birth of her first child. She was married to John Whitelamb, who had been employed by Samuel Wesley and had been a student of John Wesley's. Indeed, the Wesleys financed Whitelamb's studies at Oxford.

The sole companion of her joyless days.
   Nor was thy form unfair (tho' heav'n confin'd
30   To scanty limits thy exalted mind)
Witness the brow so faultless, open, clear,
That none cou'd ask if honesty was there;
Witness the taintless lustre of thy skin,
Bright emblem of the brighter soul within!
That soul which easy, unaffected, mild,
Thro' jetty[23] eyes with cheerful sweetness smil'd.
But oh! cou'd fancy reach, or language speak
The living beauties of thy lip and cheek,
Where nature's pencil, leaving art no room,
40   Touch'd to a miracle the vernal bloom,
Lost tho' thou art, in STELLA's faithful line
Thy face immortal as thy fame shou'd shine.
   To soundest prudence (life's unerring guide)
To love sincere, religion void of pride,
To friendship perfect in a female mind,
Which I nor wish, nor hope, on earth to find,
To mirth (the balm of care) from lightness free,
To stedfast truth, unwearied industry,
To ev'ry charm and grace compriz'd in you,
50   Most worthy friend, a long and last adieu.

(1736)

On Mrs Sybil Egerton's Singing an Anthem
in Wrexham Church, June 21, 1730

Jane Brereton

In *Maro's* Fiction, the *Cumean* Maid
Conducts *Æneas* to the *Elizian* Shade;
The *Sybil's* pow'rful Call soon gains Access,
To their imagin'd Realms of Harmony and Bliss.[24]

---

23. Black.

24. In Book 6 of Virgil's (Maro's) *Aeneid,* Aeneas is told his future by the prophetess the Cumean Sybil. Then, following her instructions, he takes a trip to the underworld, where he is able to visit Elysium, where the blest enjoy a carefree life, and see his father, Anchises. The Cumean Sybil also appears in Ovid's *Metamorphoses* 13.11.155–82.

What Thanks do we our real *Sybil* owe,
For giving us a Taste of Heav'n, below?
No gloomy Paths, or Caves, for her we trod,[25]
She shone an Angel in the House of God.
When to her Maker's Praise, she tunes her Voice;
What Soul's not rapt, what Heart does not rejoyce!   10
She, on the Royal Poet's Words[26] bestows,
Such moving Airs, as he did erst compose,
When to his God he strung the living Lyre,
And *Sion*'s[27] Daughters joyn'd th' harmonious Choir.

While her celestial Strains our Ears invade,
Methinks, I see the venerable[28] Shade,
Charm'd with the Notes she so divinely sings,
Strive to awake his Harp, and animate the Strings.

Sure, Angels joy'd to hear their Heav'nly Song,
In Heav'nly Strains, flow from a mortal Tongue!   20
Blest Maid! to God thy tuneful Voice devote,
Let *Alleluja's* ever grace thy each melodious Note.

(1744)

To a Lady Singing
Charlotte Lennox

Still sing, bright Maid, nor cease the pleasing Charm,
Each Soul subdue, each tender Bosom warm;
Such magick Sweetness to thy Voice is giv'n,

---

25. Aeneas goes through the cave of Avernus, believed to be the entrance to the underworld.

26. A reference to an unnamed hymn by Nahum Tate (1652–1715), who served as poet laureate, or "royal poet," from 1692 to 1715. In 1694 Tate published *A New Version of the Psalms of David, Fitted to the Tunes Used in Churches* (published in revised versions throughout the century), which was intended to replace the Elizabethan versified Psalter.

27. In *Paradise Lost* Milton claims Mount Sion and its brooks, Kidron and Siloa, as an alternative to Parnassus: "if Sion hill / Delight thee more ..." (1.10–11).

28. King *David's* Picture. *Brereton.* [King David was a harpist, musician to Saul: "And it came to pass, when the evil spirit from God was upon Saul, that David took an harp, and played with his hand: so Saul was refreshed, and was well, and the evil spirit departed from him" (1 Sam. 16:23). Pictures of King David, often playing the harp, frequently adorned churches at this time. *Eds.*]

We hear a Seraph,[29] and we taste of Heav'n:
Strange force of Harmony, whose Power controuls,
The warring Passions, and informs our Souls,
Soft soothing Sounds, by whose enchantment blest,
Anger and Grief forsake the tranquil Breast;
While soft Ideas rising in the Mind,
10   Bids us in Love a gentle Tyrant find, ⎫
And to his Sway the softned Soul's resign'd. ⎭
Thus sung the *Thracian* Bard,[30] while all around,
The list'ning Beasts confess'd the magick Sound:
Less sweet the Harmony *Amphion* made,
When dancing Stones mov'd to the Notes he play'd;[31]
Or him,[32] who bore by Dolphins to the Shore,
Made Winds and Waves confess his magick Pow'r:
Thou no less pow'rful o'er the Human Mind,
As great a Triumph from thy Songs can find;
20   Love and its pleasing Pains at once inspire,
And fix in ev'ry Breast the latent Fire.

(1747)

On Friendship
Elizabeth Teft

Friendship, thou common Word, rarest of Things:
Great *Cowley* writes, There's fewer Friends than Kings.[33]
Ev'ry Tongue can babble forth its Name;
One Soul in Thousands don't the Thing contain.
That must be noble to a high Degree,
Abound in Truth and Generosity,
A liberal, open, disinterested Mind,

---

29. Angel.

30. Ovid refers to Orpheus as the "Thracian Bard" in *Metamorphoses* 11.1.

31. Amphion, who ruled Thebes with his twin brother, Zethus, was a harpist of such skill that the stones to build the walls of Thebes were drawn into their places by his music.

32. Arion, semimythical poet to whom the creation of the dithyramb is attributed. While sailing from Italy, having amassed great wealth, Arion is thrown overboard by mutinous sailors who want his treasure. He is carried to shore by dolphins charmed by the song he was allowed to sing before being thrown into the sea.

33. This line appears in *Davideis,* bk. 2, line 124, Abraham Cowley's (1618–67) four-book epic fragment published in 1656. Based on the life of the young David before he became king of Judah, the text explores the intense friendship between David and Jonathan, the eldest son of Saul.

All resolutely good and gently kind;
Wou'd have his Power commanded by his Friend,
His Gifts receiv'd, all other Joys transcend: 10
To keep one Joy he strait commences Thief,
Niggard[34] in nothing but dispensing Grief.
The Friend traduc'd,[35] his Care rubs off the Stain,
Uses all Efforts to protect his Fame:
His self he but esteems his second Part,
The Friend has strongest Int'rest in his Heart:
If great Necessity require he shou'd,
Wou'd heal his Wounds with Balsam[36] of his Blood.
If such strong Faith this Title must attend,
Where find we one deserv'dly call'd a Friend?   20
'Tis difficult, indeed, to find one true,
But for pretended ones they're not a few,
Will strongly claim under a false Pretence,
Whilst dear Self-Interest governs ev'ry Sense.
From Motives vile, some gracious Acts proceed,
And we, mistaken, judge them by the Deed;
Make by these guileful Means their Int'rest strong,
And give them Pow'r the Innocent to wrong.

(1747)

Essay on Friendship
Mary Leapor

To *Artemisia*.[37]—'Tis to her we sing,
For her once more we touch the sounding String.
'Tis not to *Cythera*'s[38] Reign nor *Cupid*'s Fires,
But sacred Friendship that our Muse inspires.

34. Miserly.
35. Defamed.
36. Soothing healing agent.
37. Bridget Freemantle (1698–1779), Leapor's friend and patron. The daughter of a clergyman, Freemantle took an avid interest in Leapor. She proposed the subscription edition of her poems, wrote the brief biography of Leapor that appeared in the second volume, and supported her poetic efforts. The name Artemisia alludes to Artemis, the virgin goddess of the hunt, which, as Donna Landry suggests, points toward a "both militant, if not amazonian, singleness and the cult of unfettered female friendship." *The Muses of Resistance: Labouring-Class Women's Poetry in Britain, 1739–1796* (Cambridge: Cambridge University Press, 1990), 94.
38. Venus, the goddess of love.

A Theme that suits *Æmilia*'s pleasing Tongue:
So to the Fair Ones I devote my Song.

The Wise will seldom credit all they hear,
Tho' saucy Wits shou'd tell them with a Sneer,
That Womens Friendships, like a certain Fly,
Are hatch'd i'th Morning and at Ev'ning die.[39]
'Tis true, our Sex has been from early Time
A constant Topick for Satirick Rhyme:
Nor without Reason——since we're often found,
Or lost in Passion, or in Pleasures drown'd:
And the fierce Winds that bid the Ocean roll,
Are less inconstant than a Woman's Soul:
Yet some there are who keep the mod'rate Way,
Can think an Hour, and be calm a Day:
Who ne'er were known to start into a Flame,
Turn Pale or tremble at a losing Game.
Run *Chloe*'s Shape or *Delia*'s Features down,
Or change Complexion at *Celinda*'s Gown:
But still serene, compassionate and kind,
Walk through Life's Circuit with an equal Mind.

Of all Companions I would choose to shun
Such, whose blunt Truths are like a bursting Gun,
Who in a Breath count all your Follies o'er,
And close their Lectures with a mirthful Roar:
But Reason here will prove the safest Guide,
Extremes are dang'rous plac'd on either Side.
A Friend too soft will hardly prove sincere;
The Wit's inconstant, and the Learn'd severe.

Good-Breeding, Wit, and Learning, all conspire
To charm Mankind and make the World admire:
Yet in a Friend but serve an under Part,
The main Ingredient is an honest Heart:
By this can *Urs'la* all our Souls subdue
Which wanting, this, not *Sylvia*'s Charms, can do.

---

39. Leapor is referring to the mayfly, which usually lives less than twenty-four hours.

Now let the Muse (who takes no Courtier's Fee) ⎫
Point to her Friend——and future Ages see   ⎬   40
(If this shall live 'till future Ages be)   ⎭
One Line devoted to *Fidelia's*[40] Praise,
The lov'd Companion of my early Days:
Whouse harmless Thoughts are sprightly as her Eyes,
By Nature chearful, and by Nature wise.

To have them last, the social Laws decree;
We choose our Friendships in the same degree:
What mighty Pleasure, if we might presume,
To strut with Freedom in *Arvida's* Room,
Or share the Table what supreme Delight?   50
With some proud Dutchess or a scornful Knight,
To sit with formal and assenting Face?
For who shall dare to contradict her Grace?

Our free-born Nature hates to be confin'd,
Where State and Power check the speaking Mind;
Where heavy Pomp and sullen Form withholds
That chearful Ease and Sympathy of Souls.

But yet the Soul whate'er its Partner do,
Must lift its Head above the baser Crew.
Celestial Friendship with its nicer Rules,   60
Frequents not Dunghills nor the Clubs of Fools.
It asks, to make this Union soft and long,
A Mind susceptible, and Judgment strong;
And then a Taste: But let that Taste be giv'n
By mighty Nature and the Stamp of Heav'n:
Possest of these, the justly temper'd Flame
Will glow incessant, and be still the same:
Not mov'd by Sorrow, Sickness, or by Age
To sullen Coldness or distemper'd Rage.
The Soul unstain'd with Envy or with Pride,   70
Pleas'd with itself and all the World beside,
Unmov'd can see gilt Chariots whirling by,
Or view the wretched with a melting Eye,

40. A childhood friend whom Leapor met at Weston Hall, the first home in which she worked upon entering domestic service.

Discern a Failing and forgive it too:
Such, *Artemisia,* we may find in you.

    Be seldom sour, or your Friends will fly
From the hung Forehead and the scornful Eye:
Nor, like *Aurelia,*[41] in the Morning kind,
And soft as Summer or the western Wind:
But round ere night her giddy Passions wheel,
She'll clap the Door against your parting Heel.
An even Temper will be sure to please,
With cool Reflexion and a chearful Ease.

    But see *Armida's* unfrequented Rooms,
How vainly spread with Carpets and Perfumes:
All shun her like the Cocatrice's Beams,[42]
And for no other Reason but her loath'd Extremes.
To-day more holy than a cloister'd Nun,
Almost an Atheist by to-morrow's Sun:
Now speaks to Heaven with a lifted Eye:
Now to her Footman, You're a Rogue, and lye.
O say, from what strange Principles begin
These odd Compounds of Piety and Sin?
A sickly Fair may some Excuses find,
(What grieves the Body will affect the Mind)
But not the Creatures who have learn'd to screen
Their own Ill-nature in the name of Spleen.
What the black Mists afflict the aking Skull,
The Spirits tremble and the Heart be dull:
Have you from thence a Licence to offend,
Affront a Patron or abuse a Friend?
And ape[43] the Manners of a surly Beast,
Because 'tis cloudy and the Wind's i'th' East?

    But all have Failings, not the best are free,
Or in a greater or a less Degree.
What follows then?—Forgive, or unforgiven

80

90

100

---

41. Chrysalis or pupa of an insect, especially of a butterfly.
42. Serpent or reptile, said to be hatched by a serpent from a cock's egg and to kill by its mere glance.
43. Imitate.

Expect no Passage at the Gate of Heav'n.
Kind Nature gave, in Pity to Mankind,
This social Virtue to the human Mind:
This gives our Pleasures a more easy Flow,   110
And helps to blunt the Edge of smarting Woe:
The Soul's Relief, with Grief or Cares opprest,
Is to disclose them to a faithful Breast;
And then how lovely in a Friend appear,
The mournful Sigh and sympathizing Tear.
When changing Fortune with propitious Ray,
Gilds the brown Ev'ning or the smiling Day;
The pleas'd Companion shares the welcome Tide,
And wrap'd in Joy the happy Minutes glide.

Grave Authors differ—Men of Sense incline   120
This Way or that—Opinions rarely join:
Their Thoughts will vary. Why? Because they're free,
But most in this and only this agree;
That our chief Task is seldom to offend,
And Life's great Blessing a well-chosen Friend.

(1748)

To Miss Clayton. Occasion'd by her breaking an appointment to visit the Author

Mary Jones

Now ponder well, Miss CLAYTON[44] dear,
    And read your Bible book;
Lest you one day should rue the time
    That you your promise broke.

'Twas on that bed where you have lain
    Full many a restless night,
That you did say, nay swear it too——
    But you've forgot it quite.

44. Charlotte Clayton was Jones's longtime friend and the subject of many of her poems. She became Lady Sundon in 1735 and was a member of Queen Caroline's household.

Your tender mother eke[45] also,
     Did ratify the same;
10 And stroked me o'er the face, and vow'd—
     Much more than I will name.

But what are women's oaths, and vows,
     With which we make such pother?[46]
Ah, trust us not, ye faithful swains!
     Who cannot trust each other.

The swain may vow eternal love,
     And yet that vow revoke;
For lovers vows alas! are made
20   On purpose to be broke.

The courtier breaks his word, 'tis true,
     Or keeps it but in part;
But you, whene'er you break your word,
     Perhaps may break a heart.

The chemist[47] says he'll turn to gold
     Each thing he lights upon;
And so he will, whene'er he finds
     The philosophic stone.

The lawyer says he'll get your cause,
30   Then loses cause, and cost;
But there's a maxim in the law,
     Says, *Fees must not be lost.*

Allegiance firm to gracious King
     Swear parsons one and all:
Pity! Christ's vicars, or of *Bray*,[48]
     Should ever swear at all.

45. Added.
46. Turmoil, bustle.
47. During this time chemistry and alchemy were closely aligned terms and pursuits.
48. Thomas Bray (d. 1730) was a Church of England clergyman who published a series of lectures and devotional manuals designed to aid in the regular catechizing of children.

Physicians too can promise fair,
   In figures and in tropes——
Then let your faith and fees be great,
   And while there's life, there's hopes.   40

But when all confidence is lost,
   Small comfort hopes afford;
For whom hereafter can I trust,
   Now *You* have broke your Word?

(1750)

I shall keep your Correspondence as Misers do their Gold
Mary Masters

A shining Treasure from the World conceal'd,
A Treasure only to my self reveal'd:
Like them, I too shall frequently retire,
Count my rich Store, and secretly admire;
They GEORGE's Image in his Coin approve,[49]
Thy pictur'd Mind I in thy Letters love.
But here, indeed, we something disagree,
'Tis Money pleases them, and Paper me.

(1755)

On Friendship
Mary Masters

FRIENDSHIP is *Love* from all its Dross[50] refin'd
The chaste Enjoyment of th' immortal Mind:
A Passion warm, benevolent, sincere,
'Tis such as Angels do to Angels bear.
Unmix'd with wanton Thoughts and loose Desires,
The purer Flame to nobler Heights aspires;

---

49. An image of King George II would have appeared on any coin minted in the kingdom during his reign (1727–60).

50. Impure or foreign matter that detracts from the purity of a substance.

To ease the Bosom that is deep distress'd,
And raise the Transport of the joyful Breast;
This Gift Divine the Pow'r supreme bestows,
10   To aid our joys and dissipate our Woes:
To make the chearful Hours of Life more gay,
And drive the melancholy Shades away.

(1755)

To [*Miss Lynch*]. April the 9th
Elizabeth Carter

Still may this Morn with fairest Lustre rise,
And find thee still more happy and more wise:
The smiling Year with some new Pleasure crown;
And add some Virtue to the past unknown;
E'en that, whose future Progress shall deface
The transient Pride of each external Grace,
Survey the Soul more beauteous, young, and gay,
And chearful to the latest natal Day,
Which gilds the Ruins of declining Age,
10   And lights it safely to it's farthest Stage.
    Where Roses blush, and soft-wing'd Zephyrs play,
Thro' *Pleasure*'s walks if *Youth* unbounded stray,
Enjoy each Product of the vernal Hour,
Seize ev'ry Green, and rifle ev'ry Flow'r;
Tho' with each smiling Hue the Garland bloom,
And Fortune add her variegated Plume,
How soon, alas! the gay fantastic Wreath
Must wither on the pallid Brow of *Death!*
It's languid Sweets in mournful Dust be laid,
20   And all it's unreviving Colours fade!
    Thus the false Forms of Vanity descend,
And in the Gloom of long Oblivion end:
Unreal Fantoms, empty, void of Pow'r,
Borne on the fleeting Pinions of an Hour!
Desert in Death the disappointed Mind,
Nor leave a Trace of Happiness behind!
    O blest with Talents fitted to obtain
What wild unthinking Folly seeks in vain,

To whom, peculiarly indulgent, Heav'n
The noblest Means of Happiness has giv'n,   30
From Joys unfixt, that in Possession die
From *Falshood*'s Path my dear *Narcissa* fly.
See Faith with steady Light direct the Road
That leads unerring to the sov'reign *Good*:
See Virtue's Hand immortal Joys bestow,
That ever new in fair Succession blow,
Nor dread, secure of undecaying Bloom,
The ineffectual Winter of the Tomb.
    Such sure Rewards the happy Choice attend
Form'd on our Nature's Origin and End.   40
Pure from th' eternal Source of Being came
That Ray divine that lights the human Frame:
Yet oft, forgetful of it's heav'nly Birth,
It sinks obscur'd beneath the Weight of Earth:
Mechanic[51] Pow'rs retard it's Flight, and hence
The Storms of *Passion,* and the Clouds of *Sense:*
'Tis Life's great Task their Influence to controul,
And keep the native Splendor of the Soul:
From false Desires which wild *Opinion* frames,
From raging *Folly*'s inconsistent Schemes,   50
To guard it safe by those unerring Laws
That re-unite it to its first Great Cause.
    To this bright Mark may all thy Actions tend,
And Heav'n succeed the Wishes of a Friend,
Whose faithful Love directs its tender Cares
Beyond the Flight of momentary Years:
Beyond the Grave, where vulgar Passions end,
To future Worlds it's nobler Views extend,
Which soon each Imperfection must remove,
And ev'ry Charm of Friendship shall improve.   60
'Till then, the Muse essays[52] the tuneful Art,
To fix her moral Lesson on thy Heart,
Illume thy Soul with Virtue's brightest Flame,
And point it to that Heav'n from whence it came.

(1762)

51. Coarse.
52. Attempts.

Sonnet, To Mrs. Bates[53]

Helen Maria Williams

Oh, thou whose melody the heart obeys,
Thou who can'st all its subject passions move,
Whose notes to heav'n the list'ning soul can raise,
Can thrill with pity, or can melt with love!
Happy! whom nature lent this native charm;
Whose melting tones can shed with magic power,
A sweeter pleasure o'er the social hour,
The breast to softness sooth, to virtue warm——
But yet more happy! that thy life as clear
From discord, as thy perfect cadence flows;
That tun'd to sympathy, thy faithful tear,
In mild accordance falls for others woes;
That all the tender, pure affections bind
In chains of harmony, thy willing mind!

10

(1786)

Sonnet XXVIII: To Friendship

Charlotte Smith

Oh thou! whose name too often is profan'd!
    Whose charms, celestial! few have hearts to feel!
Unknown to folly—and by pride disdain'd;
    —To thy soft solace may my sorrows steal!
Like the fair Moon, thy mild and genuine ray,
    Thro' life's long evening shall unclouded last;
While the frail summer-friendship fleets away,
    As fades the rainbow from the northern blast.
'Tis thine, oh Nymph! with[54] 'balmy hands to bind'[55]
    The wounds inflicted in misfortunes storm,
        And blunt severe afflictions sharpest dart.

10

53. Sarah Bates (c. 1755–1811), a successful concert singer whose chief success was in sacred music.
    54. Collins. *Smith*. [William Collins (1721–59), poet known for his odes. His poems of sensibility captured his mid-century poetic generation. *Eds.*]
    55. Collins's *Ode to Pity*, line 2, reads, "With balmy Hands his Wounds to bind."

—'Tis thy pure spirit warms my Anna's[56] mind!
  Beams thro' the pensive softness of her form,
    And holds its altar——on her spotless heart.

(1786)

An Epistle
Elizabeth Hands

My dear Maria,[57] my long absent friend,
If you can spare one moment to attend,
The plaintive strains of your Belinda hear,
Who is your friend, and as yourself sincere.
Let love-sick nymphs their faithful shepherds prove,
Maria's friendship's more to me than love;
When you were here, I smil'd throughout the day,
No rustic shepherdess was half so gay;
But now, alas! I can no pleasure know,
The tedious hours of absence move so slow;   10
I secret mourn, not daring to complain,
Still seeking for relief, but seek in vain.

   When I walk forth to take the morning air,
I quickly to some rising hill repair,
From whence I may survey your village spire,
Then sigh to you, and languish with desire.

   At sultry noon retiring to the groves,
In search of you, my wand'ring fancy roves,
From shade to shade, pleas'd with the vain delight,
Imagination brings you to my sight;   20
Fatigu'd I sink into my painted chair,
And your ideal form attends me there.

---

56. Anna Augusta was the eighth of Smith's twelve children and her favorite.
57. A Miss Maria Bird, of Coleshill, is listed among the subscribers to Hands's edition. Coleshill is about fifteen miles from Rowington, in Warwickshire, where Hands was raised.

My garden claims one solitary hour,
When sober ev'ning closes ev'ry flow'r;
The drooping lily my resemblance bears,
Each pensive bloom a shining dew-drop wears;
Such shining drops my closing eyes bedew,
While I am absent from the sight of you.

When on my couch reclin'd my eyes I close,
30   The God of Sleep refuses me repose;
I 'rise half dress'd, and wander to and fro
Along my room, or to my window go:
Enraptur'd I behold the moon shine clear,
While falling waters murmur in my ear;
My thoughts to you then in a moment fly,
The moon shines misty, and my raptures die.

Thus ev'ry scene a gloomy prospect wears,
And ev'ry object prompts Belinda's tears:
'Tis you, Maria, and 'tis only you,
40   That can the wonted face of things renew:
Come to my groves; command the birds to sing,
And o'er the meadows bid fresh daisies spring:
No! rather come and chase my gloom away,
That I may sing like birds, and look like daisies gay.

(1789)

To Miranda, on Her Leaving Me
Maria Frances Cecilia Cowper

With joy, Miranda, could I pass
    The live-long day with thee;
Refreshing as the falling dews
    Thy presence is to me.

My heart, with sweet complacency,
    Attentive to thy voice,
With sympathetic ardour glows;
    I weep—and I rejoice.

How vainly Nature's liberal hand
   Thy winning form array'd!   10
Thy springing bloom, thy dawn, was veil'd
   In sorrow's gloomy shade.

Youth, beauty, song, and joy, no more
   Thy heedless hours beguil'd;
Far other hours soon follow'd those
   That had so sweetly smil'd.

I pause—I ponder and admire
   The gracious hand unseen,
That kept thee while the tempest rag'd,
   Then gave thee skies serene.   20

Thy adverse, thy mysterious fate,
   Thy labyrinth of woe,
Was all to speed the heavenly race,
   And make thy comforts grow.

Nor would'st thou now thy lot exchange
   For India's shining store:
No—all the splendour of the East,
   So won, would leave thee poor.

A pearl inestimably dear
   Within thy bosom dwells: 30
The riches of ten thousand worlds
   This precious pearl excels:

Earnest of pure, unfading bliss,
   Of life that never dies;
The bright reward on faith bestow'd,
   A portion in the skies.

(1792)

Elegy, Addressed to Mrs. Hewan[58]
Mary Whateley Darwall

Let others glory in fond fortune's smile,
  The glare of wealth, the pageantry of pow'r,—
For glitt'ring dross endure such painful toil,
  And give to pallid[59] care the midnight hour:

Let the brave hero, by ambition fir'd,
  Boast high atchievements in th'embattled field,
'Mid groves of spears, and hosts of foes untir'd,
  His gleaming sword, or deathful faulchion[60] wield;

Let the loud trumpet speak each martial deed,
10   The laurel's freshest bough his temples crown;
Gallia[61] subdu'd, his grateful country freed,
  His name invok'd by bards of fair renown:

Let the dark statesman plan his airy schemes,
  And wrap in mystic shades each deep design;
With pow'r unbounded gild his flatt'ring dreams,
  And sacrifice his peace at PLUTUS'[62] shrine:

Let the gay nymph, whom fortune's golden smile
  Allures to ev'ry elegant delight,
With festive mirth her frolic hours beguile,
20   And rove where splendor's glitt'ring scenes invite:

Be mine along the calm sequester'd vale
  Of humble life to keep my silent way,
Stranger to fame's inconstant soothing tale,
  Pour forth my unpremeditated lay.

58. Darwall identified Mrs. Hewan as a Scot with whom she had had a "short but agreeable intimacy in the year 1766." Ann Messenger, *Woman and Poet in the Eighteenth Century: The Life of Mary Whateley Darwall (1738–1825)* (New York: AMS, 1999), 81.
59. Feeble.
60. One-handed broad sword with a curved blade.
61. Gaul at the time of the Roman Empire.
62. Greek god of wealth, typically represented as blind.

When sober ev'ning draws her shadowy vest,
　　Bath'd in refreshing dews, o'er hill and plain,
When the rough sons of toil retire to rest,
　　And Philomel[63] resumes her plaintive strain;

With thee, sweet ETHELINDA, let me stray,
　　By Cynthia's[64] silv'ry light, thro' lawn and grove,　　30
Where the cool current marks its mazy way,
　　Or hold sweet converse in some green alcove.

'Tis thine, fair friend, to bless the social hour;
　　Thy breast, (the seat of virtue, peace and joy)
Can teach the Muse her lenient balm to pour,
　　And yield those pleasures that can never cloy.

(1794)

Sources

Philips: *Poems* (London, 1664), 56–59, 144–45, 189–95; Egerton: *Poems on Several Occasions, Together with a Pastoral* (London, 1703), 1–2; Finch: *Miscellany Poems, on Several Occasions* (London, 1713), 252–53; Chandler: *Miscellaneous Poems by Several Hands* (London, 1729), 328–30; Wright: *Gentleman's Magazine* 6 (December 1736): 740; Brereton: *Poems on Several Occasions* (London, 1744), 96–97; Lennox: *Poems on Several Occasions. Written by a Young Lady* (London, 1747), 11–12; Teft: *Orinthia's Miscellanies* (London, 1747), 155–56; Leapor: *Poems upon Several Occasions* (London, 1748), 74–80; Jones: *Miscellanies in Prose and Verse* (Oxford, 1750), 52–54; Masters: *Familiar Letters and Poems on Several Occasions* (London, 1755), 91–92, 123–24; Carter: *Poems on Several Occasions* (London, 1762), 18–21; Williams: *Poems*, 2 vols. (London, 1786), 1:15–16; Smith: *Elegiac Sonnets. By Charlotte Smith With Twenty Additional Sonnets*, 3rd ed. (London, [1786]), 29; Hands: *The Death of Amnon. A Poem. With An Appendix: Containing Pastorals, and other Poetical Pieces* (Coventry, 1789), 91–92; Cowper: *Original Poems, on Various Occasions. By a Lady. Revised by William Cowper, Esq.* (London, 1792), 80–81; Darwall: *Poems on Several Occasions. By Mrs. Darwall (Formerly Miss Whateley) in Two Volumes*, 2 vols. (Walsall, 1794), 2:65–68.

63. After raping Philomela, Tereus, her sister Procne's husband, cut out her tongue and hid her away. She wove a narrative of her story to alert Procne, who subsequently killed their son and served him to Tereus. When he was about to kill the sisters, Philomela turned into a nightingale. See the introduction to section 3.F for an extensive discussion of the Greek and Roman versions.

64. Goddess of the moon.

Poems of Retirement and Retreat

If, in retirement poems of the eighteenth century, men sought to claim or re-claim a *physical* space, a place for solitude and (often sorrowful) contemplation, women poetically characterized retirement as an occasion for time and *intellectual* space. In the hands of women poets, retirement poems offered an opportunity for self-fashioning, for contemplation, and for finding what Octavia Walsh describes as "my own self, from whom I long have stray'd" *(On Solitude)*. Women contributed to the development of the retirement poem, refashioning it to include the experience of women and perhaps to help women reconceive time, space, and privacy. Although, as Ann Messenger notes, "in real life, the country was not always a freely chosen refuge for a woman,"[1] in this poetic life retirement provided a desirable place of self-sufficiency, an opportunity for time in nature, and, for some, a chance to interact with female companions.

The retirement poem has its roots in Roman poetry, particularly Virgil's early *Georgics,* Horace's *Epodes,* and the *beatus ille* tradition.[2] "Happy is the man" removed to his rural retreat, distanced from political conflict and urban, commercial bustle, and thus provided with secure time for introspection and, ideally, literary production. Katherine Philips suggested the appeal of removal from political strife by inviting Ardelia to enjoy a retreat where there's "no disguise nor treachery, / Nor any deep conceal'd design; / From Bloud and Plots this place is free" (*A retir'd Friendship, to Ardelia,* 2.A). The sentiment was also captured in John Dryden's translation of Horace—"Happy the man, and happy he alone, / He who can call today his own"[3]—and remained an enduring poetic trope during the eighteenth century. Alexander Pope echoed that sentiment in *Ode on Solitude:* "Happy the man, whose wish and care / A few paternal acres bound."[4] For men, retirement presupposed choice, ownership, and a life of perfect pleasure, even when their retirement corresponded to political marginalization or diminished power.[5] Often, a man's physical location was within convenient distance of London, which provided the opportunity to move between "retirement" and "the world." By mid-century, however, men's retirement poetry was often marked by what John Sitter characterizes as an "atmosphere of melancholy gloom,"[6] in which retirement escalated to something more akin to retreat from the work of politics, commerce, and history, a gesture that was fully realized with the Romantic poets.

Such gloom is almost completely absent in women's retirement poems. While Hester Mulso Chapone delights in a "pleasing woe" (*To Solitude*), the poems generally are characterized by contentment. Indeed, Mary Whateley Darwall suggests that the meditative, contemplative state is "what Men . . . miscall / Despondence" (*The Pleasures of Contemplation*). The largest regret women express is that retirement is a periodic rather than a constant state: "For 'tis almost . . . a tedious Week, / Since here we parted" (Octavia Walsh, *On Solitude*). Far from the sexual, commercial, and social dangers of the city, with its "Complaisant Pleasures," women prefer to be among "these secure Abodes" (Sarah Fyge Egerton, *The Retreat*) or at a "safe retreat" (Anne Hunter, *Ode to Conduit Vale, Blackheath*). It is fashioned as a prelapsarian state, "the Copy of lost Paradice" (Egerton, *The Retreat*). Women's retirement poems depart from the male tradition with their focus on pleasure, the contentment of solitude, and the use of retirement as an imaginative space for emotional intimacy. For women, retirement is not leisure but "contemplative ease" (Elizabeth Hands, *On Contemplative Ease*)—meditation, musing, and "calm Reflection" (Chapone, *To Solitude*). Women seek "one thinking Hour" (Sarah Dixon, *Retirement*) in order to achieve their "highest wish, a well instructed mind" (Anna Williams, *The Happy Solitude, or the Wished Retirement*). In "safe Obscurity" (Egerton, *The Retreat*), women escape the patriarchal world that potentially limits women's poetic expression, values beauty instead of intellect, and centers too often on delusions begot by ephemeral materiality—"crowds and noise and show" (Chapone, *To Solitude*)—and "Folly, continual folly" (Williams, *The Happy Solitude, or the Wished Retirement*), which increasingly characterize eighteenth-century British culture. These poems both record and construct a respite from that world. Retirement provides liberty of thought and movement and, as Ann Messenger reminds us, a rare opportunity for "real privacy."[7] "My choicest hours are pass'd alone," writes Maria Frances Cecilia Cowper (*Apology for Retirement*). Retirement promotes creativity, mindfulness, and potentially poetic creation; it is in solitude that "the lovely sorc'ress Fancy roves" (Chapone, *To Solitude*). In solitude, "tow'ring *Fancy* takes her airy Flight / Without Restraint" (Darwall, *The Pleasures of Contemplation*). The "reverie" of Ann Finch's *Nocturnal Rêverie*, though more sensual in its focus, also captures the expansive possibilities for the unfettered mind.[8] Contemplation may include a spiritual dimension; Cowper seeks to "Let Wisdom's heavenly force impart / Divine instruction to my heart" (*Apology for Retirement*). The poem expresses concern "for men at ease" who "glide, / Unthinking, down the silver tide / Of gay prosperity."

The role of nature is also central to these poems, many of which are filled with detailed, extensive descriptions of the landscape. Elizabeth Hands savors the night skies: "Amongst these fragrant trees / I walk, the twinkling stars to view, / In solitary ease" (*On Contemplative Ease*). Lennox imagines an expansive prospect from an "airy Height," where she will "entertain the wand'ring Sight, / With flow'ry Fields, and waving Woods, / Hills and Dales, and falling Floods" (*To Mira. Inviting her to a Retreat in the Country*). Finch's poem suggests an intimate, almost medicinal knowledge of various flora and fauna on her estate: "Whence springs the *Woodbind,* and the *Bramble*-Rose, / And where the sleepy *Cowslip* shelter'd grows; / Whilst now a paler Hue the *Foxglove* takes" (*Nocturnal Rêverie*). While women may not possess the landscape legally, they inhabit the landscape and possess an intimately recorded appreciation for it. (It is important to note that the ability to seek this kind of retirement is contingent on economic and personal mobility as well as freedom from domestic labor; for example, Mary Barber's satiric poem *To a Lady, Who Invited the Author into the Country* [1.A] laments that "Citizens must stay at Home.")

Yet, retirement is not always solitary. Indeed, the "Calm, humble bliss of friendship" offers a powerful alternative "Superior to the splendid joys, / That glitter round the world" (Hands, *Friendship. An Ode,* 3.B). Poems of retirement imagine new constructions of women's relationships to the world and to each other, creating a space for emotional intimacy and expressions of private sensibility. "Come * * * * * * * *, come, and with me share / The sober Pleasures of this solemn Scene," invites Elizabeth Carter (*To [Miss Talbot]*). Lennox anticipates being "together careless laid, / Beneath a Cypress spreading Shade," reading Pope, Homer, and Plato, texts "Uncommon to our Sex and Age" (*To Mira*). Removed from the world, women can explore new intellectual territory and new personal intimacies. Contemplation, tranquility, and freedom of mind and body characterize the experiences these poets record as they break from the male retirement tradition and reconceive the form.

Notes

1. Ann Messenger, *Pastoral Tradition and the Female Talent: Studies in Augustan Poetry* (New York: AMS, 2001), 60.

2. *Beatus ille* (Happy is he) is the opening clause of Horace's Epode 2, which is contemporaneous with Virgil's *Eclogues* and the commissioning of the *Georgics* (37 BC). Horace, like Virgil in the *Georgics,* balances praise of retirement and bucolic pursuits with a keen awareness of the ways in which such praise can be falsely and strategically deployed. For a discussion of the *beatus ille* tradition, see Maren-Sofie Røstvig, *The Happy Man: Studies in the Metamorphoses of a Classical Ideal,* 2 vols. (Oslo: Akademisk Forlag; Oxford: Blackwell, 1954–58). James Grantham Turner addresses the issue of the strategic rhetorical deployment of this rhetoric in reference to seventeenth-century England in *The Politics of Landscape, 1630–1660* (Oxford: Blackwell, 1979).

3. John Dryden, *The Twenty-ninth Ode of the Third Book of Horace,* lines 65–66. This 104-line translation urged one to "leave thy business and thy care, / No mortal interest can be worth thy stay" (lines 10–11), while idealizing "the pleasures of the poor" (line 21).

4. Alexander Pope, *Ode on Solitude,* lines 1–2. Pope does focus on an intellectual component to retirement: "study and ease / Together mix'd; sweet recreation, / And innocence, which most does please, / With meditation" (lines 13–16). *The Twickenham Edition of the Poems of Alexander Pope,* ed. Norman Ault and John Butt, vol. 6, *Minor Poems* (New Haven, CT: Yale University Press, 1964), 3.

5. Messenger, *Pastoral Tradition,* 62.

6. John Sitter, *Literary Loneliness in Mid-Eighteenth-Century England* (Ithaca, NY: Cornell University Press, 1982), 85. Dustin Griffin disputes this commonly accepted conception, suggesting that men's mid-century retirement poems "implicitly conceive a political or social function for the poet" and do not exist as apolitical texts. *Patriotism and Poetry in Eighteenth-Century Britain* (Cambridge: Cambridge University Press, 2002), 4–5.

7. Messenger, *Pastoral Tradition,* 61.

8. Christopher R. Miller notes how the term *reverie* "mediates between wide-awake deliberateness and extravagant sensory drift. The word implies a stream of impressions, but Finch organizes them with a lucid syntax of wakeful observation." "Staying Out Late: Anne Finch's Poetics of Evening," *Studies in English Literature* 45 (2005): 614.

The Retreat
Sarah Fyge Egerton

Adieu to all the splendid Gallantry,
Complaisant Pleasures, modish Gaiety;
Airy Delights, imaginary Joys,
Fashions, Entertainments, Wit and Noise;
To all the Follies of my former State,
All that's Genteel, or Popular, or Great.
I'll move no longer in this gaudy Sphear,
I've been gaz'd at enough, 'tis time to disappear.
Without Concern, I'll leave the glittering Seat;
10   No, not the softest Sigh shall sound retreat,
Lest Fate should over-hear, mistrust my Flight,
Pursue me now, and so undo me quite.
In these soft Shades, I no Misfortune fear,
For she will never think to find me here;
My Joys, shall be by her no more betray'd,
I'll cheat her now, in this kind Masquerade;
While she in Noise and Crowds doth search for me
I'll lie Secure in safe Obscurity.
A silent Village doth poor Pleasures yield,
20   Or harmless Sports of the delightful Field;
Then all the pageant Glories of a Throne,
Luxurious Pleasures of the wanton Town.
Here is the Copy of lost Paradice,
The pure and spotless Quintessence of Bliss:
All the safe Pastimes Mankind can enjoy,
Which Innocence delight, but not destroy:
Here I am blest in these secure Abodes,
As once in Shades were the retiring Gods:
These silvan Joys know no surprizing Strife,
30   This is to live, whilst others spend a Life:
Here is the *Summum Bonum*[1] of the Earth,
Here the renowned Poets had their Birth;
Or hither, from the noisy World retir'd,
Here their great Souls, with noble Raptures fir'd.
Philosophers of old, in Solitude,   ⎫
Their own resisting Passions first subdu'd; ⎬
Then with good Precepts civiliz'd the Rude: ⎭

1. Highest good.

They knew a Court or City would molest
The calm Conceptions of a studious Breast.
Here the *Mantuan* Swain[2] gain'd all his Bays[3] }   40
To Solitude his unmatch'd Pen doth raise,
Disserved Trophies of immortal Praise.
How many Monarchs weary of their State,
Have quit their Glories for a mean retreat;
Thought silent Shades far happier than Thrones,
That Garlands sat much easier than Crowns.
Then why's the wond'ring World amaz'd at me,
For leaving Fraud and Infidelity?
The poor mistaken World who places Joys
In splendid Popularity and Noise,   50
When after all its Search it must conclude,
'Tis in a Friend, and well-chose Solitude.

(1703)

A Nocturnal Rêverie

Anne Finch

In such a *Night*, when every louder Wind
Is to its distant Cavern safe confin'd;
And only gentle *Zephyr*[4] fans his Wings,
And lonely *Philomel*,[5] still waking, sings;
Or from some Tree, fam'd for the *Owl's* delight,
She, hollowing clear, directs the Wand'rer right:
In such a *Night*, when passing Clouds give place,
Or thinly vail the Heav'ns mysterious Face;
When in some River, overhung with Green,

---

2. The Roman poet Virgil (70–19 BC), whose period of greatest literary production occurred during his retirement at his villas (chiefly at Campania) away from Rome. He was born at Pietole, near Mantua, a town in Lombardy, northern Italy.

3. The wreath of laurels awarded for great literary achievement; often the symbol of a poet laureate.

4. God of the west wind; a soft, gentle wind or breeze.

5. A nightingale. In the Roman legend, Philomela, sister to Procne, was forced into marriage by Procne's husband, Tereus, who tricked her into believing that Procne was dead. When she learned the truth, he cut out her tongue so that she could not speak. She instead wove a tapestry recounting the events. Upon learning of his crime against Philomela, Procne killed her son by Tereus, cooked him in a stew, and served it to Tereus. He tried to kill Philomela and Procne, but the gods turned them all into birds: Tereus a hawk, Procne a swallow, and Philomela a nightingale.

10   The waving Moon and trembling Leaves are seen;
        When freshen'd Grass now bears it self upright,
        And makes cool Banks to pleasing Rest invite,
        Whence springs the *Woodbind*,[6] and the *Bramble*-Rose,[7]
        And where the sleepy *Cowslip*[8] shelter'd grows;
        Whilst now a paler Hue the *Foxglove*[9] takes,
        Yet checquers still with Red the dusky brakes:
        When scatter'd *Glow-worms*,[10] but in Twilight fine,
        Shew trivial Beauties watch their Hour to shine;
        Whilst *Salisb'ry*[11] stands the Test of every Light,
20   In perfect Charms, and perfect Virtue bright:
        When Odours, which declin'd repelling Day,
        Thro' temp'rate Air uninterrupted stray;
        When darken'd Groves their softest Shadows wear,
        And falling Waters we distinctly hear;
        When thro' the Gloom more venerable shows
        Some ancient Fabrick,[12] awful in Repose,
        While Sunburnt Hills their swarthy Looks conceal,
        And swelling Haycocks thicken up the Vale:
        When the loos'd *Horse* now, as his Pasture leads,
30   Comes slowly grazing thro' th' adjoining Meads,
        Whose stealing Pace, and lengthen'd Shade we fear,
        Till torn up Forage in his Teeth we hear:
        When nibbling *Sheep* at large pursue their Food,
        And unmolested Kine[13] rechew the Cud;
        When *Curlews*[14] cry beneath the Village-walls,
        And to her straggling Brood the *Partridge* calls;
        Their shortliv'd Jubilee the Creatures keep,
        Which but endures, whilst Tyrant-*Man* do's sleep;
        When a sedate Content the Spirit feels,

6. Honeysuckle.

7. A wild white, trailing rose also known as the dog-rose. It blooms only in early summer.

8. A common wild plant with drooping fragrant yellow flowers found in pastures and on grassy banks that blossoms in spring.

9. A flowering plant with tall yellow, pink, white or purple clusters of flowers. The purple are most common and the source of digitalis. The common name is derived from the clusters, which resemble the fingers of gloves.

10. A luminous winged insect not unlike a firefly.

11. Anne Tufton, Countess of Salisbury.

12. Building.

13. Cows.

14. Long-beaked birds.

And no fierce Light disturbs, whilst it reveals;   40
But silent Musings urge the Mind to seek
Something, too high for Syllables to speak;
Till the free Soul to a compos'dness charm'd,
Finding the Elements of Rage disarm'd,
O'er all below a solemn Quiet grown,
Joys in th' inferiour World, and thinks it like her Own:
In such a *Night* let Me abroad remain,
Till Morning breaks, and All's confus'd again;
Our Cares, our Toils, our Clamours are renew'd,
Or Pleasures, seldom reach'd, again pursu'd.   50

(1713)

On Solitude

Octavia Walsh

I.
Welcome, ye Sylvan Shades and crystal Springs,
   Where Innocence and harmless Pleasures rest,
Welcome to me, as Victory to Kings,
   Or Life and Liberty to Slaves opprest.

II.
In this Retreat permit me now to seek
   For my own self, from whom I long have stray'd;
For 'tis almost, ye Pow'rs, a tedious Week,
   Since here we parted in this sacred Shade.

III.
I to the noisy Town have been confin'd,
   Whence Innocence all sweet Contentment flies,   10
Where most, though to their greatest Follies blind,
   Yet shun themselves as much as if they'd Eyes.

IV.
Buisy Designs, and how to gain their End,
   Take up the thinking Portion of their Time;
So they the Promontory can ascend,
   They never matter by what Steps they climb.

V.

He that's in Love with Gold, seeks how to drain
   His Neighbour's Bags, and fill his own with Pelf;[15]
A second, as ridiculously vain,
20   Tramples on others to exalt himself.

VI.

Those Fame attracts are often press'd with Fear,
   Least others Worth their Tinsel should outshine,
'Tis Policy their Credit to impair,
   That their own Dross may pass for current Coin.

VII.

Ah! miserable Fate of humane Kind!
   How much deprav'd, how fall'n from that high State
Which gracious Heav'n for them at first design'd,
    'Till the curs'd Apple[16] did our Woe create?

VIII.

Society, the greatest Bliss of Life,
30   Is now to Man become the greatest Ill;
By it at first we purchase endless Strife,
   And find our Misery increasing still.

IX.

Had our first Parents[17] Company ne'er sought,
   But, bless'd in one another, liv'd alone,
The Serpent had not our Confusion wrought,
   Nor Eve's Curiosity her Race undone.

(1734)

15. Money or riches, especially when dishonestly gained.

16. When God placed Adam in the Garden of Eden, he commanded him not to eat of the fruit of the "tree of knowledge of good and evil," commonly represented as an apple. Although Adam, in turn, warned Eve to avoid the fruit, she was curious about its power. Persuaded to try it by the Serpent, Eve ate the "curs'd Apple," which resulted in what subsequently is referred to as the fall of man, that is, the introduction of sin and the loss of innocence.

17. In the Judeo-Christian tradition, Adam and Eve were the original human couple, parents of the human race.

Retirement
Sarah Dixon

Welcome, thou silent soft Retreat;
Blessing so oft deny'd the Great!
Welcome, as Ease to Men in Pain;
Or to the Miser, sordid Gain:
Welcome! as the relenting Fair,
Is to her *Lover* in Despair.
No Wretch, who long by Tempests tost,
Survives the Fright and gains the Coast,
Where Plenty, Peace, and darling *Friends,*
And every happy Wish attends,
Can feel Delight that's more sincere
Than what my *Soul* possesses here.   10
Time is a Treasure ill bestow'd
Amongst the noisey thoughtless Crowd;
A Jewel of a Price so high,
As *Crœsus*'[18] Wealth cou'd never buy.
Great *Macedon*'s[19] extensive Soul,
Had found One World enough to rule,
If (the Fatigues of Glory o're)
He'd given himself one thinking Hour.

(1740)

To Mira. Inviting her to a Retreat in the Country
Charlotte Lennox

Now Spring returning decks the Year
With all that's lovely, all that's fair;
The Fields in lively Green array'd,
With deeper Glooms the silent Shade;
Soft descends the gentle show'rs,
And wakes to Life the springing Flow'rs;

18. The Latin form of the name of a king of Lydia (Gr., Κροῖσος) in the sixth century BC, who was famous for his riches.

19. Alexander the Great.

Hence ambrosial Sweets exhale,
And various Colours paint the Vale;
Refreshing Airs the Zephyrs[20] blow,
10   The Streams with pleasing Murmurs flow;
While nightly 'midst the silent Plain
Thy fav'rite Bird renews her Strain,
Come then, my *Mira*, come and share
My Joys, and breath a purer Air.
Together let us range the Plains,
Amongst the rustick Nymphs and Swains;[21]
In rural Dress, devoid of Care,
Give to the Winds our flowing Hair,
And round the Meadows gayly roam,
20   For Youth does sober Mirth become.
Now straining up yon airy Height,
We'll entertain the wand'ring Sight,
With flow'ry Fields, and waving Woods,
Hills and Dales, and falling Floods:
Or to relieve the searching Eyes,
See distant Spires and Temples rise.

Come now, my *Mira*, let us rove
Together thro' the mazy Grove;
Here, while with gentle Pace we walk,
30   Beguile the Time with pleasing Talk:
Here show thy melting Eloquence,
Thy sprightly Wit, thy manly Sense;
Thy virtuous Notions void of Art,
And while you charm, correct the Heart.

Or now together careless laid,
Beneath a Cypress spreading Shade,
Our Thoughts to heavenly Numbers raise,
Repeating *Pope's*[22] harmonious Lays,[23]

20. Mild or gentle westerly winds.
21. Country men, lovers.
22. Alexander Pope (1688–1744), generally acknowledged as the dominant poetic voice of early eighteenth-century England.
23. Short lyric or narrative poems intended to be sung.

Now *Homer's*[24] awful Leaves turn o'er,
Or graver History explore;   40
Or study *Plato's*[25] sacred Page,
Uncommon to our Sex and Age.

   Now, wand'ring by the Moon's pale Light,
Amidst the silent Shades of Night,
Where on the late deserted Plains
A pleasing Melancholy reigns;
Softly thro' the rustling Trees
Sobs the sweetly dying Breeze;
The Echo's catch the plaintive Sound,
And gentle Murmurs breathe around.   50
Now sing, my Friend, and let thy Strain
Recount the Arts of faithless Man:
Thy Notes, sweet *Philomel,*[26] shall join,
And mix her soft Complaints with thine.

   But raise, my *Mira,* raise thy Song,
To Friendship nobler Strains belong.
Oh sing its tender chaste Desires,
Its equal, pure, and lasting Fires!
Such as in thy Bosom burns,
Such as my fond Soul returns.   60
Friendship is but Love refin'd,
Not weakens, but exalts the Mind;
And when its sacred Power we prove,
We guess how heavenly Spirits love.

(1747)

24. Name conventionally given to the ancient Greek poet or poets who composed the *Iliad* and the *Odyssey,* the first great epic poems.

25. Plato (c. 428–c. 347 BC) was a philosopher who, along with Socrates and Aristotle, belonged to the great trio of ancient Greeks who laid the philosophical foundations of Western culture.

26. A poetic name for the nightingale in allusion to the myth of the maiden Philomela's transformation into that bird.

To [Miss Talbot]
Elizabeth Carter

Ηυιδε σιγα μευ πουτος, σιΓωυται δ'αηται.[27]

Theoc.

How sweet the Calm of this sequestr'd Shore,
    Where ebbing Waters musically roll:
And Solitude, and silent Eve restore
    The philosophic Temper of the Soul.

The sighing Gale, whose Murmurs lull to Rest
    The busy Tumult of declining Day,
To sympathetic Quiet sooths the Breast,
    And ev'ry wild Emotion dies away.

Farewell the Objects of diurnal Care,
10   Your Talk be ended with the setting Sun:
Let all be undisturb'd Vacation here,
    While o'er yon Wave ascends the peaceful Moon.

What beauteous Visions o'er the soften'd Heart,
    In this still Moment all their Charms diffuse,
Serener Joys, and brighter Hopes impart,
    And chear the Soul with more than mortal Views.

Here, faithful Mem'ry wakens all her Pow'rs,
    She bids her fair ideal Forms ascend,
And quick to ev'ry gladden'd Thought restores
20   The social Virtue, and the absent Friend.

Come * * * * * * * *, come, and with me share
    The sober Pleasures of this solemn Scene,
While no rude Tempest clouds the ruffled Air,
    But all, like thee, is smiling and serene.

Come, while the cool, the solitary Hours
    Each foolish Care, and giddy Wish controul,

---

27. "Look there, the sea is still, still are the winds." Theocritus (c. 300–260 BC), *Idyll 2*, line 38. Translated by Gerald V. Lalonde in an e-mail to the editors, 18 April 2008.

With all thy soft Persuasion's wonted Pow'rs,
　　Beyond the Stars transport my listening Soul.

Oft, when on Earth detain'd by empty Show,
　　Thy Voice has taught the Trifler how to rise;　　　　　30
Taught her to look with Scorn on Things below,
　　And seek her better Portion in the Skies.

Come: and the sacred Eloquence repeat:
　　The World shall vanish at it's gentle Sound,
Angelic Forms shall visit this Retreat,
　　And op'ning Heav'n diffuse it's Glories round.

　　　　　　　　　　　　(1762)

The Pleasures of Contemplation
Mary Whateley Darwall

Queen of the Halcyon[28] Breast, and Heav'n-ward Eye,
Sweet *Contemplation*, with thy Ray benign
Light my lone Passage thro' this Vale of Life,
And raise the Siege of *Care!* this silent Hour
To thee is sacred, when the Star of Eve,[29]
Like *Dian*'s Virgins[30] trembling ere they bathe,
Shoots o'er th' Hesperian[31] Wave its quiv'ring Ray.
　　All Nature joins to fill my lab'ring Breast
With high Sensations: aweful Silence reigns
Above, around; the sounding Winds no more　　　　　10
Wild thro' the fluctuating Forest fly

28. Undisturbed, happy. *Halcyon* is the Greek word for the kingfisher, which lays its eggs on the surface of the sea before the winter solstice. According to myth, in the fourteen days while the eggs incubated, the sea was always completely calm.

29. The evening star was called Hesperus, but it was usually the planet Venus, which sometimes shines vividly in the west shortly after sunset.

30. Diana, a virgin goddess, was the goddess of the hunt, chastity, and the moon. One day, when she and her nymphs were bathing at a mountain stream sacred to her, they were surprised by the hunter Actaeon, who viewed Diana and her nymphs naked. In retribution, she turned him into a stag, and he was eaten by his own dogs.

31. The Greeks' name for Italy was Hesperia, "evening," because to them it was the land of the setting sun and the evening star.

With Gust impetuous; Zephyr[32] scarcely breathes
Upon the trembling Foliage; Flocks, and Herds,
Retir'd beneath the friendly Shade repose
Fan'd by *Oblivion*'s Wing. Ha! is not this,
This the dread Hour, as ancient Fables tell,
When flitting Spirits from their Prisons broke
By Moon-light glide along the dusky Vales,
The solemn Church-yard, or the dreary Grove;

20   Fond to revisit their once lov'd Abodes,
And view each friendly Scene of past Delight?

Satyrs,[33] and Fawns,[34] that in sequester'd Woods,
And deep-embow'ring Shades delight to dwell;
Quitting their Caves, where in the Reign of Day
They slept in Silence, o'er the daisi'd Green
Pursue their Gambols, and with printless Feet
Chase the fleet Shadows o'er the waving Plains.

Dryads,[35] and Naiads,[36] from each Spring and Grove,
Trip blithsome o'er the Lawns; or, near the Side

30   Of mossy Fountains, sport in *Cynthia*'s[37] Beams.

The Fairy Elves, attendant on their Queen,
With light Steps bound along the Velvet Mead,
And leave the green Impression of their Dance
In Rings mysterious to the passing Swain;
While the pellucid[38] Glow-worm kindly lends
Her silver lamp to light the festive Scene.

From yon majestic Pile,[39] in Ruin great,
Whose lofty Tow'rs once on approaching Foes

32. God of the west wind; a soft, gentle wind or breeze.

33. Woodland gods or demons, in form partly human and partly bestial, supposedly the companions of Bacchus. They are represented as lustful and fond of revelry.

34. "Fauns" are a class of woodland deities. At first represented as men with horns and the tail of a goat; afterwards with the legs of a goat, like the Satyrs, to whose lustful character theirs was compared. They were associated with Pan, who, like Actaeon, pursued Diana. Overtaking her on a riverbank, he embraced what he thought was her, only to discover that he was embracing a cluster of reeds. The sound they made when he sighed with disappointment was a musical sound Diana loved. To please her, Pan bound reeds of varying lengths together to create a reed instrument known as a syrinx.

35. A nymph that supposedly inhabited trees; the life of each nymph was associated with her own tree and ended when the tree died.

36. A freshwater nymph, distinct from sea nymphs, thought to inhabit rivers, streams, or lakes.

37. Cynthia is another name given to the goddess Diana, said to have been born on Mount Cynthus. It is a poetic name for the moon personified as a goddess.

38. Translucent.

39. Castle or tower.

Look'd stern Defiance, the sad Bird of Night[40]
In mournful Accent to the Moon complains: 40
Those Tow'rs with venerable Ivy crown'd,
And mould'ring into Ruin, yield no more
A safe Retirement to the hostile Bands;
But there the lonely Bat, that shuns the Day,
Dwells in dull Solitude; and screaming thence
Wheels the Night Raven shrill, with hideous Note
Portending Death to the dejected Swain.
    Each Plant and Flow'ret bath'd in Ev'ning Dews,
Exhale refreshing Sweets: from the smooth Lake,
On whose still Bosom sleeps the tall Tree's Shade,   50
The Moon's soft Rays reflected mildly shine.
    Now tow'ring *Fancy*[41] takes her airy Flight
Without Restraint, and leaves this Earth behind;
From Pole to Pole, from World to World, she flies;
Rocks, Seas, nor Skies, can interrupt her Course.
    Is this what Men, to Thought estrang'd, miscall
Despondence? this dull *Melancholy*'s Scene?
To trace th' Eternal Cause thro' all his Works,
Minutely and magnificently wise?
Mark the Gradations which thro' Nature's Plan   60
Join each to each, and form the vast Design?
And tho' Day's glorious Guide withdraws his Beams
Impartial, chearing other Skies and Shores;
Rich Intellect, that scorns corporeal Bands,
With more than Mid-day Radiance gilds the Scene:
The Mind, now rescu'd from the Cares of Day,
Roves unrestrain'd thro' the wide Realms of Space;
Where (Thought stupendous!) Systems infinite,
In regular Confusion taught to move,
Like Gems bespangle yon etherial Plains.   70
    Ye Sons of Pleasure, and ye Foes to Thought,
Who search for Bliss in the capacious Bowl,
And blindly woo *Intemperance* for *Joy;*
Durst ye retire, hold Converse with yourselves,
And in the silent Hours of Darkness court

---

40. Owl.

41. A creative faculty, usually treated as lighter and more whimsical and playful than imagination or as an assistant to it. Imagination, with the power to transform its material, was considered the higher power.

Kind *Contemplation* with her peaceful Train;
How wou'd the Minutes dance on downy Feet,
And unperceiv'd the Midnight Taper waste,
While intellectual Pleasure reign'd supreme!
80   Ye *Muses,*[42] *Graces,*[43] *Virtues,*[44] Heav'n-born Maids!
Who love in peaceful Solitude to dwell
With meek-ey'd *Innocence,* and radiant *Truth,*
And blushing *Modesty;* that frighted fly
The dark Intrigue, and Midnight Masquerade!
What is this Pleasure which inchants Mankind?
'Tis Noise, 'tis Toil, 'tis Frenzy, like the Cup
Of *Circe,*[45] fam'd of old, who tastes it finds
Th' etherial Spark divine to Brute transform'd.
And now, methinks, I hear the Libertine
90   With supercilious Leer, cry, "Preach no more
Your musty Morals; hence to Deserts fly,
And in the Gloom of solitary Caves
Austerely dwell: what's Life debarr'd from Joy?
Crown then the Bowl, let *Music* lend her Aid,
And *Beauty* her's, to soothe my wayward Cares."
Ah! little does he know the Nymph he styles
A Foe to Pleasure; Pleasure is not more
His aim than her's; with him she joins to blame
The Hermit's Gloom, and savage Penances;
100   Each social Joy approves. Oh! without thee,
Fair *Friendship,* Life were nothing; without thee,
The Page of Fancy wou'd no longer charm,
And Solitude disgust e'en pensive Minds.
Nought I condemn but that Excess which clouds
The mental Faculties, to soothe the Sense:
Let Reason, Truth, and Virtue, guide thy Steps,
And ev'ry Blessing Heav'n bestows be thine.

(1764)

---

42. The nine Muses, the daughters of Zeus and Mnemosyne (Memory), were goddesses who presided over and inspired literature and the arts.

43. The three sister-goddesses regarded as the bestowers of beauty and charm and portrayed as women of exquisite beauty.

44. "Abstract" female divinities common to the Greeks and Romans, including Arete (Excellence), Sophrosyne (Temperance), and Dikaiosyne (Righteousness).

45. Enchantress who dwelt on the island of Aea and transformed all who drank of her cup into swine.

The Happy Solitude, or the Wished Retirement
Anna Williams

Fatigu'd with life, I yet methinks would live,
Free'd from the pains that fraud or folly give;
Where'er I turn, where'er direct my flight,
Folly, continual folly, meets my sight;
Man, thoughtless man, to sacred reason blind,
Obeys the dictates of his restless mind,
Ambition, vengeance, avarice conspire,
With luxury's delights, and anger's fire.
One toils for opulence, and one for fame,
To leave a fortune, or to leave a name;   10
Each labours restless for mistaken bliss,
All the plain road of true contentment miss;
With reason's scorn, with dignity's disgrace,
There fools contend, to fill the highest place;
There they like vapours, when exhal'd too high,
Shine glaring meteors of this lower sky;
There for a while, all dazzling they amaze,
And fright the world with their portentous blaze;
Till, having wasted all their boasted light,
They sink unpity'd to the realms of night.   20

     FOR me, contented with an humble state,
'Twas ne'er my care, or fortune, to be great;
No pomp, no grandeur, no desire of fame,
No sordid wealth was ever yet my aim;
My highest wish, a well instructed mind,
Content with little, and to heav'n resign'd;
No passion but the noblest fill'd my breast,
And all I sought, and all I seek is rest,
Free from tumult'ous cares and busy strife,
May I enjoy the harmless sweets of life;   30
In rural shades, like the first fam'd abodes
Of happy men, oft visited by Gods,
There the remains of ling'ring life employ,
In holy solitude and silent joy,
No busy cares, should there my soul molest,
No past unkindness discompose my breast,
My still retreat, so pleasant, yet so low,

That all would envy, but that none should know;
Joy, peace, and love, with me should ever reign,
40   And true religion grace the godlike train;
There pleas'd and calm I'd look with pity down,
On those who bear th' incumb'rance of a crown.
Then, O great Arbiter of all below,
A ray of wisdom on my soul bestow,
That I may wisely Nature's works explore,
And thro' her works, may Nature's God adore;
Then with devotion fir'd I'd still address
My songs to thee, thy Providence to bless;
Thus calmly would my soul thy will await,
50   Nor wish a long, nor fear a shorter date;
But when death calls I'd meet him as a friend;
Thus would I live, and thus my life should end.

(1766)

To Solitude

Hester Mulso Chapone

Thou gentle nurse of pleasing woe!
To thee, from crowds and noise and show,
   With eager haste I fly.
Thrice welcome, friendly Solitude!
O let no busy foot intrude,
   Nor list'ning ear be nigh!

Soft, silent, melancholy maid!
With thee to yon sequester'd shade
   My pensive steps I bend;
10   Still, at the mild approach of night,
When Cynthia[46] lends her sober light,
   Do thou my walk attend!

To thee alone my conscious heart
Its tender sorrow dares impart,
   And ease my lab'ring breast;

46. The moon.

To thee I trust the rising sigh,
And bid the tear that swells mine eye
        No longer be supprest.

With thee among the haunted groves
The lovely sorc'ress Fancy[47] roves,   20
        O let me find her here!
For she can time and space controul,
And swift transport my fleeting soul
        To all it holds most dear!

Ah no!—ye vain delusions hence!
No more the hallow'd influence
        Of Solitude pervert!
Shall Fancy cheat the precious hour,
Sacred to Wisdom's awful pow'r
        And calm Reflection's part?   30

O Wisdom! from the sea-beat shore
Where, list'ning to the solemn roar,
        Thy lov'd[48] Eliza strays,
Vouchsafe to visit my retreat,
And teach my erring, trembling feet
        Thy heav'n-protected ways!

Oh guide me to the humble cell
Where Resignation loves to dwell,
        Contentment's bow'r in view.
Nor pining Grief with Absence drear,   40
Nor sick Suspense, nor anxious Fear,
        Shall there my steps pursue.

There let my soul to *him* aspire
Whom none e'er sought with vain desire,
        Nor lov'd in sad despair!
There, to his gracious will divine

---

47. A creative faculty, usually treated as lighter and more whimsical and playful than imagination or as an assistant to it. Imagination, with the power to transform its material, was considered the higher power.

48. Mrs. Elizabeth Carter, a lady well known to the literary world, author of a beautiful Ode to Wisdom. *Chapone.*

My dearest, fondest hope resign,
　And all my tend'rest care!

Then Peace shall heal this wounded breast,
50　That pants to see another blest,
　From selfish passion pure;
Peace, which when human wishes rise
Intense, for aught beneath the skies,
　Can never be secure.

(1775)

On Contemplative Ease
Elizabeth Hands

Rejoice ye jovial sons of mirth,
　By sparkling wine inspir'd;
A joy of more intrinsic worth
　I feel, while thus retir'd.

Excluded from the ranting crew,
　Amongst these fragrant trees
I walk, the twinkling stars to view,
　In solitary ease.

Half wrap'd in clouds, the half-form'd moon
10　Beams forth a cheering ray,
Surpassing all the pride of noon,
　Or charms of early day.

The birds are hush'd, and not a breeze
　Disturbs the pendant leaves;
My passion's hush'd as calm as these,
　No sigh my bosom heaves.

While great ones make a splendid show,
　In equipage or dress,
I'm happy here, nor wish below
20　For greater happiness.

(1789)

Apology for Retirement
Maria Frances Cecilia Cowper

I have no leisure to bestow
Where nought but sin and folly grow.
The world's society unknown,
My choicest hours are pass'd alone:—
Alone indeed I cannot be,
If God vouchsafe to dwell with me.
   Think not, my friend, I censure those
Whom Providence hath wisely chose
To shine in more conspicuous light,
As stars that gild the darksome night;   10
Such, whose high worth their deeds proclaim,
And fix them in the ranks of fame:
These to the world are blessings given,
The bounty of all-bounteous Heaven.
But I—whom no distinctions charm,
Whose breast no public praise can warm;
Who from life's gayer scenes retir'd,
Taste pleasures more to be desir'd
Than wealth, or power, or honours give—
Must live unknown, or cease to live.   20
Oh happy hours that once I knew,
Ere yet I bade thy shades adieu.
My native haunt!—yet here I find
Content, that sunshine of the mind;
Her influence my bosom fills,
Soother of life's ten thousand ills.
   Come then, Retirement, peaceful guest;
And Love, true harbinger of rest;
That "Love divine all loves excelling;"[49]
Illuminate my humble dwelling.   30
Every choicest blessing bring
From Piety's exhaustless spring:
For some delightful theme explore

---

49. Title of a 1747 hymn by Charles Wesley (1707–88), Church of England clergyman, a founder of the denomination now known as Methodist, and long regarded as the greatest English hymn writer. He was certainly one of the most prolific.

All Contemplation's richest store.
Let Wisdom's heavenly force impart
Divine instruction to my heart;
The salutary use explain
Of trials, cares, affliction, pain;
How needful each to erring Man,
40   Too ignorant himself to scan,
Too blind his interest to discern,
Too proud the ways of Heaven to learn;
In self-conceit supremely wise,
He scorns the wisdom of the skies,
Dotes on the toys of time and sense,
Nor looks beyond what those dispense.
    Tremble, my soul, for men at ease,
Whose painted bark no ruffling breeze
Impedes; but rapidly they glide,
50   Unthinking, down the silver tide
Of gay prosperity; nor know
Of other Heaven than that below.

(1792)

On Returning to Lehena, in May, MDCCLXXXVIII
Catherine Rebecca Manners

Welcome once more, my native land![50]
    What joy to breathe the perfum'd gale,
Which, as immers'd in thought I stand,
    Salutes me from the hawthorn vale![51]

O Solitude! of mind serene,
    Parent of Innocence and Peace,
Preside for ever o'er this scene,
    Nor let this grateful silence cease!

I've left the gayer paths of life,
10   Where Reason ne'er could Pleasure find,

---

50. Manners was the third daughter of Thomas Gray, of Lehena, County Cork, Ireland.
51. A valley with hawthorn, a thorny shrub used extensively to form hedges.

Where ever restless, busy Strife
    Leaves look'd-for Happiness behind.

There Flattery o'er my youthful cheek
    Has spread a momentary glow;
There Vanity has made me seek
    The gilded roofs of hidden Woe.

There have I seen neglected Worth,
    Abash'd, decline her honest head,
While Vice in gaudy robes came forth,
    By Pride and Adulation led.   20

There Envy steeps the poison'd dart,
    To strike at Merit's open breast;
There smooth, insinuating Art
    Deceives the wisest and the best.

The Nobles, who were wont to raise
    To Liberty a spotless shrine,
To Av'rice now devote their days,
    For her unhallow'd garlands twine.

The gentle Virgin, who of yore
    Thought Worth and Happiness the same,   30
Contemns what she rever'd before,
    And Truth she calls an empty name.

The Beauty, whom relentless Time
    Has robb'd of every boasted grace,
Retains the follies of her prime,
    And decks with borrow'd bloom her face.

But say, amid such scenes as these,
    Can I still hope my mind was free?
Say, in this more than Cretan maze,[52]
    Was I devoted still to thee?   40

52. According to Greek mythology, Daedalus built for King Minos on the island of Crete the maze, or labyrinth, in which the Minotaur, the half-human, half-bull creature, lived. Every year, as a forced tribute, the Athenians randomly selected seven young men and seven young women to be placed in the maze with the inevitable fate of being devoured by the Minotaur.

Did ne'er Ambition swell my breast,
　　Or sparkle in my dazzled eye?
Did ne'er offended Pride molest
　　My hours, or prompt the heaving sigh?

Yes: I have felt their baneful power,
　　Have own'd their universal sway,
Was tempted in one thoughtless hour
　　Their shameful dictates to obey.

But Reason rais'd my fainting soul,
50　　Ere I the magic draught could sip;
Ere I had touch'd the Syren's bowl,[53]
　　She turn'd it from my eager lip.

"Amoret,"[54] she cried, "for ever leave
　　This scene where Vice and Folly reign;
The time you've lost in crowds retrieve,
　　Nor hope for bliss but on the plain."

With this kind counsel I complied,
　　No longer worldly splendour prize;
Nor shall I build my nobler pride
60　　But on becoming good and wise.

Accept then, Solitude, my prayer,
　　A wearied wanderer receive;
Strengthen'd by thee, I will prepare
　　By spotless virtue for the grave.

(1793)

53. In classical mythology, the sirens, part woman, part bird, were creatures who supposedly lured sailors to destruction by their enchanting singing. *Siren* has also come to mean anything that charms, allures, or deceives as did the Sirens.

54. A female character in Spenser's *Faerie Queene* (1590–96) whose complicated narrative is the source of much scholarly debate. Raised by Venus in the Garden of Adonis with her companion Pleasure, Amoret is often read as Spenser's allegorical representation of the married state of love, yet she endures a series of abductions and subsequent rescues that complicate a simply allegorical reading. Here, Manners would seem to allude to Amoret's escape from what Dorothy Stephens characterizes as "lustful coercion in the House of Busyrane." Stephens, "Into Other Arms: Amoret's Evasion," *ELH* 58, no. 3 (1991): 525.

Ode to Conduit Vale, Blackheath[55]

Anne Hunter

Dear tranquil shades, where freedom reigns,
　　Where calm content has fix'd her seat,
Lost to the world, its joys, its pains,
　　With thee I find a safe retreat;
The shafts of scorn or envy fail,
Alike, to reach my peaceful vale.

'Tis here with friendship's soothing smile
　　The gentle charities appear,
With converse sweet the hours beguile,
　　And steal away the frowning year;　　　　　　　　　10
To you, ye kind affections hail!
Most welcome to my peaceful vale.

Though torn from those delightful ties
　　Which hold the heart to life and light,
Remembrance still the loss supplies,
　　And fancy gives them to my sight;
Her dear delusive powers prevail,
And oft they bless my peaceful vale.

The treasur'd heaps of ancient lore,
　　The page where modern genius plays,　　　　　　　20
For me shall spread their boundless store,
　　And fill with varying thought my days;
Perhaps the muse by twilight pale
May deign to seek my peaceful vale.

---

55. Blackheath is located six miles east of London and adjacent to Greenwich Park, where the Royal Hospital for Seamen (now known as the Old Royal Naval College) opened in 1706. The park had several natural sources of water, which were "filtered by gravels in the Blackheath Beds." John Bold, *Greenwich: An Architectural History of the Royal Hospital for Seamen and the Queen's House* (New Haven, CT: Yale University Press, 2000), 15. To harness this water supply, a series of conduits and conduit houses, or "heads," were built throughout the park "to ensure both water purity and safety from poisoning" (16). The conduit system, significantly rebuilt between 1707 and 1713, was "simple and picturesquely varied," forming "a delightful, Romantic complement to the blend of Baroque formality and natural irregularity which characterized the park" (18). The upper part of the Hyde Vale Conduit was known as Conduit Vale until 1896.

> Thus far from pride of wealth and show,
>   Thus far from poverty and care,
> I walk unseen, nor wish to know
>   A joy the heart disdains to share;
> Let others spread the vent'rous sail,
30   I quit no more my peaceful vale.

(1802)

Sources

Egerton: *Poems on Several Occasions, Together with a Pastoral* (London, 1703), 31–33; Finch: *Miscellany Poems, on Several Occasions* (London, 1713), 291–93; Walsh: Simon Patrick *A Collection of Select Original Poems and Translations, chiefly on divine subjects* (London, 1734), 105–7; Dixon: *Poems on Several Occasions* (Canterbury, 1740), 143–44; Lennox: *Poems on Several Occasions. Written by a Young Lady* (London, 1747), 67–71; Carter: *Poems on Several Occasions* (London, 1762), 70–71; Darwall: *Original Poems on Several Occasions. By Miss Whateley* (London, 1764), 72–77; Williams: *Miscellanies in Prose and Verse* (London, 1766), 71–73; Chapone: *Miscellanies in Prose and Verse* (London, 1775), 146–49; Hands: *The Death of Amnon. A Poem. With An Appendix: Containing Pastorals, and other Poetical Pieces* (Coventry, 1789), 100; Cowper: *Original Poems, on Various Occasions. By a Lady. Revised by William Cowper, Esq.* (London, 1792), 46–48; Manners: *Poems by Lady Manners* (London, 1793), 85–88; Hunter: *Poems* (London, 1802), 16–17.

⁓|C|⁓

Love Poems

Love is certainly one of the oldest traditional subjects in poetry. Classical lyric poetry by Catullus and Sappho, the early modern sonnet with its tradition of courtly love, and the poems of the Cavalier poets all construct cultural expectations for the language, experience, and expression of love. Although typically written from a specific (more frequently male) poetic persona, such love poems are often (mis)read as highly personal, intimate, and at times confessional. The love poetry represented in this section simultaneously resides within and defies the cultural and literary expectations for a love poem. Some of the initial poems representing love as an emotion use imagery that might just as comfortably be found in poems of male contemporaries; the poetic forms used, such as the sonnet, are as familiar as the theme. Yet, as a whole the poems in this section explore failed love and married love from a specifically feminine perspective, and they examine manifestations of love that are unique to women, such as maternal love and Sapphic love. These poems revise not only the idea that women traditionally have been primarily the recipients of love poems but also the idea that love poems reside only within a romantic relationship between a man and a woman.

The opening poems represent general attitudes toward "mighty Love" (Martha Fowke Sansom, *To My Soul's Adoration*) and construct it as a higher power, the "best of Human Joys" (Anne Finch, *A Song*); "The Poets never found a nobler Theme" than love, "Nor Beauty cannot wear a brighter Gem" (Elizabeth Teft, *On Love*). The love poems to children appropriate the language of romantic love and modify it to this context's purpose. Thus Jane Wiseman Holt imagines her six-year old friend as her "Cupid" and "charming Valentine" (*To Mr. Wren my Valentine Six Year Old*), while Maria Frances Cecilia Cowper insists, in language that echoes Petrarchan imagery, that her sleeping infant's charms do not compare to the "rosebud" or the "jocund sunbeam" (*On Viewing her Sleeping Infant*). Jane Cave Winscom, who also has a poem in section 2.L, "Poems on Motherhood," here expresses her maternal love with her wish for her infant son's wisdom, benevolence, and modesty. For her, his appropriate behavior in a love relationship, acting with "reason," "courage," and "honor," will be a tribute to her love. Charlotte Smith, using the Elizabethan sonnet form, writes a poem of love to her late beloved daughter, Anna Augusta, of whom she has no portrait. The poem becomes an expression of the "form adored" which, with grief, "enshrines thy image in thy Mother's heart" (*Sonnet XCI: Reflections on Some Drawings of Plants*); now that image is all she has. This sonnet is allusive of Shakespeare's *Sonnet XXIV,* which similarly meditates on the "true image pictured" that "lies . . . in my bosom's shop" (6–7).

Katherine Philips's poem in the subsection "Married Love" draws from a similar strain of imagery, claiming that "in my Breast thy Picture drawn shall be, / . . . / And none shal know, though they imploy their wit, / Which is the right *Antenor,* thou, or it" (*LIV. To my dearest Antenor*). Many of the poems on married love, all written at a moment of separation, allude to a visual image of the absent partner. A similar gesture informs Anna Sawyer's *Lines, Written on seeing my Husband's Picture, Painted When He was Young* (2.K) which describes both the physical portrait, and the image of her husband "For ever on my soul engrav'd / . . . / I need not thee, though painted shade, / To tell me what my Love has been." Laetitia Pilkington's poem, published in her *Memoirs,* details how she passes the time, then concludes with praise of her husband's portrait sent to her by their (then) friend James Worsdale. Finch urges her husband to leave his worldly pursuits and "rural joys persue" with her in *An Invitation to Dafnis.* The poem's refrain, "Come, and the pleasures of the feilds, survey, / And throo' the groves, with your Ardelia stray," echoes the refrain of Robert Herrick's *Corinna's Going a-Maying* ("Come, my Corinna, come, let's go a-Maying") and the masculine imagery of the *carpe diem* poems of the Cavalier poets and refigures it as a model for marital love. In the same spirit, Anna Laetitia Barbauld, fashioning herself "empress," invites her husband to "Fancy's sunny bowers" where they will "add new feathers to the wings of Time, / And make him smoothly haste away: / We'll use him as our slave." These women in a sense domesticate imagery that previously has been used in poems of seduction.

Equally striking, however, are the poems that explore love between two women or those that caution against entering into the love relationship. The poems of same-sex love are more intense, emotional, and intimate than any others in this section. They capture a physicality absent in the others. Behn's *'Twas there, I saw my Rival take* voyeuristically describes the experience of a woman watching her female lover with her male rival: "While his ravish'd Neck she twin'd / And to his Kisses, Kisses join'd." Similarly, Behn's better-known *To the fair Clarinda, who made Love to me, imagin'd more than Woman* explores androgynous constructions: "Thou beauteous Wonder of a different kind, / Soft *Cloris* with the dear *Alexis* join'd." The love is intense, and the emotion manifests itself physically. Elizabeth Carter describes a "throbbing Heart" (*To [Miss Lynch]*), and Ann Yearsley writes of "My breath," which "in shorten'd pauses fly; / I tremble, languish, burn and die" (*Song*). Unlike marital absence, which here prompts playful poems, separation as described in the poems on same-sex love is wrenching, filled with "tedious Hours" in which the solitary lover "Still feels thy Absence equally severe, / Nor tastes without thee a Delight sincere" (Carter, *To [Miss Lynch]*). Anna Seward's poems to Honora Sneyd reconfigure recognized poems in a male literary tradition, reclaiming them for her own expressions and purpose. The opening lines of *Sonnet IV. To Honora Sneyd, Whose Health Was Always Best in Winter* ("the youthful, gay, capricious Spring, / Piercing her showery clouds …") echo the opening lines of Chaucer's *Canterbury Tales* ("Whan that Aprill with his shoures soote / The droghte of March hath perced to the roote"). She too is claiming her literary control over a new (feminine) vernacular, demonstrating a complexity of form and thought, and chronicling a renewal in her relationship. Similarly, *Elegy Written at the Sea-Side, and Addressed to Miss Honora Sneyd* alludes both to Shakespeare's *Sonnet LV* ("Not marble nor the gilded monuments / Of princes shall outlive this powerful rhyme") and to Horace's *Ode III—"Exegi monumentum aere perennius."* Using these immediately recognizable literary antecedents adds power to the poetic expression and offers to immortalize the relationship. The cautionary poems warn of the perils of "hopeless Love" (Charlotte Lennox, *A Song*). Behn does so from the perspective of the empowered partner who, as the poem's title characterizes, *A thousand Martyrs I have made*: "I thus at random rove / Despise the Fools that whine for Love." Lady Mary Wortley Montagu and Lennox describe, in Montagu's words, "the Pains that jealous Fondness brings" (*On the Death of Mrs. Bowes*, I.A).

These poems offer a rich range of representations of women's experiences in love relationships—as mothers, lovers, wives, or wary observers. They amply demonstrate the imaginative range of women's expression of these intense emotions and also complicate the easy classification of love poetry as exclusively about a romantic heterosexual relationship. Women use strains of imagery and form from previous poems of love and make them their own.

GENERAL

A Song
Anne Finch

Love, thou art best of Human Joys,
　　Our chiefest Happiness below;
All other Pleasures are but Toys,[1]
Musick without Thee is but Noise,
　　And Beauty but an empty Show.

Heav'n, who knew best what Man wou'd move,
　　And raise his Thoughts above the Brute;
Said, Let him Be, and let him Love;
That must alone his Soul improve,
10　　　　Howe'er Philosophers dispute.

(1713)

On Love
Elizabeth Teft

Of all the Graces that adorn the Mind,
If I may give my Thoughts, LOVE's most refin'd.
Thou Crown of Virtue's high-born Quality,
None but great Souls are capable of thee;
This soft Perfection, active Excellence,
Gives Force to Wit, and brightens native Sense.
She from the Mind weeds all pernicious Vice, ⎫
Drains out the Follies, which obstructs the Rise ⎬
Of growing Virtue in her Paradise. ⎭
10　　She's in her Nature all Divinity,
Nor tinctur'd[2] with gross Sensuality;
Visits the deep Recesses of the Soul,
Meekness supports, Pride feels, her Fears controul,

---

1. Amorous sports; foolish or idle fancies.
2. Tinged or tainted.

Exiles that Passion which usurps her Name,
Brands her with Scorn, with Penury, and Shame.
The vicious servile Soul she can't endure,
So fair a Guest must have her Dwelling pure;
Can stand the Test of hot Temptation's Flames,
Comes forth refin'd, and all her Weight retains;
True Sorrow oft attends her shining Ring,   20
But friendly Innocence takes out her Sting.
Which done, let all her Admonitions prize,
She mends the Soul, and makes the Suff'rer wise:
A Love like this is justify'd from Blame,
Suppose the Object's worthy of the Flame;
This Love, the Love of Libertines excell,[3]
If possible, as much as Heav'n does Hell.
The Poets never found a nobler Theme,
Nor Beauty cannot wear a brighter Gem.

(1747)

To My Soul's Adoration

Martha Fowke Sansom

Every Blessing Heaven can give,
With my lovely Lover live!
Fortune, as my Heart, be kind
To thy noble thinking Mind!
Fortune, to thy Genius bend, ⎱
All thy great Designs attend; ⎰
Love already is thy Friend. ⎰
In thy charming Face he shines,
In thy Soul-commanding Lines,
On thy Love-inspiring Tongue   10
Are a Train of *Cupids* hung;
Every Word conveys a Dart,
Through the Ear, into the Heart;
Every Feature gives Desire,
Every Breath blows up the Fire,

3. Surpass.

Every Motion charms the Sight;
Oh! thou Heav'n of all Delight.
From all coarse Alloy[4] refin'd,
Thy Body is a perfect Mind
20   Ev'ry bright, transparent Vein,
Surely does a Soul contain;
Mine, at least, is there I'm sure,
From the Transports I endure.
Wonder not if every Part,
My Lips, my Eyes, and heaving Heart,
To thy dear Breast with Transport strain,
To take their Spirit back again.
All my Frame trembles with Delight,
And thy Charms swim before my Sight.
30   Sweet Extacy[5] from Earth calcin'd,[6]
Oh! heav'nly Transport of the Mind,
Then dull Mortality retires,
Mean Interest, and low Desires,
They all to mighty Love resign,
And leave my burning Wishes thine.
How little and how low appears
All my past Hopes, and mortal Fears,
To the new Heaven that I possess,
In thy exalted Tenderness!
40   And by those lovely Arms embrac'd,
I'm far above all Troubles plac'd.
Malice and Envy trembling stand,
Kept distant by thy noble Hand.
All Things grow sacred you protect,
And shining by your Passion deck'd,
Your Passion can a lasting Passport[7] give
To future Times, and make your Favourites live.

(1752)

---

4. Mixture of metals of varying values.

5. An exalted state of feeling that engrosses the mind to the exclusion of thought; intense or rapturous delight.

6. Purified or refined by consuming the grosser part.

7. Release or dispatch from this world.

CHILDREN

To Mr. Wren my Valentine Six Year Old[8]
Jane Wiseman Holt

Since the good Bishop[9] left his Name,
And Men and Maids kept up his Fame,
Since Birds in honour of his Day
Married and went no more astray,
No she cou'd boast a Valentine
Lovely and Innocent as mine,
He has such a charming Face,
A Form so faultless, such a Grace,
That with some Wax or silken Strings
Fasten but on a pair of Wings,   10
Poets and Painters wou'd mistake
And him for very *Cupid* take,
Then he has Wit at will and can
Pose the Wisest Learned'st Man,
Artful as *Cooper*[10] he can plead,
And he can bow with any Reed.

Oh when e'er you'll be as good
As if you pleas'd and try'd you cou'd,
All fretful, Childish Tears give o'er

8. Mr. Wren was the son of the woman to whom Holt's volume was dedicated.

9. At least three different Saint Valentines, all of them martyrs, are mentioned in the early martyrologies under the date 14 February. The one alluded to here is the bishop of Interamna (modern Terni), who died c. AD 269. His name is linked with love because according to legend, he was the first religious personage to oversee the celebration of marriage between a pagan man and a Christian woman.

10. Spencer Cowper (1670–1728), father of the poet Judith Cowper Madan, had a career as one of the busiest and most effective counselors in the court of chancery and the House of Lords. Yet perhaps his most persuasive "pleading" came when he and three other men were prosecuted in July 1699 for murder in the mysterious death of a young Quaker woman, Sarah Stout, who had been found floating in a river in Hertford. Stout, allegedly in love with the married Cowper, appeared to have committed suicide. However, political interests (a reaction against his family's strong influence at Hertford), coupled with Quaker repudiation of suicide, resulted in a prosecution. In his defense, Cowper called a series of expert witnesses, including the famous physicians Samuel Garth and Hans Sloane, as well as the anatomist William Cowper (not related). He and the other men were acquitted, but the case generated extensive publicity, and allusions to the "Sarah Stout" case appeared in the popular press for the next fifteen years.

20   And love your Book a little more,
Cheerful and still at Dinner sit,
Renown'd for Manners as for Wit,
And softly round the Chamber creep,
When your grand Pa Pa's asleep,
Where cou'd be found a Youth so fine,
As my charming Valentine.

(1717)

On Viewing her Sleeping Infant (C[harles] C[owper]) Written at the Park, Hertfordshire,[11] in 1767

Maria Frances Cecilia Cowper

I have seen the rosebud blow,
And in the jocund[12] sunbeam glow,
Sportive lambs on airy mound,
Skipping o'er the velvet ground;
And the sprightly-footed morn,
When every hedge and every thorn
Was decked in spring's apparel gay,
All the pride of opening May:
Yet—nor rosebud early blowing,
10   In the jocund sunbeam glowing,
Nor the sportive lambs that bound
O'er the sweet enamelled ground,
Nor the sprightly-footed morn,
When brilliants[13] hang on every thorn—
These not half thy charms display:
Thou art fairer still than they,
Still more innocent, more gay!
    Mild thou art as evening showers,
Stealing on ambrosial flowers;
20   Or the silver-shining moon
Riding near her highest noon.

11. Maria Frances Cecilia Cowper, daughter of the poet Judith Cowper Madan, married William Cowper of Hertingfordbury, her first cousin. Hertingfordbury Park was the Cowper family estate.
12. Joyful, merry.
13. Dew that glistens like diamonds.

Who, to view thy peaceful form,
Heeds the winter-blowing storm?
Thy smiles the calm of heaven bestow,
And soothe the bitterest sense of woe!
As bees, that suck the honeyed store
From silvery dews, on blushing flower,
So on thy cheek's more lovely bloom
I scent the rose's quick perfume.
Thine ivory extended arms,   30
To hold the heart—what powerful charms!
   Come, soft babe! with every grace
Glowing in thy matchless face—
Come, unconscious innocence!
Every winning charm dispense—
All thy little arts—thine own—
For thou the world hast never known!
And yet thou canst, a thousand ways,
A mother's partial fondness raise!
And all her anxious soul detain   40
With many a link of pleasing chain;
Leading captive at thy will,
Following thy little fancies still.
Though nature yet thy tongue restrains,
Nor canst thou lisp thy joys or pains!
Yet every gracious meaning lies
Within the covert of thine eyes:
Wit, and the early dawn of sense,
Live in their silent eloquence.
   May every future day impart   50
New virtues to adorn thy heart;
May gracious heaven profusely shed
Its choicest blessings o'er thy head!
Blessed, and a blessing, mayst thou prove,
Till crowned with endless joys above!

(1767; 1989)

Written About a Month after the Birth of My Son

Jane Cave Winscom

O Thomas, I hope you'll become
　　My only, my dear little boy;
A hopeful and dutiful son,
　　And fill your glad parents with joy.

When reason and knowledge shall dawn,
　　Then may I with pleasure espy,
By the rays that appear in the morn,
　　That the noon will produce a bright sky.

May kind Heaven protract my short span,
10　　Till I deeply impress on thy mind,
Thy duty to GOD, and to man,
　　With sentiments just and refin'd.

I'll bid thee adore the Great Cause,[14]
　　Who thy joys, or thy woes can increase;
Know well and then practice his laws,
　　As the only sure passage to peace.

The Volume Celestial explore,
　　For precepts transcendent thence flow,
'Twill bid thee in principle soar,
20　　From all that's disgraceful or low.

'Twill teach to each act and design,
　　Let honor and truth be your guide,
In virtue, and properly shine,
　　And thus to excel, be your pride.

By guile, or hypocrisy, try
　　To increase nor your name, nor your chest;
And for fraud, let it never come nigh,
　　Nor stain for a moment your breast.

---

14. The original cause of the universe, or God; also called the "First Cause."

Be open, and clear as the day,
    Low art and duplicity scorn;   30
For this will a meanness betray,
    But that will your conduct adorn.

If knowledge you wish to obtain,
    Let the sun seldom find you in bed;
With vigour impregnate each vein,
    And with wisdom impregnate your head.

For e'er may my THOMAS be found,
    With the wise and the good of the age;
If with these you do not abound,
    Converse with the well written page.   40

In aught that through life you pursue,
    Which reason or prudence inspire;
Be active and vigilant too,
    And conquest succeeds your desire.

Should e'er you behold the dear maid,
    Whose charms shall dispose you to love,
Bid reason come into your aid,
    And then if you fully approve,

With courage your passion disclose,
    With honor pursue till you've won,   50
But prove not her worst of all foes,
    To leave her deceiv'd or undone.

To inferiors be gentle and kind,
    Benevolent too if you can;
To equals the free unconfin'd,
    Obliging disintr'ested man.

To all whom dame Fortune shall place,
    In stations above my dear boy,
Due deference shew with a grace,
    That declares there's no guilt to annoy.   60

With modest becoming respect,
    While integrity sits on your brow;
All cringing and fawning reject,
    As dastardly sordid and low.

Act thus, and you're equal to Kings,
    In the noblest part, the interior,
And those who want emptier things,
    Deserve not the name of superior.

Thus with a countenance clear as the sun,
70   And a heart and a conduct the same,
Let your progress in life be begun,
    And conclude with as noble a flame.

(1789)

Sonnet XCI: Reflections on Some Drawings of Plants[15]
Charlotte Smith

I can in groups these mimic flowers compose,
    These bells and golden eyes, embathed in dew;
Catch the soft blush that warms the early Rose,
    Or the pale Iris cloud with veins of blue;
Copy the scallop'd leaves, and downy stems,
    And bid the pencil's varied shades arrest
Spring's humid buds, and Summer's musky gems:
    But, save the portrait on my bleeding breast,
I have no semblance of that form adored,
10   That form, expressive of a soul divine,
    So early blighted; and while life is mine,
With fond regret, and ceaseless grief deplored—
    That grief, my angel! with too faithful art
    Enshrines thy image in thy Mother's heart.

(1800)

15. Smith's daughter Anna Augusta died in 1795, an event from which, Loraine Fletcher asserts, Smith "never fully recovered" and which possibly prompted this powerful representation of maternal loss. *Charlotte Smith: A Critical Biography* (New York: St. Martin's, 1998), 239.

SAME-SEX

'Twas there, I saw my Rival take
Aphra Behn

'Twas there, I saw my Rival take
Pleasures, he knew how to make;
There he took, and there was given,
All the Joys that Rival Heaven;
Kneeling at her Feet he lay,
And in transports dy'd away:
Where the faithless suffer'd too
All the amorous Youth cou'd do.

The Ardour of his fierce desire
Set his Face and Eyes on fire.   10
All their Language was the Blisses
Of Ten thousand eager Kisses.
While his ravish'd Neck she twin'd
And to his Kisses, Kisses join'd.
Till, both inflam'd, she yeilded so
She suffer'd all the Youth cou'd do.

(1688)

To the fair Clarinda, who made Love to me, imagin'd more than Woman
Aphra Behn

Fair lovely Maid, or if that Title be
Too weak, too Feminine for Nobler thee,
Permit a Name that more Approaches Truth:
And let me call thee, Lovely Charming Youth.
This last will justifie my soft complaint,
While that may serve to lessen my constraint;
And without Blushes I the Youth persue,
When so much beauteous Woman is in view.

Against thy Charms we struggle but in vain   ⎫
10   With thy deluding Form thou giv'st us pain,   ⎬
While the bright Nymph betrays us to the Swain. ⎭
In pity to our Sex sure thou wer't sent,
That we might Love, and yet be Innocent:
For sure no Crime with thee we can commit;
Or if we shou'd——thy Form excuses it.
For who, that gathers fairest Flowers believes
A Snake lies hid beneath the Fragrant Leaves.

Thou beauteous Wonder of a different kind,
Soft *Cloris* with the dear *Alexis* join'd;
20   When e'r the Manly part of thee, wou'd plead
Thou tempts us with the Image of the Maid,
While we the noblest Passions do extend
The Love to *Hermes, Aphrodite*[16] the Friend.

(1688)

A Letter to a Lady

Jane Wiseman Holt

Not drooping Age for the reviving Spring,
Nor fading Beauty for the Wedding Ring,
Benighted Travellers for the nighest Road,
Nor rural Ladies for the newest Mode,
When the Winds Rage and the rough Billows Roar,
Not you for your lov'd Father safe to Shoar,
E'er sigh'd with truer Care, wish'd with more Pain,
Than I to see your pleasing Form again,
Let Country Squires their fellow Beadles[17] view, ⎫
10   And from the Morning to the Evening Dew,   ⎬
With hungry Joy the flying Game pursue: ⎭
Let busy Citizens be blest with Trade,
And C——l with the Midnight Masquerade,

16. In Greek mythology, Hermes is the messenger to the Gods; he is also the inventor of the lyre. Aphrodite is the goddess of love.
17. Parish constables.

More Hearts soft *Amoretta*'s[18] triumphs Crown,
Than flame or blood on her embroider'd Gown:
Charm'd with himself, before the spatious Glass
Let fair *Narcissus*[19] all his Moments pass,
Admire his Cloaths how Elegant they fit,
And Spin his Wast as slender as his Wit.
Let Misers hoard the Gold they dare not use,   20
Give *Mammon*[20] every thing his Soul will choose,
Glad Health, good Wine, loud Mirth, cheap Love, long Ease,
And *Martio*[21] give a Frolick and a Chaise,
Near Beauteous *Flavia*[22] let me ever be,
Flavia alone is every Joy to me,
Blest with her Smiles I shall grow pleas'd and proud,
And envy none of all the happy Crowd.

(1717)

To [Miss Lynch]
Elizabeth Carter

While thus my Thoughts their softest Sense express,
And strive to make the tedious Hours seem less,
Say, shall these Lines the Name, I hide, impart,
And point their Author to my *Cynthia*'s Heart?
Will she, by correspondent Friendship, own

18. In Edmund Spenser's *Faerie Queene* (1590–96) Amoret was raised by Venus in the Garden of Adonis with her companion Pleasure and is often read as Spenser's allegorical representation of the married state of love. During this period, the name Amoret or Amoretta also connoted a sweetheart or an amorous girl.

19. A person characterized by extreme self-admiration or vanity. In Greek mythology, Narcissus was a beautiful youth who shunned all the maids who pursued him, including Echo. One maiden rejected by Narcissus prayed that he too would experience unrequited love. That occurred when he fell in love with his own reflection in water, met no response, pined away, and died.

20. In an abstract sense, Mammon is a false god who personifies the overwhelming desire for wealth or material pleasures. Mammon is also the name given to literary characters who embody these qualities. For example, in Ben Jonson's *The Alchemist* (1610) Mammon is a voluptuous, hedonistic knight. In Edmund Spenser's *Faerie Queene* the Cave of Mammon is a treasure house of the god of wealth.

21. Informal or literary designation for a soldier. Martio is another in the series of social "types" the poem details.

22. The name Flavia, from the Latin *flavus*, meaning "golden," is the feminine form of Flavius, the family name of the first-century Roman emperors.

A Verse the Muse directs to her alone?
　　Dear Object of a Love whose fond Excess
No studied Forms of Language can express,
How vain those Arts which vulgar Cares controul
To banish thy Remembrance from my Soul!
Which fixt and constant to it's fav'rite Theme,
In spite of Time and Distance is the same:
Still feels thy Absence equally severe,
Nor tastes without thee a Delight sincere.
　　Now cold *Aquarius* rules the frozen Sky,
And with pale Horrors strikes the chearless Eye;
Sooth'd by the melancholy Gloom I rove,
With lonely Footsteps thro' the leafless Grove;
While sullen Clouds the Face of Heav'n invest,
And, in rude Murmurs, howls the bleak *North-east:*
Ev'n here thy Image rises to my Sight,
And gilds the Shade with momentary Light:
It's magic Pow'r transforms the wintry Scene,
And gay as *Eden* blooms the faded Plain.
　　From Solitude to busy Crowds I fly,
And there each wild Amusement idly try:
Where laughing Folly sports in various Play,
And leads the Chorus of the Young and Gay.
But here the Fancy only takes a Part,
The giddy Mirth ne'er penetrates my Heart,
Which, cold, unmov'd, by all I hear or see,
Steals from the Circle to converse with thee.
　　To calm Philosophy I next retire,
And seek the Joys, her sacred Arts inspire,
Renounce the Frolics of unthinking Youth,
To court the more engaging Charms of Truth:
With *Plato*[23] soar on Contemplation's Wing,
And trace Perfection to th' eternal Spring:
Observe the vital Emanations flow,
That animate each fair Degree below:
Whence Order, Elegance, and Beauty move
Each finer Sense, that tunes the Mind to Love;
Whence all that Harmony and Fire that join,

___

23. Plato (c. 428–c. 347 BC) was a philosopher who, along with Socrates and Aristotle, laid the philosophical foundations of Western culture.

To form a Temper, and a Soul like thine.
   Thus thro' each diff'rent Track my Thoughts pursue,
Thy lov'd Idea ever meets my View,
Of ev'ry Joy, of ev'ry Wish a Part,
And rules each varying Motion of my Heart.
   May Angels guard thee with distinguish'd Care,
And ev'ry Blessing be my *Cynthia*'s share!   50
Thro' flow'ry Paths securely may she tread,
By Fortune follow'd, and by Virtue led;
While Health and Ease, in ev'ry Look express,
The Glow of Beauty, and the Calm of Peace.
Let one bright Sunshine form Life's vernal Day,
And clear and smiling be its Ev'ning Ray.
Late may she feel the softest Blast of Death,
As Roses droop beneath a Zephyr's[24] Breath.
Thus gently fading, peaceful rest in Earth,
'Till the glad Spring of Nature's second Birth: 60
Then quit the transient Winter of the Tomb
To rise and flourish in immortal Bloom.

                                     (1762)

To ———[25]

Elizabeth Carter

The Midnight Moon serenely smiles,
   O'er Nature's soft Repose;
No low'ring Cloud obscures the Sky,
   Nor ruffling Tempest blows.

Now ev'ry Passion sinks to Rest,
   The throbbing Heart lies still:
And varying Schemes of Life no more
   Distract the lab'ring Will.

In Silence hush'd, to Reason's Voice,
   Attends each mental Pow'r: 10

---

24. A soft, gentle wind or breeze. Zephyr was the god of the west wind.
25. This poem is the only one of Carter's for which the recipient has not been identified.

Come dear *Emilia,* and enjoy
    Reflexion's fav'rite Hour.

Come: while the peaceful Scene invites,
    Let's search this ample Round,
Where shall the lovely fleeting Form
    Of *Happiness* be found?

Does it amidst the frolic Mirth
    Of gay Assemblies dwell?
Or hide beneath the solemn Gloom,
20   That Shades the Hermit's Cell?

How oft the laughing Brow of Joy
    A sick'ning Heart conceals!
And thro' the Cloister's deep Recess,
    Invading Sorrow steals.

In vain thro' Beauty, Fortune, Wit,
    The Fugitive we trace:
It dwells not in the faithless Smile,
    That brightens *Clodio's*[26] Face.

Perhaps the Joy to these deny'd,
30   The Heart in Friendship finds:
Ah! dear Delusion! gay Conceit
    Of visionary Minds!

Howe'er our varying Notions rove,
    Yet all agree in one,
To place it's Being in some State,
    At Distance from our own.

---

26. Name frequently given to faithless lovers or otherwise unworthy men in texts of the period. For example, in Colley Cibber's *Love Makes a Man* (1701), Clodio is characterized as a "pert coxcomb" in the list of characters. In *The History of Jenny and Jemmy Jessamy*, Eliza Haywood describes Celandine as "like Clodio in the play": "he was gay, spirituous, had some wit, and . . . with the affectation of great good humour, made him pass for a very agreeable companion." Haywood, *Jemmy and Jenny Jessamy*, 3 vols. (London, 1753), 1:248. The name may derive from the infamously profligate Clodia, a lover of the Roman poet Catullus, who celebrated her as "Lesbia" in his poetic accounting of their disastrous, adulterous affair.

O blind to each indulgent Aim,
   Of Pow'r supremely wise,
Who fancy Happiness in ought
   The Hand of Heav'n denies!   40

Vain is alike the Joy we seek,
   And vain what we possess,
Unless harmonious Reason tunes
   The Passions into Peace.

To temper'd Wishes, just Desires
   Is Happiness confin'd,
And deaf to Folly's Call, attends
   The Music of the Mind.

(1762)

Sonnet IV. To Honora Sneyd,[27] Whose Health Was Always Best in Winter

Anna Seward

And now the youthful, gay, capricious Spring,
   Piercing her showery clouds with crystal light,
   And with their hues reflected streaking bright
   Her radiant bow, bids all her Warblers sing;
The Lark, shrill caroling on soaring wing;
   The lonely Thrush, in brake,[28] with blossoms white,
   That tunes his pipe so loud; while, from the sight
   Coy bending their dropt heads, young Cowslips[29] fling
Rich perfume o'er the fields.—It is the prime
   Of Hours that Beauty robes:—yet all they gild,   10
   Cheer, and delight in this their fragrant time,
For thy dear sake, to me less pleasure yield

---

27. Afterwards Mrs. Edgeworth. *Seward.* [Honora Sneyd was the second wife of Richard Lovell Edgeworth (1744–1817) and the stepmother of Maria Edgeworth (1768–1849), the Irish novelist, essayist, and author of didactic texts for children. *Eds.*]

28. Thicket.

29. A common wild plant with drooping fragrant yellow flowers found in pastures and on grassy banks, blossoming in spring.

Than, veil'd in sleet, and rain, and hoary rime,[30]
Dim Winter's naked hedge and plashy[31] field.

                              (May 1770; 1799)

Song
Ann Yearsley

What ails my heart when thou art nigh?
Why heaves the tender rising sigh?
          Ah, Delia, is it love?
My breath in shorten'd pauses fly;
I tremble, languish, burn and die;
              Dost thou those tremors prove?

Does thy fond bosom beat for me?
Dost thou my form in absence see,
          Still wishing to be near?
10   Does melting languor fill thy breast?
That something, which was ne'er exprest,
              Ah! tell me—if you dare.

But tho' my soul, soft, fond and kind,
Could in thy arms a refuge find,
          Secur'd from ev'ry woe;
Yet, strict to Honour's louder strains,
A last adieu alone remains,
              'Tis all the Fates bestow.

Then blame me not, if doom'd to prove
20   The endless pangs of hopeless love,
              And live by thee unblest:
My joyless hours fly fast away;
Let them fly on, I chide their stay,
              For sure 'tis Heav'n to rest.

                              (1787)

30. Frozen mist or fog.
31. Boggy or swampy.

Elegy Written at the Sea-Side, and Addressed to Miss Honora Sneyd

Anna Seward

I write, HONORA, on the sparkling sand!—
The envious waves forbid the trace to stay:
HONORA's name again adorns the strand!
Again the waters bear their prize away!

So Nature wrote her charms upon thy face,
The cheek's light bloom, the lip's envermeil'd[32] dye,
And every gay, and every witching grace,
That Youth's warm hours, and Beauty's stores supply.

But Time's stern tide, with cold Oblivion's wave,
Shall soon dissolve each fair, each fading charm;   10
E'en Nature's self, so powerful, cannot save
Her own rich gifts from this o'erwhelming harm.

Love and the Muse can boast superior power,
Indelible the letters they shall frame;
They yield to no inevitable hour,
But will on lasting tablets write thy name.[33]

(1810)

CAUTIONARY

A thousand Martyrs I have made

Aphra Behn

A thousand Martyrs I have made,
    All sacrific'd to my desire:

---

32. Roseate, ruddy.

33. These lines allude both to the first two lines of William Shakespeare's *Sonnet LV* ("Not marble nor the gilded monuments / Of princes shall outlive this powerful rhyme") and to the first line of Horace's *Ode III*—"*Exegi monumentum aere perennius*" (30), which translates, "I have built a monument more lasting than bronze."

A thousand Beauties have betray'd,
   That languish in resistless Fire.
The untam'd Heart to hand I brought,
   And fixt the wild and wandring Thought.

I never vow'd nor sigh'd in vain
   But both, thô false, were well receiv'd.
The Fair are pleas'd to give us pain,
    And what they wish is soon believ'd.
And thô I talk'd of Wounds and Smart,
   Loves Pleasures only toucht my Heart.

Alone the Glory and the Spoil
   I always Laughing bore away;
The Triumphs, without Pain or Toil,
   Without the Hell, the Heav'n of Joy.
And while I thus at random rove
   Despise the Fools that whine for Love.

(1688)

A Song

Charlotte Lennox

I.

WHAT Torments must the Virgin prove
That feels the Pangs of hopeless Love?
What endless Cares must rack the Breast
That is by sure Despair possest.

II.

When Love in tender Bosoms reigns,
With all its soft, its pleasing Pains,
Why should it be a Crime to own
The fatal Flame we cannot shun.

III.

The Soul by Nature form'd sincere,
A slavish forc'd Disguise must wear;
Lest the unthinking World reprove
The Heart that glows with generous Love.

IV.

But oh in vain the Sigh's represt,
That gently heaves the pensive Breast;
The glowing Blush, the falling Tear,
The conscious Wish, and silent Fear.

V.

Ye soft Betrayers aid my Flame,
And give my new Desires a Name:
Some Power my gentle Griefs redress,
Reveal, or make my Passion less.   20

(1747)

Epilogue to *Mary, Queen of Scots.*
Design'd to be spoken by Mrs. Oldfield[34]

Lady Mary Wortley Montagu

What cou'd luxurious woman wish for more,
To fix her joys, or to extend her pow'r?
Their ev'ry wish was in this Mary[35] seen,
Gay, witty, youthful, beauteous, and a queen!
Vain useless blessings with ill conduct join'd!
Light as the air, and fleeting as the wind.
Whatever poets write, or lovers vow,
Beauty, what poor omnipotence hast thou!
    Queen Bess[36] had wisdom, council, power, and laws;
How few espous'd a wretched beauty's cause!   10
Learn hence, ye fair, more solid charms to prize,
Contemn the idle flatt'rers of your eyes.
The brightest object shines but while 'tis new;
That influence lessens by familiar view.

---

34. Anne Oldfield (1683–1730) was one of the dominant actresses of the period. The play for which Montagu wrote this epilogue was never produced.

35. Mary Stuart, or Mary, Queen of Scots (1542–87), whose unwise marital and political actions provoked rebellion among the Scottish nobles, forcing her to flee to England, where she was eventually beheaded as a Roman Catholic threat to the English throne. In literary representations of this period, she was figured as both the "unfortunate" victim and an empowered, attractive (if doomed) woman.

36. Elizabeth I (1533–1603), often known as the "Virgin Queen," who reigned over England from 1558 to 1603. During her reign England experienced tremendous commercial and cultural growth, as well as increased international power.

Monarchs and beauties rule with equal sway,
All strive to serve, and glory to obey:
Alike unpitied when depos'd they grow,
Men mock the idol of their former vow.
  Two great examples have been shown to-day,
20 To what sure ruin passion does betray;
What long repentance to short joys is due;
When reason rules, what glory does ensue.
  If you will love, love like Eliza then;
Love for amusement, like those traytors men.
Think that the pastime of a leisure hour
She favour'd oft—but never shar'd her pow'r.
The traveller by desert wolves pursu'd,
If by his art the savage foe's subdu'd,
The world will still the noble act applaud,
30 Tho' victory was gain'd by needful fraud.
  Such is, my tender sex, our helpless case;
And such the barbarous heart, hid by the begging face.
By passion fir'd, and not withheld by shame,
They cruel hunters are; we, trembling game.
Trust me, dear ladies, (for I know 'em well) ⎫
They burn to triumph, and they sigh to tell: ⎬
Cruel to them that yield, Cullies[37] to them that sell.⎭
Believe me, 'tis by far the wiser course,
Superior art should meet superior force:
40 Hear, but be faithful to your int'rest still:
Secure your hearts—then fool with who you will.

             (1748)

MARRIED LOVE

LIV. To my dearest Antenor, on his Parting[38]
Katherine Philips

Though it be just to grieve when I must part
With him that is the Guardian of my Heart;

---

37. Those who are cheated or imposed upon.
38. Antenor was Philips's poetic name for her husband.

Yet by an happy change the loss of mine
Is with advantage paid in having thine.
And I (by that dear Guest instructed) find
Absence can doe no hurt to Souls combin'd.
As we were born to love, brought to agree
By the impressions of Divine Decree:
So when united nearer we became,
It did not weaken, but increase, our Flame.   10
Unlike to those who distant joys admire,
But slight them when possest of their desire.
Each of our Souls did in its temper fit,
And in the other's Mould so fashion'd it,
That now our Inclinations both are grown,
Like to our Interests and Persons, one;
And Souls whom such an Union fortifies,
Passion can ne're destroy, nor Fate surprize.
Now as in Watches, though we do not know
When the Hand moves, we find it still doth go: 20
So I, by secret Sympathy inclin'd,
Will absent meet, and understand thy mind;
And thou at thy return shalt find thy Heart
Still safe, with all the love thou didst impart.
For though that treasure I have ne're deserv'd,
It shall with strong Religion be preserv'd.
And besides this thou shalt in me survey
Thy self reflected while thou art away.
For what some forward Arts do undertake,
The Images of absent Friends to make,   30
And represent their actions in a Glass,
Friendship it self can onely bring to pass,
That Magick which both Fate and Time beguiles,[39]
And in a moment runs a thousand miles.
So in my Breast thy Picture drawn shall be,
My Guide, Life, Object, Friend and Destiny:
And none shal know, though they imploy their wit,
Which is the right *Antenor*, thou, or it.

(1664)

---

39. "Seventeenth-century 'cunning-men,' wizards and sorcerers used mirrors as a means of divi-
nation," notes Patrick Thomas, "though most commonly their purpose in doing so was to catch
thieves." *The Collected Works of Katherine Philips, "The Matchless Orinda,"* ed. Patrick Thomas, 3 vols.
(Stump Cross, UK: Stump Cross Books, 1990–93), 1:359.

An Invitation to Dafnis
Anne Finch

To leave his study and usual Employments,—
   Mathematicks Paintings, etc. and to take the
   Pleasures of the feilds with Ardelia[40]

When such a day, blesst the Arcadian[41] plaine,
Warm without Sun, and shady without rain,
Fann'd by an air, that scarsly bent the flowers,
Or wav'd the woodbines,[42] on the summer bowers,
The Nymphs disorder'd beauty cou'd not fear,
Nor ruffling winds uncurl'd the Shepheards hair,
On the fresh grasse, they trod their measures light,
And a long Evening made, from noon, to night.
Come then my Dafnis, from those cares descend
Which better may the winter season spend.
   Come, and the pleasures of the feilds, survey,
   And throo' the groves, with your Ardelia stray.

Reading the softest Poetry, refuse,
To veiw the subjects of each rural muse;
Nor lett the busy compasses go round,
When faery Cercles better mark the ground.
Rich Colours on the Vellum cease to lay,
When ev'ry lawne much nobler can display,
When on the daz'ling poppy may be seen
A glowing red, exceeding your carmine;[43]
And for the blew that o're the Sea is borne,
A brighter rises in our standing corn.
   Come then, my Dafnis, and the feilds survey,
   And throo' the groves, with your Ardelia stray.

Come, and lett Sansons[44] World, no more engage,
Altho' he gives a Kingdom in a page;

10

20

40. Dafnis was Finch's poetic name for her husband, and Ardelia was her name for herself.
41. Ideally rural; the terms comes from Sir Philip Sidney's *The Arcadia* (1581), a prose romance with poems and pastoral eclogues recounting life in Arcadia.
42. A climbing vine, a kind of honeysuckle.
43. A beautiful red or crimson.
44. Nicolas Sanson (1600–1667) was a French cartographer; Finch wants her husband to leave the world of maps.

O're all the Universe his lines may goe,
And not a clime, like temp'rate brittan show,
    Come then, my Dafnis, and her feilds survey,
    And throo' the groves, with your Ardelia stray.   30

Nor plead that you're immur'd, and cannot yield,
That mighty Bastions[45] keep you from the feild,
Think not tho' lodg'd in Mons, or in Namur,[46]
You're from my dangerous attacks secure.
No, Louis shall his falling Conquests fear,
When by succeeding Courriers he shall hear
Appollo, and the Muses, are drawn down,
To storm each fort, and take in ev'ry Town.
Vauban,[47] the Orphean Lyre, to mind shall call,
That drew the stones to the old Theban Wall,[48]   40
And make no doubt, if itt against him play,
They, from his works, will fly as fast away,
Which to prevent, he shall to peace persuade,
Of strong, confederate Syllables, affraid.
    Come then, my Dafnis, and the fields survey,
    And throo' the Groves, with your Ardelia stray.

Come, and attend, how as we walk along,
Each chearfull bird, shall treat us with a song,
Nott such as Fopps[49] compose, where witt, nor art,
Nor plainer Nature, ever bear a part;   50
The Cristall springs, shall murmure as we passe,
But not like Courtiers, sinking to disgrace;
Nor, shall the louder Rivers, in their fall,
Like unpaid Saylers, or hoarse Pleaders[50] brawle;
But all shall form a concert to delight,
And all to peace, and all to love envite.

45. Forts.

46. Mons and Namur were two Belgium towns taken by Louis XIV's armies in 1691 and 1692, respectively.

47. Sebastien Le Prestre, Seigneur de Vauban (1633–1707), was a marshal of France and the foremost military engineer of his age, famed for his skill in both designing fortifications and breaking through them. He also advised Louis XIV on how to consolidate France's borders in order to make them more defensible.

48. Thebes was a Greek city ultimately razed by Alexander the Great.

49. A fop is a foolish person, a pretender to wisdom, wit, or accomplishments.

50. Persons who plead in a law court; advocates.

Come then, my Dafnis, and the feilds survey,
And throo' the Groves, with your Ardelia stray.

As Baucis and Philemon spent their lives,[51]
60   Of husbands he, the happyest she, of wives,
When throo' the painted meads, their way they sought,
Harmlesse in act, and unperplext in thought,
Lett us my Dafnis, rural joys persue,
And Courts, or Camps, not ev'n in fancy view.
    So, lett us throo' the Groves, my Dafnis stray,
    And so, the pleasures of the feilds, survey.

(before 1689; 1903)

These Lines, dear Partner of my Life
Laetitia Pilkington

These Lines, dear Partner of my Life,[52]
Come from a tender faithful Wife;
Happy when you her Thoughts approve,
Supremely happy in your Love:
O may the blissful Flame endure!
Uninjur'd, lasting, bright, and pure.
Thus far in Verse, but can the Muse
Descend so low as telling News?
Or can I easily in Rhime
10   Inform you how I pass my Time?

    To sooth my Woe and banish Care,
I to the Theatre repair,
Where charm'd with *Shakespear's* lofty Scenes,
And pure inimitable Strains,
My Rapture rais'd so high appears,
It seeks to hide itself in Tears.

51. In Greek mythology, Baucis and Philemon, a long-married couple in Phrygia, were the only ones in their town to welcome the disguised gods Zeus and Hermes. When the gods destroyed the rest of the inhospitable town, Baucis and Philemon's cottage was turned into a temple. They were granted their wish: to care for the temple and to die simultaneously.

52. In 1725 Pilkington had married Matthew Pilkington (1701–74), from whom she had had a very acrimonious divorce in 1737.

On *Tuesday* last all Day I stray'd
In *Delville's* sweet inspiring Shade;[53]
There all was easy, gay, polite,
The Weather and the Guests were bright: 20
My lov'd *Constantia*[54] there appear'd,
And *Southern*[55] long for Wit rever'd,
Who like the hoary *Pylian* Sage,[56]
Excels in Wisdom, as in Age.
'Tis thus your Absence I beguile,
And try to make Misfortune smile;
But never can my constant Mind
A real Pleasure hope or find,
Till Heav'n indulgently once more
My *Colin*[57] to my Eyes restore.   30

P.S.
Permit me here e'er I conclude
To pay a Debt of Gratitude;
To *Worsdale*,[58] your ingenious Friend,
My Praises, and my Thanks commend;
Yet all are far beneath his Due,
Who sends me[59] what resembles you.

(1748)

---

53. Dr. Patrick Delany, a member of Swift's circle, in which the Pilkingtons circulated until their divorce, spent a great deal of money improving his house and garden at Delville, just north of Dublin. Matthew Pilkington also wrote a poem about Delville.

54. Constantia Grierson (170$\frac{4}{5}$–1732) was an Irish poet, classical scholar, and editor who had been Pilkington's friend since childhood. With her husband, the publisher George Grierson (c. 1680–1753), she compiled a series of accessible editions of Latin classics. Grierson was highly regarded by Dublin's literary elite, including Jonathan Swift, for her gifts as an editor and poet.

55. Thomas Southerne (1660–1746), an Irish playwright who had a successful forty-four-year career in London. His most successful plays were adaptations of three of Aphra Behn's novels.

56. Name conventionally given to the ancient Greek poet or poets known as Homer, who composed the *Iliad* and the *Odyssey*.

57. Conventional name for a rustic. Colin Clout is the major character in Edmund Spenser's *Shepheardes Calendar* (1579) and a rustic character in John Gay's *Shepherd's Week* (1714).

58. James Worsdale (c. 1692–1767), a portrait painter and rake.

59. My Husband's Picture. *Pilkington.*

Verses from a Lady[60] at Bath,
dying with a Consumption, to her Husband
[Elizabeth Welwood Molesworth]

Thou! who dost all my worldly thoughts imploy.
Thou pleasing source of all my worldly joy!
Thou tend'rest husband! and thou truest friend!
To thee this fond, this last, adieu I send.
Since that all-conqu'ring death asserts his right,
And will for ever veil me from thy sight;
He woos me to him with a chearful grace,
And not one terror clouds his meagre face;
At length the joys of heav'n he sets in view,
10   And shows me that no other joys are true;
He promises a lasting rest from pain,
And shows me that life's flitting joys are vain.
But love, fond love, would yet resist his pow'r,
Would yet a while defer the parting hour;
He brings thy mournful image to my eyes,
And would obstruct my journey to the skies.
But say, thou dearest, thou unwearied friend!
Say, shouldst thou grieve to see my sorrows end?
Thou know'st a painful pilgrimage I've past,
20   And shouldst thou mourn that death is come at last?
Rather rejoice to see me shake off life,
And die, as I have liv'd, thy ever faithful wife.

(1750)

---

60. *Daughter to* Dr Wellwood, *and wife to Capt.* Molesworth. *Gentleman's Magazine.* [This poem has been attributed to Mary Monck, daughter of Robert, Viscount Molesworth, since it was published in *Poems by Eminent Ladies,* ed. George Colman and Bonnell Thornton, 2 vols. (London, 1755). It is not included in the posthumously collected poems of Mary Molesworth Monck (*Marinda* [1716]). Mary Monck's husband was a colonel, and her marriage was so unhappy that she was estranged and then separated from him. This previously unidentified first publication of the poem was discovered in 2005 by Suzanne Previte, then a graduate student at Auburn University. She argues in a forthcoming essay that the author was most probably Elizabeth Welwood Molesworth, who married Captain Walter "Watty" Molesworth, the fifth son of Viscount Robert Molesworth, a brother to Mary, and a veteran of the War of Spanish Succession. According to Henrietta Howard, Elizabeth's friend, the wedding between Elizabeth and Watty was a "stolen" love match. To his great grief, she died of consumption in 1725, and a few of his agonized letters survive. The poem appeared in the *Gentleman's Magazine* in September 1750, perhaps sent by Walter, who did not die until 1773, and was reprinted in *Poems by Eminent Ladies,* attributed to Mary Monck. Thus, the error began. *Eds.*]

To Mr. Barbauld,
November, 14, 1778
Anna Laetitia Barbauld

Come, clear thy studious looks awhile,
  'T is arrant treason now
  To wear that moping brow,.
When I, thy empress, bid thee smile.

  What though the fading year
  One wreath will not afford
  To grace the poet's hair,
  Or deck the festal board;[61]

A thousand pretty ways we'll find
To mock old Winter's starving reign;   10
We'll bid the violets spring again,
Bid rich poetic roses blow,
Peeping above his heaps of snow;
We'll dress his withered cheeks in flowers,
  And on his smooth bald head
  Fantastic garlands bind:
  Garlands, which we will get
From the gay blooms of that immortal year,
  Above the turning seasons set,
Where young ideas shoot in Fancy's sunny bowers.   20

  A thousand pleasant arts we'll have
To add new feathers to the wings of Time,
  And make him smoothly haste away:
    We'll use him as our slave,
  And when we please we'll bid him stay,
And clip his wings, and make him stop to view
  Our studies, and our follies too;
How sweet our follies are, how high our fancies climb.

  We'll little care what others do,
  And where they go, and what they say;   30

---

61. Feast's table.

Our bliss, all inward and our own,
Would only tarnished be, by being shown.
The talking restless world shall see,
Spite of the world we'll happy be;
But none shall know
How much we're so,
Save only Love, and we.

(14 November 1778; 1825)

Sources

General. Finch: *Miscellany Poems, on Several Occasions* (London, 1713), 270; Teft: *Orinthia's Miscellanies* (London, 1747), 52–53; Sansom: *Clio: Or, a Secret History of the Life and Amours of the Late Celebrated Mrs. S——n——m* (London, 1752), 169–71.

   Children. Holt: *A Fairy Tale Inscrib'd, to the Honourable Mrs. W—— With Other Poems* (London, 1717), 28–30; Cowper: *Eighteenth-Century Women Poets: An Oxford Anthology,* ed. Roger Lonsdale (Oxford: Clarendon, 1989), 270–71; Winscom: *Poems on Various Subjects, Entertaining, Elegiac, and Religious,* 2nd ed. (Shrewsbury, 1789), 182–87; Smith: *Elegiac Sonnets, and Other Poems,* 2 vols., 2nd ed. (London, 1800), 2:32.

   Same-Sex. Behn: *Lycidus, or the Lover of Fashion* (London, 1688), 15, 175–76; Holt: *A Fairy Tale Inscrib'd, to the Honourable Mrs. W—— With Other Poems* (London, 1717), 26–28; Carter: *Poems on Several Occasions* (London, 1762), 12–15, 65–67; Seward: *Original Sonnets on Various Subjects; and Odes Paraphrased from Horace,* 2nd ed. (London, 1799), 6; Yearsley: *Poems on Various Subjects* (London, 1787), 29–30; Seward: *The Poetical Works of Anna Seward,* ed. Walter Scott, 3 vols. (Edinburgh, 1810), 1:82–83.

   Cautionary. Behn: *Lycidus, or the Lover of Fashion* (London, 1688), 9–10; Lennox: *Poems on Several Occasions. Written by a Young Lady* (London, 1747), 35–36; Montagu: *A Collection of Poems in Three Volumes. By Several Hands,* ed. Robert Dodsley, 3 vols. (London, 1748), 3:310–11.

   Married Love. Philips: *Poems* (London, 1664), 155–57; Finch: *The Poems of Anne Countess of Winchilsea,* ed. Myra Reynolds (Chicago: University of Chicago Press, 1903), 28–30; Pilkington: *The Memoirs of Mrs. Lætitia Pilkington,* 2 vols. (Dublin, 1748), 1:103–4; [Molesworth]: *Gentleman's Magazine* 20 (September 1750): 424; Barbauld: *The Works of Anna Lætitia Barbauld. With a Memoir by Lucy Aikin,* 2 vols. (London, 1825), 1:134–36.

✣D✣

Religious Poetry

Considering the high-level critical attention that seventeenth-century religious verse has received and the amount of time devoted to it in college classrooms, the neglect of eighteenth-century religious poetry is astonishing. That it was written between that of John Milton and of William Blake might lead us to believe that we should take it more seriously and admit that it is a major type of eighteenth-century poetry. The forms that poets loved and wrote well, such as the pastoral and the ode, are found in abundance in religious poetry, as are the full range of popular kinds, such as the fable and paraphrase exercises.[1] Admittedly, it is sometimes hard to draw a firm line between religious and secular poetry, but we have selected for this section poems that are entirely on religious themes and subjects. In a time when many people felt that they were in a personal relationship with God, religious poetry can be expected to express every human emotion and record reactions to specific experiences. Religion informs, inflects, and drives a large number of the poems written by women and men in the Restoration and the eighteenth century. As Kathryn King has pointed out, religion for these poets was more than "faith, spirituality, doctrine, or devotional experience"; it was "their most basic sense of identity, the 'context within which people give *meanings* to their actions and experiences, and make sense of their lives.'"[2] It is not surprising, then, that these poems are among the most imaginative in the anthology. Hannah More wrote a satiric fable; Ann Yearsley contested her culture's characterization of God with a narrative tale; and Elizabeth Singer Rowe dramatized the most erotic book in the Bible in her Canticles and invented a form, the devout soliloquy.

A reader of these poems might first be struck by how creative the women were. Anne Killigrew reveals herself as the intellectual and aesthetically committed person whom John Dryden admired in her chilling *Herodias Daughter.* Her two strong and startlingly contrasting images of John the Baptist are countered by Elizabeth Teft's clever, teasing poem *To an Atheist.* Maria Frances Cecilia Cowper turns the countless poems that condemn ambition upside down with the opening line of her *Where Has My Ambition Led Me?* Almost every couplet is an inversion of the most formulaic ideas about ambition. The poems in this section demonstrate the various uses women put to retellings of biblical stories. Hannah More's biting but amusing *The Lady and the Pye* contrasts to the dramatic, even shocking *On Jepthah's Vow*, by Ann Yearsley. Yearsley dramatizes a minor episode in the Old Testament and gives us a self-possessed young lady who announces majestically that before allowing herself to be sacrificed she will spend two months with her girlfriends, and More turns the story of Eve's temptation and fall into a fable about a homespun, fed-up husband's revenge. She also transforms a walk with her friend the bishop Porteus into a meeting with Bishop "Bloody Bonner," who was responsible for 141 executions by burning in a short period of time (*Bishop Bonner's Ghost*). An intimate of Faustus and a reader of Jonathan Swift's *Tale of a Tub*, the bishop even takes a stand on the abolition of slavery.

In these poems, women reveal their relationships with God, their understanding of what God is like, and their very personal experiences and feelings. Anna Laetitia Barbauld's *A Summer Evening's Meditation* creates a mood of contemplation and almost breathless wonder. The poem is a record of a mind in motion and beautifully balances the sublime with the kind of natural detail that Anne Finch includes in *A Nocturnal Rêverie* (2.B). These poems are indeed an important kind of life writing and a nearly untapped source of the most difficult biographical information. The identity that King says religion supplies is everywhere evident, from the joyous lyrics in Rowe's hymn to the sober reflections in Hester Mulso Chapone's *Translation of the Foregoing Sonnet*. Poems in other sections, such as Mary Chudleigh's *On the Death of my dear Daughter Eliza Maria Chudleigh* (2.N) and Charlotte Smith's *Sonnet XCI: Reflections on Some Drawings of Plants* (2.C), give the lie to the commonplace that the death of a child was so common that parents suffered less then than now. Although much is known about Chudleigh's and especially Smith's children, some of these poems are written by women about whom little is known. These poems often leave us puzzling over questions raised by, for instance, the startling ending to Jane Cave Winscom's *Written A few Hours before the Birth of a Child*.

Chudleigh writes in *On the Death of my dear Daughter* (2.N), "A lazy Virtue no Applause will gain." Some of the women's poems in this section, including Finch's *On Affl]iction*, and those collected in section 2.G, "Poems on Pain and Illness," find a kind of consolation in the belief that suffering is a road to Heaven and testing is a sign of God's love. A frequent conclusion is an expression of submission, but they are not formulaic. These poems may come with an account of the courageous facing of illness, adversity, or the pain of childbirth. The sight of a flower, an idle conversation, the reading of a chapter in the Old Testament, and especially the moments in life when human mortality is intensely encountered, such as illness, the death of a friend, or childbirth, inspired poetry. In a time when many people set aside time for devotional exercises, writing religious poetry was an enjoyable, satisfying activity. Following the period of the greatest religious poets in England, these serious women poets were writing in a high-prestige form with many important precedents. The glory of their religious poetry is the apparently infinite creativity they brought to it.

Notes

1. The most frequently written religious poems were paraphrases of passages, poetry, and stories from the Bible. Richardson's *Pamela* (1741) includes a competition between the most popular metrical translation of Psalm 137 and a paraphrase of it by Pamela. Writing and reading such paraphrases remained popular throughout the century. See Paula R. Backscheider, *Eighteenth-Century Women Poets and Their Poetry* (Baltimore: Johns Hopkins University Press, 2005), 126–37; and David Morris, *The Religious Sublime: Christian Poetry and Critical Tradition in Eighteenth-Century England* (Lexington: University of Kentucky Press, 1972), 104–14.

2. Kathryn King, *Jane Barker, Exile: A Literary Career, 1675–1725* (Oxford: Oxford University Press, 2000), 20–21.

Herodias Daughter Presenting to Her Mother
St. John's Head in a Charger,[1] Also Painted by her self[2]

Anne Killigrew

Behold, dear Mother, who was late our Fear,
Disarm'd and Harmless, I present you here;
The Tongue ty'd up, that made all *Jury*[3] quake,
And which so often did our Greatness shake;
No Terror sits upon his Awful Brow,
Where Fierceness reign'd, there Calmness triumphs now;
As Lovers use, he gazes on my Face,
With Eyes that languish, as they sued for Grace;
Wholly subdu'd by my Victorious Charms,
10   See how his Head reposes in my Arms.
Come, joyn then with me in my just Transport,
Who thus have brought the Hermite[4] to the Court.

(1686)

On Aff[l]iction[5]

Anne Finch

Wellcome, what e're my tender flesh may say,
  Welcome affliction, to my reason, still;
Though hard, and ruged[6] on that rock I lay
  A sure foundation,[7] which if rais'd with skill,
  Shall compasse Babel's aim,[8] and reach th' Almighty's hill.

---

1. John the Baptist was a prophet of priestly descent and son of Elizabeth, who was related to Mary the mother of Jesus. He withdrew to the wilderness, where he baptized multitudes of the repentant, proclaiming the forgiveness of their sins. Herodius was a wife of Herod Antipas; he had taken her away from his half-brother, to whom she was first married. John the Baptist denounced this act. In vengeance, Salome, Herodias's daughter, performed an especially pleasing dance on her mother's birthday. Antipas, pleased, promised her a favor, and she then demanded John's head on a platter. Matt. 14:1–11.

2. John Dryden's well-known poem *To the Pious Memory of the Accomplished Young Lady Mrs. Anne Killigrew* praises her as a painter as well as a poet.

3. Jewry.

4. John the Baptist; a reference to his solitary ministry in the wilderness.

5. This poem exists in two manuscripts; the copyists inadvertently omitted the *l*.

6. Torn.

7. God is frequently described as the rock for his believers and Jesus as the rock on which the church is built; this is probably a reference to the parable in Matthew 7:24–27, "a wise man, which built his house upon a rock."

8. Encompass Babel's aim, which was to build a lasting monument that would reach to Heaven.

Wellcome the rod, that does adoption shew,
 The cup,[9] whose wholsome dregs are giv'n me here;
There is a day behind, if God be true,
 When all these Clouds shall passe, & heav'n be clear,
 When those whom most they shade, shall shine most glorious there.   10

Affliction is the line; which every Saint
 Is measur'd by, his stature taken right;
So much itt shrinks, as they repine or faint,
 But if their faith and Courage stand upright,
 By that is made the Crown, and the full robe of light.

(before 1689; 1903)

Canticle II. viii, ix.[10]
Elizabeth Singer Rowe

Is it a dream? or does my ravish'd ear
The charming voice of my beloved hear?
Is it his face? or are my eager eyes
Deluded by some vision's bright disguise?
'Tis he himself! I know his lovely face,
It's heav'nly lustre, and peculiar grace.
I know the sound, 'tis his transporting voice,
My heart assures me by its rising joys.
He comes, and wing'd with all the speed of love,
His flying feet along the mountains move;   10
He comes, and leaves the panting hart behind,
His motion swift, and fleeting as the wind.
O welcome, welcome, never more to part!
I'll lodge thee now for ever in my heart;
My doubtful heart, which trembling scarce believes,
And scarce the mighty ecstasy receives.

(1739)

9. The rod and cup were symbols of rebuke, chastisement, and suffering but also signs of God's ownership of the person. Faced with the cross, Jesus prayed, "Take away this cup from me." Mark 14:36.

10. Canticles is another name for the Song of Songs in the Old Testament. Various explanations of the book exist, including that it was designed for use in marriage celebrations and that it is primarily symbolic. Jews have interpreted it as representing the love between God and Israel, and Christians as that between Christ and the church. Rowe's Canticles were paraphrases of verses in the Song of Songs; this one is of 2:8, 9.

Soliloquy XLI[11]

Elizabeth Singer Rowe

YE lagging months and years, take swifter wings,
And bring the promis'd day, when all my hopes
Shall be fulfill'd; when that resplendent face,
Which yonder folding clouds conceal, shall dawn
With everlasting smiles, smiles that inspire
Immortal life and undecaying joy.
Blest period! why art thou so long delay'd?
O stretch thy shining wings, and leave behind
The lazy minutes in their tedious course!

10   I CALL in vain; the hours must be fulfill'd,
And all their winding circles measur'd out;
In grief and wild complaints I yet must wait
The day, and tell my sorrows to the winds;
Forlorn I thro' the gloomy woods must stray,
And teach the murm'ring streams my tender theme:
The woods and streams already know my grief,
And oft are witness to the mournful tale;
While the pale moon in silent majesty
Her midnight empire holds, and all the stars
20   In solemn order on her state attend.

        THOU moon, I cry, and all ye ling'ring stars,
How long must you these tedious circles roll!
When shall the great commission'd angel stay
Your shining course, and with uplifted hand
Swear by the dread unutterable name,
That time shall be no more?

        THEN you no more shall turn the rolling year,
Nor lead the flow'ry spring, nor gently guide
The summer on with all her various store;
30   Great nature then thro' all her diff'rent works

11. Rowe invented the form "devout soliloquy" for her own devotions. Each is spoken personally to God, but they are soliloquies because she positions herself on the stage of the world. When she left them to Isaac Watts to publish, she wrote that reading the experiences of others had "improved" her and that she hoped hers would touch others. Paula R. Backscheider, *Eighteenth-Century Women Poets and Their Poetry* (Baltimore: Johns Hopkins University Press, 2005), 169.

Shall be transform'd, the earth and those gay skies
Shall be no more the same! A brighter scene
Succeeds, and paradise in all its charms
Shall be renew'd; but far the blissful state improv'd,
And fit for minds to whom the mighty maker
Shall give the glorious vision of his face,
Unveil'd and smiling with eternal love.

   O INFINITE delight! my eager soul
Springs forward to embrace the promis'd joy
And antedates its heav'n. The lightsome fields,   40
And blissful groves are open to my view,
The songs of angels and their silver lutes
Delight me, while th' Omnipotent they sing.
On all his glorious titles long they dwell,
But love, unbounded love, commands the song;
Their darling subject this, and noblest theme.
Here let my ravish'd soul for ever dwell,
Here let me gaze, nor turn one careless look
On yonder hated world, here let me drink
Full draughts of bliss, and bathe in boundless floods   50
Of life and joy, here let me still converse.

   IT cannot be! mortality returns.
Ye radiant skies, adieu! ye starry worlds,
Ye blissful scenes, and walks of paradise!
I must fulfil my day, and wait the hour
That brings eternal liberty and rest.

   YET while I sojourn in this gloomy waste,
And trace with weary steps life's doubtful road:
Permit me, ye gay realms, permit me oft
To visit you, and meditate your joys.   60
Whether my part in this great theatre
Be joyous or severe, let the fair hopes,
The charming prospect of eternal rest
Be present with my soul, mix with my joys,
And soften all my intervals of grief.

                  (1739)

To an Atheist
Elizabeth Teft

An Atheist! say you?—view this lovely Flower,
Let it convince you of Almighty Power.
What gave it this inimitable Dye?
What less with living Sweets its Form supply?
Can Art bestow such Bloom, such balmy Due?
With more than Velvet-softness dress its Hue?
You say, 'tis the mere Product of the Earth,
That it from wildy[12] Nature took its Birth.
Most true, and were her Paths but wisely trod,
Nature wou'd lead us on to Nature's God.
What form'd and what preserves this spacious Ball,[13]
This noble Structure which contains us all?
What mighty Hand did its rare Fabrick rear?
Who rules the changing Seasons of the Year?
But more, what Power animates my Blood,
What gives this Motion to the vital Flood?
By whose Command was to my Breast assign'd
This self-condemning, self-acquitting Mind?
What gives to the most secret Crime its Sting?
From whence does Shame, Remorse and Horror spring?
Who deck'd with shining Heat the glorious Sun,
And bade the raging Tides obey the Moon?
Or drest with Stars the Firmament so fine,
And set the colour'd Rainbow for a Sign?
From whence this unseen Wind's impetuous Rage,
Bears no Controul, no human Force asswage?
To me the Secret of the Frost reveal,
Whose fierce still Rage the limpid Streams congeal?
What for the Works of Nature laid the Plan,
And gave the Air its Influence over Man?
Why's Death the Good man's Joy, the Wicked's Dread?
If Being's at a Period when we're dead?
I've read of Witchcraft and unnatural Evil,
Sure Indication that there is a Devil:
Cou'd Chance invest this Fiend with Power of Ill,
Or Nature work with supernatural Skill?

12. Truly wild, completely untouched by human hands.
13. The earth.

Who gives him Power, the same his Power restrains,
Nor can he pass the Limits of his Chains.
Did not superior Force his Force repell,
Adam's whole Race must feel his Source in Hell.   40
This Fiend malignant, once a Child of Light,[14]
Midst thousand bright ones eminently bright,
Free in his Choice, and unrestrain'd his Will,
As once, he might have been cœlestial still;
In Glory rapt next to the sacred Three,
Pride plung'd him to the Gulph of Misery:
Dazled with Bliss, all Benefits forgot
He 'gainst the Source of Power form'd a Plot,
Which prov'd; abortive of Necessity
He falls, who dares to cope with Deity.   50
None else cou'd his audacious Pride correct,
Or form good Spirits, or when form'd protect.
Nature thro' Elements, Earth, Air, and Flood,
Proclaims a God, wise, powerful, and good.
My Eyes confirm this Faith in all I see,
And thro' each Object trace the Deity.
Thro' cloudy Death, a future Life I view,
My Soul forbodes the final Judgment true,
Which the tremendous Trump shall loud proclaim;
Dust then promiscuous must unite again;   60
Subpœna'd to attend the awful Bar,[15]
Behold the Judge of Judges in the Air,
Whose shining Glory melts the trembling Skies,
And Nature all in Dissolution lies;
In heav'nly Pomp and Majesty divine
The Judgment Seat with radiant Glories shine;
Amidst bright Millions which in Order stand,
To execute their mighty Lord's Command;
This Way and that all dreadful Paths explore,
Nature and Chance can then deceive no more;   70
From that Time forth, no Atheist can there be,
Nor thou, O Chance, no more a Deity.

(1747)

---

14. Teft's account of the devil is close to Milton's in *Paradise Lost.*

15. The wooden rail at which prisoners stood for arraignment, trial, or sentence. In Christian mythology, a trumpet would summon humankind to God's judgment.

A Request to the Divine Being
Mary Leapor

I.
Thou great and sacred Lord of all,
  Of Life the only Spring,
Creator of unnumber'd Worlds,
  Immensely glorious King.

II.
Whose Image shakes the stagg'ring Mind,
  Beyond Conception high;
Crown'd with Omnipotence, and veil'd
  With dark Eternity.

III.
Drive from the Confines of my Heart,
  Impenitence and Pride:
Nor let me in erroneous Paths
  With thoughtless Idiots glide.

IV.
Whate'er thy all-discerning Eye
  Sees for thy Creature fit,
I'll bless the Good, and to the Ill
  Contentedly submit.

V.
With humane[16] Pleasure let me view
  The prosp'rous and the great;
Malignant Envy let me fly
  With odious Self-conceit.

VI.
Let not Despair nor curs'd Revenge
  Be to my Bosom known;
Oh give me Tears for others Woe,
  And Patience for my own.

10

20

16. Human.

VII.
Feed me with necessary Food,
   I ask not Wealth nor Fame:
But give me Eyes to view thy Works,
   And Sense to praise thy Name.

VIII.
And when thy Wisdom thinks it fit,
   To shake my troubled Mind;   30
Preserve my Reason with my Griefs,
   And let me not repine.

IX.
May my still Days obscurely pass,
   Without Remorse or Care;
And let me for the parting Hour,
   My trembling Ghost prepare.

(1748)

Translation of the foregoing Sonnet[17]
Hester Mulso Chapone

How like a wanton lamb that careless play'd,
   The shepherd and the fold forgotten quite,
   My vagrant soul, in search of vain delight,
Many long years from her true Shepherd stray'd!

If winding stream or flow'ry vale she spied,
   Thither her youthful wishes eager led;
   But bitter were the flow'rs on which she fed,
The turbid stream no cooling draught supplied.

Thus oft beguil'd, at length her fruitless range,
   Her heedless wand'ring steps, she deeply mourns,   10
   And back to thee and to thy fold returns.
Receive her, dearest Lord! who once didst change

---

17. The preceding sonnet is titled *Sonnetto,* the Italian word meaning "a little sound or song," from which the English *sonnet* comes. It begins, "Qual agnellina dal sentiero uscita."

Heav'n's brightest mansion for a roof of straw,
To snatch her from the wolf's devouring jaw.

(1775)

LXXXIII
Longing for Public Worship[18]
Susannah Harrison

My Soul longeth, yea even fainteth for the
Courts of the Lord.—Psalm. lxxxiv. 2.

1.
My God, how restless is my Mind!
    Pensive I lie from Day to Day,
And loth to be so much confin'd,
    I sigh my lonely Hours away.

2.
'Tis for thy Courts, O Lord, I long;
    When shall I in thy House appear?
When shall I join the waiting Throng,
    And mix in humble Worship there?

3.
I'd praise thee for the meanest place,
    To stand as Waiter at thy Gate;
Could I but there behold thy Face,
    I'd think the Favor truly great.

4.
I long to tread that happy Ground,
    Where oft my Soul has richly fed;
To hear the Gospel's joyful Sound,
    To taste substantial, living Bread.

5.
There have I often left my Fears,
    When I have gone o'erwhelm'd with Grief;

10

18. Harrison was a semi-invalid who often suffered from debilitating attacks of illness. Her poem describes the pleasures of church attendance.

There have I left my Wants and Cares,
  And in returning, sung Relief.   20

6.
But now I'm left at Home to mourn,
  While in thy Courts thy Saints rejoice;
I pass my Sabbaths quite alone,
  In sad Complaints I spend my Voice.

7.
Jesus, do thou my Strength renew;
  Remove my Weakness, heal my Pain;
That I may serve and praise Thee too,
  O bring me to thy House again!

8.
O bring Thyself thy Graces near,
  And teach my Soul to wait thy Will;   30
Then shall I serve and praise Thee here,
  And own Thee just and righteous still.

(1780)

Written A few Hours before the Birth of a Child
Jane Cave Winscom

My GOD, prepare me for that hour,
  When most thy aid I want;
Uphold me by thy mighty power,
  Nor let my spirits faint.

I ask not life, I ask not ease,
  But patience to submit
To what shall best thy goodness please;
  Then come what thou seest fit.

Come pain, or agony, or death,
  If such the will divine;   10
With joy shall I give up my breath,
  If resignation's mine.

One wish to name I'd humbly dare,
 If death thy pleasure be;
O may the harmless babe I bear
 Haply expire with me.

     (1786)

On Jephthah's Vow, Taken in a Literal Sense[19]
Ann Yearsley

What sudden impulse rushes thro' the mind,
And gives that momentary wild resolve
Which seals the binding vow? Alas, poor man!
Blind to a dark futurity, yet rash
To mad extreme; why thus, with impious soul,
Throw up to Heav'n the edict of thy will;
Erase humility, and madly call
Events thy own, which may be born in woe?

 Or what sad wretch dare lift th' accusing eye
To an insulted Deity, when torn
By dire effect, recoiling Nature feels
Those horrors he with loud presumption claim'd?

 O, Jephthah! the soft bosom melts for thee;
When stung with ardour 'mid the din of war,
Thy spirit panted for the wreath of glory,
Trembling, and eager, lest her trophies crown
The brow of Ammon's King. In blind despair
Thou bargain'dst with thy God. Ah, yet retract!
In vain! the vow is breath'd, and, awful, borne
Most rapidly to Heaven! Now the deep groan
Of dying foes reverb'rate on the ear
With pleasing horror. Israel's hero feels
Fresh inspiration from his ill-tim'd faith.
Dealing each stroke with death, the thirsty plain

19. Jephthah vowed to sacrifice the first person who greeted him should God give him the victory over the Ammonites, who were attempting to drive the Israelites out of Gilead. Judg. 11. That person turned out to be his beloved daughter.

Drinks deep of Ammonitish blood: their Chiefs
Yield with reluctance to the chance of war,
And murm'ring kiss the ground. The tawny slave,
With faithful arm, supports his dying Lord,
Heedless, in grief; while whizzing thro' the air
The arrow flies, which soon shall meet his heart.   30
'Tis come! See how it revels in the flood
That carries life away. Jephthah returns
With vict'ry nodding on his gaudy plume;
While his exulting troops, with ruthless foot,
Press out the soul, yet quiv'ring on the lip
Of Ammon's sons, disfigur'd in the dust.

    Hark! babb'ling *Echo*,[20] riding on the blast,
Bears *far* the plaudit. Ammon, sunk in death,
Heeds not the sound: hush'd as the infant babe,
The Warriour slumbers in eternal rest.   40

    Now Mizpeh's native spires[21] salute the eye;
While Jephthah's bosom swells with glowing thought,
The soft parental rapture, fond embrace,
Kind gratulation,[22] smile of filial love,
All form a deep impression; quick his soul
Dissolves in pleasing imag'ry. Arriv'd!
Behold his gates are widely thrown; the song
Of joy is louder, with the clarion shrill,
The cymbal, psalter, and the fav'rite harp.

    Hence, Jephthah! turn thine eye;—yet, yet prolong   50
The hour of Fate! for lo! thy daughter comes
Rich in the sweets of Innocence: ah, turn!
Nor meet the blooming maid. Unconscious she,
With fatal haste, now rushes to thy arms.

    He droops! the soft sensation instant dies,
And awful terrors shake his inmost soul.

---

20. Nymph deprived of speech by Hera in order to stop her chatter; she could do nothing but repeat what others said. She fell in love with Narcissus, who rejected her, and in her grief wasted away
until nothing but her voice remained.
    21. A town in Gilead.
    22. Welcome.

Swift from his brow, in anguish torn, he hurls
The laurel[23] dearly won; yet, in his arms,
For one fond moment, clasps the tender maid.

60   Short transport! Recollection blasts the scene.
He holds her from him; and with looks of woe,
In which the pangs of Pity, Love, and Death,
Alternately appear. He murmurs loud
Against assiduous Duty; wildly asks,
Why *She,* the first, to welcome Jephthah home?

Alas! the question freezes; these are sounds
Stern and unusual to her list'ning ear,
Which oft had hung on accents breath'd in love.
She stands amaz'd: her sire, with sighs, exclaims,
70   "Oh, thou hast brought me low! my soul desponds,
For I have pledg'd thee to the Lord of Hosts,
A victim to my conquest and ambition;
Yes, thou must die: the registers of Heav'n
Are ope'd, nor dare I trifle with my God."

The blush in haste forsook her lovely cheek
At the too rigid sentence: yet resign'd
To all a father ow'd, or Heav'n would ask,
She meekly cry'd, "Thy will was ever mine.
An off'ring chearful on the altar laid,
80   This frame shall soon consume; my soul to God
Shall fly with speed; yet will I slowly rove
O'er yon high mountain, till the moon hath spent
Two portions of her light.[24] Ye Virgins, come!
Let your soft notes the fatal vow deplore,
Without accusing Jephthah." On she goes,
Leaving her father fix'd in speechless grief.

Bright Cynthia[25] twice had fill'd her wasted horn:
When the sad hour approach'd, she quits the hills,
And Israel's priests lead on the charming maid.

---

23. Leaves of the laurel tree were used to make a wreath for a conqueror or a poet.
24. Two lunations, or complete cycles of the moon.
25. Cynthia is another name given to the goddess Diana, said to have been born on Mount Cynthus.

The fillet, censer, frankincense, and myrrh,   90
Are all prepar'd; the altar's blaze ascends
In curling flame; while bigots dare pronounce
The sacrifice acceptable to Heaven.

Hence, dupes! nor make a Moloch[26] of your God.
Tear not your Infants from the tender breast,
Nor throw your Virgins to consuming fires.
He asks it not; and say, what boasting fool,
To great Omnipotence a debt can owe?
Or owing, can repay it? Would'st thou dare
Barter upon equality! Oh, man!   100
Thy notion of a Deity is poor,
Contracted, curb'd, within a narrow space,
Which must on finite rest. Hark! Jephthah groans!
And 'tis the groan of horror. Virgins, sigh
For the fair victim: vain the melting tear!
She's gone, while Jewish records hold the vow
To future ages, penn'd with cruel pride.

(1787)

Bishop Bonner's Ghost[27]
Hannah More

The Argument

In the gardens of the palace at Fulham[28] is a dark recess; at the end of this
stands a chair which once belonged to bishop Bonner.[29] - - - -A certain bishop

26. The national god of Ammon, to whom human sacrifice was made.

27. The author accompanied the late Bishop Porteus when he first went to take possession of the
palace at Fulham. He complained to her that he had found no retired walk to which he might withdraw occasionally. She pointed out a spot where such a retreat might be formed, and while he was
clearing away the branches, the following verses were written. A few copies only were printed by
Horace Walpole, Earl of Orford, at his press at Strawberry Hill. *More.* [Beilby Porteus (1731–1800)
was an energetic, brilliant man noted for the quality of his sermons. He became bishop of London
in 1787 and befriended and encouraged Hannah More for many years. Horace Walpole printed elegant, special-issue books at his private press on his estate in Twickenham. *Strawberry Hill*, both
the estate and its name, became the symbol of the gothic revival, and his first publication was two
odes by Thomas Gray, *The Progress of Poetry* and *The Bard*. The printing of this poem by More gives
it special status. *Eds.*]

28. The manor house of the bishops of London, perhaps dating from the eleventh century. The surviving house was built in the early sixteenth century. The gardens had many rare trees and plants.

29. Edmund Bonner (d. 1569), bishop of London in 1541–49 and 1553–59. He was chaplain to King

of London, more than 200 years after the death of the aforesaid Bonner, just as the clock of the gothic chapel had struck six, undertook to cut with his own hand a narrow walk thro' this thicket, which is since called the *monk's walk*. He had no sooner begun to clear the way than, lo! suddenly up-started from the chair the ghost of bishop Bonner, who in a tone of just and bitter indignation uttered the following verses.

BONNER's GHOST.

Reformer, hold! ah! spare my shade,
    Respect the hallow'd dead;
Vain pray'r! I see the op'ning glade,
    See utter darkness fled.

Just so your innovating hand
    Let in the moral light;
So, chas'd from this bewilder'd land,
    Fled intellectual night.

Where now that holy gloom which hid
10   Fair truth from vulgar ken?[30]
Where now that wisdom which forbid
    To think that monks were men?

The tangled mazes of the schools
    Which spread so thick before,
Which knaves intwin'd to puzzle fools,
    Shall catch mankind no more.

Those charming intricacies where?
    Those venerable lies?
Those legends, once the church's care,
20   Those sweet perplexities?

Ah! fatal age, whose sons combin'd
    Of credit to exhaust us;

Henry VIII and traveled widely on diplomatic assignments. Edward VI had him confined to the Marshalsea Prison for preaching Catholic doctrine and failing to emphasize the authority of the king. Queen Mary pardoned him, and he became "Bloody Bonner" during her reign. One hundred forty-one burnings of heretics are recorded in his diocese. He refused to sign the Oath of Supremacy when Queen Elizabeth came to the throne and spent the rest of his life in the Marshalsea.
    30. Knowledge, the understanding of the ignorant or uneducated people.

Ah! fatal age, which gave mankind
　　A Luther[31] and a Faustus![32]

Had only Jack and Martin[33] liv'd,
　　Our pow'r had slowly fled;
Our influence longer had surviv'd
　　Had laymen never read.

For knowledge flew, like magic spell,
　　By typographic art: 30
Oh, shame! a peasant now can tell
　　If priests the truth impart.

Ye councils, pilgrimages, creeds!
　　Synods,[34] decrees, and rules!
Ye warrants of unholy deeds,
　　Indulgencies[35] and bulls![36]

Where are ye now? and where, alas!
　　The pardons we dispense?
And penances, the sponge of sins;
　　And Peter's holy pence?   40

Where now the beads,[37] which us'd to swell
　　Lean virtue's spare amount?

31. Martin Luther (1483–1546), German leader of the Protestant Reformation.

32. The same age which brought heresy into the church unhappily introduced printing among the arts, by which means the scriptures were unluckily disseminated among the vulgar. *More (in the voice of the bishop)*. [Faustus was the hero of a medieval legend in which a man sold his soul to the devil. He became identified with Dr. Faustus, a necromancer of the sixteenth century, and is best known through Christopher Marlowe's *Tragical History of Dr. Faustus*. In that play, Faustus becomes disillusioned with science and turns to magic; he makes a pact with Mephistopheles, deeding his soul to the devil after twenty-four years of magic power. *Eds.*]

33. How bishop Bonner came to have read Swift's Tale of a Tub it may now be in vain to inquire. *More*. [Jack and Martin were characters in Jonathan Swift's *A Tale of a Tub* (1710) who represented the Reformation theologian John Calvin and Martin Luther. Peter was their brother and stood for the Catholic Church. *Eds.*]

34. Council or assembly of church officials.

35. In the Roman Catholic Church, pardons of temporal punishment for sins drawn from the Treasury of Merit, won by Jesus and the saints for the church. The purchase of indulgences was one of the abuses that led Martin Luther to protest Catholic practices.

36. Papal letters, generally sealed with lead but sometimes with gold or silver. In 1520 Pope Leo X issued a bull against Martin Luther; a 1773 bull suppressed the Jesuits.

37. Beads are used as counters of the fifteen meditations of the mysteries in the rosary, a Roman Catholic prayer.

Here only faith and goodness fill
    A heretic's account.

But soft- - -what gracious form appears?
    Is this a convent's life?
Atrocious sight! by all my fears,
    A prelate with a wife![38]

Ah! sainted Mary,[39] not for this
50   Our pious labours join'd;
The witcheries of domestic bliss
    Had shook ev'n Gardiner's[40] mind.

Hence all the sinful, human ties,
    Which mar the cloyster's plan;
Hence all the weak fond charities,
    Which make man feel for man.

But tortur'd memory vainly speaks
    The projects we design'd,
While this apostate bishop seeks
60   The freedom of mankind.

Oh, born in ev'ry thing to shake
    The systems plann'd by me!
So heterodox, that he wou'd make
    Both soul and body free.

Nor clime nor colour stays his hand;
    With charity deprav'd,
He wou'd, from Thames' to Gambia's strand,[41]
    Have all be free and sav'd.

38. Porteus married Margaret Hodgson, of Stamford, in 1765. Catholic clergy were required to be celibate. Bonner had prosecuted the bishops who married during the reign of Edward VI.

39. An orthodox queen of the 16th century, who laboured with might and main, conjointly with these two venerable bishops to extinguish a dangerous heresy y-cleped [styled, called] the reformation. *More.*

40. Stephen Gardiner (c. 1498–1555) was a staunch defender of the authority of the Roman Catholic Church, and he and Bonner were friends and collaborators. He was imprisoned in the Fleet Prison and the Tower during Edward's reign. In 1554 he and Bonner collaborated on the replacement of the married bishops.

41. From the shores of the Thames River to the shores of Gambia, a country in West Africa. More and her friends were committed abolitionists.

And who shall change his wayward heart;
   His wilful spirit turn?   70
For those his labours can't convert,
   His weakness will not burn.

Ann. Dom. 1900.   A GOOD OLD PAPIST.

By the lapse of time the three last stanzas are become unintelligible. Old chronicles say, that towards the latter end of the 18th century a bill was brought into the British parliament by an active young reformer for the abolition of a pretended traffic of the human species. But this only shews how little faith is to be given to the exaggerations of history, for as no vestige of this incredible trade now remains, we look upon the whole story to have been one of those fictions, not uncommon among authors, to blacken the memory of former ages.[42]

(1789)

Where Has My Ambition Led Me?
Maria Frances Cecilia Cowper

—E'en to the height of God's eternal throne,
Where my affections, my desires, are gone.
No view of this frail, fleeting scene of things,
Pleasures that tire, or riches that have wings,
Can fill the heart, or feed th' aspiring mind,
For purer bliss, for better joys design'd.
   Though once surrounded by each fair delight
Whate'er could sooth the sense or charm the sight,
Whate'er the flattering world could best impart,
Sublimer prospects more possess'd my heart: 10
These, like the breaking of the morning sun,
O'er all my sweetest earthly comforts shone;
And still they shone with undiminish'd ray,
When all those earthly comforts died away:
Faith, join'd with humble Hope, bade sorrow cease,
And o'er my soul diffus'd the balm of peace.

(1792)

---

42. The young reformer is William Wilberforce, whose bill to abolish the slave trade was rejected in Parliament. See Anna Laetitia Barbauld's *Epistle to William Wilberforce* (2.F).

A Summer Evening's Meditation
Anna Laetitia Barbauld

One sun by day, by night ten thousand shine.[43]

YOUNG.

'Tis past! The sultry tyrant of the south[44]
Has spent his short-liv'd rage; more grateful hours
Move silent on; the skies no more repel
The dazzled sight, but with mild maiden[45] beams
Of tempered lustre, court the cherished eye
To wander o'er their sphere; where hung aloft
DIAN's[46] bright crescent, like a silver bow
New strung in heaven, lifts high its beamy horns
Impatient for the night, and seems to push
10   Her brother[47] down the sky. Fair VENUS[48] shines
Even in the eye of day; with sweetest beam
Propitious shines, and shakes a trembling flood
Of softened radiance from her dewy locks.
The shadows spread apace; while meekened Eve,[49]
Her cheek yet warm with blushes, slow retires
Thro' the Hesperian gardens of the west,[50]
And shuts the gates of day. 'Tis now the hour
When Contemplation, from her sunless haunts,
The cool damp grotto, or the lonely depth
20   Of unpierc'd woods, where wrapt in solid shade
She mused away the gaudy hours of noon,
And fed on thoughts unripened by the sun,
Moves forward; and with radiant finger points
To yon blue concave[51] swelled by breath divine,
Where, one by one, the living eyes of heaven

---

43. Epigraph from both Edward Young's *The Consolation* (1745), 39, and his *The Complaint. Or, Night Thoughts: Volume II* (1748), 211.
44. The sun.
45. The moon.
46. Diana, Roman goddess of the moon, of forests, of animals, and of childbirth.
47. Apollo, the sun god, Diana's twin brother.
48. The planet.
49. Mild or gentle evening.
50. A wondrous garden located at the western edge of the world, where the daughters of Atlas lived. The tree with the golden apples that Hercules obtained as one of his labors is located here.
51. The sky.

Awake, quick kindling o'er the face of ether[52]
One boundless blaze; ten thousand trembling fires,
And dancing lustres, where the unsteady eye,
Restless and dazzled, wanders unconfin'd
O'er all this field of glories; spacious field,   30
And worthy of the Master: he, whose hand
With hieroglyphics elder than the Nile
Inscribed the mystic tablet; hung on high
To public gaze, and said, Adore, O man!
The finger of thy GOD. From what pure wells
Of milky light, what soft o'erflowing urn,
Are all these lamps so fill'd? these friendly lamps,
For ever streaming o'er the azure deep
To point our path, and light us to our home.
How soft they slide along their lucid spheres!   40
And silent as the foot of time, fulfil
Their destined courses. Nature's self is hushed,
And, but a scattered leaf, which rustles thro'
The thick-wove foliage, not a sound is heard
To break the midnight air; tho' the raised ear,
Intensely listening, drinks in every breath.
How deep the silence, yet how loud the praise!
But are they silent all? or is there not
A tongue in every star that talks with man,
And wooes him to be wise? nor wooes in vain: 50
This dead of midnight is the noon of thought,
And wisdom mounts her zenith with the stars.
At this still hour the self-collected soul
Turns inward, and beholds a stranger there
Of high descent, and more than mortal rank;
An embryo GOD; a spark of fire divine,
Which must burn on for ages, when the sun
(Fair transitory creature of a day!)
Has closed his golden eye, and wrapt in shades
Forgets his wonted journey thro' the east.   60

Ye citadels of light, and seats of GODS!
Perhaps my future home, from whence the soul

52. A pure form of air or fire, the space beyond the sphere of the moon.

Revolving periods past, may oft look back,
With recollected tenderness, on all
The various busy scenes she left below,
Its deep laid projects and its strange events,
As on some fond and doting tale that sooth'd
Her infant hours—O be it lawful now
To tread the hallow'd circle of your courts,
70   And with mute wonder and delighted awe
Approach your burning confines. Seiz'd in thought,
On fancy's wild and roving wing I sail,
From the green borders of the peopled earth,
And the pale moon, her duteous fair attendant;
From solitary Mars;[53] from the vast orb
Of Jupiter,[54] whose huge gigantic bulk
Dances in ether like the lightest leaf;
To the dim verge, the suburbs of the system,
Where cheerless Saturn[55] 'midst his wat'ry moons
80   Girt with a lucid zone, in gloomy pomp,
Sits like an exiled monarch: fearless thence
I launch into the trackless deeps of space,
Where, burning round, ten thousand suns appear,
Of elder beam, which ask no leave to shine
Of our terrestrial star, nor borrow light
From the proud regent of our scanty day;
Sons of the morning, first-born of creation,
And only less than HIM who marks their track,
And guides their fiery wheels. Here must I stop,
90   Or is there aught beyond? What hand unseen
Impels me onward thro' the glowing orbs
Of habitable nature, far remote,
To the dread confines of eternal night,
To solitudes of vast unpeopled space,
The desarts of creation, wide and wild;
Where embryo systems and unkindled suns
Sleep in the womb of chaos? fancy[56] droops,

53. The planet.
54. The planet.
55. The planet.
56. A creative faculty, usually treated as lighter and more whimsical and playful than imagination or as an assistant to it. Imagination, with the power to transform its material, was considered the higher power.

And thought astonish'd stops her bold career.
But oh thou mighty mind! whose powerful word
Said, Thus let all things be, and thus they were,[57]   100
Where shall I seek thy presence? how unblamed
Invoke thy dread perfection?
Have the broad eye-lids of the morn beheld thee?
Or does the beamy shoulder of Orion[58]
Support thy throne? O look with pity down
On erring, guilty man; not in thy names
Of terror clad; not with those thunders armed
That conscious Sinai[59] felt, when fear appalled
The scatter'd tribes;[60] thou hast a gentler voice,
That whispers comfort to the swelling heart,   110
Abash'd, yet longing to behold her Maker.

But now my soul, unused to stretch her powers
In flight so daring, drops her weary wing,
And seeks again the known accustomed spot,
Drest up with sun, and shade, and lawns, and streams,
A mansion fair and spacious for its guest,[61]
And full replete with wonders. Let me here,
Content and grateful wait the appointed time,
And ripen for the skies: the hour will come
When all these splendors bursting on my sight   120
Shall stand unveiled, and to my ravish'd sense
Unlock the glories of the world unknown.

(1792)

57. Paraphrase of refrain in Genesis 1: "And God said, Let there be. . . ."
58. Constellation that Orion, a mythical giant of great beauty with great prowess as a hunter, became after death.
59. In Exodus 19:16, 18, Mount Sinai was the place where God revealed his presence to the Israelites with thunder, smoke, fire, a thick cloud, and quakes. Moses descended from Mount Sinai with the sealed covenant between God and the people.
60. The tribes of Israel descended from Jacob and his sons.
61. Allusion to John 2:1–2: "In my Father's house are many mansions. . . . I go to prepare a place for you."

The Lady and the Pye; Or, Know Thyself[62]

Hannah More

A worthy Squire[63] of sober life,
Had a conceited boasting wife;
Of *him* she daily made complaint,
Herself she thought a very saint.
She lov'd to load mankind with blame,
And on their errors build her fame.
Her favourite subject of dispute
Was Eve and the forbidden fruit.[64]
"Had I been Eve," she often cried,
10   "Man had not fall'n nor woman died;
I still had kept the orders given,
Nor for an apple[65] lost my heaven;
To gratify my curious mind,
I ne'er had ruin'd all mankind;
Nor from a vain desire to know,
Entail'd on all my race such woe."
     The Squire reply'd, "I fear 'tis true,
The same ill spirit lives in you:
Tempted alike, I dare believe,
20   You would have disobey'd like Eve."
The lady storm'd and still deny'd
Both curiosity and pride.
     The Squire some future day at dinner,
Resolv'd to try this boastful sinner;
He griev'd such vanity possest her,
And thus in serious terms address'd her.
"Madam, the usual splendid feast,
With which our wedding day is grac'd,
With you I must not share to-day,
30   For business summons me away.

62. This fable was first published in the series *Cheap Repository for Moral and Religious Tracts*, the project initiated to provide moral reading in schools, Sunday schools, and Sunday evening village gatherings.

63. Country gentleman; chief property owner in a district.

64. In Genesis 3:1–16, Eve eats the fruit of the forbidden tree, and Adam and Eve are banished from the Garden of Eden.

65. Although the forbidden fruit is not identified in the Old Testament, popular culture usually identifies it as an apple.

Of all the dainties on the table,
Pray eat as long as you are able;
Indulge in every costly dish;
Enjoy, 'tis what I really wish;
Only observe one prohibition,
Nor think it a severe condition;
On one small dish which cover'd stands,
You must not dare to lay your hands;
Go—disobey not on your life,
Or henceforth you're no more my wife."   40
 The treat was serv'd, the Squire was gone,
The murm'ring lady din'd alone:
She saw whate'er could grace a feast,
Or charm the eye, or please the taste.
But while she rang'd from this to that,
From ven'son haunch to turtle fat;
On one small dish she chanc'd to light,
By a deep cover hid from sight.
"Oh! here it is—yet not for me!
I must not taste, nay, dare not see.   50
Why place it there? or why forbid
That I so much as lift the lid?
Prohibited of this to eat,
I care not for the sumptuous treat.
I wonder if 'tis fowl or fish,
To know what's there I merely wish.
I'll look—O no, I lose for ever,
If I'm betray'd my husband's favour.
I own I think it vastly hard,
Nay, tyranny, to be debarr'd.   60
John[66] you may go—the wine's decanted
I'll ring or call you when you're wanted."
 Now left alone, she waits no longer,
Temptation presses more and stronger.
"I'll peep—the harm can ne'er be much,
For tho' I peep I will not touch;
Why I'm forbid to lift this cover
One glance will tell, and then 'tis over.
My husband's absent, so is John,

66. Generic name for a manservant.

70   My peeping never can be known."
            Trembling, she yielded to her wish,
        And rais'd the cover from the dish:
        She starts—for lo! an open pye
        From which six living sparrows fly.
        She calls, she screams, with wild surprise,
        "Haste John and catch these birds," she cries;
        John hears not, but to crown her shame,
        In at her call, her husband came.
        Sternly he frown'd as thus he spoke,
80   "Thus is your vow'd allegiance broke!
        Self-ign'rance led you to believe
        You did not share the sin of Eve.
        Like her's, how blest was your condition!
        How small my gentle prohibition!
        Yet you, tho' fed with every dainty,
        Sat pining in the midst of plenty.
        This dish, thus singled from the rest,
        Of your obedience was the test.
        Your mind, unbroke by self denial,
90   Cou'd not sustain this slender trial.
        Humility from hence be taught,
        Learn candour to another's fault;
        Go now, like Eve, from this sad dinner,
        You're both a vain and curious sinner."

                                    ([1796])

Sources

Killigrew: *Poems* (London, 1686), 27–28; Finch: *The Poems of Anne Countess of Winchilsea*, ed. Myra Reynolds (Chicago: University of Chicago Press, 1903), 19; Rowe: *The Miscellaneous Works in Prose and Verse of Mrs. Elizabeth Rowe*, 2 vols. (London, 1739), 1:172–73, 242–45; Teft: *Orinthia's Miscellanies* (London, 1747), 48–51; Leapor: *Poems upon Several Occasions* (London, 1748), 280–82; Chapone: *Miscellanies in Prose and Verse* (London, 1775), 171; Harrison: *Songs in the Night* (London, 1780), 80–81; Winscom: *Poems on Various Subjects, Entertaining, Elegiac, and Religious* (Bristol, 1786), 151–52; for Winscom Yearsley: *Poems on Various Subjects* (London, 1787), 131–38; More: *Bishop Bonner's Ghost* (Twickenham, 1789), 1–4; Cowper: *Original Poems, on Various Occasions. by a Lady.* Revised by William Cowper, Esq. (London, 1792), 28; Barbauld: *Poems by Anna Laetitia Barbauld* (London, 1792), 137–44; More: *The Lady and the Pye* (London, [1796]), 3–8.

✦E✦

The Poetry of War

How does a culture process the effects of war? How does it give voice to the personal loss of a beloved son, father, or husband or to the domestic effects of the war? How does it express anxieties about invasion or defeat or discomfort about the treatment of prisoners of war or captured troops? And how does it reconcile feelings of patriotism engendered by expanding imperial power with concerns about what James Winn terms the "moral ambiguity of empire."[1] Poets from Homer and Virgil to those of the present day have wrestled with these questions. The poems in this section, like many of the poems in section 2.F, on the public sphere, that deal with war and its consequences suggest how in eighteenth-century England the poetry of war simultaneously provides a vehicle for celebration and critique, quiet reflection and exultation. Beginning with the English Civil War and continuing through the ongoing struggles with France culminating in the Napoleonic Wars (1792–1815), England, during the expansion of its empire, was a martial nation.[2] As Linda Colley reminds us, "in a very real sense, war—recurrent, protracted, and increasingly demanding war—had been the making of Great Britain."[3] The poems in this section address three different though interrelated aspects of war. Some poems treat the military event with a description of soldiers in the theater of war or offer encomiums for victorious generals. Other poems explore the effects of war on those remaining at home; they capture the domestic moods of war. Finally, many poems depict the effects of war in both a material and a moral sense and question the cost of the war to the soldier and the nation, to England's power and humanity. Some poems, such as Anna Laetitia Barbauld's *Eighteen Hundred and Eleven* (2.F), range widely and address all these concerns simultaneously; others, such as Anne Bannerman's *Sonnet II. The Soldier*, concentrate fourteen lines on one compelling element. While we have collected poems explicitly about war in this section, tellingly, many more poems throughout this volume, in almost every poetic form, directly deal with or allude to war. Collectively these poems demonstrate what an insistent cultural presence war was in the lives, and life writing, of female poets and the culture of eighteenth-century England.

As was common in the eighteenth century, many poems celebrate the accomplishments of prominent military figures or specific naval or land victories. Such poems allowed poets to display their patriotism or political allegiances and to capitalize on the market for these poems. Key victories like Marlborough's at Blenheim sparked public celebrations: bonfires, bell ringings, and illuminations were held all over the country, and dozens of poems were published. Following Vice-Admiral Edward Vernon's victory at Porto Bello (the same campaign that resulted in the death of Aubrey Beauclerk, memorialized in Mary Jones's poem *In Memory of the Rt. Hon. Lord Aubrey Beauclerk,* 2.F), "enterprising manufacturers were quick to exploit it" among a patriotically predisposed populace.[4] The market for poems and ballads was matched by that for medals, badges, and commemorative pieces of ceramics. Poems in this vein often tap into the fervent nationalism and excitement that could follow a victory. "When I hear thy conquests told," writes Mary Whateley Darwall, "Glory fires me, / Fame inspires me, / E'en a woman's heart grows bold" (*Ode on the Peace*). Elizabeth Teft asks "Reason" to "moderate my Bliss" at the news of a successfully suppressed Jacobite Rebellion (*On hearing the Duke of Cumberland had defeated the Rebels,* 2.F). Esther Lewis Clark describes how "with assur'd success each English heart, / Beats high . . ." (*On hearing of the defeat of our Troops at the Battle of Val, 1747*). The enthusiasm is extended by the poems' often hyperbolic language. For example, Marlborough's stature is so exalted (surpassing even that of Aeneas) that the "coming Age" would "Suspect Invention, and Poetick Strain, / . . . / And well might *Marlb'rough* seem a Fiction of the Brain" (Catharine Trotter Cockburn, *On his Grace the Duke of Marlborough*). Similarly, Elizabeth's Boyd's *Sacred Hymn to the Victory,* on the battle of Dettingen, during the War of the Austrian Succession, unusual because King George II led his troops in the field (the last time a sitting monarch took the field), praises "GREAT-BRITAIN's King, in full Array, / . . . / . . . aiding by the High Supreme."[5] The hymn is a notable form for this triumphal poem (for a history of the hymn, see 1.G) and suggests the collective celebration and national pride, as does Eliza Tuite's *Song. In the Year 1794,* with the exhortation "Awake, arise, defend your laws, / Your monarch's rights maintain." The frequent mention of specific details of battles and individual officers, such as Honywood and Clayton in Boyd's *Sacred Hymn to the Victory,* heightens the poems' topicality and immediacy.

However, even poems of victory bear the weight of the dead. Clark's *On hearing of the defeat of our Troops* captures the aural, visual, and olfactory effects of battle, describing the "heaps on heaps" of "slaughter'd soldiers" whose "dying groans, and prayers" can be heard; the "mangl'd limbs," the "reeking torrent," and the battlefield "drench'd with English blood" conjure the image of dying soldiers. Catherine Rebecca Manners describes the "sanguine plain" (*Eugenio and Eliza,* 1.J), and Mary Masters writes of the staining of "Hostile Field with human Gore" (*On the Peace*). The graphic imagery reflects the changing reality of warfare and vividly reminds readers of the human price of war.[6] Women, often figured as latter-day Penelopes, lament that their loved one "was not born to live in Peace," although they are ostensibly comforted by the thought that "Th' Ignoble only live secure from Harms" (Anne Killigrew, *To My Lady Berkeley*). Concerns for the fate of British soldiers increased when the French government decreed in 1794 that no British or Hanoverian soldiers were to be taken alive but rather killed in the field. The policy spurred the British no-ransom policy, which resulted in the taking of 102,000 French prisoners during the Napoleonic Wars. These prisoners, living on decommissioned ships, or "hulks" (commonly referred to as "floating tombs"), or in the nine concentration camps established in England, were a domestic reminder of the ongoing struggle. That situation is the context for Anna Seward's poem, which represents a woman poetically creating a nostalgic domestic space while her husband is held a prisoner of war: "All things around me seem to expect him here; / My husband's favourite robe . . . / the books he lov'd, . . . / . . . the selected chair" (*Elegy, Written as from a French Lady*). She too is a kind of prisoner of war and of "life-exhausting Time!" Her "faded face," like the poem, becomes a readable history of the conflict, on which "Thy absence [is] written."

According to J. E. Cookson, the inhumane treatment of these captured soldiers, like the reality of battle, "challenged the optimism of the Enlightenment at a fundamental level," giving rise to cultural despair, questions about morality, and "the concern for British liberty."[7] The ongoing struggles also had an effect on the domestic lives of British citizens. Julian Hoppit notes that "it was not merely that battles were won and lost, but that at times the burden upon domestic resources produced a chaos that many found hard to bear."[8] To fund military efforts over the century, the government increased levels of taxation, established the permanent national debt, and created a growing state bureaucracy.[9] Citizens were asked to symbolically demonstrate their support for the war with a series of "fast days," the subject of poems by Jane Cave Winscom and Anna Seward, among others. Seward's satiric representation of the self-righteous "Patriot" (*Verses, Inviting Stella to Tea on the Public Fast-Day*, 1.L) contrasts with Winscom's earnest appeal for "all the nation" to "thus with fasting turn, / And heart sincere, their past transgressions mourn" (*On the First General-Fast*). Read together, the poems illustrate a diversity of opinions on war and politics.

Fears of "a violent French invasion of Britain"[10] remained. At the closest point, the nations were separated by only twenty miles of the English Channel, and militias were strategically stationed along the English coast in case of attack. Charlotte Smith conveys the proximity of France—and battle—as a shepherd watching the calm channel views an incursion between warships: "The mangled dead / And dying victims then pollute the flood" (*Sonnet LXXXIII. The Sea View*). In contrast, Ann Thomas suggests the excitement of stationed troops and the possibility of invasion. The attractive Scottish soldiers "with Legs quite bare up to their Knee; / They look'd as we are often told / Brave Roman Warriors did of old," provide a welcome diversion: "We'd such Amusements every Day; / . . . from the Country tramp / To see the Manners of the Camp" (*To Laura, on the French Fleet parading before Plymouth in August 1779*). The promise of domestic pleasures and commercial possibilities after the war also loom large. China broken during an evacuation from the coast is "a Loss we may regain, / When India Ships come home again" (*To Laura*). "Merchants, look round, the joyful Prospect see, / Send out your Ships, for ev'ry Port is free," writes Mary Masters. "No murd'ring Foes molest the trading Main" (*On the Peace*).

Not all face the end of conflict with such optimism. A soldier's "fancy" rushed "on the scene of home," imagining his loved one, "who chas'd / With looks of anxious tenderness, thy woes." Yet home is nothing but a "dreary waste." His wife dead, nothing "met thee on thy native soil, / And all thy country gave, for years of blood and toil" (Anne Bannerman, *Sonnet II. The Soldier*). Much like Joanna Baillie's *A Winter's Day* (1.c), with its image of the homeless soldier, Bannerman's *The Soldier*, in a sonnet form, laments the "stifled sigh" of the "sick, and wounded" veteran begging for his "bitter bread." Moments of public celebration seem inappropriate in the face of such need and the loss of so many. "Is this a time for triumph and applause," asks Bannerman. "Wide o'er the bloody scene, while glory flies / To heap the pile of human sacrifice; / Hid in some dark retreat, the widow weeps / Her heart's best treasure buried in the deeps" (*Verses on an Illumination for a Naval Victory*). After 1780 more than 1 million men were serving in the army and the navy, leaving many behind to await their return or mourn their absence.

The treatment of prisoners of war, the impressing of men into naval service (see *Disconsolate Judy's Lamentation*, 1.e), and the abysmal conditions on ships and in the field, along with the attendant problems of decommissioned soldiers, unemployed, often homeless veterans, or impoverished, pensionless widows (see Mary Barber, *The Widow Gordon's Petition*, 2.f), raised the question "whether the wars were producing domestic changes threatening the very society the nation had gone to war to defend."[11] Pride in British nationalism was tempered by concerns about the direction of England, the price of imperial power, and the behavior at home, where "luxury'd destructive band, / Thus locust-like, pollute the land" (Eliza Tuite, *Written at the Close of the Year 1794*). "Our black crimes, a monstrous full-grown brood," writes Esther Lewis Clark, "lays the soldier weltering in his blood" (*On hearing of the defeat of our Troops*). These poems begin to suggest the fiercely held, sometimes ambivalent attitudes toward armed conflict. Some glory in the highly visible trappings of victorious generals, patriotism, and imperial power; more often they reveal the potentially eclipsed or obscured sacrifices made by women, children, and unnamed soldiers. Together, they comprise the poetry of war.

Notes

1. James Anderson Winn, *The Poetry of War* (Cambridge: Cambridge University Press, 2008), 94.

2. England was at war in 1702–13, 1715, 1718–29, 1739–48, 1756–63, 1775–83, and 1793–1815. Dustin Griffin suggests that the names of wars "obscure the fact the Britain's chief adversary in each of these wars was France. Britain and France had become rivals for European—and worldwide—hegemony." *Patriotism and Poetry in Eighteenth-Century Britain* (Cambridge: Cambridge University Press, 2002), 10.

3. Linda Colley, *Britons: Forging the Nation, 1701–1837* (New Haven, CT: Yale University Press, 1992), 322.

4. Kathleen Wilson, *The Sense of the People: Politics, Culture and Imperialism in England, 1715–1785* (Cambridge: Cambridge University Press, 1998), 146.

5. Some of these poems elevated the identifiable hero to obscure an inconclusive battle that fell short of complete victory. For example, writing of Dettingen, Griffin notes that battle "inspires British poets to make the most of what was in fact an inconclusive battle in which the British forces avoided defeat." *Patriotism and Poetry*, 38.

6. Important changes in weaponry increased casualties. The "development of canon boring . . . . the replacement of the matchlock firing mechanisms with flintlocks, and the lightening of field guns and their carriages," along with the proliferation of artillery in terms of types and caliber, improved accuracy. Keith Krause, *Arms and the State: Patterns of Military Production and Trade* (Cambridge: Cambridge University Press, 2005), 54.

7. J. E. Cookson, *The Friends of Peace: Anti-War Liberalism in England, 1793–1815* (Cambridge: Cambridge University Press, 1982), 30, 121.

8. Julian Hoppit, *A Land of Liberty? England, 1689–1727* (Oxford: Clarendon, 2000), 4. "In the best of circumstances eighteenth-century economic life was still remarkably capricious and unpredictable," observes John Brewer. "War, the main business of the state, only compounded the problem." *The Sinews of Power: War, Money and the English State, 1688–1783* (Cambridge, MA: Harvard University Press, 1988), 199.

9. "Politicians, investors, and taxpayers certainly became vocally concerned in the aftermath of every war about the scale of accumulated debt and the burden of taxes required for its service," writes Patrick K. O'Brien in "Inseparable Connections: Trade, Economy, Fiscal State, and the Expansion of Empire, 1688–1815," in *The Oxford History of the British Empire*, vol. 2, *The Eighteenth Century*, ed. P. J. Marshall (Oxford: Oxford University Press, 1998), 66.

10. Colley, *Britons*, 306. Colley goes on to note, "Nerves were kept at fever pitch by preparations for evacuation, by long lines of wagons in village streets waiting to transport women, children and the infirm away from the scene of battle, and by instructions distributed by local clergymen and constables, urging people to prepare . . . in readiness for when the order came to flee or fight."

11. Hoppit, *A Land of Liberty?* 4.

To My Lady Berkeley, Afflicted upon her Son, My Lord Berkeley's Early Engaging in the Sea-Service[1]

Anne Killigrew

So the renown'd *Ithacensian* Queen
In Tears for her *Telemachus* was seen,
When leaving Home, he did attempt the Ire
Of rageing Seas, to seek his absent Sire:[2]
Such bitter Sighs her tender Breast did rend;
But had she known a God did him attend,
And would with Glory bring him safe again,
Bright Thoughts would then have dispossess't her Pain.

Ah Noblest Lady! You that her excel
10   In every Vertue, may in Prudence well
Suspend your Care; knowing what power befriends
Your Hopes, and what on Vertue still attends.
In bloody Conflicts he will Armour find,
In strongest Tempests he will rule the Wind,
He will through Thousand Dangers force a way,
And still Triumphant will his Charge convey.
And the All-ruling power that can act thus,
Will safe return your Dear *Telemachus*.

Alas, he was not born to live in Peace,
20   Souls of his Temper were not made for Ease,
Th' Ignoble only live secure from Harms,
The Generous tempt, and seek out fierce Alarms.
Huge Labours were for *Hercules*[3] design'd,

1. Lady Berkeley was Christiana, the wife of John Berkeley, first Baron Berkeley of Stratton. Two of Lady Berkeley's sons served in the navy: Charles (1662–82) and John, third Baron Berkeley of Stratton (1663–97), who succeeded to the title on the death of Charles. As Patricia Hoffmann detailed in a 25 June 2007 e-mail to the editors sharing her original research, Charles went to sea first, at seventeen, prompting the composition of the poem. On 2 July 1681, after two years' service, he was given the command of the *Tyger;* he died of smallpox the next year. We are grateful to Dr. Hoffmann for sharing her specialized knowledge of the poem.

2. In the *Odyssey,* Telemachus, son of Penelope and Odysseus, who live in Ithaca, goes off in search of news of his father ("absent sire") when he is twenty.

3. In Roman mythology, Hercules was the son of the god Jupiter and Alemana, a mortal. The goddess Juno, resentful of her husband's children by mortal women, made Hercules subject to the commands of Eurystheus, who devised twelve extraordinary "labours" that Hercules completed.

Jason,[4] to fetch the Gold Fleece, enjoyn'd,
The *Minotaure* by Noble *Theseus* dy'd,[5]
In vain were Valour, if it were not try'd,
Should the admir'd and far-sought Diamond lye,
As in its Bed, unpolisht to the Eye,
It would be slighted like a common stone,
Its Value would be small, its Glory none.   30
But when't has pass'd the Wheel and Cutters hand,
Then it is meet[6] in Monarchs Crowns to stand.

  Upon the Noble Object of your Care
Heaven has bestow'd, of Worth, so large a share,
That unastonisht none can him behold,
Or credit all the Wonders of him told!
When others, at his Years were turning o're,
The Acts of Heroes that had liv'd before,
Their Valour to excite, when time should fit,
He then did Things, were Worthy to be writ!   40
Stayd not for Time, his Courage that out-ran
In Actions, far before in Years, a Man.
Two *French* Campagnes he boldly courted Fame,
While his Face more the Maid, than Youth became
Adde then to these a Soul so truly Mild,
Though more than Man, Obedient as a Child.
And (ah) should one Small Isle all these confine,
Vertues created through the World to shine?
Heaven that forbids, and Madam so should you;
Remember he but bravely does pursue   50
His Noble Fathers steps; with your own Hand
Then Gird his Armour on, like him he'll stand,
His Countries Champion, and Worthy be
Of your High Vertue, and his Memory.

(1686)

---

4. Jason was the son of the Argonaut king Aeson, who, tired of ruling, allowed his brother Pelias to assume the throne until Jason reached the age of majority. Pelias was reluctant to yield the crown and persuaded Jason to seek the Golden Fleece of the mythical ram Chrysomallos.

5. The Greek hero Theseus was the son of Aegeus, the king of Athens. At this time, as a forced tribute to Minos, king of Crete, Athenians annually sent seven young men and seven young women to be eaten by the Minotaur, a half-man, half-bull beast, in King Minos's labyrinth. Theseus volunteered to go, and with the help of Minos's daughter, who provided him with a sword and thread so that he might escape the labyrinth, he killed the Minotaur.

6. Suitable or fitting.

On His Grace the Duke of Marlborough,[7] a Poem
Catharine Trotter Cockburn

Durst[8] thou attempt to sing of *Blenheim's* Plain,[9] ⎫
Too strongly mov'd thy Transport to restrain, ⎬
(Nor *Marlb'rough* did thy humble Verse disdain?) ⎭
And can'st thou now behold his Toils encrease,
Thy Countries Glory, *Europe's* Happiness,
Adding new Lustre to thy Queens lov'd Name
Yet thus desponding, check thy kindling Flame?
A *Sapho* shou'd for *ANNA* tune her Lyre,
And *ANNA* may with nobler Verse inspire.[10]

10   Or, tho' thy Genius justly thou esteem
Too mean, Oh far unequal to thy Theme,
Worthy a Master Hand! yet bear a part,
The worthiest Theme needs least the Poets Art.
The Hero comes, no longer then delay,
Loud as the publick Joy thy Tribute pay;
Shou'd none below a *Virgil,*[11] sing his Name,
The coming Age wou'd give him doubtful Fame,
Suspect Invention, and Poetick Strain,   ⎫
In all the wond'rous Truths of *ANNA's* Reign, ⎬
20   And well might *Marlb'rough* seem a Fiction of the Brain? ⎭

---

7. John Churchill, first Duke of Marlborough (1650–1722), one of the most important figures in military and diplomatic affairs between 1702 and 1710, was regarded as one of the greatest military strategists in history. A major victory in the 1706 campaign of the War of Spanish Succession (1701–14), the battle of Ramillies (Ramillia in the poem), provided tremendous momentum for the remaining conquests on the Continent. Richard Kane writes that "the Duke of *Marlborough* acted the Part of a most consummate General, not only in gaining so great a Victory over the Enemy, who had so great Advantage both in their Situation concerted, as well as Number of Troops; but also in pursuing the Advantage that accrued thereby: The Consequence of which was, the Conquest of all the *Spanish* Netherlands." *Campaigns of King William and the Duke of Marlborough*, 2nd ed. (London, 1747), 68.

8. Past tense of *dare;* here used in the sense of being so bold as to do something.

9. Marlborough's victory against the Franco-Bavarian forces in the 1704 battle of Blenheim in the War of Spanish Succession was the first major defeat for the French in forty years. It brought Marlborough tremendous financial and popular recognition both domestically and abroad and was a turning point in the war.

10. Queen Anne ("Anna") reigned from 1702 to 1714. Sappho was a female poet from the seventh century BC and remains a resonant image of female creative power.

11. Virgil (70–19 BC) was a Roman epic poet whose national epic the *Aeneid* (written between 30 and 19 BC) justified the origins of the Roman Empire. Virgil remained a powerful literary model for much of the eighteenth century.

If when the labour'd *Æneid* we peruse
The *Trojans* thought a Creature of the Muse,
Or most ascribing to the sacred Fire,
We less the Hero, than the Bard, admire;
What lofty Song, wou'd then Belief obtain
Of such a Chief as *Virgil* durst not feign?

   Among the Greatest then in Arms renown'd,
The searching *Mantuan*[12] none had perfect found,
But with some failing Shades each Character,
That all like Truth, and Nature, might appear;   30
Had he our *Marlb'rough* drawn, he must with Art
Have vail'd some Bright some most surprizing Part,
Not have describ'd in one excelling Mind
The Virtues of his varying Heroes join'd,
So temper'd each, that none the rest controul,
Such active Fire, in so compos'd a Soul,
Resenting tenderly each Soldier's Fate,
Yet in the direst chance of War, sedate;
Whilst griev'd[13] a valu'd Servant, at his Feet
A stroke the Foe for him design'd, shou'd meet.   40
Unlike *Æneas, Marlb'rough* still the same
Pursues not Vengeance, with intemp'rate Flame,[14]
Righting the Injur'd, bounds his juster Aim;
On Conquest bent, yet pleas'd the Foe to spare,
Then most desiring Peace, when dreaded most in War.

   Thus drawn ——
With those stupenduous Actions that compleat
A Hero's Character, so truly great,
In flowing Numbers dress'd, sublimer Sense,
And all the Pomp of dazling Eloquence,   50
Who wou'd not think the Poet's obvious Art
Had trespass'd on the just Historian's Part?
That he contracted into one Campaign

12. Epithet for the Roman poet Virgil, who was born near the city of Mantua, in northern Italy.
13. Col. Bingfield, his Gentleman of the Horse. *Cockburn.* [According to contemporary accounts, Colonel Bingfield "had his Head taken off with a Cannon Ball" while helping Marlborough remount during the battle of Ramillies. John Macky, *A Journey through the Austrian Netherlands* (London, 1725), 117. *Eds.*]
14. In book 12 of the *Aeneid,* Aeneas wounds his enemy Turnus and, in a fit of vengeance, kills him.

A Hero's Life, a long successful Reign,
Such cause of doubt those Toils may justly yield
That raise the Glories of *Ramillia*'s Field:
Yet more, that *A N N A* cou'd one Subject find
Greatly to act the Wonders she design'd,
Empires to save, Nations enslav'd, to free,
60   Securing *Britain*'s Peace, and *Europe*'s Liberty.

But when each ruder, untaught Voice, we raise,
And *Marlb'rough* sing with one tumultuous Praise,
All must confess, the Good, the Glorious Cause,
Unfeign'd, and Universal as th'Applause;
That native Gratitude the Croud had fir'd,
And Truth alone, such Artless Strains inspir'd.

So in adoring Heav'n, Mankind agree,
And wild Barbarian Worship, proves the Deity.

(1706)

A Sacred Hymn to the Victory[15]
Elizabeth Boyd

I.
Victorious Generals, Laud the Lord,
    The Sacred Lord of Might.
The God who sits enthron'd on High,
    In Orbs Seraphic, Bright.
Hal, Hal, Hal, Hallelujah, Hallelujah.

II.
ALL Glory be to God on High,
    Let BRITAIN's Monarch Sing,
Glory to God, his Subjects Chaunt,
    And Honour to the King.
10   *Hal, Hal, &c.*

---

15. The battle of Dettingen (27 June 1743), during the War of the Austrian Succession (1740–48), also known in England as King George's War, was a British victory. Dettingen is of considerable importance in British history almost solely because of the sovereign's presence on the battlefield. The famous composer George Frederic Handel wrote a *Te Deum* and an anthem in celebration of the victory.

III.

THY God implore, meer Mortal Man,
    Thy Cause to Justify,
Inferior Number's, then shall win,
    Immortal Victory.
Hal, Hal, &c.

IV.

NOR FRANCE, nor SPAIN, can give us Dread,
    Nor Legions fast, in League,
On the Almighty's Name, we Call,
    Who spoils, their deep Intrigue.
Hal, Hal, &c.   20

V.

BROGLIO,[16] and NOAILLES,[17] may unite,
    And eager follow Slaughter,
We've yet a STAIR's[18] and CARTERET,[19]
    Who look for a Hereafter.
Hal, Hal, &c.

VI.

GREAT-BRITAIN's King, in full Array,[20]
    Once more shall Face the Foe,
And aiding by the High Supreme,
    Cease Wars intestine[21] Woe.
Hall. Hall., &c.   30

16. François-Marie, first Duke de Broglie (1671–1745), appointed to command the French army in Germany during the War of the Austrian Succession. After the loss at Dettingen, *The Lamentations of The French Marshals, Broglio and Noailles* (London, 1743) appeared, suggesting the marshals' notoriety in England.

17. French marshal Adrien-Maurice, third Duke de Noailles (1678–1766), who served in all the most important wars of the reign of Louis XV, becoming marshal in 1734. After taking the town of Dettingen, Noailles's troops charged the British and Hanoverian infantry "with great impetuosity." But the allied troops, "animated by the presence of their sovereign . . . poured forth an incessant fire, which nothing could resist." Although the French cavalry "rushed on in desperation," they experienced a stunning defeat and the loss of more than five thousand men. William Russell, *The History of Modern Europe*, 5 vols. (London, 1786), 5:92. The battle of Dettingen was Noailles's last command.

18. John Dalrymple, the second Earl of Stair (1673–1747), colonel of the Inniskilling dragoons, who executed much of the tactical control in the battle of Dettingen, where he was second in command to George II.

19. At this time, John Carteret, second Earl Granville (1690–1763), was secretary of state and generally counseled a strong exertion of British power.

20. The battle was notable in part because George II himself led his men in battle.

21. Internal or civil.

VII.

Tho' Honywood,[22] and Clayton[23] Fell,
 And many Chief's, Beside,
In Paradice they still Excell,
 No Glory here deny'd.
Hal, Hal, &c.

VIII.

In Letter'd Gold, or Marble Bust,
 To endless Time enduring
They shall on Record with the Just,
 Be endless Fame ensuing.
40 *Hal, Hal,* &c.

IX.

The Bleeding Captive, well we Use,
 On our great Lord, Relying,
Should France, then the Allies Abuse,
 And purchase Peace by Dying.
Hal, Hal, &c.

X.

Tho' Spain and France in one should Blend,
 The Sacred Three will Guard us,
Victorious then, will be our End,
 Our God will still Reward us.
50 *Hal, Hal,* &c.

XI.

All Glory to the Three, in One,
 Who'll peacefully unite us,
And When our Work on Earth is Done,
 In blest Abodes delight us.
Hal, Hal, &c.

(1743)

---

22. Sir Philip Honywood (or Honeywood) (c. 1677–1752). At the battle of Dettingen he was senior commander after George II and Lord Stair. He did not die in battle, but his regiment, in turning away from the enemy to regroup, ploughed into the Royal Horse Guards and broke up their formation. He is listed as wounded in *The Annals of Europe for the Year 1743,* 6 vols. (London: T. Astley and George Hawkins, 1745), 6:379.

23. Lieutenant General Clayton is listed among the killed in *The Annals of Europe for the Year 1743,* 379.

On hearing of the defeat of our Troops at the Battle of Val, 1747[24]
Esther Lewis Clark

Conquer'd again, O fatal, deadly sound!
Shall we with laurels never more be crown'd?
Tho' justice does our glitt'ring swords unshield;
And pours our legions o'er the martial field;
Yet our high hopes of conquest all are cross'd;
And battle after battle now is lost.

   O say, ye pow'rs above, whence springs the cause,
That British troops, who once with loud applause,
Were wont to quit the purple breathing field,
Nor knew what 'twas to puny Gaul to yield,   10
O'er bleeding foes all bath'd in crimson dye
Still forward press'd, and ever scorn'd to fly,
Should now not know what blooming laurels are,
But sink beneath the foe or fly the war?
Tho' army after army now is sent,
'Till half our bleeding nation's wealth is spent;[25]
Tho' with assur'd success each English heart,
Beats high, nor fear'd of France the strength, or art;
Yet these high hopes sad disappointments meet;
Some fly, some fall low at their conqueror's feet;   20
Of slaughter'd soldiers heaps on heaps arise,
And dying groans, and prayers pierce the skies;
The horse and rider both together slain,
Promiscuous strew with mangl'd limbs the plain:
From mingl'd heaps of undistinguish'd clay,
A boiling, reeking torrent flows away;
The gaping sluices pour a crimson flood,
And foreign soils are drench'd with English blood;
The piercing sword has lost its wonted power;
The whizzing ball forgets how to devour;   30
Some unseen pow'r forbids our arms to kill,
And baffles all our prudence, strength, and skill.

24. At the battle of Val, also known as the battle of Lauffeldt, which took place on 2 July 1747, in the War of the Austrian Succession, the British suffered a severe defeat, losing about two thousand men.

25. In addition to losses on the battlefield, the nation was "bled" financially through the extensive taxes that were increasingly levied to support the war efforts.

Oh! whence this fatal source, this baleful spring,
Which clogs with weights unseen fair vict'ry's wing?

Behold the latent spring explor'd to light,
Which clips her wings and stops her soaring flight;
'Tis our black crimes, a monstrous full-grown brood,
That lays the soldier weltering in his blood;
'Tis sin, which makes the once strong sinews shake,
40   From that dire fiend our foes their vigour take;
'Tis sin forbids the lifted sword to slay,
Blunts the keen edge, and robs it of its prey;
'Tis sin misguides the once unerring ball,
When death unseen made ranks on ranks to fall.

In vain the horse for battle we prepare;
In vain the soldier's train'd in arts of war;
In vain the nations richest stores are drain'd;
In vain unnumber'd armies are maintain'd;
While 'gainst ourselves, O cruel management,
50   We arm with sin a foe omnipotent.
Fruitless shall all our preparations be,
As were the labours of Penelope:
Whose ever-faithful hand each night destroy'd,
What the preceding day that hand employ'd;[26]
Virtuous was this chaste fair one's nice deceit;
Unblameable and innocent the cheat.

Ours is a policy before unknown,
As one hand builds, the other still pulls down; ⎫
Industrious to destroy our own renown,   ⎬
60   Fair schemes we frame with vast expence and art, ⎭
Then with our vices stab 'em to the heart.

Offended heav'n with angry eye surveys,
Our black transgressions, our corrupted ways;
Our monst'rous sins to such a height are grown,
From a just God they must call vengeance down;

26. As recounted in the *Odyssey,* Penelope, while waiting twenty years for the return of her husband, Odysseus, from the Trojan War, was besieged by suitors in his absence. She claimed that she would choose one of them when she completed her weaving. To delay her suitors, every night she unraveled what she had woven that day, ensuring that her weaving would never be finished.

His laws we trample on, his pow'r despise, ⎫
On his great word our wit we exercise, ⎬
And flatly tell him to his face, he lies. ⎭
Don't we in ev'ry loathsome vice excel?
Don't ev'ry nation's crimes among us dwell?   70
From court to cot[27] the black contagion's spread;
Virtue despis'd, with all her train is fled.
Has not our God us'd ev'ry means to draw,
Our hearts once more to reverence his law?
With fond paternal love light strokes lets fall,
This long offending nation to recal:
But if regardless quite we still go on,
'Till patient mercy long abus'd is gone,
And justice takes its place; 'twill be too late,
To cry to heav'n against determin'd fate.   80
Long has th' almighty's glittering sword been whet,[28]
And all his terrors in array been set:
But mercy still withheld th' uplifted sword,
Or hopeless woes we had e'er now deplor'd:
At length the blow from that stupendous height,
From th' immortal arm with pond'rous weight,
Will crush us low in pains, no more to rise,
If all his calls we slight, his threats despise.
O then in time ward off the threaten'd blow,
Repent, amend, and fear no pow'rful foe.   90

   Defer no more: but let each Briton lay,
His hand upon his conscious heart and say,
What have I done, what crimes have I thrown in
To the preponderating scale of sin,
To weigh my native, sinking country down;
Or how provoke th' Almighty's angry frown?
And when you once the fatal dart have found,
Whose mortal edge widen'd Britannia's wound;
With fortitude, fearless of present smart,   ⎫
Draw with unpitying hand the poison'd dart,   ⎬   100
Which pierc'd thro' your own souls your country's heart. ⎭

27. Cottage.
28. Sharpened.

See at your feet your bleeding parent lies,
Your aid imploring with uplifted eyes;
O then in tender pity lend your hand,
To raise once more your low-fall'n native land;
Timely consider then, timely repent,
And conquest by your crimes no more prevent, ⎫
Nor rend those breasts which gave you nourishment, ⎬
O turn your feet while mercy yet does wait, ⎭
110   And save in your own souls a sinking state.

And you, ye great ones, who in courts preside,
Whose virtues, or whose vices downward glide,
'Till it arrives where lowest meanness dwells,
And taints, or brightens cottages and cells;
Think how severe a punishment's your due,
If boldly you the paths of vice pursue,
And by your foul examples lead astray, ⎫
The multitude from virtues radiant way, ⎬
And thousand, thousand souls to sin betray; ⎭
120   Who blindly follow the dark rules you set,
Thinking your wisdom as your fortunes great;
As are the high, so always are the low:
If those to virtue give a cruel blow,
These instantly the fatal strokes repeat,
To drive the lovely goddess from her seat;
'Till by degrees at length to earth she's crush'd,
Laught at, despis'd, and trampl'd low in dust.

But if fair virtue's reverenc'd at the helm,
She spreads her beamy rays o'er all the realm;
130   The gazing throng with gentle influence draws,
'Till from admiring, they obey her laws.
Then turn, ye great ones, turn and seek to God;
Mercy may yet withdraw th' uplifted rod.
No more the paths of vicious pleasures tread;
No more be with the fatal madness led;
Follow fair virtue's ever radiant light,
Nor let the lovely virgin quit your sight;
Still let her reign supreme within your heart,
And never from your charming guide depart;
140   Her steps pursue, with chearful, vig'rous pace,
Nor droop, nor tire in the glorious chace;

If follow'd close she'll a reward bestow,
Such as you'll ne'er from vicious pleasures know;
Not such rewards are given by fame or wealth,
The heavenly maid will pay you with herself:
The secret, conscious, self approving mind, ⎫
Will give you joys you can't in pleasures find, ⎬
Blest in yourselves, and blessings to mankind. ⎭
Then bring by bright examples back the croud,
You have misled in sin's pernicious road.   150

   O where's Britannia's native virtue fled, ⎫
Whose beams our troops to certain conquest led; ⎬
And with fresh laurels ever crown'd her head! ⎭
Rouse, Britons, rouse you from this sink of sin,
This maze of crimes so long you've wander'd in:
Think on the ne'er to be forgotten fame, ⎫
Your noble fathers won, then blush for shame, ⎬
And let their bright examples you inflame. ⎭

   From court to cot now let us all amend,
Repent what's past, and make our God our friend;   160
That God omnipotent, whose pow'rful breath,
Can speak unnumber'd armies into death;
And when the host goes forth the foe to meet,
Low let us fall at th' Almighty's feet,
Implore his aid, and guard our hearts from sin,
Nor cherish any latent foe within.
Then let us meet their pow'rs, devoid of fear,
Secure of conquest, if our God be near.

(1747; 1789)

On the Peace[29]

Mary Masters

Stern War is past, the Soldier now no more,
Dis-tains the Hostile Field with human Gore;

---

29. Written during a rare interlude of peace between the War of the Austrian Succession, ended by the Peace of Aix-la-Chapelle in October 1748, and the Seven Years' War, which began on 29 August 1756.

Safe rests his Sword within its peaceful Sheath,
And he no longer dreads the sudden Death:
Loud Cannons now with harmless Thunder roar,
And Peals of Joy salute the neighb'ring Shore;
No murd'ring Foes molest the trading Main,
But friendly are the Courts of *France* and *Spain*.
Merchants, look round, the joyful Prospect see,
Send out your Ships, for ev'ry Port is free;
Peace comes with gracious look and bounteous Hand,
That promise Blessings to a happy Land:
May *Britain* long the promis'd Blessings share,
Un-vex'd with foreign or domestic War.

                        (1755)

10 (line 10 marker at left)

To Laura, on the French Fleet parading before Plymouth in August 1779[30]

Ann Thomas

Our Ears were stun'd with noisy Drum,
That beats to Arms—the Foe is come!
The combin'd Fleets plain did appear,
The Van, the Center, and the Rear;
You cannot think what horrid Rout,
And how the People ran about;
For fear my Spirits shou'd grow damp,
I thought I'd go and view the Camp;[31]
And LAURA, if you had been there,
You'd had no Thought of Dread or Fear;
The good old FRAZER[32] march'd along,

10 (line 10 marker at left)

30. In August 1779 a Franco-Spanish fleet was spotted off the Devonshire coast. As Robert W. Jones notes, "Such was the extent of Britain's vulnerability, that by the summer of 1779, when Thomas composed her poem, the coastal towns of Plymouth and Portsmouth had been fearful of invasion for nearly a year." "Sheridan and the Theatre of Patriotism: Staging Dissent during the War for America," *Eighteenth-Century Life* 26 (Winter 2002): 25.

31. The government, to assuage fears among the local population and to defend against invasion, established several large military encampments at strategic points along the coast early in 1778. The English Channel was crucial to England's domestic and foreign prosperity, for it was the primary throughway for all vessels and was thus pivotal to trade and supplies.

32. Simon Fraser, master of Lovat (1726–82), a Scottish army officer who served in North America, the Caribbean, and Portugal. With the start of the American war, he raised a new two-battalion

Like Hector brave—Achilles strong;[33]
His Royal first Battalion too
Look'd as brave Soldiers ought to do;
And Highlanders you there might see
With Legs quite bare up to their Knee;
They look'd as we are often told
Brave Roman Warriors did of old;[34]
Each County Band in Armour bright,[35]
Seem'd well dispos'd the Foe to fight: 20
So when I'd seen the Martial Plain,
Contented I went home again;
All thro' the Streets, the Waggons creak,
They jumble—and the Dishes break;
Twill take some Time sure to repair
The Loss sustain'd in China Ware;
Yet that's a Loss we may regain,
When India Ships[36] come home again;
But as for me, I thought I'd stay,
And see the Fortune of the Day;   30
For LAURA, very well you know,
I need not fear the plund'ring Foe;
I had no Money—had no Plate,
Nor Title Deeds for an Estate,
So at the last I cou'd but pack,
And take my Fortune on my Back:
But when the Foe had made this Rout,
They took one Ship—and so went out;
A mighty Victory sure was won,
An hundred Ships have captur'd one;   40

Highland regiment, the "Highlanders," mentioned below. Fraser's Highlanders served with some distinction in America, and he was highly regarded as a hero.

33. During the Trojan War, as recounted in the *Iliad* and the *Aeneid,* Hector was the Trojans' greatest warrior, and Achilles was the Greeks'. Their battle, during which Achilles slayed Hector, was the turning point of the Trojan War.

34. A Roman soldier was attired in a tunic that came to his knees; similarly, Highlander soldiers would have been in kilts that revealed their knees. During this period, as Robert Jones notes, great military camps such as the one at Coxheath, near Maidstone in Kent, "soon proved to be a destination for parties of society ladies eager to see the garrisoned battalions and their officers." The poem represents a similar dynamic. Jones, "Sheridan and the Theatre of Patriotism," 26.

35. By this point in the century, counties were responsible for generating and outfitting a militia, or "county bands."

36. The potential loss of naval control over the English Channel had huge implications for British trade, including, of course, goods and raw materials imported from India.

And now we are from Danger free,
And all the Folks are in high Glee,
I wonder you so long can stay?
We'd such Amusements every Day;
The People from the Country tramp
To see the Manners of the Camp,
And when of that they'd had a View,
Then they consult our Conjurer too;
Poor Man—indeed he cannot see,
But reads the Stars like A B C;
He tells them all what will betide,
And when each Lass shall be a Bride;
And when the destin'd Youth appears,
Describes the very Coat he wears;
He'd tell her too, if he may prove,
An Object worthy of her Love:
When these important Things they know,
Then home again contented go:
LAURA, if you shou'd longer stay,
I think I'll come some Holiday;
And JENNY call a thousand Sluts,
Unless she gives me store of Nuts;
And when I come, I hope her Hoard,
Good red-streak'd Apples will afford:
LAURA, I think it's Time to end,
I'll only say I am thy Friend.

(1784)

On the First General-Fast after the Commencement of the late War[37]
Jane Cave Winscom

When direful judgments pour in like flood,
And fields, alas! are drench'd with human blood,

37. Throughout the seventeenth and eighteenth centuries it was common for Parliament to declare a general fast, a day of prayer and fasting to recognize anything from the earthquake in Lisbon to the "trouble in America." Frequently, specific prayers were issued to be used in all churches on that day, and the nation participated in a day of recognition. This poem commemorates the first general fast after the beginning of the American war.

When armies after armies prostrate lie,
And brother, by his brother's hand must die,
When kingdoms seem to rise, or empire fall,
One great Omnipotent conducts it all,
And those have but a superficial scan,
Who view no higher origin than Man.

    Be still, methinks I hear JEHOVAH cry,
Be still before your GOD, and know 'tis I!   10
'Tis I make peace, and I create stern war,
And ride to battle in my flaming car,[38]
I guide the bullet, point the glitt'ring sword
Defeat, or conquest, wait my awful word.
But do I pleasure in destruction take,
Or have your sins not bid the sword awake?
Do not a nation's sad offences call
For national calamities to fall?

    Great Sov'reign Lord, we own thy judgments just,
And hide our guilty faces in the dust;   20
Rejoice to hear a day is sanctify'd
T' implore thy aid, and humble BRITAIN's pride.
But may we not in this incur the rod,
And make a solemn mockery of GOD?
T'abstain from food, to take our prayer-books,
And walk to church with evangelic looks;
To bend the knee, or move the lips in pray'r,
If all the heart be not engaged there,
Is empty shew, a poor external part,
While GOD, the Omniscient GOD, demands the heart;   30
And should we fail in this grand sacrifice,
The whole will be offensive in his eyes.

    Descend, celestial dove, with holy fire,
And pure devotion ev'ry soul inspire.
May vital pray'r, express'd by ardent sighs,
Ascend to GOD, and penetrate the skies.
Let all the nation thus with fasting turn,

38. Chariot of war or triumph, often associated with Phaëton, whose father was the Greek sun god, Helios.

And heart sincere, their past transgressions mourn;
Then is eternal truth engag'd to bless,
40   And crown our just petitions with success.

(1783)

Ode on the Peace.
Mary Whateley Darwall

Written January 3rd. 1783.

Long the bleeding world has groan'd,
  Long has madd'ning discord rag'd,
Long have Albion's sons bemoan'd
  The hateful war with brothers wag'd.[39]
Bourbon and Belgia aid th'insurgent's claim,
Proud to diminish Britain's envy'd fame.

    Unequal task! to cope with foreign foes,
While faithless friends at home each scheme oppose,
While children, nurtur'd with maternal care,
10   Spread for their country the insidious snare,
Disguis'd in patriotism's flaming robe;—
Tho' long they scatter'd firebrands[40] o'er the globe:
Still a brave honest few the cause maintain'd,
And in the people's hearts with their lov'd monarch reign'd.

    RODNEY[41]—oh! name to England ever dear—
Who but must honor, love, revere!
    When I hear thy conquests told,
      Glory fires me,

---

39. The Treaty of Paris, also known as the Peace of Paris, a collection of treaties between England on one side and America, France, and Spain on the other, was signed in 1783. The British failure to hold the colonies, the aid given to the American colonies by France and the Netherlands, and the on-going conflicts with "foreign foes" tempers the notion of peace conveyed in the poem.

40. Literally, a piece of wood kindled in a fire, but figuratively, and here, anything that kindles strife or mischief or inflames passions.

41. Admiral Sir George Brydges Rodney (bap. 1718, d. 1792) won a decisive victory against the French at the Battle of the Saints in the West Indies in April 1782, capturing nine French ships and essentially saving Jamaica for England. The popular response and representation of this victory was overwhelming (multiple illuminations, Rodney's image on mugs and teapots), in part because of recent British defeats abroad.

    Fame inspires me,
       E'en a woman's heart grows bold.   20
ELLIOT[42] claims an HOMER's strain,
    Deathless deeds like his to tell,
Encircled by the boist'rous main,
And stern Iberia's hostile train,
    On the drear sterile rock[43] constrain'd to dwell,
With his few friends, a faithful band;—
Firm as Gib'raltar's solid base they stand,
    Smiling at the num'rous foes,
    That dare their vet'ran arms oppose.
Had ELLIOT rul'd in Troy, the Greeks had fail'd,   30
Their ten years toil had nought avail'd;
    ACHILLES[44] here had fought in vain,
    Vainly brav'd the force of Spain;
    Where ELLIOT calmly brave succeeds:—
    Who can recount his matchless deeds?
    Vain were th' attempt each gallant chief to sing,
Who dauntless serv'd his country and his king.
But see! Bellona,[45] cloy'd with carnage, flies,
Bearing her bloody torch to Asia's torrid skies:—
And lo! from yonder azure cloud,   40
    A fair angelic form descends;
Tho' some dark tints her beauties shroud,
    Each blessing on her step attends.
The cheerful olive wreaths her brow,
    Plenty smiles beneath her eye,
Mars[46] unbends his sanguine bow,
    The furies from her presence fly.
'Tis heav'n-born Peace, long wish'd-for guest!

42. General George Augustus Eliott (1717–90) was responsible for holding the British position and ending the three-year siege of Gibraltar in September 1782. The Strait of Gibraltar, lying between southernmost Spain and northwesternmost Africa, is the channel connecting the Mediterranean Sea with the Atlantic Ocean. The only passageway from the Mediterranean to the Atlantic, it was thus central to British interests.

43. The "sterile rock" of Gibraltar is a three-mile-long peninsula surrounded by water ("the boist'rous main") and connected to the Spanish (Iberian) Peninsula. A limestone and shale ridge, it measures 1,396 feet at its highest point.

44. Premier Greek warrior. The Trojans were held under siege by the Greeks during the ten-year period of the Trojan War, recounted in the *Iliad* and the *Aeneid*.

45. Roman goddess of war.

46. Roman god of war.

Thrice welcome to this war-worn isle!
50   Thou bring'st a balm to sooth each breast,
And make dull care and anguish smile.
Beneath thy sacred influence benign,
Commerce shall raise her languid head,
Joy in each bright'ning eye shall shine,
Nor industry despair of bread.
'Tis thine, sweet Peace, to bless a mourning land,
And heal a nation's sorrows with thy lenient hand.

(3 January 1783; 1794)

Henry and Lucy,
Or the Loss of the Royal George at Spithead[47]
Ann Thomas

No Village sure could boast a brighter Maid,
In native Charms, and Innocence array'd,
Then Lucy was—for her each Village Swain
Tried every rustic Art her Love to gain,
But all in vain, still Lucy's Heart was free,
That Conquest Henry, was reserv'd for thee:
The gentle Youth who to his native Plain,
From distant Climes, was safe return'd again,
With joy the Village Youths around him crowd,
10   And of the hopeful, blooming Hero proud;
For he behav'd amidst the Shock of War
Like an intrepid, gallant, British Tar;[48]
Merit like his, soon call'd for some Regard,
And due Promotion was the Youth's Reward;

47. The *Royal George* was a 100-gun royal ship under the command of Richard Kempenfelt that went down on Thursday, 29 August 1782, in the harbor at Spithead, the stretch of water off the naval base at Portsmouth, England. "Built on dangerously top-heavy lines," with a 114-foot main mast, the *Royal George* was in for repairs when a squall caused it to heel slightly. Douglas Ford, *Admiral Vernon and the Navy: A Memoir and Vindication* (London: T. Fisher Unwin, 1907), 180. Her ports had been left open, so the ship filled with water and sank, drowning Captain Kempenfelt and much of the crew. The amount of iron ballast in the hold when the ship sank was 126 tons. William Cowper also wrote a poem about the event—*Loss of the Royal George*—in part to urge recovery of the ship and its contents.

48. Colloquial term for a sailor derived from *tarpaulin,* the name of the waterproof fabric used to make sailors' hats.

And HENRY promis'd fair to add his Name
To British Heroes, on the List of Fame;
To hear him speak, the aged and the young
Delighted hear, and on his Accents hung;
With Eloquence he'd tell the pleasing Story,
Of various Climes, and of Britannia's Glory: 20
Such HENRY was—and who cou'd Lucy blame,
If for the Youth she felt a mutual Flame?
Nor yet the Swains behold with jealous Eyes,
But to superior Merit yield the Prize;
Their Friends united, praise the happy Choice,
And in their promis'd Union all rejoice;
But soon the Royal George prepar'd for Sea,
When Duty calls, sure HENRY must obey.
Poor LUCY mourns, the Tears bedew her Cheek,
And HENRY dreads the sad adieu to speak;   30
The Morn arrives that bids him to depart,
Adieu, he cries, my ever constant Heart;
Amidst the Din of Arms, or Tempests roar,
I'll think on LUCY and this happy Shore.
Now HENRY quits the peaceful rural Plain,
His Duty calls—no longer can remain
In rural Shades, but joins the busy Scene:
He comes! the Ship is order'd to Careen;
Each busy Sailor now his Strength apply'd,
To heave the pond'rous Vessel on her Side;   40
Whilst cruel Fate tremendous hovers o'er,
Alas! she heel'd—but heel'd to rise no more!
She sinks! the Royal George, our Navy's Pride,
Shall o'er the Seas no more triumphant ride.
O! KEMPENFELT, thou much lamented Chief,
For thee the Muse can scarce express her Grief;
She oft along the Shore shall pensive mourn,
Whilst Rocks responsive shall her Plaints return.
O! KEMPENFELT, for thee and for thy Crew,
Soft Pity shall the generous Cheek bedew;   50
And oft the gallant Sailor steering nigh,
Shall point—and heave the sympathetic Sigh.
For such sad Fate even Foes themselves might mourn,
And look with Pity on their wat'ry Urn:
Britons be kind, and from the Widow's Eye,

O! wipe the Tear, and sooth the heart-felt Sigh,
And let the wretched helpless Orphans share
Your kind Protection, and your generous Care.
But O! no Words nor Language can explain
60   Poor LUCY's Grief—th' Attempt were only vain.
Thus have you seen full many a fragrant Rose,
The Garden grace, and ev'ry Sweet disclose;
But soon the Northern Blast with chilling Pow'r,
Severely seizes on the beauteous Flow'r;
It binds its Stalk, reclines its fragrant Head,
And soon—too soon—its ev'ry Sweet is fled.
So LUCY droop'd, and so her Head reclin'd,
In Death, soon with her much-lov'd HENRY join'd;
The Village all assemble round the Bier,
70   Bemoan her Loss with many an honest Tear;
And whilst thy mourn the Maiden's hapless Lot,
Nor is her HENRY's dreadful Fate forgot:
Farewell sweet Pair, the mournful Shepherds cry,
More worth than yours could never live nor die.

(1784)

The Horse and His Rider
Joanna Baillie

Brac'd in the sinewy vigour of thy breed,
In pride of gen'rous strength, thou stately steed,
Thy broad chest to the battle's front is given,
Thy mane fair floating to the winds of heaven.
Thy champing hoofs the flinty pebbles break;
Graceful the rising of thine arched neck.
White churning foam thy chaffed bits enlock;
And from thy nostril bursts the curling smoke.
Thy kindling eye-balls brave the glaring south;
10   And dreadful is the thunder of thy mouth:
Whilst low to earth thy curving haunches bend,
Thy sweepy tail involv'd in clouds of sand;
Erect in air thou rear'st thy front of pride,
And ring'st the plated harness on thy side.

But, lo! what creature, goodly to the sight,
Dares thus bestride thee, chaffing in thy might?
Of portly stature, and determin'd mien?
Whose dark eye dwells beneath a brow serene?
And forward looks unmov'd to fields of death:
And smiling, gently strokes thee in thy wrath?   20
Whose brandish'd falch'on[49] dreaded gleams afar?
It is a British soldier, arm'd for war!

(1790)

Written at the Close of the Year 1794
Eliza Tuite

Just this time thirty years ago
I came into this world of woe;
And sure of all the years I've past,
Few have been equal to the last.
But of this fatal Ninety-four,
By treason blasted, steep'd in gore,
Impartial let me take review,
Ere it receives my last adieu.[50]
Oh could the page by horror stain'd,
But shew one step, by virtue gain'd,   10
Then would I grieve, the scene was o'er,
And bless departing Ninety-four;
But vain the fruitless wish appears,
(As idle, as most hopes and fears)
Thro' private life, where'er we glance,
'Tis all the same unmeaning dance,
Change part'ners, skip from side to side,
But still no ebb, to folly's tide.

49. Falchion, a curved broad sword with the edge on the convex side. The word can also mean a sword of any kind.

50. In addition to the British military losses noted above, in 1794 the Dissenter and radical Thomas Hardy (1752–1832) was prosecuted for leading an effort to organize a convention of reformers to demand voting rights for a wider population in Parliament, but the jury acquitted him, supporting the right to peaceably assemble to petition for redress of grievances.

Our women, of all shame bereft,
20   Have scarce more form, than feeling left;
To please the vary'ng eye of taste,
They sport, just half an inch of waist,
Their shapes, ambitious to display,
No beggar's thinner clad than they;
Their limbs expos'd, their bosoms bare,
Still so reserv'd, the British fair
That many deem it a disgrace,
To let one see a *naked face;*
And art, with lavish hand, supplies
30   The blushes, modesty denies;
Our men (but here I am to blame,
To give to forward boys the name,
Our beaux then) we must all confess,
Do not take too much pains to dress,
(For that they have not time to spare,
A *Beau* disdains to comb his hair)
With breeches, half-way down their legs,
Coats loose, as tho' they hung on pegs,
Huge stocks their beardless chins to hide,
40   Huge cudgels, dangling by their side,
Gigantic hats, on pigmy shoulders,
Enough to frighten all beholders,
In short, their follies to expose,
Seems the *whole* study of our *beaux,*
And she who most in art excels,
Now leads the ton, 'midst modern belles:
With beating heart, as I explore,
The blotted page of Ninety-four,
In vain I seek, some cause to find,
50   Of triumph to a British mind;
What tho' our armies undismay'd,
Their wonted valor have display'd?
Tho' How e,[51] and his victorious fleet,

51. Richard, Earl Howe (1726–99), was commander-in-chief of the Channel Fleet. On 1 June 1794, leading a line of thirty-four battle ships, he successfully defeated a French fleet of twenty-six ships under the command of Rear Admiral Louis Villaret-Joyeuse (1750–1812). It was the first great battle between the British and French fleets in the French Revolutionary War. Seven thousand French soldiers were killed, wounded, or captured, while only one thousand British soldiers were wounded or killed.

Again their country's foes should meet,
Useless their triumphs o'er the main,
Our gallant soldiers, bleed in vain,
While luxury's destructive band,
Thus locust-like, pollute the land;
While fashion's idle, motley, crew,
The same unthinking course pursue;   60
'Tis the long files, of bills unpaid,
That ruin industry, and trade,
While sharpers, rogues, and pimps, are fed,
With what *should* give, the *artist bread;*
To dissipation, cards, and dice,
See health, and peace, the sacrifice;
From willing dupes, and titled cheats,
Morality appall'd retreats;
Reflection, from the croud has fled,
To hide in shades her sober head,   70
Friendship (of fashion's slaves the jest,
The pride of ev'ry honest breast);
Resolv'd no more to be the tool,
Or sport, of ev'ry knave and fool,
Indignant quits the busy stage,
And seeks the peaceful hermitage.
Oh England thou wouldst be too blest,
Were but thy *noblest* sons, thy best,
Thou hadst not then been bought or sold,
For thirst of pow'r, or thirst of gold.   80
Did but thy lovely daughters try,
In virtue, as in charms to vie;
Would *they,* the course of vice restrain,
Our foreign foes might threat in vain;
Suspended then, 'twixt hope and fear,
We should not wait th' approaching year,
Nor children yet unborn deplore,
The sad events of Ninety-four.

(1796)

Song. In the Year 1794[52]

Eliza Tuite

Tho' still triumphant o'er the main,
　　Britannia's thunders roar;
She fondly mourns her warriors slain,
　　On yonder hostile shore.
　　　　　　Britons.[53]

She grieves, that while on foreign ground,
　　They bleed at honor's call,
At home one traitor should be found,
　　Exulting in their fall.
10　　　　　　Britons.

Such alien children, lost to shame,
　　She views with aching heart;
Who under Freedom's sacred name,
　　Would play a tyrant's part.
　　　　　　Britons.

They do but flatter to ensnare,
　　And sell her to her foe;
O may her gen'rous sons beware,
　　And timely ward the blow.
20　　　　　　Britons.

Awake, arise, defend your laws,
　　Your monarch's rights maintain;
So may your blood, in England's cause,
　　No more be shed in vain.
　　　　　　Britons.

52. As J. E. Cookson notes, "The campaign of 1794 was one of the most unsuccessful England had ever fought on the Continent." *The Friends of Peace: Anti-War Liberalism in England, 1793–1815* (Cambridge: Cambridge University Press, 1982), 142.

53. The reader should imagine the singing of *Britons, Strike Home* at the end of each verse. Henry Purcell (1659–95) made John Fletcher's *Bonduca* into an opera (published in 1695) and set the words to music: "*Britains*, Strike Home: Revenge your Country's Wrongs: / Fight and Record your selves in *Druids* Songs." Throughout the eighteenth century his music was played on board British ships as they sailed into battle and before the Horse Guards charged into battle; it was a more popular military inspirational song than James Thomson's *Rule Britannia*. It was also frequently requested along with *God Save the King* in theaters. *Bonduca* and the better-known *Boadicea* are corrupt forms of *Boudicca*, the name of the queen of the Iceni who led a revolt against the Romans.

So may fair Peace, round Albion's throne,
   Her choicest blessings shed;
While Heav'n approving guards its own,
   And shields your Brunswick's head.[54]
        Britons.   30

(1796)

Sonnet LXXXIII. The Sea View
Charlotte Smith

The upland Shepherd, as reclined he lies[55]
   On the soft turf that clothes the mountain brow,
Marks the bright Sea-line mingling with the skies;
   Or from his course celestial, sinking slow,
   The Summer-Sun in purple radiance low,
Blaze on the western waters; the wide scene
   Magnificent, and tranquil, seems to spread
Even o'er the Rustic's breast a joy serene,
   When, like dark plague-spots by the Demons shed,
Charged deep with death, upon the waves, far seen,   10
   Move the war-freighted ships; and fierce and red,
   Flash their destructive fires—The mangled dead
And dying victims then pollute the flood.
Ah! thus man spoils Heaven's glorious works with blood!

(1797)

Sonnet II. The Soldier[56]
Anne Bannerman

With swelling heart I hear thy stifled sigh,
   Poor time-worn vet'ran! on thy hoary head

---

54. Reference to King George III. His grandfather, George I, originator of the Hanoverian succession, was an heir in the Brunswick-Lüneburg inheritance. Thus the appellation Brunswick is used.

55. Suggested by the recollection of having seen, some years since, on a beautiful evening of Summer, an engagement between two armed ships, from the high down called the Beacon Hill, near Brighthelmstone. *Smith*. [Brighthelmstone is Brighton, a seaside town on the English Channel, about fifty miles south of London and less than a hundred miles from the French coast. *Eds.*]

56. The demobilization of soldiers found them returning to what Linda Colley describes as "pov-

Beats the keen fury of the winter's sky,
    And slow thou mov'st, "to beg thy bitter bread,"[57]

While heaves impetuous thine indignant breast;
    O! when the vessel cut the Atlantic foam,
And bore thee, sick, and wounded, and opprest,
    Then rush'd thy fancy on the scene of home;

On all its guiltless pleasures;—her, who chas'd
10   With looks of anxious tenderness, thy woes.
Eternal Heaven! that home—a dreary waste!
    And the cold grave, where thy fond hopes repose,
Were all that met thee on thy native soil,
And all thy country gave, for years of blood and toil.

(1800)

Verses on an Illumination for a Naval Victory[58]
Anne Bannerman

Quels traits me présentent vos fastes,
    Impitoyables conquerans?
—Des murs, que la flamme ravage,
—Des vainqueurs, fumans de carnage,
    Un peuple au fér abandonné.
Juges insensés que nous sommes,
Nous admirons de tels exploits.   J. B. ROUSSEAU.[59]

Hark! 'tis the note of joy; the trumpet's voice
Swells in the wind, and bids the world rejoice;

---

erty and neglect," causing a rise in the homelessness and unemployment of many veterans. *Britons: Forging the Nation, 1707–1837* (New Haven, CT: Yale University Press, 1992), 321.

57. The refrain was probably quoted from memory from *Night the First,* lines 249–50, in Edward Young's *The Complaint: or Night-Thoughts:* "In battle lopt away, with half their limbs, / Beg bitter bread thro' realms their Valour sav'd."

58. Probably General Howe's defeat of the French fleet on 1 June 1794. Andrew Ashfield notes that the victory to which she refers could be General Nelson's over Napoleon's navy in the Nile River in 1798, "but the early position of the text in the [original] volume seems to favour Howe's victory." *Romantic Women Poets: 1788–1848,* 2 vols. (New York: Manchester University Press, 1997–98), 2:270.

59. Jean-Baptiste Rousseau (1671–1741), a popular French dramatist and poet, known for his topical often satiric verse. The text is from *Ode VI: A la Fortune,* published in his *Oeuvres diverses* (London,

From street to street, in artificial light,
The blaze of torches glitters on the night;
Loud peals of triumph rend the startled sky:
Rejoice; it is the shout of victory!
Rejoice o'er thousands in untimely graves;
Rejoice! for Conquest rides the crimson'd waves.
    Is this a time for triumph and applause,
When shrinking Nature mourns her broken laws?   10
Wide o'er the bloody scene, while glory flies
To heap the pile of human sacrifice;
Hid in some dark retreat, the widow weeps
Her heart's best treasure buried in the deeps;
The frantic mother's cries of Heaven implore
Some youthful warrior—she shall meet no more:
From the first beam, that wakes the golden day,
To ling'ring twilight's melancholy ray,
No respite comes, their breaking hearts to cheer,
Or, from the fount of misery, steal a tear!   20
    Rough as the storm that rends the icy seas,
Th' uncultur'd savage spurns the arts of peace;
Impell'd by hatred, and revenge his guide,
He leaves[60] his native mountain's shelt'ring side,
Thro' trackless deserts holds his bloody way,
With toil unwearied, thro' the tedious day;
At night, reposing on the blasted heath,
In dreams, his fancy points the stroke of death,
Exults horrific o'er his prostrate foe,
And aims anew the visionary blow.   30
Starting he wakes: afar he sees a form,
Half-viewless, stalking thro' the misty storm;
Nearer he comes; his frantic eye-balls glare,

1723), 1:86. Bannerman omits five lines, which appear in brackets in the translation: "In such scenes do your splendours appear, / Merciless conquerors? / [Unbounded desires, vast schemes, / Kings vanquished by Titans.] / City walls ablaze, / Victors steeped in blood, / A people put to the sword. / [Mothers ashen and bloody, / Snatching their trembling daughters / From the arms of a soldier.] / Bewildered spectators that we are, / We admire such exploits." Ashfield, *Romantic Women Poets*, 2:270.

    60. "A single warrior, prompted by caprice or revenge, will take the field alone, and march several hundred miles to surprise and cut off a straggling enemy." ROB. HIST. AMER. VOL. II. *Bannerman*. [William Robertson, *The History of America*, 2 vols. (Dublin, 1777), 2:106. Robertson notes that he takes his information from James Adair, *The History of the American Indians* (London, 1775), 150. *Eds.*]

And yells inhuman ring along the air:
They meet, engage; affrighted Nature flies;
A fearful darkness dims the low'ring skies;
Revenge beside them points th' envenom'd stings,
And murder shrouds them, with his gory wings!
   "Accurs'd the deed!" the Sons of Europe cry,
40   While the tear starting, trembles in their eye;
Yes! ye may boast, from feeling's source sublime,
That milder mercy gilds your favour'd clime;
With eager joy, you bid oppression cease,
And lull the jarring universe to peace!
Alas! Humanity would shroud the sight,
And wrap Destruction in his native night;
With breasts begirt with steel, in dread array,
The glitt'ring legions flash upon the day;
Brothers in Science, at the trumpet's sound,
50   Like dæmons meet, and scatter death around.
Unmov'd they stand, and view the living tide
Pour, with a torrent's force, on every side.
On Andes' cliffs, untutor'd Murder low'rs,
But all its keener, deadlier arts——are ours.
   O! could some Spirit, from the fields of day,
To this fair planet wing his vent'rous way,
Inhale the freshness of the vernal breeze,
And mark the sun, reflected in the seas,
View where, abundant, on a thousand shores,
60   The waving harvests yield their golden stores;
Gay Beauty smiling in the sweets of morn,
The op'ning violet, and the flow'ring thorn,
Th' expanding fields of every varied hue,
And the clear concave of unclouded blue!
   Then let Him stand, where hostile armies join,
By the red waters of the rushing Rhine,
Amid thick darkness, hear the trumpets blow,
And the last shriek of Nature quiver low,
Mark the full tide of Desolation spread,
70   And count, at eve, the dying and the dead:
How would he pause! How seek, in vain, to find
Some trace, in Man, of an immortal mind;
Man, who can glory in a scene like this,

Yet look to brighter worlds, for endless bliss!
    O! for a lodge,[61] where Peace might love to dwell,
In some sequester'd, solitary dell!
Some fairy isle, beyond the Southern wave,
Where War ne'er led his victims to the grave;
Where, mid the tufted groves, when twilight pale
Peoples with shadowy forms the dewy dale,   80
The lone Enthusiast, wrapt in trance sublime,
Might soar, unfetter'd by the bounds of time,
Might bask in Fancy's reign, where scenes appear
Of blooms perpetual, thro' the vernal year;
Where heav'nly odours scent the zephyr's wing,
And fruits and flow'rs, in wild luxuriance spring!
    Such were the dreams, that sooth'd the pensive breast,
And lull'd the soul to visionary rest.
    Such were the scenes, the poet's fancy drew,
While Rapture hail'd the moments, as they flew: 90
Till mad Ambition bade the battle rage,
And Man with Man eternal warfare wage.
    Ah! did our years thro' circling ages flow,
Or Fate secure the heart from private woe;
Did strength for ever in the arm reside,
Or the firm frame retain its youthful pride;
The eye that saw th' embattled hosts extend,
Might also hope to see their discord end;
The heart, which Sorrow never taught to feel,
Might point, with surer aim, th' avenging steel: 100
Ah! when a few short years have roll'd away,
The foes shall rest, unjarring, in the clay.
The Tartar-Chief,[62] expiring on the plain,
Amid the multitudes his arm has slain,
Yields his fierce soul, ere half his years are run,
And ends his fiery course, when scarce begun.
The polish'd youth, whom Europe rears to arms,
And glory flatters, with deceitful charms,

61. Oh! for a lodge in some vast wilderness, / Some boundless contiguity of shade. COWPER'S TASK. *Bannerman*. [William Cowper, *The Task* (London, 1785), bk. 2, lines 1–2. *Eds.*]

62. The leader of an army of Tartar warriors, that is, soldiers of Mongolian, Turkish, or Chinese descent native to the Central Asia region. Tartar people first became known to the western European world because of the victories of the Mongol conqueror Genghis Khan's armies.

Chills each fine impulse of the glowing soul,
110   And, pressing onward to the laurel'd goal,
Forgets that feeling ever warm'd his breast,
Or Pity pleaded for the heart opprest.
    All hail, ye joys! to genuine feeling dear,
The heart's warm transport, and the gushing tear!
Welcome the sigh, from pity's altar stole,
Ye calm the tumult of the troubled soul.
O! on whatever shore, by fortune cast,
My shatter'd bosom finds a home at last;
Whatever ills, in sorrow's ample reign,
120   May wring my heart, with aggravated pain;
Still, at those hours, when, hush'd in deep repose,
The happy lose their joys, the sad their woes,
May fancy lead me to the desert steep,
Stupendous frowning o'er the sullen deep;
To hear the ship-wreck'd mariner deplore
His doom relentless, on the rocky shore!
Even when the winds their awful fury urge,
And, heap'd like mountains, raves the foaming surge,
Less dread the terrors of the turbid main,
130   Than Carnage, stalking o'er th' ensanguin'd plain!
    And ye, who, bending o'er the untimely urn,
Will see nor joy, nor happiness return;
Thro' your chang'd homes, who wildly seek in vain
For those who slumber in the stormy main;
May piercing anguish spare his arrows keen,
And pity soothe you, as ye weep unseen!
May peace pervade, where faithful sorrow reigns,
And charm the grief, that not an eye profanes!
Ah! think, tho' ling'ring years unblest decay,
140   To troubled night succeeds untroubled day!
Time's feeble barrier bounds the painful course,
But joy shall reign, eternal as its source.

(1800)

Elegy, Written as from a French Lady, Whose Husband Had Been Three Years Prisoner of War at Lichfield[63]
Anna Seward

Fled are the years Love should have call'd his own,
Bearing my wasted youth they roll'd away;
Dost thou conceive, my husband, how I moan
Thro' the long, lonely, disappointed day?

Night comes.—Ah! every instant, as it flies,
Feeds my impatience to behold thee here.—
Morning will soon relume[64] the darken'd skies,
But when shall my soul's morning re-appear?

Each separated moment dost thou count
With a regret solicitous as mine?   10
Ruthless the foe who swells their vast amount,
And bids thee in unransom'd bondage pine!

For thee, I judge thee by myself, and know,
Dear, hapless Exile! all thou must endure;
The cheerless days, and every heart-sick woe
That Liberty might chase, and Love should cure.

Yet, O! when absence all my soul o'er-powers,
Why does thy pen with-hold the only aid?
When gales blow homeward from the hostile shores,
Why are th' expected lines of Love delay'd?   20

Question unwise!—Does not this heart require
Trust in my husband's tenderness and truth?

---

63. During the Napoleonic Wars with Britain (1792–1815) thousands of French prisoners of war were held captive in Britain. In a departure from previous wars, these soldiers were subjected to long-term captivity and remained prisoners for the duration of the conflict—the "unransom'd bondage" to which the poem refers. In addition to keeping prisoners on decommissioned ships, the British built nine prison camps throughout England, including the one at Lichfield. Seward spent seven years in Eyam and then, beginning at age thirteen, in 1755, lived the rest of her life in Lichfield. For a discussion of French prisoners of war, see Gavin Daly, "Napoleon's Lost Legions: French Prisoners of War in Britain, 1803–1814," *History* 89 (July 2004): 361–80.

64. Make bright again.

What else can slake[65] the slow-consuming fire
My peace that scorches, and that wastes my youth?

Trust in his love my heart demands,—and, Oh!
Another confidence blest power obtains,
Rescuing my senses from severer woe,
Than e'en this cruel banishment ordains;

Reliance that kind Heaven preserves his life,
30   His health from wasting by Disease's brands;[66]
That not to their restraints his faithful wife
Owes her late baffled hopes and vacant hands.

If she may judge his feelings by her own,
And grateful Memory urges that she may,
He numbers tear for tear, and groan for groan,
Thro' the slow progress of the joyless day.

With sweet remembrances my thrilling heart
Full of the Past surrounds itself in vain;
They rise!—they charm!—but soon, alas! impart,
40   By sad comparison, increase of pain.

No fond deception, nor yet Hope, nor Fear
Arrest the pace of life-exhausting Time!—
He might return!—one word, and he is here!—
Ah! why are bonds for him who knows not crime?

Fierce War ordains them!—Fiend of human kind!—
Fetters and death one murder overtake;
From thee the Guiltless no exemption find,
Thy murder'd millions glut the vulture's beak!

And from such fate remember, O my soul,
50   Exile and bonds severe redemption prove;
That thought drops sweetness in the bitter bowl
Quaff'd to the dregs[67] by long-divided love.

---

65. Quench, modify.
66. As Gavin Daly details, the "brutal and inhumane conditions of imprisonment" were widely known and documented. "Napoleon's Lost Legions," 373.
67. Drained down to the thick sediment.

Oft to my aid this consciousness I call,
To close the eyes, which still have op'd to weep.—
When Night and Sorrow spread their mingled pall,
That thought distills th' oblivious balm of sleep.

All things around me seem to expect him here;
My Husband's favourite robe enfolds me still;
Here have I rang'd the books he lov'd,—and there
Placed the selected chair he us'd to fill.   60

Again to be resum'd, if yielding Fate,
At length, would give him back to love and me;
Then should I see him there reclin'd sedate,
Our darling children clinging round his knee!

And lo! at yonder table where they stand!—
Their glances o'er the map of England stray;
Ah! on the too, too interesting land
How bends thy ANNISE her intense survey!

And now she smiles, and to her brother turns,
Her finger placed on Lichfield!—there, she says,   70
There is our dear, dear father!—O! how yearns
My very soul to mark their ardent gaze!

Frequent, this killing absence to beguile,
Anxious I watch, as traits of thee arise,
I see them playing in my ANNISE' smile,
I meet them in thy FREDERIC's candid eyes.

Their strengthen'd bloom, their much expanded mind
Shall recompense my beauty's vanish'd trace;
Yet thou wilt love me more, when thou shalt find
Thy absence written on my faded face.   80

Dearest, farewell!—tho' misery now be ours,
Slow time will bring the re-uniting day,
When Thou, and Joy, shall bless these lonely bowers,
By sweet excess o'er-paying long delay!

(1810)

Sources

Killigrew: *Poems* (London, 1686), 24–26; Cockburn: *On his Grace the Duke of Marlborough. A Poem* (London, 1706), 1–2; Boyd: *Glory to the Highest, a Thanksgiving Poem* (London, 1743), 6–8; Clark: *Poems Moral and Entertaining* (Bath, 1789), 329–35; Masters: *Familiar Letters and Poems on Several Occasions* (London, 1755), 208–9; Thomas: *Poems, on Various Subjects* (Plymouth, 1784), 4–7; Winscom: *Poems on Various Subjects, Entertaining, Elegiac, and Religious* (Winchester, 1783), 111–14; Darwall: *Poems on Several Occasions. By Mrs. Darwall. (Formerly Miss Whateley) in Two Volumes*, 2 vols. (Walsall, 1794), 2:24–28; Thomas: *Poems, on Various Subjects* (Plymouth, 1784), 7–11; Baillie: *Poems; Wherein It Is Attempted to Describe Certain Views of Nature and of Rustic Manners* (London, 1790), 178–79; Tuite: *Poems by Lady Tuite* (London, 1796), 7–12, 160–62; Smith: *Elegiac Sonnets, and Other Poems*, 8th ed., 2 vols. (London, 1797), 2:24; Bannerman: *Poems by Anne Bannerman* (Edinburgh, 1800), 78, 25–34; Seward: *The Poetical Works of Anna Seward*, ed. Walter Scott, 3 vols. (Edinburgh, 1810), 3:375–79.

✢F✢

Poems on the Public Sphere

In the preface to her 1734 collection, *Poems on Several Occasions*, Mary Barber describes how "the Distress of an Officer's Widow set me upon drawing a Petition in Verse, having found that other Methods had proved ineffectual for her Relief."[1] The poem, *The Widow Gordon's Petition: To the Right Hon. the Lady Carteret*, transforms the legal discourse of a petition into a literary form and seeks assistance from the wife of the Lord Lieutenant of Ireland in securing the rightful pension for a war widow "who hears the Want she never can relieve!" Like other poems in this section, *The Widow Gordon's Petition* creates a compelling narrative to illustrate a larger social problem; it publicizes what might be considered a domestic issue in a manner consistent with the emergence of a public sphere in which women (and men of all classes) contributed to ongoing discussions about social, military, or cultural issues.[2] "Matters once considered 'private'... and those considered 'political'... were transformed," writes Charlotte Sussman, "into public issues, about which any rational citizen might have an opinion," and about which many published that opinion.[3] Susannah Centlivre captures the brimming literary marketplace in which "Daily we see Plays, Pamphlets, Libels, Rhimes" (*Prologue [to "Love's Contrivance"]*). Women wrote with the belief that published texts generally, and poetry specifically, possessed efficacy and resonance; they viewed them as a vehicle through which they could prompt change, express strong opinions, or reenvisage their world. Thus Elizabeth Teft, an ardent opponent of the Jacobite Rebellion of 1745, poetically figures herself on the battlefield at Culloden, transforming her pen into a sword, "Some memorable glorious Deed to do" (*On the Times*): "I'd be the Victim, see my Bosom bleed, /.../... shew them how a Woman dare to Dye; / Dye like a Hero for the publick Good." Passion about military victory or royal figures reveals an intensity rivaling that found in love poems. Elizabeth Singer Rowe recounts her "Raptures" and describes "What *mighty genious* thus excites my Breast" (*Upon King William's Passing the Boyn*) when describing King William's victory at the battle of the Boyne. Teft describes "this Torrent of extatick Joy," which leaves her gasping "for more Breathing room" (*On hearing the Duke of Cumberland had defeated the Rebels*). The poems also display a keen sensitivity about the degree to

459

which the public impinged profoundly on the domestic. In a time of global military conflict, women learn of personal loss through published information: "Oft o'er the daily page some soft-one bends / To learn the fate of husband, brothers, friends" (Barbauld, *Eighteen Hundred and Eleven*). In the late eighteenth century, even the very consumer goods on women's tables become politically marked during campaigns urging abstinence from West Indian sugar.

Written at different historical moments of the eighteenth century and with alternately conservative and more radical postures, the poems in this section nevertheless share three overarching and ultimately intertwined concerns: the legitimacy of monarchal authority; the appropriate use of civil, legal, and military power; and the threats to liberty and the human rights of marginalized, disenfranchised, or enslaved persons. The poems in this section contradict essentializing discussions that look at women's poetry as primarily autobiographical.[4] Although often personal responses to public issues, these poems constitute another form of life writing and demonstrate women's deep engagement in imagining their world, and their position in it, differently. They illustrate women's awareness of the complexities of domestic and foreign policies and the implications of the same for the lives of citizens, adding a new dimension to our understanding of women's poetry and the cultural history of the time.

The legitimacy of monarchal authority was a pressing concern for British citizens throughout the long eighteenth century. The execution of Charles I during the English Civil War and the subsequent restoration of the monarchy with his son Charles II, the Bloodless Revolution of 1688, and then the Hanoverian succession of 1714 marked the ascension to the throne of three different royal houses, only one of them British.[5] Some poems nostalgically depict Charles I, a Stuart king, contributing to the cult of his martyrdom, maintaining his presence in the public consciousness, and endorsing the legitimacy of the Stuart line. Katherine Philips, a royalist appalled by the king's execution and the subsequent treatment of his body, lamented the "breach of Nature's laws": "Oh! to what height of horrour are they come / Who dare pull down a Crown, tear up a Tomb!" (*Upon the double Murther of K. Charles I*). Efforts to canonize Charles began at the moment of his execution on 30 January, and a prayer on that date was one of three added to the Book of Common Prayer in 1662.[6] Sarah Dixon's *On the XXXth of January*, written in 1740, reflects on this day of sermons and remembrance, labeling him "The Christian HERO *perfected.*" Praising King William in his defeat of the Stuarts at the battle of the Boyne, Elizabeth Singer Rowe has the same intensity as she glorifies the *"Hero and the King,"* praises the *"Martial God,"* and makes a calculated statement of solidarity with her final line, *"And long, and long, and long, let WILLIAM live"* (*Upon King William's Passing the Boyn*). These royalist poems share the fervor Anne Finch expresses in *Upon an improbable undertaking*, where she casts the Hanoverian succession of 1714 as an unnatural or inorganic grafting: "To think this Timber cou'd maintain / Like what you've lost a stable reign / . . . / A Scion from the home-bred tree / May grow in time to fill the place."

The Hanoverian succession exacerbated concerns about the perceived threat from the "Jacobites," the loyal supporters of the exiled house of Stuart. James II was the last Stuart king; he, his son, and then his grandson, "Bonnie Prince Charles," lived in France and figured in the cultural imagination alternately as nostalgically desirable and rightful heirs to the throne or as persistent threats to the nation's stability.[7] We include poems on the Jacobite Rebellion of 1745 that represent both perspectives. Bonnie Prince Charlie, or the "Young Pretender" to the throne of England, arrived in Scotland in 1745 to organize support from the Highland clans in a rebellion. He rallied about five thousand mostly Catholic men, who made it to Edinburgh without any resistance. The ballads of Carolina Oliphant Nairne capture the appeal to Charlie's supporters and his central claim to the throne: "He should be king, ye ken wha I mean, / . . . / He's waiting us there where heather grows fair, / And the clans they are gath'ring strong and strong" (*Gathering Song*). Charlie inspires men to leave their wives and children "To draw the sword for Scotland's Lord, / The young Chevalier" (*Charlie is My Darling*), men who, though "few, their hearts are true, / They'll live or die for Charlie" (*Charlie's Landing*). By contrast, Teft's poems relish the "Grim Slaughter" of the rebels at the hands of the Duke of Cumberland (1721–65), the third son of George II, recalled from his responsibilities on the Continent in the War of the Austrian Succession. Teft praises Cumberland's "Voracious" and "rapacious" nature as he brutally defeated the poorly led and under-supplied Highlanders (*On hearing the Duke of Cumberland had defeated the Rebels*). In the subsequent months, royal troops searched the Highlands for remaining rebels and treated loyalists and rebels indiscriminately. "These expeditions," notes W. A. Speck, "have become legendary for their brutality and bloodlust,"[8] a brutality to which Teft's poems clearly allude.

The widespread allegations of British atrocities after Culloden were followed by escalating questions about England's future, the treatment of its citizens, and the use of civil and military power. When and to what degree should civil or military force be used against citizens? What national interests justify the deployment and sacrifice of troops on foreign soil? What is the appropriate balance between personal liberty and national security? These questions, central to many of the poems about war (2.E), run through the poems in this section in subtle and complicated ways. Mary Jones's monody *In Memory of the Rt. Hon. Lord Aubrey Beauclerk* praises the "many gallant warriors *Britain* lost," yet its portrait of a world where "the coward with the brave promiscuous lie" implicitly questions the worth of this military effort. The poem poses a series of questions ("Virtue!—What is it?" "Say, what is Life? and wherefore was it giv'n?") designed to prompt greater reflection. Jones writes both to preserve Beauclerk's memory and to remind others of the dangers of forgetting the issues his loss should raise: "Shall so much worth in silence pass away, / ... / Shall public spirit like the private die, ... ?" Ultimately, imperial war disrupts the boundaries between the public and the domestic. Domestic reproduction becomes fodder for public death as women are "Fruitful in vain," finding their "fallen blossoms strew a foreign strand" (Barbauld, *Eighteen Hundred and Eleven*).

Domestic actions by British authorities were also questioned as, at the end of the century, the emergent concern for British liberty "became overwhelming,"[9] especially as the French had highlighted Britain's claims to be the land of liberty during France's own revolution. Mary Alcock's *Instructions, Supposed to Be Written in Paris, for the Mob in England* ironically recontextualizes the galvanizing language of the French Revolution to express a pervasive cultural anxiety about the power of the "mob," governmental reaction, and the rule of law. The most sustained exploration of the tensions between citizens' rights and the abuses of civil and military power is Jane Cave Winscom's intricate poem recounting the Bristol Bridge riot, "the most deadly disturbance of the 1790s."[10] Winscom's poem, like contemporaneous accounts of the event, contrasts a citizen's right to peaceful assembly with the magisterial responsibility to follow the Riot Act. Without ordering the crowd at the bridge to disperse, the Bristol militia fired "directly up High-Street" upon "that gaping populace," killing eleven and wounding forty-five men, women, and children.[11] The killing of English citizens by their own soldiers, like England's failure to abolish the slave trade, raised questions about the country's moral stature, indeed about its very humanity. It anticipates Barbauld's nearly apocalyptic vision of England's future in *Eighteen Hundred and Eleven:* "The worm is in thy core, thy glories pass away." Ultimately Winscom, like other poets in this section, seeks justice from a higher authority. Just as Barbauld reminds Wilberforce he will be favorably judged by "faithful History," so too Winscom asserts that "vengeance belongs alone to GOD!" a transcendent morality removed from the contingencies of misunderstood military orders or mediated interactions.

The plight of disenfranchised soldiers, "rioting" citizens, and questionable military incursions eroded England's moral authority. Yet nothing undermined it as completely as England's role in the slave trade: "By foreign wealth are British morals chang'd" (Barbauld, *Epistle to William Wilberforce*). The British concept of liberty allegedly distinguished England from other nations, and abolition writers appealed directly to liberty in making their case. For example, Hannah More's *Slavery, A Poem* (not included), written, according to Clare Midgley, "explicitly to aid Wilberforce at his opening of the Parliamentary Campaign against the slave trade in 1788,"[12] begins: "IF Heaven has into being deign'd to call / Thy light, O LIBERTY! to shine on all; / ... why does thy ray / To earth distribute only partial day?" William Fox's enormously influential pamphlet *An Address to the People of Great-Britain on the Propriety of Abstaining from West-India Sugar and Rum* (1791), which launched a public abstinence campaign, made liberty a central part of the argument. "In demanding liberty then for the persons called slaves in our islands," writes Fox, "we demand no more than they are entitled to by the common law of the land."[13] Organized abstinence efforts, spurred by Fox's pamphlet, involved women in the abolition movement as public figures. The sugar abstinence was appealing to women because it "exposed their power as domestic consumers to have a direct effect on commerce and an indirect influence on politics."[14] Fox described the particularly brutal conditions on sugar plantations, what Philip Freneau's *To Sir Toby, A Sugar-Planter in the Interior Parts of Jamaica* describes as "a HELL .../ Here are no blazing brimstone lakes—'tis true, / But kindled RUM full often burns as blue."[15] Amelia Opie's *Black Man's Lament; or, How to Make Sugar* details the complete cycle of sugar production and dramatizes the situation of the enslaved, who were considered "expendable units of labor";[16] so-called gangs worked at times in a twenty-four-hour production schedule during the height of the sugarcane season. As with earlier poets such as William Cowper in *The Negro's Complaint* or Freneau in *To Sir Toby*, Opie uses the lament form to provide graphic detail about the life of the enslaved while constructing a compelling personal narrative. Like Barber's *Widow Gordon's Petition* and Mary Alcock's *Chimney-Sweeper's Complaint* (1.c), *The Black Man's Lament* makes a public issue accessible and compelling. Opie's poem was accompanied by a visual narrative of detailed woodcuts illustrating work on the plantation.

These abolition poems, like the majority of the poems in this section, seek to "rent the veil" off Britons' eyes and compel people to confront issues that can be ignored or avoided (Barbauld, *Epistle to William Wilberforce*); Barbauld wants to force "averted eyes ... to scan" the images she constructs. There was the risk that England would become, in Winscom's words, "inur'd" as "we send our *ships* abroad, / To *buy* and *sell*, and *sport* with HUMAN BLOOD!" (*An Address to the Inhabitants of Bristol*, not included). Like the poetry of war (2.E), the poems on the public sphere demonstrate the wide reaches of the subject of women's poetry and their unflinching treatment of some of the most pressing issues of the day; for these women historical "facts" were material reality. Ultimately they sought not just to function within the public sphere as a spur to social change or a voice of cultural memory; they also sought to reveal the discrepancy between the cultural ideal—the high standard demanded in the age of enlightenment—and the many different cultural realities these poems present. Even in a poem vigorously endorsing the nation, Teft integrates a critique of the status of women—"My State and Slav'ry differ but in Name; / No Rights, no Privilege, no fertile Land, / My very Will subservient to Command" (*On the Times*). The myriad power relationships revolving around different forms of authority in place in the public sphere are deeply imbricated, increasing the complexity of these poems.

Notes

1. Mary Barber, *Poems on Several Occasions* (London, 1734), xviii.

2. The notion of the so-called bourgeois public sphere comes from Jürgen Habermas, *The Structural Transformation of the Public Sphere: An Inquiry into a Category of Bourgeois Society,* trans. Thomas Burger (Boston: MIT Press, 1991).

3. Charlotte Sussman, *Consuming Anxieties: Consumer Protest, Gender, and British Slavery, 1713–1833* (Stanford, CA: Stanford University Press, 2000), 2. Lawrence Klein observes that eighteenth-century women had "public dimensions to their lives . . . [and] a consciousness that they were behaving publicly." "Gender and the Public/Private Distinction in the Eighteenth Century: Some Questions about Evidence and Analytic Procedure," *Eighteenth-Century Studies* 29 (1996): 102.

4. Carol Barash reminds us that "if we look only for the private meanings . . . or assume that their public self-constructions accurately describe their private lives, we ignore many of the most interesting tensions in their works." *English Women's Poetry, 1649–1714: Politics, Community, and Linguistic Authority* (Oxford: Clarendon, 1996), 8.

5. In 1688 William, Prince of Orange, a Dutch-speaking Protestant married to James's daughter Mary, came to the throne at Parliament's request in what was known as the Glorious (or Bloodless) Revolution of 1688. Upon Willam's death in 1702, Anne, James's Protestant daughter, peacefully assumed the throne. Childless, Anne had agreed to the Hanoverian succession, which determined in 1701 to settle the succession of the throne to the Protestant Sophia of Hanover, granddaughter of James I. Since Sophia died before Anne, her son, Georg, Elector of Hanover, became George I of Great Britain in 1714. He spoke English reluctantly and was fifty-second in line to the throne, but he was the nearest Protestant according to the Act of Settlement. He was succeeded by his son, George II (r. 1727–60), whose grandson, George III (r. 1760–1820), followed him onto the throne.

6. "A Form of Prayer with Fasting, to be us'd Yearly upon the Thirtieth of *January,* being the Day of the Martyrdom of the Blessed King *Charles* the First: To Implore the Mercy of God, That neither the Guilt of that Sacred and Innocent Blood, nor those other Sins, by which God was provoked to deliver up both us and our King into the hands of cruel and unreasonable Men, may at any time hereafter be visited upon us, or our Posterity." *Book of Common Prayer and administration of the sacraments, . . . together with the Psalter* (London, 1702).

7. The Jacobite "pretenders" to the throne were James's son James Francis Edward Stuart (1688–1766), the "Old Pretender," and his grandson, Charles Edward Stuart (1720–88), the "Young Pretender" or "Bonnie Prince Charlie."

8. W. A. Speck, *The Butcher: The Duke of Cumberland and the Suppression of the 45* (Oxford: Blackwell, 1981), 155.

9. J. E. Cookson, *The Friends of Peace: Anti-War Liberalism in England, 1793–1815* (Cambridge: Cambridge University Press, 1982), 121.

10. Ian Gilmour, *Riot, Risings, and Revolution: Governance and Violence in Eighteenth-*

Century England (London: Pimlico, 1992), 407. Certainly the Gordon Riots, of the previous decade, had resulted in a greater loss of life.

11. John Rose, *An Impartial History of the Late Disturbances in Bristol: Interspersed with Occasional Remarks. To Which are Added a List of the Killed* (Bristol, 1793), 12.

12. Clare Midgley, *Women against Slavery: The British Campaigns, 1780–1870* (London: Routledge, 1992), 32. For related discussions, see Moira Ferguson's classic study, *Subject to Others: British Women Writers and Colonial Slavery, 1670–1834* (New York: Routledge, 1992) or, more recently, George Boulukos, *The Grateful Slave: The Emergence of Race in Eighteenth-Century British and American Culture* (Cambridge: Cambridge University Press, 2008).

13. William Fox, *An Address to the People of Great-Britain on the Propriety of Abstaining from West-India Sugar and Rum* (London, 1792), 32.

14. Midgley, *Women against Slavery,* 40.

15. Philip Freneau, *Poems Written between the Years 1768 and 1794* (Monmouth, NJ, 1795), 391.

16. Bernard Moitt, introduction to *Sugar, Slavery, and Society: Perspectives on the Caribbean, India, the Mascarenes, and the United States* (Gainesville: University of Florida Press, 2004), 6.

Upon the double Murther of K. Charles I. in Answer to a Libellous Copy of Rimes Made by Vavasor Powell[1]

Katherine Philips

I think not on the State, nor am concern'd
Which way soever the great helm[2] is turn'd:
But as that son whose father's dangers nigh
Did force his native dumbness,[3] and untie
The fetter'd organs; so here's a fair cause
That will excuse the breach of Nature's laws.
Silence were now a sin, nay Passion now
Wise men themselves for Merit would allow.
What noble eye could see (and careless pass)
10   The dying Lion kick'd by every Ass?[4]
Has *Charles* so broke God's Laws, he must not have
A quiet Crown nor yet a quiet Grave?[5]
Tombs have been Sanctuaries; Thieves lie there
Secure from all their penalty and fear.
Great *Charles* his double misery was this,
Unfaithful Friends, ignoble Enemies.
Had any Heathen been this Prince's foe,
He would have wept to see him injur'd so.
His Title was his Crime, they'd reason good
20   To quarrel at the Right they had withstood.

1. The double murder refers to both the physical murder and the subsequent libelous words. Vavasor Powell (1617–70), a radical Welsh Puritan preacher, was very vocal in his opposition to the restoration of the monarchy, refusing to swear allegiance to the king. He was imprisoned almost immediately after the Restoration and spent eight of the last ten years of his life in thirteen jails. He published primarily polemical pieces, sermons, and evangelical tracts. Philips's husband, also Welsh and a Cromwellian, knew Powell, who had been a guest in the Philips's home. Indeed, Philips wrote *Upon the Double Murther of K. Charles* in response to a poem by Powell, *On the late K. Charles Blessed Memory* (by some accounts written in her home), in which he attacked the dead king.

2. Ship of state.

3. As Patrick Thomas notes, "In Herodotus, King Croesus has a mute son and the Delphic oracle has prophesied that if he should ever speak, it would be the sign of doom for his father. When Croesus is in danger from Persian forces, the son cries out a warning, and the Persians capture Croesus." *The Collected Works of Katherine Philips, "The Matchless Orinda,"* ed. Thomas, 3 vols. (Stump Cross, UK: Stump Cross Books, 1990–93), 1:261.

4. "In the fable by Phaedrus," notes Patrick Thomas, "the dying lion can endure attacks by a boar and a bull, but 'seem[s] to die a second death' when attacked by an ass." Thomas, *Collected Works of Katherine Philips,* 1:261.

5. Charles I was beheaded, and following the common practice for traitors, his head was exhibited to the crowd. Then the king's head was sewn back on his body, and he was privately buried a week later in St. George's Chapel, home of the Order of the Garter, within the closed walls of the castle.

He broke God's Laws, and therefore he must die;
And what shall then become of thee and I?
Slander must follow Treason; but yet stay,
Take not our Reason with our King away.
Though you have seiz'd upon all our defence,
Yet do not sequester[6] our common Sense.
But I admire not at this new supply:
No bounds will hold those who at Sceptres fly.
Christ will be King, but I ne're understood
His Subjects built his Kingdom up with bloud,   30
Except their own; or that he would dispence
With his commands, though for his own defence.
Oh! to what height of horrour are they come
Who dare pull down a Crown, tear up a Tomb!

                                        (1664)

On the Birth-Day of Queen Katherine[7]
Anne Killigrew

While yet it was the Empire of the Night,
And Stars still check'r'd Darkness with their Light,
From Temples round the cheerful Bells did ring,
But with the Peales[8] a churlish Storm did sing.
I slumbr'd; and the Heavens like things did show,
Like things which I had seen and heard below.
Playing on Harps Angels did singing fly,
But through a cloudy and a troubl'd Sky,
Some fixt a Throne, and Royal Robes display'd,
And then a Massie[9] Cross upon it laid.   10
I wept: and earnestly implor'd to know,
Why Royal Ensigns were disposed so.
An Angel said, The Emblem thou hast seen,
Denotes the Birth-Day of a Saint and Queen.

6. Set aside, appropriate. *Sequester* had a topical resonance during and after the English Civil War (1642–51), during which many lands were confiscated from Royalists and Cromwellians alike.

7. Written for Catherine of Brazanga (1638–1705), wife of Charles II. Her birthdate was 25 November.

8. The ringing of bells.

9. Having great mass and depth, substantial.

Ah, Glorious Minister, I then reply'd,
Goodness and Bliss together do reside
In Heaven and thee, why then on Earth below
These two combin'd so rarely do we know?
He said, Heaven so decrees: and such a Sable Morne
20   Was that, in which the *Son of God* was borne.
Then Mortal wipe thine Eyes, and cease to rave,
God darkn'd Heaven,[10] when He the World did save.

(1686)

Upon King William's Passing the Boyn, &c.[11]
Elizabeth Singer Rowe

What *mighty genious* thus excites my Breast
With flames too great to manage or resist;
And prompts my humbler Muse at once to Sing,
(Unequal Task) the *Hero and the King.*
Oh were the potent inspiration less!
I might find words its Raptures to express;
But now I neither can its force controul,
Nor paint the *great Ideas* of my Soul:
Even so the *Priests Inspir'd,* left half the Mind
10   Of the *unutterable* God behind.
Too soft's my Voice the *Hero* to express;
Or, like himself, the War-like Prince to dress;
Or, speak him Acting in the dreadful Field,
As Brave Exploits as e'r the Sun beheld;
(Secure, and Threatning as a *Martial*[12] God,
Among the thickest of his Foes he Rode;[13]

10. An allusion to the darkening of the sky at the moment when Jesus died.

11. The battle of the Boyne, between the Protestant king William III and his father-in-law, King James II, a Catholic, was fought on 11 July 1690 just outside the Irish town of Drogheda. During the battle, William's soldiers forded the river Boyne, while James's army, outflanked and outnumbered, retreated. Although not militarily decisive, it symbolically marked the triumph of Protestantism in Ireland, consolidated the political structure ushered in by the Glorious Revolution, and cemented William and Mary's royal power. It was "the greatest single success on land in William's reign . . . . [and] reassured Englishmen of the military prowess of Williamite armies." *Poems on Affairs of State: Augustan Satirical Verse, 1660–1714,* vol. 5, *1688–1697,* ed. William J. Cameron (New Haven, CT: Yale University Press, 1971), 226–27.

12. Warlike.

13. Both kings led their own troops into battle, William crossing the river with thirty-five hundred of his thirty-six thousand troops.

And, like an Angry *Torrent* forc't his way
Through all the Horrors that in Ambush lay:)
Or at the *Boyne* describe him as he stood
Resolv'd, upon the edges of the Flood: 20
𝕺n, on, 𝕲reat 𝖂illiam; for no Breast but Thine,
Was ever urg'd with such a Bold Design:
Indulge the Motions of this Sacred Heat;
For none but thee *can weild a thought so great.*
He's lanch'd, he's lanch'd; the foremost from the Shore;
The Noblest Weight that e'r the River Bore.
To smooth their Streams, the smiling *Naides*[14] hast;
And, Rising, did him Homage as he pass'd:
And all the shapes of Death and Horror[15]——
𝕹o more—ah stay—though in a cause so good;   30
'Tis pitty to expend that Sacred Blood.
Why wilt thou thus the boldest Dangers seek,
And foremost through the Hostile Squadrons break?
Why wilt thou thus so bravely venture all?
Oh, where's unhappy *Albion,*[16] should'st thou fall?
Keep near him still, you *kind Æthereal Powers,*
That Guard him, and are pleas'd, the Task is yours.

All the Ill Fate that threatens him oppose; ⎫
Confound the Forces of his Foreign Foes,[17] ⎬
And Treacherous Friends less generous then those; ⎭   40
May Heaven success to all his Actions give,
And long, and long, and long, let WILLIAM live.

(1696)

Prologue [to *Love's Contrivance*]
Susanna Centlivre

Poets like Mushroms rise and fall of late,
Or as th' uncertain Favourites of State,
Inventions rack'd to please both Eye and Ear,
But no Scene takes without the moving Player:

---

14. Freshwater nymphs, distinct from sea nymphs, thought to inhabit rivers, streams, or lakes.
15. Approximately fifteen hundred men were killed.
16. Great Britain.
17. Louis XIV sent sixty-five hundred French troops to support James.

Daily we see Plays, Pamphlets, Libels, Rhimes,
Become the Falling-Sickness[18] of the Times;
So feavourish is the Humor of the Town,
It surfeits of a Play e'er three Days run.
At *Locket's, Brown's,* and at *Pontack's*[19] enquire,
What modish Kick-shaws[20] the nice Beaus desire,
What fam'd Ragoust,[21] what new invented Salate[22]
Has best Pretensions to regale the Palate.
If we present you with a Medly here,
A hodge podge Dish serv'd up in *China* Ware,
We hope 'twill please, 'cause like your Bills of Fare.[23]
To please you all we shou'd attempt in vain,
In diff'rent Persons diff'rent Humors reign.
The Soldier's for the rattling Scenes of War,
The peaceful Beau hates shedding Blood so near.
Courtiers in Com'dy place their chief Delight,
'Cause Love's the proper Bus'ness of the Night.
The Clown for Pastoral his half Crown bestows,
But t'other House by sad Experience knows,
This polish'd Town produces few of those.
The Merchant is for Traffick ev'ry where,
And values not the best, but cheapest Ware:
Since various Humors are pleas'd various ways,
A Critick's but a Fool to judge of Plays.
Fool, did I say? 'Tis difficult to know
Who 'tis that's so indeed, or is not so:
If that be then a Point so hard to gain,
Wit's sure a most profound unfathom'd Main.[24]
He that sits Judge, the Trident ought to sway,
To know who's greatest Fool, or Wit to Day,
The Audience, or the Author of the Play.

(1703)

---

18. Epilepsy.
19. All three were ordinaries, or taverns, frequented by a sophisticated theatrical crowd.
20. Fancy but insubstantial dishes.
21. Highly seasoned stew.
22. Salad.
23. Menus.
24. A fathom is a nautical measure of depth; the main is the open sea. Thus the phrase doubles the incomprehensibility of wit.

Upon an improbable undertaking[25]
Anne Finch

A tree the fairest in the wood
That long in Majesty had stood
A gracefull prospect to the plains
And shelter to the flocks and Swains
Up by the roots a tempest tore
And to a neighbouring meadow bore
The Country sorrow for the Oak[26]
And meaner trees bewail'd the stroak
But when the tenants of the Land
This general grief did understand   10
They bid all be of better chear
Who soon shou'd have another there
Which shou'd be found as large and high
And satisfy both use and eye
Next day to make their promise good
No gap was seen throughout the wood
But fixt within the vacant place
With verdant bough and mimick grace
Another Oak its body rais'd
And for a while was own'd and prais'd   20
But time which all discovery brings
Distinguishing 'twixt knaves and Kings
Withers the bough and drys the trunk
The planters grieved to see it shrunk
Totring and tending to decay
More strongly prop it every day
And wet it whilst their grounds lye dry
With all their rivulets supply
At length in spite of cost and art
Since nature in it had no part   30
Down fell the bough which by a rope
Was only fasten'd to the top

25. Written at the time of the Hanoverian succession, when, following the death of Queen Anne, George I ascended the throne.

26. The royal oak was one of the key symbols of the monarchy and was especially identified with King Charles II, who had hidden in an oak tree during his retreat following the battle of Worcester in 1651. Charles and others planted trees from the acorns of this tree to commemorate his restoration.

The trunk into the air was flung
From whence no sprig or fiber sprung
Friends quoth a man who came to see
The ruine of the bough and tree
How cou'd your folly be so staunch
When it had neither root or branch
To think this Timber cou'd maintain
Like what you've lost a stable reign
But yet if you'd successfull be
A Scion from the home-bred tree[27]
May grow in time to fill the place
And Royal Oaks be of his race.
    Application
Your project seems as wild as this
Then 'twere not strange if it shou'd miss
But if you wou'd that fate prevent
With solid maxims be content.

40

(1714; 1998)

The Widow Gordon's Petition:[28]
To the Right Hon. the Lady Carteret
Mary Barber

Weary'd with long Attendance on the Court,
You, Madam, are the Wretch's last Resort.
Eternal King! if Here in vain I cry,
Where shall the Fatherless, and Widow fly?

27. George I, from Hanover, was believed to speak no English or only rudimentary English and was therefore clearly not a "home-bred" English king.

28. Written for an Officer's Widow. *Barber*. [The poem is written to Frances Worsley Carteret (1694–1743), the wife of John Carteret (1690–1763), second Earl of Granville, and Lord Lieutenant of Ireland. In the preface to the collection of poems in which it appeared, Barber wrote, "THE Petition was to my Lady CARTERET, during the Time of my Lord CARTERET's Government in *Ireland*, and sent inclosed to Mr. TICKELL, in a Letter without a Name. It was my Felicity, as well as the Petitioner's, to have the Petition recommended with great Generosity, and received with uncommon Goodness; that excellent Lady interested herself with so much Zeal for the distressed Widow, that a considerable Sum was raised for her Relief." *Poems on Several Occasions* (London, 1734), xviii. Carteret subsequently became a patron of Barber's, as did her husband. Both are listed as subscribers to her *Poems on Several Occasions,* and Lord Carteret is listed as purchasing five books. *Eds.*]

How blest are they, who sleep among the Dead,
Nor hear their Childrens piercing Cries for Bread!

WHEN your lov'd Off-spring gives your Soul Delight,
Reflect, how mine are irksome to my Sight:
O think, how must a wretched Mother grieve,
Who hears the Want she never can relieve!   10

AN *Evil* preys upon my helpless Son,
(How many ways the Wretched are undone!)
Cruel Distemper, to assault his Sight,
And rob him of his only Joy, the Light!
His Anguish makes my wearied Eyes o'erflow,
And loads me with unutterable Woe.

No Friendly Voice my lonely Mansion cheers,
All fly th' Infection of the Widow's Tears:
Ev'n those, whose Pity eas'd my Wants with Bread,
Are now, O sad Reverse! my greatest Dread.   20
My mournful Story will no more prevail,
And ev'ry Hour I dread a dismal Jail:[29]
I start at each imaginary Sound,
And *Horrors have encompass'd me around.*

TREMBLE, ye Daughters, who at Ease recline,
Lest ye should know a Misery like mine.
Ye now, unmov'd, can hear the Wretched moan,
And feel no Wants, yourselves oppress'd by none;
Fly from the Sight of Woes, ye will not share,
And leave the helpless Orphan to despair.   30
But know, that dreadful Hour is drawing near,
When you'll be treated, as you've acted here:
To you no more the Wretched shall complain,
'Twill be *your* Turn to weep, and sue in vain.

NOT so the Fair, with God-like Mercy bless'd,
Who feels another's Anguish in her Breast;
Who never hears the Wretched sigh in vain,
Herself distress'd, till she relieves their Pain.

29. Debtor's prison.

THIS, Fame reports, Fair CARTERET, of You;
40   This blest Report encourag'd me to sue.
O Angel Goodness, hear, and ease my Moan,
Nor let your Mercy fail in *me* alone!
So at the last Tribunal will I stand,
With my poor Orphans, plac'd on either Hand;
There, with my Cries, my SAVIOUR I'll assail;
(For at *His* Bar[30] the Widow's Tears prevail)
That she, who made the Fatherless her Care,
The Fulness of Cœlestial Joys may share;
That She a Crown of Glory may receive,
50   Who snatch'd me from Destruction and the Grave.

(1734)

On the XXXth *of* JANUARY[31]
Sarah Dixon

Whilst shining Characters from *Greece* or *Rome*,
By learned Authors, are transmitted Home;
We trace the Glories of each distant Age,
And read with Pleasure the *instructive* Page.
The gen'rous Soul expands, and ardent feels
The innate Joys, consummate Virtue yields.
But when the Prince, the Patriot, or the Saint,
In every Ornament of *Truth* they paint,
Let conscious *Britain*, blushing, make her Claim,
10   Of all united, in one deathless Name;
And call him *CHARLES*,—read him with Candour through,
You'll find inimitable Goodness flow;
Pride of his Friends, the Envy of his Foes;
Whose Soul above the *common* Standard rose.
Undaunted Champion of our Church and Laws;

---

30. The wooden rail at which prisoners stood for arraignment, trial, or sentence.

31. The thirtieth of January was observed to be the day of martyrdom of King Charles I, who was executed on that date in 1648. The date was added to the Book of Common Prayer upon the Restoration, and throughout the eighteenth century it was a day of sermons and remembrance. The cult of the martyrdom of Charles was further enhanced when, within hours of his death, his alleged final thoughts were published in *Eikon Basilike* (Royal Portrait) (1648). The frontispiece had Charles in a Christlike apotheosis with purple robe and crown of thorns.

Impartial Friend, to every noble Cause:
Humble in Royal, Great in Abject State,
As truly Pious as Unfortunate;
Conspicuous in thy Actions, all may see,
The Christian HERO *perfected* in Thee!   20
Is it too much, with the revolving Year,
To offer for our selves and Thee a Tear?
The Tears thy Virtues and thy Sufferings claim;
The only Tribute we can pay thy Fame.
Tho' circling Ocean do's embrace our Shores,
And rich returning Fleets increase our Stores;
Tho' Theologick Truths are purely taught,
And Civil Sanctions accurately wrought;
Wars dreadful Din, confin'd to foreign Climes,
Reflect, O *Britain!* on thy *Native* Crimes;   30
In all thy Boast of Peace and Plenty, bring
To thy Remembrance, thy Martyr'd KING.
Then fell the Saint, the Patriot, and the Prince;
Victim to Honour, and to Innocence:
Erase our Annals, or our Griefs renew,
Give to his Memory, at least, its Due.

(1740)

In Memory of the Rt. Hon. Lord Aubrey Beauclerk, Who was slain at Carthagena (Written in the year 1743, at the request of his Lady)[32]
Mary Jones

Shall so much worth in silence pass away,
And no recording muse that worth display?
Shall public spirit like the private die,
The coward with the brave promiscuous[33] lie?

32. Beauclerk (c. 1710–41), a naval officer, was born into a prominent English family as the eighth son of Charles Beauclerk, illegitimate son of the actress Nell Gwyn and King Charles II. Jones was a friend of Martha Lovelace, who married Henry Beauclerk, Aubrey's brother. Aubrey Beauclerk was married to Catherine Newton Alexander, also a friend of Jones, although she published these verses without Jones's permission. Beauclerk was killed on 24 March 1741, in the attack on the Boca Chica in Carthagena, now known as Cartagena.
33. Confused, contradictory.

The hero's toils should be the muses care,
In peace their guardian, and their shield in war:
Alike inspir'd, they mutual succours lend;
The Muses His, and He the Muses friend.

To me the solemn lyre you reach in vain,
10   The simple warbler of some idle strain.
What tho' the hero's fate the lay demands,
What tho' impell'd and urg'd by your commands;
Yet, weak of flight, in vain I prune the wing,
And, diffident of voice, attempt to sing.

What dreadful slaughter on the western coast!
How many gallant warriors *Britain* lost,
A *British* muse would willingly conceal;
But what the muse would hide, our tears reveal.
Pensive, we oft recal those fatal shores,
20   Where *Carthagena*[34] lifts her warlike tow'rs.
High o'er the deep th' embattl'd fortress heaves
Its awful front, its basis in the waves;
Without impregnable by nature's care,
And arm'd within with all the rage of war.

Deep in oblivion sink th' ill-omen'd hour,
That call'd our legions to the baneful shore!
Where death, in all her horrid pomp array'd,
O'er the pale clime her direful influ'nce shed.
Want, famine, war, and pestilential breath,
30   All act subservient to the rage of death.
Those whom the wave, or fiercer war would spare,
Yeild to the clime, and sink in silence there:
No friend to close their eyes, no pitying guest
To drop the silent tear, or strike the pensive breast.

---

34. Cartagena is a port town in what is now Colombia, in the very western part of the Caribbean; at the time of the poem it was a Spanish colony. Boca Chica was the fortification at the entrance to the harbor in which Cartagena was located. Although the British were able to secure Boca Chica, they were unsuccessful in their attempts to capture Cartagena. Their attack was, according to W. A. Speck, "a dismal failure." *Stability and Strife: England, 1714–1760* (Cambridge, MA: Harvard University Press, 1979), 234. Military incompetence, disease, and fierce fighting led to a large number of casualties. By one estimate, the naval force was reduced by two-thirds, and colonial soldiers by four-fifths.

Here *Douglas*[35] fell, the gallant and the brave!
Here much-lamented *Watson*[36] found a grave.
Here, early try'd, and acting but too well,
The lov'd, ennobled, gen'rous BEAUCLERK fell.
Just as the spring of life began to bloom,
When ev'ry grace grew softer on the tomb;   40
In all that health and energy of youth,
Which promis'd honours of maturer growth;
When round his head the warriour laurel sprung,
And temp'rance brac'd the nerve which valour strung;
When his full heart expanded to the goal,
And promis'd victory had flush'd his soul,
He fell!—His country lost her earliest boast;
His family a faithful guardian lost;
His friend a safe companion; and his wife,
Her last resource, her happiness in life.   50

O ever honour'd, ever happy shade!
How well hast thou thy debt to virtue paid!
Brave, active, undismay'd in all the past;
Compos'd, intrepid, steady to the last.
When half thy limbs, and more than half was lost
Of life, thy valour still maintain'd it's post:
Gave the last signal[37] for thy country's good,
And, dying, seal'd it with thy purest blood.

Say, what is Life? and wherefore was it giv'n?
What the design, the purpose mark'd by Heav'n?   60
Was it in lux'ry to dissolve the span,
To raise the animal, and sink the man?
In the soft bands of pleasure, idly gay,
To frolic the immortal gift away?
To tell the tale, or flow'ry wreath to bind,
Then shoot away, and leave no track behind?

35. *The Authentic Papers Relating to the Expedition against Carthagena,* 2nd ed. (London, 1744), identifies a Captain Douglas as a crewmate on a ship engaged in the assault (13).

36. Colonel Jonas Watson, killed at the siege of Cartagena on 30 March 1741.

37. After both his legs were shot off. See the account of his death in the prose inscription in
Westminster-Abbey, written by the author, under his Lady's directions. The verse by Dr. *Young. Jones.*
[The poet, playwright, and writer Edward Young (bap. 1683, d. 1765), whose most famous poem was
The Complaint: or, Night-Thoughts on Life, Death and Immortality (1742–45). *Eds.*]

Arise no duties from the social tie?
No kindred virtues from our native sky?
No truths from reason, and the thought intense?
70   Nothing result from soul, but all from sense?

   O thoughtless reptile, Man!—Born! yet ask why?
Truly, for something serious—*Born to die.*
Knowing this truth, can we be wise too soon?
And this once known, sure something's to be done—
To live's to suffer; *act,* is to exist;
And life, at best, a trial, not a feast:
Our bus'ness virtue; and when that is done,
We cannot sit too late, or rise too soon.

   "Virtue!—What is it?—Whence does it arise!"
80   Ask of the brave, the social, and the wise;
Of those who study'd for the gen'ral good,
Of those who fought, and purchas'd it with blood;
Of those who build, or plant, or who design,
Ev'n those who dig the soil, or work the mine.
If yet not clearly seen, or understood;
Ask the humane, the pious, and the good.
To no one station, stage, or part confin'd,
No single act of body, or of mind;
But whate'er lovely, just, or fit we call,
90   The fair result, the congregate of all.

   The active mind, ascending by degrees,
Its various ties, relations, duties sees:
Examines parts, thence rising to the whole,
Sees the connexion, chain, and spring of soul;
Th' eternal source! from whose pervading ray
We caught the flame, and kindled into day.
Hence the collected truths *coercive* rise,
Oblige as nat'ral, or as moral ties.
Son, brother, country, friend demand our care;
100   The common bounty all partake, must share.
Hence virtue in its source, and in its end,
To God as relative, to Man as friend.

   O friend to truth! to virtue! to thy kind!
O early call'd to leave these ties behind!

How shall the muse her vary'd tribute pay,
Indulge the tear, and not debase the lay!
Come, fair example of heroic truth!
Descend, and animate the *British* youth:
Now, when their country's wrongs demand their care,
And proud *Iberia*[38] meditates[39] the war: 110
Now, while the trumpet sounds her shrill alarms,
And calls forth all her gen'rous sons to arms;
Pour all thy genius, all thy martial fire
O'er the brave youth, and ev'ry breast inspire.
Say, *this* is virtue, glory, honour, fame,
To rise from sloth, and catch the martial flame.
When fair occasion calls their vigour forth,
To *meet* the call, and vindicate its worth:
To rouse, to kindle, animate, combine,
Revenge their country's wrongs, and think on Thine. 120

Go, happy shade! to where the good, and blest
Enjoy eternal scenes of bliss and rest:
While we below thy sudden farewel mourn,
Collect thy virtues, weeping o'er the urn;
Recal their scatter'd lustre as they past,
And see them all united in the last.

So the bright orb, which gilds the groves and streams,
Mildly diffusive of his golden beams;
Drawn to a point, his strong concenter'd[40] rays
More fulgent[41] glow, and more intensely blaze. 130

And Thou! late partner of his softer hour,
Ordain'd but just to meet, and meet no more;
Say, with the virtues how each grace combin'd!
How brave, yet social! how resolv'd, yet kind!
With manners how sincere! polite with ease!
How diffident! and yet how sure to please!
Was he of ought but infamy afraid?
Was he not modest as the blushing maid?
Asham'd to flatter, eager to commend;

38. Spain and Portugal united.
39. Plans.
40. Concentrated.
41. Brightly shining.

140   A gen'rous master, and a steady friend.
Humane to all, but warm'd when virtuous grief,
Or silent modesty, imply'd relief.
Pure in his principles, unshaken, just;
True to his God, and faithful to his trust.

BEAUCLERK, farewel!——If, with thy virtues warm'd,
And not too fondly, or too rashly charm'd,
I strive the tributary dirge[42] to pay,
And form the pinion[43] to the hasty lay;
The feeble, but well-meaning flight excuse:
150   Perhaps hereafter some more gen'rous muse,
Touch'd with thy fate, with genius at command,
May snatch the pencil from the female hand;
And give the perfect portrait, bold and free,
In numbers such as *Young*'s,[44] and worthy *Thee*.

(1743; 1750)

On hearing the Duke of CUMBERLAND had defeated the Rebels[45]

Elizabeth Teft

Stop, stop this Torrent of extatick Joy,
Lest its O'erflow this happy Land destroy;
Oh for more Breathing room, the World's too small!

---

42. Song of mourning.
43. Wing.
44. Edward Young wrote the epitaph that appeared on Beauclerk's urn in Westminster Abbey:
Whilst Britain boasts her empire o'er the deep,
This marble shall compel the brave to weep:
As men, as Britons, and as soldiers, mourn;
'Tis dauntless, loyal, virtuous Beauclerk's urn.
Sweet were his manners, as his soul was great,
And ripe his worth, though immature his fate;
Each tender grace that joy and love inspires,
Living, he mingled with his martial fires:
Dying, he bid Britannia's thunders roar;
And Spain still felt him, when he breath'd no more.
45. The Duke of Cumberland, William Augustus (1721–65), was known as "the Butcher," and there were allegations about his brutal treatment of the Scots following their defeat at the battle of Culloden on 16 April 1745, the final blow to the Jacobite Rebellion of 1745. An estimated thirty-six hundred Jacobite soldiers died during the battle or retreat. After the victory, Cumberland issued a

Its rapid Force will more than Deluge all:
Reason, thy Aid, to moderate my Bliss,
'Ere I expire in the profound Abyss.
   CUMBERLAND!
That Name the City, Vales and Woods resound,
Its ev'ry Letter has a Martial Sound.
Fame, blow thy Trump, sound loud his high Renown,   10
Thro' jarring Nations, reach the Triple Crown;
Say, of more Conquests *Britons* can't distrust,
With such a Leader in a Cause so Just.
Ne'er blest was any Country, any Land,
With such a Gen'ral as our CUMBERLAND.
You'll say, there's *Cæsar*,[46] and great *Philip's* Son;[47]
Ah! but Thirst of Pow'r drove those Victors on;
Far Nobler Motives draw our Hero's Sword,
He'd be the World's Deliv'rer, not its Lord.
Sought with intrepid Vigilance the Foe,   20
His Road to Glory lay thro' Mounts of Snow:[48]
The Followers caught the animating Fire,
His generous noble Conduct did inspire.
The Battle's Plan, the private Orders giv'n,
Speak him in Wisdom near ally'd to Heaven:
Grim Slaughter issu'd from his Princely Sword,
And Conquest seem'd dependent on his Word.
When Death stalk'd forth amongst the Rebel Crew, ⎫
Was more and more Voracious as he Slew,   ⎬
By theirs his Nature more rapacious grew.   ⎭   30
Others with great Precipitation run,
From the triumphant Sword of *George's* Son.[49]

---

policy of "no quarter," resulting in the English army's killing Highlanders regardless of their political affiliation. Allegedly, even women and children were murdered.

    Within the context of this poem, the rebels are those Highlanders who were considered Jacobites, loyal supporters of the exiled royal house of Stuart. Charles Stuart, "Bonnie Prince Charlie," was the Jacobite claimant, or "Young Pretender," to the throne. When he arrived in Scotland in 1745, most of the Highland clans gave him their support.

    46. Julius Caesar (c. 102–44 BC), celebrated Roman general, statesman, and, from 46 BC until his assassination, dictator.

    47. Alexander the Great (356–323 BC), king of Macedonia who overthrew the Persian Empire during his reign.

    48. The Jacobite army, led by Prince Charles, retreated through thick snow to Inverness. Cumberland caught them at Culloden and killed one-fifth of the five thousand rebels on 16 April 1746. He pursued the survivors to remote corners of the Highlands, parts of which were still snow covered.

    49. The Duke of Cumberland was the third son of King George II.

Be always, O Great GOD, his sure Defence,
And stamp on him the Seal of Providence;
Let this record, and future Ages tell,
Glory's top Height he Soar'd, nor ever Fell.

(1747)

On the Times. Wrote during the late Rebellion[50]
Elizabeth Teft

O *Britain!* once high-favour'd happy Isle,
When Wealth with Peace, Freedom with Concord smile,
Bless'd in thy Clime, in Product and in State,
Strength, Courage, Conduct, did thy Natives wait.
All *Europe* homag'd thy judicious Nod,
Envy of Nations, Darling of thy GOD:
But now how fall'n! how lost the glorious Boast!
Abject, forlorn, Jest of the rival Host!
Methinks I hear *Cato's* sententious[51] Breath
10 Cry Chains or Conquest, Liberty or Death:[52]
To Arms, to Arms, unanimously rise,
As your Progenitors be bravely wise:
Record can't shew a more illust'rious Cause,
Religion, Liberty, and well-plann'd Laws,
Demand the Sword, and court you to the Field,
To stab Rebellion, make proud Discord yield.
Now turn your Eyes on suff'ring Majesty,
Pre-eminent in virtuous Degree;
The general Father, anxious in Defence
20 Of publick Safety, at his Life's Expence:
In Danger eminent he stands confest,
The Crown is but a shining Grief at best;
Each Jewel weighs its treble[53] Worth of Care;
The sacred Wearer much we should revere,

---

50. The Jacobite Rebellion of 1745.

51. Full of intelligence or wisdom. The word can also have a more negative sense, as in one addicted to pompous moralizing.

52. These lines appear in Joseph Addison's play *Cato* (London, 1713): "It is not now a time to talk of aught / But Chains, or Conquest; Liberty, or Death" (2.4.314–15).

53. Three times.

As Heaven's Vicegerent,[54] our anointed King.
Fly, *British* Worthies, fly to succour him.
Great self-existing GOD, in Mercy thou
Preserve thy Representative below:
Speak Safety to him and his Royal Line,
Whilst Time meets Period let his Issue[55] shine: 30
And you ye Angels, Ministers of Light, ⎫
Who to obey Omnipotence delight, ⎬
Guard *Britain,* till the non-succeeding Night. ⎭
Next those high Bless'd ones, happy most are those
Who honest Courage, Faction dare oppose;
O! animating Thought, thrice envy'd Men,
That to a Sword I cou'd transform my Pen,
Some memorable glorious Deed to do,
Destroy the Treason, yet preserve the Foe,
To juster Thoughts his stubborn Nature bend,   40
Transform this Enemy to a faithful Friend;
Strictly adhere to our Religious Laws,[56]
Turn Proselyte[57] in Royal *George's*[58] Cause,
His Schemes to legal Justice sacrifice,
Use all his Pow'r the State to aggrandize;
Wake from Ambition as a frightful Dream,
And pay glad Homage, where he wants to reign.
Extatic Thought! and since that cannot be,
Wou'd they accept a Sacrifice from me,
Preparatives and proper Times, be given,   50
To fill my Soul with stedfast hopes of Heaven,
I'd be the Victim, see my Bosom bleed,
My Thoughts suggest I'd glory in the Deed;
Nor the fierce Pain extort a murm'ring Sigh,
But shew them how a Woman dare to Dye;
Dye like a Hero for the publick Good,
Buy off their Ruin with my vital Blood.
Yet why am I thus anxious for the State?
It better wou'd become the Rich and Great.

---

54. Representative of the Deity; the use of this word alludes to the divine right of kings.
55. Offspring.
56. Charles Stuart, "Bonnie Prince Charlie," was Catholic.
57. Convert.
58. King George II.

60 Tho' *England* triumphs, slender is my claim,
My State and Slav'ry differ but in Name;
No Rights, no Privilege, no fertile Land,
My very Will subservient to Command.
Need there these Motives to excite a Flame?
What'ere my State, *Britannia's* still the same,
Dear to my Soul, as Infants witty Prate[59]
To a fond Mother, think how dear is that.
Then thus to dye, perhaps it wou'd be said,
Orinthia[60] was a brave Heroick Maid;
70 Love to her Country was severely try'd,
Honour'd it living, then its Martyr dy'd.
This, or this not, merits but small Regard,
Generous Virtue is its own Reward.
'Tis here I fix, God's Glory shou'd
 Be the grand Aim of Breath;
Second to that the General Good:
Then meet Reward in Death.

(1747)

Sonnet XLVI: Written at Penshurst, in Autumn 1788[61]
Charlotte Smith

Ye Towers sublime, deserted now and drear,
 Ye woods, deep sighing to the hollow blast,
The musing wanderer loves to linger near,
 While History points to all your glories past:
And startling from their haunts the timid deer,
 To trace the walks obscured by matted fern,
Which Waller's[62] soothing lyre were wont to hear,

59. Prattle; childish talk.
60. Teft's poetic name for herself.
61. Penshurst, in Kent, was the ancestral home of the Sidney family since 1552 and the birthplace of the poet Sir Philip Sidney (1554–86). The estate retained its association with literary achievement in part because of tributes such as Ben Jonson's *To Penshurst* (1616), which praised it as the place "where all the *Muses* met" when Sidney was born.
62. The lyric poet and politician Edmund Waller (1606–87). He spent lengthy periods of time at Penshurst between 1635 and 1638 while pursuing a courtship with Dorothy Sidney (1617–84), who, raised at Penshurst, appears as "Sacharissa" in Waller's poetic courtship. In his poem *At Penshurst* (1645) Waller praises her "more than humane grace."

But where now clamours the discordant heron![63]
The spoiling hand of Time may overturn
 These lofty battlements, and quite deface   10
The fading canvas whence we love to learn
 Sydney's[64] keen look, and Sacharissa's grace;
But fame and beauty still defy decay,
Saved by the historic page——the poet's tender lay!

(1788; 1789)

Epistle to William Wilberforce, Esq., on the Rejection of the Bill for Abolishing the Slave Trade[65]

Anna Laetitia Barbauld

Cease, Wilberforce, to urge thy generous aim!
Thy Country knows the sin, and stands the shame!
The Preacher, Poet, Senator in vain
Has rattled in her sight the Negro's chain;
With his deep groans assail'd her startled ear,
And rent[66] the veil that hid his constant tear;
Forc'd her averted eyes his stripes to scan,
Beneath the bloody scourge laid bare the man,
Claim'd Pity's tear, urg'd Conscience's strong controul,
And flash'd conviction on her shrinking soul.   10
The Muse, too soon awak'd, with ready tongue
At Mercy's shrine applausive peans[67] rung;
And Freedom's eager sons, in vain foretold
A new Astrean[68] reign, an age of gold:

63. In the park at Penshurst is an heronry. The house is at present uninhabited, and the windows of the galleries and other rooms, in which there are many invaluable pictures, are never opened but when strangers visit it. *Smith.*

64. Algernon Sidney. *Smith.* [Algernon Sidney (1623–83) was Dorothy Sidney's younger brother. The author of *Discourses Concerning Government,* written from 1681 to 1683, he vindicated armed resistance to oppression and Machiavellian militarism. He was tried, convicted, and beheaded in 1683 for "treasonable" advocacy of rebellion. Today he is regarded with John Locke (1632–1704) as a champion of freedom and a theorist of the Glorious Revolution. *Eds.*]

65. In April 1790 William Wilberforce (1759–1833), MP from Yorkshire, introduced an abolition bill in Parliament that was defeated by a vote of 163 to 88. Parliament did not approve an abolition bill until 1807.

66. Torn.

67. Variant spelling of *paean,* heartfelt song of praise or thanksgiving.

68. Related to the stars.

She knows and she persists—Still Afric bleeds,
Uncheck'd, the human traffic still proceeds;[69]
She stamps her infamy to future time,
And on her harden'd forehead seals the crime.

   In vain, to thy white standard gathering round,
20   Wit, Worth, and Parts and Eloquence are found:
In vain, to push to birth thy great design,
Contending chiefs, and hostile virtues join;
All, from conflicting ranks, of power possest
To rouse, to melt, or to inform the breast.
Where seasoned tools of Avarice prevail,
A Nation's eloquence, combined, must fail:
Each flimsy sophistry[70] by turns they try;
The plausive[71] argument, the daring lye,
The artful gloss, that moral sense confounds,
30   Th' acknowledged thirst of gain that honour wounds:
Bane of ingenuous[72] minds, th' unfeeling sneer,
Which, sudden, turns to stone the falling tear:
They search assiduous, with inverted skill,
For forms of wrong, and precedents of ill;
With impious mockery wrest the sacred page,
And glean up crimes from each remoter age:
Wrung Nature's tortures, shuddering, while you tell,
From scoffing fiends bursts forth the laugh of hell;
In Britain's senate, Misery's pangs give birth
40   To jests unseemly, and to horrid mirth——
Forbear!—thy virtues but provoke our doom,
And swell th' account of vengeance yet to come;
For, not unmark'd in Heaven's impartial plan,
Shall man, proud worm, contemn[73] his fellow-man?
And injur'd Afric, by herself redrest,
Darts her own serpents at her Tyrant's breast.
Each vice, to minds deprav'd by bondage known,
With sure contagion fastens on his own;

---

69. By the 1790s the capital from the slave trade constituted 11 percent of the national income in England.
70. Specious, fallacious reasoning.
71. Plausible.
72. Noble or honorable.
73. Treat with contemptuous disregard.

In sickly languors[74] melts his nerveless frame,
And blows to rage impetuous Passion's flame: 50
Fermenting swift, the fiery venom gains
The milky innocence of infant veins;
There swells the stubborn will, damps learning's fire,
The whirlwind wakes of uncontroul'd desire,
Sears the young heart to images of woe,
And blasts the buds of Virtue as they blow.

   Lo! where reclin'd, pale Beauty courts the breeze,
Diffus'd on sofas of voluptuous ease;
With anxious awe, her menial train around,
Catch her faint whispers of half-utter'd sound;   60
See her, in monstrous fellowship, unite
At once the Scythian, and the Sybarite;[75]
Blending repugnant vices, misally'd,
Which *frugal* nature purpos'd to divide;
See her, with indolence to fierceness join'd,
Of body delicate, infirm of mind,
With languid tones imperious mandates urge;
With arm recumbent wield the household scourge;
And with unruffled mien, and placid sounds,
Contriving torture, and inflicting wounds.   70

   Nor, in their palmy walks and spicy groves,
The form benign of rural Pleasure roves;
No milk-maids' song, or hum of village talk,
Sooths the lone Poet in his evening walk:
No willing arm the flail unweary'd plies,
Where the mix'd sounds of cheerful labour rise;
No blooming maids, and frolic swains are seen
To pay gay homage to their harvest queen:
No heart-expanding scenes their eyes must prove
Of thriving industry, and faithful love: 80

74. Fatigue.

75. Scythians were a nomadic people inhabiting a large section of what are now eastern Europe and Asiatic Russia; they were known for their barbarity. By contrast, the Sybarites were citizens of Sybaris, an ancient Greek city in what is now southern Italy traditionally noted for the effeminacy and wealth of its inhabitants; the term generally alludes to any person devoted to luxury or pleasure. Barbauld here characterizes the barbarity of the slave trade that feeds the luxuries desired by the British nation.

But shrieks and yells disturb the balmy air,
Dumb sullen looks of woe announce despair,
And angry eyes thro' dusky features glare.
Far from the sounding lash the Muses fly,
And sensual riot drowns each finer joy.

    Nor less from the gay East, on essenc'd wings,
Breathing unnam'd perfumes, Contagion springs;
The soft luxurious plague alike pervades
The marble palaces, and rural shades;
90   Hence, throng'd Augusta[76] builds her rosy bowers,
And decks in summer wreaths her smoky towers;
And hence, in summer bow'rs, Art's costly hand
Pours courtly splendours o'er the dazzled land:
The manners melt—One undistinguish'd blaze
O'erwhelms the sober pomp of elder days;
Corruption follows with gigantic stride,
And scarce vouchsafes his shameless front to hide:
The spreading leprosy taints ev'ry part,
Infects each limb, and sickens at the heart.
100   Simplicity! most dear of rural maids,
Weeping resigns her violated shades:
Stern Independence from his glebe[77] retires,
And anxious Freedom eyes her drooping fires;
By foreign wealth are British morals chang'd,
And Afric's sons, and India's, smile aveng'd.

    For you,[78] whose temper'd ardour long has borne
Untir'd the labour, and unmov'd the scorn;
In Virtue's fasti[79] be inscrib'd your fame,
And utter'd your's with Howard's[80] honour'd name,
110   Friends of the friendless—Hail, ye generous band!
Whose efforts yet arrest Heav'n's lifted hand,
Around whose steady brows, in union bright,
The civic wreath, and Christian's palm unite:

76. England.
77. Land.
78. Wilberforce.
79. Annals.
80. John Howard (c. 1726–90), philanthropist and prison reformer, also praised in Barbauld's *Eighteen Hundred and Eleven*.

Your merit stands, no greater and no less,
Without, or with the varnish of success;
But seek no more to break a Nation's fall,
For ye have sav'd yourselves—and that is all.
Succeeding times your struggles, and their fate,
With mingled shame and triumph shall relate,
While faithful History, in her various page,   120
Marking the features of this motley age,
To shed a glory, and to fix a stain,
Tells how you strove, and that you strove in vain.

(1791)

THOUGHTS

OCCASIONED BY THE PROCEEDINGS ON
BRISTOL-BRIDGE,
AND THE
Melancholy Consequences,
On the AWFUL NIGHT of MONDAY,
The 30th of SEPTEMBER, 1793,
When the Military were ordered to fire on the Populace, in
Consequence of their collecting together, to obstruct the
Continuance of the BRIDGE TOLLS, by which Means many
innocent People passing by lost their Lives.[81]

Jane Cave Winscom

Pause, reader! and admire the grace,
Which still protracts thy chequer'd race;
Thy husband, neighbour, friend, or son
All tranquil stood as thou hast done:
When lo! they met the awful doom!
Which now consigns them to the tomb.

81. The Bristol Bridge spanned the Avon River and connected two parts of Bristol. John Rose wrote that "the average number of persons who pass over Bristol Bridge in a minute is more than sixty . . . every interruption, even of a few minutes, must, therefore, make a crowd." *An Impartial History of the Late Disturbances in Bristol: Interspersed with Occasional Remarks. To Which are Added a List of the Killed* (Bristol, 1793), 11. The riot was a two-day occurrence that began on Saturday, 28 September 1793, with an attempt to reinstate the bridge toll. The first citizens' protest occurred the next day, culminating on 30 September with the shooting that occurred at 8:15 PM.

How spake the MAGISTRATE on high?
CAPTAIN in chief of earth and sky,[82]
Carnage and woe had not prevail'd,
Nor horror ev'ry face assail'd,
While bullets flew from street to street,
Leaving no moment for retreat;[83]

The honest tradesman homeward bound,
Would not have met the mortal wound;
Nor inoffensive stander-by
Drop by his neighbour's side, and die;
No amputated legs or arms,
(As tho' amid dire war's alarms)
The hapless woman, boy, or man,
Had mourn'd through life's protracted span:
Nor widow wept her husband gone,
While orphan's tears the groan prolong!

My Friend,[84] alas! whose peaceful mind
Riot[85] abhors of every kind,
Had pass'd the street in *duty's* call,

---

82. *But he said nay, lest while ye gather up the Tares, ye root up also the Wheat with them.* (Mat. xiii. 29.) *Winscom.*

83. According to John Rose, the militia "fired upon their assailants and the gaping populace: some oyster-shells being that instant thrown from that part of the Back near St. Nicholas-church, the rear faced about, and fired directly up High-street." *Impartial History,* 12. According to another account, "The front rank fired up High street, the mob instantly fell back and jammed up every street; the angry soldiers, it is said, left their ranks in order to single out individuals, whilst others of them kept a desultory fire up every street that radiated from the bridge. Nor were those safe who had kept at a distance, one shot entered the house at the corner of Wine street and passed through the headboard of the bedstead." J. F. Nicholls and John Taylor, *Bristol Past and Present,* 3 vols. (Bristol: J. W. Arrowsmith, 1881–82), 3:218.

84. The AUTHOR's Husband, returning from the Duties of his Office. *Winscom.* [Winscom's husband, Thomas Winscom, was an exciseman, and the couple lived in Bristol from 1792 to 1797. Her husband is not included in the list of those killed or wounded. *Eds.*]

85. The use of this term in relation to the poem and the event is loaded. One of the primary complaints related to the incident was the magistrates' failure to follow the Riot Act. Enacted in 1714, the Riot Act allowed any official to disperse a crowd of twelve or more people by stating, "OUR Sovereign Lord the King chargeth and commandeth all Persons, being assembled, immediately to disperse themselves, and peaceably to depart to their Habitations, or to their lawful Business, upon the Pains contained in the Act made in the first Year of King George, for preventing Tumults and riotous Assemblies. God save the King." Individuals then had one hour to disperse before action was taken. While John Rose acknowledged that the Riot Act was read the day before the shootings, he noted that it was "not heard by many (comparatively) and supposed by most to allude only to the rioters, in which class peaceable citizens could not think of including themselves." *Impartial History,* 8. While the Riot Act was read three times the morning of 30 September, it was not read immediately prior to the shooting; thus participants asserted that they had not been given sufficient opportunity to disperse.

Where whistled through the deadly ball,
Not *two* short minutes e'er began
The fire! which levell'd man by man:
He! who with warmth espous'd the cause
Of those who fought t'inforce the laws.   30
("The legal pow'r should be obey'd,⎫
And due investigation made;   ⎬
If wrong,—to law apply for aid,   ⎭
And not by riot seek redress,
Or hope an evil to suppress.
'Tis seeking demons to expel,
By Belzebub,[86] the prince of hell.")
Yet he! with ball in breast or head,
Perchance had sunk among the dead!

How spake the patriarch of old!   40
When Sodom's[87] judgment was foretold:
"Ah! wilt thou not the city spare[88]
If fifty righteous souls are there?"
Thou can'st not *sport* with human blood,
And with the *wicked* slay the *good*.
Or fire promiscuously[89] *on all*,
Lest guiltless with the guilty fall:
This *deed* were *odious* in thy sight,
Shall not the Judge of all do right?

E'er fell the dread devouring flame,   50
How cautious was the great I AM![90]

86. Beelzebub, "Prince of the devils," or Satan.

87. One of two notoriously sinful cities in the Old Testament book of Genesis, the other being Gomorrah. In Genesis 19:24 Sodom and Gomorrah are represented as being destroyed because of their depravity: "Then the LORD rained upon Sodom and upon Gomorrah brimstone and fire from the LORD out of heaven."

88. Gen. xviii. 24–27. *Winscom.* [The verses from the King James translation of the Bible read, "Peradventure there be fifty righteous within the city: wilt thou also destroy and not spare the place for the fifty righteous that are therein? That be far from thee to do after this manner, to slay the righteous with the wicked: and that the righteous should be as the wicked, that be far from thee: Shall not the Judge of all the earth do right? And the LORD said, 'If I find in Sodom fifty righteous within the city, then I will spare all the place for their sakes.' And Abraham answered and said, 'Behold now, I have taken upon me to speak unto the Lord, which am but dust and ashes.'" *Eds.*]

89. Indiscriminately, randomly.

90. An allusion to God from Exodus 3:14. When Moses asks God what his reply should be when the Israelites ask him who sent Moses to them, God replies, "'I AM THAT I AM': and he said, 'Thus shalt you say unto the children of Israel, "I AM hath sent me unto you."'"

Though thousands soon must burning lie,
That not *one* righteous man should die,
For thus he spake,[91] with angel's tongue,
'I can do nothing till thou'rt gone!'
For better *fifty* justice fly,
Than *one* should innocently die.

If such the language of the good,
Of Abraham, and Abram's GOD,[92]
60   Then how speaks conscience, Sirs! to YOU,
By whose *command* the bullets flew?[93]——
But what can this fell spectre say,
In our reformed enlighten'd day!
Then let old conscience take her flight,
And view it in a moral light;
If ought attack the human frame,
Should we not think the *man* to blame,
Or say *his* intellects were bad,
If not conclude *him* really mad;
70   Suppose our toe or finger swell,
Who thus prescrib'd to make them well;
"Cut off the foot, or leg, or arm,
And to prevent all future harm;
If these by amputation bleed,
Cut off the head with utmost speed."
Thus cure the swelling of the toe,
By the whole body's overthrow.

Permit me, e'er I drop my pen,
To add a line for injur'd men:—
80   O why, in common sense's name,
Should each his folly thus proclaim,
By treating with unjust abuse,

91. To Lot, Gen. xix. 22. *Winscom.* [These verses read: "Haste thee, escape thither; for I cannot do any thing till thou be come thither. Therefore the name of the city was called Zoar." *Eds.*]

92. Abraham, whose original name was Abram (meaning "exalted father"), was viewed to have a very favorable relationship with God. Abraham's generations are presented as part of the crowning explanation of how the world has been fashioned by the hand of God and how the boundaries and relationships of peoples were established by him. In the New Testament the phrase is "God of Abram."

93. The question "by whose command" shots were fired was also raised in relation to the incident.

The *men*[94] who cannot want excuse!
What private soldier durst withstand,
His stern superior's dread command?
Ah! what had been his wretched lot?
Himself had met the fatal shot!
Or with his arms to halberds[95] ty'd,
In streaming blood had soon been dy'd,
While lash succeeding lash had flown,   90
And stript the culprit to the bone!
Why, in the name of justice then,
Each day insult the private men?

   The BOOK[96] we call our rule of life,
Promotes no bloodshed, noise, or strife;
'Tis long forbearance! kindness! love!
The page celestial deigns t' approve:
Then let this Page your minds impress,
Who by revenge would seek redress;
For limbs or friends that's torn away,   100
JUSTICE the evil will repay,
In this or some more distant day!
Calmly to heav'n submit your cause,
Nor violate its sacred laws,
By fell revenge seek not for blood,
Vengeance belongs alone to GOD!

(1794)

Song. Fidelle; or, the Negro Child
Mary R. Stockdale

An outcast from my native home,
   A helpless maid forlorn,

---

94. After this melancholy Event, so great was the Resentment of the People against the Military, that the private Men were grossly insulted. *Winscom.*

95. A weapon consisting of a sharp-edged blade ending in a point and a spearhead, mounted on a handle five to seven feet long.

96. The HOLY BIBLE. *Winscom.*

O'er dangerous seas I'm doom'd to roam,
   From friends and country torn.
No mother's smile now sooths my grief;
   A Christian me beguil'd;
But, ah! he scorns to give relief,
   Or ease a poor black child.

My father now, unhappy man!
10   Weeps for his lov'd Fidelle,
And wonders much that Christians can
   Poor negroes buy and sell:
O had you heard him beg and pray,
   And seen his looks so wild!
He cried, "O let me bless this day;
   O spare my darling child!"

But, O! their hearts were hearts of stone;
   They tore me from his arms;
A Christian savage scoffs the groan
20   Caus'd by a black's alarms.
They chain'd me in this dungeon deep,
   And on my sorrows smil'd,
Then left, alas! to sigh and weep,
   The slave! the negro child!

(1798)

Instructions, Supposed to Be Written in Paris, for the Mob in England[97]

Mary Alcock

Of Liberty, Reform, and Rights I sing,
Freedom I mean, without or Church or King;
Freedom to seize and keep whate'er I can,
And boldly claim my right—The Rights of Man:[98]

97. The phrase *the mob*, connoting an unruly, violent, and disruptive group, had very specifically contemptuous and political meanings during this time.

98. Throughout the poem, Alcock appropriates the politicized terms, used both by Mary Wollstonecraft in *Vindication of the Rights of Men* (1790) and by Thomas Paine in *The Rights of Man* (1791). Both texts were radical responses to Edmund Burke's conservative apologia for the *ancien régime, Re-*

Such is the blessed liberty in vogue,
The envied liberty to be a rogue;
The right to pay no taxes, tithes, or dues;[99]
The liberty to do whate'er I chuse;
The right to take by violence and strife
My neighbour's goods, and, if I please, his life;   10
The liberty to raise a mob or riot,
For spoil and plunder ne'er were got by quiet;
The right to level and reform the great;
The liberty to overturn the state;
The right to break through all the nation's laws,
And boldly dare to take rebellion's cause:
Let all be equal, every man my brother;
Why one have property, and not another?
Why suffer titles to give awe and fear?
There shall not long remain one British peer;   20
Nor shall the criminal appalled stand
Before the mighty judges of the land;
Nor judge, nor jury shall there longer be,
Nor any jail, but every pris'ner free;
All law abolish'd, and with sword in hand
We'll seize the property of all the land.
Then hail to Liberty, Reform, and Riot!
Adieu Contentment, Safety, Peace, and Quiet!

(1799)

Eighteen Hundred and Eleven, a Poem[100]
Anna Laetitia Barbauld

Still the loud death drum, thundering from afar,
O'er the vext nations pours the storm of war:[101]
To the stern call still Britain bends her ear,
Feeds the fierce strife, the alternate hope and fear;

---

flections on the Revolution in France (1790), and were part of the larger pamphlet war known as the
"revolution controversy."

99. Tolls or legal charges.

100. The year 1811 was pivotal in England's global conflicts—the continuing Napoleonic Wars, the
looming War of 1812—as well as in its domestic unrest.

101. England and France had been at war for the last seventeen years.

Bravely, though vainly, dares to strive with Fate,
And seeks by turns to prop each sinking state.
Colossal Power with overwhelming force
Bears down each fort of Freedom in its course;
Prostrate she lies beneath the Despot's sway,
10 While the hushed nations curse him—and obey.[102]

Bounteous in vain, with frantic man at strife,
Glad Nature pours the means—the joys of life;
In vain with orange blossoms scents the gale,
The hills with olives clothes, with corn the vale;
Man calls to Famine, nor invokes in vain,
Disease and Rapine follow in her train;
The tramp of marching hosts disturbs the plough,
The sword, not sickle, reaps the harvest now,
And where the Soldier gleans the scant supply,
20 The helpless Peasant but retires to die;[103]
No laws his hut from licensed outrage shield,
And war's least horror is the ensanguined[104] field.

Fruitful in vain, the matron counts with pride
The blooming youths that grace her honoured side;
No son returns to press her widow'd hand,
Her fallen blossoms strew a foreign strand.
—Fruitful in vain, she boasts her virgin race,
Whom cultured arts adorn and gentlest grace;
Defrauded of its homage, Beauty mourns,
30 And the rose withers on its virgin thorns.
Frequent, some stream obscure, some uncouth name
By deeds of blood is lifted into fame;
Oft o'er the daily page some soft-one bends
To learn the fate of husband, brothers, friends,
Or spread the map with anxious eye explores,
Its dotted boundaries and penciled shores,
Asks *where* the spot that wrecked her bliss is found,
And learns its name but to detest the sound.

102. The "Despot" is Napoleon, who by 1811 had been victorious over Poland, Austria, Prussia, Italy, and Russia.
103. Allusion to the complaint that resources were diverted from domestic needs to support soldiers in foreign wars.
104. Bloody.

And thinks't thou, Britain, still to sit at ease,
An island Queen amidst thy subject seas,   40
While the vext billows, in their distant roar,
But soothe thy slumbers, and but kiss thy shore?
To sport in wars, while danger keeps aloof,
Thy grassy turf unbruised by hostile hoof?
So sing thy flatterers; but, Britain, know,
Thou who hast shared the guilt must share the woe.
Nor distant is the hour; low murmurs spread,
And whispered fears, creating what they dread;[105]
Ruin, as with an earthquake shock, is here,
There, the heart-witherings of unuttered fear,   50
And that sad death, whence most affection bleeds,
Which sickness, only of the soul, precedes.
Thy baseless wealth dissolves in air away,
Like mists that melt before the morning ray:
No more on crowded mart or busy street
Friends, meeting friends, with cheerful hurry greet;
Sad, on the ground thy princely merchants bend
Their altered looks, and evil days portend,
And fold their arms, and watch with anxious breast
The tempest blackening in the distant West.[106]   60

  Yes, thou must dröop; thy Midas dream is o'er;
The golden tide of Commerce leaves thy shore,
Leaves thee to prove the alternate ills that haunt
Enfeebling Luxury and ghastly Want;
Leaves thee, perhaps, to visit distant lands,
And deal the gifts of Heaven with equal hands.

  Yet, O my Country, name beloved, revered,
By every tie that binds the soul endeared,
Whose image to my infant senses came
Mixt with Religion's light and Freedom's holy flame!   70

---

105. British fears of an invasion by the French had escalated during this period. Linda Colley details "how common nightmares of a violent French invasion of Britain were." *Britons: Forging the Nation, 1707–1837* (New Haven, CT: Yale University Press, 1992), 306.

106. Nicholas Birns suggests that Barbauld alludes to the impending War of 1812, between Britain and America, placing North America as a central reference point for the poem. "'Thy World Columbus!': Barbauld and Global Space, 1803, '1811,' 1812, 2003," *European Romantic Review* 16 (December 2005): 545–62.

If prayers may not avert, if 'tis thy fate
To rank amongst the names that once were great,
Not like the dim cold Crescent[107] shalt thou fade,
Thy debt to Science and the Muse unpaid;
Thine are the laws surrounding states revere,
Thine the full harvest of the mental year,
Thine the bright stars in Glory's sky that shine,
And arts that make it life to live are thine.
If westward streams the light that leaves thy shores,
80   Still from thy lamp the streaming radiance pours.
Wide spreads thy race from Ganges to the pole,
O'er half the western world thy accents roll:
Nations beyond the Apalachian hills
Thy hand has planted and thy spirit fills:
Soon as their gradual progress shall impart
The finer sense of morals and of art,
Thy stores of knowledge the new states shall know,
And think thy thoughts, and with thy fancy glow;
Thy Lockes,[108] thy Paleys[109] shall instruct their youth,
90   Thy leading star direct their search for truth;
Beneath the spreading Platan's[110] tent-like shade,
Or by Missouri's[111] rushing waters laid,
"Old father Thames" shall be the Poets' theme,
Of Hagley's[112] woods the enamoured virgin dream,

---

107. Symbol for the Ottoman Empire, which, while still in existence in 1811, had been at the height of its powers in the sixteenth and seventeenth centuries.

108. John Locke (1632–1704), one of the most influential philosophers of the Enlightenment, whose *Essay Concerning Human Understanding* (1690) was a cornerstone of epistemology. He also wrote *Some Thoughts Concerning Education* (1692), likely referred to here, which explores new didactic practices for the young.

109. William Paley (1743–1805) was among the most influential philosophers and theologians of the eighteenth century. He was a master at making complex philosophical positions accessible to a wider audience. In fact his book *The Principles of Moral and Political Philosophy* (1785), containing a revised version of a series of lectures on morality, was so clearly written and understandable that it was adopted as a textbook at Cambridge, where it profoundly informed the teaching of morality.

110. The plantain tree, known for its broad leaves, was common in the Caribbean and grew as far north as Florida and as far south as southern Brazil.

111. The Missouri River, the longest tributary of the Mississippi, flows centrally through the North American lands acquired during the Louisiana Purchase (1803). Meriwether Lewis and William Clark navigated its headwaters during their expedition in 1804–6.

112. Hagley Hall, improved by George, first Baron Lyttelton (1709–73), is in the West Midlands and has a 350-acre wooded park. John Brown's *Essay on Satire, Occasioned by the Death of Mr Pope* alludes to "HAGLEY's honour'd Shade." *The Works of Alexander Pope*, ed. William Warburton, 9 vols. (London, 1751), 3:xxiii.

And Milton's[113] tones the raptured ear enthrall,
Mixt with the roar of Niagara's fall;
In Thomson's[114] glass the ingenuous youth shall learn
A fairer face of Nature to discern;
Nor of the Bards that swept the British lyre
Shall fade one laurel, or one note expire.   100
Then, loved Joanna,[115] to admiring eyes
Thy storied groups in scenic pomp shall rise;
Their high soul'd strains and Shakespear's noble rage
Shall with alternate passion shake the stage.
Some youthful Basil[116] from thy moral lay
With stricter hand his fond desires shall sway;
Some Ethwald,[117] as the fleeting shadows pass,
Start at his likeness in the mystic glass;
The tragic Muse resume her just controul,
With pity and with terror purge the soul,   110
While wide o'er transatlantic realms thy name
Shall live in light, and gather *all* its fame.

    Where wanders Fancy down the lapse of years
Shedding o'er imaged woes untimely tears?
Fond moody Power! as hopes—as fears prevail,
She longs, or dreads, to lift the awful veil,
On visions of delight now loves to dwell,
Now hears the shriek of woe or Freedom's knell:
Perhaps, she says, long ages past away,
And set in western waves our closing day,   120
Night, Gothic night, again may shade the plains
Where Power is seated, and where Science reigns;

113. The poet and polemicist John Milton (1608–74), whose *Paradise Lost* (1667) remains one of the most influential texts in the English language.

114. Allusion to James Thomson's *The Seasons* (1730).

115. Joanna Baillie (1762–1851), poet and playwright.

116. Baillie's *Count Basil: A Tragedy* (1798) is one of several plays she wrote about the military. Basil is an effective soldier, but he is unable to curb his private desires. His passion for his lover Victoria delays his arrival at a key battle, resulting in a significant loss of men.

117. Baillie's *Ethwald. A Tragedy in Five Acts* (1802) has two parts. *Part First* resembles *Macbeth*, with Ethwald soliciting the aid of three mystics who show him the future—a vision of himself wearing a crown—which compels him to move successfully from soldier to king. *Part Second* illustrates the results of his power: he is now a callous, brutal king whose military ambitions have exacted a high toll from his people, and the world has been destroyed by war. We are grateful to Dr. Judy Slagle for sharing her extensive knowledge of Baillie.

England, the seat of arts, be only known
By the gray ruin and the mouldering stone;
That Time may tear the garland from her brow,
And Europe sit in dust, as Asia now.

    Yet then the ingenuous youth whom Fancy fires
With pictured glories of illustrious sires,
With duteous zeal their pilgrimage shall take
130   From the blue mountains, or Ontario's lake,[118]
With fond adoring steps to press the sod
By statesmen, sages, poets, heroes trod;
On Isis'[119] banks to draw inspiring air,
From Runnymede[120] to send the patriot's prayer;
In pensive thought, where Cam's[121] slow waters wind,
To meet those shades that ruled the realms of mind;
In silent halls to sculptured marbles bow,
And hang fresh wreaths round Newton's[122] awful brow.
Oft shall they seek some peasant's homely shed,
140   Who toils, unconscious of the mighty dead,
To ask where Avon's[123] winding waters stray,
And thence a knot of wild flowers bear away;
Anxious enquire where Clarkson,[124] friend of man,
Or all-accomplished Jones[125] his race began;
If of the modest mansion aught remains
Where Heaven and Nature prompted Cowper's[126] strains;

118. In travel narratives of the later eighteenth century, such as Thomas Anburey's *Travels through the Interior Parts of America*, 2 vols. (London: William Lane, 1789), the Alleghany Mountains in Pennsylvania were known as the Blue Mountains. Lake Ontario is one of the Great Lakes forming the boundary between Canada and the United States. Elizabeth Kraft and William McCarthy suggest that Barbauld was familiar with William Winterbotham's four-volume *View of the American United States* (London: J. Ridgway & H. D. Symonds, 1795), as well as with the Blue Mountains in Jamaica, then a British colony, from reading William Beckford's *Descriptive Account of the Island of Jamaica*, 2 vols. (London: T. and J. Egerton, 1790). William McCarthy and Elizabeth Kraft, *The Poems of Anna Letitia Barbauld*, ed. McCarthy and Kraft (Athens: University of Georgia Press, 1994), 313.

119. The part of the river Thames that flows through the city of Oxford.

120. Riverside site of the sealing of the Magna Carta in 1215, the cornerstone of English constitutional principles.

121. The river Cam, which runs through Cambridge.

122. Isaac Newton (1642–1727), a mathematician, studied at Cambridge.

123. The river Avon, which runs through Stratford, the birthplace of Shakespeare.

124. Thomas Clarkson (1760–1846), abolitionist.

125. William Jones (1746–94), Sanskrit scholar, Orientalist, and Whig radical.

126. William Cowper (1731–1800), poet.

Where Roscoe,[127] to whose patriot breast belong
The Roman virtue and the Tuscan song,
Led Ceres[128] to the black and barren moor
Where Ceres never gained a wreath before:[129]   150
With curious search their pilgrim steps shall rove
By many a ruined tower and proud alcove,
Shall listen for those strains that soothed of yore
Thy rock, stern Skiddaw, and thy fall, Lodore;[130]
Feast with Dun Edin's[131] classic brow their sight,
And visit "Melross by the pale moonlight."[132]

    But who their mingled feelings shall pursue
When London's faded glories rise to view?
The mighty city, which by every road,
In floods of people poured itself abroad;   160
Ungirt by walls, irregularly great,
No jealous drawbridge, and no closing gate;
Whose merchants (such the state which commerce brings)
Sent forth their mandates to dependant kings;
Streets, where the turban'd Moslem, bearded Jew,
And woolly Afric, met the brown Hindu;
Where through each vein spontaneous plenty flowed,
Where Wealth enjoyed, and Charity bestowed.
Pensive and thoughtful shall the wanderers greet
Each splendid square, and still, untrodden street;   170
Or of some crumbling turret, mined by time,
The broken stair with perilous step shall climb,
Thence stretch their view the wide horizon round,
By scattered hamlets trace its antient bound,

127. William Roscoe (1753–1831), historian, abolitionist, and author who was read widely in America. He was also an amateur agriculturalist.

128. Roman goddess of agriculture.

129. The Historian of the age of Leo has brought into cultivation the extensive tract of Chatmoss. *Barbauld.* ["William Roscoe of Liverpool (1753–1831), scholar, poet, and agriculturalist, wrote *The History of the Life and Pontificate of Leo the Tenth* (1805). At Chat Moss in Lancashire he demonstrated that moorland could yield high-quality crops." A friend of Barbauld's family, Roscoe was also fiercely opposed to the war. McCarthy and Kraft, *Poems of Anna Letitia Barbauld,* 313. *Eds.*]

130. A mountain and a waterfall in the Lake District.

131. Dun Edin, meaning "hill of Edwin," is the ancient name for Edinburgh.

132. Melrose Abbey, near the border of Scotland. The quotation from Sir Walter Scott's *The Lay of the Last Minstrel* (1805) reads, "If thou wouldst view fair Melrose aright, / Go visit it by the pale moonlight" (2.1–2).

And, choked no more with fleets, fair Thames survey
Through reeds and sedge pursue his idle way.

With throbbing bosoms shall the wanderers tread
The hallowed mansions of the silent dead,
Shall enter the long isle and vaulted dome
180   Where Genius and where Valour find a home;
Awe-struck, midst chill sepulchral marbles breathe,
Where all above is still, as all beneath;
Bend at each antique shrine, and frequent turn
To clasp with fond delight some sculptured urn,
The ponderous mass of Johnson's[133] form to greet,
Or breathe the prayer at Howard's[134] sainted feet.

Perhaps some Briton, in whose musing mind
Those ages live which Time has cast behind,
To every spot shall lead his wondering guests
190   On whose known site the beam of glory rests:
Here Chatham's[135] eloquence in thunder broke,
Here Fox[136] persuaded, or here Garrick[137] spoke;
Shall boast how Nelson,[138] fame and death in view,
To wonted victory led his ardent crew,
In England's name enforced, with loftiest tone,[139]
Their duty,—and too well fulfilled his own:
How gallant Moore,[140] as ebbing life dissolved,

133. Samuel Johnson (1709–84), essayist, poet, and author of *Dictionary of the English Language* (1755). His statue is in St. Paul's Cathedral, London, where it has stood at the entrance of the North Quire Aisle since 1796.

134. John Howard, noted in *Epistle to William Wilberforce, Esq.*, was a tireless prison reformer. His statue also is in St. Paul's Cathedral, outside the South Transept.

135. William Pitt, first Earl of Chatham (1708–78), prime minister during the Seven Years' War.

136. Charles Fox (1749–1806), liberal Whig political figure whose influence lasted throughout the nineteenth century.

137. David Garrick (1717–79), the greatest actor-manager of the eighteenth century.

138. Horatio Nelson (1758–1805), naval officer immortalized for his victory and death at the battle of Trafalgar.

139. Every reader will recollect the sublime telegraphic dispatch, "England expects every man to do his duty." *Barbauld.* [These are the words Nelson dispatched (by flags) at the beginning of the battle of Trafalgar, on 21 October 1805. It is the most famous dispatch in British naval history, although some questions arose subsequently about the exact wording. Nevertheless, this utterance entered the public's consciousness, was inscribed on Nelson's monument as well as on his tomb, and was used in a number of patriotic prints and publications of the time. *Eds.*]

140. "I hope England will be satisfied," were the last words of General Moore. *Barbauld.* [Sir John Moore (1761–1809), a military officer who died in battle after leading his men on retreat on the Span-

But hoped his country had his fame absolved.
Or call up sages whose capacious mind
Left in its course a track of light behind;   200
Point where mute crowds on Davy's[141] lips reposed,
And Nature's coyest secrets were disclosed;
Join with their Franklin, Priestley's[142] injured name,
Whom, then, each continent shall proudly claim.

Oft shall the strangers turn their eager feet
The rich remains of antient art to greet,
The pictured walls with critic eye explore,
And Reynolds[143] be what Raphael was before.
On spoils from every clime their eyes shall gaze,
Ægyptian granites and the Etruscan vase;[144]   210
And when midst fallen London, they survey
The stone where Alexander's ashes lay,
Shall own with humbled pride the lesson just
By Time's slow finger written in the dust.

There walks a Spirit o'er the peopled earth,
Secret his progress is, unknown his birth;
Moody and viewless as the changing wind,
No force arrests his foot, no chains can bind;
Where'er he turns, the human brute awakes,
And, roused to better life, his sordid hut forsakes: 220
He thinks, he reasons, glows with purer fires,
Feels finer wants, and burns with new desires:
Obedient Nature follows where he leads;
The steaming marsh is changed to fruitful meads;
The beasts retire from man's asserted reign,
And prove his kingdom was not given in vain.
Then from its bed is drawn the ponderous ore,
Then Commerce pours her gifts on every shore,

---

ish peninsula. After his death, a general order from the Horse Guards stated that "his fame remains the strongest incentive to great and glorious actions." *Eds.*]

141. Sir Humphry Davy (1778–1829), chemist who discovered laughing gas.

142. Benjamin Franklin (1706–90), American inventor, author, and politician, and Joseph Priestley (1733–1804), Unitarian whose home, laboratory, and library were destroyed in the Priestley Riots of 1791. Priestley emigrated to America in 1794.

143. Joshua Reynolds (1723–92), premier portrait artist of the eighteenth century.

144. Reference to the British Museum, established in 1753, where a sarcophagus thought to hold the ashes of Alexander the Great was housed.

Then Babel's towers[145] and terrassed gardens rise,
230   And pointed obelisks invade the skies;
The prince commands, in Tyrian purple[146] drest,
And Ægypt's virgins weave the linen vest.
Then spans the graceful arch the roaring tide,
And stricter bounds the cultured fields divide.
Then kindles Fancy, then expands the heart,
Then blow the flowers of Genius and of Art;
Saints, Heroes, Sages, who the land adorn,
Seem rather to descend than to be born;
Whilst History, midst the rolls consigned to fame,
240   With pen of adamant inscribes their name.

      The Genius now forsakes the favoured shore,
And hates, capricious, what he loved before;
Then empires fall to dust, then arts decay,
And wasted realms enfeebled despots sway;
Even Nature's changed; without his fostering smile
Ophir,[147] no gold, no plenty yields the Nile;
The thirsty sand absorbs the useless rill,[148]
And spotted plagues from putrid fens[149] distill.
In desert solitudes then Tadmor[150] sleeps,
250   Stern Marius then o'er fallen Carthage weeps;[151]
Then with enthusiast love the pilgrim roves
To seek his footsteps in forsaken groves,
Explores the fractured arch, the ruined tower,
Those limbs disjointed of gigantic power;
Still at each step he dreads the adder's sting,

145. Babel was a biblical city whose citizens came together to build a mighty tower to the heavens. In response, God bestowed upon the people different languages so that they could not communicate and therefore could not complete their project. Gen. 11:1–9.

146. The famous royal purple dye of Greece and Rome, perfected in Tyre. A commercial center in early times, the city of Tyre still exists on the eastern banks of the Mediterranean Sea in modern Lebanon.

147. In the Old Testament, a famous gold-producing region.

148. Trickle of water.

149. Marshes.

150. City built by Solomon in the wilderness.

151. Gaius Marius (157–86 BC), chronicled in Plutarch's *Lives*, took refuge in Carthage upon his political defeat in Rome. When he was ordered to leave Carthage, he allegedly said to the messenger, "Tell the praetor you have seen Gaius Marius, fugitive, amid the ruins of Carthage." Barbauld might also have been familiar with the American artist John Vanderlyn's painting *Marius Viewing the Ruins of Carthage* (1807), which won a gold medal in Paris in 1808. Another commonly known representation of Marius was Thomas Otway's *History and Fall of Caius Marius* (1679).

The Arab's javelin, or the tiger's spring;
With doubtful caution treads the echoing ground,
And asks where Troy or Babylon[152] is found.

And now the vagrant Power no more detains
The vale of Tempe,[153] or Ausonian[154] plains;   260
Northward he throws the animating ray,
O'er Celtic nations bursts the mental day:
And, as some playful child the mirror turns,
Now here now there the moving lustre burns;
Now o'er his changeful fancy more prevail
Batavia's[155] dykes than Arno's[156] purple vale,
And stinted suns, and rivers bound with frost,
Than Enna's[157] plains or Baia's[158] viny coast;
Venice the Adriatic weds in vain,
And Death sits brooding o'er Campania's[159] plain;   270
O'er Baltic shores and through Hercynian groves,[160]
Stirring the soul, the mighty impulse moves;
Art plies his tools, and Commerce spreads her sail,
And wealth is wafted in each shifting gale.
The sons of Odin[161] tread on Persian looms,
And Odin's daughters breathe distilled perfumes;
Loud minstrel Bards, in Gothic halls, rehearse
The Runic[162] rhyme, and "build the lofty verse:"[163]
The Muse, whose liquid notes were wont to swell
To the soft breathings of the' Æolian shell,[164]   280
Submits, reluctant, to the harsher tone,

152. Famous ancient cities in Anatolia and Mesopotamia, respectively.

153. Valley in Thessaly, Greece.

154. Poetic name for Italy from the Greek *ausones,* the ancient name for inhabitants of southern Italy.

155. When the French army invaded the Netherlands in 1795, the country was designated the Batavian Republic, which lasted until 1806.

156. River in Tuscany. By 1800 Napoleon had successfully conquered Italy.

157. Sicilian province.

158. During the Roman Empire a resort area located slightly west of Naples.

159. Region in southern Italy.

160. Hercynian was an ancient, dense forest that stretched eastward from the Rhine River.

161. The Norse god of death, war, poetry, and music.

162. Runes are symbols in a non-Germanic alphabet. Runic rhymes were incantations and magic.

163. A reference to Milton's *Lycidas* (1638): "Who would not sing for Lycidas? he knew / Himself to sing, and build the lofty rhyme" (lines 10–11).

164. A reference to the phenomenon of humans' being able to hear the sounds of the ocean in an empty seashell. Aeolus was the Greek god of the winds.

And scarce believes the altered voice her own.
And now, where Cæsar saw with proud disdain
The wattled hut and skin of azure stain,
Corinthian columns rear their graceful forms,
And light varandas brave the wintry storms,
While British tongues the fading fame prolong
Of Tully's[165] eloquence and Maro's[166] song.
Where once Bonduca[167] whirled the scythed car,
And the fierce matrons raised the shriek of war,
Light forms beneath transparent muslins float,
And tutored voices swell the artful note.
Light-leaved acacias[168] and the shady plane
And spreading cedar grace the woodland reign;
While crystal walls the tenderer plants confine,
The fragrant orange and the nectared pine;
The Syrian grape there hangs her rich festoons,
Nor asks for purer air, or brighter noons:
Science and Art urge on the useful toil,
New mould a climate and create the soil,
Subdue the rigour of the northern Bear,[169]
O'er polar climes shed aromatic air,
On yielding Nature urge their new demands,
And ask not gifts but tribute at her hands.

London exults:—on London Art bestows
Her summer ices and her winter rose;
Gems of the East her mural crown adorn,
And Plenty at her feet pours forth her horn;
While even the exiles her just laws disclaim,
People a continent, and build a name:[170]

290

300

310

165. Roman orator and statesman Cicero (106–43 BC).

166. Roman poet Virgil (70–19 BC).

167. *Bonduca* and the better-known *Boadicea* are corrupt forms of *Boudicca,* the name of the queen of the Iceni who led a revolt against the Romans in AD 60–61.

168. Ornamental trees with sweet-scented white flowers.

169. Ursa Major, a large constellation in the Northern Hemisphere more commonly known as the "Big Dipper" or the "Great Bear." In Roman mythology, Callisto, desired by Jupiter, who disguised himself as Minerva in order to seduce her, was turned into a bear by his jealous wife, Juno, in the hope that she would be hunted and killed. At the moment when Callisto was about to be killed by her son Arcas (who of course did not recognize her as a bear) Jupiter sent her to the heavens. Outraged at Callisto's position of honor, Juno asked the powers of the ocean to prevent Callisto from ever touching the water. In central Europe the constellation never touches the horizon.

170. An allusion to Britain's exiled criminals building new societies in America and Australia.

August she sits, and with extended hands
Holds forth the book of life to distant lands.[171]

 But fairest flowers expand but to decay;
The worm is in thy core, thy glories pass away;
Arts, arms and wealth destroy the fruits they bring;
Commerce, like beauty, knows no second spring.
Crime walks thy streets, Fraud earns her unblest bread,
O'er want and woe thy gorgeous robe is spread,
And angel charities in vain oppose:
With grandeur's growth the mass of misery grows.   320
For see,—to other climes the Genius soars,
He turns from Europe's desolated shores;
And lo, even now, midst mountains wrapt in storm,
On Andes'[172] heights he shrouds his awful form;
On Chimborazo's[173] summits treads sublime,
Measuring in lofty thought the march of Time;
Sudden he calls:—"'Tis now the hour!" he cries,
Spreads his broad hand, and bids the nations rise.
La Plata[174] hears amidst her torrents' roar,
Potosi[175] hears it, as she digs the ore: 330
Ardent, the Genius fans the noble strife,
And pours through feeble souls a higher life,
Shouts to the mingled tribes from sea to sea,
And swears—Thy world, Columbus,[176] shall be free.

     (1812)

171. Reference to British Christian evangelism overseas.
172. South American mountain range.
173. Ecuador's highest mountain.
174. Rio de la Plata, large river on the southeastern coast of South America; its major ports are Buenos Aires and Montevideo. The viceroyalty of Rio de la Plata was established in 1776 and corresponds to modern Argentina.
175. Bolivian city that was one of the largest and wealthiest in South America at the time because of its vast silver mines.
176. Christopher Columbus, or Cristoforo Colombo (1451–1506), the Italian explorer credited with first arriving in North America. His four transatlantic voyages were central to further exploration and colonization.

Charlie is My Darling[177]

Carolina Oliphant Nairne

'Twas on a Monday morning,
    Right early in the year,
When Charlie came to our town,
    The young Chevalier.
        Oh! Charlie is my darling,
            My darling, my darling;
        Oh! Charlie is my darling,
            The young Chevalier.

As he came marching up the street,
10   The pipes play'd loud and clear,
And a' the folk came running out
    To meet the Chevalier.
        Oh! Charlie is my darling, &c.

Wi' hieland bonnets on their heads,
    And claymores[178] bright and clear,
They came to fight for Scotland's right
    And the young Chevalier.
        Oh! Charlie is my darling, &c.

They've left their bonny hielands hills,
20   Their wives and bairnies[179] dear,
To draw the sword for Scotland's Lord,
    The young Chevalier.
        Oh! Charlie is my darling, &c.

---

177. Charles Edward Stuart (1720–88), "Bonnie Prince Charlie," arrived in Scotland in July 1745 seeking support from the Highland clans to invade England and reinstate the Stuart succession. He rallied about twenty-five hundred Highlanders of all ranks, moved toward the lowlands and Edinburgh (which he took), and then amassed another twenty-five hundred troops by December. He and his army advanced as far south as Derby, their efforts ending in the resounding defeat at the battle of Culloden in April. This poem and the two that follow capture the idealism, romanticism, and optimism that accompanied this almost mythical figure. Linda Colley reminds us that "the romantic aura that still hovers around his memory should not obscure the seriousness of his invasion. That it had achieved so much with such minimal resources was a testament to the Jacobite army's mettle and leadership, and to the ineptitude of much of the formal machinery of the British state." *Britons,* 80.

178. Broad swords used by Scottish Highlanders.

179. Children.

Oh! there were mony[180] beating hearts,
   And mony hopes and fears;
And mony were the prayers put up
   For the young Chevalier.
     Oh! Charlie is my darling, &c.

(1820)

Gathering Song
Carolina Oliphant Nairne

Oh come, come along, and join in our song,
And march wi' our lads, along an' along;
He's waiting us there where heather grows fair,
And the clans they are gath'ring strong and strong.

He should be king, ye ken[181] wha I mean,
Tho' Whigs that winna allow, allow;
We daurna speak out, but ye needna doubt,
That a' that we tell is true is true.
    Oh come, come along, &c.

On the steep mountains' breast, where shadows oft rest,   10
An' burnies[182] are tumblin' down, and down;
In that deep recess, there's *ane* we can guess,
That is heir to our ain Scottish crown.
    Oh come, come along, &c.

Like a sunbeam to cheer, he soon will appear,
Gracefu' and fleet, like a mountain deer;
Come gather, a' gather, along and along,
The clans and the echoes will join in our song.

Oh come, come along, and join in our song,
And march wi' our lads, along an' along;   20

180. Many.
181. Know.
182. Streams.

He's waiting us there where heather grows fair,
And the clans they are gath'ring strong and strong.

(1869)

Charlie's Landing
Carolina Oliphant Nairne

Air — "When Wild Wars."

There cam' a wee boatie owre the sea,
   Wi' the winds an' waves it strove sairlie;[183]
But oh! it brought great joy to me,
   For wha was there but Prince Charlie.
The wind was hie, and unco[184] chill,
   An' a' things luiket barely;[185]
Bu oh! we come with right good-will,
   To welcome bonnie Charlie.

Wae's[186] me, puir lad, yere thinly clad,
10   The waves yere fair hair weeting;[187]
We'll row ye in a tartan plaid,
   An' gie ye Scotland's greeting.
Tho' wild an' bleak the prospect round,
   We'll cheer yere heart, dear Charlie;
Ye're landed now on Scottish grund,
   Wi' them wha lo'e ye dearly.

O lang we've prayed to see this day;
   True hearts they maist[188] were breaking;
Now clouds an' storms will flee away,
20   Young hope again is waking.
We'll sound the Gathering, lang an' loud,
   Yere friends will greet ye fairlie;

183. Sorely.
184. Unusually, uncommonly.
185. Looked barren.
186. Woe's.
187. Wetting.
188. Most.

Tho' now they're few, their hearts are true;
   They'll live or die for Charlie.

(1869)

On the Deserted Village[189]
Anna Laetitia Barbauld

In vain fair Auburn weeps her desert plains,
She moves our envy who so well complains;
In vain has proud oppression laid her low,
So sweet a garland on her faded brow.
Now, Auburn, now absolve impartial fate,
Which if it made thee wretched, makes thee great:—
So, unobserved, some humble plant may bloom,
Till crushed it fills the air with sweet perfume;
So, had thy swains in ease and plenty slept,
Thy Poet had not sung, nor Britain wept.   10
Nor let Britannia mourn her drooping bay,
Unhonoured genius, and her swift decay;
O Patron of the poor! it cannot be,
While one—one Poet yet remains like thee!
Nor can the Muse desert our favoured isle,
Till thou desert the Muse and scorn her smile.

(1825)

The Black Man's Lament; or, How to Make Sugar
Amelia Opie

Come, listen to my plaintive ditty,
   Ye tender hearts, and children dear!
And, should it move your souls to pity,
   Oh! try to *end* the griefs you hear.

---

189. A poem by Oliver Goldsmith (c. 1728–74), *The Deserted Village* (London: W. Griffin, 1770), details the fate of "sweet Auburn," a fictional village. As Goldsmith details in the prefatory letter, the poem explores the dangers of rural "depopulation" and the increase of "those luxuries prejudicial to states, by which so many vices are introduced, and so many kingdoms have been undone" (vi).

There is a *beauteous plant*,[190] that grows
   In western India's sultry clime,
Which makes, alas! the Black man's woes,
   And also makes the White man's crime.

For know, its tall gold stems contain
10   A sweet rich juice,[191] which White men prize;
And that they may this *sugar* gain,
   The Negro toils, and bleeds, and *dies*.

But, Negro slave! *thyself* shall tell,
   Of past and present wrongs the story;
And would all British hearts could feel,
   To *end* those wrongs were *Britain's glory*.

Negro speaks.

First to our own dear Negro land,
   His ships the cruel White man sends;
And there contrives, by armed band,
20   To tear us from our homes and friends;

From parents, brethren's fond embrace;
   From tender wife, and child to tear;
Then in a darksome ship to place,
   Pack'd close, like bales of cotton there.[192]

---

190. "A field of canes, when standing in the month of November, when it is in arrow or full blossom, (says Beckford, in his descriptive account of the Island of Jamaica,) is one of the most beautiful productions that the pen or pencil can possibly describe. It, in common, rises from three to eight feet, or more, in height; a difference of growth that very strongly marks the difference of soil, or the varieties of culture. It is, when ripe, of a bright and golden yellow; and, where obvious to the sun, is in many parts very beautifully streaked with red. The top is of a darkish green; but the more dry it becomes, (from either an excess of ripeness, or a continuance of drought,) of a russet yellow, with long and narrow leaves depending; from the centre of which, shoots up an arrow, like a silver wand, from two to six feet in height; and, from the summit of which, grows out a plume of white feathers, which are delicately fringed with a lilac dye, and indeed is, in its appearance, not much unlike the tuft that adorns this particular and elegant tree." *Opie.* [William Beckford, *A Descriptive Account of the Island of Jamaica,* 2 vols. (London: T. and J. Egerton, 1790), 1:50–51. Beckford (1744–99) wrote the work while incarcerated for debt in Fleet Prison following misfortune in the affairs of his Jamaican sugar estates. *Eds.*]

191. The juice extracted from the sugarcane during the processing cycle was the basis for white sugar, brown sugar, molasses, and rum.

192. Reference to the conditions of enslaved Africans during their transport across the Atlantic.

Oh! happy those, who, in that hour,
   Die from their prison's putrid breath!
Since they escape from White man's pow'r,
   From toils and stripes, and lingering death!

For what awaited us on shore,
   Soon as the ship had reach'd the strand,   30
Unloading its degraded store
   Of freemen, forc'd from Negro land?

See! eager White men come around,
   To choose and claim us for their slaves;
And make us envy those who found
   In the dark ship their early graves.

They bid black men and women stand
   In lines, the drivers in the rear:
Poor Negroes hold a *hoe* in hand,
   But they the wicked cart-whip bear.   40

Then we, in gangs, like beasts in droves,
   Swift to the cane-fields driven are;
There first our toil the weeds removes,
   And next we holes for plants prepare.[193]

But woe to all, both old and young,
   Women and men, or strong or weak,
Worn out or fresh, those gangs among,
   That dare the toilsome line to break!

As holes must all *at once* be made,
   Together we must work or stop;   50
Therefore, the whip our strength must aid,
   And lash us when we pause or drop!

193. Slaves on sugar plantations worked in groups, or "gangs." The cane was planted by the excavation of a grid of four-foot squares to a depth of six to nine inches, with holes in the center into which either a cutting of old cane stalk or cuttings of old cane laid end to end were placed. "Cane holing was generally regarded as the heaviest work required," writes B. W. Higman. *Slave Populations of the British Caribbean, 1807–1834* (Baltimore: Johns Hopkins University Press, 1984), 163.

When we have dug sufficient space,
    The bright-eye top[194] of many a cane,
Lengthways, we in the trenches place,
    And *then* we trenches dig again.

We cover next the plants with mould;
    And e'en, ere fifteen days come round,
We can the slender sprouts behold,
60   Just shooting greenly from the ground.

The weeds about them clear'd away,
    Then mould again by hand we throw;
And, at no very distant day,
    Here Negroes plough, and there they hoe.

But when the crops are ripen'd quite,
    'Tis then begin our saddest pains;
For then we toil both day and night,[195]
    Though fever burns within our veins.

When 18 months complete their growth,
70   Then the tall canes rich juices fill;
And we, to bring their liquor forth,
    Convey them to the bruising-mill.[196]

That mill, our labour, every hour,
    Must with fresh loads of canes supply;
And if we faint, the cart-whip's power,
    Gives force which *nature's* powers *deny*.

Our task is next to catch the juice
    In leaden bed, soon as it flows;

194. The top shoots are *full of eyes,* or *gems,* as they are called. *Opie.*

195. Once the sugar cane ripens, after fourteen to eighteen months, the next stages required "careful timing" to ensure the successful processing of the sugar and resulted in sugar mills' operating nearly twenty-four hours a day. Richard Dunn, *Sugar and Slaves: The Rise of the Planter Class in the English West Indies, 1624–1713* (New York: Norton, 1973), 190.

196. After the cane was harvested, it was taken to a sugar mill, where it was ground down to extract the juice, which flowed into a cistern.

And instant, lest it spoil for use,
   It into boiling vessels goes.[197]   80

Nor one alone: four vessels more
   Receive and clear the sugar-tide.
Six coolers next receive the store;
   Long vessels, shallow, wooden, *wide*.[198]

While cooling, it begins to grain,
   Or form in crystals white and clear;
Then we remove the whole again,
   And to the *curing-house* we bear.

Molasses there is drain'd away;
   The liquor is through hogsheads pour'd;   90
The scum falls through, the crystals stay;
   The casks are clos'd, and soon on board.

The ships to English country go,
   And bear the hardly-gotten treasure.
Oh! that good Englishmen could know
   How Negroes suffer for their pleasure!

Five months, we, every week, alas!
   Save when we eat, to work are driven:
Six days, three nights; then, to each class,
   Just twenty hours of rest are given.   100

But when the Sabbath-eve comes round,
   That eve which White men sacred keep,
Again we at our toil are found,
   And six days more we work and weep.

197. In the boiling houses, "which became so hot that slaves were often employed to spray water on their shingled roofs to prevent them from catching fire" (Higman, *Slave Populations*, 166), the cane juice was clarified and evaporated, leaving sugar crystal.

198. Once the sugar was boiled, it was cured into muscovado, or golden brown sugar. The curing house contained a series of sugar pots; the molasses drained through a hole in the bottom of the vessels, leaving the processed sugar. The molasses was subsequently taken to the distillery for the production of rum.

"But, Negro slave, some men must toil.
    The English peasant works all day;
Turns up, and sows, and ploughs the soil.
    Thou wouldst not, sure, have Negroes play?"

"Ah! no. But Englishmen can work
    Whene'er they like, and stop for breath;
No driver dares, like any Turk,[199]
    Flog peasants on almost to death.

"Who dares an English peasant flog,
    Or buy, or sell, or steal away?
Who sheds his blood? treats him like dog,
    Or fetters him like beasts of prey?

"He has a cottage, he a wife;
    If child he has, that child is free.
I am depriv'd of married life,
    And my poor child were *slave* like *me*.

"Unlike his home, ours is a shed
    Of pine-tree trunks, unsquar'd, ill-clos'd;
Blanket we have, but not a bed,
    Whene'er to short, chill sleep dispos'd.

"Our clothing's ragged. All our food
    Is rice, dried fish, and Indian meal.
Hard, scanty fare! Oh, would I could
    Make White men Negroes' miseries feel!"

"But could you not, your huts around,
    Raise plants for food, and poultry rear?
You might, if willing, till your ground,
    And then some wants would disappear."

110

120

130

199. "Slavery in Ottoman Turkey met a certain indulgence," writes Reinhold Schiffer. "A minority of [British] travellers even believed that Turkish slavery meant no denigration but in name. . . . Lady [Mary Wortley] Montagu . . . saw little difference between servitude in other parts of the world and slavery in Turkey." *Oriental Panorama: British Travellers in Nineteenth-Century Turkey* (Atlanta: Rodopi, 1999), 191–92.

"Work for ourselves and others too?
    When all our master's work is o'er,
How could we bear our own to do?
    Poor, weary slaves, hot, scourg'd, and sore!

"Sometimes, 'tis true, when Sabbath-bell
    Calls White man to the house of pray'r,
And makes poor blacks more sadly feel
    'Tis thought *slaves* have no *business* there: 140

"Then Negroes try the earth to till,
    And raise their food on Sabbath-day;
But Envy's pangs poor Negroes fill,
    That we must *work* while others *pray*.

"Then, where have we *one* legal right?
    White men may bind, whip, torture slave.
But oh! if we but strike one White,
    Who can poor Negro help or save?

"There are, I'm told, upon some isles,
    Masters who gentle deign to be;   150
And there, perhaps, the Negro *smiles,*
    But *smiling* Negroes *few* can see.

"Well, I must learn to bear my pain;
    And, lately, I am grown more calm;
For Christian men come o'er the main,
    To pour in Negro souls a balm.

"They tell us there is one above
    Who died to save both bond and free;
And who, with eyes of equal love,
    Beholds White man, and *humble me.*   160

"They tell me if, with patient heart,
    I bear my wrongs from day to day,
I shall, at death, to realms depart,
    Where God wipes every tear away!

"Yet still, at times, with fear I shrink;
　　For, when with sense of injury prest,
I burn with rage! and *then* I think
　　I ne'er can *gain* that place of rest."

He ceas'd; for here his tears would flow,
170　　　　And ne'er resum'd his tale of *ruth.*[200]
Alas! it rends my heart to know
　　He only told a *tale of truth.*

(1826)

Sources

Philips: *Poems* (London, 1664), 1–3. Killigrew: *Poems* (London, 1686), 47–48. Rowe: *Poems on Several Occasions. Written by Philomela* (London, 1696), 30–33. Centlivre: *Love's Contrivance, or, Le Medecin malgre Lui* (London, 1703), viii–ix. Finch: *The Anne Finch Wellesley Manuscript Poems: A Critical Edition,* ed. Barbara McGovern and Charles H. Hinnant (Athens: University of Georgia Press, 1998), 45–46. Barber: *Poems on Several Occasions* (London, 1734), 2–5. Dixon: *Poems on Several Occasions* (Canterbury, 1740), 126–27. Jones: *Miscellanies in Prose and Verse* (Oxford, 1750), 36–44. Teft: *Orinthia's Miscellanies* (London, 1747), 156–58, 135–39. Smith: *Elegiac Sonnets . . . With additional Sonnets and Other Poems,* 5th ed. (London, 1789), 46. Barbauld: *Epistle to William Wilberforce* (London, 1791), 5–14. Winscom: *Poems on Various Subjects, Entertaining, Elegiac, and Religious,* 4th ed. (Bristol, 1794), 181–87. Stockdale: *The Effusions of the Heart: Poems* (London, 1798), 145–46. Alcock: *Poems, &c. &c. By the Late Mrs. Mary Alcock* (London, 1799), 48–49. Barbauld: *Eighteen Hundred and Eleven* (London, 1812), 1–25. Nairne: *The Scotish Minstrel: A Selection from the Vocal Melodies of Scotland,* ed. Robert Archibald Smith, 4 vols. (Edinburgh, 1820), 1:86–87; *Life and Songs of the Baroness Nairne with a Memoir and Poems of Carolina Oliphant the Younger,* ed. Charles Rogers, 2nd ed. (London: Griffin, 1869), 202–3, 198–99. Barbauld: *The Works of Anna Lætitia Barbauld. With a Memoir by Lucy Aikin,* 2 vols. (London, 1825), 1:60. Opie: *The Black Man's Lament* (London, 1826), 2–25.

200. Distress or lamentation.

⋈G⋈

Poems on Pain and Illness

In the Restoration and eighteenth century almost any illness could result in death. Without antibiotics, anesthesia, x-ray, or detailed knowledge of the human body, medical practitioners often made terrible mistakes, and some of the treatments, such as bleeding and harsh laxatives, weakened and even killed patients. Daniel Defoe wrote of being "torn and mangled by the merciless Surgeons, cut open alive, and bound Hand and Foot to force him to bear it."[1] Frances Burney recounted feeling the knife "describing a curve— cutting against the grain . . . while the flesh resisted" during her operation for breast cancer. "When the knife went in . . . 'I began a scream that lasted unintermittingly during the whole time of the incision.'"[2] Vaccines did not exist, and several poems mention the fear of infecting others. Anne Finch in *To Death*, for example, mentions as one of her terrors, "contagious Darts, that wound the Heads / Of weeping Friends, who wait at dying Beds" (2.N). There are harrowing accounts of illness, surgery, and near death and fervent prayers for deliverance. In these poems, public policy, the state of medical arts, religion, and personal experience meet.

Three of the seven poems in this section are about the most feared illness— smallpox. It often killed, and it almost invariably mutilated survivors. About one-fourth of the people who contracted it died; Esther Lewis Clark, in her *On Recovery from the Small-Pox by Inoculation*, mentions knowing many "all their hopes and comforts cross'd, / Weep a lov'd partner, child, or parent lost." The disease, which often lasted several weeks, began with high fever, vomiting, constipation, backaches, and pouring sweat. Next pustules filled with clear liquid broke out, and the mucous membranes of mouth, throat, eyes, nostrils, and genitals swelled. At this stage some sufferers died of choking or suffocation, and some were blinded or developed permanent vision impairments, such as sensitivity to light. Nearly unbearable itching continued, and pustules broke as the patient moved; the pus had a nauseous smell, and spikes of fever sent the person into delirium. Contemporary treatment was torture. The most common was to wrap the patient in layers of bedding and blankets and keep the windows closed and a fire blazing even in summer. The patient was bled, purged, and kept in darkness. Finally, the pustules scabbed, the itching got worse, and the scabs began to drop off, leaving white spots and pits.[3] How badly the person would be marked would not be known for months.

Smallpox was a common poetic subject, and Lady Mary Wortley Montagu's poem *Saturday: The Small-Pox* (not included) is one of the most frequently anthologized poems by an eighteenth-century woman. Mary Jones's subtle verse *After the Small Pox* offers consolation to women like Montagu, who had been one of the most beautiful women at court and was badly marked by the disease and even lost her eyelashes. Catharine Trotter Cockburn also offers comfort, specifically to a family friend, Bevil Higgons, in *Verses sent to Mr. Bevil Higgons*. Clark's 1789 poem is particularly interesting because it is an early account of experience with innoculation.[4] Most people considered their survival largely dependent on God's will, and Clark begins by thanking the God "who blest those means, which reason's voice / Bade human prudence make its choice, / To free the mind from anxious fears, / And easier make my future years." She gives us unusual access to her thinking at the time of the decision. First, she yielded to "reason" and "prudence," and her fervent hope was a future free from the fear of contracting the disease. This fear was reasonable, since the virus is airborne, and people could communicate it before they showed signs of having it; even the fallen scabs remained infectious, and people who washed sheets and blankets often caught it. She tells us that inoculation is "A *blessing* gave to human skill" (emphasis ours), yet she still writes of needing to place her trust in God. The hope, fear, and calling upon God for strength and recovery give us unusual insight into the experience.

The importance and seriousness of the experience and Clark's feelings are reflected in her decision to write her poem as a Great Ode. She praises her physician, and Mary Chandler thanks God for the skill of hers. Chandler begins *On My Recovery* with the traditional strong opening of hymns, "God of my Life and lengthen'd Days!" The second line, however, turns the poem firmly into a personal lyric: "To Thee my Breath I owe." She brings us to her bedside, and she ends with a renewed commitment to serving God. In contrast to her simple quatrains with their occasional use of breaks in rhyme, Finch's hymn is more Hebraic in form. She too begins by thanking God for lengthening her life and includes a pledge to serve God. Writing before the time of widespread congregational singing, she uses imagery more common to the hymns of the earlier century. The picture of angels camped around her bed while she is ill flows into her expression of her desire to join their choir in time. The concluding verses are highly personal and include a mention of the ailment that tortured her throughout her life and a striking statement of what her ability to write poetry means. In these poems high artistic merit and invaluable life writing come together.

The final poems, which are from the end of the century, in contrast to Clark's *On Recovery,* suggest that medical science had not advanced a great deal. Bannerman, who suffered from some serious deformity, amasses images of pain as she describes it and her efforts to cope with it in *Ode III: To Pain*. In a lighter poem, *To-Morrow: Written During Sickness*, Susanna Blamire expresses the common hope of any ailing human being, that the next day "will ease and serenity bring." All of these poems mention death and the poets' hopes for salvation, but perhaps the most striking features are their tough-mindedness and their unsentimental appreciation of life. There are many speculations about how eighteenth-century women, who were often so close to death, felt about it. These poems tell us, and they challenge many of the existing common opinions.

Notes

1. *Applebee's Original Weekly Journal,* 25 September 1725, quoted in William Lee, *Daniel Defoe,* 3 vols. (London: Hotten, 1869), 3:430.

2. Margaret Anne Doody, *Frances Burney: The Life in the Works* (New Brunswick, NJ: Rutgers University Press, 1988), 315.

3. This account is based on Isobel Grundy's narrative in *Lady Mary Wortley Montagu: Comet of the Enlightenment* (Oxford: Oxford University Press, 1999), 99–101; and Lise Wilkinson, "Smallpox: The Great Killers," in *Oxford Companion to Medicine,* ed. Stephen Lock, John Last, and George Dunea, Oxford Reference Online, http://www.oxfordreference.com/views/ENTRY.html?subview=Main+entry=t185.e455 (accessed 24 May 2007).

4. After her time in Turkey, where inoculation had been common for centuries, Lady Mary became a powerful advocate for the procedure. Sources such as the *Oxford Companion to Medicine* and the *Encyclopedia Britannica* give her considerable credit for its adoption in Great Britain. Grundy gives a good account of her efforts in *Lady Mary Wortley Montagu.*

Verses sent to Mr. Bevil Higgons,
On his sickness and recovery from the Small-pox, in the Year 1693[1]

Catharine Trotter Cockburn

Cruel disease! can there for beauty be
Against thy malice no security?
Must thou pursue her to this choice retreat?
Enough thy triumphs in her wonted seat,
The softer sex, whose epithet is fair;
How couldst thou follow or suspect her here?
But beauty does, like light, itself reveal;
No place can either's glorious beams conceal.

Thine, as destructive flames, too fatal shin'd,
10   And left no peace in either sex's mind.
The men with envy burn'd, and ev'n the fair,
When with their own, thy matchless charms compare,
Doubt, if they should or love, or envy, most, ⎫
A finer form than they themselves can boast: ⎬
Repine not, lovely youth, if that be lost. ⎭
What hearts it gain'd thee! 'Twas no pride to please, ⎫
To whom that part was lost, which no disease, ⎬
Nor time, nor age, nor death itself can seize. ⎭
That part, which thou for ever wilt retain,
20   Fewer, but nobler victories will gain.
And what all felt, when you in danger were,
Shews us how needful to our peace you are.

When death stood menacing the stroke so near,
That as on certain ills, we left to fear,
Grief seem'd to dart at once a speedier blow,
For less of life appear'd in us, than you;
Nor could you doubt our truth, all hearts were known,
Artless and open to you as your own.
Who feign'd to love you, now no longer would,

---

1. A historian and poet, Higgons (1670–1736) was nine years older than Trotter. He had returned to England in 1692 to help raise Jacobite regiments to support James II's French-backed restoration. Trotter's connections to him were various: her father was also a Jacobite, and Higgons wrote for the stage at the same time that she did.

And who had hid their love no longer could,   30
What prudence, fear, or modesty conceal'd,
The force of grief like tortures soon reveal'd:
Nor was the highest blam'd for an excess,
All own'd the moving cause deserv'd no less.
Whate'er philosophers of old had taught,
Here the most sensible was wisest thought.
Silent they wept, nor ceas'd their flowing tears,
Unless to offer more availing prayers,
To which thy life the gracious powers grant,
For fears and prayers make threat'ning heav'n relent.   40

   Go on, brave youth, in all the noblest arts,
And every virtue; exercise thy parts.
The world much will expect, and claim from thee,
But most thy gratitude is due to me,
Who tho' of numbers, that thy friendship claim,
The least recorded in the leaves of fame,
The last in worth, am yet the first to show
What for thy safety we to heav'n owe,
Perhaps the only: less mankind incline
T' acknowledge favours, than at ills repine.   50

   Of ten diseas'd, who heav'nly medicine gain'd,⎤
Tho' all importunate alike complain'd,   ⎬
And equal all the cure they sought, obtain'd,   ⎦
But one return'd, and he like me unknown,
The blessing giv'n with grateful joy to own.

(1693; 1751)

An Hymn of Thanksgiving after a Dangerous fit of sickness in the year 1715

Anne Finch

1.
To thee encreaser of my days
My ransom'd Soul my voice I raise
   O may thy love
   My warmth improve
And guide my future days.

2.
With Allelujahs now I come
From terrours rescued and the tomb
   To pay my thanks
   Amidst the ranks
10 Devoted from the womb.

3.
With Allelujahs let me try
To penetrate the vaulted sky
   Till all thy train
   Endulge the vein
And Allelujah cry.

4.
For health restored and will to please
For softened passions and for ease
   O let me give
   Whilst I shall live
20 In Allelujahs praise.

5.
By Angels who their tents display'd
Around my curtains gloomy shade
   Now I their charge
   Am set at large,
By Allelujahs paid.

6.
With Allelujahs I aspire
To mix with that Celestial choire
   Accept my heart
   Without the art
30 Which does their songs inspire.

7.
Till to thy Courts thou dost me bring
Where I like them shall touch the string
   With zeal and will
   And equal skill
Their Allelujahs sing.

8.

For Providence my ample feild
My food my raiment and my shield
   Thro' life my trust
   Rejoice I must
And Allelujahs yeild.   40

9.

For scaping dangers in my way
The deadly shaft which flys by day
   The hasty fright
   That comes by night
I Allelujahs pay.

10.

For this the gift by Heaven assign'd
With verse to sooth my active mind
   To every thought
   Which there is wrought
Be Allelujah join'd.   50

11.

In Allelujahs who'l proceed
Shall find all objects praises breed
   Nor fear the spleen[2]
   Shou'd come between
By Allelujahs freed.

12.

To Allelujahs till I dye
May I my chearfull hours apply
   Then to the blest
   In ceasless rest
With Allelujahs fly.   60

(1715; 1998)

2. Finch's great poem *The Spleen* (I.D) unites the personal, the topical, and the universal, and her reference here is to the condition from which she believed she suffered, the spleen, meaning melancholy. The condition was believed to be caused by the organ and the production of black bile. *Spleen* was also a catchall term for depression, moodiness, and irritability, and it came to be known as "the English malady."

On My Recovery
Mary Chandler

God of my Life and lengthen'd Days!
   To Thee my Breath I owe.
Teach me my grateful Voice to raise,
   In Sounds that sweetly flow.

When sinking to the silent Grave,
   My Spirits dy'd away;
Thy quick'ning Word new Vigour gave,
   Thy Voice commands my Stay.

In my Distress to Thee I cry'd,
   When tossing in my Bed;
Thou sent'st thy Mercy to my Aid,
   And eas'd my aking Head.

Thou bidd'st the vital Current flow
   In a less rapid Tide;
My dancing Pulse beat calm and low,
   And fev'rish Heats subside:

Thou lend'st to my Physician Skill,
   Right Med'cines to apply;
And my Disease obey'd thy Will,
   The painful Symptoms die.

That Life, which thou hast longer spar'd,
   I would devote to Thee.
O let thy Spirit be my Guard,
   Till I thy Face shall see!

(1736)

After the Small Pox
Mary Jones

When skillful traders first set up,
To draw the people to their shop,

They strait hang out some gaudy sign,
Expressive of the goods within.
The Vintner[3] has his boy and grapes,
The Haberdasher[4] thread and tapes,
The Shoemaker exposes boots,
And Monmouth Street[5] old tatter'd suits.

So fares it with the nymph divine;
For what is Beauty but a Sign?   10
A face hung out, thro' which is seen
The nature of the goods within.[6]
   Thus the coquet her beau ensnares
With study'd smiles, and forward airs;
The graver prude hangs out a frown
To strike th' audacious gazer down;
But she alone, whose temp'rate wit
Each nicer medium can hit,
Is still adorn'd with ev'ry grace,
And wears a sample in her face.   20

   What tho' some envious folks have said,
That *Stella*[7] now must hide her head,
That all her stock of beauty's gone,
And ev'n the very sign took down:
Yet grieve not at the fatal blow;   ⎫
For if you break[8] a while, we know,   ⎬
'Tis bankrupt like, more rich to grow. ⎭
A fairer sign you'll soon hang up,
And with fresh credit open shop:
For nature's pencil soon shall trace,   30
And once more finish off your face,

---

3. Wine merchant.

4. Dealer in men's clothing, including socks and shirts.

5. Street famous for its shops selling secondhand (or older) clothes.

6. The trope of the face as the wooden sign hung out to identify types of business establishments had been used in many literary works, including Aphra Behn's *The Rover* (1677) and Jonathan Swift's *Stella's Birthday, 1721* (1728), a particular favorite of women poets.

7. Latin word for "star" and conventional name for a virtuous, beautiful maiden, derived from Philip Sidney's chaste Stella, loved by Astrophel, in the sonnet sequence *Astrophel and Stella*. Significantly, it was the name Swift gave Esther Johnson, the subject and addressee of his birthday poems.

8. Go bankrupt, to fail commercially.

Which all your neighbours shall out-shine,
And of your Mind remain the Sign.[9]

(1750)

On Recovery from the Small-Pox by Inoculation[10]
Esther Lewis Clark

I.

Awake my muse, and tune thy lyre,
   Let joyous gratitude thy strains inspire;
   Let all my soul ascend in praise,
   And all her pow'rs with ardour raise
To HIM, who blest those means, which reason's voice
   Bade human prudence make its choice,
   To free the mind from anxious fears,
   And easier make my future years;
Years, if my GOD permit my glass[11] to run;
10   If not, his heav'nly will be done.
   Be it my constant care to keep
My lamp still burning, if I 'wake or sleep;
   Then shall my soul be free from fears,
Nor does it matter when pale death appears.

II.

O thou benign, whose all-directing hand
   A blessing gave to human skill,
   And bad'st success attendant stand,
   How shall my full o'er-flowing heart
   Its thankful sentiments impart!
20   Firm in thy strength I plac'd my trust,
   Nor rested on frail, feeble dust;

9. A reworking of lines 53–56 from Swift's *Stella's Birthday, 1721:* "No bloom of youth can ever blind / The cracks and wrinkles of your mind / All men of sense will pass your door, / And crowd to Stella's at fourscore."

10. Throughout the eighteenth century, epidemics of smallpox killed thousands of British people. Inoculation to prevent smallpox at that time involved the use of the live virus and remained controversial among medical men and frightening to the population at large. An important advance was Edward Jenner's introduction of the use of the cowpox, rather than smallpox pus, at the end of the century.

11. Hourglass.

With low submission to thy will
   My fervent pray'rs arose,
To bless those means which prudence chose,
Nor did my sins or frailties interpose
   To blast those pray'rs, they reach'd the skies,
   Propitious mercy on them smil'd;
Nor didst thou leave me, nor forsake thy child.
   For this my soul shall ev'ry day
   Her grateful adorations pay;   30
   And praise sincere, tho' lowly, rise.
   And O! let all the world agree
   To place their confidence in thee:
   On each design thy blessing crave,
Since none against thy will can kill, or save.

III.
   Nature, thy substitute below,
   Which wisest councils does bestow,
Thus spoke, behold where gracious providence,
With pity mov'd, and full of love immense,
   Benignly merciful, and kind,   40
   Points out a way by which mankind
With safety o'er that dreadful gulf may steer,
Where myriads perish each revolving year:
   Then since thy Maker smooths the wave,
   Don't thou refuse thyself to save,
But wisely trust him with the life he gave;
   If to that trust in pow'r divine,
   By judgment led, thou wisely join
   For christian graces, constant pray'r,
   The danger vanishes in air.   50

IV.
   But O! my strains unequal rise,
And with my grateful heart too poorly sympathize,
   To praise that pow'r whose gracious hand,
   In mercy wasted to my natal land,[12]

---

12. Immunization by use of the live virus had been practiced for centuries in China and in southwestern Asia. Lady Mary Wortley Montagu, who saw the benefits in Turkey and had her young children successfully inoculated there, publicized the procedure when she returned to England.

This salutary way to shun
The fatal fury of a dire disease,
 And that malignant rage appease
 Which its ten thousands has undone.
How many, all their hopes and comforts cross'd,
Weep a lov'd partner, child, or parent lost?
Beauty's fair field 't has oft' in ruins laid,
And kill'd the peace of many a lovely maid;
 For O! few females can despise
 Those charms which catch the gazer's eyes.

V.
Nor thou, O B-wd-n,[13] nor yet J-n-s[14] refuse
 The tribute of a grateful muse.
 The first by nature form'd, and art
 To act the wise physician's part,
Prescrib'd the way to make the dire disease
 With soften'd symptoms gently seize;
The other fraught with judgment, care and skill,
From present danger free, and future ill,
 Safe led me thro' an easy road
 Again to health's serene abode.

        (1789)

60

70

To-Morrow
Written During Sickness
Susanna Blamire

How sweet to the heart is the thought of to-morrow,
 When Hopes fairy pictures bright colours display;
How sweet when we can from Futurity[15] borrow
 A balm for the griefs which afflict us to-day!

---

 13. Samuel Bowden, Frome physician and poet, who was also a friend of Elizabeth Singer Rowe's. Like Clark, he published in the *Bath Journal.*
 14. Probably Edward Jenner (1749–1823), the surgeon who experimented with and pioneered small-pox vaccination from animal virus.
 15. The future.

When wearisome sickness has taught me to languish
   For Health, and the blessings it bears on its wing;
Let me hope (ah! how soon would it lessen my anguish),
   That to-morrow will ease and serenity bring.

The pilgrim sojourning alone, unbefriended,
   Hopes, joyful, to-morrow his wanderings shall cease;   10
That at home, and with care sympathetic attended,
   He shall rest unmolested, and slumber in peace.

When six days of labour each other succeeding,
   The husbandman toils with his spirits depress'd;
What pleasure to think, as the last is receding,
   To-morrow will be a sweet Sabbath of rest!

And when the vain shadows of Time are retiring,
   When life is fast fleeting, and death is in sight,
The Christian believing, exulting, expiring,
   Beholds a to-morrow of endless delight!   20

The Infidel then sees no joyous to-morrow,
   Yet he knows that his moments must hasten away;
Poor wretch! can he feel without heart-rending sorrow,
   That his joys and his life must expire with to-day!

            (d. 1794; 1842)

Ode III: To Pain

Anne Bannerman

I.
Hail! fiercest herald of a power,
   Whose harsh controul each nerve obeys!
I call thee, at this fearful hour;
   To thee my feeble voice I raise.
Say, does compassion never glow
Within thy soul, and bid thee know
   The pangs, with which thou fir'st[16] the breast?

16. *Firest,* that is, burns.

Or dost thou never, never mourn,
To plant so deep the hidden thorn,
   Forbidding aid, and blasting rest?

10

II.
Think'st thou my wavering fickle mind
   Requires so much, to break her chain?
Alas! what earthly joys can bind
   The wretch, who sees thy figure, Pain!
For ever fleet before his eyes;
For him, no glories gild the skies;
   No beauties shine in nature's bound,
In vain with verdure[17] glows the spring,
If, from within, thy gnawing sting
   Bid only demons scowl around.

20

III.
Too sure, I feel, in every vein,
   With thee soft Pity ne'er can dwell.
Shall pleasure never smile again
   Or health thro' ev'ry channel swell?
Yes! tho' thy hand hath crush'd the rose
Before its prime, another blows,
   Whose blooms thy breath can ne'er destroy;
Say, can thy keen and cruel chains
Corrode, where bliss seraphic reigns,
   Where all is peace, and all is joy.

30

IV.
Then, wherefore sighs my fearful heart,
   And trembles thus my tottering frame?
Alas! I feel thy deadly dart,
   More potent far than fancy's flame:
I bend, grim tyrant! at thy throne;
But spare, ah! spare that sullen frown,
   Relax the horrors of thy brow!
O! lead me, with a softer hand,

17. Fresh green grass and other plants.

And lo! I come at thy command,
    And, unrepining, follow through.   40

(1800)

Sources

Cockburn: *The Works of Mrs. Catharine Cockburn,* 2 vols. (London, 1751), 2:557–59; Finch: *The Anne Finch Wellesley Manuscript Poems: A Critical Edition,* ed. Barbara McGovern and Charles H. Hinnant (Athens: University of Georgia Press, 1998), 37–38; Chandler: *The Description of Bath. A Poem,* 3rd ed. (London, 1736), 63–64; Jones: *Miscellanies in Prose and Verse* (Oxford, 1750), 79–80; Clark: *Poems Moral and Entertaining* (Bath, 1789), 96–98; Blamire: *The Poetical Works of Miss Susanna Blamire* (Edinburgh, 1842), 71–72; Bannerman: *Poems by Anne Bannerman* (Edinburgh, 1800), 66–68.

⊁{H}⊱

Poems on Nature

During the Restoration and eighteenth century a number of compelling and contradictory conceptions of the relationship between humankind and nature coexisted, many developed within the poetic kinds.[1] The most influential were related to Christianity, whether invocations of nature as God's second book for the enlightenment of humankind (the first book being the Bible) or portrayals of nature as sources of inspiration ("I will lift up mine eyes unto the hills, / From whence cometh my help ...," *Psalms* 121:1–2). In these interpretations God's nature and laws evidenced themselves in the physical world. Nature was also portrayed contradictorily as a law unto itself, as part of the Great Chain of Being, or as "pathetic fallacy," which depicted nature as responding to human events.[2] Native Americans were portrayed as both "savages" (even in the U.S. Declaration of Independence) and also in harmony with the earth, the "ecological Indian." Other powerful representations of nature were pastoral, depicting simple people as part of the landscape, and georgic, advocating patriotic cultivation of the land. The imagery, ideologies, and modes of all of these conceptions of the relationship between nature and humankind flowed into and through the poetry of the period. Women's poetry, however, does not always fit into familiar categories, and, as with other poetic kinds, their adaptations and revisions sometimes fuel new poetic movements.

More often than other kinds of poetry, nature poetry is ridiculed and even reviled, and that by women often insulted as sentimental, mawkish, trivial, and hackneyed. Even Roger Lonsdale, who did so much for eighteenth-century women's poetry, congratulates himself for "underrepresenting" "laments for dead birds and small animals."[3] Men and women are dismissed for brief, general descriptions marred by repeated conventions, such as representing a breeze as "gentle Zephyr" and all meadows as "verdant meads." Rather charitably, Bonamy Dobrée explains, "The setting was given, and the reader was expected to fill in the details with whatever attendant delights he might associate with them."[4]

The phrase *nature poetry* oversimplifies and flattens the reality of the diverse kinds poets wrote and the work the poems do. It even erases the fact that some poetry emphasizes nature as the totality of the physical universe, while other poetry is devoted to flora and fauna. Social practices, thoughts about nature, and fashions involving it changed considerably during the long eighteenth century, and the poems demand discriminating reading within specific sociohistorical situations. Although, as Karla Armbruster and Kathleen R. Wallace write, "most environmental history, philosophy, and criticism tends to characterize Western thought through the Enlightenment as profoundly antienvironmental and deeply invested in the notion of human beings as separate from and superior to nonhuman nature," this generalization is also flattening and misleading.[5] As Myra Reynolds correctly observes, there came to be "a real and vital love for the out-door world, and . . . this new attitude toward Nature is marked by first-hand observation, by artistic sensitiveness to beauty, by personal enthusiasm for Nature, by a recognition of the effect of Nature on man [*sic*]."[6] In fact, even the early women poets writing on nature outpace most male nature poets, as demonstrated by Anne Finch's *Nocturnal Rêverie* (2.B) and Jane Barker's poetry, of which *On the Death of my Dear Friend and Play-fellow* (2.N) is an example. As metaphoric, even allegorical, as Barker's *Sitting by a Rivulet,* in this section, is, the specific details about the stream are quite extraordinary, as she compares it to tidal water and describes it in different lights.

Indicative of the kinds of changes in perception and taste are the gardens, which evolved from rigidly geometric formal gardens to carefully designed spaces that were, in fact, highly artificial but conceived to imitate natural settings and, as country estates proliferated, "prospects," views from various vantage points that looked over settings cultivated to replicate popular landscape paintings. The great public gardens in London and other places attracted increasingly diverse pleasure seekers, and the gardens at country estates became tourist attractions. Botany as science and hobby engaged a wide spectrum of men and women, and access to the Richmond Lodge and Kew Gardens, the Royal Botanic Gardens, with more than thirty-four hundred plant species, turned botany into a national passion.[7] Gardens become major topics of description and discussion in letters. With the decided shift away from the geometric formal gardens to "natural" walks and gardens, even carefully constructed "wildernesses" were fashionable for a brief period. At the time when American colonists were struggling with a vast, real wilderness, these manicured walks that opened into various kinds of cultivated gardens, clumps of architecturally arranged flowers, and carefully crafted seats were the height of fashion.[8] The gardens of this time became aesthetic spaces and places of reflection and renewal. The politeness, or gentility, movement, which Lawrence Klein dates as rising to prominence between 1660 and 1730, reinforced their importance for individuals and the nation.[9]

Nature poetry is usually more than an effective description of the natural world, as six diverse poems in this section illustrate. Elizabeth Carter's beautifully conceived poem correlates the spaciousness of contemplation with that of the heavenly universe. Hester Mulso Chapone finds a thunderstorm spark for reflection, while Charlotte Smith takes a tiny spider and the missel thrush as her impetus. Jane West catalogs with exquisite, close observation the yielding of winter to the signs of spring. One of the most delightful poems is Ann Yearsley's creative *To Miss Eliza Dawson*. Yearsley, a milkwoman, to whom many kinds of weather were no friends, portrays Eliza as identified with some kinds of weather and reacting to others. As a "phantom" presence, one heard "in the whisp'ring gale" and sensed in the "tints" of sunrise, Eliza becomes the means to touch upon youth and death, pleasure and endurance.

Two poems in the center of this section are pure fun. Mary Savage's *The Disaster* begins with a description of her pet birds. Playing with an idea in a friend's invitation to visit, she imagines training them to pull her chariot. Nature, in the form of a cat following its natural instinct, interferes. Hannah More's *Inscription: In a beautiful Retreat called Fairy Bower* is part of a group of her writings on the attainment of human happiness. She invites those who share her enjoyment of nature and her sensibility into her bower, while she admonishes, "Mortals! form'd of grosser clay, / From our haunts keep far away." The poem is filled with delightful details, such as the discovery of violets or a bird's nest, and inflected with More's seriousness. For instance, she compliments those who see but "spare" the nest. The taming and keeping of wild birds and the creation of "fairy bowers" were both popular in the century, and these poems introduce to twenty-first-century readers the imaginative playfulness that added to the enjoyment.

The final poems in this section are examples of ekphrasis, the representation of a work of art in literature. Famous examples are Ovid's description of Minerva's tapestry in the *Metamorphoses* and John Keats's *Ode on a Grecian Urn*. Two of the poems here are on needlework, a women's art that came to be appreciated in the feminist movement of the late twentieth century. Both Jane Brereton and Ann Thomas praise the detail and "lifelike" qualities of their friends' work. Brereton "reads" what the embroidery reveals about her friend. Thomas's poem is double ekphrasis, a poem describing a tapestry based on a painting, as is Helen Maria Williams's *Sonnet, On reading the Poem upon the Mountain-Daisy*, a poem praising a poem describing a flower. Mary Whateley Darwall's *Lines, Occasioned by Seeing a Beautiful Print of the River Clyde* is the most common kind of ekphrasis poem in the century, a poem about a painting or print. These poems are especially interesting because they combine recollections of things in nature that the poet enjoys with an appreciation of a form of art other than poetry.

Each of the kinds of poetry represented in this section could be multiplied, and together they introduce the reader to the variety and creativity of women's nature poetry. Some include evidence about popular pastimes and women's occupations and lifestyles. Each offers delightful descriptions of the natural world, and each has levels of meanings woven into the fabric of the poems. They give us access to what nature meant to these women and also suggest the ways women influenced observing and thinking about the world around them.

Notes

1. A. O. Lovejoy has identified sixty-six meanings of *nature*. Arthur Oncken Lovejoy and George Boas, *Primitivism and Related Ideas in Antiquity* (Baltimore: Johns Hopkins Press, 1935), 447–56.

2. Sylvia Bowerbank helpfully substitutes the term *pathetic stylistics* for the pejorative *fallacy* in *Speaking for Nature: Women and Ecologies of Early Modern England* (Baltimore: Johns Hopkins University Press, 2004), 35.

3. Roger Lonsdale, ed., *Eighteenth-Century Women Poets: An Oxford Anthology* (Oxford: Oxford University Press, 1990), xxxvi.

4. Bonamy Dobrée, *English Literature in the Early Eighteenth Century, 1700–1740* (Oxford: Clarendon, 1959), 146.

5. For the history of this conception and a challenge to it, see Karla Armbruster and Kathleen R. Wallace, eds., *Beyond Nature Writing: Expanding the Boundaries of Ecocriticism* (Charlottesville: University Press of Virginia, 2000), 7–9, quotation from 8.

6. Myra Reynolds, *The Treatment of Nature in English Poetry between Pope and Wordsworth* (Chicago: University of Chicago Press, 1909), 87; see also 58.

7. Beginning in 1763 the gardens were open sporadically, depending on royal whim; one or both gardens were most commonly open on Sundays and Thursdays. Despite the expense of getting to Richmond, gardeners and casual sightseers flocked to the gardens. There were designated paths for viewing the gardens, and expert gardeners quickly clamored for better, separate access. Richard Mabey, *The Flowering of Kew* (London: Century, 1988), 19; Ray Desmond, *Kew: The History of the Royal Botanic Gardens* (London: Harvill, 1995), 59, 167–68; Mary Soderstrom, *Recreating Eden: A Natural History of Botanical Gardens* (Montreal: Véhicule, 2001), 71. We would like to thank Micaela Ellson for her research on this topic.

8. This fact underscores that "nature" is a human idea with a long and complicated history; our perception of it is culturally shaped and mediated through language and literature. This is one of the premises of William Cronon's groundbreaking *Uncommon Ground: Rethinking the Human Place in Nature,* ed. Cronon (New York: Norton, 1996), 20. He emphasized recognition of both the construction and the reality of nature, and his approach has encouraged books such as Robert N. Watson's *Back to Nature: The Green and the Real in the Late Renaissance* (note the subtitle) (Philadelphia: University of Pennsylvania Press, 2006).

9. Discussions of this movement are numerous. See, for example, Lawrence Klein, "Shaftesbury and the Progress of Politeness," *Eighteenth-Century Studies* 18 (1984–85): 186–214; Klein, "Politeness for Plebes," in *The Consumption of Culture, 1600–1800: Image, Object, Text,* ed. Ann Bermingham and John Brewer (New York: Routledge, 1995), 63–82

(what Defoe and the earlier guides for "gentleman," Klein's subject here, are doing seems quite different from the agenda of the midcentury gentility novel); and John Brewer, "'The most polite age and the most vicious': Attitudes towards culture as a commodity, 1660–1800," in Bermingham and Brewer, *Consumption of Culture, 1600–1800*, 341–45. Helen Sard Hughes reports that Rowe enjoyed Shaftesbury's *Characteristics* and Berkeley's *Minute Philosopher*. "Thomson and the Countess of Hertford," *Modern Philology* 25 (1928): 445.

· Sitting by a Rivulet
Jane Barker

I.

Ah lovely stream, how fitly may'st thou be,
    By thy *immutability,*
Thy gentle motion and *perennity,*
     To us the Emblem of *Eternity:*
      And to us thou do'st no less
    A kind of *Omnipresence* too express.
  For always at the *Ocean* thou
Art always here, and at thy *Fountain* too;
    Always thou go'st thy proper Course,
     Spontaneously, and yet by force,   10
     Each Wave forcing his *Precursor* on;
   Yet each one runs with equal haste,
    As though each fear'd to be the last.
With mutual strife, void of contention,
In Troops they march, till thousands, thousands past.
     Yet gentle stream, thou'rt still the same,
      Always going, never gone;
     Yet do'st all Constancy disclaim,
Wildly dancing to thine own murmuring tunefull Song;
     Old as Time, as Love and Beauty young.   20

II.

But chiefly thou to *Unity* lay'st claim,
    For though in thee,
   Innumerable drops there be,
    Yet still thou art but one,
Th' Original of which from Heav'n came:
    The purest Transcript thereof we
I'th' *Church* may wish, but never hope to see,
  Whilst each Pretender thinks himself alone
    The Holy *Catholick Church*[1] Militant;

---

1. The Christian church throughout the world, not just the Roman Catholic Church. The term is usually traced to Cyril of Jerusalem, who wrote: "It is called Catholic because it extends over all the world . . . and because it teaches universally . . . and because it brings into subjection to godliness the whole race of mankind." George A. Buttrick et al., eds., *Interpreter's Dictionary of the Bible,* 4 vols. (New York: Abingdon, 1962), s.v. "Catholic Letters."

30   Nay, well it is if such will grant,
                That there is one elsewhere Triumphant.

III.
                But gentle stream, if they,
        As thou do'st Nature, would their *God* obey;
        And as they run their course of life, would try
                Their consciences to purify:
        From *self-love, pride,* and *avaricy,*
                Stubbornness equal to *Idolatry;*
                They'd find opinion of themselves,
                To be but dang'rous sandy Shelves,
40   To found or build their *Faith* upon,
                Unable to resist the force
        Of Prosperity's swelling violent *sorce,*[2]
                Or storms of Persecution:
        Whose own *voracity* (were't in their power)
                Wou'd not only Ornaments devour,
        But the whole *Fabrick* of Religion.

IV.
                But gentle stream, thou'rt nothing so,
                A Child in thee may safely go
                To rifle thy rich Cabinet;
50   And his Knees be scarcely wet,
                Whilst thou wantonly do'st glide,
        By thy Enamell'd Banks most beauteous side;
                Nor is sweet stream thy peacefull tyde,
        Disturbed by pale *Cynthia's* influence;[3]
                Like us thou do'st not swell with pride
                Of Chastity or Innocence.

        But thou remain'st still unconcern'd,
        Whether her Brows be smooth or horn'd;
        Whether her Lights extinguish'd or renew'd,
60   In her thou mindest no *Vicissitude.*

2. Source.

3. Cynthia is another name given to the goddess Diana, said to have been born on Mount Cynthus. It is a poetic name for the moon personified as a goddess. The moon controls the tides, not the movement of streams.

Happy if we, in our more noble State,
Could so slight all *Vicissitudes* of Fate.

(1688)

While Clear the Night
Elizabeth Carter

Felices animæ quibus hæc cognoscere primis,
Inque domos superas scandere, cura fuit.
Credibile est illas, pariter vitiisque locisque
Altius humanis, exeruisse caput.

OVID. FAST.[4]

While clear the Night, and ev'ry Thought serene,
  Let Fancy[5] wander o'er the solemn Scene:
And, wing'd by active Contemplation, rise
Amidst the radiant Wonders of the Skies.
  Here, *Cassiopeia*[6] fills a lucid Throne,
There blaze the Splendors of the *Northern Crown:*[7]
While the slow Car[8] the cold *Triones*[9] roll
O'er the pale Countries of the frozen Pole,
With faithful Beams conduct the wand'ring Ship,
O'er the wide Desart[10] of the pathless Deep.   10
Throughout the *Galaxy*'s extended Line,

4. Ovid's *Fasti,* his incomplete calendar of the Roman year. The opening lines for 3 January read, "Who says me nay if I would tell also of the stars, their risings and their settings? That was part of my promise." Carter's epigraph is the next lines: "Ah happy souls, who first took thought to know these things and scale the heavenly mansions! Well may we believe they lifted up their heads alike above the frailties and the homes of men." *Ovid's Fasti,* trans. Sir James George Frazer (London: Heinemann, 1931), 23. An early and significantly different version of this poem appeared in *Gentleman's Magazine* 8 (June 1738): 315–16.

5. A creative faculty, usually treated as lighter and more whimsical and playful than imagination or as an assistant to it. Imagination, with the power to transform its material, was considered the higher power.

6. Five bright stars form a constellation across the north celestial pole from the Big Dipper that is thought to look like a chair and therefore is called Cassiopeia's Chair.

7. Corona Borealis, a constellation of small bright stars. Its name derives from the legend of Bacchus giving a crown to Ariadne after she was deserted by Theseus.

8. Chariot. The sun, moon, and planets were described as processing across the sky in chariots.

9. The Great Bear and Little Bear constellations.

10. Desert.

Unnumber'd Orbs in gay Confusion shine:
Where ev'ry Star that gilds the Gloom of Night
With the faint Tremblings of a distant Light,
Perhaps illumes some System of it's own
With the strong Influence of a radiant Sun.
    Plac'd on the Verge, which *Titan*'s Realm[11] confines,
The slow revolving Orb of *Saturn*[12] shines;
Where the bright Pow'r whose near approaching Ray

20   Gilds our gay Climates with the Blaze of Day,
On those dark Regions glimmers from afar,
With the pale Lustre of a twinkling Star.
While, glowing with unmitigated Day,
The nearer Planets roll their rapid Way.
    Let stupid Atheists boast th' atomic Dance,[13]
And call these beauteous Worlds the Work of Chance:
But nobler Minds, from Guilt and Passion free,
Where Truth unclouded darts her heav'nly Ray,
Or on the Earth, or in th' ætherial Road,

30   Survey the Footsteps of a ruling GOD:
Sole LORD of Nature's universal Frame,
Thro' endless Years unchangeably the same:
Whose Presence, unconfin'd by Time or Place,
Fills all the vast Immensity of Space.
He saw while Matter yet a Chaos lay:[14]
The shapeless Chaos own'd his potent Sway.
His single Fiat[15] form'd th' amazing Whole,
And taught the new-born Planets where to roll:
With wise Direction curv'd their steady Course,

40   Imprest the central and projectile Force,
Left in one Mass their Orbs confus'd should run,
Drawn by th' attractive Virtue of the Sun,
Or quit the harmonious Round, and wildly stray
Beyond the Limits of his genial Ray.

---

11. Titan is the largest of Saturn's moons, discovered in 1655.

12. The sixth planet from the sun, distinctive because of its ring system.

13. An early Greek theory was that creation and change were the result of the combination and separation of an unchanging set of atoms.

14. In Greek mythology, the earth, sea, and air were mixed together; according to the first chapter of the Judeo-Christian book of Genesis, "the earth was without form" and God divided the earth and waters.

15. Authoritative decree. Genesis 1:3 in the Vulgate, the most ancient version of the entire Bible, contains the phrase *Fiat lux;* thus *fiat* is a command for creation.

To thee, *Endymion*,[16] I devote my Song;
To Minds like thee, these Subjects best belong;
Whose curious Thoughts with active Freedom fear,
And trace the Wonders of creating Pow'r.
For this, some nobler Pen shall speak thy Fame;
But let the Muse indulge a gentler Theme,   50
While pleas'd she tells thy more engaging Part,
Thy social Temper and diffusive Heart.
Unless these Charms their soft-ning Aid bestow,
Science[17] turns Pride, and common Wit a Foe.

(1738; 1762)

Written during a violent Storm at Midnight, 1749
Hester Mulso Chapone

In gloomy pomp whilst awful Midnight reigns,
    And wide o'er earth her mournful mantle spreads,
    Whilst deep-voic'd thunders threaten guilty heads,
And rushing torrents drown the frighted plains,
And quick-glanced lightnings, to my dazzled sight
Betray the double horrors of the night;

A solemn stillness creeps upon my soul,
    And all its pow'rs in deep attention die;
    My heart forgets to beat; my stedfast eye
Catches the flying gleam; the distant roll,   10
Advancing gradual, swells upon my ear
With louder peals, more dreadful as more near.

Awake, my soul, from thy forgetful trance!
    The storm calls loud, and Meditation wakes;
    How at the sound pale Superstition shakes,
Whilst all her train of frantic Fears advance!
Children of Darkness, hence! fly far from me!
And dwell with Guilt and Infidelity!

16. Endymion, a shepherd boy loved by the moon, asked Zeus for perpetual youth. Zeus granted
his request, but on the condition that Endymion remain eternally asleep.
    17. Knowledge.

But come, with look composed and sober pace,
20   Calm Contemplation, come! and hither lead
Devotion, that on earth disdains to tread;
Her inward flame illumes her glowing face,
Her upcast eye, and spreading wings, prepare
Her flight for heav'n, to find her treasure there.

She sees, enraptur'd, thro' the thickest gloom,
Celestial beauty beam, and, midst the howl
Of warring winds, sweet music charms her soul;
She sees, while rifted oaks in flames consume,[18]
A Father-God, that o'er the storm presides,
30   Threatens, to save, and loves, when most he chides.

(1749; 1775)

Inscription
In a beautiful Retreat called Fairy Bower[19]
Hannah More

Airy spirits, you who love
Cooling bower, or shady grove,
Streams, that murmur as they flow,
Zephyrs[20] bland, that softly blow,

Babbling echo, or the tale
Of the love-lorn Nightingale,[21]
Hither, airy spirits, come,
This is your peculiar home.

If you love a verdant glade,
10   If you love a noon-tide shade,
Hither Sylphs,[22] and Fairies, fly,
Unobserv'd of earthly eye.

18. Oaks split by lightning.
19. This poem was first published in a collection of poems that were added to the fourth edition (1774) of More's *Search after Happiness: A Pastoral Drama*.
20. Any soft, warm wind.
21. See section 3.F, "The Nightingale in Poetry." There are numerous legends about the nightingale's beautiful, sad songs.
22. Sylphs were spirits of the air, each one assigned to guard a single person or thing.

Come, and wander every night
By the moon-beam's glimmering light,
And again at early day
Brush the silver dews away.

Mark where first the daisies blow,
Where the bluest violets grow,
Where the sweetest linnet sings,
Where the earliest cowslip springs: 20

Where the largest acorn lies,
Precious in a Fairy's eyes;
Sylphs, tho' unconfin'd to place
Love to fill an acorn's space.

Come, and mark within what bush
Builds the blackbird or the thrush,
Great *his* joy who first *espies*,
Greater his who *spares* the prize.

Come, and watch the hallow'd bow'r,
Chase the insect from the flower;   30
Little offices like these
Gentle souls and Fairies please.

Mortals! form'd of grosser clay,
From our haunts keep far away,
Or, if you shou'd dare appear
See that you from vice are clear.

Folly's minion, Fashion's fool,
Mad Ambition's restless tool,
Slave of passion, slave of power,
Fly, ah! fly this tranquil bower.   40

Son of Avarice, soul of frost,
Wretch, of Heaven abhorr'd the most,
Learn to pity others wants,
Or avoid these hallow'd haunts.

Eye, unconscious of a tear
When Affliction's train appear,

Heart, that never heav'd a sigh
For another, come not nigh.

But, ye darling sons of Heaven,
50   Giving freely what was given,
Who, like Providence, dispense
Blessings of benevolence.

You, who wipe the tearful eye,
You, who stop the rising sigh,
You, who well have understood
The luxury of doing good;

Come, ye happy virtuous few,
Open is my bower to you;
You, the mossy banks may press,
60   You, each guardian Fay[23] shall bless.

(1774)

The Disaster

Mary Savage

The Author had informed her Friend, that among other amusements she had diverted her self with taming two Sparrows—in answer to which her Friend sent the following paragraph in her next letter—

"What a whimsical account do you give of the avocations that take up your time; among which taming of Sparrows seems to be one part—if you can bring them to draw your chariot, I beseech you to direct their flight our way—with what pleasure shall I see them fluttering their little wings and gently descending for you to alight at our door—"

By Sparrows drawn, there's now no chance,
To see your car-born[24] friend advance.
A dire disaster—hang the cat;
Far better had she kill'd a rat.

23. Fairy.
24. Chariot-borne, carried in a chariot.

Supinely seated in my chair,
And building castles in the air,
Contriving how to form the traces,
And where to fix the springs and braces,[25]
To make my car secure and tight,
And guide the little flutt'rers right;   10
A buzzing fly sports round my head,
And strait the airy castle fled.

　My son with arm of mighty force,
Soon stopt the fly's progressive course,
The trembling insect fast he held,
With joy elate his bosom swell'd,
And thus he spoke to Dick and Phill,
I give this victim to your will.
Then op'd the cage, that each might vie,
To seize the half expireing fly;   20
With wings out spread to try their chance,
The little chirpers soon advance:
With tail erect, and back raised high, ⎫
The cat appeared—her sparkling eye, ⎬
As green as is the emerald's dye: ⎭
With out stretch'd paw, and lofty bound,
She gave poor Dick a fatal wound.

　Oh! dire mishap oh! fell despair
His fleeting breath was lost in air;
Struck with the sight, fix'd pale and dumb,   30
(Like coward when he hears a drum.)
The youth remain'd—but kindled rage,
Glows on my cheeks—and war I wage;
While puss exulting o'er the prey,
Essays[26] in vain to break away;
With hand of force, I grip'd her throat,
(Her life was then not worth a groat.)[27]
Unfeeling wretch, declare I say,
Deep mischief brooding, where you lay;

25. Parts of a chariot. The traces, for instance, are the side straps connecting the horses (here, sparrows) to the chariot.
26. Attempts.
27. A silver coin worth four pence.

40   Unloose thy hold, release the corse,[28]
      Nor tear those limbs with brutal force;
      'Twas impious theft, that prompts the deed,
      But impious theft, shall ne'er succeed;
      Nor shalt thou bear the prize away,
      Grimalkin[29] hold—I charge thee stay.
      Life now no longer swells his breast,
      Yet safe entoomb'd my bird shall rest.

          But Cailif[30] vile, live thou disgrac'd,
      Nor ever more of sparrow taste,
50   Thy share of toast, and cream shall fail,
      Or e'er in mirth pursue thy tail.
      No tender mouse shall grace thy dish,
      Nor shalt thou ever taste of fish;
      At dreary eve of winters day,
      Warm by the fire each cat shall lay,
      Whilst thou shut out, shall mew in vain,
      Expos'd to storms of wind and rain;
      Through pools of wet be forc'd to tramp,
      Thy limbs benumb'd with painful cramp.

60   With trembling nerves and glaring eye,
      She heard my threats without reply.

          Firm in my hand I held her still,
      To show I had the power to kill;
      Then rais'd her high, to strike the blow,
      And lay the sprawling victim low;
      But rage subsides—to give her pain,
      Would not bring back poor Dick again.
      Grimalkin go—thy life I spare,
      But never more my friendship share.

70   His mate poor Phill, in silence mourns,
      And pensive to the cage returns.

---

28. Corpse.
    29. The spirit of a witch. According to legend, any witch could assume the body of a cat nine times.
Cats who misbehaved were often called Grimalkin. See Mary Robinson's *Mistress Gurton's Cat* (1.H).
    30. Probably a misspelling of *caitiff,* meaning a captive or contemptible or cowardly person.

While I lament the fatal day,
That snatch'd my flatt'ring hopes away;
For never yet in one horse chair,
Did god or goddess mount in air;
And shall a mortal dare to fly,
With single sparrow thro' the sky,
No—rather let me wait my doom
And in my husband's chariot come.

(1777)

Spring: An Ode
Jane West

And now, obedient to divine command,
   Reluctant winter yields his rigid reign;
Exulting Nature breaks his cruel band,
   And welcomes Flora[31] to her old domain;
She from her chariot strews ambrosial flowers;
'Tis she, that decks the vales, and renovates the bowers.

The pendent isicle perceives the thaw,
   Then quits the straw-roof'd cot, and melts away;
The snow beholds, and hastens to withdraw,
   But loses first its innocent array: 10
Assuming now, a robe of murky hue
More soil'd, as more receding from our view.

Ice in its northern magazine[32] lies chain'd,
   And all the furious hurricanes are bound;
Zephyr,[33] by Eurus[34] fierce too long restrain'd,
   Now claps his pinions[35] at the joyful sound;
The gentle shower descends; earth opens wide
Her jaws, and thirsty sucks the copious tide.

31. Goddess of flowers and fertility.
32. Storehouse.
33. The west wind, lover of Flora, goddess of flowers; any soft, warm wind.
34. The east wind.
35. The distal segment of a bird's wing where the feathers fan out beautifully; corresponds to the human forearm.

The glorious sun with vegetative powers
  Endues the air, resolving to unchain

20

The willing world, while in his noon-tide hours:
  Well knowing, that his sister Queen[36] again,
When she resum'd her silver throne, would freeze
The brooks and rills, and hardly spare the seas.

And now alternate, what bright Phœbus[37] thaws
  By day, by night the Queen of shade congeals:
Nature, subservient to discordant laws,
  In all her springs the dire commotion feels:
The bud, that noon-tide suns inspir'd to rise,

30

Lies dead at evening, chill'd by frosty skies.

Mid the confusion, whilst we scarce can tell
  If winter stays or flies, the snow-drop rears
Her humid head, and fills each drooping bell
  With incense pure and odoriferous tears:
Safe in its native innocence it stands,
Nor dreads keen Boreas,[38] nor the wintry bands.

Yet, but a herald to the crocus proud,
  Who peers a King in golden arms array'd,
Around him daffodils and violets crowd,

40

  And primroses dear to the wood-land maid;
Succeeded quickly by a thousand flowers,
All that delight in meadows, hills, and bowers.

Behold, the elm puts on its dark array
  Of dusky green; forth shoots the alder dun;[39]
In the light breeze the leaves of aspin play;
  The bushy sycamore defies the sun;
And last, as if the sylvan band to close,
The regal oak his ample foliage shows.

But see, the young creation is awake;

50

  The houshold bee forsakes her waxen cell;

36. The moon.
37. Apollo, the sun god, here the personification of the sun.
38. The north wind.
39. Small birch trees that grow well in moist soil; their grayish-brown bark is used to create dyes.

The finny nations wanton in the lake;
  The gentle birds their pleasing descants[40] tell;
The lordly steed indignant paws the ground;
And o'er green thymy banks the lambkins bound.

And now the etherial ram the zenith leaves,
  The ram of old surcharg'd with Helle's fate;[41]
This, the proud bull,[42] his rival stern, perceives,
  And issues forth in all his radiant state,
He bends his starry horns, enwreath'd with light,
As if to rend the dusky veil of night.   60

The blessed sun his beams benignly pours
  On the glad earth, and bids creation smile:
Exuberant nature pours forth all her stores,
  And chearful swains[43] renew their annual toil:
War too, by intermission unsubdu'd,
Resumes its rage for violence and blood!

But that I fear my mortal muse would faint,
  And leave me aidless in th' unbounded space,
My song the starry firmament should paint,
  How planets run their vast eliptic race,   70
Arcturus[44] urging on his starry team,
Orion's sword,[45] and Ursa's[46] guiding beam.

But let me stop the thought, nor strive to rein
  This fiery steed, nor compass heights divine;
Lest I, dismounted on the Lycian plain,[47]
  Mourn like Bellerophon[48] the rash design;

40. Songs in which the birds seem to be creating a two-part melody.
41. In Greek mythology, Helle and her brother were flying through the air on the back of a ram with the Golden Fleece when Helle fell off into the sea; the Hellespont is named for her.
42. The zodiacal sign Aries, the ram, gives way to Taurus, the bull. Both are constellations.
43. Country men; lovers.
44. The fourth brightest star in the sky and the brightest in the northern sky.
45. The Sword of Orion is a region of sky around the Orion Nebula; its double, single, and multiple stars hang from the constellation known as Orion's Belt. Part of the magnificent constellation Orion on the celestial equator. Ian Ridpath, "Sword of Orion," in *Oxford Dictionary of Astronomy*, ed. Ridpath, 2nd ed. (New York: Oxford University Press, 2007).
46. Ursa Major, the Great Bear, a constellation that includes the stars in the Big Dipper.
47. Lycia was an ancient country in southwest Asia Minor; it was mentioned by Homer.
48. Ancient Corinthian hero who tried to ride his winged horse, Pegasus, to heaven. The horse threw him, and the gods were angered.

Enough that I with rude and doric strain,[49]
Oh genial spring! have hail'd thy welcome reign.

(1786)

To Miss Eliza Dawson, of Oxton, Yorkshire[50]
Ann Yearsley

Come, fair ELIZA! bless the vale,
    And realize what fancy[51] forms:
I hear thee in the whisp'ring gale;
    I see thee weep the wint'ry storms,

Which on Lactilla's[52] bosom beat,
    While fleecy snows in haste descend:
They seek my heart-melting retreat,
    For *there*'s the image of my friend.

All glowing,'mid immortal fire,
10   Eliza owns my rustic soul,
Before her light'nings pale expire,
    And thunders seek the distant pole.

Oh! thou canst cheer the dreary wild;
    Rememb'ring thee, my sorrows die:
Thy friendship renders horror mild,
    And calms the rude inclement sky.

When wand'ring o'er yon rugged rocks
    Unseen, Eliza hovers near.
Ah, no!—the lovely phantom mocks
20   My eager soul—she is not there!

49. The Dorians invaded Greece about 1100 BC, and their art and architecture remained distinct within the Greek world.

50. Eliza Dawson, a poet and autobiographer, was seventeen at the time this poem was published. Prior to her marriage to Archibald Fletcher in 1791, Dawson helped gather five hundred subscriptions for Ann Yearsley's poetry, and later she established herself as a leading hostess in Edinburgh literary circles. Her autobiography was not published until 1875, seventeen years after her death.

51. A creative faculty, usually treated as lighter and more whimsical and playful than imagination or as an assistant to it. Imagination, with the power to transform its material, was considered the higher power.

52. Yearsley delivered milk door to door and was known as Lactilla, "the poetical milk woman."

Idea,[53] die, nor falsely play
   With tints which my Eliza grace;
Yon Eastern blush must sure display
   A guiltless emblem of her face.

Yet deathless Fancy, near me live!
   Lo! grateful Ardour lends her flame,
Bidding Eliza's charms survive,
   And dying accents *sigh* her name.

(1787)

Sonnet LXXVII
To the Insect of the Gossamer[54]
Charlotte Smith

Small, viewless Æronaut,[55] that by the line
   Of Gossamer suspended, in mid air
   Float'st on a sun beam—Living Atom, where
Ends thy breeze-guided voyage;—with what design
In Æther[56] dost thou launch thy form minute,
   Mocking the eye?—Alas! before the veil
Of denser clouds shall hide thee, the pursuit
   Of the keen Swift[57] may end thy fairy sail!—
Thus on the golden thread that Fancy[58] weaves
   Buoyant, as Hope's illusive flattery breathes,   10
The young and visionary Poet leaves
   Life's dull realities, while sevenfold wreaths
Of rainbow-light around his head revolve.
Ah! soon at Sorrow's touch the radiant dreams dissolve!

(1797)

53. The Platonic ideal, the personification of the ideal person and friend.

54. A spider. Gossamer is a fine, filmy substance spun by small spiders; it is seen floating in the air or spread over a grassy surface. Smith first published this sonnet in the 1797 *Elegiac Sonnets* and then made it part of *Conversations Introducing Poetry* (1804).

55. One who sails through the air.

56. A pure form of air or fire, the space beyond the sphere of the moon.

57. One of the fastest flyers among birds and similar to the swallow. It has a short bill and a gaping mouth in order to feed on insects while flying.

58. A creative faculty, usually treated as lighter and more whimsical and playful than imagination or as an assistant to it. Imagination, with the power to transform its material, was considered the higher power.

Ode to the missel thrush[59]

Charlotte Smith

The Winter Solstice[60] scarce is past,
Loud is the wind, and hoarsely sound
The mill-streams in the swelling blast,
And cold and humid is the ground[;]
When, to the ivy, that embowers
Some pollard tree, or sheltering rock,
The troop of timid warblers flock,
And shuddering wait for milder hours.

    While thou! the leader of their band,
10   Fearless salut'st the opening year;
Nor stay'st, till blow the breeze bland
That bid the tender leaves appear:
But, on some towering elm or pine,
Waving elate thy dauntless wing,
Thou joy'st thy love notes wild to sing,
Impatient of St. Valentine!

Oh, herald of the Spring! while yet
No harebell[61] scents the woodland lane,
Nor starwort[62] fair, nor violet,
20   Braves the bleak gust and driving rain,
'Tis thine, as thro' the copses[63] rude

---

59. Missel Thrush. *Turdus visivorous* [*sic*]. Mr. White, in his account of singing birds [in the *Natural History of Selborne* (London, 1789)], puts this among those whose song ceases before Midsummer. It is certainly an error. This remarkable bird, which cannot be mistaken for any other, began to sing so early as the second week of January; and now I hear him uttering a more clamorous song, the 8th of July, between the flying showers. Whenever the weather is windy or changeable, he announces it by a variety of loud notes. There is only one bird of this kind within hearing, who sang last year to the beginning of August. His food consists of berries and insects, but principally, the former. The fruit of the Hawthorn, *Mesphilus*, Elder, *Sambucus*, Spindletree, *Euonymus*, Sloe, *Prunus*, and Holly, *Ilex*, occasionally supply him; but the Missletoe, *Viscum*, from whence he takes his name of *viscivorous*, is his favourite food. As bird-lime is often made of its glutinous berries, and this thrush is supposed to encrease the Missletoe by depositing the seeds he has swallowed on other trees, he is said in a Latin proverb to propagate the means of his own destruction. *Smith*.
60. About 22 December, one of the two times when the sun is farthest from the equator and appears to stand still (the other is, of course, the summer solstice, about 21 June).
61. Slender, delicate plant with clusters of bell-shaped, blue flowers.
62. Plant with white, starry flowers.
63. Thickets of small trees and shrubs.

Some pensive wanderer sighs along,
To soothe him with thy cheerful song,
And tell of Hope and Fortitude!

For thee then, may the hawthorn bush,
The elder, and the spindle tree,
With all their various berries blush,
And the blue sloe[64] abound for thee!
For thee, the coral holly glow   30
Its arm'd and glossy leaves among,
And many a branched oak be hung
With thy pellucid missletoe.[65]

Still may thy nest, with lichen[66] lin'd,
Be hidden from the invading jay,
Nor truant boy its covert find,
To bear thy callow young away;
So thou, precursor still of good,
O, herald of approaching Spring,
Shalt to the pensive wanderer sing
Thy song of Hope and Fortitude.   40

(1804)

On seeing Mrs. Eliz. Owen, now Lady Longueville,[67] in an embroider'd Suit, all her own Work

Jane Brereton

Sure, this glorious Lady's the fair Queen of *May!*[68]
Tho' a Goddess, e'en *Flora*[69] was never so gay,

64. Small, plumlike fruit of the blackthorn that is so blue as to appear almost black.

65. The "pellucid," translucent white berries of the mistletoe are a favorite food of the thrush.

66. Small plant, part algae and part fungus, that sticks to rocks, wood, and soil and creates spongy patches of color.

67. Probably the wife of George Augustus Yelverton, Earl of Sussex, Viscount de Longueville, Lord Gray, who held the title from 1731 to 1758. It is said that after Brereton's death, Lady Longueville "could not mention her Name without Floods of Tears . . . and in the sincerest Manner regretted the Loss . . . of so wise, and entertaining a Friend." "An Account of the Life of Mrs. Brereton," in Brereton, *Poems on Several Occasions* (London, 1744), xiv.

68. Young woman chosen to be queen of the May Day (1 May) festivities.

69. Goddess of flowers and fertility.

With her Robe adorn'd, with the brightest of Flow'rs,
Which enamel the Meads,[70] or encircle the Bow'rs.
Had *Eliza* been seen by the Folks of old *Rome*,
They had sworn 'twas the Goddess appear'd in her Bloom;
At the Sight of her Garments with Flow'rets strew'd o'er,
From gazing, and wond'ring—they'd bow and adore.

    Behold, with what Skill she has damask'd the Rose![71]
10   The charming Carnation how crimson'd it glows!
There, the Lilly discloses its snowy white Head,
And here, their rich Purple the Violets spread;
In fine Party-colours the Tulip is shown,
The Jonquills, and Jess'mines appear newly blown.
Th' Auricula,[72] there, its Perfection displays;
And here, bright Anemonies gloriously blaze.

    So fair a Creation, the Work of her Hands,
First attracts my Regard, then my Wonder commands:
So verdant[73] the Ground is, the Flow'rs are so gay,
20   In the Midst of *December,* you'd swear it was *May*!
When thus we behold her, we needs must confess,
Her Fancy and Judgment are seen in her Dress;
In her Converse, good Sense, and good Humour we find,
And own her fine Outside excell'd by her Mind.

                                    (1744)

On Birds, Butterflies, a Deer, &c.
Another Piece of NEEDLE-WORK, in Imitation of Painting
Ann Thomas

Sure Anna here delighted could I stand,
And view the Piece, form'd by thy lovely Hand;
The Picture true to Nature doth appear,
Surpriz'd mine Eye, surveys the bounding Deer;

70. Meadows.
71. Woven a rose into damask cloth.
72. A variety of primrose.
73. Rich in fresh green grass and vegetation.

Well pleas'd he seems to crop the verdant Mead,[74]
And toss the branching Honors of his Head.[75]
On the gay Pheasants next I turn mine Eye,
Both seem contending for a single Fly;
With eager Haste they seem to stretch their Bill,
The flutt'ring Insect both resolve to Kill.   10
The Butterflies their painted Wings display,
With many a Spot and silken Colour gay.
The tow'ring Hawk displays such matchless Skill,
His Plumage, Talons, and his crooked Bill.
Whilst on the verdant Ground mine Eye I keep,
I almost see the scarlet Locust leap.
O! could the humble Muse as well declare,
The Merits of each all-accomplish'd Fair;
On you and Delia ev'ry fleeting Hour,
O! may kind Heav'n each earthly Blessing show'r.   20

(1784)

Sonnet, On reading the Poem upon the Mountain-Daisy, By Mr. Burns[76]

Helen Maria Williams

While soon the "Garden's flaunting flowers" decay,[77]
And, scatter'd on the earth, neglected lie,
The "Mountain Daisy," cherish'd by the ray
A Poet drew from heav'n, shall never die.—
Ah! like that lonely flower the Poet rose
'Mid Penury's bare soil, and bitter gale;
He felt each storm that on the mountain blows,
Nor ever knew the shelter of the vale.—
By Genius[78] in her native vigor nurst,

---

74. Meadow with fresh green grass and vegetation.

75. Antlers.

76. Robert Burns, Scottish poet (1759–96); the poem is *To a Mountain-Daisy, On turning one down, with the Plough, in April—1786.*

77. "The flaunting *flow'rs* our Gardens yield" is a line from Burns's poem that begins a comparison between a cultivated flower and the wild "unseen" solitary daisy.

78. The spirit of Scotland.

10   On Nature with impassion'd look he gaz'd,
      Then thro' the cloud of adverse fortune burst
      Indignant, and in light unborrow'd blaz'd.
      SCOTIA! from rude affliction shield thy Bard;
      His heav'n-taught numbers Fame herself will guard.

                                        (1791)

Lines, Occasioned by Seeing a Beautiful Print of the River Clyde[79]

Mary Whateley Darwall

      Give me to range with mind serene
      The heath-clad hills, the pastures green,
      That deck the sweetly-varied side
      Of Errick's boast,[80] romantic CLYDE:
      Where, by the mould'ring gothic tow'rs,
      The rapid stream resistless pours
      Thro' rocky chasms, wild and rude,
      In all the pomp of solitude.
      Fair stream! I trace thee thro' the meads,
10   Where bleating flocks, and shepherd's reeds,
      And every warbler of the wood,
      Pay their glad tribute to thy flood.

      Well pleas'd I see the rural lass,
      Bleaching her web[81] upon the grass,
      Or, bending o'er thy lucid wave,
      From ev'ry soil her linen lave;[82]

---

79. Engraved prints of landscapes and river sonnets were very popular. Connoisseurs and ordinary people collected prints after improvements in engraving raised their quality. Stipple engravings became more popular than mezzotints or line engravings, and "furniture prints," designed to be framed and displayed, joined the portfolio collections. John Brewer, *The Pleasures of the Imagination: English Culture in the Eighteenth Century* (New York: Farrar Straus Giroux, 1997), 458–63. The Clyde is the principal river in southwestern Scotland; it runs through Glasgow.

80. Strath Errick, a district of valleys and mountains in northwestern Scotland, leads to a famous waterfall. *Strath* is the Scottish word for river or mountain valley. Sarah Murray's *A Companion, and Useful Guide to the Beauties of Scotland* (London, 1799) contains a good description.

81. Crocheted or woven fabric was put in the sun to bleach it.

82. Wash.

Whilst blithe she carols many a lay[83]
Of Tiviot's banks,[84] or winding Tay.[85]

Now, from thy varied scenes so bland,
I turn to views august and grand,   20
Where Glasgow's sacred fanes[86] arise,
And point our wishes to the skies.

See, on the bosom of the stream,
Illum'd with Cynthia's[87] trembling beam,
Inverted edifices lie,
With all the glories of the sky.

Enraptur'd with the scene, I lay
Where Tame[88] his gently-winding way
Steals thro' the osier-fringed vales,[89]
Fann'd by soft zephyr's balmy gales;[90]   30
When (deeply musing) Morpheus[91] shed
His magic influence round my head,
And fancy form'd the pleasing dream:—

Methought a Naiad[92] from the stream
Arose; loose flow'd her sea-green vest,
An amber clasp adorn'd her breast;
Her pearly brow, her coral lip,
Whence Venus' doves[93] might nectar sip,

---

83. Ballad; lyric or narrative poem meant to be sung.

84. The Teviot, a river in the Borders region of Scotland, intersects with the river Tweed, a natural boundary between Scotland and England. Rich in trout, the Teviot winds through farmland and hills of grazing sheep.

85. The largest river (in terms of flow) in the United Kingdom, located in east-central Tayside, Scotland. The Tay runs from Loch Tay in the west to the Firth of Tay in the east and through the city of Perth.

86. Temples.

87. Cynthia is another name given to the goddess Diana, said to have been born on Mount Cynthus. It is a poetic name for the moon personified as a goddess.

88. Once a fast-moving, powerful river, the Tame now runs through some of the most urbanized areas of the United Kingdom, including Birmingham, and exists mostly in culverts and ditches.

89. Valleys with many willow trees.

90. Warm breezes from the west wind.

91. Ovid's name for the son of Sleep and the god of dreams.

92. Nymphs of rivers, streams, and lakes.

93. Venus was the Roman goddess of beauty and love, mother of Cupid. Doves drew her chariot and were sacred creatures to her because they came from Cyprus, her sacred island. "Cyprus" means

Her soft blue eye, that beam'd a ray
40   Mild as the blush of orient day,
Her modest, glowing, damask cheek,
"Where Cupids lurk in dimples sleek,"—[94]
Were such as beauty's goddess chose,
When blooming from the sea she rose;
Or such as heav'n, t'enslave mankind,
In MYRA's face has sweetly join'd:—
Her auburn tresses wav'd beneath
A wildly graceful sedgy wreath.[95]

"Mortal," she cry'd, "the wish give o'er,
50   Thine eye shall ne'er the banks explore
Of CLYDE's clear stream, where joyous rove
The sons of freedom, peace, and love.
Can'st thou the glen,[96] or pine-topp'd hill,
Like BURNS, with strains ecstatic fill?
Or dare to touch thy humble wire,
Where beauteous HELEN's[97] sweet-ton'd lyre
Breathes harmony in every gale,
That cheers the grove, or fans the dale
Where gentle Leven's silver tide[98]
60   Flows swift to mingle with the CLYDE.
Content, amid thy native plains,
Breathe to the woods thy rural strains."

I started, rose, and sighing cry'd,
Adieu, vain wish! adieu, sweet CLYDE!

(1794)

"copper," which is linked to the planet through the goddess. Doves were also known as the birds of Venus because of their excessive lust.

94. The god of love, Cupid was usually depicted as a winged boy with a bow and a quiver of arrows. Eighteenth-century writers referred to his darts or arrows as "cupids." The danger of attractive dimples, where Cupid might hide with his arrows, was a commonplace. It seems to date from the French romances of the early modern period and is even found in Gothic novels. Cf. Matthew Lewis, *The Monk*, 3 vols. (London, 1797), 1:136. We are grateful to Lacy Marschalk for her research on this note.

95. Wreath made from coarse grasses and rushes found along riverbanks.

96. Valley.

97. Miss H. M. Williams, Author of a Vol. of Sonnets, &c. *Darwall.* [*Poems by Helen Maria Williams, in two volumes,* esp. the 1791 second edition, included a number of sonnets. *Eds.*]

98. The Leven, a river approximately six miles long in West Dunbartonshire, Scotland, flows out of Loch Lomond in the north and into the Clyde in the south.

Sources

Barker: *Poetical Recreations* (London, 1688), 24–27. Carter: *Poems on Several Occasions* (London, 1762), 5–7. Chapone: *Miscellanies in Prose and Verse* (London, 1775), 125–26. More: *The Search after Happiness: A Pastoral Drama,* 4th ed. (Bristol, 1774), 45–47. Savage: *Poems on Various Subjects and Occasions,* 2 vols. (London, 1777), 2:79–85. West: *Miscellaneous Poetry by Mrs. West* (London, 1786), 37–40. Yearsley: *Poems on Various Subjects* (London, 1787), 45–47. Smith: *Elegiac Sonnets, and Other Poems,* 8th ed., 2 vols. (London, 1797), 2:18; *The Poems of Charlotte Smith,* ed. Stuart Curran (New York: Oxford University Press, 1993), 200–202. Brereton: *Poems on Several Occasions* (London, 1744), 37–38. Thomas: *Poems on Various Subjects* (Plymouth, 1784), 41–42. Williams: *Poems,* 2 vols., 2nd ed. (London, 1791), 1:55–56. Darwall: *Poems on Several Occasions. By Mrs. Darwall (Formerly Miss Whateley),* 2 vols. (Walsall, 1794), 1:14–18.

☀I☀

Poems on Ecology

"Ecocriticism seems to be booming in its test markets (British Romanticism and the literature of the American West)," Robert N. Watson wrote in 2006.[1] In fact, ecocriticism is booming in many literary periods and has already been institutionalized by the formation of the Association for the Study of Literature and the Environment, now an organization affiliated with the Modern Language Association, and featured in the *PMLA* series The Changing Profession.[2] The poems in this section have been selected in an attempt to invite ecocritical analyses to poetry and, indeed, to a historical period that has rarely been approached this way or even seen as appropriate for such criticism. By *ecocriticism* we mean "the study of the relationship between literature, humankind, and the physical environment"; the term reflects the recognition that environment and environmental issues often draw together or put in opposition biology, geography, philosophy, engineering, politics, history, commerce, and cultural theory.[3] Ecocriticism combines study, even appreciation, of cultural representations of the nonhuman with analysis of scientific, literary, economic, and political factors and implications. It emphasizes the relationships between humans and nonhumans and identifies environmental awarenesses, which may include recognition of the universe as ecosphere or attention to plants and living creatures in ways distinct from, for instance, descriptive settings. Increasingly it recognizes the part language plays in the sociopolitics of nature writing, including shaping our conception of what "nature" and "natural" are, creating and maintaining fashions in what is appreciated and valued, and manipulating opinion, as Rachel Carson famously did in *Silent Spring* (1962) with metaphors of nuclear destruction and biblical apocalypse.

The long eighteenth century was a time in which new kinds of nature poetry emerged as the result of philosophical movements (notably sensibility), new ways of enjoying nature and apprehending the world, and the needs created by growing populations, the industrial revolution, and military and imperial ambitions. To varying degrees people became increasingly aware of being both the guardians of the earth and the exploiters of it ("replenish the earth, and subdue it: and have dominion over the fish of the sea ...").[4] At the same time that formal and botanical gardens were becoming tourist sites, England was greatly concerned with managing fields and forests, as well as controlling the seas. The carefully structured and severely pruned formal or geometric gardens writ domination large, as did the later planting to, for instance, turn the Thames into "a number of separate water features in different pictures" rather than the "silvery streak" it naturally appeared as.[5] Parks, wildernesses, prospects, and the construction of artificial ruins usually involved rather drastic altering of the natural features of the land.[6] The second half of the century came to be marked by sharp conflicts about enclosure, land management, land use, and even the cutting of small groves of trees. Elizabeth Carter protests the cutting of an entire stand of trees in *To [Dr. Walwyn]*. From the different titles she gave the poem, it is clear that she first used the poem to protest the fashion for creating "prospects." Like so many women, Carter loved the "shady walk" that encouraged solitary contemplation, and she contrasts her active, intellectual engagement to mere admiration.

Some inherited traditions that encouraged ecocritical attitudes survived. Among them was the conception of nature as part of an animate world, a trope if not a belief that continued throughout the century. For example, in her 1769 novel *The History of Emily Montague* Frances Brooke has a character write to a friend that "the cascade of Montmorenci . . . . almost breathes; I no longer wonder at the enthusiasm of Greece and Rome, 'twas from objects resembling this their mythology took its rise."[7] This statement acknowledges the influence of classical thought, and the animation of the landscape has been traced through the Romantic movement, especially in Wordsworth's poetry. This representation of nature allowed identification or comparison and anthropomorphism. Katherine Philips, in *Upon the Graving of her Name Upon a Tree in Barnelmes Walks,* a witty poem that finds the tree superior to men, pays tribute to the tree's "generous" qualities, including its "broad shade." A tree that compares itself to a bashful virgin is the narrator in Aphra Behn's *On a Juniper-Tree,* and in Anna Laetitia Barbauld's poem *The Mouse's Petition* the mouse is the purported author. Behn's poem begins with a seduction story and then describes the pleasures shared by the lovers and the tree, which is shelter, observer, pillow, and canopy. In the poem's ending, rather than destruction, the expiring juniper receives surprising tributes.

Ecocritics note that attitudes toward science are often ambivalent. Science is, after all, the means of knowing and then exploiting nature, but it often provides the arguments that legitimate sociopolitical environmentalism.[8] Just as Carter both amasses positive allusions to specific kinds of trees and criticizes a "Son of Science," Barbauld presents the mice's desires in terms familiar to all humans and rebukes a powerful man of science, in this case Joseph Priestley, who conducted his experiments with gases on mice and birds, which he put in bell jars and watched suffocate. Barbauld's poem *The Caterpillar* is based upon the same identification of creature with human. She begins with the speaker addressing the caterpillar, which is in stark contrast to the violence with which she has been annihilating "thy race" "with persecuting zeal," crushing "whole families beneath my foot." This activity comes to symbolize "horrid war, o'erwhelming cities, fields, / And peaceful villages." As in *The Mouse's Petition,* she concludes with a recognition of "fellowship of sense with all that breathes" and a hopeful fantasy of a warrior "grown human."

The poems in this section provide a sketchy history of responses to the treatment of the nonhuman. Occasional references to the repair of damaged land appear, and a shared commitment to ending incidents of public cruelty to animals became a movement. In an age when bearbaiting and cockfighting were acceptable forms of public entertainment, these poems express concern for a public indifferent to cruelty. People witnessed gangs of boys torturing pets, often little girls' kittens, and kicking small wild animals, as Charlotte Smith describes in *Conversations Introducing Poetry.* Some of the poems, like Smith's *To a Hedgehog* (not included) and Mary Whateley Darwall's *To a Cricket,* were aimed at correcting superstitions and educating people. Jane Cave Winscom's *Poem for Children: On Cruelty to the Irrational Creation* speaks from the perspectives of snakes, insects, birds, and animals and, showing her degree of outrage, threatens the children with hell. As the politeness movement spread, the condemnation of violence toward living creatures was taken for granted, as it is in Helen Maria Williams's *The Linnet,* one of the happiest poems in this section. Molly, a servant girl who shares her mistress's sensibility, rescues the bird from a cat. With an image that unites the humans with the bird, Molly can feel its heart beating against hers.

Anna Seward's two poems on Colebrooke Dale close this group of poems, and unusually detailed notes are provided to encourage an ecocritical approach. The intensity of her feelings about the effect of the Colebrooke Dale blast furnaces and ironworks on an entire region of England is part protest and part lament. In the earlier poem, the sonnet, the "sulphureous smoke" is a funeral omen. The later poem describes Colebrooke as "violated," and the third quarter of the poem rises to an expansive essay on Britain's commercial and imperial ambitions within her overarching ecological understanding.

Some of the women seem to approach what we know as "deep ecology," as Seward does in what is really a unifying vision of an ecosystem of which she is but a small part. Deep ecology presents the universe as an ecosphere, in which everything is valuable, everything is dependent on other parts of the system, and everything is useful. Nonhuman things are thus valuable in and of themselves, and environmentalism is the realization of a self that harmonizes the individual within the ecosphere, which includes the cosmos. Barbauld's *Caterpillar* hopefully imagines such a thing. In the third letter of Elizabeth Singer Rowe's *Friendship in Death,* the child speaking from Heaven says, " 'Tis unintelligible to me, that Hills and Vallies, Trees and Rivers, the Mines and Caverns under their Feet, any more than the Clouds that fly over their Heads, should be the wealth of reasonable Creatures."[9] This attitude toward the physical universe, that it cannot be possessed, that it is fragile, and that it is also *whole,* an inextricable ecosystem, permeates some poems and anticipates the moving conclusion to Jonathan Bate's *Song of the Earth,* in which he asks readers to remember a photograph of the earth taken from space.[10] A subtle signal of this attitude is whether the speaker or human subject is part of or even encompassed by the scene and landscape in contrast to beholding it, therefore outside of the physical world.[11]

In the poems in this section, women express strong opinions through a variety of tones and technical strategies. They speak variously as observers, as immersed in or inseparable from the scene, and as animals, trees, and other nonhuman things. They focus on process as well as on goal and outcome, on uses as well as on destruction. Above all, their work counters the stereotype that nature poetry was trivial and repetitious.

Notes

1. Robert N. Watson, *Back to Nature: The Green and the Real in the Late Renaissance* (Philadelphia: University of Pennsylvania Press, 2006), 3.

2. Ursula K. Heise, "The Hitchhiker's Guide to Ecocriticism," *PMLA* 121 (2006): 503–16. For a list of ways it has been institutionalized, see *Beyond Nature Writing: Expanding the Boundaries of Ecocriticism,* ed. Karla Armbruster and Kathleen R. Wallace (Charlottesville: University Press of Virginia, 2001), 1.

3. This is an expansion of Cheryll Glotfelty's much-quoted definition in *The Ecocriticism Reader: Landmarks in Literary Ecology,* ed. Glotfelty and Harold Fromm (Athens: University of Georgia Press, 1996), xviii. On challenges to disciplinary boundaries, see George Myerson and Yvonne Rydin, *The Language of Environment: A New Rhetoric* (London: UCL Press, 1996), v. Although *environmental criticism* is a popular term, we are in agreement with John Elder that *ecocriticism* is preferable. Not only does it escape the current American sense of *environmentalism* but it foregrounds dialogues between literature and the sciences of ecology and ecospheres. See John Elder, "The Poetry of Experience," in Armbruster and Wallace, *Beyond Nature Writing,* 313. Ursula Heise sees *ecocriticism* as more inclusive, "a convenient shorthand" for a number of terms, including *literary ecology* and *green cultural studies.* "Hitchhiker's Guide to Ecocriticism," 506.

4. Quoted by Arne Naess from Gen. 1:28 in *Ecology, Community, and Lifestyle,* trans. and ed. David Rothenberg (Cambridge: Cambridge University Press, 1989), 183; on the contradictions in the Bible, see 183–89. For a balanced drawing together of relevant biblical passages, see Steven Bouma-Prediger, "Earthkeeping and the Bible," *Reflections* 94 (2007): 28–32.

5. Description of Nuneham Courtenay as commissioned by the second Earl Harcourt, Mavis Batey. "The High Phase of English Landscape Gardening," in *British and American Gardens in the Eighteenth Century,* ed. Robert P. Maccubbin and Peter Martin (Williamsburg, VA: Colonial Williamsburg Foundation, 1984), 45.

6. Among the many studies are Walter J. Hopple, *The Beautiful, the Sublime, and the Picturesque in Eighteenth-Century British Aesthetic Theory* (Carbondale: Southern Illinois University Press, 1957); Mario Praz, *The Romantic Agony,* trans. Angus Davidson (1979; Oxford: Oxford University Press, 1970); and J. R. Watson, *Picturesque Landscape and Romantic Poetry* (London: Hutchinson, 1970).

7. Frances Brooke, *The History of Emily Montague* (Toronto: McClelland & Stewart, 1995), 33.

8. Heise, "Hitchhiker's Guide to Ecocriticism," 509.

9. Elizabeth Singer Rowe, *Friendship in Death* (London, 1728), 11.

10. Jonathan Bate, *The Song of the Earth* (Cambridge, MA: Harvard University Press, 2000), 282. Our discussion of deep ecology has benefited from Bate's book.

11. See Brigette Weltman-Aron, *On Other Grounds: Landscape Gardening and Nationalism in Eighteenth-Century England and France* (Albany: State University of New York Press, 2001), 109–23.

Upon the Graving of Her Name Upon a Tree in Barnelmes Walks[1]

Katherine Philips

Alas how barbarous are we,
Thus to reward the courteous Tree,
Who its broad shade affording us,
Deserves not to be wounded thus;
See how the Yielding Bark complies
With our ungrateful injuries.
And seeing this, say how much then
Trees are more generous then Men,
Who by a Nobleness so pure
Can first oblige and then endure.   10

(1667)

On a Juniper-Tree, Cut Down to Make Busks

Aphra Behn

Whilst happy I Triumphant stood,
The Pride and Glory of the Wood;
My Aromatick Boughs and Fruit,[2]
Did with all other Trees dispute.
Had right by Nature to excel,
In pleasing both the taste and smell:
But to the touch I must confess,
Bore an Ungrateful Sullenness.
My Wealth, like bashful Virgins, I
Yielded with some Reluctancy;   10
For which my vallue should be more,
Not giving easily my store.

---

1. The gardens of Barn Elms, with their ornamental lake system, were a fashionable place to walk on Rocks Lane in London. Formerly they were part of a manor house and estate.

2. Members of the cypress family, junipers are lovely evergreen shrubs and small trees with needle-sharp leaves. Fragrant, their boughs were used to purify the air. The seed cones have a berrylike structure; these "berries" are usually blue, although they can be orange or dark red, and are used to make gin.

My verdant[3] Branches all the year⎫
Did an Eternal Beauty wear;   ⎬
Did ever young and gay appear. ⎭
Nor needed any tribute pay,
For bounties from the God of Day:
Nor do I hold Supremacy,
(In all the Wood) o'er every Tree.
20   But even those too of my own Race,
That grow not in this happy place.
But that in which I glory most,
And do my self with Reason boast,
Beneath my shade the other day,
Young *Philocles* and *Cloris* lay,
Upon my Root she lean'd her head,   ⎫
And where I grew, he made their Bed ⎬
Whilst I the Canopy more largely spread.⎭
Their trembling Limbs did gently press,
30   The kind supporting yielding Grass:
Ne'er half so blest as now, to bear
A Swain[4] so Young, a Nimph so fair:
My Grateful Shade I kindly lent,
And every aiding Bough I bent.
So low, as sometimes had the blisse,
To rob the Shepherd of a kiss,
Whilst he in Pleasures far above
The Sence of that degree of Love:
Permitted every stealth I made,
40   Unjealous of his Rival Shade.
I saw 'em kindle to desire.
Whilst with soft sighs they blew the fire:
Saw the approaches of their joy,
He growing more fierce, and she less Coy,
Saw how they mingled melting Rays,
Exchanging Love a thousand ways.
Kind was the force on every side,   ⎫
Her new desire she could not hide: ⎬
Nor wou'd the Shepherd be deny'd. ⎭
50   Impatient he waits no consent

3. Rich green.
4. Country man; lover.

But what she gave by Languishment,[5]
The blessed Minute he pursu'd;
While Love and Shame her Soul Subdu'd.
And now transported in his Arms,
Yeilds to the Conqueror all her Charmes,
His panting Breast, to hers now join'd,
They feast on Raptures unconfin'd;
Vast and Luxuriant, such as prove
The Immortality of Love.
For who but a Divinitie,   60
Could mingle Souls to that Degree?
Now like the *Phenix*,[6] both Expire, ⎤
While from the Ashes of their fire,   ⎬
Sprung up a new, and soft desire.   ⎦
Like Charmers,[7] thrice they did invoke,
The God! and thrice new vigor took.
Nor had the Mysterie[8] ended there,
But *Cloris* reassum'd her fear,
And chid the Swain, for having prest,
What she alas cou'd not resist: 70
Whilst he in whom Loves sacred flame,
Before and after was the same,
Fondly implor'd she wou'd forget
A fault, which he wou'd yet repeat.
From Active Joyes with some they hast,
To a Reflexion on the past;
A thousand times my Covert[9] bless,
That did secure their Happiness:
Their Gratitude to every Tree
They pay, but most to happy me;   80
The Shepherdess my Bark carest,
Whilst he my Root, Love's Pillow, kist;
And did with sighs, their Fate deplore,
Since I must shelter them no more;

---

5. One of the flirtatious arts women practiced, a languish was a tender, melting glance.

6. In classical mythology, the phoenix is a bird resembling an eagle but with sumptuous red and gold plumage. Said to live for five or six hundred years in the deserts of Arabia, it makes a nest of spices, sings a beautiful dirge, and burns itself to ashes on a funeral pyre ignited by the sun and fanned by its own wings, only to rise from its ashes with renewed youth to repeat the cycle.

7. Magicians, spell-casters.

8. Rite.

9. Shelter; thick undergrowth serving as a hiding place for game.

And if before my Joyes were such,
In having heard, and seen too much,
My Grief must be as great and high, ⎫
When all abandon'd I shall be,   ⎬
Doom'd to a silent Destinie.   ⎭
90   No more the Charming strife to hear,
The Shepherds Vows, the Virgins fear:
No more a joyful looker on,
Whilst Loves soft Battel's lost and won.
 With grief I bow'd my murmering Head,
And all my Christal Dew I shed.
Which did in *Cloris* Pity move,
(*Cloris* whose Soul is made of Love;)
She cut me down, and did translate,
My being to a happier state.
100   No Martyr for Religion di'd
With half that Unconsidering Pride;
My top was on that Altar laid,
Where Love his softest Offerings paid:
And was as fragrant Incense burn'd,[10]
My body into Busks[11] was turn'd:
Where I still guard the Sacred Store,
And of Loves Temple keep the Door.

(1684)

To [Dr. Walwyn][12]
On his Design of cutting down a Shady Walk[13]
Elizabeth Carter

In plaintive Notes, that tun'd to Woe
 The sadly sighing Breeze,

---

10. Twigs and branches too small for any use were burned on the spot. "Behn's conceit turns this utilitarian bonfire into a sacred ritual celebrating the fulfilment of love," writes Janet Todd. *Works of Aphra Behn,* ed. Todd, 7 vols. (Columbus: Ohio State University Press, 1992–96), 1:387, note to line 105.

 11. Strips of wood sewn into the front of a corset to stiffen it.

 12. Francis Walwyn (b. 1713), received his doctorate of divinity from Oxford University in 1745. Shortly after moving to his position as rector of East Peckham, Kent, he cut down trees to give his fruit trees more sun. He became a prebendary of Canterbury.

 13. This poem was titled *To a Gentleman, On his intending to cut down a Grove, to enlarge his Prospect* when it was first published, in Robert Dodsley's *Collection of Poems in Three Volumes. By Several Hands* (London, 1748), but Dodsley is known to have edited poems he published.

A weeping Hamadryad[14] mourn'd,
   Her Fate-devoted Trees.

Ah! Stop thy sacrilegious Hand,
   Nor violate the Shade,
Where Nature form'd a silent Haunt,
   For Contemplation's Aid.

Canst thou, the Son of Science,[15] train'd
   Where learned *Isis*[16] flows,   10
Forget, that nurs'd in shelt'ring Groves
   The *Grecian* Genius[17] rose.

Beneath the *Plantane's*[18] spreading Branch,
   Immortal *Plato*[19] taught:
And fair *Lyceum*[20] form'd the Depth
   Of *Aristotle's*[21] Thought.

To *Latian*[22] Groves reflect thy View,
   And bless the *Tuscan*[23] Gloom:
Where *Eloquence* deplor'd the Fate
   Of Liberty and *Rome*.   20

Within the *Beechen* Shade retir'd,
   From each inspiring Bough,
The Muses wove unfading Wreaths,
   To circle *Virgil's*[24] Brow.

Reflect, before the fatal Ax
   My threatned Doom has wrought:

14. Tree nymph. A tree nymph's life began and ended with the life of a particular tree.
15. Knowledge.
16. North of and around Oxford the Thames River is called the Isis.
17. Comparisons were often made between the creativity of those living in Grecian liberty and those in Turkish slavery. Greek genius in the arts, government, and architecture was highly respected in Great Britain.
18. Plane tree, a kind of sycamore with thin, pale bark and a distinctive elevated crown.
19. Greek philosopher who wrote the Socratic dialogues, the *Republic*, and other influential works.
20. The school outside Athens where Aristotle taught from 335 to 323 BC.
21. Greek philosopher who wrote the *Poetics*, the *Nicomachean Ethics*, and other dialogues. Among his students was Alexander the Great.
22. Latium or ancient Roman groves; strictly speaking, Latium is a region in central Italy.
23. Tuscany is a region in north-central Italy.
24. Roman poet (70–19 BC) who wrote the *Aeneid*, the *Georgics*, and the *Eclogues*.

Nor sacrifice to sensual Taste,
    The nobler Growth of Thought.

Not all the glowing Fruits, that blush
30   On *India*'s sunny Coast,
Can recompense thee for the Worth
    Of one Idea lost.

My Shade a Produce may supply,
    Unknown to solar Fire:
And what excludes *Apollo*'s Rays,
    Shall harmonize his Lyre.[25]

(c. 1745; 1762)

The Mouse's Petition,[26] Found in the Trap
where he had been confin'd all Night
Anna Laetitia Barbauld

Parcere subjectis, & debellare superbos.[27]
    Virgil

Oh! hear a pensive captive's prayer,
For liberty that sighs;
And never let thine heart be shut
Against the prisoner's cries.

For here forlorn and sad I sit,
Within the wiry grate;
And tremble at th' approaching morn,
Which brings impending fate.

25. A clever play on the myth that Apollo was the god of the sun and of music and poetry.

26. To Doctor Priestley. *Barbauld.* [A later note to the poem by Barbauld explains that the mouse was trapped "for the sake of making experiments with different kinds of air." Joseph Priestley (1733–1804), a distinguished theologian, philosopher, and chemist, discovered oxygen. His experiments with birds, mice, and other small creatures in bell jars were both science and entertainment. *Eds.*]

27. "To spare the humbled, and to tame in war the proud!" *Aeneid* 6:853, translated in *The Poems of Anna Letitia Barbauld,* ed. William McCarthy and Elizabeth Kraft (Athens: University of Georgia Press, 1994), 245.

If e'er thy breast with freedom glow'd,
And spurn'd a tyrant's chain,   10
Let not thy strong oppressive force
A free-born mouse detain.[28]

Oh! do not stain with guiltless blood
Thy hospitable hearth;
Nor triumph that thy wiles betray'd
A prize so little worth.

The scatter'd gleanings of a feast
My scanty meals supply;
But if thine unrelenting heart
That slender boon deny,   20

The chearful light, the vital air,
Are blessings widely given;
Let nature's commoners enjoy
The common gifts of heaven.

The well taught philosophic mind
To all compassion gives;
Casts round the world an equal eye,
And feels for all that lives.

If mind, as ancient sages taught,
A never dying flame,   30
Still shifts thro' matter's varying forms,
In every form the same,

Beware, lest in the worm you crush
A brother's soul you find;
And tremble lest thy luckless hand
Dislodge a kindred mind.

---

28. From the time of the publication of Daniel Defoe's *Free-Born Englishman,* the phrase *free born* had been a unifying phrase for the disparate people who lived in or migrated to Great Britain. William McCarthy and Elizabeth Kraft call it "a cant phrase of popular politics" without identifying the origin. McCarthy and Kraft, *Poems of Anna Letitia Barbauld,* 245. As many ecologists do, Barbauld grants the mouse sibling status.

Or, if this transient gleam of day
Be *all* of life we share,
Let pity plead within thy breast
40   That little *all* to spare.

So may thy hospitable board[29]
With health and peace be crown'd;
And every charm of heartfelt ease
Beneath thy roof be found.

So when unseen destruction lurks,
Which men like mice may share,
May some kind angel clear thy path,
And break the hidden snare.

(1773)

The Caterpillar
Anna Laetitia Barbauld

No, helpless thing, I cannot harm thee now;
Depart in peace, thy little life is safe,
For I have scanned thy form with curious eye,
Noted the silver line that streaks thy back,
The azure and the orange that divide
Thy velvet sides; thee, houseless wanderer,
My garment has enfolded, and my arm
Felt the light pressure of thy hairy feet;
Thou hast curled round my finger; from its tip,
10   Precipitous descent! with stretched out neck,
Bending thy head in airy vacancy,
This way and that, inquiring, thou hast seemed
To ask protection; now, I cannot kill thee.
Yet I have sworn perdition to thy race,
And recent from the slaughter am I come
Of tribes and embryo nations: I have sought
With sharpened eye and persecuting zeal,
Where, folded in their silken webs they lay

---

29. A table set for serving food.

Thriving and happy; swept them from the tree
And crushed whole families beneath my foot;   20
Or, sudden, poured on their devoted heads
The vials of destruction.[30]——This I've done,
Nor felt the touch of pity: but when thou,——
A single wretch, escaped the general doom,
Making me feel and clearly recognise
Thine individual existence, life,
And fellowship of sense with all that breathes,——
Present'st thyself before me, I relent,
And cannot hurt thy weakness.—So the storm
Of horrid war, o'erwhelming cities, fields,   30
And peaceful villages, rolls dreadful on:
The victor shouts triumphant; he enjoys
The roar of cannon and the clang of arms,
And urges, by no soft relentings stopped,
The work of death and carnage. Yet should one,
A single sufferer from the field escaped,
Panting and pale, and bleeding at his feet,
Lift his imploring eyes,——the hero weeps;
He is grown human, and capricious Pity,
Which would not stir for thousands, melts for one   40
With sympathy spontaneous:——'Tis not Virtue,
Yet 'tis the weakness of a virtuous mind.

(c. 1816; 1825)

A Poem for Children
On Cruelty to the Irrational Creation
Jane Cave Winscom

Oh! what a cruel wicked thing,
For me who am a little King,[31]
To give my hapless subjects pain,
And make them groan beneath my reign.

30. Pesticide.

31. See Psalm viii.vi. *Winscom.* [The lines from Psalms 8:6 are "Thou madest him to have dominion over the works of thy hands; / Thou hast put all *things* under his feet." *Eds.*]

Were I a chafer,[32] and could fly,
Ah! should I not with anguish cry,
Should naughty children take a pin,
And run me through to make me spin?

Were I a bird, took from my nest,
Should I not think myself opprest,
If toss'd about in wanton play,
'Till maim'd and faint I die away?

Now, and when I'm a bigger boy,
Let cruelty my heart annoy,
Because it is a dreadful evil,
That only fits me for the Devil.

If I must ought of life deprive,
The quickest way I will contrive,
To stop the tremb'ling victim's breath,
And give it little pain in death.

I'll not torment a dog or cat,
A toad, a viper, or a rat;
They're form'd by an Almighty hand,
And sprung to life at his command.

A bull, a horse, yea every creature,
Of the most mild or savage nature,
Were kindly given for my use,
But never meant for my abuse.

Good men, thy holy word attests,
Are kind and tender to their beasts;
May I be merciful and kind,
That I with thee may mercy find.

(1783)

32. Beetle.

The Linnet[33]

Helen Maria Williams

When fading Autumn's latest hours
Strip the brown wood, and chill the flowers;
When Evening, wintry, short, and pale,
Expires in many an hollow gale;
And only Morn herself looks gay,
When first she throws her quiv'ring ray
Where the light frost congeals the dew,
Flushing the turf with purple hue;
Gay bloom, whose transient glow can shed
A charm like Summer, when 'tis fled!   10
A Linnet, among leafless trees,
Sung, in the pauses of the breeze,
His farewell note, to fancy[34] dear,
That ends the music of the year.
The short'ning day, the sad'ning sky,
With frost and famine low'ring nigh,
The summer's dirge he seemed to sing,
And droop'd his elegiac wing.
Poor bird! he read amiss his fate,
Nor saw the horrors of his state.   20
A prowling cat, with jetty skin,
Dark emblem of the mind within,
Who feels no sympathetic pain,
Who hears, unmov'd, the sweetest strain,
Quite "fit for stratagem and spoil,"[35]
Mischief his pleasure and his toil,
Drew near—and shook the wither'd leaves—
The linnet's flutt'ring bosom heaves—
Alarm'd he hears the rustling sound,

---

33. This poem appears in Williams's *Julia, A Novel; Interspersed with Some Poetical Pieces*, 2 vols. (London, 1790), 1:69–71. Julia has been listening to the linnet when a cat seizes it. Julia cries out, and a servant maid runs and catches the cat "with great intrepidity" and rescues the bird.

34. A creative faculty, usually treated as lighter and more whimsical and playful than imagination or as an assistant to it. Imagination, with the power to transform its material, was considered the higher power.

35. Williams is quoting Lorenzo in William Shakespeare's *Merchant of Venice* 5.1.83–85. "The man that hath no music in himself, / Nor is not moved with concord of sweet sounds, / Is fit for treasons, stratagems, and spoils."

30 He starts—he pauses—looks around—
Too late—more near the savage draws,
And grasps the victim in his jaws.
The linnet's muse,[36] a tim'rous maid,
Saw, and to Molly[37] scream'd for aid;
A tear then fill'd her earnest eye,
Useless as dews on desarts[38] lie:
But Molly's pity fell like showers
That feed the plants and wake the flowers:
Heroic Molly dauntless flew,
40 And, scorning all his claws could do,
Snatch'd from Grimalkin's[39] teeth his prey,
And bore him in her breast away.
His beating heart, and wings, declare
How small his hope of safety there:
Still the dire foe he seem'd to see,
And scarce could fancy he was free.
Awhile he cowr'd on Molly's breast,
Then upward sprang and sought his nest.
 Dear Molly! for thy tender speed,
50 Thy fearless pity's gentle deed,
My purple gown, still bright and clear,
And meant to last another year;
That purple lutestring[40] I decree,
With yellow knots,[41] a gift to thee;
The well-earn'd prize, at Whitsun'-fair,[42]
Shalt thou, lov'd maid, in triumph wear;
And may the graceful dress obtain
The youth thy heart desires to gain.
And thou, sweet bird, whom rapture fills,
60 Who feel'st no sense of future ills;
That sense which human peace destroys,

36. Julia, the heroine of the novel and the "writer" of the poem.
37. A maid-servant. *Williams.*
38. Deserts.
39. The spirit of a witch; according to legend, any witch could assume the body of a cat nine times. Cats who misbehaved were often called Grimalkin. See Mary Robinson's *Mistress Gurton's Cat* (I.H).
40. A glossy silk fabric.
41. Decorative fringes.
42. White Sunday, the seventh Sunday after Easter, celebrates the descent of the Holy Ghost. Another tradition is that it is Wit, or Wisdom, Sunday, the day when the Apostles were filled with wisdom by the Holy Ghost. A few British communities included "trysting fairs" on that day.

And murders all our present joys,
Still sooth with song th' autumnal hours:
And, when the wintry tempest low'rs,
When snow thy shiv'ring plumes shall fill,
And icicles shall load thy bill,
Come fearless to my friendly shed,
This careful hand the crumbs shall spread;
Then peck secure, these watchful eyes
Shall guard my linnet from surprize.   70

(1790)

To a Cricket
Mary Whateley Darwall

Little chirping, cheerful thing,
   Say, for what cause do mortals fear thee?[43]
Canst not thou thy vespers[44] sing,
Blithe as the birds that wake the spring,
   But we suspect misfortune's near thee?

Cricket, raven, bat and owl,
   Idly deem'd of ills foretellers,
Or the dog that haps to howl,[45]
Draw each forehead to a scowl,
   And shake with fear the cottage dwellers.   10

Folly,[46] say, did not the hand
   That form'd us all, form these dread creatures?
Each link in nature's chain[47] was scann'd,

43. The house cricket chirped around ovens and fireplaces. It was a common superstition that the cricket was a sign that someone in the house would die; there is a reference to this superstition in Shakespeare's *Macbeth* 2.2.16. It was also considered bad luck to kill a house cricket.

44. Evening prayers.

45. The superstitious believed that all were omens of evil, tragedy, or bad luck.

46. Foolish one; Darwall is referring to the person who believes the superstitions.

47. The Great Chain of Being theory, accepted by most scientists, philosophers, and other educated people in the eighteenth century, conceived the universe as composed of a continuous chain that linked all natural things, organic and inorganic, in an immense, infinite number of links ranging in hierarchical order up to the Creator.

And universal fitness plann'd
   Throughout creation's countless features.

Sure the voice that nature gave,
   Expresses nature's pure sensation,
Be it shrill, or hoarse and grave
As surges that the sea-beach lave;—[48]
20   Then who shall frown disapprobation?

Little chirping, cheerful thing,
Sing as thou art wont to sing.

(1794)

Sonnet LXIII
To Colebrooke Dale
Anna Seward

Thy GENIUS,[49] Colebrooke,[50] faithless to his charge,
   Amid thy woods and vales, thy rocks and streams,
   Form'd for the Train[51] that haunt poetic dreams,
   Naiads,[52] and Nymphs,[53]—now hears the toiling Barge
And the swart Cyclops[54] ever-clanging forge
   Din in thy dells;[55]—permits the dark-red gleams,
   From umber'd[56] fires on all thy hills, the beams,
   Solar and pure, to shroud with columns large
Of black sulphureous smoke, that spread their veils
10   Like funeral crape[57] upon the sylvan robe[58]

---

48. Bathes, washes.

49. The spirit of a place, here the Severn River.

50. Town in scenic Shropshire near the Severn and Tern rivers. Abraham Darby (1678–1717) built blast furnaces there in the 1710s, and his son, grandson, and partners continued to develop the iron-works in Seward's lifetime. His grandson, Abraham Darby (1750–89), built the first iron bridge, over the Severn River, in 1773.

51. Current, flow of the river.

52. Nymphs of rivers, streams, and lakes.

53. In Greek mythology, an infinite variety of female divinities associated with natural objects.

54. A race of giants with only one eye, placed in the middle of the forehead. They forged iron for Vulcan, the god of fire and metalworking.

55. Small, secluded wooded valleys.

56. Brown-hued.

57. Black band of thin, light cloth worn on the sleeve or hat as a sign of mourning.

58. Forest's flowing garment.

Of thy romantic rocks, pollute thy gales,[59]
And stain thy glassy floods;—while o'er the globe
  To spread thy stores metallic, this rude yell
  Drowns the wild woodland song, and breaks the Poet's spell.

(1799)

Colebrook Dale[60]
Anna Seward

Scene of superfluous grace, and wasted bloom,
O, violated COLEBROOK! in an hour,
  To beauty unpropitious and to song,
  The Genius[61] of thy shades, by Plutus[62] brib'd,
Amid thy grassy lanes, thy woodwild glens,
Thy knolls and bubbling wells, thy rocks, and streams,
Slumbers!—while tribes fuliginous[63] invade
  The soft, romantic, consecrated scenes;
Haunt of the wood-nymph, who with airy step,
In times long vanish'd, through thy pathless groves   10
Rang'd;—while the pearly-wristed Naiads[64] lean'd,
  Braiding their light locks o'er thy crystal flood,
Shadowy and smooth. What, though to vulgar eye
  Invisible, yet oft the lucid gaze
Of the rapt Bard, in every dell and glade
Beheld them wander;—saw, from the clear wave
Emerging, all the watry sisters rise,
  Weaving the aqueous lily, and the flag,
In wreaths fantastic, for the tresses bright
Of amber-hair'd SABRINA.[65]—Now we view   20
Their fresh, their fragrant, and their silent reign

59. Breezes.
60. Town in scenic Shropshire near the Severn and Tern rivers where Colebrook Dale iron-works was established in 1710. The Darbys and their partners continued to develop the ironworks in Seward's lifetime. See nn. 50 and 75 in this section.
61. The spirit or soul of a place.
62. The god of riches. In Greek mythology, he was blinded by Zeus so that his gifts would be distributed randomly rather than only to those who merited them.
63. Sooty.
64. Nymphs of rivers, streams, and lakes.
65. Latin name of the Severn River. According to a British legend, Sabrina was the goddess of the Severn because she jumped into it to avoid a vengeful enemy.

Usurpt by Cyclops;[66]—hear, in mingled tones,
Shout their throng'd barge, their pond'rous engines clang
Through thy coy dales; while red the countless fires,
With umber'd[67] flames, bicker on all thy hills,
Dark'ning the Summer's sun with columns large
Of thick, sulphureous smoke, which spread, like palls,
That screen the dead, upon the sylvan robe[68]
Of thy aspiring rocks; pollute thy gales,
30   And stain thy glassy waters.—See, in troops,
The dusk artificers, with brazen throats,
Swarm on thy cliffs, and clamour in thy glens,
Steepy and wild, ill suited to such guests.

Ah! what avails it to the poet's sense,
That the large stores of thy metallic veins
Gleam over Europe; transatlantic shores
Illumine wide;—are chang'd in either Ind[69]
For all they boast, hot Ceylon's breathing spice;
Peruvian gums; Brazilia's golden ore;
40   And odorous gums, which Persia's white-rob'd seer,
With warbled orisons,[70] on Ganges' brink,
Kindles, when first his MITHRA's[71] living ray
Purples the Orient.—Ah! the traffic rich,
With equal 'vantage, might Britannia send
From regions better suited to such aims,
Than from her Colebrook's muse-devoted vales,
To far resounding BIRMINGHAM,[72] the boast,
The growing LONDON of the MERCIAN realm;[73]

---

66. A race of giants with only one eye, placed in the middle of the foreheads. They forged iron for Vulcan, the god of fire and metalworking.

67. *Umber'd* flames——"Each battle sees the other's *umber'd* face."—SHAKESPEAR. *Seward.* [Spoken by the Chorus, "Fire answers fire, and through their paly flames / Each battle sees the other's umbered face." *The Life of King Henry the Fifth* 4, prologue, lines 8–9. *Umbered* means "brown-hued." *Eds.*]

68. Forest's flowing garment.

69. The East or West Indies.

70. Prayers.

71. The ancient Persians' god of light and ruler of the universe, who cares for humankind in life and after death. The word means "friend."

72. City in the Midlands (central England) equidistant from England's major ports. It led the Industrial Revolution; for example, the steam engine was designed there, and in 1762 a factory to build them opened there. Birmingham was already the second largest city in Great Britain.

73. The Anglo-Saxon kingdom in the Midlands.

Thence to be wafted o'er our subject seas
To every port;—yes, from that town, the mart   50
Of rich inventive Commerce. Science[74] there
Leads her enlighten'd sons, to guide the hand
Of the prompt artist, and with great design
Plan the vast engine, whose extended arms,
Heavy and huge, on the soft-seeming breath
Of the hot steam, rise slowly;—till, by cold
Condens'd, it leaves them soon, with clanging roar,
Down, down, to fall precipitant. Nor yet
Her fam'd Triumvirate,[75] in every land
Known and rever'd, not they the only boast,   60
Of this our second London; the rapt sage,
Who trac'd the viewless Aura's[76] subtle breath
Through all its various powers, there bending feeds
The lamp of Science[77] with the richest oils
Which the arch-chemist, Genius, knows to draw
From Nature's stores, or latent, or reveal'd.

---

74. Knowledge.

75. *Fam'd triumvirate*—Messrs. Bolton, Watt, and Kier. *Seward.* [Seward creates a modern trio with James Watt (1736–1819), James Keir (1735–1820), and Matthew Boulton (1728–1819). Boulton inherited a hardware-manufacturing business from his father; part of the "toy" trade, he specialized in steel products, including buckles. He and Josiah Wedgwood (1730–95) collaborated to make cameo jewelry on steel mounts. Boulton developed Soho Manufactory in order to expand his business exponentially. He added many more steel products, including engine parts. Watt was the inventor of the cost-effective steam engine and, with Samuel Garbett (1717–1803), of Birmingham, the lead-chamber process of sulfuric-acid manufacture. He moved to Birmingham in 1774 and entered into a partnership with Boulton to produce steam engines. Keir settled in Birmingham in 1769. Over the next forty years he opened six distinct businesses, including alkali manufacture, and he developed the first soap factory in the world. Although he refused to invest in the manufacture of steam engines, he effectively became the manager of the Manufactory. Companies in Coalbrooke were important customers for the engines from the beginning, and the Soho Foundry, devoted exclusively to steam engines, opened in 1796 as Boulton, Watt & Co. *Eds.*]

76. *Rapt Sage*—Doctor Priestley, then residing at Birmingham, and the event wholly unforeseen, which drove him thence in the year 1791, with so much loss of property, and induced him to quit his native country. It is to be regretted that he drew upon himself the hatred of the hierarchy, and the fury of the populace, by quitting his philosophic studies for the thorny paths of schismatic controversy, and republican politics. *Seward.* [Joseph Priestley (1733–1804) was the discoverer of oxygen and a distinguished clergyman, philosopher, and chemist. His home in Birmingham was burned by a mob infuriated by his sympathy with the French Revolution; his library and laboratory were destroyed, and he moved to the United States. Seward's reference to "schismatic controversy" alludes to his Arian and Unitarian sentiments, made evident in such publications as *An History of the Corruptions of Christianity* (1782). He angered powerful clergymen, who tried to silence him and preached against him. *Eds.*]

77. Knowledge.

While neighbouring cities waste the fleeting hours,
Careless of art and knowledge, and the smile
Of every Muse, expanding BIRMINGHAM,
70   Illum'd by intellect, as gay in wealth,
Commands her aye-accumulating walls,[78]
From month to month, to climb the adjacent hills;
Creep on the circling plains, now here, now there,
Divergent—change the hedges, thickets, trees,
Upturn'd, disrooted, into mortar'd piles,
The street elongate, and the statelier square.

So, with intent transmutant, Chemists bruise
The shrinking leaves and flowers, whose steams saline,
Congealing swift on the recipient's sides,
80   Shoot into crystals;—and the night-frost thus
Insidious creeping on the watry plain,
Wave after wave incrusts, till liquid change
To solid, and support the volant[79] foot.

Warn'd by the Muse, if Birmingham should draw,
In future years, from more congenial climes
Her massy[80] ore, her labouring sons recall,
And sylvan Colebrook's winding vales restore
To beauty and to song, content to draw
From unpoetic scenes her rattling stores,
90   Massy and dun;[81] if, thence supplied, she fail,
Britain, to glut thy rage commercial, see
Grim WOLVERHAMPTON[82] lights her smouldering fires,
And SHEFFIELD,[83] smoke-involv'd; dim where she stands
Circled by lofty mountains, which condense
Her dark and spiral wreaths to drizzling rains,
Frequent and sullied; as the neighbouring hills

78. Ever-multiplying buildings.
79. Flying; moving quickly and agilely.
80. Massive.
81. Dull brownish gray.
82. Highly industrialized city in the "Black Country" of the West Midlands. The name Black Country comes from the black smoke from the factories that blanket the area. The region was rich in coal, iron, clay, and limestone and was a center for iron, steel, brass, and copper manufacture beginning in the mid-eighteenth century.
83. Heavily industrialized city in northern Yorkshire located at the confluence of several rivers.

Ope their deep veins, and feed her cavern'd flames;
While, to her dusky sister, Ketley[84] yields,
From her long-desolate, and livid breast,
The ponderous metal. No aerial forms   100
On Sheffield's arid moor,[85] or Ketley's heath,
E'er wove the floral crowns, or smiling stretch'd
The shelly scepter;—there no Poet rov'd
To catch bright inspirations. Blush, ah, blush,
Thou venal[86] Genius of these outraged groves,
And thy apostate head with thy soil'd wings
Veil!—who hast thus thy beauteous charge resign'd
To habitants ill-suited; hast allow'd
Their rattling forges, and their hammer's din,
And hoarse, rude throats, to fright the gentle train,   110
Dryads,[87] and fair hair'd Naiades;[88]—the song,
Once loud as sweet, of the wild woodland choir
To silence;—disenchant the poet's spell,
And to a gloomy Erebus[89] transform
The destined rival of Tempean vales.[90]

(1810)

84. *Dusky sister*—Wolverhampton has the greatest part of her iron from Ketley, a dreary and barren wold [hilly area] in her vicinity. *Seward.* [In the late eighteenth century, the township of Ketley,
in Shropshire, began to attract settlements of colliers. The area was rich in coal. In 1788 the Ketley
Canal had been completed, and coal and ironstone were brought to expanding and new ironworks in
Ketley, Horsehay, and Coalbrookdale. *Eds.*]

85. *Arid moor*—The East-moor, near Sheffield, which is dreary, though the rest of the country surrounding that town, is very fine. *Seward.*

86. Corrupt, subject to bribery.

87. Tree nymphs.

88. *Fair-hair'd Naiades*—In Milton's Comus we find the plural of Naiad made three syllables, thus
"Amid the flowery kirtled Naiades." And the old pastoral poet, [William] Browne [1591–c. 1643] so
pluralizes the word Nereid, thus, "Call to a dance the fair Nereides." *Seward.* [Nymphs of rivers,
streams, and lakes. *Eds.*]

89. In classical mythology, the gloomy cavern through which the Shades, or the disembodied spirits of the dead, pass on their way to Hades, or the underworld; named after Erebus, son of Chaos
and the brother of Night.

90. Tempe is a valley in Greece; its name is used by poets for any beautiful valley filled with singing birds, pleasant shade, and romantic scenery.

Sources

Philips: *Poems by the Most Deservedly Admired Mrs. Katherine Philips, the Matchless Orinda* (London, 1667), 137. Behn: *Poems upon Several Occasions* (London, 1684), 19–24. Carter: *Poems on Several Occasions* (London, 1762), 39–41. Barbauld: *Poems* (London, 1773), 37–40; *The Poems of Anna Letitia Barbauld,* ed. William McCarthy and Elizabeth Kraft (Athens: University of Georgia Press, 1994), 172–73. Winscom: *Poems on Various Subjects, Entertaining, Elegiac, and Religious* (Winchester, 1783), 47–49. Williams: *Julia, A Novel,* 2 vols. (London, 1790), 2: 69–71. Darwall: *Poems on Several Occasions. By Mrs. Darwall (Formerly Miss Whateley),* 2 vols. (Walsall, 1794), 2:59–60. Seward: *Original Sonnets on Various Subjects,* 2nd ed. (London, 1799), 65; *The Poetical Works of Anna Seward,* ed. Walter Scott, 3 vols. (Edinburgh, 1810), 2:314–19.

⊁J⊁

Poems on Seeking
Personal Happiness

The poems in this section are some of the most revealing in this anthology. Women's hopes and fantasies, their fears and satisfactions, are laid open before us. The advice they are given and the pressures society puts on them are baldly stated. "Custom" is the monster stalking and imprisoning them. Happy, defiant, contented, frustrated, courageous, resigned, and fearful—the many moods of these poems shift like patterns of clouds and sun on a summer day. The situations and experiences of the women are diverse, and in some cases the challenges they faced in their pursuit of happiness or at least contentment are stark. Jane Barker was a royalist exile in France; Anna Williams was blind at age forty; Frances Greville suffered ill health and had to move from friend to friend in Ireland during the time when her husband was attempting to take her fortune. At least three of the women, Sarah Fyge Egerton, Mary Alcock, and Greville, were unhappily married, and Laetitia Pilkington was divorced, a rarity and a disgrace in the century. (Although we can surmise that Mary Savage was married, almost nothing is known of her life.) Elizabeth Singer Rowe was widowed after a short, satisfying marriage. Three of the poets, Barker, Williams, and Eliza Tuite, were lifelong singlewomen.[1]

These poems and others in the anthology show the tensions inherent in women's positions, regardless of what those were. Egerton gives a shocking list of women's relationships to men: nurse to a parent, mistress to a "swain," wife to a person with tyrannical power. Marital status dramatically influenced women's lives, and as Judith Bennett and Amy Froide note, "wives, widows, and singlewomen generally faced quite different opportunities and limitations."[2] For much of history, and certainly in the long eighteenth century, singleness was "an identity issue," "a negative—something missing, incomplete, or damaged, something without, even something pitied."[3] Neither Rowe nor Pilkington remarried, and at moments in their poetry we can discern all five poets cognitively and emotionally feeling through the meaning of their status. Single and widowed women had more freedom of choice, but they also reveal anxieties tied to stereotypes. "Ungoverned" by men, with the implication that they needed restraint and "coverture," they sometimes emphasize their moral principles and lifestyles and even argue their social usefulness.[4]

That the poets represented in this section were either financially comfortable or in secure living situations cannot be overlooked. To have time to write poems and to be able to imagine securing a satisfying life were not options for the majority of women, including some represented in sections 1.c, "Poems of Common Life," and 2.E, "The Poetry of War." It is also telling that the happiest poem in this section may be the most fanciful, Rowe's *To Chloe. An Epistle.* Felicity Nussbaum explains that "women's self-writing in eighteenth-century England ventriloquates [*sic*] male ideologies of gender while it allows alternative discourses of 'experience' to erupt at the margins of meanings. [It] is one location of these contradictions that both produce and reflect historicized concepts of self and gender while sometimes threatening to disrupt or transform them."[5] The poems in this section are proof of her insight.

We begin with Barker's *A Virgin Life,* in which she declares that she has no fear of being called an old maid and would make as "good a Subject as the stoutest Man." Next is the poem that may have introduced the equation of wife and slave, Egerton's *The Emulation,* which begins, "Say Tyrant Custom." Poems by Savage, Tuite, and Alcock take up this theme. Savage modernizes it in *On the Tyranny of Custom,* and Alcock revises the name of the tyrant in the language of the end-of-the-century newspaper-gossip mode: *On What the World Will Say.*

The styles the women chose varied as much as the moods. Appropriate to poems about the happy life, several invoke the *beatus ille* tradition. They title the poems *On Happiness* and reexamine each of the conventional delusionary sources of happiness. Janet Little, for instance, includes revelry, riches, martial success, fame, and love in her poem with that title (not included). Often beginning, "Ah! happy the man . . . ," the poems followed Virgil's *Georgics,* Book 2, and Horace's Ode 29, Book 3. Anna Williams's *The Happy Life* and Tuite's *On Being Teazed to Go More into Company* deliberately adapt the Horatian and Virgilian ideas. Williams uses what had become the most popular metrics for Horatian poems, heroic couplets, and Tuite chooses lighter tetrameter quatrains. Rowe's poem is a creative variant of the many poems comparing the pleasures of the city with those of the country. Her smooth pastoral epistle draws her friend into a beautiful, idyllic scene where they can live the life of dryads, or tree nymphs. This poem contrasts markedly with Savage's pungent yet comic hexameters.[6] "Serene and free"—the phrase appears over and over in women's wishes for themselves. Sometimes they imagine themselves alone, and sometimes with a friend or lover, as Rowe does in *To Chloe* when she writes, "Serene and free, we spend the lightsome hours." In these poems and others scattered throughout this anthology, women wish for time to enjoy their books and friends, as Barker does in *A Virgin Life.* Pilkington celebrates her free time in *Verses wrote in a Library,* and, in *Epistle, from Fern-Hill* (1.c), Mary Jones creates a homey scene in which her friend Charlotte plays with a cat while she reads, sloshily spilling her tea now and then. Her self-deprecating humor insists that it is a dull evening scene, but their contentment is clear.

Because of its remarkable reception, Frances Greville's *Ode to Indifference* and two responses to it close this section. In eighteenth-century biographical dictionaries, Greville was described, as one put it, as "a lady of fashion, and author of an Ode of Indifference, together with some other fugitive poetical pieces."[7] Greville's ode, probably first published in the *Edinburgh Chronicle* on 19 April 1759, had circulated widely in manuscript earlier. It focused on an important contemporary debate about happiness and states of mind (sensibility vs. indifference) and was reprinted almost as often as Thomas Gray's *Elegy in a Country Church Yard.* Roger Lonsdale identifies it as "the most celebrated poem by a woman in the period,"[8] and it was cited and quoted countless times. Many women poets took up the debate. Hannah Cowley, under the pseudonym Anna Matilda, published a poem in the *World* that compared the nymph Indifference to deceptive Sensibility (16 January 1788); Ann Yearsley wrote *Addressed to Sensibility* and *To Indifference* (both 1787); and in *Sensibility: A Poem* (1782) Hannah More wrote, "No, Greville, no!"[9] Entire verses are in poems such as Eliza Day's *To Leander* (1796), and other poems refer to the sentiments in the poem or to "tuneful" or "elegant" Greville. Mary Scott writes in her important work *The Female Advocate: A Poem* (1774):

> But hark! what softly-plaintive strains I hear!
> How sweet they vibrate on my list'ning ear!
> Sure *Greville*'s Muse must ev'ry bosom please
> That finds a Charm in elegance or ease:
> Hers were those nice sensations of the heart,
> Whose magic pow'r can pain to joy impart;
> A feeling "heart, that like the needle true,
> Turn'd at each touch, and turning trembled too!"[10]

This exquisite image of the feeling yet discerning heart and the verse in which it appeared was quoted innumerable times. For a surprisingly long time it was recommended in a variety of moral works, both serious and popular, such as *Divine Revelation Impartial and Universal; or, An humble Attempt to defend Christianity,* by John Bennett and John Courtenay (1783), and *Select Essays, from the Batchelor,* by Robert Jephson (1772).

As the answers to the poem suggest, the ode was read variously—as a repudiation of romantic love, as a critique of sensibility, and as a fine representation of sensibility itself.[11] Isobel Grundy expresses our intrigued fascination: "Something about it, either its pessimism, or its silence about the standard consolations of Christianity or of sensibility, or its hint of unfeminine hard-heartedness, was immensely provocative."[12] The two answering poems in this section take two different approaches. Savage considers what happens to a feeling heart over a lifetime and concludes with her idea of happiness, while Tuite's poem is a more direct answer and the more common response, a defense of sensibility. The popularity of *Ode to Indifference* has intrigued modern critics, and it deserves to be read as an acute expression of the sources of unhappiness in women's lives and a nuanced exploration of the limits of human response to them. The early poems in this section depict various ways of living life—single, solitary or seeking company, reading—and the later poems turn to the ways women can exert their minds to create the life they want to lead.

Notes

1. Judith Bennett and Amy Froide discuss the use of *singlewoman* in British legal and social history in "A Singular Past," in *Singlewomen in the European Past, 1250–1800,* ed. Bennett and Froide (Philadelphia: University of Pennsylvania Press, 1999), 2–3.

2. Bennett and Froide, "Singular Past," 13. In a sample of one hundred urban and rural communities, Froide found that widows made up approximately 14.9% of the population, and single women 30.2%. Only 1.1% of heads of household were never-married women, while 12.9% of households were headed by widows. Amy Froide, "Marital Status as a Category of Difference," in Bennett and Froide, *Singlewomen,* 237, 239; see also the statistics in tables on 278–79.

3. Rudolph M. Bell and Virginia Yans, introduction to *Women on Their Own: Interdisciplinary Perspectives on Being Single,* ed. Bell and Yans (New Brunswick: Rutgers University Press, 2008), 5, 1.

4. Susan Lanser demonstrates that "old maids" came to be seen as a "national detriment" because they were portrayed as refusing to "propagate the Species of Mankind," a duty "to God and Country." She ties this stigmatizing to the national desire to increase the British population. "Singular Politics: The Rise of the British Nation and the Production of the Old Maid," in Bennett and Froide, *Singlewomen,* 308–9.

5. Felicity Nussbaum, "Eighteenth-Century Women's Autobiographical Commonplaces," in *The Private Self,* ed. Shari Benstock (Chapel Hill: University of North Carolina Press, 1988), 149.

6. Margaret Doody describes the meter's usefulness to women and compares it to iambic pentameter in "Women Poets of the Eighteenth Century," in *Women and Literature in Britain, 1700–1800,* ed. Vivien Jones (Cambridge: Cambridge University Press, 2000), 222–23.

7. The quotation is from *A Catalogue of Five Hundred Celebrated Authors of Great Britain, Now Living* (London, 1788), s.v. "Greville."

8. Roger Lonsdale, ed., *Eighteenth-Century Women Poets: An Oxford Anthology* (Oxford: Oxford University Press, 1990), 190.

9. For these examples we are indebted to the late Betty Rizzo, who compiled a list of poetic responses to the poem.

10. Mary Scott, *The Female Advocate. A Poem* (London, 1774), 26. None of the poems mentioned in this paragraph is included in this anthology.

11. Betty Rizzo cites some of the most in-depth responses to the poem in *Companions without Vows: Relationships among Eighteenth-Century British Women* (Athens: University of Georgia Press, 1994), 371n. 9; for her discussion of the poem, see 244–49.

12. Isobel Grundy, "Indifference and Attachment: An Eighteenth-Century Poetic Debate," *Factotum* 26 (1988): 15.

A Virgin Life
Jane Barker

Since, O ye Pow'rs, ye have bestow'd on me
So great a kindness[1] for Virginity,
Suffer me not to fall into the Pow'rs
Of Mens almost Omnipotent Amours;
But in this happy Life let me remain,
Fearless of Twenty five and all its train,
Of slights and scorns, or being call'd Old Maid,
Those Goblings which so many have betray'd:
Like harmless Kids, that are pursu'd by Men,
10   For safety run into a Lyon's Den.
Ah lovely State how strange it is to see,
What mad conceptions some have made of thee,
As though thy Being was all wretchedness,
Or foul deformity i'th' ugliest dress;
Whereas thy Beauty's pure, Celestial,
Thy thoughts Divine, thy words Angelical:
And such ought all thy Votaries[2] to be,
Or else they're so, but for necessity.
A Virgin bears the impress[3] of all good,
20   In that dread Name all Vertue's understood:
So equal all her looks, her mien, her dress,
That nought but modesty seems in excess.
And when she any treats or visits make,
'Tis not for tattle, but for Friendship's sake;
Her Neighb'ring Poor she do's adopt her Heirs,
And less she cares for her own good than theirs;
And by Obedience testifies she can
Be's good a Subject as the stoutest Man.
She to her Church such filial duty pays,
30   That one would think she'd liv'd i'th pristine days.
Her Closet,[4] where she do's much time bestow,
Is both her Library and Chappel too,

---

1. Kinship, natural affection.
2. Those bound by a special vow; devoted or zealous believers.
3. Stamp, seal.
4. Private room for retirement. Many held a small library and writing materials.

Where she enjoys society alone,
I'th' Great Three-One——⁵
She drives her whole Lives business to these Ends,
To serve her God, enjoy her Books and Friends.

(1688)

The Emulation⁶

Sarah Fyge Egerton

Say Tyrant Custom, why must we obey,
The impositions of thy haughty Sway;
From the first dawn of Life, unto the Grave,
Poor Womankind's in every State, a Slave.
The Nurse, the Mistress, Parent and the Swain,⁷
For Love she must, there's none escape that Pain;
Then comes the last, the fatal Slavery,
The Husband with insulting Tyranny
Can have ill Manners justify'd by Law;
For Men all join to keep the Wife in awe.   10
Moses who first our Freedom did rebuke,
Was Marry'd when he writ the Pentateuch;⁸
They're Wise to keep us Slaves, for well they know,
If we were loose, we soon should make them, so.
We yeild like vanquish'd Kings whom Fetters bind,
When chance of War is to Usurpers kind;
Submit in Form; but they'd our Thoughts controul,
And lay restraints on the impassive Soul:
They fear we should excel their sluggish Parts,
Should we attempt the Sciences and Arts.   20
Pretend they were design'd for them alone,
So keep us Fools to raise their own Renown;
Thus Priests of old their Grandeur to maintain,
Cry'd vulgar Eyes would sacred Laws Prophane.

5. In the Christian religion, the Trinity: Father, Son, and Holy Ghost.
6. Desire to imitate, rival, or surpass others.
7. Country man; lover.
8. Moses was married to Zipporah, and the Pentateuch, the first five books of the Old Testament, contains many references to women being subject to their husbands.

So kept the Mysteries[9] behind a Screen,
There Homage and the Name were lost had they been seen:
But in this blessed Age, such Freedom's given,
That every Man explains the Will of Heaven;
And shall we Women now sit tamely by, ⎫
30   Make no excursions in Philosophy,   ⎬
Or grace our Thoughts in tuneful Poetry? ⎭
We will our Rights in Learning's World maintain,
Wits Empire, now, shall know a Female Reign;
Come all ye Fair, the great Attempt improve,
Divinely imitate the Realms above:
There's ten celestial Females govern Wit,[10]
And but two Gods[11] that dare pretend to it;
And shall these finite Males reverse their Rules,
No, we'll be Wits, and then Men must be Fools.

(1703)

To Chloe. An Epistle.

Elizabeth Singer Rowe

FAIR *Chloe*, leave the noisy town, and try
What artless sweets the country scenes supply:
While the young year in all its pride invites,
And promises a thousand gay delights;
While the glad sun his fairest light displays,
And op'ning blossoms court his chearful rays.
The nymphs[12] for thee shall deck some rural bow'r
With ev'ry verdant branch and painted flow'r;
To thee the swains[13] full canisters shall bring,
10   Of all the fragrant treasures of the spring:
While some young shepherd in the sounding grove

9. The mystic rites, open only to a special group, included initiation and purification rites, viewing sacred objects, and acting out sacred dramas.

10. Mnemosyne and her nine daughters, the Muses.

11. Apollo, god of poetry and music, and Mercury, god of science and commerce.

12. In Greek mythology, an infinite variety of female divinities associated with natural objects. Nymphs were represented as young, beautiful, graceful, musical, amorous, and gentle. Some nymphs were also mischievous. In pastoral poetry, women called nymphs had these characteristics.

13. Country men; lovers.

Shall tune his reed for thee to strains of love.
Nor from the soft, enchanting accents run,
For who the pleasing charms of love would shun?
Such love as in these guiltless seats is known,
Such as a state of innocence might own.
No frauds, no treach'rous arts are practis'd here,
No perjur'd vows deluded virgins fear.
The gentle god with mild indulgence sways,
And ev'ry willing heart his laws obeys.   20

    ALL hail, ye fields and ev'ry happy grove!
How your soft scenes the tender flame improve, ⎫
And melt the thoughts, and turn the soul to love! ⎬
'Twas here *Mirtillo's*[14] charms my bosom fir'd,
While all the gods th' am'rous youth inspir'd;
Divine his art, prevailing was his tongue,
While in the shades the skilful shepherd sung:
On downy wings young *Zephyrs*[15] took the sound,
And chear'd the plains, and all the valleys round.
The list'ning streams were conscious of his flame,   30
And ev'ry grove acquainted with my name.
No nymph but envy'd me *Mirtillo's* praise,
For I had all his vows and tender lays.[16]
Nor could such truth and merit plead in vain,
I heard his sighs, and pity'd all his pain;
While *Venus* smil'd propitious from above,
And crown'd our vows, and blest our mutual love.
May prosp'rous fates attend the happy day,
And circling joys for ever make it gay!
From thence we date our bliss, and still improve   40
Our soft delights, as thro' the woods we rove:
In flow'ry meadows, groves, and fragrant bow'rs,
Serene and free, we spend the lightsome hours.

14. A character in George Frideric Handel's opera *Il Pastor Fido* (*The Faithful Shepherd*, 1712), which was very popular in 1734. The opera is set in Arcadia, where the Arcadians are oppressed by the goddess Diana, who can only be appeased by the marriage of "two of a heavenly race." The Arcadians believe the shepherdess Amarilli and the huntsman Silvio are the two who can appease Diana. Amarilli, however, declares her love for Mirtillo and is condemned to death for breaking her vow to Silvio. Mirtillo demands to die in Amarilli's place, the two lovers are pardoned and allowed to marry, and peace is restored to Arcadia.

15. The west wind, lover of Flora, goddess of flowers; any soft, warm wind.

16. Short lyric or narrative poems intended to be sung.

THUS live the *Dryads*,[17] thus the sacred race
That haunt the valleys, and the fountains grace;
The rural scenes indulge their warm desires,
Heighten their joys, and feed immortal fires.
Diana, who in heav'n could guard her breast,
In *Latmos'* flow'ry fields the god confest.[18]

50 No name but his among the swains is known,
Superior love is all the pow'r they own;
Their willing tribute to his shrine they bring,
Turtles, and lambs, and all the blooming spring,
While to their tuneful harps his praise they sing.
Young *Zephyrs* bear the charming accents round,
And rocks and mossy caves retain the sound;
Tigers and wolves grow wild, the tim'rous fawns,
Undaunted, skip along the open lawns;
Roses and myrtles bloom, the am'rous doves,

60 And all the warbling chorus own their loves;
The nodding groves, and falling floods reply,
And all confess the pow'rful deity.

(1739)

Verses wrote in a Library
Laetitia Pilkington

Seat for Contemplation fit,
Sacred Nursery of Wit!
Let me here enwrap'd in Pleasure,
Taste the Sweets of learned Leisure:
Vain, deceitful World, adieu;
I more solid Bliss pursue.

Faithful Friends, surround me here,
Wise, delightful, and sincere;
Friends, who never yet betray'd
10 Those who trusted in their Aid;
Friends, who ne'er were known to shun
Those by adverse Fate undone.

17. Tree nymphs.
18. Diana, goddess of the moon, loved Endymion, the shepherd boy of Mount Latmos.

Calm Philosophy and Truth
Crown'd with undecaying Youth,
Glowing with celestial Charms,
Fondly woo me to their Arms.
Here immortal Bards dispense
Polish'd Numbers,[19] nervous Sense;[20]
While the just Historian's Page
Back recals the distant Age;   20
In whose Paintings we behold
All the wond'rous Men of old;
Heroes fill each finish'd Piece,
Once the Pride of *Rome* and *Greece.*

Nor shall *Greece* and *Rome* alone,
Boast the Virtues all their own;
Thou, *Ierne,*[21] too shalt claim
Sons amongst the Heirs of Fame;
Patriots who undaunted stood,
To defend the public good;   30
Foremost in the sacred Line,
Ever shall the D R A P E R[22] shine:
Next be virtuous S T A N N A R D[23] plac'd,
With unfading Honours grac'd;
Godlike Men! accept my Praise,
Guard, and elevate, my Lays.[24]

Learning can the Soul refine,
Raise from human to divine.
Come then, all ye sacred Dead,
Who for Virtue wrote or bled;   40
On my Mind intensely beam,
Touch it with your hallow'd Flame.
And thou chaste and lovely Muse,

19. Polished, masterful metrics, rhythmical lines and verses.

20. Strong, direct meaning. "Nervous" describes the way emotions traveled and caused actions.

21. Ancient name for Ireland, Pilkington's native country.

22. Jonathan Swift (1667–1745), whose *Drapier's Letters* (1724) made him a national hero.

23. Eaton Stannard, recorder of Dublin, was very popular, perhaps because he opposed a bill to prevent smuggling. He became a member of Jonathan Swift's Lunacy Commission and was in the circle that included Barber. He also became a member of the House of Commons and represented a borough in Cork. In the year Pilkington's *Memoirs* appeared, he published *The Honest Man's Speech* (1749).

24. Short lyric or narrative poems intended to be sung.

Who didst once thy Dwelling chuse
In *Orinda*'s[25] spotless Breast,
Condescend to be my Guest;
Bring with thee the bloomy Pair,
Young-ey'd Health, and Virtue fair;
Here your purest Rays impart,
50   So direct and guard my Heart,
That it may a Temple be
Worthy Heav'n, and worthy thee.

(1748)

The Happy Life[26]
Anna Williams

Las d' esperer, et de me plaindre
De l' amour des Grands et de sort,
C'est ici que j' attends la mort,
Sans la desirer ou la craindre.   St. Amand[27]

Thrice happy they, who in an humble state
Contented live, and aim not to be great;
Whose life not sunk in sloth is free from care,
Nor tost by change, nor stagnant in despair;
Who chearfully receive each mercy given,
And bless the lib'ral hand of bounteous Heaven;
Who with wise authors pass the instructive day,
And wonder how the moments stole away;
Who gently taught by calm experience find

25. Katherine Philips, known as "the Matchless Orinda."

26. Following Virgil's *Georgics,* Book 2, and Horace's Epode 2d and Ode 29, Book 3, poets used the conventional line, "Happy the man . . . ," and this poem's title and opening lines clearly invoke the poetic kind. Especially popular were echoes of Dryden's translation of Horace's Ode 29, Book 3: "Happy the Man, and happy he alone, / He, who can call to day his own" (lines 65–66). See also section 2.B, in which the image is also frequently invoked.

27. "Weary from hoping, and from complaining / Of the love of the powerful and of Fate, / It is here that I await death, / Without desiring it or fearing it." The lines are by Marc-Antoine de Gérard, Sieur de Saint-Amant (1594–1661), a French poet who made his fame reading in Parisian cabarets. He performed in courts and other venues in Warsaw, Rome, and London. In fact, the lines are an adaptation of an inscription that Francis Maynard (1582–1646), one of the forty members of the French Academy, put above the door to his closet, or private room: "Las d' esperer, et de me plaindre / Des Muses, des Grands, et du Sort; / C'est ici que j'attends la mort, / Sans la desirer, ni la craindre."

No riches equal to a well form'd mind;   10
Who not retir'd beyond the sight of life,
Behold its weary cares, its noisy strife;
And safe in virtue's philosophick cell,
Content with thinking right, and acting well,
Mark rashness sporting on perdition's brink,
And see the turrets of ambition sink;
Of life without a pang dissolve the tie,
In peace decay, with resignation die.
Breathe out the vital flame in humble trust,
And mingle blameless with their native dust.   20

(1766)

On the Tyranny of Custom
Mary Savage

Of tyrants I've read, who have made Nations mourn,
And of husbands and wives, being tyrants in turn;
That Love is a tyrant, is oftentimes said,
Sometimes to the lover, sometimes to the maid;
That Anger's a tyrant we cannot dispute,
From his pow'r of changing the man to a brute;
Of tyrants like these, each would shake off the chain,
And tho' forc'd to submit, that submission is pain;
But a tyrant there is, more pow'rful than these,
Who instead of opposing, we all strive to please.   10
His name to your mind, sure I need not recall;
Is not Custom, the tyrant, who governs them all?
'Tis he makes the man with six hundred a year,
Like him with six thousand attempt to appear;
He fills the assembly,[28] the ball, and the play,
With those, who attending their business should stay;
He teaches to wed—for the sake of an heir,
While love is bestow'd on some favourite fair;
He employs ev'ry female, who would be polite,
In diversions all day, and in cards all the night;   20

---

28. Social gathering of both sexes for conversation, flirtation, news, and cards.

He commands debts of honor both sexes should pay,
But judges it proper that tradesmen should stay;
He dictates our words, on our books he attends,
And scarcely allows us, the choice of our friends.

   But in vain the attempt, half his powers to name,
And still harder the task, to throw off his chain;
For judgment, and reason, must learn to obey,
Whilst CUSTOM's the tyrant, who governs the day.

(1777)

On Being Teazed to Go More into Company
Eliza Tuite

Let others follow Fame and Wealth,
   Their choice I'll ne'er upbraid;
Give me but Competence[29] and Health,
   And Freedom in the shade!

Let those who sigh for plays or balls,
   Those pleasures still pursue;
While I awake to Friendship's calls,
   But seek to please a *few.*

Those *few,* from prejudices free,
10   Who outward forms despise,
Who for myself, will value *me,*
   Nor like me in disguise.

'Tis such alone that I revere,
   Who (scorning ev'ry art)
Can justly prize regard sincere,
   They'll find it in my heart.

For *them* still may I string the lyre,
   For *them* my song renew,

---

29. Adequate money.

With them from busy crouds retire,
   Content to please a few.   20

(1796)

On What the World Will Say
Mary Alcock

Of all the foolish vain pretences,
That mortals use to cheat their senses,
   This has the greatest sway—
Not that, which conscience dictates right,
Tho' clearly mark'd as day from night,
   But what the World will say.

To this, as to some idol god,
Who rules us with an iron rod,
   We sacrifice each day;
Our time, our judgment, and our ease   10
Alike bow down this shrine to please
   Thro' fear what it might say.

Thus subject to it's base control,
We check each motion of the soul,
   Which points to Reason's way,
Lest, varying from the giddy throng,
We rudely shew them they are wrong,
   What would they then not say?

While motives weak as these prevail,
We turn with every shifting sail   20
   Of Fashion's pow'rful sway,
Down her impetuous tide we're hurl'd,
Lost to each comfort in the world,
   Thro' fear what it might say.

Thus like some heedless bark[30] we're tost,
Till foundering on that very coast

30. Small boat.

Where all our treasure lay,
Deserted and forlorn we lie,
Unpitied by each stander-by,
 Nor cheer'd by what they say.

30

Oh could the World that peace bestow,
Which, courting it, we all forego,
 Our toils it well would pay;
But since the sad reverse we find,
'Tis nought but madness e'er to mind
 What such a World can say.

(1799)

Ode to Indifference[31]

Frances Greville

Oft I've implor'd the Gods in vain,
 And pray'd till I've been weary.
For once I'll seek my suit to gain
 Of Oberon the Fairy.[32]

Sweet airy being Wanton Sprite
 Who liv'st in woods unseen
And oft by Cynthia's[33] silver light
 Trip'st gaily o'er the Green

If e'er thy pitying Heart was mov'd
 As Ancient Stories tell
And for th'Athenian maid who lov'd
 Thou sought'st a Wondrous Spell

10

31. This ode has a complex publication history and was reprinted about as often as Thomas Gray's *Elegy Written in a Country Church Yard*. This version is from Greville's own notebook of poems. We thank Betty Rizzo for providing it: "The Frances Greville Letters," *Eighteenth-Century Women* 4 (2006): 316–17.

32. King of the Fairies from the medieval French romance *Huon de Bordeaux* and an important character in William Shakespeare's *Midsummer Night's Dream*. He has the gift of insight into others' thoughts and the power to transport himself anywhere instantly.

33. The moon's.

Oh Deign once more t'exert thy pow'r
    Haply some Herb or Tree
Sov'reign as Juice from Western Flow'r
    Conceals a Balm for me.

I ask no kind return in Love,
    No tempting Charm to please
Far from the Heart such gifts remove
    That sighs for Peace and Ease.   20

Nor ease nor peace that Heart can know,
    Which like the Needle true,[34]
Turns at the touch of Joy or Woe,
    But turning trembles too.

Far as distress the Soul can wound
    'Tis pain in each degree.
'Tis Bliss but to a certain bound;
    Beyond is Agony.

Then take this treach'rous sense of mine
    Which dooms me still to Smart   30
Which pleasure can to pain refine
    To pain new pangs impart.

Oh haste to shed the Sov'reign Balm
    My shatter'd nerves new string
And for my Guest serenely calm,
    The nymph Indifference bring.[35]

At her approach see Hope see Fear,
    See Expectation Fly.
With disappointment in the rear,
    That blasts the promis'd Joy.   40

The tears which pity taught to flow,
    My Eyes shall then disown.

34. A compass needle. This is the best-known image in the poem.

35. She asks for a nymph who will give her Indifference and guard it rather than for one of the nymphs of rivers, forests, etc.

The Heart that throb'd at others woe
    Shall then scarce feel its own.

The Wounds that now each moment bleed
    For ever then shall close
And tranquil days shall still succeed
    To nights of sweet repose.

O Fairy Elf but grant me this,
    This one kind Comfort lend
50 And so may never fading Bliss
    Thy Flow'ry paths attend.

So may the Glow worms glim'ring light
    Thy tiny footsteps lead
To some new Region of Delight,
    Unknown to Mortal tread.

And be thy Acorn Goblet fill'd
    With Heavn's ambrosial dew
From sweetest freshest Flowers distill'd
60   That shed fresh sweets for you.

And what of life remains for me,
    I'll pass in sober ease,
Half pleas'd Contented will I be,
    Content but half to please.

(c. 1757; 2006)

A Transient Thought
Mary Savage

I.
    I aim not to decide the case,
What most declare, full sure I know:
"The feeling heart must bear distress;
And ease must from indifference flow."

II.

   Tell me then, ye minds serene,
Whose ease doth from indifference flow,
When first began the happy scene,
And how ye conquer'd every woe.

III.

   For never yet, from nature's hand,
Was destin'd thro' the world to go,   10
A heart, with feelings at command,
To take its choice, of joy, or woe.

IV.

   Witness the infant's poignant grief,
When from its eye the nurse is hid,
With scorn, it slights your fond relief,
And sobbing hangs its drooping head.

V.

   Or if perchance, with wiley art,
She but affects some sad distress,
Quick throbbings move its little heart,
And vain attempts, speak wish'd redress.   20

VI.

   Emotions kind, design'd thro' life,
To constitute the faithful friend,
To form the father, husband, wife,
And make each joy, on all depend.

VII.

   Unless repeated ills intrude,
To check kind nature's first intent,
And wearied by ingratitude,
The heart grows steel'd to each event.

VIII.

   Then haughty pride in man presides,
To brave the ills he cannot cure;   30
And art, the tear of pity hides,
When others feel what we endure.

IX.

External mirth employs each hour,
With false pretence the world to please,
While habit; (borrowing nature's pow'r,)
Indifference gains, and calls it ease.

X.

Free then they leave our claim to joy,
As free they leave our sad distress,
Nor can another's ills annoy,
40   The heart, which asks not here to bless.

XI.

But Oh! to me those moments spare
By which the feeling heart can live,
To take of grief and joy my share,
And blest by others, blessings give.

(1777)

Answer to Mrs. Greville's "Ode to Indifference"
Eliza Tuite

I.

While tuneful GREVILLE sweetly sings
The joy that cold Indifference brings,
    A nobler theme I'll chuse;
As tender feeling shall inspire,
I'll string my long neglected lyre,
    And court once more the Muse.

II.

I seek not fame, I want not praise,
Nor envy all the verdant bays,[36]
    That blooms round GREVILLE's head;
10   May laurels too her brows entwine,[37]

---

36. The fresh green leaves of the laurel tree.
37. In classical times, leaves from the laurel were made into wreaths for poets and conquerors.

More suited to my Muse, o'er *mine*
    Be fonder myrtles[38] spread.

III.

Sweet type of constancy and love,
Its emblematic charms will prove,
    The hope I'll ne'er resign;
In friendship warm, in love sincere,
To *me* affections bonds are dear,
    Oh, may they still be mine.

IV.

And pardon, GREVILLE, tho' I dare,
(While I admire) reprove a pray'r,   20
    So little worthy *thee;*
How could a heart thus form'd to know,
The transports that from feelings flow,
    E'er sigh for Apathy?

V.

You "ask no kind return in Love,"
Its hopes and fears, you would not prove,
    But scorn a lover's name;
You "seek no tempting charm to please,"
And sigh for that insipid ease,
    That ev'ry brute may claim.   30

VI.

Oh! GREVILLE *could* that heart of thine,
Whose feeling glows, thro' ev'ry line,
    The sacred touch disown,
That bids the tear of pity flow,
And melts the soul, at others woe,
    Or makes their joy its own?

---

38. Myrtle was sacred to Aphrodite, Greek goddess of love and beauty, and to Venus, her Roman equivalent, who has the additional characteristics of marriage and fertility. Generals received a crown of myrtle to commemorate the union of Sabine and Roman tribes at the foundation of Rome.

VII.

Could she, who as the needle[39] true,
Was form'd to "turn, and tremble too,"
　　A gift so rare despise?
40　Could she, by nature taught to please,
(Whose smiles, might sorrow's bondage ease)
　　Would *she* Indiff'rence prize?

VIII.

Distress the mind may often wound,
While bliss can scarce e'er reach the bound[40]
　　'Twixt joy and agony;
But who that bound'ry to attain,
Would not endure whole years of pain,
　　Can never feel like *me.*

IX.

Should I a lover's fondness claim,
50　I hope to feel an equal flame,
　　Will seek each charm to please;
Be blest, in blessing what I love,
And each illib'ral thought reprove,
　　That tends to selfish ease;

X.

Hence cold Indiff'rence far from me,
'Tis tender Sensibility[41]
　　Alone true pleasure yields;
My days, I would not have serene,
So hope but paint the varying scene
60　　That expectation gilds.

XI.

Regret may oft extort a sigh,
Or disappointment cloud the sky,

39. The slender magnetic pointer on a compass. Reference to Greville's image.
40. Boundary.
41. One of the most complicated terms in intellectual history, *sensibility* refers to a heightened consciousness of feelings. These feelings began in the nervous system but were informed by reason and by moral values. Thus, the ideal person of sensibility recognized and was moved by worthy objects of feeling.

And blast my promis'd joys;
But hope, again may warm my breast,
And others bliss can make *me* blest,
Tho' care my own destroys.

(1796)

Sources

Barker: *Poetical Recreations* (London, 1688), 12–13; Egerton: *Poems on Several Occasions* (London, 1703), 108–9; Rowe: *The Miscellaneous Works in Prose and Verse of Mrs. Elizabeth Rowe,* 2 vols. (London, 1739), 1:84–86; Pilkington: *The Memoirs of Mrs. Laetitia Pilkington,* 3 vols. (London, 1748), 1:143–45; Williams: *Miscellanies in Prose and Verse* (London, 1766), 18–19; Savage: *Poems on Various Subjects and Occasions,* 2 vols. (London, 1777), 1:82–84; Tuite: *Poems by Lady Tuite* (London, 1796), 142–43; Alcock: *Poems, &c. &c. By the Late Mrs. Mary Alcock* (London, 1799), 37–39; Greville: Betty Rizzo, "The Frances Greville Letters," *Eighteenth-Century Women* 4 (2006): 316–17; Savage: *Poems on Various Subjects and Occasions,* 2: 25–30; Tuite: *Poems by Lady Tuite,* 1–6.

⸙ K ⸙

Poems on Marriage

Recounting the experience of married life in eighteenth-century England is very different from exploring the institution of marriage itself. Some poems about married life capture the intimacy, affection, playfulness, and joy that can accompany the union. Poets write warmly of their married lives. Elizabeth Molesworth addresses her spouse as "tend'rest husband! and . . . truest friend!" (*Verses from a Lady at Bath,* 2.c). Anne Finch invites her husband, "my Dafnis," to leave his business concerns and "stray / And so, the pleasures of the feilds, survey" (*An Invitation to Dafnis,* 2.c). Anna Laetitia Barbauld describes intense privacy afforded by marriage: "We'll little care what others do, / . . . / . . . none shall know / How much we're so, / Save only Love, and we" (*To Mr. Barbauld,* 2.c). Many women record personal pleasure found in their relationships with their spouses. Others convey the equally vivid realities of a less successful union and the legal, economic, and cultural implications of marriage for a woman. Anger, loneliness, frustration, jealousy, and disappointment in an unhappy marriage, concern for a friend who marries, and resistance to the strictures of the position of "wife" find voice in the poetry in this section. These poems emphasize the institutional challenges marriage presented for women in eighteenth-century England, while also alluding to the companionate ideal of marriage, against which all these unions are implicitly measured.[1] The poems in this section are of three general kinds: poems written on the occasion of marriage, poems describing the pains or challenges of marriage as institution or lived experience, and poems reflecting upon a happy union. However, all these poems share a profound ambivalence toward marriage. Those unequivocally praising a union simultaneously acknowledge its constricting force or the possibilities for subsequent disappointment, while those critiquing the institutional inequalities of marriage often display hope for a rewarding relationship. Read with the poems on married love in section 2.c, the poems in this section capture the many dimensions of marriage in eighteenth-century England and illustrate why it is an important subject for life writing.

The alteration of status between a married and an unmarried woman was profound, and many poets look at the "change of life" (Elizabeth Teft, *On the Marriage of a Young Lady*) and its implications. Wives legally did not breathe what Mary Wollstonecraft described as "the sharp invigorating air of freedom."[2] George Saville, Earl of Halifax, reminds his daughter in *The Lady's New-year's Gift: or, Advice to a Daughter* "that the *Laws* of *Marriage* run in a harsher Stile toward your *Sex*."[3] When a woman married, she was no longer a *feme sole*, a woman who could act legally on her own behalf. With marriage, a woman became a *feme covert;* that is, she ceased to exist legally. As William Blackstone described in the first volume of his *Commentaries on the Laws of England* (1765), "By marriage the husband and wife are one person in law ... the very being or legal existence of the woman is suspended during this marriage, or at least is incorporated and consolidated into that of the husband.... For this reason, a man cannot grant his wife anything, ... for the grant would be to suppose her separate existence."[4] It is perhaps that alteration to which Millamant alludes in William Congreve's *The Way of the World* (1700) when she agrees to "by degrees dwindle into a Wife" while Mirabelle is "beyond Measure enlarg'd into a Husband."[5] Given that the dominant cultural expectation for women at this time was to marry and have children, the implications of this legal reality are hard to exaggerate. Elizabeth Foyster has suggested that during this period "The institution of marriage was intended to be the bedrock of the patriarchal ideal where women were subordinated to men, and husbands ruled over and dominated their wives."[6]

Lady Mary Chudleigh marks the transition between courtship and marriage, a moment when "all that's kind is laid aside." "When she the word *obey* has said," she observes, "Man by Law supreme" is made (*To the Ladies*). The dangers of choosing the wrong mate were high (and essentially irrevocable), for "'tis hard amongst Mankind, / A Heart of real Worth to find" (Mary Masters, *May you with Freedom still be Blest*). Jane Cave Winscom trusts that she has found in her spouse "A friend, an husband—faithful, wise and true" (*An Elegy on a Maiden Name*). Elizabeth Teft celebrates her friend's nuptials—"Gay blooming Joys attend your Change of Life, / At once commence true Happiness and Wife"— with the wish that the new husband may "augment the Lover in the Spouse" (*On the Marriage of a Young Lady*). Yet, many celebratory poems strategically deploy images associated with the dangers of marriage. Will the "tempting ... Connubial State" "reclaim the railing Libertine" (Teft, *On the Marriage of a Young Lady*)? What is the consequence of a husband's "fluctuating mind" (Winscom, *On the Marriage of a Lady*)? While wishing her friend may sweetly "pass your future life," Winscom simultaneously hopes that she may not "once repent that you became a wife."

Teft's final wish in *On the Marriage of a Young Lady*, "Long be the Chain of your united Years," uses an image of chains and fetters that consistently appears in poems on marriage. The possibility exists for "Hymen's chains" to be "silken bands" (Winscom, *On the Marriage of a Lady*); a happy marriage will "gently fix the lasting Chain of Love" (Mary Masters, *May you with Freedom still be blest*). Yet those chains can quickly transform into the "eternal Chains" of oppressive matrimony (Lady Mary Wortley Montagu, *Epistle from Mrs. Y—— to Her Husband*, 1.L), which can victimize women. Anne Finch describes how marriage creates "unequal fetters" that make women "Slaves of Hymen / Still . . . begging Love again / At the full length of all their chain" (*The Unequal Fetters*). Elizabeth Thomas's account of jealousy in a marriage likens spouses to pet monkeys, who in captivity come to "hug the *Chain*" of their oppression; marriage to a man who does not reciprocate the emotion makes women "Slaves to *Passion*" (*The Monkey Dance*). Interestingly, even the typographic appearance of Mary Jones's experimental poem *Matrimony* consists of a series of dashes that visually creates a kind of "chain" within the poem.

This ambivalence of imagery and attitude and the tension between the experience of marriage and its institutional structures are vividly illustrated by Mehetabel Wright. Compelled, after her two elopements, to marry a man of her parents' choosing, Wright describes to her father the elements lacking in her marriage: "a mutual affection and desire of pleasing, something near an equality of mind and person, either earthly or heavenly wisdom, and any thing to keep love warm between a young couple."[7] While expressing her personal unhappiness, she simultaneously projects an ideal of marriage. Her paired poems do the same. The first, *Mrs. Mehetabel Wright to her Husband*, is a very intimate plea to her husband, with the hope that a poem "may try, / By saddest softest strains, to move / My wedded latest dearest love." "Tell me why I cease to please," she implores. She questions what is responsible for the failure of a relationship—age, differing interests, incompatibility—and how she can connect with him "on whom my earthly bliss depend." In contrast, *Wedlock* projects the profound anger Wright, like many other women poets, feels toward the institution of marriage. Personifying "wedlock" as a "tyrant," Wright summons her "rage and grief" to attack the "eternal foe to soft desires, / Inflamer of forbidden fires." She projects what Mary Jones describes as "unwonted fury" that can subsume a woman and a relationship *(Matrimony)*.

Embedded within these poems of anger and disappointment is the companionate ideal of marriage, which seems elusive for many and the focus for others. In *The Conclusion of a Letter to the Rev. Mr. C——* (1.F) Mary Barber explicitly advises her son to "Chuse a Woman of Wisdom, as well as good Breeding," while reminding him of his responsibility to be "a *Friend* and *Protector:* / . . . not . . . *Tyrant* and *Hector*." Similarly, Priscilla Poynton offers advice to a "gay Bachelor," creating an image of marriage guided by mutuality, reciprocity, and friendship (*The Following Advice to a gay Bachelor*). The most sustained depiction of a successful marriage is Anna Sawyer's *Lines, Written on seeing my Husband's*

Picture. Using a kind of ekphrastic gesture to describe the picture of her husband in his youth—"the smiles, / That first engag'd my virgin heart"—she initiates her own verbal portrait, capturing the age, disappointment, and misfortune that colors him now. She writes with great affection and respect, but with a realistic assessment of their marriage. This poem represents married life as completely subsuming. Sawyer can admire and remember the portrait, yet her initial viewing of the portrait and her poem mark her only points of individuation from her spouse. Her "very being," in Blackstone's words, "is suspended."[8]

These poems begin to represent the range of experiences and capture the limitations and possibilities of women's married life during the long eighteenth century. They represent the love, hope, and desire with which some women enter marriage, as well as the disappointment, anger, and discontent that might follow or occur simultaneously. They capture the vacillations and intensity of emotion—"One Hour we *love,* and *hate* the next" (Thomas, *The Monkey Dance*)—that can characterize marriage. They also underscore the mixed emotions with which many women may have approached a union. Though delighting in her new "dear spouse," Winscom cannot help but shed an "ill-tim'd tear or two" at the loss of her maiden name (*An Elegy on a Maiden Name*), which, interestingly, she retained in some form on the title page of her publications.[9] The poems convey the complex and shifting perspectives, emotions, and experiences marriage produced in women during the long eighteenth century.

Notes

1. Nearly two decades ago, historians such a Lawrence Stone, Randolph Trumbach, and Alan Macfarlane suggested a shift in the basis of marriage from a union of purely financial, contractual, or political advantage to one of (controlled) emotions, a "companionate" ideal of marriage. The decline in patriarchal authority such a shift suggested has been challenged by subsequent feminist historians and literary critics such as Susan Staves, whose study illustrates the financial implications of women's legal status during this period. *Women's Separate Property in England, 1660–1833* (Cambridge, MA: Harvard University Press, 1990).

2. Mary Wollstonecraft, *A Vindication of the Rights of Woman* (London, 1792), 73.

3. George Saville, Marquis of Halifax, *The Lady's New-year's Gift: or, Advice to a Daughter,* 7th ed. (London, 1701), 21–22.

4. William Blackstone, *Commentaries on the Laws of England,* 4 vols. (Oxford, 1765–69), 1:430.

5. William Congreve, *The Way of the World* (London, 1706), 46.

6. Elizabeth Foyster, *Marital Violence: An English Family History, 1660–1857* (Cambridge: Cambridge University Press, 2005), 9.

7. Quoted in Roger Lonsdale, ed., *Eighteenth-Century Women's Poetry: An Oxford Anthology* (Oxford: Oxford University Press, 1990), 110.

8. For a discussion of the cultural value of portraits in ways that inform this poem, see Kelly McGuire, "Mourning and Material Culture in Eliza Haywood's *The History of Miss Betsy Thoughtless*," *Eighteenth-Century Fiction* 18, no. 3 (2006): 281–304.

9. Her name typically appeared as "By Miss Cave, Now Mrs. Winscom" on the title page of her texts. While it may have been designed to identify her to her audience, that decision may have had personal significance as well.

->->->->->•<-<-<-<-<-

To the Ladies
Mary Chudleigh

Wife and Servant are the same,
But only differ in the Name:
For when that fatal Knot is ty'd,
Which nothing, nothing can divide:
When she the word *obey* has said,
And Man by Law supreme has made,
Then all that's kind is laid aside,
And nothing left but State and Pride:
Fierce as an Eastern Prince he grows,
And all his innate Rigor shows: 10
Then but to look, to laugh, or speak,
Will the Nuptial Contract break.
Like Mutes she Signs alone must make,
And never any Freedom take:
But still be govern'd by a Nod,
And fear her Husband as her God:
Him still must serve, him still obey,
And nothing act, and nothing say,
But what her haughty Lord thinks fit,
Who with the Pow'r, has all the Wit.   20
Then shun, oh! shun that wretched State,
And all the fawning Flatt'rers hate:
Value your selves, and Men despise,
You must be proud, if you'll be wise.

(1703)

The Unequal Fetters[1]
Anne Finch

Cou'd we stop the time that's flying
   Or recall itt when 'tis past
Put far off the day of Dying

---

1. As Barbara McGovern notes, this unusual form of quintet stanzas with alternating eight- and seven-syllable lines was apparently Finch's own invention. *Anne Finch and Her Poetry: A Critical Biography* (Athens: University of Georgia Press, 1992), 50.

Or make Youth for ever last
To Love wou'd then be worth our cost.

But since we must loose those Graces
   Which at first your hearts have wonne
And you seek for in new Faces
   When our Spring of Life is done
10   It wou'd but urdge our ruine on.

Free as Nature's first intention
   Was to make us, I'll be found
Nor by subtle Man's invention
   Yeild to be in Fetters bound
By one that walks a freer round.

Mariage does but slightly tye Men
   Whil'st close Pris'ners we remain
They the larger Slaves of Hymen[2]
   Still are begging Love again
20   At the full length of all their chain.

(c. 1706–9; 1903)

The Monkey Dance.[3] To a jealous Wife
Elizabeth Thomas

Let those who think a *Man* sincere,
Devote themselves to *Hope* and *Fear,*
With all the curs'd *Inquietude,*
Which on those *Passions* still intrude.

2. In Greek and Roman mythology, Hymen was the god of marriage, represented as a young man carrying a torch and veil. The term also signified marriage generally.

3. Monkeys were popular as exhibits at fairs or as exotic pets, particularly for women. *Spectator* 343, of 3 April 1712, recounts Jack Freelove's visit to a lady whose "favourite monkey . . . was chained in one of the windows." Often dressed up to resemble humans (as in plate 2 of Hogarth's *Harlot's Progress,* among many other examples), monkeys were familiar objects of curiosity and affection throughout the eighteenth century. As Louise E. Robbins observes in connection with exotic pets in France during the same period, "Their status as expensive consumer items and their association with women provoked critical comments that tied in with contemporary concerns about changing social and gender roles." *Elephant Slaves and Pampered Parrots: Exotic Animals in Eighteenth-Century Paris* (Baltimore: Johns Hopkins University Press, 2002), 123.

False Joys and *Griefs* alternative
Are all the Pleasures *Love* can give.
With endless *Doubts,* and *Fears* perplext,
One Hour we *love,* and *hate* the next:
Yet Slaves to *Passion* still remain,
As *Monkey* drags his *Clog*[4] and *Chain:*   10
With antick *Grins* he hopps about,
    And fondly thinks him free,
    But when he would go further out,
       Pug[5] has no Liberty.
The *Clog* and *Chain* his Motions bound,
    And *Monkey* at his Post is found.
So jealous *Lovers,* without starting,
Can *huff,* and *rage,* and *threaten* Parting:
But when to *Practice* they descend,
The boasted *Pow'r* is at an End: 20
Their *Fury* on themselves they wreak,
And hug the *Chain* they strive to break.[6]

(1722)

Mrs. Mehetabel Wright to her Husband[7]
Mehetabel Wright

The ardent lover cannot find
A coldness in his fair unkind,
But blaming what he cannot hate
He mildly chides the dear ingrate;
And though dispairing of relief,
In soft complaining vents his grief.

Then what should hinder but that I,
Impatient of my wrongs, may try,
By saddest softest strains, to move
My wedded latest dearest love?   10

---

4. A block or heavy piece of wood, or the like, attached to the leg or neck of a man or beast to impede motion or prevent escape.

5. Term of endearment for a person; also, another term for a monkey.

6. To "hug the chain" is to delight in bondage. *OED.*

7. Mehetabel Wright married William Wright of Louth, a plumber and glazier, on 12 October 1725.

To throw his cold neglect aside
And cheer once more his injur'd bride.

O! thou whom sacred rites design'd,
My guide and husband ever kind;
My sov'reign master, best of friends,
On whom my earthly bliss depends;
If e'er thou didst in Hetty[8] see
Ought[9] fair, or good, or dear to thee;
If gentle speech can ever move

20 The cold remains of former love,
Turn thee at last—my bosom ease,
Or tell me why I cease to please.

Is it because revolving years,
Heart-breaking sighs, and fruitless tears,
Have quite depriv'd this form of mine
Of all that once thou fanci'dst fine?
Ah no! what once allur'd thy sight,
Is still in its meridian[10] height:
These eyes their usual lustre shew,

30 When un-eclips'd by flowing woe.
Old age and wrinkles in this face
As yet could never find a place;
A youthful grace adorns the lines,
Where still the purple current[11] shines;
Unless by thy ungentle art,
It flies to aid my wretched heart:
Nor does this slighted bosom shew
The thousand hours it spends in woe.

Or is it that oppress'd with care

40 I stun with loud complaints thine ear,
And make thy home, for quiet meant,
The seat of noise and discontent?
Oh no! those ears were ever free

8. Mehetabel was known as "Hetty" to her family. Her use of the familiar term here may summon the intimacy she is attempting to restore to her own marriage.

9. Aught: anything whatever, anything at all.

10. Period of highest development or splendor.

11. Reference to blood, suggesting that her cheeks are rosy.

From matrimonial melody.
For though thine absence I lament,
When half the lonely night is spent;[12]
Yet when the watch or early morn,[13]
Has brought me hopes of thy return,
I oft have wip'd these watchful eyes,
Conceal'd my cares, and curb'd my sighs,   50
In spite of grief, to let thee see
I wore an endless smile for thee.

   Had I not practis'd ev'ry art
T' oblige, divert, and cheer thy heart,
To make me pleasing in thine eyes,
And turn thy home to paradise,
I had not ask'd, why dost thou shun
These faithful arms, and eager run
To some obscure unclean retreat,
With fiends incarnate[14] glad to meet,   60
The vile companions of thy mirth,
The scum and refuse of the earth?
Who when inspir'd with beer can grin
At witless oaths, and jests obscene;
Till the most learned of the throng
Begin a tale of ten hours long,
Whilst thou in raptures, with stretch'd jaws,
Crownest each joke with loud applause.

   Depriv'd of freedom, health, and ease,
And rival'd by such *things* as these,   70
This latest effort will I try,
Or to regain thine heart, or die:
Soft as I am, I'll make thee see,
I will not brook[15] contempt from thee.
Then quit the shuffling doubtful sense,
Nor hold me longer in suspense.

---

12. Allegedly, William Wright spent his evenings "drinking with low company." Roger Lonsdale, ed., *Eighteenth-Century Women Poets: An Oxford Anthology* (Oxford: Clarendon, 1989), 111.

13. A watchman was appointed to keep watch in all towns from sunset to sunrise. His arrival marked sunset, and his departure, sunrise.

14. Play on the very common saying "He's the devil incarnate!"

15. Tolerate.

Unkind, ungrateful as thou art,
Say, must I ne'er regain thy heart?
Must all attempts to please thee prove
80   Unable to regain thy love?
If so, by truth itself I swear,
The sad reverse I cannot bear;
No rest, no pleasure will I see,
My whole of bliss is lost with thee.
I'll give all thought of patience o'er,
(A gift I never lost before)
Indulge at once my rage and grief,
Mourn obstinate, disdain relief;
And call that wretch my mortal foe,
90   Who tries to mitigate my woe;
Till life, on terms severe as these,
Shall ebbing leave my heart at ease;
To thee thy liberty restore,
To laugh when Hetty is no more.

(1730; 1793)

Wedlock: A Satire

Mehetabel Wright

Thou tyrant, whom I will not name,
Whom heaven and hell alike disclaim;
Abhorr'd and shunn'd, for different ends,
By angels, Jesuits, beasts, and fiends!
What terms to curse thee shall I find,
Thou plague peculiar to mankind?
O may my verse excel in spite
The wiliest, wittiest imps of night!
Then lend me for a while your rage,
10   You maidens old and matrons sage:
So may my terms in railing seem
As vile and hateful as my theme.
     Eternal foe to soft desires,
Inflamer of forbidden fires,
Thou source of discord, pain, and care,
Thou sure forerunner of despair,

Thou scorpion with a double face,
Thou lawful plague of human race,
Thou bane of freedom, ease, and mirth,
Thou deep damnation upon earth,   20
Thou serpent which the angels fly,
Thou monster whom the beasts defy,
Whom wily Jesuits sneer at too;
And Satan (let him have his due)
Was never so confirm'd a dunce
To risk damnation more than once.
That wretch, if such a wretch there be,
Who hopes for happiness from thee,
May search successfully as well
For truth in whores and ease in hell.   30

(1730; 1862)

On the Marriage of a Young Lady
Elizabeth Teft

It gives me Pleasure, to congratulate
You on the Alteration of your State;
Gay blooming Joys attend your Change of Life,
At once commence true Happiness and Wife.
May he with whom you plight your ardent Vows,
Greatly augment the Lover in the Spouse:
As do your Days, so may your Bliss increase,
In shining Affluence, and easy Peace.
Each Wish prevented by indulgent Fate,
Hymen's[16] best Comforts on your Nuptials wait;   10
Paternal Fondness many Thoughts imploy,
Return'd with duteous Love and grateful Joy;
Ever exulting in these darling Cares,
The Spouse unequal'd, and your Virtue's Airs.
Gay rapturous Love in the Fruition dies,
Esteem's the Author of substantial Joys;
Not to esteem the Object of our Flame,

16. In Greek and Roman mythology, Hymen was the god of marriage, represented as a young man carrying a torch and veil. The term also signified marriage generally.

Is blindfold Passion, Love's fictitious Name.
But you've a Judgment too profound to err,
20   And real Bliss to fancy'd will prefer.
Merit alone can captivate your Heart,
The favour'd Youth is rich in true Desert:
Oh! can he boast with you an equal Worth,
I hail you the most perfect Pair on Earth:
So tempting the Connubial State will shine,
As may reclaim the railing Libertine.
In vast Effusion Heav'n its Joys dispense
To you, the Pattern of all Excellence;
I shall be blest in knowing you are so,
30   Each Minute multiply those Joys ye know.
Long be the Chain of your united Years,
No distant Ill, anticipate through Fears.
Meet Life's last Stage with chearful Peace of Mind,
Nature a gentle Dissolution find.
Mingl'd by Fate your last-expiring Breath,
And as in Life, so Union find in Death.
When the great Retribution Morn appear,
May each a Crown of Deathless Glory wear.

(1747)

Matrimony[17]

Mary Jones

Cloe, coquet and debon - - - - - - - *air,*
Haughty, flatter'd, vain, and - - - - - *fair;*
No longer obstinately - - - - - - - - - *coy,*
Let loose her soul to dreams of - - - *joy.*
She took the husband to her - - - - *arms,*
Resign'd her freedom and her - - - - *charms;*
Grew tame, and passive to his - - - - *will,*
And bid her eyes forbear to - - - - - *kill.*

---

17. The rhymes first put down by a gentleman, for the author to fill up as she pleas'd. *Jones.* [The poem's form, with dashes designating the blank spaces, underscores its collaborative and subversive nature. *Eds.*]

But mighty happy still at - - - - - - - - - *heart,*
Nor room was there for pain, or - - - - - - *smart.*   10

   At length she found the name of - - - - *wife*
Was but another word for - - - - - - - - - - *strife.*
That cheek, which late out-blush'd the - - *rose,*
Now with unwonted fury - - - - - - - - - - *glows.*
Those tender words, "my dear, I - - - - - - *die,"*
The moving tear, and melting - - - - - - - *sigh,*
Were now exchang'd for something - - - - *new,*
And feign'd emotions yeild to - - - - - - - *true.*
Reproach, debate, and loss of - - - - - - - - *fame,*
Intrigues, diseases, duns,[18] and - - - - - - *shame.*   20
No single fault He strives to - - - - - - - *hide;*
Madam has virtue, therefore - - - - - - - - *pride.*
Thus both resent, while neither - - - - - *spares,*
And curse, but cannot break their - - - - - *snares.*

         (1750)

May you with Freedom still be blest[19]
Mary Masters

[I was glad to find that you as well as your Friend]

Had, hitherto, escap'd those Darts,
That wound, unseen, poor Virgin's Hearts,
May you with Freedom still be blest,
Or of a worthy Heart possest;
But, Oh, 'tis hard amongst Mankind,
A Heart of real Worth to find,
Full of Merit, kind and true,
Wise and good, and fit for you.

---

18. Importunate creditors.

19. The poem appears in the same letter as *I Shall Keep Your Correspondence as Misers Do Their Gold* (2.A). In the letter, Masters observes that "the Happiness of that State [Marriage] is not connected with the Violence or Moderation of the Passion preceding the Union, but depends in a great Measure, I believe I may venture to say entirely, on a prudent Conduct afterward; but it must be seasoned with Affection on both Sides, or there can be no true Felicity. The Coldness and Indifference which sometimes happen between married People, I believe it is greatly in a Woman's Power to guard

10   . . . . .²⁰

> Ye lovely Nymphs of *Britain's* beauteous Race,
> Let no false Shews your native Charms disgrace,
> Ape not the vain Coquette, too kind or rude,
> Nor imitate the stiff dissembling Prude.
> A Heart to Pride unknown, a Smile sincere;
> A mild Address, an unaffected Air
> Will make Mankind your pleasing Worth approve,
> And gently fix the lasting Chain of Love.

. . . .

20

> For early will the treach'rous Tempters come:
> They spread their Nets for Beauty in its Bloom.
> O happy she that can *betimes* beware,
> And shun the sly Deluder's gilded Snare.

(1755)

The following Advice to a gay Bachelor, upon the Marriage State
Priscilla Poynton

> Know, Strephon, this is my advice,
> You make a virtuous Fair your choice;
> Each day will then you pleasure lend,
> In her you'll find the wife and friend:
> Her converse, Sir, tho' not refin'd,
> May sweetly sooth to rest your mind;
> She'll be a part'ner in each pain,
> And chearful half your wrongs sustain:
> The hours she'll make glide soft away,

10

> And crown with virtuous love the day;
> As flow'rets raise their drooping heads,
> When SOL[21] his orient beams he spreads,
> So she with smiles your heart shall chear,
> And make your spirits debonair:

---

against. . . . Good-Nature, Neatness of Person, Delicacy both in Sentiment and Expression, with a modest Reserve, is infinitely engaging, and will not only render a Woman amiable and dear to her Husband, but command Respect from all that know her." *Familiar Letters and Poems on Several Occasions* (London, 1755), 95–96.

    20. The poem is interrupted here and again after the following eight lines by prose.

    21. Personification of the sun.

But whilst you emulate the Bee,[22]
Real happiness you ne'er will see;
Wed, STREPHON, then, ere 'tis too late,
And you shall own, in single state,
A joy that's true you never found,
'Till you in HYMEN's bands were bound;   20
There mutual friendship ever dwell,
Beyond what I have skill to tell:
Shou'd I attempt this bliss to paint,
My humble Muse wou'd prove too faint.
Methinks I hear you peevish say,
"Can she expect I'll her obey,
Who never was herself a wife!
What knows she then of wedded life?"
Yet frown not, if too much I've said,
But pardon, Sir, a blushing Maid.   30

(1770)

On the Marriage of a Lady, to whom the Author was Bride-Maid
Jane Cave Winscom

As the light bark[23] on the tempestuous sea,
Toss'd to and fro, from dangers never free;
Dismay'd with fear, and mov'd with ev'ry blast,
Till in a port her anchor's firmly cast;
So oft is mov'd Man's fluctuating mind,
Till it in wedlock a safe anchor find;
Here, if the soul but meets her destin'd mate,
Her joys are full, her happiness compleat.

   Be this your happy lot, my lovely friend,
Whose nuptial rites I this glad morn attend;   10
Whose humble, gentle mind for peace was born,
Whom virtue, love, and innocence adorn.
Celestial graces dignify thy soul,

---

22. Male bees live a life of ease: their sole purpose is mating; they are not responsible for gathering pollen or creating honey.
   23. Small sailboat with three to five masts.

While pure religion all thy ways controul.
These noble virtues, which in thee abound,
Are haply in thy lov'd PHILANDER[24] found.
His heart sincere, his temper soft and mild,
Nor torn by anger, nor with art beguil'd.
Such gentle hearts alone should join their hands,
20   And find that Hymen's chains are silken bands.
Their emulation's not who'll reign supreme,
But who shall love the most,—be most serene.
Remote from vanity and worldly toys,
Each seeks with each for more substantial joys.
Tranquillity shall in their borders dwell,
Nor discord once approach their peaceful cell,
But mutually each other's grief they'll bear,
As mutually each other's joys will share.

  Thus, thus, my friend, may you for ever prove,
30   The soft delight of harmony and love;
May ev'ry blessing you can ask of Heav'n,
To constitute your happiness be giv'n.
If Heav'n bestows, with joy receive the prize,
If Heav'n witholds, 'tis best what Heav'n denies.
Thus sweetly may you pass your future life,
Nor once repent that you became a wife;
That you declin'd the pleasing name of B——M,
And that alone preferr'd of H—RAG—M.[25]

                                        (1783)

An Elegy on a Maiden Name
Jane Cave Winscom

Adieu, dear name, which birth and nature gave— ⎫
Lo! at the altar I've interr'd dear Cave,   ⎬
For there she fell, expir'd, and found a grave. ⎭

24. Male lover.

25. The fourth edition (Bristol, 1794) of Winscom's *Poems on Various Subjects, Entertaining, Elegiac, and Religious* includes the full (and likely disguised) maiden and married names of her friend, Bloom and Harragoom.

Forgive, dear spouse, this ill-tim'd tear or two,
They are not meant in disrespect to you.
I hope the name, which you have lately giv'n,
Was kindly meant, and sent to me by heav'n.
But, ah! the loss of Cave I must deplore,
For that dear name the tend'rest mother bore.
With that she pass'd full forty years of life,   10
Adorn'd th' important character of wife.
Then meet for bliss, from earth to heav'n retir'd,
With holy zeal and true devotion fir'd.

In me what blest my father may you find,
A wife domestic, virtuous, meek and kind.
What blest my mother may I meet in you,
A friend, an husband—faithful, wise and true.

Then be our voyage prosperous or adverse,
No keen upbraidings shall our tongues rehearse;
But mutually we'll brave against the storm,   20
Remembering still for help-mates we were born:
Then let rough torrents roar or skies look dark,
If love commands the helm which guides our bark,
No shipwreck will we fear, but to the end,
Each find in each a just, unshaken friend.

(1786)

Lines, Written on seeing my Husband's Picture, painted when he was young

Anna Sawyer

1.
Those are the features, those the smiles,
    That first engag'd my virgin heart:
I feel the pencil'd image true,
    I feel the mimic pow'r of art.

2.
For ever on my soul engrav'd
    His glowing cheek, his manly mien;

I need not thee, thou painted shade,
   To tell me what my Love has been.

3.
O dearer now, tho' bent with age,
   Than in the pride of blooming youth!
I knew not then his constant heart,
   I knew not then his matchless truth.

4.
Full many a year, at random tost,
   The sport of many an adverse gale,
Together, hand in hand, we've stray'd,
   O'er dreary hill, and lonely vale.

5.
Hope only flattered to betray,
   Her keenest shafts misfortune shot:
In spite of prudence, spite of care,
   Dependence was our bitter lot.

6.
Ill can'st thou bear the sneer of wealth,
   Averted looks, and rustic scorn;
For thou wert born to better hopes,
   And brighter rose thy vernal morn.

7.
Thy ev'ning hours to want expos'd,
   I cannot, cannot bear to see:
Were but thy honest heart at ease,
   I care not what becomes of me.

8.
But tho', my Love, the winds of woe,
   Beat cold upon thy silver hairs,
Thy ANNA's bosom still is warm;
   Affection still shall soothe thy cares.

10

20

30

9.

And Conscience, with unclouded ray,
    The cottage of our age will chear;
Friendship will lift our humble latch,
    And Pity pour her healing tear.

(1796; 1801)

Sources

Chudleigh: *Poems on Several Occasions* (London, 1703), 40. Finch: *The Poems of Anne Countess of Winchilsea,* ed. Myra Reynolds (Chicago: University of Chicago Press, 1903), 150–51. Thomas: *Miscellany Poems on Several Subjects* (London, 1722), 263–64. Wright: John Whitehead, *The Life of the Rev. John Wesley, M. A.,* 2 vols. (London, 1793, 1796), 1:63–66; Samuel Wesley, Jr. *Poems on Several Occasions,* ed. James Nichols (London, 1862), 553–54. Teft: *Orinthia's Miscellanies* (London, 1747), 71–73. Jones: *Miscellanies in Prose and Verse* (Oxford, 1750), 49–50. Masters: *Familiar Letters and Poems on Several Occasions* (London, 1755), 94–98. Poynton: *Poems on Several Occasions* (Birmingham, 1770), 45–46. Winscom: *Poems on Various Subjects, Entertaining, Elegiac, and Religious* (Winchester, 1783), 21–24; *Poems on Various Subjects, Entertaining, Elegiac, and Religious* (Bristol, 1786), 149–51. Sawyer: *Poems on Various Subjects* (Birmingham, 1801), 37–39.

⊀L⊁

Poems on Motherhood

The child's physical presence and always feared absence compel the poems in this section. These poems are intimate, emotional, and personal, though rarely sentimental. They convey the fragility of the lives of children and mothers. Complex in form and meaning, they provide an unflinching portrait of maternity. Poems about children and mothers appear in most sections of this anthology and complement the ones gathered here; together they create a dialogue about the complicated construction and performance of maternity during the long eighteenth century. As is frequently discussed in connection with the novel, the period saw the rise of what Felicity Nussbaum terms "the cult of domestic maternity."[1] The perceived power of maternal influence, new ideologies of maternal affection, and increasingly codified models of femininity brought motherhood and the practices of maternal behavior under close scrutiny.[2] Some poems convey the more idealized aspects of domestic maternity. Martha Rigby Hale's argument in favor of breastfeeding ("the little bleating Lamb, / Who close attends the fost'ring dam; / She ne'er gives up the mother's part" (*The Infant's Petition to Be Nursed at Home*) echoes the language of William Cadogan's popular 1748 breast-feeding manual: "When was there a Lamb, a Bird, or a Tree that died because it was young? These are under the immediate Nursing of unerring nature, and they thrive accordingly."[3] Throughout her poetry Mary Barber discusses her sons' lives, poetically offers "my own boys" advice and education, and muses affectionately on their dual roles as inspiration and distraction (*To a Lady, who Invited the Author into the Country*, 1.A). Maria Frances Celia Cowper likens herself to a "captive . . . / Following [the] little fancies" of her infant son; the sight of him sleeping is infatuating: "thou canst, a thousand ways, / A mother's partial fondness raise!" (*On Viewing her Sleeping Infant*, 2.C). Joanna Baillie, although never a mother herself, captures a mother's fascination with an infant's "curled nose . . . , / . . . / And little chin with crystal spread" (*A Mother to Her Waking Infant*). Such poems express the joy, hope, and laughter that can accompany mothering.

Yet most of the poems in this section have a different cadence, as they focus primarily on loss, death, or separation. The possible death of an infant or mother during childbirth was "a pervasive and painful fact of life for most women."[4] Though notoriously difficult to quantify precisely, the maternal and infant mortality rates were high at this time. Roy Porter estimates that "a fifth of all babies died in their first year; perhaps one in three died ... before the age of five."[5] Primitive obstetrics, unanaesthetized deliveries, and the potential for postpartum infection also made pregnancy "a precarious and anxious undertaking."[6] Poems reflect the trepidation that women felt. Many poets represent childbirth as a liminal moment "at which, poised with their children in the threshold between life and death, they glimpse a prolepsis of child loss"[7] or loss of their own life. Jane Cave Winscom questions whether her unborn child "should'st ... live," or, if it does, whether she will: "Perhaps the day, which gives you life, / Deprives Eusebius of his wife; / And you ... / ... ne'er will know a mother's care" (*To My Dear Child*). She explores a similar uncertainty in *Written A few Hours before the Birth of a Child* (2.D): "If death thy pleasure be; / O may the harmless babe I bear / Haply expire with me." In *On the Author's Lying-In* Elizabeth Hands seems surprised to have survived childbirth: "I live! my God be prais'd ... , / ... / I live within my arms to clasp, / My infant with endearing grasp." Other poems record the death of a young child. Mourning her son, "boy too dear to live," Katherine Philips must leave "the unconcerned World alone" (*Orinda upon little Hector Philips*, 2.N). In her "anguish," Mehetabel Wright—whose four children all died—attempts to preserve the visual image of the infant: "Transient luster, beauteous clay, / Smiling wonder of a day" (*To an Infant expiring the second day of its Birth*). In the title of her poem, Wright marks her choice of the meter known as "Namby Pamby," typically used in children's verse; the musical form aurally echoes the children's poems that she will never share with her child, creating a dissonance between sound and sense.[8]

The poems addressing loss display a visceral quality. The response is intense, physical, and emotionally raw. "Why throbs my breast?" asks Charlotte Brereton (*To the Memory of a Mother*). Philips writes in "gasping numbers" (*Orinda upon little Hector Philips*). Wright describes "a mother's moan" in *To an Infant expiring the second day of its Birth*. Even at a time when maternal duty was aligned with pursuits of empire and, in turn, the sacrifice of a son to war was portrayed as ennobling, the loss is profound. "The frantic mother's cries of Heaven implore / Some youthful warrior—she shall meet no more" (Anne Bannerman, *Verses on an Illumination*, 2.E). Indeed, the loss of an adult child for any reason exacts a high price; Charlotte Smith will lament the loss of Anna Augusta, the "form adored," as long as "life is mine, / With fond regret, and ceaseless grief deplored— / That grief, my angel!" (*Sonnet XCI: Reflections on Some Drawings of Plants*, 2.C).

The depth of Smith's grief suggests the intimacy of the mother-daughter relationship, which shares qualities with the female communities discussed in the introduction to section 2.A, "Friendship Poems." Writing of her mother, "that all-gracious, all victorious friend," Winscom seeks to "weep and sigh!" to "mourn, and wail my loss until I die!" (*On the Death of the Author's Mother,* not included). Charlotte Brereton regards her mother, the poet Jane Brereton, as a poetic and personal model whose memory has a talismanic effect: "Long as I wander thro' the maze of life, / . . . / Fix'd in my breast thy mem'ry shall reside, / Thy virtue fire me, and thy precept guide" (*To the Memory of a Mother*). Anne Hunter, anticipating her daughter's separation upon her marriage, describes their intimacy in language similar to that of female friendship: "Twin'd ev'ry joy, and care, and thought, / And o'er our minds one mantle cast / Of kind affections finely wrought." Hunter essentially casts the new husband as an emotional competitor of sorts: "May he who claims thy tender heart / Deserve its love, as I have done!" (*To My Daughter*). Representations of motherhood may at first glance seem predictable, but these poems confound expectation. They display an unusual depth of feeling, use original imagery and perspective, and experiment metrically. Ultimately the poems offer another kind of life writing that elevates domestic maternity and enriches our understanding of women's lives in the long eighteenth century.

Notes

1. Felicity Nussbaum, *Torrid Zones: Maternity, Sexuality, and Empire in Eighteenth-Century English Narratives* (Baltimore: Johns Hopkins University Press, 1995), 48. Susan C. Greenfield asserts, similarly, that maternity was "invented and re-invented" during the long eighteenth century, a period of contested and shifting maternal constructions. Introduction to *Inventing Maternity: Politics, Science, and Literature, 1650–1865,* ed. Susan C. Greenfield and Carol Barash (Lexington: University Press of Kentucky, 1999), 1. However, some scholars, such as Naomi J. Miller and Naomi Yavneh, in *Maternal Measures: Figuring Caregiving in the Early Modern Period,* ed. Miller and Yavneh (Aldershot: Ashgate, 2000), and Kathryn M. Moncrief and Kathryn R. McPherson, in *Performing Maternity in Early Modern England,* ed. Moncrief and McPherson (Aldershot: Ashgate, 2007), see similar constructions and emphases as originating in the early modern period.

2. The public and contradictory constructions of motherhood during the Augustan period are explored by Toni Bowers in *The Politics of Motherhood: British Writing and Culture, 1680–1760* (Cambridge: Cambridge University Press, 1996). She, like Nussbaum, focuses on the numerous representations of bad mothers, as well as on the expectations for exemplary behavior.

3. William Cadogan, *An Essay upon Nursing, and the Management of Children, from their Birth to Three Years of Age* (London, 1748), 7.

4. Patricia Phillippy, "London's Mourning Garment: Maternity, Mourning, and Royal Succession," in Miller and Yavneh, *Maternal Measures,* 321.

5. Roy Porter, *English Society in the Eighteenth Century* (London: Penguin, 1990), 13.

6. Bowers, *Politics of Motherhood,* 26.

7. Phillippy, "London's Mourning Garment," 320.

8. All the poems written to or in the persona of an infant are written in tetrameter, a less formal meter commonly used for nursery rhymes that Margaret Doody describes as "a measure less official, more comic, more pungent" than iambic pentameter, which is used in many of the maternal monodies for more formal effect. "Women Poets of the Eighteenth Century," in *Women and Literature in Britain, 1700–1800,* ed. Vivien Jones (Cambridge: Cambridge University Press, 2000), 222–23.

To an Infant expiring the second day of its Birth. Written by its Mother, in Imitation of NAMBY PAMBY[1]

Mehetabel Wright[2]

> Tender softness, infant mild,
> Perfect, purest, brightest child;
> Transient lustre, beauteous clay,
> Smiling wonder of a day:
> E're the last convulsive start
> Bends thy *unresisting* heart:
> E'er the long enduring swoon
> Weighs thy precious eyes-lids down,
> Oh regard a mother's moan,
> Anguish deeper than thy own!
> Fairest eyes, whose dawning light
> Late with rapture blest my sight,
> E're your orbs extinguish'd be,
> Bend their trembling beams on me:
> Drooping sweetness, verdant flow'r
> Blooming, with'ring in an hour;
> E're thy gentle breast sustains
> Latest, fiercest, vital pains,
> Hear a suppliant! Let me be
> Partner in thy Destiny.

10

20

(1733)

---

1. The title refers to the seven-syllable line—three trochees followed by an extra-stressed mono-syllabic foot—that Wright uses in the poem, first introduced by Ambrose Philips and parodied by Henry Carey in *Namby Pamby: or, A Panegyrick on the New Versification, Address'd to A—— P——* (1725). Carey's poem was so popular that people began to refer to Philips himself as Namby Pamby.

2. Wright was married to William Wright, a plumber and glazier described as "by no means a fit husband for such a woman." She attributed her children's failing health to her husband's leadworks on the property. William Duncombe recounts that when asked about her children, she replied, "I have had several; but the white lead killed them all." William Duncombe to Elizabeth Carter, 20 November 1752, quoted in Elspeth Knights, "A 'Licensuous' Daughter: Mehetabel Wesley, 1697–1750," *Women's Writing* 4 (1997): 37.

To the Memory of a Mother[3]
Charlotte Brereton

Why sinks my heart beneath a weight of woe?
Why throbs my breast? my tears incessant flow?
Why flies the slumber from my aching eyes?
What prompts the sigh when morning gilds the skies?
Day's chearful orb, why hateful to my sight?
Why seeks my soul the mournful gloom of night?
Ask death the cause- - -too well the tyrant knows,
From his relentless hand proceed my woes.
   To thee, blest shade![4] I chearless tune the lay
All, for thy love, my bleeding heart can pay;   10
As now that love a sad remembrance brings
The Muse must weep- - -yet while she weeps, she sings!
   How did her care, her tenderness engage
The artless fondness of my infant age?
And when advancing in the years of youth
Teach me the ways of wisdom and of truth?
The happy hours flew unperceiv'd along,
While native wit flow'd, tuneful, from her tongue:
Her gentle numbers charm'd the list'ning ear,
MELISSA's[5] name was to the Muses dear.   20
Nature, in her, with care unwonted join'd
The beauteous frame and still more beauteous mind;
Neither diminish'd by affected art,
Nor guile deform'd, nor pride debased her heart;
Above her sex's foibles was her aim,
Too just, too good, to flatter or defame;
To friendship ever true, in converse free,
And dear to all—but oh! most dear to me.
With every virtue was her bosom warm,
And pure religion brighten'd every charm.   30
But say, lamented shade, should I repine
That thou has chang'd the mortal for divine?

---

3. Charlotte Brereton wrote this poem, published in *Gentleman's Magazine* under the name Carolina, for her mother, poet Jane Brereton, upon her death in 1740.

4. Ghost or disembodied spirit.

5. From 1734 on, Jane Brereton published some verse in the *Gentleman's Magazine* under the pseudonym Melissa.

More than I've lost in thee, to thee is giv'n:
I've lost a parent——thou has gain'd a heav'n.- - -
With spotless *Rowe*[6] you tread th' etherial plains,
And wake the golden lyre to heav'nly strains;
Harmonious join the blest angelick choirs,
God all the theme- - -while God the song inspires.
   Long as I wander thro' the maze of life,
40   Amidst delusive joys, and care, and strife,
Fix'd in my breast thy mem'ry shall reside,
Thy virtue fire me, and thy precept guide,
Thus shall I fearless feel the hand of death,
Like thee, in peace, resign my trembling breath,
My soul exulting meet her pitying God,
And join thy raptures in the blest abode.

(1740)

To My Dear Child[7]
Jane Cave Winscom

Dear sinless babe, whose peaceful room
Centers within thy mother's womb;
Whose mind's unspotted, spirit pure,
As happy (doubtless) as obscure.

Whom having never seen, I love,
And breath my ardent soul above,
That Heav'n its richest gifts may give
To thee, my infant, should'st thou live.[8]

   What unknown cares obstruct my rest,
10   What new emotions fill my breast!

---

6. Poet Elizabeth Singer Rowe (1674–1737).

7. Winscom offers the following preface to this poem in her collection: "The following lines were not intended for publication, nor would they have been inserted here, but in compliance with the request of several friends. They were composed by the Author, previous to the birth of her first child;— written and sealed with her own hand, and committed to the care of her friends, that in the case of the mother's death, and the child's living till a proper age, it might be presented therewith." *Poems on Various Subjects, Entertaining, Elegiac, and Religious* (Bristol, 1786), 153.

8. Winscom had two sons and perhaps other children who did not survive.

I count the days so oft retold,
E'er I my infant can behold.
Thought after thought intrudes a dart,
And strange forbodings fill my heart.

Perhaps the day, which gives you life,
Deprives Eusebius of his wife;[9]
And you for circling years may spare,
Who ne'er will know a mother's care.
Perhaps some rude ungentle hand
Thy infant footsteps may command;   20
Who, void of tenderness and thought,
Too harshly menaces each fault.
Oh; thought too poignant! may'st thou die,
And breathless with thy mother lie.
But dare I Heav'n designs o'er throw;
Come, resignation, quickly flow;
Say, to fond Nature's fears be still,
And bow me to the Almighty will.

Perhaps I yet may live to see
My child grow up, and comfort me.   30
And if I die—perhaps my shade
My darling footsteps may pervade.
Sleepless myself, thy eye-lids close,
And guard thee whilst in soft repose:
And if you e'er attain thirteen,
These lines may by my child be seen;
For then your mind may comprehend
What once your anxious mother penn'd.
Here I would ev'ry wish impart,
And ope[10] my darling all my heart.   40

I wish the child, I call my own,
A soul that would adorn a throne!
With keen sensations, soft, refin'd,
A noble, but an humble mind.

9. *Eusebius* is the Latinate form of the Greek *Eusebios*, which means "pious." Eusebius of Caesarea is known as the father of ecclesiastical history, and his simple baptismal creed became the basis for the Nicaean or, later, Nicene Creed.

10. Open.

Be courteous, prudent, humble, wise,
Each friend's instruction always prize.
And if you're cast in learning's way,
Improve each moment of the day,
And grasp at knowledge whilst you may.
50 With richest freight your memory store
And prize it more than golden ore.
For riches you may loose and spend,
But knowledge is a lasting friend.

Be strictly honest, strictly just,
On no pretence betray your trust.
If any to your breast confide
A secret—there let it abide.
Whate'er you promise bear in mind,
Each promise should to action bind.
60 From low deceits and falshoods fly,
Nor dread a serpent as a lie.
For should you e'er the name acquire
As some I've known,—a common liar,
A common thief, my child, would be
By far more excellent than thee.

In some you'll find a constant flame
To vilify their neighbour's name;
But mark that woman, mark the man,
And shun their converse if you can:
70 For such, as thus dispos'd, you see
When thou art gone, speak ill of thee.
But, if with such obliged to meet,
Like prudence, shew yourself discreet;
And if you're urg'd, as oft I've known,
To join with them to cast a stone.
Rather appear to know it not
Than help thy neighbour's name to blot.
Thus you may find evasions good,
Well tim'd, and rightly understood;
80 But 'twould be wrong should you conceal
Faults which obstruct your neighbour's weal;[11]
And doubly wrong if you evade,

---

11. Welfare, happiness, prosperity, general good.

What known would honour—not degrade.
Hence your own judgment must disclose
When to conceal, and when expose.

    Are any plac'd beneath your care,
Of proud austerities beware;
Let ev'ry word and action prove
You'd win their services by love.
Be soft and gentle, tender, mild,   90
E'en from the servant to the child;
Yea, let each insect, bird, and beast
Within your sphere, your goodness, taste.
Must you destroy a worm or fly?
With quickest motion let it die:
Nor let a creature e'er complain
You gave one moment's needless pain.

    They but a savage heart expose,
Who trifle with a reptile's woes.

    What e'er you want, to God make known, ⎫   100
If meet,—your wishes are your own;   ⎬
Make him your confidant alone.   ⎭
His laws obey, his voice attend,
And then you'll never want a friend.

                    (1786)

On the Author's Lying-In,[12] August, 1785
Elizabeth Hands

O God, the giver of all joy,
Whose gifts no mortal can destroy,
    Accept my grateful lays:[13]
My tongue did almost ask for death,
But thou did'st spare my lab'ring breath,
    To sing thy future praise.

---

12. The state of being in labor with a child.
13. Short lyric or narrative poems intended to be sung.

I live! my God be prais'd, I live,
And do most thankfully receive,
   The bounty of my life:
I live, still longer to improve,
The fondest husband's tender love,
   To the most happy wife.

I live within my arms to clasp,
My infant with endearing grasp,
   And feel my fondness grow:
O God endow her with thy grace,
And heav'nly gifts, to hold a place
   Among thy Saints below.

May she in duty, as she ought,
By thy unerring precepts taught,
   To us a blessing prove:
And thus prepar'd for greater joys,
May she, with thine elect arise
   To taste the joys above.

                  (1785; 1789)

A Mother to Her Waking Infant
Joanna Baillie

Now in thy dazzling half-op'd eye,
Thy curled nose, and lip awry,
Thy up-hoist arms, and noddling head,
And little chin with crystal[14] spread,
Poor helpless thing! what do I see,
   That I should sing of thee?

From thy poor tongue no accents come,
Which can but rub thy toothless gum:
Small understanding boast thy face,
Thy shapeless limbs nor step, nor grace:

14. Drool.

A few short words thy feats may tell,
    And yet I love thee well.

When sudden wakes the bitter shriek,
And redder swells thy little cheek;
When rattled keys thy woe beguile,
And thro' the wet eye gleams the smile,
Still for thy weakly self is spent
    Thy little silly plaint.[15]

But when thy friends are in distress,
Thou'lt laugh and chuckle ne'er the less;   20
Nor e'en with sympathy be smitten,
Tho' all are sad but thee and kitten;
Yet little varlet[16] that thou art,
    Thou twitchest at the heart.

Thy rosy cheek so soft and warm;
Thy pinky hand, and dimpled arm;
Thy silken locks that scantly peep,
With gold-tip'd ends, where circle deep
Around thy neck in harmless grace
So soft and sleekly hold their place,   30
Might harder hearts with kindness fill,
    And gain our right good will.

Each passing clown[17] bestows his blessing,
Thy mouth is worn with old wives' kissing:
E'en lighter looks the gloomy eye
Of surly sense, when thou art by;
And yet I think whoe'er they be,
    They love thee not like me.

Perhaps when time shall add a few
Short years to thee, thou'lt love me too.   40
Then wilt thou thro' life's weary way
Become my sure and cheering stay:

15. Audible expression of sorrow, wailing.
16. Rascal, here used affectionately.
17. Rustic, countryman.

Wilt care for me, and be my hold,
    When I am weak and old.

Thou'lt listen to my lengthen'd tale,
And pity me when I am frail——
But see, the sweepy spinning fly
Upon the window takes thine eye.
Go to thy little senseless play—
50   Thou doest not heed my lay.[18]

(1790)

Verses in Memory of the Author's Mother[19]
Maria Frances Cecilia Cowper

Kind parent, faithful friend! O names how sweet!
How precious each! how lovely when they meet!
Friendship, when join'd with Nature's fondest tie,
Gives to the soul a taste of perfect joy.
A joy so rare, a fervour so refin'd,
Was for this life's peculiar bliss design'd:
"Tho' fann'd by adverse winds, a constant flame,
In every intercourse of life the same."
    Rear'd by her hand, and to an early share
10   Advanc'd of Sappho's love and tender care,
How blest was I through childhood's little scene!
Her soothing smiles made every day serene;
And in maturer life, ne'er seen in vain,
My joy augmented, or assuag'd my pain.
    Her steady judgment and discerning sense,
And truth, that nurse of mutual confidence,
In every feature eminently shone,
While each distinguish'd virtue was her own.
Grace from her lips distill'd like early dew,
20   Sparkling her wit, her converse ever new;
With unaffected ease her wisdom charm'd,
And her sweet counsel every bosom warm'd.

18. Short lyric or narrative poem intended to be sung.
19 Judith Cowper Madan (1702–81). Maria Frances Cecilia Cowper was her oldest daughter.

Such was my parent, such my boasted birth;
And though myself of less conspicuous worth,
Attentive let me still the pattern view,
With humble hope her shining course pursue,
And, steering by her precepts, safely guide
My little bark[20] through life's tempestuous tide.
Oh! to my soul be given that zeal divine,
Sweet saint! that ever animated thine;   30
That constant fire that brighten'd all thy way
To the blest regions of eternal day!
   But ah! how rare such worth as thine to see!
Such innocence! such genuine piety!
All we can frame of human excellence,
And every charm that virtue can dispense,
By sacred chymistry improv'd, refin'd,
Adorn'd my parent's evangelic mind.
   Thou early saint! thy God's peculiar care,
Who gave thee wisdom, goodness, knowledge rare,   40
Taught thee thro' life's perplexing scene to shine,
And prov'd by every mark the work divine,
Farewell!—but only till, my voyage o'er,
Grace join us yet again, to part no more.

(1792)

The Infant's Petition to Be Nursed at Home[21]
Martha Rigby Hale

What! banish me my native home:
Thus early sent abroad to roam!
Commit me to a stranger's care,
Who in my pains will feel no share!
Should fits disturb my midnight rest,

---

20. Small sailboat with three to five masts.

21. In *Emile; or, On Education* (1762) Jean-Jacques Rousseau (1712–78) makes a powerful plea for women to breastfeed their own children; his arguments are similar to Hale's. Eighteenth-century culture's growing preference for breastfeeding created a "virulent outcry against wet nursing" as "moralists, philosophers, physicians, and scientists . . . set out to prove that what was natural in the human body was basically good for the body politic." Marilyn Yalom, *A History of the Breast* (New York: Knopf, 1997), 106.

She'd scold that I her dreams molest;
And with rude hands, and ruder strains,
Add to my misery and pains.—
Was it for this I saw the light,
10   To be debarr'd my parent's sight?
    Not so the little bleating Lamb,
Who close attends the fost'ring dam;[22]
She ne'er gives up the mother's part,
But leaves to man this cruel art.
    Then hear me when I fondly sue
For what e'en nature makes my due.
Think what must be the mother's pleasure,
Who fondly sees her infant treasure
With laughing eye her arms employ,
20   And, crowing with unconscious joy,
Seems from a grateful heart to say,
"A parent's care no thanks can pay."
Think what a father's soft delight,
When gay I gambol[23] in his sight;
Think his fond heart what rapture warms,
When pleas'd I spring into his arms,
My little hands smooth o'er his face,
And in my likeness speak my race;
For want of words gay looks employ,
30   —Such looks! as give fond parents joy—
In which they fancy they can see
A soul from vice and folly free.
Indeed, I'll try your lives to cheer, ⎫
My cries shall cease when you appear, ⎬
Your kiss shall dry the falling tear. ⎭
    Should nurse bestow, with scanty care,
My morn's repast, my ev'ning's fare,
Mama, attentive to my cry,
Will all my infant wants supply,
40   *Her* watchful eye my surest guard,
My fondest love her best reward.
    Then let not nature plead in vain,
Deaf to her cries no more remain;

22. Female parent.
23. To leap or spring, in dancing or sporting.

My growing years I will employ
To give my parents peace and joy;
Attentive to their wish or will,
With pleasure each command fulfil,
And time shall only serve to prove
How well I will deserve their love.

(1800)

To My Daughter, on Being Separated from Her on Her Marriage
Anne Hunter

Dear to my heart as life's warm stream,
   Which animates this mortal clay,
For thee I court the waking dream,
   And deck with smiles the future day;
And thus beguile the present pain
With hopes that we shall meet again.[24]

Yet will it be, as when the past
   Twin'd ev'ry joy, and care, and thought,
And o'er our minds one mantle[25] cast
   Of kind affections finely wrought?   10
Ah no! the groundless hope were vain,
For so we ne'er can meet again!

May he who claims thy tender heart
   Deserve its love, as I have done!
For, kind and gentle as thou art,
   If so belov'd, thou'rt fairly won.
Bright may the sacred torch remain,
And cheer thee till we meet again!

(1802)

24. Though Hunter was estranged from her son, her daughter, Agnes Margaretta, who married
first Sir James Campbell and then, after his death, Benjamin Charlewood, was one of her main supports in her old age.
25. Cloak, sheltering garment.

Sources

Wright: *Gentleman's Magazine* 3 (October 1733): 542; Brereton: *Gentleman's Magazine* 10 (October 1740): 518; Winscom: *Poems on Various Subjects, Entertaining, Elegiac, and Religious* (Bristol, 1786), 153–60; Hands: *The Death of Amnon: A Poem with An Appendix: Containing Pastorals, and other Poetical Pieces* (Coventry, 1789), 123–24; Baillie: *Poems; Wherein It Is Attempted to Describe Certain Views of Nature and of Rustic Manners* (London, 1790), 170–73; Cowper: *Original Poems, on Various Occasions. By a Lady. Revised by William Cowper, Esq.* (London, 1792), 96–98; Hale: *Poetical Attempts* (London, 1800), 16–18; Hunter: *Poems* (London, 1802), 33–34.

⊹M⊱

Poems on the New Year,
Birthdays, and Aging

The poems in this section mark the passage of time—the New Year, the birthday of a friend, the poet's own birthday, or the coming of old age. They address the complicated relationship between women and time and in a variety of tones and forms shatter commonplace opinions such as Alexander Pope's in *Epistle to a Lady* that "Time and Thought" are the "foes" of women. Perhaps most striking are the poems women write in reflection upon their own lives and the past and coming year. The poem Katherine Philips writes on her twenty-sixth birthday muses both on the events she has witnessed, "change of Empire, and the chance of War," and on her poetic potential with her allusion of "future Candidates to wear the Bay" *(On the 1. of January 1657)*. More than one hundred years later, in *Written at the Close of the Year 1794* (2.E), Eliza Tuite also observes the world of war and turmoil that characterized the entire period. The New Year, her thirtieth birthday, and "this fatal Ninety-four, / By treason blasted, steep'd in gore," converge. Susannah Harrison's *New Year* has a prayerlike quality as it expresses concern for those things "neglected by my soul!" and seeks "Heart," "Strength" and "Wisdom" in order to serve God more effectively in the coming year. Anne Hunter's *To a Friend on New Year's Day* is a dignified Horatian epistle that pays tribute to the unchanging affection between herself and her friend and lists what she hopes will be unchanged in herself as the years pass.

The birthday poems vary in mood and draw upon many poetic kinds. Some, as occasional poems written to commemorate a specific event, also share characteristics of the friendship poem in their celebration of the woman's accomplishments and friendships. These poems generally reflect upon the passage of time as an opportunity to recognize achievements, growth, and accumulated wisdom. They embrace qualities that are valuable in the feminine world of women poets rather than lament the loss of power in the patriarchal world of compulsory heterosexuality, where youth and beauty are the dominant commodities. Some of these poets celebrate both the achievements and personal characteristics of their friends. For example, in a richly allusive poem, *To Mrs Roberts on her Spinning*, Jane Brereton compliments her friend's skill with the loom and with life. Similarly, Mary Jones in her poem to her friend Charlotte Clayton praises Clayton's continued kindness and modesty even though she is "now among the nymphs of *Britain*'s Queen" *(Birth-day. To the same)*. Charlotte Smith more playfully explores the passage of time in *Thirty-eight* and more fully identifies the friends with each other. The poem mentions three ages—eighteen, thirty-eight, and forty-eight—thereby playing with past, present, and future and weighing losses and gains. As in a number of these poems, the poet's identity as a poet is a minor theme. Eliza Tuite's *Written on the Birthday of my Best Friend* opens with an echo of Alexander Pope's stance as an honest, discriminating portrayer of deserving friends and, like Anne Hunter's New Year's Day poem, offers a protracted image of the inevitability of mortality. The poem, however, affirms the contrast to the friends' devotion: "Whether adorn'd as now, in beauty's bloom, / Or in old age ... , / Still shall that friendship ... / Preserve to life's *last* gasp its native truth."

Mary Jones, as a few others did, wrote a birthday poem for herself almost every year. These vary considerably, and because they are marked by personal allusions, they challenge interpretation. The metaphoric meaning of Jones's *Birthday*, for instance, may be illuminated only in relation to her other poetic observations on gender power relations. Esther Lewis Clark's poem *A Birth-Day Soliloquy* is a long, searching poem that takes stock of her life, a puritan tradition on birthdays and at the new year. The series of questions—"What passion ... ?" "What fault ... ?" "What vanity ... ?"—makes the first section of the poem a kind of catechism. With skillful alliteration that underscores the passage of time, she cites "Follies on follies, faults on faults arise" and expresses concern that she has misspent her time: " ... our squander'd moments to regain, / With ardent groans we wish, but wish in vain." The poem affirms puritan orthodoxy and offers no relief: "Eternity's begun, and time's no more." As a group the poems completely eschew the dominant cultural values for women—youth and beauty—and construct an alternative system. By focusing on personal accomplishments, intellectual and moral development, and the possibility for the immortality of the soul, the poets offer an empowering way to regard the passage of time.

Many, many poets wrote verses to wish friends a happy birthday, and these poems give clear and rather poignant images of their ideas of happiness. Mary Masters wrote nearly a dozen of them, many with witty statements about age: "Be long preserv'd, free from uneasy Cares, / And not grow old in any thing but Years" (*To Clemene on her Birth-day*, not included). These poems often end with a benediction or a hopeful vision of grace and tranquillity lasting through death. The poems in the final group in this section, poems about age and aging, continue these themes and structures. For example, in *On the Difficulty of Growing Old* Mary Savage writes, "To-morrow, and to-morrow, steals a joy" and "Each, for a while, defer the mighty change." Thus her poem records the contrast between past and present, youth and age, that is present in many of the poems in this section. Also like the others, it portrays a future; in this case one that is something of the ideal for many in her culture. Some of the best poems take women through the stages of their lives and, like those by Masters, Harrison, Clark, Tuite, and Hunter, are original, valuable examples of life writing.

Few have said it better than Anne Finch does in the poem that opens the final group of poems, *An Epilogue to the Tragedy of Jane Shore:* women "dwindle" from *"fair* and *young"* to *"fine"* to *"well as yet"* to *"well enough"* to *"good,"* when it is time to "retire," to avoid being one of the "Ghosts of Beauty" who "glide, / And haunt the places where their Honour dy'd."[1] She was almost certainly fifty-three when she wrote these lines for Anne Oldfield to speak about a play representing Jane Shore, and she would be dead at fifty-nine. In our time, "ageism," prejudice and discrimination against the old, has been documented to be as pervasive and at least as destructive as sexism and racism.[2] In her prodigious book *The Coming of Age* Simone de Beauvoir quotes Johann Wolfgang von Goethe (1749–1832) and continues, "'Age takes hold of us by surprise'. . . . and we are often astonished when the common fate becomes our own." She gives examples of people, including herself, who were startled by matter-of-fact observations: "'It comes as a shock . . . the first time he hears himself called "old,"' observed Oliver Wendell Holmes."[3] Even before eyesight changes and the joints ache, a matter-of-fact statement suddenly forces people to begin to submit to the outside point of view. As de Beauvoir says, "Within me it is the Other—that is to say the person I am for the outsider—who is old. . . . Yet our private, inward experience does not tell us the number of our years. . . . Old age is more apparent to others than to the subject" (284).

The women poets in this section have experienced this disjuncture. They are self-assured, confident of their minds and writing lives, and formidable social critics, wonderful commentators positioned to disrupt male ideologies of gender and age. In a classic satiric move, Finch's poem holds up a mirror to Nicholas Rowe: "Whate'er he makes us women do or say, / . . . [we won't] go fast and pray." Savage's *On the Difficulty of Growing Old* makes many of the same points that Finch does, including the different experiences of old men and old women. Her dignified poem uses Pope's metonymy of women's reluctance to "quit the former scene," but she firmly refutes society's "sentence" as she summarizes it: "Age of itself can render life despised." Instead, she takes Pope's verb, *glide,* and turns woman's old age into the possibility of "Gliding, with chearful ease, thro' length of days." Three of these poems use the trope of woman's nemesis, the mirror, as the central image. As de Beauvoir says, it is the mirror that confirms the outside judgment. Maria Frances Cecilia Cowper's little gem of a poem, *On Seeing a Certain Advertisement,* expresses the surprise of realizing that youth is past. Like Finch's, Sarah Dixon's poem *The Looking-Glass* begins as a familiar kind of satire, but its ending is far from conventional. Janet Little titles her poem *Celia and*

Her Looking Glass and also gives her heroine a surprising, happy ending. The final poem, Susanna Blamire's *When the Sunbeams of Joy,* picks up Cowper's image of an eye-catching bauble as it traces the ages of life in three beautiful images. In these poems on aging, women confront the insulting expectations of their society and substitute their own experiences and alternative stories. They create characters, such as Jane Shore, whom their male contemporaries seem to be falsifying, and other characters, such as Evadne, who begin as stereotypes but turn temper tantrums into self-possessed triumphs.

Because the poems in this section are filled with memories, assessments, and details of lived lives, they are valuable as life writing. However, they are especially important because they provide evidence about identity construction and imaginings of different ways of thinking and living that lead to the development of philosophies of life that give serenity. De Beauvoir quotes Madame de Sévigné: "Providence leads us so kindly through all these different stages of our life that we hardly feel them at all. The slope runs gently down" (287). These poems are some of the strongest examples of women cocking their heads and saying decidedly, "Here's another way of thinking."

Notes

1. The "Ghosts of Beauty" image is from Alexander Pope's *Epistle II. To a Lady,* lines 241–42.

2. Margaret M. Gullette, *Aged by Culture* (Chicago: University of Chicago Press, 2004), 21–39, 79–97; Bernice L. Neugarten, "Adult Personality: Toward a Psychology of the Life Cycle," in *Middle Age and Aging* (Chicago: University of Chicago Press, 1968), 139–43.

3. Simone de Beauvoir, *The Coming of Age,* trans. Patrick O'Brian (New York: G. P. Putnam's Sons, 1972), 283, 288.

THE NEW YEAR

On the *1.* of *January 1657*
Katherine Philips

Th' Eternal Centre of my life and me,
Who when I was not gave me room to be,
Hath since (my time preserving in his hands)
By moments numbred out the precious sand,
Till it is swell'd to six and twenty years,
Checquer'd by Providence with smiles and tears.
I have observ'd how vain all glories are,
The change of Empire, and the chance of War:
Seen Faction with its native venom burst,
And Treason struck, by what it self had nurs'd.   10
Seen useless Crimes, whose Owners but made way,
For future Candidates to wear the Bay.[1]

(1667)

New Year
Susannah Harrison

1 Rapid my Days and Months run on,
   How soon another Year is gone!
   How swift my golden Moments roll,
   How much neglected by my Soul!

2 Let me begin with holy Fear
   This new, this fleeting, flying Year;
   Too many unimprov'd have pass'd,
   This Year, perhaps, may be my last!

3 Give me, Great God, an Heart to pray;
   Let all old things be done away;   10
   Give me new Strength to conquer Sin,
   And plant new Holiness within.

1.Wreath of woven laurel worn by a poet.

4 I ask new Wisdom for this Year,
New Fitness for my Trials here;
Of ev'ry Grace a richer Store,
My God to love and honour more.

5 This Year, O sheath War's direful Sword!
Let ev'ry Nation serve the LORD:
Visit thy Church, and may she bear
20   Much glorious Fruit, this blessed Year!

(1780)

To a Friend on New Year's Day
Anne Hunter

Dear friend, for thee, through ev'ry changing year,
Unchang'd affection draws the tie more near;
Treasure most precious, dearest to the heart,
Increas'd in value as the rest depart.
Tho' kindred bonds may break, and love must fade,
Friendship still brightens in the deep'ning shade.
Time, silent and unseen, pursues his course,
And wearied nature sickens at her source.
Methinks I see the season onward roll,
10   When age, like winter, comes to chill the soul:
I tremble at that pow'r's resistless sway
Who bears the flowers and fruit of life away.
   Sudden to cease, or gently to decline,
O, Power of Mercy! may the lot be mine:
Let me not linger on the verge of fate,
Nor weary duty to its utmost date;
Losing, in pain's impatient gloom confin'd,
Freedom of thought, and dignity of mind;
Till pity views untouch'd the parting breath,
20   And cold indiff'rence adds a pang to death.
Yet if to suffer long my doom is past,
Let me preserve this temper to the last:
O let me still from self my feelings bear,
To sympathise with sorrow's starting tear,

Nor sadden at the smile which joy bestows,
Though far from me her beam ethereal glows:
Let me remember, in the gloom of age,
To smile at follies happier youth engage;
See them fallacious, but indulgent spare
The fairy dreams experience cannot share.   30
Nor view the rising morn with jaundice eye,
Because for me no more the sparkling moments fly.

(1802)

BIRTHDAYS

To Mrs *Roberts* on her Spinning.
Written on her Birth-day, Jan. 6, 1731.
Jane Brereton

Penelope did thus her Time employ,
Till her lov'd wand'ring Lord return'd from *Troy*;[2]
While He was fated thro' strange Realms to roam,
The prudent Queen play'd the good Wife at Home;
While he the various Turns of Fortune knew,
She ply'd the Loom, and th' Ivory Shuttle[3] threw.

So the dull Hours you at your Wheel deceive,
And draw a Web, fit for a Queen to weave.

Wise the Resolve, when to your Wheel you sate,
The Wheel, best Emblem of our worldly State;   10
Still changing, varying, always moving found,
Where high and low, alternate, take their round,
With skilful Hand you manage this Machine,
May like Success thro' all your Life be seen!

2. Penelope waited twenty years for Odysseus to return from the Trojan War; his travels are recounted in the *Odyssey*.
3. An instrument used in weaving for passing the thread of the weft to and fro, from one edge of
the cloth to the other, between the threads of the warp.

May each revolving Year with Joy be crown'd,
And this your Natal Day still happy found!

Let no proud Dame the Spinning Art despise,
Which from the wise *Minerva*[4] took its Rise;
And which *Aliza* for Amusement chose
20   To lighten Absence, and to soften Woes.

(1744)

Birth-day

Mary Jones

Come, my Muse, prepare the lay,[5]
Once more hail this happy Day.
Bid it shine o'er all the past;
Brightest, since it is the last.
For her full meridian ray,
Soon must sicken, and decay:
See ! she hastens down the skies,
In another sphere to rise;
In a world unknown, untry'd,
10   Sets a Maid, to rise a Bride.

So the sun, with splendid ray,
Having shone his summer's day,
Gilding all the groves and plains,
Drops at length the golden reins,
And night's curtain round him spread,
Hides his beams in *Thetis*'[6] bed.

(1750)

4. Roman goddess of wisdom and of handicrafts and the arts.
5. Song, poetic offering.
6. Thetis, daughter of Nereus, was a Nereid, a demi-goddess. Beloved by Zeus, Thetis was fated to have a son more powerful than his father. Thus, Zeus determined that she should be the wife of a mortal, and she was married to Peleus. The Greek hero Achilles was her son.

Birth-day. To the same [Charlotte Clayton], on Richmond Green, Soon after her being Maid of Honour to Queen Caroline.[7]

Mary Jones

Bring, bring the lyre,[8] to usher in the morn;
Delia, the gentlest Maid, to day was born:
And tho' she twenty summer suns has seen,
Tho' now among the nymphs of *Britain*'s Queen, ⎫
Is still the gentlest Maid upon the green. ⎭
Sure guardian Sylphs around her paths attend!
Without a foe, and worthy ev'ry Friend.

   In one bright calm may each succeeding year
Roll guiltless on, unruffled by a care!
Till future Maids of Honour have approv'd   10
The grove she haunted, and the stream she lov'd:
And each bright Sister, emulous, proclaim,
That *Innocence* and *Pleasure* are the same.

                                     (1750)

A Birth-Day Soliloquy

Esther Lewis Clark

'Tis past, another year is roll'd away,
And time, once more has brought my natal day.
All these past circling hours heav'n's bounty lent,
But say, my soul, how have these hours been spent,
What conquest o'er myself have I obtain'd?
What passion is subdu'd, what virtue gain'd?
What fault is crush'd, what error is abjur'd?
What vanity cashier'd,[9] what folly cur'd?

---

7. Charlotte Clayton (1679–1742), Jones's close friend, was appointed a Woman of the Bedchamber to Caroline, Princess of Wales, in 1714. Caroline became queen in 1727.

8. A stringed instrument of the harp kind, used by the Greeks for accompanying song and recitation; the symbol of lyric poetry.

9. Discarded, put aside.

Have I with industry improv'd the share
10   Of talents heav'n committed to my care?
Have I been faithful in th' important trust,
Both to my GOD, myself, and neighbour just?
Have I been careful to preserve from sin
That spark of heav'nly fire, which burns within?
Daily adorn'd that best immortal part,
And kept a jealous eye upon my heart?
And does my breast no thought or wish conceal,
For which, if known, my cheeks a blush might feel?
Have I that precious talent, time, well us'd,
20   And ne'er th' invaluable gift abus'd?
Have I, with care, for heav'nly wisdom sought?
And have I practis'd what that wisdom taught?
Hath reason still been victor of the field,
Nor did it once to rebel passion yield?

My conscious heart declines the strict survey,
A blush without, the blots within betray;
Follies on follies, faults on faults arise,
Some lesser spots, and some of larger size.

O time, thou precious treasure, how have I,
30   Regardless of thy value, let thee fly?
How have I lavish'd thee, thou costly store!
How many years are sunk to rise no more!
Another year has now begun its race,
While time glides on, unseen, with rapid pace;
Let me regard each future hour as given
By the Supreme, to make me ripe for heav'n;
Seize ev'ry rising moment as it springs,
Eternity and heav'n are on their wings.

How many in the gaudy spring of life,
40   E'er rack'd by secret anguish, care, or strife,
Have I beheld, like morning clouds, decay,
And set just in the dawn of rising day;
Upon the stage of life appear'd, look round,
But in another scene were never found.

Say then, my soul, what cause canst thou assign,
Why he, who cut their thread,[10] has lengthen'd thine.
Was it for worth, or merit of thy own?
Ah no! 'twas heav'n's indulgent love alone.
Ten thousand times have I deserv'd like fate,
But heav'n was patient and compassionate;   50
While I, regardless of the mighty loan,
Took the intrusted talent as my own;
And on a thousand trifles vainly spent
That time, which heav'n, to be improv'd, had lent.

How do mankind this best of talents use?
Nine parts in ten the precious gift abuse;
Squander the ne'er-to-be-recover'd store,
More worth than all the wealth of India's shore.
Nor crowns, nor kingdoms, nor whole world's can buy,
O time, one hour, from thy vast treasury;   60
Immense thy worth, each hour's the grant of heav'n,
If well improv'd, eternal life is giv'n.
Yet mortals, who enjoy this mighty loan,
Beneath the cumb'rous burden tire and groan,
And gen'rously upon their friends bestow
A heavy load, they know not where to throw,
Scatter the costly treasure thoughtless round
On all, who to accept it can be found;
Nor its inestimable worth perceive,
'Till 'tis too late that treasure to retrieve.   70

In vain the preacher speaks, in vain he writes,
In vain the sage philosopher indites;[11]
We hear, we feel; the bright conviction's clear,
Yet still in vain we b'lieve, in vain we hear;
We still go on, tho' still they write, and preach,
And rarely practice what their precepts teach.
Th' important truths, tho' prest with moving art,
Make but a slight impression on the heart;

---

10. Allusion to the continued course of life, represented in classical mythology as a thread that is spun and cut off by the Fates. Klotho spins the thread of life, Lakhesis determines the length of the thread, and Atropos cuts the thread when the proper time has come for death.

11. Pronounces or writes.

A tide of pleasures, or a tide of care,
80   Erase the imperfect characters writ there:
'Tis death alone (pathetic preacher) can
Imprint those truths deep in the heart of man.
One single sentence spoke by him does more,
Than all their oratory did before.
But ah? too late he speaks, we hear too late,
Our glass[12] is run, determin'd is our fate.

And now, our squander'd moments to regain,
With ardent groans we wish, but wish in vain;
Whole worlds we'd freely give, if worlds we had,
90   But one poor hour to parting life to add,
Nor wealth, nor world's can purchase that poor hour
We've now the will to mend, but not the pow'r.
Revers'd our case by death's emphatic skill,
Before we had the pow'r, but not the will.

Time long abus'd now rings our passing knell,
Death ope's the eternal gates to heav'n or hell.
Amaz'd we view the deep, the dark abyss,
Which leads to everlasting woe, or bliss.
Fears press on fears, in ghastly horrors drest,
100   Within, without, on ev'ry side distrest;
Black scenes before, if back we turn our eyes,
The ghosts of our departed days arise;
Those slaughter'd friends, who by our folly bled,
Call loud for vengeance on their murd'rers' head.
Conscience pleads guilty to the heavy bill,
Conscience, just judge, and faithful witness still.
Full of distracting horrors pale we stand,
Aghast, and trembling on the dreary strand;
Death drags us headlong down the dreadful steep,
110   Amaz'd we plunge into the boundless deep;
One instant lands us on the unknown shore,
Eternity's begun, and time's no more.

(1789)

12. Hourglass, a reference to the passage of time.

Thirty-eight
Address'd to Mrs. H[ayle]y [13]

Charlotte Smith

In early youth's unclouded scene,
The brilliant morning of eighteen,
With health and sprightly joy elate
   We gaz'd on life's enchanting spring,
   Nor thought how quickly time would bring
The mournful period——Thirty-eight.

Then the starch maid, or matron sage,
Already of that sober age,
We view'd with mingled scorn and hate;
   In whose sharp words, or sharper face,   10
   With thoughtless mirth we lov'd to trace
The sad effects of——Thirty-eight.

Till saddening, sickening at the view,
We learn'd to dread what time might do;
And then preferr'd a prayer to Fate
   To end our days ere that arriv'd;
   When (pow'r and pleasure long surviv'd)
We met neglect and——Thirty-eight.

But Time, in spite of wishes flies,
And Fate our simple prayer denies,   20
And bids us Death's own hour await:
   The auburn locks are mix'd with grey,
   The transient roses fade away,
But Reason comes at——Thirty-eight.

Her voice the anguish contradicts
That dying vanity inflicts;
Her hand new pleasures can create,

13. Eliza Ball Hayley (1750–97) married the poet William Hayley when she was nineteen, and by all accounts the marriage was difficult. Mr. Hayley fathered an illegitimate child born in 1780, and Eliza had chronic health problems, which, in part, prompted Hayley to send her to Derby in the 1780s. Shortly after this poem was written, she separated from him permanently. The marriage ended acrimoniously in 1795.

For us she opens to the view
Prospects less bright—but far more true,
30 And bids us smile at——Thirty-eight.

No more shall *Scandal*'s breath destroy
The social converse we enjoy
With bard or critic tête à tête;—
  O'er Youth's bright blooms her blights shall pour,
  But spare the improving friendly hour
That Science gives to —— Thirty-eight.

Stripp'd of their gaudy hues by truth,
We view the glitt'ring toys of youth,
And blush to think how poor the bait
40 For which to public scenes we ran
  And scorn'd of sober sense the plan
Which gives content at——Thirty-eight.

Tho' Time's inexorable sway
Has torn the myrtle bands[14] away,
For other wreaths 'tis not too late,
  The amaranth's[15] purple glow survives,
  And still Minerva's olive[16] lives
On the calm brow of——Thirty-eight.

With eye more steady we engage
50 To contemplate approaching age,
And life more justly estimate;
  With firmer souls, and stronger powers,
  With reason, faith, and friendship ours,
  We'll not regret the stealing hours
That lead from Thirty—even to Forty-eight.

(1792)

14. A garland of myrtle is associated with love and honor.

15. A flower reputed never to fade; the name derives from the Greek adjective *amarantus*, meaning "everlasting."

16. Minerva is the Roman name for the Greek goddess Pallas Athena, goddess of wisdom, poetry, useful and ornamental arts, and, within Rome itself, war. She sprang from the head of Jupiter mature and fully armed. The plant sacred to her is the olive, and in statuary and art she is frequently represented with a wreath of olive leaves on her head.

Written on the Birth-Day of my Best Friend
Eliza Tuite

Peace to the Bard, whose Muse well-tutor'd sings
On each returning year the birth of kings;[17]
May royal gifts reward his duteous lays,[18]
And crown with well-earn'd wealth his fruitful bays.[19]
For *me* to whom the monarch's smile's unknown,
(Tho' few more loyal hearts surround his throne)
Who *scorn* to bow before Ambition's shrine,
And seek no wealth beyond what's *freely mine;*
My artless song the great ones may deride,
(The voice of *flatt'ry* suits the ear of *pride*)   10
But white-rob'd *Truth* inspires my humble strains,
And guides them to the heart, wherein *she* reigns;
At Friendship's feet my willing vows I'll pay,
And greet with *unbought* zeal, this welcome day:
This day to orphans did a *parent* lend,
To sorrow comfort, and to *me* a *friend;*
This day (if prescience is to mortals given)
Was *Laura* born, to guide my steps to heaven;
Come, welcome day, thy glad return I hail,
This day may joy in ev'ry heart prevail,   20
May anguish meet relief, may trouble rest,
And hope returning, cheer each aching breast;
And *thou,* for whose dear sake I daily raise,
My feeble voice in pray'r, my heart in praise;
(If gracious heav'n will deign that pray'r to hear;)
Oh may *this day,* thro' each revolving year,
With Peace (fair inmate of the spotless breast),
And Health, and calm Contentment find thee blest,
May Love unchang'd, and Hope for ever new,
Thy joys perpetuate, thy cares subdue;   30
Till like the ev'ning of a summer's day,
Thy life by slow degrees shall ebb away:
Meanwhile, Remembrance pointing to the past,
Shall gild the present scene, and cheer the *last.*

17. Writing birthday poems for members of the royal family was a duty of the poet laureate.
18. Short lyric or narrative poems intended to be sung.
19. The wreath of laurels symbolizing the poet laureate's status.

Still thro' each varying season will thy friend,
With constant care, upon thy couch attend;
Whether adorn'd as now, in beauty's bloom,
Or in old age descending to the tomb,
Still shall that friendship form'd in earliest youth,
40   Preserve to life's *last* gasp its native truth,
Devote to *thee* and *thine* its latest breath,
By Time unmov'd, nor yet destroy'd by Death.

(1796)

AGE AND AGING

An Epilogue to the Tragedy of Jane Shore[20]
Anne Finch

To be spoken by Mrs. Oldfield[21] *the night before the Poet's Day*[22]

The audience seems tonight so very kind,
I fancy I may freely speak my mind,
And tell you, when the author nam'd Jane Shore,

20. Nicholas Rowe's *Tragedy of Jane Shore* was one of the two longest-running plays of the century. Finch's epilogue may have been written to encourage attendance at the second benefit for Rowe, on 8 February 1714. Her epilogue has been interpreted as a rejoinder to Alexander Pope's for the first benefit, on 4 February. Pope praised Jane Shore's wronged husband, and he called attention to the actress's conduct, implying that the women in the audience might also "sin" in lines such as "So from a sister sinner you shall hear, / 'How strangely you expose your self, my dear!'" In contrast, Finch's epilogue is a witty exposé of the fact that Rowe and Pope have turned the mesmerizing Jane into a spectacle of female repentance and virtue. Both epilogues end with appeals: "Come here in crowds," writes Pope, but Finch's appeal is ironic.

21. Anne Oldfield (1683–1730), one of the greatest actresses in the century, created the role of Jane Shore. Finch's epilogue takes full advantage of her lively personality and complete power over her audience. Oldfield was known for being part of a tradition in which actresses addressed audiences in their own voices in prologues and epilogues, and parts of Finch's poem acknowledge her love affairs, first with Arthur Mainwaring until his death and then, just beginning, with Charles Churchill. She was also one of the most highly paid actresses of the century; one of her benefits, in 1729, brought her £500.

22. The "Poet's Day" was the benefit for the playwright, when he or she received all of the profits for the evening as well as monetary gifts from special supporters. Rowe's benefits in February were unusual in that entrance was by advanced ticket purchase only, and tickets were half a guinea, an unusually high price. Finch's biographers note that she had a longstanding friendship with Rowe, and the success of her book the year before the play opened would have made her epilogue a draw. Barbara McGovern, *Anne Finch and Her Poetry: A Critical Biography* (Athens: University of Georgia Press, 1992), 46–47; Charles H. Hinnant, *The Poetry of Anne Finch: An Essay in Interpretation* (Newark: University of Delaware Press, 1994), 62.

I all her glorious history run o'er,[23]
And thought he would have shewn her on the stage,
In the first triumphs of her blooming age;
Edward in public at her feet a slave,
The jealous Queen in private left to rave;
Yet *Jane* superior still in all the strife,
For sure that mistress leads a wretched life,   10
Who can't insult the Keeper and the wife.
This I concluded was his right design,
To make her lavish, careless, gay and fine;
Not bring her here to mortify and whine.
I hate such parts as we have plaid today,
Before I promis'd, had I read the play,
I wou'd have staid at home, and drank my Tea.
Then why the husband shou'd at last be brought
To hear her own and aggravate her fault,
Puzzled as much my discontented thought.   20
For were I to transgress, for all the Poet,
I'll swear no friend of mine should ever know it.
But you perhaps are pleas'd to see her mended,
And so should I; had all her charms been ended.
But whilst another lover might be had,
The woman or the Poet must be mad.
There is a season, which too fast approaches,
And every list'ning beauty nearly touches;
When handsome Ladies, falling to decay,
Pass thro' new epithets to smooth the way: 30
From *fair* and *young* transportedly confess'd,
Dwindle to *fine, well fashion'd,* and *well dress'd.*
Thence as their fortitude's extremest proof,
To *well as yet;* from *well* to *well enough;*
Till having on such weak foundation stood,
Deplorably at last they sink to *good.*
Abandon'd then, 'tis time to be retir'd,
And seen no more, when not alas! admir'd.

23. When Rowe wrote his play, the story of Jane Shore was familiar, having long been retold in ballads and featured in plays, such as Thomas Heywood's *King Edward the Fourth.* Jane, the only child of a mercer, married William Shore, a goldsmith. William Hastings, Edward's Lord Chamberlain, was unable to seduce her but told King Edward, "the handsomest man in Europe," about her. She resisted, but in 1476 became she became his royal mistress. The play opens shortly after Edward dies, when Jane is at the mercy of various competitors for the crown and her person. For an account of the story's fame, see Maria M. Scott, *Re-Presenting "Jane" Shore* (Burlington, VT: Ashgate, 2005).

By men indeed a better fate is known.
40   The pretty fellow, that has youth outgrown,
Who nothing knew, but how his cloaths did sit,
Transforms to a *Free-thinker*[24] and a *Wit;*[25]
At Operas becomes a skill'd Musician;
Ends in a partyman and politician;
Maintains some figure, while he keeps his breath,
And is a fop of consequence till death.
And so would I have had our mistress Shore
To make a figure, till she pleas'd no more.
But if you better like her present sorrow,
50   Pray let me see you here again to-morrow,
And should the house be throng'd the Poets' day,
Whate'er he makes us women do or say,
You'll not believe, that he'll go fast and pray.

(1714; 1741)

The Looking-Glass

Sarah Dixon

1.

Evadne[26] once a flaming Toast,
    Perceiv'd her Power decay;
Never consider'd Time rides Post,[27]
    Nor will be brib'd to stay.

2.

Poor *Jenny*[28] oft' was in Disgrace
    When Things succeeded ill;
No Fault there cou'd be in her Face,
    'Twas *Jenny*'s want of Skill.

3.

Madam, says *Jenny*, all in Tears,
10   You can't be better drest;

24. Person who refuses to subordinate his or her reason to any authority or religious belief.
25. Person who is quick with clever repartee and observations, a socially desirable appellation.
26. In Greek legend, the wife of Capaneus. She threw herself on the funeral pyre of her husband.
27. Carriers of news or mail rode horses on fixed routes, often speedily.
28. Common name for a maidservant.

Your Ladyship to me appears
   A *Venus*,[29] I protest.

4.

New place the Glass, *Evadne* cries,
   What can the Matter be?
Aminta[30] now has all those Eyes,
   Which once were fixt on me!

5.

The Toy was mov'd from Side to Side,
   Yet gave us no Content;
At length to break it both agreed,
   By way of Punishment.   20

6.

The Guardian *Silph*[31] who lay conceal'd
   Within the Mirror's Frame,
Soon as their Mischief was reveal'd
   Accosted thus the Dame:

7.

Evadne! darling of my Care,
   Your Anger is in vain;
The innocent Reflector spare,
   Of what do'st thou complain?

8.

Was not an early Homage paid
   Those Charms you now deplore?   30
Remember, thou ungrateful Maid,
   Thy past despotick Power.

9.

Art thou, *Evadne,* yet to learn
   There is no second Spring,

---

29. Roman goddess of beauty and love, mother of Cupid.

30. The name is from Torquato Tasso's pastoral play *Aminta* (1573).

31. Sylphs were said to be spirits inhabiting the air; in myths and stories, they often became guardians. Here probably a poetic device borrowed from Alexander Pope's *Rape of the Lock,* in which Belinda has guardian sylphs.

For that which gives thee this Concern,
  And all this Trifling.

10.

Partial to thee, my darling Care!
  Beyond frail Nature's Date;
I have preserv'd thee still so fair,
40   But now 'tis not in Fate.

11.

No Flower so sweet, so fresh, so gay,
  Can stand the Winter's Blast;
Their Bloom goes off, they soon decay,
  And wither thus at last.

12.

Jane,—bring my Night-Dress, put it on,
  And set the Glass aside;
When once a Woman's Beauty's gone,
  How needless is her Pride?

(1740)

On the Difficulty of Growing Old
Mary Savage

I am convinced that dotage, tho' the usual, is
not a necessary effect of age;—but the mind
grows indolent about the middle stage of life;
and the exercise of reading and reflection,
which is requisite to prevent our sense and
apprehension from stagnating becomes too great
a labour to us, unless a happy and more early
habit should have rendered it easy and familiar.
    Ninon de L'Enclos,[32] Vol. I. page 45,
    Translator to the Reader

---

32. Anne "Ninon" de L'Enclos (1620–1705) was a French writer known for her liaisons with important men. She was also a patron of the arts, and her salon was frequented by writers, artists, scientists,
and other distinguished visitors to Paris. She wrote poetry, and her letters were published, but her

When memory recals our infant hours,
Remark, my friend, how trifling they appear;
How lightly we esteem those gilded toys,
Which, then possess'd, bestow'd supreme delight.
Then eager, pressing forward into life,
We blam'd the slow-pac'd minutes as they ran,
And fancy'd joy annexed to life's gay prime.

By inclination led to different schemes,
Grandeur, and pow'r, soft love, or mighty gold,
Exert their sway, and rule the anxious throng;   10
And self-applause, approving every act,
Gives flattering hope each wish shall be possess'd.

Reflect, (alas! how common is the thought
By sad experience taught) how few have reach'd,
The wish'd for state.

To-morrow, and to-morrow, steals a joy,
And each day mourns a disappointed former:
By unperceiv'd degrees life's prime decays,
Neglected passing, and regreted past.

But when, from added years, we first perceive   20
The loss of youth, how slow the steps we take;
With what reluctance quit the former scene!
No longer lightly we esteem past joys;
No longer drive the tardy minutes on;
But fondly wishing for past hours again,
Pursue youth's paths, nor feel that time still flies.

At rising life we scorn'd our infant joys,
At its decline, with timid glance, we view
Approaching age,—and blush at mem'ry's length.

But chief the fair (forbid to mourn, or boast   30
Their conquests past) regret their loss of charms,

---

most noted literary work is *La Coquette vengée* (1659), a response to Félix de Juvenel's (b. 1617) attack on the feminist movement, *Le Portrait de la Coquette*. This quotation is taken from the "Translator to the Reader" prefacing *The Life and Character of Ninon de L'Enclos*, which is the middle part of Douxménil, *The Memoirs of Ninon de L'Enclos, with Her Letters to Monsr. de St. Evremond and to the Marquis de Sevigné*, trans. Elizabeth Griffith, 2 vols. (London, 1761), 1:45–46.

When reason rising, as the form decays,
Serves but to strongly point their empire lost.

  Lord of his words, man longer may conceal
His date of age,—and fancy conquests still.

  Each, for a while, defer the mighty change;
Making an uncouth pause; 'twixt youth and age;
'Till tir'd with trying to retard the hour,
At length they follow nature's great behests,[33]
40   And from reflection of a youth misused,
Brag out a churlish age, devoid of ease;
And ill judged alms, with grudging hand dispense,
To bribe a pardon for a life of sin.

  Yet hard the sentence that shall dare pronounce,
Age of itself can render life despised.
There are, who happy in a mind serene,
With conscious pleasure scan their actions past,
Nor find a cause to bid their blushes rise,
But for the errors of unguarded youth;
50   Whose thoughts rais'd high, depend on heav'n for joy,
Gliding, with chearful ease, thro' length of days,
Nor hope aught here but what content can give.

(1777)

Celia and Her Looking Glass
Janet Little

As Celia,[34] who a coquette was,
  O'er fading charms lamented,
She frown'd upon her looking-glass,
  And thus her spleen[35] she vented.

33. Commands.
34. In Renaissance literature, a name for a ladylove.
35. Irritation, depression.

"Thou silly, stupid, worthless thing,
    Of all discretion empty,
I o'er the window will thee sling,
    If any more you tempt me.

"Thou'rt incorrigible and bold,
    Unworthy my attention: 10
What! must I ever more be told,
    The thing I dread to mention?

"A maiden old, kind heaven avert;
    I hate the appellation.
The blood runs chill about my heart,
    I'm choak'd with sore vexation.

"Last night when at the ball I danc'd,
    My air[36] was counted charming;
My eyes gave pain where'er they glanc'd,
    Each gesture prov'd alarming.   20

"Philander[37] saw, their pow'r confest,
    And with love tales did tease me!
I sigh'd, I frown'd, he was distress'd,
    But with my smiles seem'd easy.

"But Chloe[38] mark'd, that new made toast,
    By other flirts surrounded,
Poor Celia now her charms had lost,
    Which in last cent'ry wounded.

"A whisper then and laugh went round,
    Such scoffing I endured,   30
Nor did Philander heed my frown,
    But by the jest was cured.

36. Bearing, often affected movement and poses.

37. Trifling, promiscuous lover, a male coquette named after the Dutch knight in Ariosto's *Orlando Furioso*. A number of texts made the name conventional, including Beaumont and Fletcher's *Laws of Candy* and Aphra Behn's *Love Letters between a Nobleman and his Sister*.

38. Another name common in romances and pastorals.

"An easy passage through the crowd
　I found, none did escort me;
No gallant youth my presence su'd,
　Nor flatter'd to support me.

"Now Morpheus[39] next I did address,
　For slumbers more delightful;
But in my dreams I found distress,
40　　With apes[40] and spectres frightful.

"Then unto thee, thou base ingrate,
　I su'd for consolation,
Who rudely now foretels my fate
　Without alleviation.

"Though I'm abandon'd on that score,
　Though fools and fops are changed,
Of thy impertinence no more,
　Else sure I'll be revenged."

Its head the looking-glass did bow,
50　　With reverent low submission,
And to its angry mistress now,
　Did utter this petition.

"O madam, deign[41] to hear my tale,
　And let my sorrows move ye;
My plain sincerity can't fail
　To shew how much I love you.

"Nor lap-dog, bird, or powder'd beau
　Was more by you regarded,
Than I full fifteen years ago,
60　　Though basely now discarded.

"Each hour you paid me visits ten,
　My counsel well you trusted;

39. Ovid's name for the son of Sleep and the god of dreams.
40. Old maids were said to lead apes to hell. A medieval legend pronounced this fate for women married neither to God as nuns nor to men.
41. Condescend.

Without my approbation then
  No curls you e'er adjusted.

"An artless smile adorn'd your cheek,
  And grac'd each lovely feature,
Which I observe now, once a-week,
  Distorted by ill nature.

"The pallid cheek and wrinkl'd brow
  Announce your charms declining;   70
And wont you take the vestal vow[42]
  Without so much repining?

"The truth, though in unwelcome strain,
  To you I must discover;
While youth or beauty sways the swain,[43]
  You'll never find a lover."

Poor Celia now could bear no more,
  Her stars malignant cursed;
Her looking-glass cast on the floor,
  And into tears she bursted.   80

She would have died, but Claudia[44] came,
  Preventing all her fears;
He wed the pensive, weeping dame,
  And wip'd away her tears.

                                    (1792)

On Seeing a Certain Advertisement
Maria Frances Cecilia Cowper

So then—farewell ye fugitive delights,
Ye glassy splendours, once so much enjoy'd,

---

42. Vow to be a virgin. The term is from the vestal virgins, the priestesses who tended the sacred fire in the temple of Vesta, virgin goddess of the hearth, in Rome.

43. Country man; lover.

44. Perhaps she has in mind Claudio, in Shakespeare's *Measure for Measure,* whose best-known speech is on the fear of death.

And hop'd more lasting—O my halcyon days,[45]
Whose pleasing round of gay felicities
The wisest had beguil'd—farewell for ever!
　So the pleas'd child who hath a bubble rais'd,
Joys in the airy globe, and views, surpris'd,
The gaudy colours that its surface shews;
But ere his raptur'd eye beholds his face
In the slight mirror, with a sudden burst
It vanishes, and can be found no more.

(1792)

When the Sunbeams of Joy
Susanna Blamire

When the sunbeams of joy gild the morn of our days,
And the soft heart is warm'd both with hope and with praise,
New pleasures, new prospects, still burst on the view,
And the phantom of bliss in our walks we pursue:
What tho' tangl'd in brakes,[46] or withheld by the thorn,
Such sorrows of youth are but pearls of the morn;
As they "gem the light leaf"[47] in the fervour of day,
The warmth of the season dissolves them away.

In the noon-tide of life, though not robb'd of their fire,
The warm wishes abate, and the spirits retire;
Thus pictures less glowing give equal delight,
When reason just tints them with shades of the night;
Reflection's slow shadow steals down the gay hill,
Though as yet you may shun the soft shade as you will,
And on hope fix your eye, till the brightness, so clear,
Shall hang on its lid a dim trembling tear.

Next, the shades of mild evening close gently around,
And lengthen'd reflection must stalk o'er the ground;

45. Period of peace and tranquility; especially days of fine weather occurring near the time of the winter solstice.

46. Dense, tangled brushwood, briers, and undergrowth.

47. Adorn as with gems. Quotation from Anna Seward's wildly popular *Louisa, A Poetical Novel* (1784): "The plenteous dews, that in the early ray / Gem the light leaf, and tremble on the spray."

Through her lantern of magic[48] past pleasures are seen,
And we then only know what our day-dreams have been: 20
On the painted illusion we gaze while we can,
Though we often exclaim, What a bauble[49] is man!—
In youth but a gewgaw[50]—in age but a toy—
The same empty trifle as man and as boy!

(before 1794; 1842)

Sources

The New Year. Philips: *Poems by the Most Deservedly Admired Mrs. Katherine Philips, the Matchless Orinda* (London, 1667), 141–42; Harrison: *Songs in the Night* (London, 1780), 1; Hunter: *Poems* (London, 1802), 69–70.

  Birthdays. Brereton: *Poems on Several Occasions* (London, 1744), 100–101; Jones: *Miscellanies in Prose and Verse* (Oxford, 1750), 151–52, 117; Clark: *Poems Moral and Entertaining* (Bath, 1789), 41–45; Smith: *Elegiac Sonnets, With Additional Sonnets and Other Poems,* 6th ed. (London, 1792), 82–85; Tuite: *Poems by Lady Tuite* (London, 1796), 108–10.

  Age and Aging. Finch: *The Poems of Anne Countess of Winchilsea,* ed. Myra Reynolds (Chicago: University of Chicago Press, 1903), 100–101; Dixon: *Poems on Several Occasions* (Canterbury, 1740), 15–18; Savage: *Poems on Various Subjects and Occasions,* 2 vols. (London, 1777), 2:16–21; Little: *The Poetical Works of Janet Little, the Scotch Milkmaid* (Air [Ayr], 1792), 86–90; Cowper: *Original Poems, on Various Occasions. By a Lady. Revised by William Cowper, Esq.* (London, 1792), 23; Blamire: *The Poetical Works of Miss Susanna Blamire* (Edinburgh, 1842), 181.

48. Optical device used to project an enlarged image of a picture.
49. Small, showy trinket.
50. Decorative, showy trinket.

Poems on Death

Death. "King of Terrors." "Thou'art slave to Fate, chance, kings, and desperate men, / And dost with poyson, warre, and sicknesse dwell." "Aye, but to die, and go we know not where, / To lie in cold obstruction and to rot."[1] Narratives of life inevitably conclude with thoughts of death, and if the first confrontations with age surprise, that with death begins a long, slow coming to a philosophy of life. Anne Wharton's highly metaphoric poem *On the Storm between Gravesend and Diepe* concludes with an observation and a philosophical statement, a conclusion about death that seems less settled than exploratory. Other poems seek, in Mary Chudleigh's terms, "a truce" with grief and death. Life writing is traditionally studied as evidence about identity construction and as access to cultural mores; poems about death give valuable insights to both. They are also compelling individual utterances.

This anthology includes many excellent poems about death. Some of them are in the most respected, classical forms, as are Elizabeth Thomas's *A Pastoral Elegy* (1.1); Mary Jones's tribute to a public figure, *In Memory of the Rt. Hon. Lord Aubrey Beauclerk* (2.F), and, in this section, Elizabeth Tollet's luminous Horatian ode, *Imitation of Horace.* Some are about the deaths of friends or famous men in the country's many wars; others are about private griefs, and there are commemorative poems on the anniversaries of deaths of spouses, friends, and children. The poems in this section, like the ones in section 2.D, "Religious Poetry," however, concentrate specifically on the topic and illustrate original kinds of life writing.

Two of them are epitaphs, assessments of the lives the poets were still leading. Mary Chandler's opening to *My Own Epitaph* surprises and arrests the reader: "Here lies a true Maid, deformed and old." In balanced hexameters, she tallies her disappointments and pleasures in pairings such as never having had a lover but having had "much Friendship." She concludes with the certainties of her credo, and a final pairing, "she lost not her Soul with her Breath." In contrast to the courageous optimism of Chandler's poem, Mehetabel Wright reveals a quite different feeling about her life. The brilliant but wild daughter of Susanna Annesley Wesley and Samuel Wesley, sister to Charles and John, she was forced into marriage with a plumber and glazier who was much her inferior; she died at age fifty-three, still showing traces of her former beauty and "great refinement of manners."[2] She confesses, "Without complaint, she learnt to bear / A living death, a long despair." Most of her poetry reveals private feelings and was published posthumously, as this poem was.

Equally intimate are the revelations in Mary Chudleigh's *On the Death of my dear Daughter Eliza Maria Chudleigh*. The middle section of the poem describes Eliza Maria's final days and her mother's haunting helplessness: "Rack'd by Convulsive Pains she meekly lies, / And gazes on me with imploring Eyes, / With Eyes which beg Relief, but all in vain, / I see, but cannot, cannot ease her Pain." These verses are so detailed in their movement from what the mother observes the child experiencing to what the mother is thinking and feeling that the effect is a gripping immediacy. Including the child's full name in the title is unusual and suggests that her mother is lingering over it, even as the form of the poem seems to provide a means to control grief so overwhelming that suicide is contemplated. The friend's consolation in the dialogue comes from understanding as well as from the reminder of the culture's belief in the sources of consolation. The friend offers, "Your Sorrow is of the severest kind." Mary Barber's *Occasion'd by seeing some Verses written by Mrs. Constantia Grierson* is also cast as friend consoling friend. In Barber's poem, the poet, rather than the grieving mother, is the friend speaking to the bereaved, Constantia Grierson, and her presentation of this familiar consolation is among the most imaginative. Perhaps drawing upon Elizabeth Singer Rowe's prose fiction *Letters from the Dead to the Living*, in which children compare Heaven with their time on earth, the poet asks that the boy's guardian angel come to Grierson and describes the angel leading her "lovely Boy" to Paradise. Grierson is to imagine the course of human life from the "dang'rous Paths of Youth" through troubled old age as a contrast to this vision. These poems and most others wish for "resignation" for their friends. The access they give to the most intimate thoughts of the poets is hardly equaled in diaries and letters of the time.

While the abovementioned poems are rather long and narrative, others are severely compressed. The section opens with Katherine Philips's dignified twenty-line poem on the death of little Hector Philips. In an understated way, she tells us that she waited almost seven years to bear a child and that his death was "A sorrow unforeseen and scarcely fear'd." Philips writes, "I did but see him and he dis-appear'd, / I did but pluck the Rose-bud and it fell." Mehetebel Wright muses, "Drooping sweetness, verdant flow'r / Blooming, with'ring in an hour" (*To an Infant expiring the second day of its Birth*, 2.L). Her poem too is but twenty lines. Certainly these poems, as well as others in this anthology, give the lie to the commonplace statement that parents felt the death of children less than we do today because such deaths were so common then.

Memory plays an important part in all life writing, and some of the most memorable sections of the poems that follow draw upon it. Repeatedly the poet recreates a past experience or impression through a detailed visual image, often one that seems veridical. Jane West's *Elegy: Occasioned by a great Mortality* vividly recreates a young person's first experience of death on a large scale. She seems to have known the young people who died and contrasts the dismay that greets the deaths of those with "vig'rous boast of florid health" with the rightness of "when old Eliza paid / The debt of death, to time and nature due." Barker's *On the Death of my Dear Friend and Play-fellow, Mrs. E.D.* takes us back to the days when the two were girls enjoying the freedom and privacy of the outdoors, playing games, and eating plums and apples. The opening of the poem is Barker's most trenchant definition of friendship. The sincerity and depth of feeling is clear in this poem and in lines such as Brereton's "Methinks, I see her—as she late was seen, / Humble and free, obliging and serene" (*On the Death of a Lady*, 1.1). The face, the form, the "idea"—the essence of the person—come to the poet's mind just as vividly as Barker's summer days with her friend did. Sometimes there is even a recollection of touch, as there are in several of Anna Seward's poems about Honora Sneyd.

All told, death is mundane more than it is tragic or profound. D. J. Enright, the editor of *The Oxford Book of Death*, writes, "The certain knowledge that death is universal, and not a fate reserved for you or me, suggests that we oughtn't to fuss too much about it—on the night we die a thousand others go with us. . . . Anyone can do it; it can be done to anyone."[3] Poets have always tried to make death profound, but the best poets accept the ordinariness of death and know that for each death only a small group of people grieve. They avoid the bombast, the inflation, and, finally, the pretentiousness of a failed attempt at profundity. The poems in this section are startlingly direct and about mundane deaths, yet the repertory of emotions is as varied and thought-provoking as in any other section of the anthology. The forceful voices in the poems bring cultural and individual attitudes to the surface. Chudleigh, for instance, admits into her poem statements of extreme grief, grief that makes us uncomfortable even three hundred years later and would have struck her contemporaries as sinful. Elizabeth Tollet gathers the accumulated wisdom of Western culture in her poem, and the two women demonstrate in very different ways that life writing is the place where the enabling constructions we live by emerge. The autobiographical details in a number of the poems invite us to look at other poems by these authors for more extended life narratives. Wright's poem in this section and her other poems in the anthology record her crushed hopes and spirit, what she describes as the breaking of her heart. The union of content and form in these poems seems exceptionally strong, and they are an extraordinarily rich kind of life writing.

Notes

1. The first quotation is from Anne Finch's *To Death,* in this section; the second, from John Donne's familiar *Holy Sonnet X, Death be not Proud;* and the third, from William Shakespeare's *Measure for Measure* (spoken by Claudio, 3.1.117–18).

2. Adam Clarke, *Memoirs of the Wesley Family* (London, 1823), 498.

3. D. J. Enright, ed., *The Oxford Book of Death* (Oxford: Oxford University Press, 1983), 22.

Orinda[1] upon little Hector Philips

Katherine Philips

I.

Twice forty months of Wedlock I did stay,
Then had my vows crown'd with a Lovely boy,
And yet in forty days he dropt away,
O swift Visissitude of humane[2] joy.

2.

I did but see him and he dis-appear'd,
I did but pluck the Rose-bud and it fell,
A sorrow unforeseen and scarcely fear'd,
For ill can mortals their afflictions spell.

3.

And now (sweet Babe) what can my trembling heart
10 Suggest to right my doleful fate or thee,
Tears are my Muse and sorrow all my Art,
So piercing groans must be thy Elogy.

4.

Thus whilst no eye is witness of my mone,[3]
I grieve thy loss (Ah boy too dear to live)
And let the unconcerned World alone,
Who neither will, nor can refreshment give.

5.

An Off'ring too for thy sad Tomb I have,
Too just a tribute to thy early Herse,[4]
Receive these gasping numbers to thy grave,
20 The last of thy unhappy Mothers Verse.

(1667)

---

1. Both men and women often wrote and corresponded under pastoral pseudonyms that everyone knew. "Orinda" was Philips's choice.
2. Human.
3. Obsolete form of *moan*.
4. Hearse; carriage for the dead.

On the Death of my Dear Friend and Play-fellow, Mrs. E.D. having Dream'd the night before I heard thereof, that I had lost a Pearl

Jane Barker

I Dream'd I lost a Pearl,[5] and so it prov'd;
I lost a Friend much above Pearls belov'd:
A Pearl perhaps adorns some outward part,
But Friendship decks each corner of the heart:
Friendship's a *Gem,* whose Lustre do's out-shine
All that's below the heav'nly *Crystaline:*[6]
Friendship is that mysterious thing alone,
Which can unite, and make two Hearts but one;
It purifies our Love, and makes it flow
I'th' clearest stream that's found in Love below;   10
It *sublimates*[7] the Soul, and makes it move
Towards Perfection and *Celestial* Love.
We had no by-designs, nor hop'd to get
Each by the other place amongst the great;
Nor *Riches* hop'd, nor *Poverty* we fear'd,
'Twas *Innocence* in both, which both rever'd.
Witness this truth the *Wilsthorp-Fields,*[8] where we
So oft enjoy'd a harmless *Luxurie;*
Where we indulg'd our easie Appetites,
With Pocket-Apples, Plumbs, and such delights.   20
Then we contriv'd to spend the rest o'th' day,
In making Chaplets,[9] or at Check-stone play;[10]

5. In a series of comparisons that Jesus used to explain the kingdom of Heaven, a merchant "when he had found one pearl of great price, went and sold all that he had and bought it." Matt. 14.46; for the value of pearls, see also Matt. 7.6 and Rev. 21:21. Pearls were also sacred to Aphrodite Marina as Pearl of the Sea and symbolized sexual paradise. In legend, Cleopatra bet Antony that she could host the most expensive banquet in history; when at the end of it he was unimpressed, she removed one of her earrings (reputed to have the value of fifteen countries), dissolved it in vinegar, and drank it. Because of the pearl's association with Aphrodite and since both were born in the ocean, it was considered an aphrodisiac.

6. In the Ptolemaic astronomical system, the crystalline heaven was supposed to exist between the *primum mobile* (the outermost, or tenth, sphere) and the firmament (the arch or vault of the sky, where the clouds and stars appear).

7. Term adopted from the emergent science of chemistry meaning to act upon and refine.

8. Wilsthorpe, Lincolnshire, where Barker grew up. She probably lived there from 1662 until the early 1680s and returned in 1727.

9. Wreaths or garlands of flowers for the head.

10. Children's game played with smooth, round pebbles.

When weary, we our selves supinely laid
On Beds of *Vi'lets* under some cool shade,
Where th' *Sun* in vain strove to dart through his *Rays;*
Whilst *Birds* around us chanted Forth their *Lays;*[11]
Ev'n those we had bereaved of their young,
Would greet us with a *Querimonious*[12] Song.
Stay here, my *Muse,* and of these let us learn,
30   The loss of our deceased Friend to Mourn:
Learn did I say? alas, that cannot be,
We can teach Clouds to weep, and Winds to sigh at Sea,
Teach *Brooks* to murmur, *Rivers* to o're-flow,
We can add Solitude to Shades of *Yeaugh.*[13]
Were *Turtles*[14] to be witness of our moan,
They'd in compassion quite forget their own:
Nor shall hereafter *Heraclitus* be,
Fam'd for his Tears,[15] but to my *Muse* and Me;
Fate shall give all that *Fame* can comprehend,
40   Ah poor repair for th' loss of such a *Friend.*

(1688)

On the Storm between Gravesend and Diepe;[16] Made at That Time.

Anne Wharton

When the Tempestuous Sea did foam and roar,
Tossing the Bark[17] from the long-wish'd for Shore;
With false affected fondness it betray'd,
Striving to keep what Perish'd, if it stay'd.

11. Ballads; lyric or narrative poems meant to be sung.
12. Complaining.
13. Yew, tree with thick, dark green foliage, often planted in churchyards and symbolic of sadness.
14. The turtledove, a common European dove known for its affection for its mate.
15. Greek known as "the Weeping Philosopher."
16 Gravesend, in southern Kent, is the last port on the Thames before the open water of the English Channel. Historically, it was the place from which important expeditions began and where important dignitaries were received. Dieppe, in northern Normandy, France, was the harbor for a resort area and manufacturing center and was a common port for ships crossing the Channel. Because of several natural conditions, including the narrowness of the Channel, which acted as a wind funnel, storms between Gravesend and Dieppe were especially severe.
17. Small sailboat with three to five masts.

Such is the Love of Impious Men, where e're
Their cruel Kindness lights, 'tis to ensnare:
I, toss'd in tedious Storms of troubled Thought,
Was careless of the Waves the Ocean brought.
My Anchor *Hope* was lost, and too too near
On either hand were Rocks of sad Despair.   10
Mistaken Seamen prais'd my fearless Mind,
Which, sunk in Seas of Grief, could dare the Wind.
In Life, tempestuous Life is dread and harm, ⎫
Approaching Death had no unpleasing Form; ⎬
Approaching Death appeases ev'ry Storm. ⎭

(1695)

On the Death of my dear Daughter Eliza Maria Chudleigh[18]
A Dialogue between Lucinda and Marissa[19]
Mary Chudleigh

Marissa. O My *Lucinda!* O my dearest Friend!
Must my Afflictions never, never End!
Has Heav'n for me no Pity left in Store,
Must I! O must I ne'er be happy more,
Philinda's Loss[20] had almost broke my Heart,
From her, Alas! I did but lately part:
And must there still be new Occasions found
To try my Patience, and my Soul to wound?
Must my lov'd Daughter too be snatch'd away,
Must she so soon the Call of Fate obey?   10
In her first Dawn, replete with youthful Charms,
She's fled, she's fled from my deserted Arms.
Long did she struggle, long the War maintain,
But all th' Efforts of Life, alas! were vain.
Could Art have sav'd her she had still been mine, ⎫
Both Art and Care together did combine, ⎬
But what is Proof against the Will Divine! ⎭

18. Eliza Maria was Chudleigh's younger daughter. Chudleigh had six children, only two of whom reached adulthood.

19. Women in Chudleigh's literary circle took pastoral pen names. The name Lucinda appears frequently but has not been identified; Marissa was Chudleigh's pastoral pen name.

20. Philinda was Mary Sydenham Lee (1632–1701), Mary Chudleigh's mother.

Methinks I still her dying Conflict view,
And the sad Sight does all my Grief renew:
20 Rack'd by Convulsive Pains she meekly lies,
And gazes on me with imploring Eyes,
With Eyes which beg Relief, but all in vain,
I see, but cannot, cannot ease her Pain:
She must the Burthen unassisted bear,
I cannot with her in her Tortures share:
Wou'd they were mine, and she stood easie by;
For what one loves, sure 'twere not hard to die.

 See, how she labours, how she pants for Breath,
She's lovely still, she's sweet, she's sweet in Death!
30 Pale as she is, she beauteous does remain,
Her closing Eyes their Lustre still retain:
Like setting Suns, with undiminish'd Light,
They hide themselves within the Verge of Night.

 She's gone! she's gone! she sigh'd her Soul away!
And can I! can I any longer stay!
My Life, alas! has ever tiresome been,
And I few happy, easie Days have seen;
But now it does a greater Burthen grow, ⎫
I'll throw it off and no more Sorrow know, ⎬
40 But with her to calm peaceful Regions go. ⎭

 Stay thou, dear Innocence, retard thy Flight,
O stop thy Journy to the Realms of Light,
Stay till I come: To thee I'll swiftly move,
Attracted by the strongest Passion, Love.

 Lucinda. No more, no more let me such Language hear,
I can't, I can't the piercing Accents bear:
Each Word you utter stabs me to the Heart:
I cou'd from Life, not from *Marissa* part:
And were your Tenderness as great as mine,
50 While I were left, you would not thus repine.
My Friends are Riches, Health, and all to me,
And while they're mine, I cannot wretched be.

 Marissa. If I on you cou'd Happiness bestow,
I still the Toils of Life wou'd undergo,
Wou'd still contentedly my Lot sustain,

And never more of my hard Fate complain:
But since my Life to you will useless prove,
O let me hasten to the Joys above:
Farewel, farewel, take, take my last adieu,
May Heav'n be more propitious still to you   60
May you live happy when I'm in my Grave,
And no Misfortunes, no Afflictions have:
If to sad Objects you'll some Pity lend,
And give a Sigh to an unhappy Friend,
Think of *Marissa,* and her wretched State,
How she's been us'd by her malicious Fate,
Recount those Storms which she has long sustain'd,[21]
And then rejoice that she the Port has gain'd,
The welcome Haven of eternal Rest,
Where she shall be for ever, ever blest;   70
And in her Mother's, and her Daughter's Arms,
Shall meet with new, with unexperienc'd Charms.
O how I long those dear Delights to taste;
Farewel, farewel; my Soul is much in haste.
Come Death and give the kind releasing Blow;
I'm tir'd with Life, and over-charg'd with Woe:
In thy cool, silent, unmolested Shade,
O let me be by their dear Relicks laid;
And there with them from all my Troubles free,
Enjoy the Blessings of a long Tranquillity.   80

    Lucinda. O thou dear Suff'rer, on my Breast recline
Thy drooping Head, and mix thy Tears with mine:
Here rest a while, and make a Truce with Grief,
Consider; Sorrow brings you no Relief.
In the great Play of Life we must not chuse,
Nor yet the meanest Character refuse.
Like Soldiers we our Gen'ral must obey, ⎫
Must stand our Ground, and not to Fear give way, ⎬
But go undaunted on till we have won the Day. ⎭
Honour is ever the Reward of Pain,   90
A lazy Virtue no Applause will gain,

---

21. In addition to the deaths of four of her children, Chudleigh lived a lonely life and suffered from a long illness.

All such as to uncommon Heights would rise, ⎫
And on the Wings of Fame ascend the Skies, ⎬
Must learn the Gifts of Fortune to despise. ⎭
They to themselves their Bliss must still confine,
Must be unmov'd, and never once repine:
But few to this Perfection can attain, ⎫
Our Passions often will th' Ascendant gain, ⎬
And Reason but alternately does reign; ⎭

100   Disguis'd by Pride, we sometimes seem to bear
A haughty Port, and scorn to shed a Tear;
While Grief within still acts a tragick Part,
And plays the Tyrant in the bleeding Heart.
Your Sorrow is of the severest kind,
And can't be wholly to your Soul confin'd:
Losses like yours, may be allow'd to move
A gen'rous Mind, that knows what 'tis to love.
Who that her innate Worth had understood,
Wou'd not lament a Mother so divinely good?

110   And who, alas! without a Flood of Tears,
Cou'd lose a Daughter in her blooming Years:
An only Daughter, such a Daughter too,
As did deserve to be belov'd by you;
Who'd all that cou'd her to the World commend,
A Wit that did her tender Age transcend,
Inviting Sweetness, and a sprightly Air, ⎫
Looks that had something pleasingly severe, ⎬
The Serious and the Gay were mingl'd there: ⎭
These merit all the Tears that you have shed,

120   And could Complaints recall them from the Dead,
Could Sorrow their dear Lives again restore,
I here with you for ever would deplore:
But since th' intensest Grief will prove in vain,
And these lost Blessings can't be yours again,
Recal your wand'ring Reason to your Aid,
And hear it calmly when it does persuade;
'Twill teach you Patience, and the useful Skill
To rule your Passions, and command your Will;
To bear Afflictions with a steady Mind, ⎫
130   Still to be easie, pleas'd, and still resign'd, ⎬
And look as if you did no inward Trouble find. ⎭

Marissa. I know, *Lucinda,* this I ought to do,
But oh! 'tis hard my Frailties to subdue:
My Head-strong Passions will Resistance make,
And all my firmest Resolutions shake:
I for my Daughter's Death did long prepare,
And hop'd I shou'd the Stroke with Temper bear,
But when it came, Grief quickly did prevail,
And I soon found my boasted Courage fail:
Yet still I strove, but 'twas, alas! in vain,   140
My Sorrow did at length th'Ascendant gain:
But I'm resolv'd I will no longer yield;
By Reason led, I'll once more take the Field,
And there from my insulting Passions try
To gain a full, a glorious Victory:
Which till I've done, I never will give o'er,
But still fight on, and think of Peace no more;
With an unweary'd Courage still contend,
Till Death, or Conquest, does my Labour end.

(1703)

To Death

Anne Finch

O King of Terrors, whose unbounded Sway
All that have Life, must certainly Obey;
The King, the Priest, the Prophet, all are Thine,
Nor wou'd ev'n *God* (in Flesh) thy Stroke decline.
My Name is on thy Roll, and sure I must
Encrease thy gloomy Kingdom in the Dust.
My soul at this no Apprehension feels,
But trembles at thy Swords, thy Racks, thy Wheels;[22]
Thy scorching Fevers, which distract the Sense,
And snatch us raving, unprepar'd from hence;   10
At thy contagious Darts, that wound the Heads
Of weeping Friends, who wait at dying Beds.
Spare these, and let thy Time be when it will;

22. Instruments of torture.

My Bus'ness is to Dye, and Thine to Kill.
Gently thy fatal Sceptre[23] on me lay,
And take to thy cold Arms, insensibly, thy Prey.

(1713)

Imitation of Horace, Lib. II. Ode 3[24]
Elizabeth Tollet

Æquam memento rebus in arduis
Servare mentem—[25]

I.

Why thus dejected? can you hope a Cure
    In mourning Ills which you endure?
        Without Redress you grieve:
    A melancholy Thought may sour
    The Pleasures of the present Hour.
    But never can the Past retrieve.
Who knows if more remain for Fate to give?
Unerring Death alike on all attends;
    Alike our Hopes and Fears destroys:
10   Alike one silent Period ends.
All our repining Griefs and our insulting Joys.

II.

Not thy Expence, nor thy Physicians Skill
    Can guard thee from the Stroak of Fate:
Thou yield'st to some imaginary Ill
    Thy very Fears of Death create.
    With the fantastick Spleen[26] oppress'd,

23. Staff held by a monarch or person in authority on ceremonial occasions as a mark of his or her status.

24. Horace's three books of odes (23 BC) made him the premier Roman poet. *Lib.* is the abbreviation for the Latin *liber,* "book."

25. The opening lines of the ode: "Remember, when life's path is steep, to keep an even mind. . . ." *Horace: The Odes and Epodes,* trans. C. E. Bennett (London: Heinemann, 1914), 113.

26. Condition believed to be caused by the organ of the same name and by the production of black bile that came to be known as "the English malady." Also a catchall term for depression, moodiness, irritability.

With Vapours[27] wilder Indolence possess'd,
　　Thy stagnant Blood forgets to roll,
And Fate attacks thee from thy inward Soul,
　　Vain is Resistance, let's retreat   20
　　To some remote, some rural Seat;
　　Where on the Grass reclin'd we may,
　　Make ev'ry Day an Holy-day:
　　Where all to our Delights combine,
　　With Friendship, Wit, and chearful Wine.

III.
Where the tall Poplar and aspiring Pine
　　Their hospitable Branches twine:
Among their Roots a silver Current strays,
Which wand'ring here and there, its Course delays,
And in *Meanders* forms its winding Ways,   30
　　Perfumes, and Wine, and Roses bring!
　　The short-liv'd Treasures of the Spring!
　　While Wealth can give, or Youth can use,
　　While that can purchase, this excuse,
　　Let's live the present Now!
'Tis all the fatal Sisters[28] may allow,
Tho' thou should'st purchase an immense Estate,
Tho' the clear Mirror of the rolling Tide
　　Reflect thy *Villa's*[29] rising Pride,
　　And Forest shading either side;   40
　　　Yet must thou yield to Fate:
To these shall thy unthankful Heir succeed;
And waste the heapy Treasures of the Dead.

IV.
　　Nor shall it aid thee then to trace
　　Thy Ancestors beyond the *Norman* Race:[30]

27. Depression, boredom; occasionally more severe symptoms such as hypochondria, hysteria, and fainting were attributed to the vapors.

28. The Fates, three sisters who arbitrarily control birth, life, and death. Clotho holds the distaff, Lachesis spins the thread of life, and Atropos cuts the thread.

29. Spacious, luxurious house, often on a large estate.

30. William, Duke of Normandy, defeated King Harold of England in 1066. The victory was quick and brutal; almost all of the Anglo-Saxon aristocracy were killed or driven from their land, and a Norman aristocracy replaced them.

Death, the great Leveller of all Degrees,
Does on Mankind without Distinction seize.
Undaunted Guards attend in vain
The mighty Tyrant to repel;
50   Nor does his Cruelty disdain
The lab'ring Hind[31] and weary Swain,[32]
Who in obscure Oblivion dwell.
When from the fated Urn the Lot is cast,
The Doom irrevocable past,
Still on the Brink the shiv'ring Ghosts wou'd stay:
Imperious Fate brooks no Delay;
The Steersman[33] calls, away! away!

(1724)

In Answer to a Lady
Who Advised Retirement
Lady Mary Wortley Montagu

You little know the heart that you advise;
I view this various scene with equal eyes,
In crowded courts I find myself alone,
And pay my worship to a nobler throne.
Long since the value of this world I know,
Pity the madness, and despise the show.
Well as I can my tedious part I bear,
And wait for my dismission without fear.
Seldom I mark mankind's detested ways,
10   Not hearing censure, nor affecting Praise,
And, unconcern'd, my future fate I trust
To that sole Being, merciful and just.

(1730; 1750)

31. Farm servant.
32. Country man; lover.
33. In Greek and Roman mythology, the dead were carried in boats across the river Styx.

Occasion'd by seeing some Verses written by Mrs. Constantia Grierson, upon the Death of her Son

Mary Barber

THIS Mourning Mother can with Ease explore
The Arts of *Latium*, and the *Grecian* Store:[34]
Was early learn'd, nay more, was early wise;
And knew, the Pride of Science[35] to despise;
Left Men to take assuming Airs from thence,
And seem'd unconscious of superior Sense.
Yet ah! how vain to guard the Soul, we see,
Are the best Precepts of Philosophy!
See Nature triumph o'er the boasted Art,
Ev'n in a SOLON's,[36] and CONSTANTIA's, Heart.   10
See how she mourns her Son's untimely Doom,
And pours her Woes o'er the relentless Tomb.

SOFTEN, kind Heav'n, her seeming rigid Fate,
With frequent Visions of his blissful State.
Oft let the Guardian Angel of her Son
Tell her in faithful Dreams, his Task is done;
Shew, how he kindly led her lovely Boy
To Realms of Peace, and never-fading Joy.

THEN, for a while, reverse his happy Fate;
Shew him still here, still in this wretched State: 20
Shew the false World, seducing him from Truth;
And paint the slipp'ry, dang'rous Paths of Youth:
Shew him, in riper Years, beset with Snares,
Wearied with struggling thro' unnumber'd Cares.
Convey him thence to Life's remotest Stage,
To feel the dire Calamities of Age;
Opprest with Sorrows, with Distempers torn,
Or rack'd with Guilt, much harder to be born.

34. Constantia Grierson had been apprenticed to Laetitia Pilkington's father, who was an obstetrician. She was part of a circle of friends that included Barber, Laetitia Pilkington, and Jonathan Swift. She married George Grierson, the King's Printer in Dublin. A highly learned woman, she was responsible for editions of Terence and Tacitus.

35. Knowledge.

36. See Plutarch's *Life of Solon*. Athenian statesman, reformer, poet, and military hero (630?–660? BC). *Barber.*

Raise the Distress, and let her darling Care,
30   Distracted in the Horrors of Despair,
The dreadful Scene of Judgment op'ning see,
And, trembling, plunge into Eternity.

THEN ask her, Wou'd she call him down from Bliss,
To hazard such a dismal Doom as this?
That she may learn to be resign'd from thence,
And bless the Guardian Hand, that snatch'd him hence.

(1734)

My Own Epitaph
Mary Chandler

Here lies a true Maid, deformed[37] and old;
Who, that she never was handsome, ne'er needed be told.
Tho' she ne'er had a Lover, much Friendship had met;
And thought all Mankind quite out of her Debt.
She ne'er could forgive, for she ne'er had resented;
As she ne'er had deny'd, so she never repented.
She lov'd the whole Species, but some had distinguish'd;
But Time and much Thought had all Passion extinguish'd.
Tho' not fond of her Station,[38] content with her Lot;
10   A Favour receiv'd she had never forgot.
She rejoic'd in the Good that her Neighbour possess'd,
And Piety, Purity, Truth she profess'd.
She liv'd in much Peace, but ne'er courted Pleasure;
Her Book and her Pen had her Moments of Leisure.
Pleas'd with Life, fond of Health, yet fearless of Death;
Believing she lost not her Soul with her Breath.

(1736)

37. Chandler occasionally refers to her crooked spine, which she believed ruled out marriage.
38. Chandler ran a milliner's shop in Bath.

An Epitaph on Herself
Mehetabel Wright

Destin'd, while living, to sustain
An equal share of grief and pain;
All various ills of human race
Within this breast had once a place:
Without complaint, she learnt to bear
A living death, a long despair,
Till, hard opprest by adverse fate,
O'ercharg'd, she sunk beneath its weight;
And to this peaceful tomb retir'd,
So much esteem'd, so long desir'd!   10
The painful mortal conflict o'er,   ·
A broken heart can bleed no more.

(1750; 1763)

An Elegy
Occasioned by a great Mortality in the Village where the Author resided. Written at the Age of Eighteen[39]
Jane West

The knell of death, tremendous, strikes again
   On aw'd mortality's awaken'd ear!
Slow down the village move the sable train,
   The silent followers of the lifeless bier!

To day! perchance, the young with streaming eyes
   Lament the parent and the guardian dead!
To-morrow! feeble age, with hopeless sighs
   Upholds expiring manhood's languid head!

39. The village of Desborough, in Northamptonshire, where West's family moved when she was eleven. She turned eighteen on 30 April 1776. Although the "great Mortality" has not been identified, cases of influenza and scarlet fever were prevalent in English villages during this time and proved especially fatal to children. See Mary J. Dobson, *Contours of Death and Disease in Early Modern England* (Cambridge: Cambridge University Press, 1997), 442.

Plead on, ye charmers, with persuasive tongue!
Death, the deaf adder,[40] will not hear ye pray;
Ye sons of music, try the soothing song!
He strikes! tho' angels tuned the pleading lay![41]

How dread my song! thy triumphs, Death, I sing!
Since the fierce tyrant ne'er was known to spare,
Ere yet my bosom feels the mortal sting,
To his Director I'll prefer my prayer.

My life, the safety of my friends, I owe
To heav'n's omniscient providence alone;
That buckler[42] warded the impending blow,
Or heal'd the sickness, when the shaft[43] was thrown.

Amid the gen'ral ruin, safe I stand,
And breath uninjur'd, pestilential air!
The King of Kings, displays his powr'ful hand,
And health and vigor at his word I share.

In pleasing childhood's inoffensive morn,
I saw the playful Mary-Ann decline,
Ere keen malevolence, or wounding scorn,
Distain'd her robe of innocence divine.

These hands to dust her kindred relics bore,
With flowers adorn'd; herself the sweetest flower!
Happy advent'rer! soon thy talk was o'er!
Now carol anthems to th' eternal power!

Calistus next, sunk to the silent tomb!
With him, Jemima clos'd her heavy eyes!
Within one grave, the kindred forms consume,
Beside the youth, the lovely sister lies!

The vig'rous boast of florid health, how vain!
See wasting sickness instantaneous seize!

40. The common venomous viper.
41. Ballad; lyric or narrative poem meant to be sung.
42. Small round shield carried or worn on the arm.
43. Spear bearing death.

Fast boils the blood in every turgid vein,
    And tortur'd nature calls on death for ease!   40

And now, Sin's offspring with impetuous speed,
    Enthrones destruction in a livid car;[44]
Resolv'd the av'rice of the grave to feed,
    He spreads the putrid exhalation far.

A groan succeeds! ah! spare the gen'rous friend,
    In him, the neighbour, husband, father dies!
From yon low dwelling, what loud shrieks ascend?
    There, on his death-bed, good Artemon lies!

Oft was he wont, the blazing hearth beside,
    To cheer the social hour with moral lore: 50
His mild benevolence, diffusing wide,
    To all imparted from his little store.

Still, as the rustic banquet is prepar'd,
    His loss, impassion'd mem'ry shall supply;
There, his repeated jests shall oft be heard;
    The tale concluding with a thrilling sigh.

Not so we wept, when old Eliza paid
    The debt of death, to time and nature due:
See Virtue, crown'd with hoary hairs, we said!
    So may we die with blessed hope in view!   60

Yet cease the song;—descriptive lays are vain;
    When heaps on heaps around promiscuous[45] die!
Still through the village moves the funeral train,
    And the hard Sexton[46] learns at last to sigh!

Nor is the raging fever here confin'd;
    Through all the realm, the flaming javelin flies;
Whilst war its twin destroyer of mankind,
    Lifts its red banners, waving to the skies.[47]

44. Carriage.

45. Randomly; death is undiscriminating.

46. Gravedigger or maintenance man responsible for the care of church property and usually charged with supervising burials.

47. The English were fighting the American Rebellion.

Eternal God! in thee alone we trust!
70   Our foes discomfit, mitigate our pains!
Can thy great acts be chaunted in the dust?
Or sounds thy glory where oblivion reigns?

(1776; 1786)

Sources

Philips: *Poems* (London, 1667), 148–49; Barker: *Poetical Recreations* (London, 1688), 18–19; Wharton: *The Temple of Death; a Poem,* 2nd ed. (London, 1695), 240–41; Chudleigh: *Poems on Several Occasions* (London, 1703), 94–99; Finch: *Miscellany Poems, on Several Occasions* (London, 1713), 122–23; Tollet: *Poems on Several Occasions* (London, 1724), 11–12; Montagu: *In Answer to a Lady Who Advised Retirement,* in *London Magazine* 19 (May 1750): 230; Barber: *Poems on Several Occasions* (London, 1734), 38–40; Chandler: *The Description of Bath. A poem,* 3rd ed. (London, 1736), 40–41; Wright: Francis Fawkes and William Woty, *The Poetical Calendar. Containing a Collection of Scarce and Valuable Pieces of Poetry,* 2nd ed., 12 vols. (London, 1763), 6:89; West: *Miscellaneous Poetry by Mrs. West* (London, 1786), 14–17.

PART THREE

Writing on Writing

Introduction

To speak in generalizations about women writing as poets or about their relationship with print culture in the long eighteenth century is to risk flattening the distinct differences among these poets, essentializing them, and ultimately diminishing the rich range of their experiences and contributions. The material and symbolic economies in which women's poetry circulated changed over the century, and the poets in this volume represent a diverse set of positions in terms of class, region, and cultural status. Many women were professional poets, in the sense that they received money for their work, sold it in a commercial marketplace, wrote with an awareness of an existing literary culture, and developed a literary network in London, the provinces, or both. However, even those common threads were realized very differently. Some poets, such as Anne Finch and Lady Mary Wortley Montagu, wrote over the span of their lives and published strategically, although their wealth and cultural status largely freed them from concerns about the marketplace; they were perhaps more focused on establishing and maintaining a highly valued literary reputation and protecting themselves against unauthorized publication of their work. Other poets, such as Mary Whateley Darwall and Mary Barber, published only one volume of poetry by subscription or two volumes many years apart, often with a provincial bookseller; while they wrote throughout their lives and published in the growing periodical press, they were not "career" or "professional" poets for a commercial market, and they struggled financially, often looking to the print trade to relieve that situation. They, like most, seriously studied poetry, striving to realize their ambition of writing excellent verse. The work of some poets, such as Anne Killigrew and Mary Leapor, was published posthumously. Some women, such as Charlotte Lennox, Helen Maria Williams, and Charlotte Smith, were not only poets but professional writers, writing in multiple genres through most of their adult lives and using the high cultural value of their poetry to add prestige to their other publications. Smith, Susannah Harrison, Jane Cave Winscom, and Anna Laetitia Barbauld published volumes of poetry that went through multiple editions; other women never saw their work issued a second time. Given the diversity of poets and poetic paths, what common patterns and contexts can we identify for women, poetry, and print culture?

The eighteenth century saw the development of a commercial literary marketplace that enabled women to publish a significant amount of poetry. As noted in the introduction to this anthology, in the period from 1660 and 1800, 243 women published books of poetry, 28.8 percent of all books of poetry published in the period, and more than 800 women poets in England and America published 1,402 first editions in the years 1770–1835.[1] At the beginning of the century, the growing middling classes created a market for literary commodities in which poetry was simultaneously accessible and of high cultural value. Poetry was published widely and in a variety of forms. The periodical press provided an important venue for female poets. For example, Edmund Cave's *Gentleman's Magazine,* begun in 1731, published eight pages of poetry in every issue; realizing "the market potential of the provinces . . . provincial women . . . were well represented,"[2] and the entrepreneurial Cave published their work regularly. For many women, the periodical was their first point of entry into the literary marketplace. Collections, anthologies, and miscellanies of poetry, marketed to the nascent reading public and designed to construct taste and cultivate readers, also highlighted the work of women poets. Some anthologies, such as Robert Dodsley's *Collection of Poems by Several Hands* (1748–58), offered elite poetry for literary consumers, while George Colman and Bonnell Thornton's *Poems by Eminent Ladies* (1755, reprinted in 1773 and 1780) was designed specifically for women of the middle classes. In addition to anthologies or periodicals, women also published individual poems responding to specific cultural events, such as Catharine Trotter Cockburn's *On His Grace the Duke of Marlborough, a Poem* (2.E). Although less profitable for publishers, highly topical poems were often a kind of "news" and thus highly marketable.[3] Booksellers had to balance their desire to preserve the

1. The information about English women writing appears in Judith Phillips Stanton, "Statistical Profile of Women Writing in English from 1660–1800," in *Eighteenth-Century Women and the Arts,* ed. Frederick M. Keener and Susan B. Lorsch (Westport, CT: Greenwood, 1988), 250–51. The information about British and American women writing appears in James Robert de J. Jackson, *Annals of English Verse, 1770–1835: A Preliminary Survey of the Volumes Published* (New York: Garland, 1985). These statistics and a wider discussion of the publishing industry in the eighteenth century can be found in Paula R. Backscheider, *Eighteenth-Century Women Poets and Their Poetry* (Baltimore: Johns Hopkins University Press, 2005), xvii.

2. Sarah Prescott, "Provincial Networks, Dissenting Connections, and Noble Friends: Elizabeth Singer Rowe and Female Authorship in Early Eighteenth-Century England," *Eighteenth-Century Life* 25 (Winter 2001): 41n. 11.

3. As Barbara Benedict writes, "In addition, booksellers began to publish fixed catalogues of books that were always available, and distribute them all over the country. This innovation presented literature as both topical and timeless. It may even have helped to create an audience receptive to the idea of a fixed canon of superior literature that yet coexists with topical verse." "Publishing and Reading Poetry," in *The Cambridge Companion to Eighteenth-Century Poetry,* ed. John Sitter (Cambridge: Cambridge University Press, 2001), 65.

high cultural value of poetry and the sense of permanence it conveyed with the need to offer fresh, timely verse in the marketplace. Finally, contemporaneous with the professionalization of the literary marketplace was the development of an extensive system of reviewing, which was nearly nonexistent at the beginning of the century but quite comprehensive by the end. The cultural apparatus for discussing poetry in publications such as the *Monthly Review* or the *Critical Review*, including reviews by professional critics, had the potential to assign literary value to women poets, to engender a greater knowledge among readers, and to institute a professional literary discourse.

The prestige of women's poetry was high by the end of the century. Roger Lonsdale notes that "in the 1780s women virtually took over, as writers and readers, the territories most readily conceded to them, of popular fiction and fashionable poetry."[4] But the remuneration was not generous even then. Publishers were savvy about holding on to copyright, repackaging material in increasingly marketable ways, and ensuring that they retained the majority of profits. It was a period in which almost no poet could earn even a modest living. Women had to negotiate the material reality of the marketplace and the need to accrue the literary value so desirable to booksellers, critics, and readers while maintaining a reputation that preserved their high cultural value. These women also actively traded in a symbolic economy of reputation, recognition, and worth within established communities of often predominately female readers and writers. Women's ability to compete in these multiple economies varied over the course of the century.

Restoration poets such as Katherine Philips and Anne Finch, both writing from an elite cultural position, were removed from the literary marketplace in the sense that they did not need to publish to survive. Although they were "career" poets who were focused, skilled, and deliberate in their work, they did not support themselves financially. Philips wrote and circulated her work within her literary coterie, and her reputation as the fair "Orinda" relied as much on the circulation of her poems among friends as it did on their eventual publication.[5] When published, Philips's poetry was, in Paula McDowell's words, "marketed" for its virtue and high cultural value.[6] Finch, who did not write out of financial need, possessed a great deal of creative freedom and published her poems selec-

4. Roger Lonsdale, ed., *Eighteenth-Century Women Poets: An Oxford Anthology* (Oxford: Oxford University Press, 1990), xxxv.

5. For discussions of manuscript "publication," see Kathryn R. King, "Elizabeth Singer Rowe's Tactical Use of Print and Manuscript," in *Women's Writing and the Circulation of Ideas: Manuscript Publication in England, 1550–1800,* ed. George L. Justice and Nathan Tinker (Cambridge: Cambridge University Press, 2002), 158–81; and Margaret J. M. Ezell, "From Manuscript to Print: A Volume of Their Own?" in *Women and Poetry, 1660–1750,* ed. Sarah Prescott and David E. Shuttleton (Basingstoke: Palgrave Macmillan, 2003), 140–60.

6. Paula McDowell, *The Women of Grub Street: Press, Politics, and Gender in the London Literary Marketplace, 1678–1730* (Oxford: Clarendon, 1998), 232.

tively. Finch returned to London in 1709 after living in Kent. That year Dela-rivière Manley included two of Finch's poems in *The New Atalantis,* and Jacob Tonson published three of her pastorals in *Poetical Miscellanies,* where they appeared between Alexander Pope's *Pastorals* and two poems by Jonathan Swift, who had helped Finch secure a spot in the high-prestige collection. Swift, in fact, was instrumental in the publication of her volume *Miscellany Poems, on Several Occasions* (1713), which was published by his "own publisher and friend, John Barber."[7] Finch's friendship with Swift and Pope, to whom she was introduced in 1713, placed her in a premiere literary network that "nurtured her talent,"[8] praised her poems, and encouraged her to continue publishing. In contrast to Philips and Finch were clearly professional writers such as Aphra Behn and Delarivière Manley, who lived in London, circulated in the literary marketplace, and used their existing literary connections to get their material into print. Their geographic location, coupled with a clear professional identity cultivated across different genres, allowed them to publish poetry with relative ease, although their poetry often failed to achieve the same high cultural value as that of Philips and Finch, in part because of their other highly political or "scandalous" texts.

By contrast, their contemporary Elizabeth Singer Rowe[9] illustrates the importance of the provincial literary network, the periodic press, and miscellanies in establishing a literary reputation and belies the notion that living in London was essential for success. Rowe, publishing as "Philomela" or "Pindarick Lady," made significant contributions to John Dunton's commercially successful *Athenian Mercury,* and her work comprised "the majority of its poetical content" after 19 May 1694. The editor's comments suggested "that the popularity of Rowe's verses was so great that she could sustain a whole issue independently."[10] Dunton sought to capitalize on Rowe's popularity and the high cultural value of her poetry by publishing *Poems on Several Occasions: Written by Philomela* (1696), which brought Rowe into an established network of writers who shared her literary and religious interests. Her collection, coupled with the appearance of her poetry in prestige collections such as Tonson's *Poetical Miscellanies* (1704), which included poems by Matthew Prior, and Bernard Lintot's *Poems on Several Occasions* (1717), which included poems by Pope, established her reputation and credibility as a poet. "Miscellanies manifested the connection between writers in

---

7. Barbara McGovern, "Finch, Pope, and Swift: The Bond of Displacement," in *Pope, Swift, and Women Writers,* ed. Donald Mell (Newark: University of Delaware Press, 1996), 108.

8. McGovern, "Finch, Pope, and Swift," 122.

9. To avoid confusion, throughout this introduction we use the full published names of the authors. Thus, although Rowe initially published under "Singer," we refer to her as Elizabeth Singer Rowe; although Mary Whateley Darwall's first volume was published under "Whateley," we use "Darwall"; and so on.

10. Prescott, "Provincial Networks, Dissenting Connections, and Noble Friends," 31.

print" and "became an important way of establishing a reputation," writes Barbara Benedict.[11] Rowe was circulating with Pope and Prior, benefiting from their cultural currency. Her relationship with Prior also gave her another point of access to greater control over the publication of her poems. The correspondence between Rowe and Prior indicates "that she was very much involved with the publication of her work," notes Sarah Prescott, using "Prior for her negotiations with Tonson" so that he would include some of her friends' poems in his next miscellany.[12] Women like Rowe could act as both poets and patrons, leveraging their literary success or their financial, social, or literary position to advance themselves and others. Rowe's career provides an excellent example of the growing power of the periodical press in the marketing and circulation of poetry, the intimate participation of women in male literary circles, and the power of the provincial literary network.

However, the commercialization of the print trade did not mean the elimination of the patronage system that had previously dominated literary culture. Rather, as Dustin Griffin observes, "the period is characterized by overlapping 'economies' of patronage *and* marketplace."[13] Women did not only operate in an "author-bookseller dynamic" that exchanged copy for copyright; it was a more "complex network" of "patrons and subscribers, as well as booksellers and printers," both in the provinces and in London.[14] Patronage took many forms: a patron might offer money, accommodations, or sponsorship of a new publication; he or she might also provide specific items or "necessities" for an impecunious author. A 1730 letter written by the long-struggling Elizabeth Thomas while in Fleet Street debtor's prison details the range of support she received: "Lady Frances Clifton clothed me, my Lord Delaware sent me four guineas toward paying my prison debts. . . . The Duchess of Somerset (who has been long a great support to me) had the bounty last week to give me a stock of stationary ware, and to buy of me after, with a gracious promise of future custom at her return. My Lady Delaware has given me leave to hope for a recommendation among her acquaintance, when I am out of this place; so that I now begin to hope I shall live by my honest industry."[15] She receives both the supplies she needs to write,

---

11. Benedict, "Publishing and Reading Poetry," 68.

12. Prescott, "Provincial Networks, Dissenting Connections, and Noble Friends," 37.

13. Dustin Griffin, *Literary Patronage in England, 1650–1800* (Cambridge: Cambridge University Press, 1996), 10.

14. Sarah Prescott, *Women, Authorship and Literary Culture, 1690–1740* (Houndmills: Palgrave Macmillan, 2003), 138.

15. *Report on the manuscripts of his Grace the Duke of Portland, K.G., Preserved at Welbeck Abbey*, vol. vi (London: His Majesty's Stationary Office, 1901). Harley Letters and Papers, "Mrs. E[lizabeth] Thomas ('Corinna') to [the Earl of Oxford]," 5 June 1730, Fleet Prison, quoted in Prescott, *Women, Authorship and Literary Culture*, 114.

"a stock of stationary ware," and the promise of a potential patron in the form of "recommendations among acquaintances."

The recommendation of a patron and the ability to capitalize on an existing network of social and literary connections were essential when publishing a volume by subscription, an important way for women to get their work into print. After 1730 the average number of books published by subscription per decade was about 250.[16] When a volume of poetry was brought out by subscription, individuals agreed to purchase one or more copies of the proposed text. They paid half the price at the time of subscription and promised to pay the other half upon receipt of the book. Their names, location of residence, and the number of books they had purchased were published on the subscription list, which usually appeared at the front of the book. Subscribing to a book, as Thomas Lockwood details, "did not necessarily make you a reader of that book," however. Nor did it mean "that you knew the writer, or had any interest in the subject, or shared a political outlook, or planned to read the book someday."[17] Rather, subscription was itself a social practice demonstrating any number of things, including fashionability, gentility, pity, political affiliation, or a desire to see one's name published in a volume of high cultural status. Priscilla Poynton's sponsor confesses "I have but little knowledge in the art of poetry, and less in the art of criticism." He was moved by the force of her personal characteristics: the poet and her poetry are described as "modest, meek, and instructive."[18] Poynton is established as an appropriate object of charity, a "helpless maid," who needs others to "alleviate the afflictions to which her misfortune must necessarily explore her future life."[19] The prefaces to volumes sold by subscription often position the female poet as the object of charitable benevolence, and she, in turn, expresses gratitude for the assistance received. This economy of patron and subscriber depends on the delicate balance of virtuous need, charitable benevolence, and literary value.

Subscription as a form of charity enabled the publication of laboring-class women poets such as Mary Leapor, Mary Collier, and Anne Yearsley, as well as women of the lower or middling classes such as Elizabeth Hands and Mary Chandler. Laboring-class women poets attracted literary attention (or at least curiosity on the part of the reader) and gained social or literary currency, although their class and provincial origins were always highlighted on the title page of their volumes and in the rhetoric of the prefaces. Designed to provide these women with some economic relief, the volumes did not always benefit them

16. Thomas Lockwood, "Subscription-Hunters and Their Prey," *Studies in the Literary Imagination* 34, no. 1 (2001): 121.

17. Lockwood, "Subscription-Hunters and Their Prey," 122.

18. Poynton, *Poems on Several Occasions* (Birmingham, 1770), ix.

19. Poynton, *Poems on Several Occasions*, x.

financially. Leapor's poetry was published posthumously, having been sold by subscription through the efforts of Bridget Freemantle.[20] The proceeds went to Leapor's impoverished father. Mary Collier's *The Woman's Labour* (not included), written in response to Stephen Duck's *The Thresher's Labour* (1730), while a compelling poem, was, more importantly, a marketable one that could capitalize on the public's preoccupation with the "thresher poet"; her identity as "a washerwoman" appeared prominently on the title page of her poem. In her *Poems, on Several Occasions* (1762), published by subscription, she recounts how little profit she received from the poem that initially made her name. Many advised "me to have it printed and at length comply'd to have it done at my own charge," she writes. "I lost nothing, neither did I gain much, others run away with the profit."[21] Although she attempted to capitalize on the currency of her previous poem by identifying herself on the title page as "Author of the Washerwoman's Labour," she likely benefited little from the collected poems; the subscriber list includes only 165 subscribers for 174 books. She worked as a washerwoman for most of her life. The most famous laboring-class poet was Ann Yearsley, or, as she was named, "Lactilla the milk-maid poet." Her career and the subscription to her 1785 collection *Poems on Several Occasions* were facilitated by the author Hannah More, who "offered to be Yearsley's patron, a gesture that assumed the milkmaid's unconditional gratitude and reflected a fashionable eighteenth-century welcome for 'untutored genius.'"[22] However, Yearsley bristled under More's control of the money raised by subscription and her treatment of Yearsley and her husband as, in Margaret Doody's words, "dependent children."[23] Yearsley severed the relationship by January 1786, and she used the incident as material for subsequent poems.

While some laboring-class poets had one well-known advocate who advanced their subscriptions, others benefited from the mobilization of an extended social network. For example, Elizabeth Hands did not have a highly visible literary figure such as More as her sponsor, yet through the assiduous efforts of two local clergymen, Henry Homer, the vicar of Birdingbury, and his son, the

20. For a discussion of Leapor's subscription and her relationship with Freemantle, see Richard Greene, *Mary Leapor: A Study in Eighteenth-Century Women's Poetry* (Oxford: Clarendon, 1993), chap. 1.

21. Mary Collier, *Poems, on Several Occasions, by Mary Collier, . . . With some remarks on her life* (Winchester, 1762), iv.

22. Moira Ferguson, *Eighteenth-Century Women Poets: Nation, Class, and Gender* (Albany: State University of New York Press, 1995), 46.

23. Margaret Doody, "Women Poets of the Eighteenth Century," in *Women and Literature in Britain, 1700–1800*, ed. Vivien Jones (Cambridge: Cambridge University Press, 2000), 234. For a full discussion of the financial relationship between More and Yearsley and Yearsley's break from More, see Mary Waldron, *Lactilla, Milkwoman of Clifton: The Life and Writings of Ann Yearsley, 1753–1806* (Athens: University of Georgia Press, 1996), chap. 3; and Ferguson, *Eighteenth-Century Women Poets*, chap. 4.

Reverend Philip Bracebridge Homer, and a "network of rural social contacts," she had twelve hundred names on her subscription list.[24] A comparison of "the lists of sponsors or godparents" of Homer's children with the subscription list for the poems reveals that "very few of the Homer family friends ... had not been contacted and persuaded to sign up to sponsor the volume of poems."[25] Subscribing could provide an opportunity to perform a charitable act, demonstrate literary taste, or establish a position within a social network revealed through the published subscription list.[26] Mary Chandler, a physically disabled woman who owned a milliner's shop in Bath, did not publish her poetry by subscription, yet she clearly benefited from the literary network that read her poetry and from the encouragement of her wide social network in Bath. The popularity of her first poem, *A Description of Bath* (1733, not included), prompted her to republish it with additional poems. Dedicating the new edition, for which the title page reads *Poems by Mary Chandler* (1736), to her brother John, she circumscribes the scope of her audience, claiming not to write "to the World," but only to "the small Circle of my Acquaintance, and those of my Superiors, to whom I have the Honour to appear in a favourable Light." She eschews a sponsor, asserting that "it would be impertinent in me to look out for a noble Patron to recommend my Trifles."[27] Her "small circle" grew appreciatively; Elizabeth Singer Rowe, the Countess of Herford, Samuel Richardson, who printed her volume, and, ultimately, Alexander Pope helped generate sufficient interest to warrant eight editions.

Any author's association with members of the social elite, no matter how tangential, could be the basis for a successful subscription list, as evidenced by Mary Jones and Mary Barber. Mary Jones published her 1750 *Miscellanies in Prose and Verse* by subscription and capitalized on her close friendship with two women of Queen Caroline's household, Martha Lovelace and Charlotte Clayton. Their assistance doubtless helped her garner fourteen hundred subscribers, including numerous members of the court, many individuals requesting the volume on "royal paper." A poem within her volume, *An Epistle to Lady Bowyer* (3.D), satirizes the

24. Cynthia Dereli, "In Search of a Poet: The Life and Work of Elizabeth Hands," *Women's Writing* 8 (2001): 173.

25. Dereli, "In Search of a Poet," 172. Dereli goes on to note that "rivalry may even have played a part, for not all the people listed were on the best of terms with each other" (173).

26. Mary Masters, though not belonging to the laboring class per se, casts herself as a rural maid whose "Genius to Poetry was always brow-beat and discountenanc'd by her Parents, and ... she was shut out from all Commerce with the more knowing and polite Part of the World." The "knowing and polite" world took an interest in her subscription, as evidenced by the volume's subscription list, "which lists 879 copies for 721 patrons, twenty-nine of whom were titled nobility of baronets, with a large number of subscribers from Masters's native Norwich." Adam Budd, "'Merit in Distress': The Troubled Success of Mary Barber," *Review of English Studies*, n.s., 53 (2002): 205n. 3.

27. Mary Chandler, *Poems* (London, 1736).

process of seeking support in this "easy trade," while the preface to the collection offers the requisite humility and gratitude to "her numerous and generous subscribers," who had "put it into her power" to "effectually assist" "a relation, grown old and helpless thro' a series of misfortunes." Recognizing that public (and published) recognition is part of the implicit patron-poet exchange, Jones "cannot but take the public opportunity of giving them their share of the satisfaction."[28] In the preface as in the poem, she negotiates the dual economies of deserving need and literary worth.

Mary Barber, a woolen draper's wife, was part of the Dublin literary circle around writer Jonathan Swift, upon whose extensive network of connections in London she depended to construct her subscription list. Her situation illustrates the possibilities and pitfalls of the subscription process. It took nearly five years from the initial proposal of *Poems on Several Occasions* in 1730 to its final publication in 1735, in part because of Barber's ill health and her occasional missteps in the soliciting of subscribers. Barber ultimately mustered a list of 918 subscribers for 1,106 copies of her book,[29] more names than for any volume since Matthew Prior's 1718 folio. That impressive list of subscribers, however, did not result in significant financial remuneration. With publication by subscription, when subscribers died, decided not to collect the volume, "or simply forgot to do so, then the author and her bookseller would be accountable for the cost of printing."[30] The time lag between initial proposal and actual publication meant that not all of Barber's subscribers accepted receipt of the book, leaving her with a financial liability. The opportunity to market them separately probably yielded few additional funds; in 1735 the average price for a book of poetry sold was only 6s. Although Barber's situation was perhaps extreme in terms of the extensive list of sponsors and her financial liability, it highlights the complex, often precarious nature of publishing even in an arrangement ostensibly removed from the pressures of the marketplace.

While Mary Barber's entrance into a social network was assisted by one well-known author, Mary Whateley Darwall's experience illustrates how a provincial social network mobilized by clergy could fill a subscription list. Darwall, living in Walsall, West Midlands, published four poems in the *Gentleman's Magazine* and two more in the *Royal Female Magazine* under the pseudonym Harriott Airy, an experience that helped her grow "wiser in the ways of the publishing world."[31]

28. Mary Jones, *Miscellanies in Prose and Verse* (Oxford, 1750), v.

29. Adam Budd notes that 249 of Barber's subscribers "were aristocracy and other nobles representing 183 titled families—more than one-third of the entire British nobility and baronetage." "Merit in Distress," 205.

30. Budd, "Merit in Distress," 213.

31. Ann Messenger, *Woman and Poet in the Eighteenth Century: The Life of Mary Whateley Darwall (1738–1825)* (New York: AMS, 1999), 30.

A male supporter, Dr. John Wall, sent one of her poems, *Liberty* (not included), along with a brief biographical note, to four additional magazines and newspapers within a two-month period, generating the interest in her poetry that became the springboard for bringing out a volume by subscription with a London publisher. A farmer's daughter who had strong connections with the local clergy and with the poet William Shenstone, who lived nearby, Darwall was not a servant plucked from obscurity; she was an educated woman who would go on to marry the clergyman who was one of the champions of her subscription list. But her experience illustrates that a single woman confined to the country "could not have managed such a feat without a great deal of help from friends."[32] Darwall ended up with 761 names on her subscription list, mostly drawn from her regional network, and *Original Poems on Several Occasions* was published in 1764.

Thirty years later, with pressing financial needs, Darwall attempted to replicate her earlier success. The son of her initial sponsor, Dr. Wall, who was practicing medicine in Oxford, secured Oxonian subscribers; Darwall's old friend Reverend Luke Booker enlisted some clerical support. But without the kind of advocates she had found for her first volume, Darwall could not secure a patron, and only 359 people subscribed to the volume. The volume itself suggests the limited control an author had over the production and distribution of her text. Published by Darwall's friend, the bookseller Frederick Milward, from Walsall, the book was "poorly proofread"; Ann Messenger notes that although it was offered for sale by a London printer, H. Lowndes Milward "neglected to arrange for advertising, so the sales, apart from subscriptions, were probably small."[33] That result is revealing of the contingencies of print culture for women. The patronage/subscription system depended on a combination of patronal support, personal charms, poetical ability, political affiliation, and, often, intangible network connections. Although seeking subscribers for a volume was not the same as selling it in an open marketplace, sale by subscription still required the author to negotiate the shifting values of notoriety, literary worth, reputation, and social credibility. It could prove more unpredictable than a commercial marketplace. For example, Charlotte Lennox was initially championed by Lady Finch, to whom she dedicated *Poems on Several Occasions* (1747), and was comfortably part of an established literary network. Yet her relative success was followed by extreme misfortune because of her inability to retain existing patrons or cultivate new ones. Thus, "after 1761 Lennox in effect stood outside the patronage system," and she ended her life in poverty.[34]

Sarah Prescott correctly asserts that "it was extremely difficult for a woman to have complete control over her authorial image, her poetic voice, or her texts,

---

32. Messenger, *Woman and Poet*, 38.
33. Messenger, *Woman and Poet*, 181.
34. See Griffin, *Literary Patronage in England*, 205–9, quotation on 209.

if she wanted to enter print and/or receive patronal support";[35] control could be absent in the open market as well. The competitive nature of the print trade and porous notions of copyright introduced the possibility of unlawful proliferation or duplication of a poem in the marketplace in a way that could potentially devalue the poet's work. An extreme although perhaps not anomalous example is Elizabeth Carter's poem *To Wisdom: A nocturnal Ode* (1.D), which was initially published in Samuel Richardson's *Clarissa* (1747) in unauthorized form without her knowledge or permission after Richardson saw the poem in manuscript. Carter subsequently gave Richardson permission to include the poem in "a book which I greatly esteem," recognizing the additional cultural currency she could accrue through her attachment with that novel. However, Richardson's appropriation of her text made it vulnerable to subsequent pirating: it "has flown post through the kingdom upon a hackney newspaper." She is distressed about the poem's inappropriate and potentially devaluing circulation in lesser venues: "I have more reason to resent the very unfair dealing in the person, whoever it was, who gave away copies without my leave, or any restriction. . . . to see it fluttering in two or three journals is beyond all sufferance. 'Tis well for me that the farthing post is supprest, or to be sure it would cut a figure there too."[36] While Carter used the mechanism of the marketplace to recuperate and authorize the poem by publishing it in the *Gentleman's Magazine,* the episode illustrates the vagaries of the marketplace that were often beyond an authorial control.

Charlotte Smith understood the mechanisms of print culture as well as any other poet included in this volume. A career author who supported herself and twelve children exclusively through her writing, Smith knew how to negotiate the twin economies of the commercial marketplace and literary value and reputation. Publishing nine editions of *Elegiac Sonnets* over sixteen years after its initial publication in 1784, Smith used the successive editions, with complicated revisions and additional poems, to refine her aesthetic vision, remain current and competitive in the marketplace, and increase her cultural capital. Smith obscured her financial situation and the need to publish for profit by identifying herself on the title page as "Charlotte Smith of Bignor Park, in Sussex," distancing the marketplace and cultivating a persona as a cultured, refined, learned purveyor of poetry.[37] Smith's poetry was not as financially lucrative for her as her fiction. In her twenty-four-year publishing career Smith earned £2,660 from her prose,

35. Prescott, *Women, Authorship and Literary Culture,* 138.

36. Elizabeth Carter to Catherine Talbot, 20 January 1748, in *Elizabeth Carter,* ed. Judith Hawley, *Bluestocking Feminism: Writings of the Bluestocking Circle, 1738–1785,* vol. 2 (London: Pickering & Chatto, 1999), 389. Some of Carter's poems were also published without her authorization in Robert Dodsley's *Collection of Poems in Three Volumes. By Several Hands* (London, 1748).

37. Stuart Curran suggests that "Smith would not hide her name behind a cloak of anonymity nor would she deny herself the estate where she grew up." Introduction to *The Poems of Charlotte Smith,* ed. Curran (New York: Oxford University Press, 1993), xxiii.

708   PART III. WRITING ON WRITING

£650 from children's books, and £930 from her poetry.[38] However, her "sense of her genteel heritage and her claims to artistry never allowed her to abandon a commitment to poetry,"[39] which she valued "more for her reputation ... her own estimation of her worth as a writer ... poetry made her other work more respectable."[40]

Smith's correspondence indicates her savvy resilience in negotiating with her publishers, Thomas Cadell and William Davies. She balances her need for their continued financial support with her desire to control the circulation of her poetic currency. Responding to their "intimation" that she has "kept back some verses that I might have added to the Subscription volume" in order "to make a farther & unfair advantage of them" or "defraud" them of poetry, Smith denies the accusation. In fact, Smith strategically placed poetry in her novels and then moved those sonnets and poems into her subsequent volumes of verse. She was not alone in recognizing the value of publishing the same poem in different literary contexts. Early in the century, Jane Barker moved poems that had previously received little attention into *The Galesia Trilogy* (1713–26), Laetitia Pilkington interspersed poems throughout her *Memoirs* (1748), and Helen Maria Williams inserted original poetry into *Julia* (1789). For Smith, that shared technique generated increased interest in both the fiction and the poetry and further enhanced the construction of herself as an author. She also understands how to time the market ("I did not intend to publish the Sonnets till Spring") and recognizes that poetry's value can shift according to what she terms "the fashion at this moment." While threatening her publishers—"you will not take it amiss if I engage another publisher"—she reveals her considerable knowledge about packaging and marketing her own poems.[41] Her control over the publication of her poetry, her understanding of the financial implications of different publication decisions, her sense of its cultural value, and her commitment to authorship as the primary means of supporting her family distinguish her.

Each poet in this volume negotiated a unique relationship with print culture, the literary marketplace, her own literary and social network, and the economy of reputation; all their stories differ in some way. In contrast to Smith's actively discussing details of publication, Anna Laetitia Barbauld's level of involvement with the 1773 publication of her *Poems* seems limited; she apparently allowed

---

38. All figures are from Judith Phillips Stanton, "Charlotte Smith's 'Literary Business'; Income, Patronage, and Indigence," *Age of Johnson* 1 (1987): 375–401.

39. Curran, Introduction to *Poems of Charlotte Smith*, xxiii.

40. Stanton, "Charlotte Smith's 'Literary Business,'" 392–93.

41. Charlotte Smith to Thomas Cadell Jr. and William Davies, 20 October 1797, in *The Collected Letters of Charlotte Smith*, ed. Judith Phillips Stanton (Bloomington: Indiana University Press, 2003), 295, 297.

her brother John to make editorial decisions.[42] Although many of the poems in section 3.B, "The Muses," celebrate a supportive female community of writers, Anna Seward, who was instrumental in the revitalization of the sonnet form, famously dismisses Charlotte Smith's sonnets as "pretty tuneful centos from our various poets, without any thing original. . . . It makes one sick."[43] Within this varied context the poems about writing are situated. The pressures of the literary marketplace and the power of the patronage and subscription process influenced women's access to publication. The growth of the provincial press and its importance in the publication of women's poetry is evident. The significance of social networks—in London or the provinces—and of communities of readers cannot be underestimated. Many of these poems represent the material economy in which women operated—the search for a patron, the process of review by critics, the voices of the critics reviewing their works, the interactions with potential patrons or subscribers to their volumes, the logistics of bringing a volume to market, and the difficulty of supporting oneself by poetry. Others focus on the social situations women had to address: the domestic demands, the financial exigencies, the disapproval from friends and family, the defiance of social norms, what Elizabeth Thomas calls "Customs *Tyranny*" (*On Sir J——S—— saying in a sarcastick Manner, My Books would make me Mad*, 3.E). Still other poems represent the alternative economy of friendship, virtue, and transcendent literary value; they explore the metaphors of women's poetic composition and poetically construct an idealized community of women. It is clear that both the symbolic and the material economy could be challenged by class conflict, professional jealousy, and marketplace competition, but that was part of the experience of writing. The reader will learn much about women's relationship with writing in the long eighteenth century from the rich selection of poems in this section.

42. For a discussion of Barbauld's publication of her poems and the involvement of her brother John, see the introduction to *The Poems of Anna Letitia Barbauld*, ed. William McCarthy and Elizabeth Kraft (Athens: University of Georgia Press, 1994).

43. Anna Seward to Miss Weston, 20 July 1786, *The Letters of Anna Seward: Written Between the Years 1784 and 1807*, ed. A. Constable, 6 vols. (Edinburgh, 1811), 1:163.

❀A❀

Alternative Traditions

A large number of poets, male and female, left progress-of-poetry and circuit-of-Apollo poems, and they are telling guides to canon making. Many, like Judith Madan's *Progress of Poetry* (1721) and Joseph Addison's *Account of the Greatest English Poets* (1694), were written when the poets were young. Like Matthew Prior's *Sessions of the Poets* (1688) and Mary Barber's *A True Tale* (1734), some record both changing literary tastes and the part politics plays in a poet's popularity. Chaucer is sometimes excluded, sometimes not. Until the last quarter of the eighteenth century, Aphra Behn is unfailingly included and often given high honors, but mentions of her explicit language and subject matter and then her own questionable lifestyle begin to creep in by the 1720s. The reputations of Katherine Philips, Matthew Prior, Thomas Chatterton, William Shenstone, and Robert Merry rise and fade.

The forms and stories these poems tell are highly imaginative. Mary Barber's *Apollo's Edict* (1734) forbids hackneyed phrases and creates an anti-canon; Jane Brereton's *The Dream* (1744) imitates Chaucer's *House of Fame* and has the orderly line of poets become a chaotic struggle between true geniuses and crowds of pretenders, and Mary Leapor's *Proclamation of Apollo* (1748) features a fight among poets that ends in feasting (not included). Anne Finch observes wittily in *The Circuit of Apollo* that when Apollo surveyed Kent, he "saw there that Poets were not very common, / But most that pretended to Verse, were the Women." The poem begins with a tribute to Behn, "amongst Femens was not on the earth / Her superiour in fancy, in language, or witt." The conclusion is as witty as the opening, for Apollo, unwilling to choose among women, hastens to consult with the Muses concerning "Who of their own sex, best the title might try." An impetus for the alternative traditions that women envision is the desire to create a collaborative, generative relationship. Dominant poems such as Dryden's *Mac-Flecknoe* or Pope's *Essay on Criticism* and *Dunciad* are firmly situated within hierarchical relationships, whether born of literary (or commercial) competition or aesthetic considerations. The male recipients of these poems are worthy readers rather than empowering examples engaged in the same endeavors.

The poems in this section trace changing shapes and purposes for the progress poem and illustrate the construction of a variety of alternate traditions that form canons. The first poems are women's explorations of the history of women's poetry, and they assemble an enabling line of sister poets. While perhaps written to a personal friend, they are more pointedly written to a literary model whom the poet aspires to emulate. Anne Wharton, niece of John Wilmot, Earl of Rochester, commends Aphra Behn on her verses in praise of her uncle. Although the poem ostensibly commemorates his poetic worth, it is more powerfully an exhortation for Behn to continue her own work: "If you do this, what Glory will insue, / To all our Sex, to Poesie, and you? / Write on, and may your Numbers ever flow, / Soft as the Wishes that I make for you" (*To Mrs. A. Behn, on What She Writ of the Earl of Rochester*). Delarivière Manley does the same thing in her poem to Catharine Trotter (later Cockburn), then sixteen, upon the success of her first play, *Agnes de Castro*. Cockburn becomes the woman poet "to fill the Vacant Throne." As with the Wharton poem, one woman's success is significant for its own sake. More powerfully, however, it provides an aspirational model for her female colleagues. Thus, "Fired by the bold Example," writes Manley, "I would try / To turn our Sexes weaker Destiny." As in Finch's *Circuit of Appollo,* in the "Poetick Race" one woman's success is every woman's success: "Encourag'd, and thus led by you, / Methinks we might more Crowns than theirs Subdue" (*To the Author of "Agnes de Castro"*). Mary Chudleigh is also a powerful model. Elizabeth Thomas, in her effort to pay "duteous Homage," writes three poems celebrating Chudleigh, two in this section and one in section I.D, "The Ode." In all three poems Chudleigh and her work function as an important touchstone. Her poetry is marked by "*Eloquence* divine" and "solid *Judgment*"; she is the "*fair Defender*" whom the "Foes *subdues*."

Part of this construction was a trend to encourage women to write virtuous poetry, a movement paralleled by society's growing consensus about how virtuous women spoke and behaved and their importance to the nation's wellbeing. A central element of Chudleigh's appeal was her work's unassailably virtuous message: "own the Force of *Virtue's* sovereign Pow'r" (Thomas, *To the Lady Chudleigh*). The female poets in this section included morality as a value in their work, as Finch did when she mentioned that Behn "a little too loosly she writt" and when she praised other qualities in the other poets. Mary Whateley Darwall and Anna Williams, for example, both made this argument. Williams sought the power to "emulate [the] pious art" of Moses, Deborah, and David (*An Ode*). Similarly Darwall, in *Elegy on the Uses of Poetry,* detailed how the Muse helped to "harmonize, instruct, and charm Mankind": "Her pleasing Task, . . . / . . . / To vindicate the Ways of God to Man." This Popean allusion—his stated purpose in *Essay on Man* was to "vindicate the ways of God to Man"[1]—popularized an argument for the virtues of moral verse.

By mid-century it was conventional to construct "a politico-historical account of Western literature" in which literature's and liberty's superiority progressed from classical Greece and Rome to Britain.[2] These accounts usually included at least Homer and Virgil but moved quickly to Shakespeare, to Milton, and, depending on the detail, to Abraham Cowley, Edmund Waller, and an orderly line of poets up to the writer's time. That arts, arms, and civilization are interwoven is clear from titles such as James Thomson's *Liberty* (1735–36). These poems, like Thomas Gray's *Progress of Poetry* and *The Bard* (both 1757), are deeply concerned with the purposes of poetry and its value for the nation. Mary Darwall's *Elegy on the Uses of Poetry*, Anna Williams's *Ode*, and Helen Maria Williams's *Address to Poetry* are in this tradition, and in form and content they are serious and elevated. Darwall depends heavily upon classical structures, imagery, language, and tensions. Through personifications, she touches almost every note in the mid-century reflective elegy on poetry: "Where Heav'n-born *Truth*, and keen-ey'd *Genius* rove, / Where *Peace* resides in *Freedom*'s Moss-roof'd Dome." For these poets Britain is the epitome of liberty, Milton is the noble poet of religious inspiration, and poetry has social and moral responsibilities to maintain a tradition of artistic and civic ideals.

Helen Maria Williams's *Address to Poetry* and Mary Robinson's *Ainsi Va le Monde, A Poem* continues this tradition but constructs yet another canon based upon an alternate reading of tradition. Writing from the perspective of a poet, Williams explains what poetry means to her, and one of the most remarkable sections of the poem is her assertion of what poetry means to people in her specific culture, including the poor. Rather than following the earlier pattern of chronological order, she works with a hierarchy of modes and moods. She places the mixed audience listening to a minstrel entertain with Homer's "native art" beside, in the next verse, the poor who "Spare one small coin, the ballad's price; / Admire their poet's quaint device, / And marvel much as all his rhymes unfold." Her conclusion draws out what Thomson, Pope, and Gray have in common. Robinson includes the call for freedom and virtue and breaks with the other poems by including canons of dramatic writers (including Shakespeare, Thomas Otway, and Garrick) and painters (Raphael, Godfrey Kneller, Peter Lely, and Joshua Reynolds, among others). Her poem is addressed to Robert Merry (1755–98), who was a leader of the Della Cruscans, a coterie of English poets formed in Italy in 1785, who were at the height of their popularity in 1790. Their poetry was sentimental, highly ornamented, and stylized. Thus, in Robinson's view, Thomas Chatterton and Otway are regrettably ignored; "coarser flow'rs" succeed where "sweet blossoms" fail. Robinson laments the "fantastic folly o'er the land" as "True Wit recedes" and "blushing Reason views / This spurious offspring of the banish'd Muse." The Muse must help liberate "The Arts," who have "Toil'd without fame, in sordid chains confin'd." The "native Genius" of Britain causes worthy poets to go unrecognized. Especially in the second half of the century, poetic fads inflected the canons constructed in poems by men and women.

Robinson and Williams move closer to Romantic themes and prosody with their exuberant celebrations of the beauty of nature and its power to inspire. The turn of the century has been associated with the expunging of women from the canon, and neither Williams nor Robinson includes earlier women poets.[3] Their contemporary Rebecca Manners excluded all women but Sappho in her *Review of Poetry* (1799) although she praised thirty-four male British poets and twenty-nine classical and Renaissance Italian poets. Yet the continuity of the socio-political and nationalistic-literary emphases in the progress-of-poetry poems remains. Although ostensibly focusing on poetic expression and the value of Merry's work, Robinson sounds a libratory note that goes beyond the poetic. She writes eloquently and extensively in the final stanzas about the "nat'ral Rights of Man," alluding both to the recent events of the French Revolution and to Robert Merry's 1790 poem *The Laurel of Liberty*.[4] Robinson was initially a supporter of the French Revolution, and this poem moves from the Muse to the "blithe Goddess," Freedom. The concepts of freedom and liberation, although deeply political within the immediate context of 1790, are actually central to all the poems in this section. The tradition of British liberty, the line of poets who have called Britain to its highest ideals, and the poet's continued high calling, ability to see Truth, and liberty to speak it are woven inextricably together. That the women poets weave themselves so firmly into these poems suggests that they did not see themselves as outside the republic of letters.

Notes

1. Alexander Pope, *Essay on Man,* 1.16. Pope is also, of course, alluding to Milton's stated purpose in *Paradise Lost,* to "justify the ways of God to man" (1.26).

2. Abigail Williams, "Whig and Tory Poetics," in *A Companion to Eighteenth-Century Poetry,* ed. Christine Gerrard (Oxford: Blackwell, 2006), 451.

3. Most scholars date canon formation to 1770–1880, and the "national" collections compiled at the beginning of the nineteenth century largely omitted women. Richard Terry speaks of women "quarantined" in one anthology and surveys these collections in *Poetry and the Making of the English Literary Past, 1660–1781* (Oxford: Oxford University Press, 2001), 252–59, 277. See also Elizabeth Eger, "Fashioning a Female Canon: Eighteenth-Century Women Poets and the Politics of the Anthology," in *Women's Poetry in the Enlightenment: The Making of the Canon, 1730–1820,* ed. Isobel Armstrong and Virginia Blain (New York: St. Martin's, 1999), 201–15.

4. Robert Merry, *The Laurel of Liberty, A Poem* (London, 1790), 36. Dedicated to "the National Assembly of France, the true and zealous representatives of a Free People," the poem celebrates the revolution and envisions a day when "earth becomes a temporary Heav'n."

To Mrs. A. Behn, on What She Writ of the Earl of Rochester[1]

Anne Wharton

> In pleasing Transport rap't, my Thoughts aspire
> With humble Verse to Praise what you Admire:
> Few living Poets may the Laurel claim,
> Most pass thro' Death, to reach at Living Fame.
> Fame, Phoenix like,[2] still rises from a Tomb;
> But bravely you this Custom have o'ercome.
> You force an Homage from each Generous Heart,
> Such as you always pay to just Desert.
> You prais'd him Living, whom you Dead bemoan,
> And now your Tears afresh his Laurel crown.
> It is this Flight of yours excites my Art,
> Weak as it is, to take your Muse's part,
> And pay loud Thanks back from my bleeding Heart.[3]
> May you in every pleasing Grace excel,
> May Bright *Apollo*[4] in your Bosome dwell;
> May yours excel the Matchless *Sappho*'s[5] Name;
> May you have all her Wit, without her Shame:

10

1. Wharton was the niece of the poet John Wilmot, the Earl of Rochester (1647–80). He was twelve years her senior, and by all accounts the two apparently were very close. In her will she left three thousand pounds to Rochester's illegitimate daughter by Elizabeth Barry. Following Rochester's death in 1680, the poet Aphra Behn wrote *On the Death of the late Earl of Rochester* (not included). The opening lines read: "Mourn, Mourn, ye Muses, all your loss deplore, / The Young, the Noble *Strephon* is no more." Wharton responded with this poem, which Behn, in turn, answered with *Lines to Mrs. Wharton* (not included). Wharton subsequently composed *Elegy on the Earle of Rochester* (1685, not included), which includes the following lines: "His lively Wit was of himself a part, / Not, as in other men, the Work of Art; / For, tho his Learning like his Wit was great, / Yet sure all Learning came below his Wit; / . . . / . . . he did Mankind excel" (lines 23–27, 30).

2. In classical mythology, the phoenix is a bird resembling an eagle but with sumptuous red and gold plumage. Said to live for five or six hundred years in the deserts of Arabia, it makes a nest of spices, sings a beautiful dirge, and burns itself to ashes on a funeral pyre ignited by the sun and fanned by its own wings, only to rise from its ashes with renewed youth and repeat the cycle.

3. Wharton returned to this bleeding-heart imagery in *Elegy on the Earle of Rochester:* "Weep drops of Blood, my Heart, thou'st lost thy Pride."

4. In Greek mythology, Apollo was the god of music and poetry, archery, and prophecy; indeed, the oracular shrine at Delphi was the precinct of Apollo. He was also the god of light and the sun, which is why he is often referred to as Phoebus, which means "bright."

5. Lyric poet who lived on the island of Lesbos in the seventh and sixth centuries BC. Her intensely personal lyric poetry recounted the emotions, hopes, and knowledge of women of her privileged class. She also developed a unique intricate meter that is known as Sapphic verse. In addition to being a poet, Sappho also operated a prestigious *thiasos,* an academy for young unmarried women. Two attitudes toward Sappho explain the "shame" to which Wharton refers in the next line. The first stems from the Roman poet Ovid's fictional representation of Sappho in *Heroides* 15. He writes a letter from Sappho's perspective, recounting her allegedly failed love affair with the boatman Phaon, which drives her to suicide. Second, in the centuries after her death, questions emerged regarding the

Tho' she to Honour gave a fatal Wound,
Employ your Hand to raise it from the ground.
Right its wrong'd Cause with your Inticing Strain,   20
Its ruin'd Temples try to build again.
Scorn meaner Theams, declining low desire,
And bid your Muse maintain a Vestal Fire.
If you do this, what Glory will insue,
To all our Sex, to Poesie, and you?
Write on, and may your Numbers ever flow,
Soft as the Wishes that I make for you.

(1680; 1695)

To the Author of *Agnes de Castro*[6]
Delarivière Manley

Orinda, and the Fair *Astrea* gone,[7]
Not one was found to fill the Vacant Throne:
Aspiring Man had quite regain'd the Sway,
Again had Taught us humbly to Obey;
Till you (Natures third start, in favour of our Kind)
With stronger Arms, their Empire have disjoyn'd,
And snatcht a Lawrel[8] which they thought their Prize,
Thus Conqu'ror, with your Wit, as with your Eyes.
Fired by the bold Example, I would try
To turn our Sexes weaker Destiny.   10
O! How I long in the Poetick Race,
To loose the Reins, and give their Glory Chase;
For thus Encourag'd, and thus led by you,
Methinks we might more Crowns than theirs Subdue.

(1696)

---

degree and nature of the intimacy within her female community. Although her poems remain only in fragments, she was commonly regarded as the greatest female classical poet (Plato dubbed her the "Tenth Muse"); as such, she represented a powerful originating female poetic voice.

6. Catharine Trotter Cockburn was only sixteen when her first play, *Agnes de Castro,* adapted from Aphra Behn's novel *Agnes de Castro, or The Force of Generous Love,* debuted at the Theatre Royal in late 1695 or early 1696.

7. Katherine Philips and Aphra Behn, respectively.

8. Reference to the wreath of laurels that marks great poetic achievement or is a symbol of the poet laureate.

The Circuit of Appollo
Anne Finch

Appollo[9] as lately a Circuit[10] he made,
Throo' the lands of the Muses when Kent[11] he survey'd
And saw there that Poets were not very common,
But most that pretended to Verse, were the Women
Resolv'd to encourage, the few that he found,
And she that writt best, with a wreath shou'd be crown'd.
A summons sent out, was obey'd but by four,
When Phebus,[12] afflicted, to meet with no more,
And standing, where sadly, he now might descry,
From the banks of the Stoure the desolate Wye,[13]
He lamented for Behn o're that place of her birth,
And said amongst Fem̄ens[14] was not on the earth
Her superiour in fancy,[15] in language, or witt,
Yett own'd that a little too loosly she writt;
Since the art of the Muse is to stirr up soft thoughts,
Yett to make all hearts beat, without blushes, or faults.
But now to proceed, and their merritts to know,
Before he on any, the Bay's wou'd bestow,
He order'd them each in their several[16] way,
To show him their papers, to sing, or to say,
What 'ere they thought best, their pretention's might prove,
When Alinda,[17] began, with a song upon Love.
So easy the Verse, yett compos'd with such art,
That not one expression fell short of the heart;

10

20

9. In Greek mythology, Apollo was the god of music, archery, and the sun. Everyday he drove the golden chariot made by Vulcan that carried the sun across the sky.

10. Reference both to the daily trip made by Apollo in his chariot and to the journey of a judge through certain appointed areas, or "circuits," for the purpose of holding courts or performing other stated duties at various places in succession.

11. County in southeastern England.

12. A name meaning "brightness," given to Apollo because of his association with the sun.

13. The Stour River and the village of Wye are both located in Kent.

14. *Femmens*, a French word for women, usually mature and/or married; the macron doubles the *m*.

15. A creative faculty, usually treated as lighter and more whimsical and playful than imagination or as an assistant to it. Imagination, with the power to transform its material, was considered the higher power.

16. Distinct, separate.

17. Not identified.

Apollo himself, did their influence obey,
He catch'd up his Lyre, and a part he wou'd play,
Declaring, no harmony else, cou'd be found,
Fitt to wait upon words, of so moving a sound.
The Wreath, he reach'd out, to have plac'd on her head,
If Laura[18] not quickly a paper had read,   30
Wherin She Orinda[19] has praised so high,
He own'd itt had reach'd him, while yett in the sky,
That he thought with himself, when itt first struck his ear,
Who e're cou'd write that, ought the Laurel to wear.
Betwixt them he stood, in a musing suspence,
Till Valeria[20] withdrew him a little from thence,
And told him, as soon as she'd gott him aside,
Her works, by no other, but him shou'd be try'd;
Which so often he read, and with still new delight,
That Iudgment t'was thought wou'd not passe till twas 'night;   40
Yet at length, he restor'd them, but told her withall
If she kept itt still close, he'd the Talent recall.
Ardelia,[21] came last as expecting least praise,
Who writt for her pleasure and not for the Bays,[22]
But yett, as occasion, or fancy should sway,
Wou'd sometimes endeavour to passe a dull day,
In composing a song, or a Scene of a Play
Not seeking for Fame, which so little does last,
That e're we can taste itt, the Pleasure is Past.

18. Not identified, although the subject of speculation. The best guess is probably an obscure poet known only as "Mrs. Randolph," who had sent Finch a poem praising her as the heir to Orinda, Katherine Philips. Barbara McGovern, *Anne Finch and Her Poetry: A Critical Biography* (Athens: University of Georgia Press, 1992), 121–23. A. Harriette Andreadis identifies Laura as Mary of Modena (1658–1718) in *Sappho in Early Modern England: Female Same-Sex Literary Erotics, 1550–1714* (Chicago: University of Chicago Press, 2001), 125.

19. Katherine Philips.

20. Not identified, but speculated by Edmund Gosse to be Lady Ann Boyle and by Ellen Moody to be a woman referred to in a poem in the Wellesley manuscript or Mary Astell (1666–1731), the author of *A Serious Proposal to the Ladies* (1694) and *Some Reflections on Marriage* (1700), which made her the most influential feminist before Mary Wollstonecraft (1759–97). According to Gosse, Valeria was the name Katherine Philips gave to Lady Ann, sister of Roger Boyle, first Earl of Orrery. *Seventeenth-Century Studies: A Contribution to the History of English Poetry* (New York: Charles Scribner's Sons, 1897), 233. There are problems with all of these identifications, as evidence about origins or homes in Kent or dates of acquaintance with Finch needs further scrutiny.

21. Finch.

22. Another term for the wreath of laurels awarded for poetic achievement and often associated with the poet laureate.

50   But Appollo reply'd, tho' so carelesse she seemd,
        Yett the Bays, if her share, wou'd be highly esteem'd.

        And now, he was going to make an Oration,
        Had thrown by one lock, with a delicate fassion,
        Upon the left foot, most genteely did stand,
        Had drawn back the other, and wav'd his white hand,
        When calling to mind, how the Prize alltho' given
        By Paris, to her, who was fairest in Heaven,
        Had pull'd on the rash, inconsiderate Boy,
        The fall of his House, with the ruine of Troy,[23]
60   Since in Witt, or in Beauty, itt never was heard,
        One female cou'd yield t' have another preferr'd,
        He changed his dessign, and devided his praise,
        And said that they all had a right to the Bay's,
        And that t'were injustice, one brow to adorn,
        With a wreath, which so fittly by each might be worn.
        Then smil'd to himself, and applauded his art,
        Who thus nicely has acted so suttle a part,
        Four Women to wheedle, but found 'em too many,
        For who wou'd please all, can never please any.
70   In vain then, he thought itt, there longer to stay,
        But told them, he now must go drive on the day,
        Yett the case to Parnassus,[24] shou'd soon be referr'd,
        And there in a councill of Muses,[25] be heard,
        Who of their own sex, best the title might try,
        Since no man upon earth, nor Himself in the sky,
        Wou'd be so imprudent, so dull, or so blind,
        To loose three parts in four from amongst woman kind.

                                    (c. 1713; 1903)

23. In the Judgment of Paris, Priam's son Paris gave the golden apple inscribed "to the fairest" to Aphrodite rather than to Hera or Athena. His action unwittingly initiated a chain of events that resulted in the Trojan War and the fall of the house of Priam.

24. In Greek mythology, the mountain that is home to the nine Muses; regarded as the source of literary and poetic inspiration.

25. The nine daughters of Jupiter and Mnemosyne (Memory), they presided over song, prompted memory, and were regarded as the sources of poetic inspiration.

To the Lady Chudleigh, the Anonymous Author of the Lady's Defence[26]

Elizabeth Thomas

MADAM,

Long since we heard of *One*, who mighty *wise*,
Would needs pretend to give us *sage Advice;*
The *pompous* Title Page I view'd with Awe,
And thought he might expound the *sacred Law;*[27]
Inform our *Minds,* mysterious *Precepts* clear,
And by good Rules our future Conduct steer:
But when I found, instead of *Truth*'s divine,
Malignant Humour lurk'd in ev'ry Line,[28]
Each Period void of *Charity* and *Sense,*
Yet varnish'd over with the dull Pretence;   10
'Twas then, with just *Disdain* and *Anger* fir'd,
I to a lonesome gloomy Shade retir'd;
Wishing I could some happy Means invent,
Which might betimes the *Moral Plague* prevent.

　Poor Sex, cried I, with *Malice* still opprest,
By Knaves, and Fools, on ev'ry Side *distrest!*
Long have we drag'd a servile heavy Chain,
Yet were our Souls *too noble* to complain:
For *Quiet Sake,* we own'd the barb'rous Sway,
And tamely did their rigid Laws obey.   20
Such mild Submission, *gen'rous Minds* would own,
But *savage Men* are not with Mildness won;

---

26. Chudleigh published *The Ladies Defence* (London, 1701), which went through four editions in her lifetime. The text was a response to John Sprint's *The Bride-Woman's Counseller* (London, 1699). Chudleigh's dialogue poem contrasts the boorish attitudes of a parson, Sir John Brute, and Sir William Loveall, who assert that women should regard their husbands "like wise Eastern Slaves with trembling Awe" (ix), with the enlightened view of Melissa. Thomas initiated her relationship with Chudleigh by sending her some of her own work.

27. The full title of Sprint's text reads, *The Bride-Woman's Counseller. Being a Sermon Preach'd at a Wedding, May the 11th, 1699, at Sherbourn, in Dorsetshire.* Additionally, the following epigraph appears on the title page: "I COR. Chap. 7 Ver. 34. But she that is Married careth for the things of the World, how she may please her Husband."

28. Sprint's tract begins with the assumption, "Women are of weaker Capacities to learn than Men, and therefore when they have a hard and difficult Lesson, and but weak Abilities to learn it, . . . it behoves us not only to tell them their Duty in Conjunction with their Husbands, but also to teach them singly and by themselves." *Bride-Woman's Counseller,* 2.

Our *Duty* cannot calm their brutal Rage,
Nor silent *Virtue,* Thirst of Rule asswage.

Rise! Rise ye *Heroins,* secure the Field,
Truth be your Guide, and *Innocence* your Shield;
Confute the Maxims of these sordid Tools,
And make them know, we follow *Virtue's* Rules.
Crush but this Hope forlorn of *hireling Wit,*
30   The num'rous *Rebel Fry*[29] will soon submit.

What! all asleep!
No *gen'rous Soul* with noble *Ardour* fir'd,
No *free-born Muse* with Sense of *Wrong* inspir'd?
Not one *Zenobia* to maintain our *Right,*[30]
And meet their *Champion* in an equal Fight.
Oh were my *Power* but equal to my *Will,*
In listed[31] Combat would I prove my Skill;
This infant Muse her callow Wings[32] should try,
      And bravely Conquer, or as bravely Die.[33]
40   Ye Pow'rs above, some worthy Mind inspire,
Let *Truth* advance, and *Calumny*[34] retire.
This said, with Wrongs and Insolence opprest,
A balmy Slumber lull'd my Mind to rest.

When Lo! a sudden Voice I heard,
And looking up, a youthful Swain appear'd.
Awake, cry'd he, shake off this dull Despair,
For I O *Peans,*[35] let thy Muse prepare:
See here, what Wonders *Eloquence* can do,
When join'd with *Harmony* and *Beauty* too:
50   Whilst thou in lazy Wishes pass'd the Day,

29. Offspring.
30. Zenobia was the queen of Palmyra who fought against the Romans and invaded Asia Minor and Egypt. In *The Ladies Defence* Melissa, listing examples of "Women remarkable for Virtue," writes, "A Place with them does Great *Zenobia* claim" (19).
31. Enlisted.
32. Without feathers and, in this case, inexperienced.
33. In Alexander Fyfe's *The Royal Martyr* the Duke of Richmond pledges his allegiance to Charles I, stating, "The Work with Expedition, I will ply / And bravely conquer, or as bravely die." *The Royal Martyr, K. Charles I. An Opera* (Edinburgh, 1705), 11.
34. Slander, false charge.
35. Paeans, heartfelt songs of praise or thanksgiving.

And sigh'd ingloriously thy Time away,
This gen'rous Nymph in *Action* spoke her Mind,
She *came*, she *saw*, and *gain'd* what she design'd:[36]
By dint of *Reason*, she your Foes *subdues*,
See how they trembling fly, and *she alone* pursues.

    Marissa[37] Hail! hail *Eloquence* divine!
What solid *Judgment* sparkles in each Line! }
What *strenuous* Proofs in ev'ry Period shine!
With such Success the happy *Goal* you reach,
Not *Wisdom's self* could better Lessons teach;   60
Could more impartially the Case decide,
And solve the Doubts that rose on either Side.

    Fly! brutal Wretches fly! no more proclaim
Your want of *Candour*, and your Love of *Shame:*
No more the Foibles of the Sex explore,
But own the Force of *Virtue*'s sovereign Pow'r:
Let bright *Marissa!* now your Rage disarm,
Whose Eyes are Darts, whose ev'ry Word's a *Charm*.

    He said——
Yet I delay'd the *Blessing* to receive,   70
And scarcely could the welcome News believe:
Wav'ring I stood, with *Hope* and *Fear* opprest,
Such diff'rent Passions strove within my Breast;
Lest he had utter'd more than was your *Due*,
For sure I thought it could not all be true.

    Forgive this *Doubt;* my Error soon I found,
And was in Wonder and Amazement drown'd;
Such *Wit*, and *Learning*, shin'd in ev'ry Part;
Such serious *Piety*, so free from Art:
Entranc'd with *Joy*, I found his Words were true,   80
And freely own'd, he scarce had spoke your *Due*.
'Twas then in rural Notes I sung your Fame;
'Twas then I bless'd our *fair Defender*'s Name.

36. Allusion to *Veni, vidi, vici* (I came, I saw, I conquered), uttered by Julius Caesar in 47 BC, proclaiming total military victory over Pharnaces, enemy of the Roman Republic.
37. Chudleigh's name for herself in correspondence with Thomas.

But while in artless, humble Lays,[38] I strove
T' express my *Duty, Gratitude,* and *Love;*
I heard a joyful Murmur eccho round,
And all the beauteous Quire[39] *Marissa's* Name resound.

(1722)

To the Lady Chudleigh, On Printing Her Excellent Poems
Elizabeth Thomas

MADAM,
Could I the Wonders of your *Pen* rehearse,
In Notes, as sweet, and lofty as your *Verse,*
With eager Haste I would this Volume meet,
And pay my *duteous Homage* at your Feet.
Extol your great, your generous Design,
And praise the *Beauties* of each sparkling Line:
Show, with what solid Pleasures they delight,
How *Wit,* and *Learning,* in your Works *unite:*
With what illustrious Charms you *Friendship* dress,
10   And slighted *Virtue's* lovely Form express.
What pious *Zeal,* your sacred Lines inspire,
And how you raise our Souls with true *Seraphick*[40] Fire,
But oh! *too Conscious* of the Want of Art,
I dare not write the Dictates of my Heart;
Lest my unskilful *Muse* should rudely *praise*
A *Theam,*[41] deserving of the noblest Lays.[42]

(1722)

---

38. Short lyric or narrative poems intended to be sung.
39. Thomas would seem to be punning here: *quire* is not only a variant spelling of *choir* but also a publishing term referring to twenty-four sheets of writing paper.
40. Angelic.
41. Variant spelling of *theme.*
42. Short lyric or narrative poems intended to be sung.

Elegy on the Uses of Poetry
Inscribed to the Rev. Randle Darwall, M.A.[43]

Mary Whateley Darwall

Hail! gentle *Evening,* clad in sober grey,
   Mild Mother, Thou, of *Fancy's*[44] airy Train;
How sweet to fly the vain Pursuits of Day,
   And range with Thee the solitary Plain!

Far from the Dome, where splendid *Anguish* weeps,
   Where *Guilt,* or *Envy,* blast the Midnight Hour;
Lead me, where Poppy-crown'd[45] *Contentment* sleeps,
   To the light Breeze, that fans the Dew-bath'd Flow'r.

Slow-winding near yon Osier-fringed Stream,[46]
   On whose green Marge[47] soft *Silence* loves to stray;   10
O modest *Eve!* indulge my Muse-rapt Dream,
   That breathes no light-tun'd Air, or wanton Lay.

At this still Hour oft thro' the high-arch'd Grove,
   Where dwells sage *Contemplation,* let me roam;
Where Heav'n-born *Truth,* and keen-ey'd *Genius* rove,
   Where *Peace* resides in *Freedom*'s Moss-roof'd Dome.

These Heaven ordain'd the Guardians of the Muse;
   Beneath their sacred Influence unconfin'd

43. Randall Darwall, who would become Darwall's father-in-law when she married his son John in 1766, graduated from Brazen Nose (now Brasenose) College, Oxford, on 28 June 1726 and from 1726 to 1777 was rector of Haughton, in Staffordshire, where Darwall (then Whateley) lived from 1760 to 1763. Ann Messenger writes, "A versifier himself (some of his efforts appeared in the *London Magazine*), he apparently sent her a poem" to which this poem responds. *Woman and Poet in the Eighteenth Century: The Life of Mary Whateley Darwall (1738–1825)* (New York: AMS, 1999), 43. Throughout his life, Darwall was an active subscriber to works of poetry, including Darwall's—he, his wife, and their daughter each subscribed, and he apparently secured eighty subscribers for Darwall's first volume of poetry—and clearly he had an active engagement with poetry.

44. A creative faculty, usually treated as lighter and more whimsical and playful than imagination or as an assistant to it. Imagination, with the power to transform its material, was considered the higher power.

45. Poppies are flowers long valued for their medicinal and narcotic properties. In eighteenth-century poetry the poppy is associated with soporific powers; thus dozing Contentment has a wreath of poppies.

46. Stream lined by willows.

47. Riverbank.

She soars, superior to terrestrial Views,
20   To harmonize, instruct, and charm Mankind.

Her pleasing Task, thro' Nature's varied Plan,
     To trace the Goodness of Almighty Power;
To vindicate the Ways of God to Man,[48]
     Soothe *Care*'s deep Gloom, and chear the lonely Hour.

Nor scorn'd she mild, to sing of Swains[49] and Flocks,
     In simple Elegance to haunt the Plains;
In *Dorian*[50] Mood beneath impending Rocks
     To breathe the rural Reed to softest Strains;

To paint the Scenes, which sportive *Fancy* drew,
30   To *Love* and *Truth* attune the tender Lyre;
While her chaste Steps fair *Virtue*'s Paths pursue,
     Scorning each sordid Wish and low Desire.

Shame to the Hand, that first *Her* Pow'r abus'd,
     And with licentious Freedom stain'd the Page;
Whose Wit infectious Poison wide diffus'd,
     Of sacrific'd to Gold the noble Rage.

When *Vice* wou'd taint the Morals of Mankind,
     When *Pride* or *Envy* wou'd debase a Name;
When *Flattery* has her venal Chaplet[51] twin'd,
40   Shall these degrade the Muse's sacred Flame?

When *Beauty* from the chaste-rob'd *Graces*[52] flies
     To hold light Converse with the *Cyprian* Queen;[53]
While blushing *Modesty* with down-cast Eyes,
     Gives place to *Mirth*'s loud Laugh, or Jest obscene.

---

48. Here and in the third stanza the poem alludes to *Paradise Lost.*
49. Country men; lovers.
50. One of the ancient Grecian modes, characterized by simplicity and solemnity; also, the first of the "authentic" ecclesiastical modes.
51. Flower garland.
52. The goddesses Euphrosyne, Aglaia, and Thalia, presiding over all social enjoyments and elegant arts.
53. Aphrodite, the goddess of love; Cyprus was known for the worship of Aphrodite.

Shall these a Place in *Fame*'s fair Records gain,
    Who strew *Pierian*[54] Flow'rs on *Vice*'s Shrine?
No, let Oblivion shrowd each guilty Strain,
    Tho' *Wit* and *Learning* all their Pow'rs combine.

For me, the meanest of the tuneful Throng,
    If e'er to Themes like these my Voice I raise;   50
If venal *Flatt'ry* e'er debase my Song,
    Or aught but Merit gain my honest Praise;

Perish the Blooms, which from the Vernal Field[55]
    This Hand has cull'd fair *Friendship*'s Brows to wreathe;
No Pleasure may the humble Off'rings yield,
    No grateful Odours, or sweet Fragrance breathe.

To *Gratitude* and *Friendship* flows this Strain;
    Accept, O *Darwall!* what your Verse inspir'd;
Else have I wak'd my Rural Reed[56] in vain,
    Else has the Muse in vain my Bosom fir'd.   60

But shou'd your Eye with wonted Candour view
    This well-meant Lay, by *Truth* and *Freedom* plan'd;
Shou'd these faint Strokes, which simple *Nature* drew,
    Pass unreprov'd beneath your judging Hand;

I ask no more; *happy*, with this poor Bough,
    This tributary Strain of artless Youth,
If gracious you shall deign to bind your Brow,
    O! Friend to *Virtue, Piety* and *Truth!*

(1764)

54. One of the four mountains of the Muses—the others were Helicon, Parnassus, and Olympus—Pierus was their birthplace. Pierian flowers represented inspiration.
55. Flowering or green field.
56. Reed made into a rustic musical pipe, the symbol of rustic or pastoral poetry.

An Ode
Anna Williams

I.

Cease, ye profane, your impious rhimes,
   Ye wanton poets of the times,
Whose wit is lavish'd in defence
Of folly, and the joys of sense;
   The mischief-spreading verse forbear,
That taints the mind, and pains the modest ear.
Too strongly is our bark[57] borne down the stream,
   By passions pow'rful gale;
Ill does it then the Muse beseem[58]

10   With modulated breath to swell the hast'ning sail.

II.

For what, ye sons of verse, was reason given,
   Illustrious donative[59] of Heaven;
For what, but with the charms of flowing lays,[60]
   To propagate the Donor's praise;
   And lead with sweetest force the mind,
   By mirth and melody combin'd,
To know and to revere the first great Cause:[61]
   Who fram'd the skies, and earth, and sea,
Gave us, and all that we behold, to be,

20   And rules the whole by wondrous laws.

III.

   How can degenerate bards excuse
   The sallies[62] of a vitious[63] Muse;
   How poor a plea 'twou'd be to say,
That ye were borne, spite of yourselves, away,
   To pen the gross or impious page,
And court the taste of a licentious age!

57. Small sailboat with three masts.
58. Befit.
59. Gift.
60. Short lyric or narrative poems intended to be sung.
61. God; the cause of the universe.
62. Sprightly or audacious utterances or literary compositions.
63. Alternate spelling of *vicious,* in this context meaning "profligate" or "wicked."

No more with conqu'ring truth debate,
Nor term your wickedness your fate;
No more with grov'ling views debase an art
Design'd to raise the thought and mend the heart.   30

IV.

Awake, ye sons of harmony,
    And string anew the silver lyre;
To themes sublime your art apply,
    And set the soul on fire:
Fear not to quit the common road,
And shew that to be wise is to be good;
Till won to virtue by persuasive lays,
All practice what all now consent to praise.

V.

When blest Religion breathes in ev'ry strain,
    And hallows the poetick vein,   40
Like tow'ring eagles soars the bard on high,
And dwells above the unpolluted sky.
Thus Moses tun'd his voice,[64] thus Deb'rah sung,[65]
And David's harp to airs divine was strung.[66]

VI.

All-gracious God, to me the power impart,
    To emulate their pious art:
Fain would I take a daring flight, and bring
From Heaven the verse that sings th' Eternal King.
Then should my zeal stop piety's decay,
And light in ev'ry heart devotion's ray;   50
Till Nature's change my thoughts and verse inspire
With sweeter musick and sublimer fire.

(1766)

---

64. Moses was the Hebrew prophet, teacher, and leader who delivered the Hebrew tribes from Egyptian slavery: "Then sang Moses and the children of Israel this song unto the LORD, and spake, saying, I will sing unto the LORD." Exod. 15:1.

65. Following the defeat of the Canaanites, Deborah, an Israelite prophetess, sang a triumphal song of praise to God. Judg. 4:1–23.

66. King David was a harpist, musician to Saul: "And it came to pass, when the evil spirit from God was upon Saul, that David took an harp, and played with his hand: so Saul was refreshed, and was well, and the evil spirit departed from him." 1 Sam. 16:23.

An Address to Poetry
Helen Maria Williams

While envious crowds the summit view,
Where danger with ambition strays;
   Or far, with anxious step, pursue
Pale av'rice, thro' his winding ways;
   The selfish passions in their train,
Whose force the social ties unbind,
   And chill the love of human kind,
And make fond Nature's best emotions vain;

   Oh Poesy! Oh nymph most dear,
10   To whom I early gave my heart,
   Whose voice is sweetest to my ear
Of aught in nature or in art;
   Thou, who canst all my breast controul,
Come, and thy harp of various cadence bring,
   And long with melting music swell the string
That suits the present temper of my soul.

   Oh! ever gild my path of woe,
And I the ills of life can bear;
   Let but thy lovely visions glow,
20   And chase the forms of real care;
   Oh still, when tempted to repine
At partial fortune's frown severe,
   Wipe from my eyes the anxious tear,
And whisper, that thy soothing joys are mine!

   When did my fancy[67] ever frame
A dream of joy by thee unblest?
   When first my lips pronounc'd thy name,
New pleasure warm'd my infant breast.
   I lov'd to form the jingling rhyme,
30   The measur'd sounds, tho' rude, my ear could please,

---

67. A creative faculty, usually treated as lighter and more whimsical and playful than imagination or as an assistant to it. Imagination, with the power to transform its material, was considered the higher power.

Could give the little pains of childhood ease,
And long have sooth'd the keener[68] pains of time.

The idle crowd in fashion's train,
Their trifling comment, pert reply,
    Who talk so much, yet talk in vain,
How pleas'd for thee, Oh nymph, I fly!
    For thine is all the wealth of mind,
Thine the unborrow'd gems of thought,
    The flash of light, by souls refin'd,
From heav'n's empyreal[69] source exulting caught.   40

And ah! when destin'd to forego
The social hour with those I love,
    That charm which brightens all below,
That joy all other joys above,
    And dearer to this breast of mine,
Oh Muse! than aught thy magic power can give;
    Then on the gloom of lonely sadness shine,
And bid thy airy forms around me live.

Thy page, Oh SHAKESPEARE! let me view,
Thine! at whose name my bosom glows;   50
    Proud that my earliest breath I drew
In that blest isle where Shakespeare rose!—
    Where shall my dazzled glances roll?
Shall I pursue gay Ariel's flight,[70]
    Or wander where those hags of night[71]
With deeds unnam'd shall freeze my trembling soul?

Plunge me, foul sisters! in the gloom
Ye wrap around yon blasted heath,
    To hear the harrowing rite I come,
That calls the angry shades from death!—   60
    Away—my frighted bosom spare!

68. Sharper.
69. Celestial.
70. Prospero's sprite in William Shakespeare's *The Tempest*.
71. Reference to the witches in Shakespeare's *Macbeth*.

Let true Cordelia pour her filial sigh,
　　Let Desdemona lift her pleading eye,
And poor Ophelia sing in wild despair![72]

　　When the bright noon of summer streams
In one wide flash of lavish day,
　　As soon shall mortal count the beams,
As tell the powers of Shakespeare's lay;[73]
　　Oh Nature's Poet![74] the untaught
70　The simple mind thy tale pursues,
　　And wonders by what art it views
The perfect image of each native thought.

　　In those still moments when the breast,
Expanded, leaves its cares behind,
　　Glows by some higher thought possest,
And feels the energies of mind;
　　Then, awful MILTON, raise the veil
That hides from human eye the heav'nly throng!
　　Immortal sons of light! I hear your song,
80　I hear your high-tun'd harps creation hail!

　　Well might creation claim your care,
And well the string of rapture move,
　　When all was perfect, good, and fair,
When all was music, joy, and love!
　　Ere evil's inauspicious birth
Chang'd nature's harmony to strife;
　　And wild remorse, abhorring life,
And deep affliction, spread their shade on earth.

　　Blest Poesy! Oh sent to calm
90　The human pains which all must feel;
　　Still shed on life thy precious balm,
And every wound of nature heal!
　　Is there a heart of human frame
Along the burning track of torrid light,

---

72. Tragic heroines in Shakespeare's *King Lear, Othello,* and *Hamlet,* respectively.

73. Short lyric or narrative poem intended to be sung.

74. Shakespeare was commonly known as "nature's poet" for his apparent ability to convey the essence of human nature.

Or 'mid the fearful waste of polar night,
That never glow'd at thy inspiring name?

Ye southern isles, emerg'd so late[75]
Where the pacific billow rolls,
    Witness, tho' rude your simple state,
How heav'n-taught verse can melt your souls: 100
    Say, when you hear the wand'ring bard,
How thrill'd ye listen to his lay,
    By what kind arts ye court his stay,
All savage life affords, his sure reward.

So, when great Homer's[76] chiefs prepare,
A while from war's rude toils releas'd,
    The pious hecatomb,[77] and share
The flowing bowl, and genial feast;
    Some heav'nly minstrel sweeps the lyre,
While all applaud the poet's native art,   110
    For him they heap the viands[78] choicest part,
And copious goblets crown the muses fire.

Ev'n *here*, in scenes of pride and gain,
Where faint each genuine feeling glows;
    Here, Nature asks, in want and pain,
The dear illusions verse bestows;
    The poor, from hunger, and from cold,
Spare one small coin, the ballad's price;
    Admire their poet's quaint device,
And marvel much at all his rhymes unfold.   120

Ye children, lost in forests drear,
Still o'er your wrongs each bosom grieves,

75. "The song of the bards or minstrels of Otaheite was unpremeditated, and accompanied with music. They were continually going about from place to place; and they were rewarded by the master of the house with such things as the one wanted, and the other could spare." Cook's Voyage. *Williams.* [The quotation appears in John Hawkesworth, *An Account of the Voyages Undertaken by the Order of His Present Majesty for Making Discoveries in the Southern Hemisphere, and Successively Performed by Commodore Byron, Captain Carteret, Captain Wallis, and Captain Cook* (London, 1773), 2:148. Otaheite is Tahiti. Captain Samuel Wallis and the H.M.S. *Dolphin* arrived on the isle of Tahiti in 1766. *Eds.*]
    76. Name given to poet or poets credited with authoring the *Iliad* and the *Odyssey*.
    77. A great public sacrifice (properly of a hundred oxen) among the ancient Greeks and Romans.
    78. Food's.

And long the red-breast shall be dear
Who strew'd each little corpse with leaves;
   For you, my earliest tears were shed,
For you the gaudy doll I pleas'd forsook,
   And heard with hands up-rais'd, and eager look,
The cruel tale, and wish'd ye were not dead!

   And still on Scotia's[79] northern shore,
130   "At times, between the rushing blast,"
   Recording mem'ry loves to pour
The mournful song of ages past;
   Come, lonely bard "of other years!"
While dim the half-seen moon of varying skies,
   While sad the wind along the grey-moss sighs,
And give my pensive heart "the joy of tears!"[80]

   The various tropes that splendour dart
Around the modern poet's line,
   Where, borrow'd from the sphere of art,
140   Unnumber'd gay allusions shine,
   Have not a charm my breast to please
Like the blue mist, the meteor's beam,
   The dark-brow'd rock, the mountain stream,
And the light thistle waving in the breeze.

   Wild Poesy, in haunts sublime,
Delights her lofty note to pour;
   She loves the hanging rock to climb,
And hear the sweeping torrent roar:
   The little scene of cultur'd grace
150   But faintly her expanded bosom warms;
   She seeks the daring stroke, the aweful charms,
Which Nature's pencil throws on Nature's face.

   Oh Nature! thou whose works divine
Such rapture in this breast inspire,

79. Scotland's.

80. Although in this stanza Williams does not directly quote James MacPherson's forged Gaelic epic *Ossian,* the language and imagery are strongly allusive to that forged text "of other years." *Fingal* was published in 1762, *Temora* in 1763, and the two-volume *Works of Ossian* in 1765; cumulatively, they generated an interest in primitivism.

As makes me dream one spark is mine
Of Poesy's celestial fire;
   When doom'd for London smoke to leave
'The kindling morn's unfolding view,
   Which ever wears some aspect new,
And all the shadowy forms of soothing eve;   160

Then, THOMSON,[81] then be ever near,
And paint whatever season reigns;
   Still let me see the varying year,
And worship Nature in thy strains;
   Now, when the wintry tempests roll,
Unfold their dark and desolating form,
   Rush in the savage madness of the storm,
And spread those horrors that exalt my soul.

And POPE,[82] the music of thy verse
Shall winter's dreary gloom dispel,   170
   And fond remembrance oft rehearse
The moral song she knows so well;
   The sportive sylphs[83] shall flutter here,
There Eloise, in anguish pale,[84]
   "Kiss with cold lips the sacred veil,
And drop with every bead too soft a tear!"[85]

When disappointment's sick'ning pain,
With chilling sadness numbs my breast,
   That feels its dearest hope was vain,
And bids its fruitless struggles rest;   180
   When those for whom I wish to live,
With cold suspicion wrong my aching heart;
   Or, doom'd from those for ever lov'd to part,
And feel a sharper pang than death can give;

81. James Thomson (1700–1748) published *The Seasons,* one of the most popular and widely read poems of the century, in parts from 1726 to 1730.

82. Alexander Pope (1688–1744), the dominant poetic voice of the early eighteenth century.

83. In the expanded, five-canto version of *Rape of the Lock* (1714) Pope added the machinery of the sylphs as supernatural creatures who tried to protect Belinda.

84. Pope published *Eloisa and Abelard* in 1717.

85. These two lines from *Eloisa and Abelard* are not successive in the poem: "As with cold lips I kiss'd the sacred veil" is line 111; "With ev'ry bead I drop too soft a tear" is line 270.

Then with the mournful bard[86] I go,
Whom "melancholy mark'd her own,"
While tolls the curfew, solemn, slow,[87]
And wander amid' graves unknown;
With yon pale orb, lov'd poet, come!
190   While from those elms long shadows spread,
And where the lines of light are shed,
Read the fond record of the rustic tomb!

Or let me o'er old Conway's flood[88]
Hang on the frowning rock, and trace
The characters, that wove in blood,
Stamp'd the dire fate of Edward's race;
Proud tyrant, tear thy laurel'd plume;
How poor thy vain pretence to deathless fame!
The injur'd muse records thy lasting shame,
200   And she has power to "ratify thy doom."[89]

Nature, when first she smiling came,
To wake within the human breast
The sacred muses hallow'd flame,
And earth, with heav'n's rich spirit blest!
Nature in that auspicious hour,
With aweful mandate, bade the bard
The register of glory guard,
And gave him o'er all mortal honours power.

Can fame on painting's aid rely,
210   Or lean on sculpture's trophy'd bust?
The faithless colours bloom to die,
The crumbling pillar mocks its trust;
But thou, oh muse, immortal maid!
Canst paint the godlike deeds that praise inspire,

86. Thomas Gray (1716–71), whose *Elegy Written in a Country Church Yard* (1751) is directly quoted in the next line and alluded to throughout the stanza.

87. The first line of Gray's *Elegy* reads, "The *Curfew* tolls the Knell of parting Day."

88. In 1775 Gray published *The Bard, A Pindaric Ode*, a story told by the surviving Bard following Edward I's violent suppression of the Welsh bards. "On a rock, whose haughty brow / Frowns o'er old Conway's foaming flood, / Rob'd in the sable garb of woe, / With haggard eyes the Poet stood" (1.2.1–4). Many admirers of the poem considered it an example of the sublime. The remaining Bard laments the slaughter of his fellow bards, and the fallen prophesize the fall of Edward.

89. From the final line of stanza 2.3 of Gray's poem *The Bard*.

Or worth that lives but in the mind's desire,
In tints that only shall with Nature fade!

Oh tell me, partial[90] nymph! what rite,
What incense sweet, what homage true,
    Draws from thy fount of purest light
The flame it lends a chosen few?   220
    Alas! these lips can never frame
The mystic vow that moves thy breast;
    Yet by thy joys my life is blest,
And my fond soul shall consecrate thy name.

(1790)

Ainsi Va le Monde, A Poem.[91]

Mary Robinson

O thou, to whom superior worth's allied,
Thy Country's honour- - -and the Muses' pride;
Whose pen gives polish to the varying line
That blends instruction with the song divine;
Whose fancy,[92] glancing o'er the hostile plain,
Plants a fond trophy o'er the mighty slain;[93]
Or to the daisied lawn directs its way,
Blithe as the songstress of returning day;

90. Biased, fond, often unfairly favoring one person over another.

91. Loosely translated, "So goes the world." The title page continues, "Inscried to Robert Merry. By Laura Maria." Merry (1755–98), the poet who initiated the Della Cruscan style of poetry, one many consider pretentious, affected, sentimental, and rhetorically too ornate. It was at the zenith of its popularity from 1787 to 1791. Laura Maria was one of Robinson's pen names; among the others were Oberon and Tabitha Bramble.

92. A creative faculty, usually treated as lighter and more whimsical and playful than imagination or as an assistant to it. Imagination, with the power to transform its material, was considered the higher power.

93. See the Elegy written on the plains of Fontenoy, by Mr. Merry. *Robinson.* [Robert Merry published *Elegy Written on the Plain of Fontenoy* (1787) under the pen name Della Crusca. The poem focuses on the defeat of the British and their allies by the French at the battle of Fontenoy on 11 May 1745 in the War of the Austrian Succession. The speaker in the poem wanders on the field of Fontenoy and muses, "when carnage here her crimson toil began; / . . . / And Man the murd'rer, met the murd'rer Man" (lines 14–16). The poem expresses clear anti-war sentiment, alluding to Napoleon at the end, while also charting the poet's reaction to the battlefield: "I can no more—an agony too keen / Absorbs my senses, and my mind subdues" (lines 117–18). *Eds.*]

Who deign'd to rove where twinkling glow-worms lead
10   The tiny legions o'er the glitt'ring mead;
Whose liquid notes in sweet meand'rings flow,
Mild as the murmurs of the Bird of Woe;[94]
Who gave to Sympathy its softest pow'r,
The charm to wing Affliction's sable hour;
Who in *Italia's* groves, with thrilling song,
Call'd mute attention from the minstrel throng;
Gave proud distinction to the Poet's name,
And claim'd, by modest worth, the wreath of fame- - -
Accept the Verse thy magic harp inspires,
20   Nor scorn the Muse that kindles at its fires.

O, JUSTLY gifted with the Sacred Lyre,
Whose sounds can more than mortal thoughts inspire,
Whether its strings HEROIC measures move,
Or lyric numbers charm the soul to love;
Whether thy fancy "pours the varying verse"
In bow'rs of bliss, or o'er the plumed hearse;
Whether of patriot zeal, or past'ral sports,
The peace of hamlets, or the pride of courts:
Still nature glows in ev'ry classic line- - -
30   Still Genius dictates—still the verse is *thine.*

Too long the Muse, in ancient garb array'd,
Has pin'd neglected in oblivion's shade;
Driv'n from the sun-shine of poetic fame,
Stripp'd of each charm,- - -she scarcely boasts a name:
Her voice no more can please the vapid throng,
No more loud Pæans consecrate her song,
Cold, faint, and sullen, to the grove she flies,
A faded garland veils her radiant eyes;
A with'ring laurel on her breast she bears,
40   Fann'd by her sighs, and spangled with her tears;
From her each fond associate early fled,

---

94. The nightingale. In the Roman legend, Philomela, sister to Procne, was forced into marriage by Procne's husband, Tereus, who tricked her into believing that Procne was dead. When she learned the truth, he cut out her tongue so that she could not speak. She instead wove a tapestry recounting the events. Upon learning of Tereus's crime against Philomela, Procne killed her son by him, cooked him in a stew, and served it to Tereus. He tried to kill Philomela and Procne, but the gods turned them all into birds: Tereus a hawk, Procne a swallow, and Philomela a nightingale.

She mourn'd a MILTON lost, a SHAKSPERE dead:
Her eye beheld a CHATTERTON[95] oppress'd,
A famish'd OTWAY[96]- - -ravish'd from her breast;
Now in their place a flutt'ring form appears,
Mocks her fall'n pow'r, and triumphs in her tears:
A flippant, senseless, aery, thing, whose eye
Glares wanton mirth and fulsome ribaldry.
While motley mumm'ry[97] holds her tinsel reign,
SHAKSPERE might write, and GARRICK[98] act in vain: 50
True Wit recedes, when blushing Reason views
This spurious offspring of the banish'd Muse.

THE task be thine to check the daring hand
That leads fantastic folly o'er the land;
The task be thine with witching spells to bind
The feath'ry shadows of the fickle mind;
To strew with deathless flow'rs the dreary waste;
To pluck the weeds of vitiated taste;
To cheer with smiles the Muse's glorious toil,
And plant perfection on her native soil: 60

95. Thomas Chatterton (1752–77), prolific Bristol poet and essayist whose brief career was over-
shadowed by his imaginative creation of "medieval" texts by a fabricated persona, Thomas Rowley;
recognized as forgeries by his contemporaries, all of his works were subsequently discredited. Chatterton's early death, long and erroneously labeled a suicide, punctuated the image of him as an unrecognized genius. While contemporary accounts suggest that Chatterton had recovered from the
Rowley affair and was on his way to a successful literary career, his contemporaries would have considered him "oppress'd." His work had a profound influence on poets of the Romantic era. Samuel
Taylor Coleridge wrote in *Monody on the Death of Chatterton*, "I weep, that heaven-born Genius so
should fall" (line 26).

96. Thomas Otway (1652–85), playwright who, despite successful plays such as *The Orphan* and
Venice Preserved, the latter of which was performed regularly in the eighteenth century, died impoverished at thirty-three. At one time he was considered second only to Shakespeare and his plays were
among the top ten most performed in the century. In *Lives of the Poets*, Theophilus Cibber claimed
that Otway choked on a roll he had purchased with money secured by begging. "Who can read Mr.
Otway's story," he concluded, "without indignation at those idols of greatness, who demand worship
from men of genius, and yet can suffer them to live miserably, and die neglected?" *The Lives of the
Poets of Great Britain and Ireland, to the Time of Dean Swift*, 5 vols. (London, 1753), 2:334.

97. Mumming plays probably developed from an ancient folk celebration. Based on the legend of
St. George and the dragon, the theme is the death and resurrection of the hero, which symbolized
the reawakening of the earth from the death of winter. They became popular in the early seventeenth
century and are still performed in some English villages at Christmas. Performed by mummers or
mimes, the plays were often referred to slightingly as superstition or low art.

98. David Garrick (1717–79), playwright, manager, and the greatest actor of the century. He revived
many of Shakespeare's plays, and his Shakespeare Jubilee, in 1769, contributed to establishing Shakespeare as the national poet and permanently associated Garrick with him.

The Arts, that thro' dark centuries have pin'd,
Toil'd without fame, in sordid chains confin'd,
Burst into light with renovated fire,
Bid Envy shrink and Ignorance expire.
No more prim KNELLER's[99] simp'ring beauties vie,
Or LELY's[100] genius droops with languid eye:
No more prepost'rous figures pain the view,
Aliens to Nature, yet to Fancy[101] true,
The wild chimeras of capricious thought,
70   Deform'd in fashion, and with errors fraught;
The gothic phantoms sick'ning fade away,
And native Genius rushes into day.

REYNOLDS,[102] 'tis thine with magic skill to trace
The perfect semblance of exterior grace;
Thy hand, by Nature guided, marks the line
That stamps perfection on the form divine.
What RAPHAEL boasted, and what TITIAN[103] knew,
Immortal REYNOLDS, is excell'd by you:
'Tis thine to tint the lip with rosy die,
80   To paint the softness of the melting eye;
With auburn curls luxuriantly display'd,
The ivory shoulders polish'd fall to shade;
To deck the well-turn'd arm with matchless grace,
To mark the dimpled smile on Beauty's face:
The task is thine, with cunning hand to throw
The veil transparent on the breast of snow:
The Statesman's thought, the Infant's cherub mien,
The Poet's fire, the Matron's eye serene,

---

99. Godfrey Kneller (1646–1723), portrait painter, was the most important court and society painter of the last two decades of the seventeenth century.

100. Peter Lely (1618–80), painter and art collector, was the dominant portrait artist for Charles II and his court. Because of the heavy demand for his portraits, he increasingly relied on studio assistants to paint all but the face, perhaps earning Robinson's characterization.

101. A creative faculty, usually treated as lighter and more whimsical and playful than imagination or as an assistant to it. Imagination, with the power to transform its material, was considered the higher power.

102. Sir Joshua Reynolds (1723–92), the dominant portrait and history painter of the eighteenth century, known for his intimate and at times innovative portraits. He painted Robinson a number of times.

103. Reynolds's portraits consistently demonstrated his vast knowledge of Renaissance painting and were particularly influenced by Raphael (1483–1520), the Italian master painter and architect, and Titian (1485–1576), the leader of the Venetian school.

Alike with animated lustre shine
Beneath thy polish'd pencil's touch divine.   90
As BRITAIN's Genius glories in thy Art,
Adores thy virtues, and reveres thy heart,
Nations unborn shall celebrate thy name,
And waft thy mem'ry on the wings of Fame.

    OFT when the mind, with sick'ning pangs oppress'd,
Flies to the Muse, and courts the balm of rest,
When Reason, sated with life's weary woes,
Turns to *itself,*- - -and finds a blest repose,
A gen'rous pride that scorns each petty art,
That feels no envy rankling in the heart,   100
No mean deceit that wings its shaft at *Fame,*
Or gives to pamper'd *Vice* a pompous *name;*
Then, calm reflection shuns the sordid crowd,
The senseless chaos of the *little* proud,
Then, indignation stealing through the breast,
Spurns the pert tribe in flimsy greatness drest;
Who, to their native nothingness consign'd,
Sink in contempt,- - -nor leave a trace behind.
Then Fancy paints, in visionary gloom,
The sainted shadows of the laurel'd tomb,   110
The Star of Virtue glist'ning on each breast,
Divine insignia of the spirit blest!
Then MILTON smiles serene, a beauteous shade,
In worth august—in lust'rous fires array'd
Immortal SHAKSPERE gleams across the sight,
Rob'd in ethereal vest of radiant light.
Wing'd Ages picture to the dazzled view
Each mark'd perfection—of the sacred few,
POPE, DRYDEN, SPENSER, all that Fame shall raise,
From CHAUCER's[104] gloom- - -till MERRY's lucid days: 120
Then emulation kindles fancy's fire,
The glorious throng poetic flights inspire;
Each sensate bosom feels the god-like flame,
The cherish'd harbinger of future fame.

104. Geoffrey Chaucer (1343–1400), author of *The Canterbury Tales* and the first great English poet. She omits John Milton from the standard list of the greatest English poets: Chaucer, Alexander Pope, John Dryden, and Edmund Spenser.

Yet timid genius, oft in conscious ease,
Steals from the world, content the few to please:
Obscur'd in shades, the modest Muse retires,
While sparkling vapours emulate her fires.
The proud enthusiast shuns promiscuous praise,
130   The Idiot's smile condemns the Poet's lays.[105]
Perfection wisely courts the lib'ral few,
The voice of kindred genius must be true.
But empty witlings sate[106] the public eye
With puny jest and low buffoonery,
The buzzing hornets swarm about the great,
The poor appendages of pamper'd state;
The trifling, flutt'ring, insects of a day,
Flit near the sun, and glitter in its ray;
Whose subtle fires with charms magnetic burn,
140   Where every servile fool *may* have his turn.
Lull'd in the lap of indolence, they boast
Who best can fawn- - -and who can flatter most;[107]
While with a cunning arrogance they blend
Sound without sense—and wit that stabs a friend;
Slanders oblique- - -that check ambition's toil,
The pois'nous weeds, that mark the barren soil.
So the sweet blossoms of salubrious[108] spring
Thro' the lone wood their spicy odours fling;
Shrink from the sun, and bow their beauteous heads
150   To scatter incense o'er their mossy beds,
While coarser flow'rs expand with gaudy ray,
Brave the rude wind, and mock the burning day.

Ah! gentle Muse, from trivial follies turn,
Where Patriot souls with god-like passions burn;
Again to Merry dedicate the line,
So shall the envied meed of taste be thine;

105. Short lyric or narrative poems intended to be sung.
106. Satisfy or gratify.
107. This line echoes the last line of Alexander Pope's *Eloisa to Abelard.* Pope's stance as a poet was as an enemy to flattery. See his *Epistle to Dr. Arbuthnot,* lines 104–8 and 333–59, and *First Satire of the Second Book of Horace Imitated,* lines 115–22.
108. Favorable or conducive to health.

So shall thy song to glorious themes aspire,
"Warm'd with a spark"[109] of his transcendent fire.

THRO' all the scenes of Nature's varying plan,
Celestial Freedom warms the breast of man;   160
Led by her daring hand, what pow'r can bind
The boundless efforts of the lab'ring mind.
The god-like fervour, thrilling thro' the heart,
Gives new creation to each vital part;
Throbs rapture thro' each palpitating vein,
Wings the rapt thought, and warms the fertile brain;
To her the noblest attributes of Heav'n,
Ambition, valour, eloquence, are giv'n.
She binds the soldier's brow with wreaths sublime,
From her, expanding reason learns to climb,   170
To her the sounds of melody belong,
She wakes the raptures of the Poet's song;
'Tis god-like Freedom bids each passion live,
That truth may boast, or patriot virtue give;
From her, the Arts enlighten'd splendors own,
She guides the peasant- - -She adorns the throne;
To mild Philanthropy extends her hand,
Gives Truth pre-eminence, and Worth command;
Her eye directs the path that leads to Fame,
Lights Valour's torch, and trims the glorious flame;   180
She scatters joy o'er Nature's endless scope,
Gives strength to Reason- - -extacy to Hope;
Tempers each pang Humanity can feel,
And binds presumptuous Power with nerves of steel;
Strangles each tyrant Phantom in its birth,
And knows no title- - -but SUPERIOR WORTH.

ENLIGHTEN'D Gallia![110] what were all your toys,
Your dazzling splendors,- - -your voluptuous joys?
What were your glitt'ring villas,- - -lofty tow'rs,

109. Probably recalled quotation from Nicholas Rowe's *Callipædie: or, the Art of Producing Beautiful Children. A Poem in Four Books* (London, 1720), bk. 4, p. 93: "warm'd with a brighter spark of heav'nly Fire."
110. Latin name for Gaul. Although originally the area comprising modern Belgium and France, Robinson means France.

190   Your perfum'd chambers, and your painted bow'rs?
       Did not insidious *Art* those gifts bestow,
       To cheat the prying eye- - -with tinsel show?
       Yes; luxury diffus'd her spells, to bind
       The deep researches of the restless mind?
       To lull the active soul with witching wiles,
       To hide pale Slav'ry[111] in a mask of smiles:
       The tow'ring wings of reason to restrain,
       And lead the victim in a flow'ry chain:
       Cold Superstition favour'd the deceit,
200   And e'en Religion lent her aid to cheat.- - -
       When warlike Louis,[112] arrogant and vain,
       Whom *worth* could never hold, or *fear* restrain;
       The soul's last refuge, in repentance sought,
       An artful MAINTENON[113] absolved each fault;
       She who had led his worldly steps astray,
       Now, "smooth'd his passage to the realms of day!"[114]
       O, monstrous hypocrite!- - -who vainly strove
       By pious fraud, to win a people's love;
       Whose coffers groan'd with reliques from the proud,
210   The pompous off'rings of the venal crowd.
       The massy hecatombs[115] of dire disgrace,
       To purchase titles, or secure a place.- - -
       And yet,- - -so sacred was the matron's fame,
       Nor truth, nor virtue, dar'd assail her name;
       None could approach but with obsequious breath,
       To *smile* was TREASON,- - -and to *speak* was DEATH.

---

111. The British consistently contrasted their Protestant nation, with liberty of conscience, to the "slavery" and "superstition" of French Catholicism.

112. Louis XIV. *Robinson.* [Louis XIV (1638–1715), king of France from 1643. He transformed the state into an absolute monarchy, expanded its commercial and military might, and was a patron of the arts. Among his wars were the Dutch Succession, the War of the Spanish Succession, and various initiatives against religious sects in France. *Eds.*]

113. Françoise d' Aubigné, Marquise de Maintenon (1635–1719), was the second wife of King Louis XIV. She was the governess for the children of the king and one of his mistresses. She was a favorite of Queen Maria Thérèse, who died in her arms. Known as a devout Catholic, she wrote treatises on education and founded a school for poor children. She is credited with raising the moral tone of the court and bringing the king to religion.

114. Slight rewording of line 322 of Alexander Pope's *Eloisa to Abelard.* The Marquise de Maintenon allegedly moderated Louis XIV's passions in his final years. These words are part of Eloisa's dying plea to Abelard.

115. Large-scale public sacrifice, a symbol of arbitrary imprisonment and absolutism. In ancient Greece and Rome one hundred oxen were offered to the gods.

In meek and humble garb, she veil'd command,
While helpless millions, shrunk beneath her hand.
And when Ambition's idle dream was o'er,
And art could blind, and beauty charm no more;   220
She, whose luxurious bosom spurn'd restraint,
Who liv'd the slave of passion,---died a saint![116]

    What were the feelings of the hapless throng,
By threats insulted, and oppressed with wrong?
While grasping avarice, with skill profound,
Spread her fell snares, and dealt destruction round;
Each rising sun some new infringement saw,
While pride was consequence,---and pow'r was law;
A people's suff'rings hop'd redress in vain,
Subjection curb'd the tongue that *dar'd* complain.   230
Imputed guilt each virtuous victim led
Where all the fiends their direst mischiefs spread;
Where, thro' long ages past, with watchful care,
THY TYRANTS, GALLIA, nurs'd the witch DESPAIR.
Where in her black BASTILE[117] the harpy[118] fed
On the warm crimson drops, her fangs had shed;
Where recreant malice mock'd the suff'rer's sigh,
While regal light'nings darted from her eye.---
Where deep mysterious whispers murmur'd round,
And death stalk'd sullen o'er the treach'rous ground.   240
O DAY—transcendent on the page of Fame!
When from her Heav'n, insulted *Freedom* came;
Glancing o'er earth's wide space, her beaming eye
Mark'd the dread scene of impious slavery,
Warm'd by her breath, the vanquish'd, trembling race,
Wake from the torpid slumber of disgrace;
Roused by oppression, *Man* his birth-right claims,
O'er the proud battlements red vengeance flames;[119]
Exulting thunders rend the turbid skies;---

---

116. Madame de Maintenon died a perfect devotee at the Convent of St. Cyr. *Robinson.* [She established a school at Saint-Cyr for impoverished young noblewomen in 1686. *Eds.*]

117. Fortress and state prison in Paris.

118. Predatory bird with a woman's face. In mythology, harpies snatched food from the blind king Phineas.

119. On 14 July 1789 a Parisian mob stormed the Bastille seeking arms and ammunition. The governor was killed, and the prisoners freed. Bastille Day is still celebrated as a day of liberation.

250   In sulph'rous clouds the gorgeous ruin lies!- - -
        The angel, PITY, now each cave explores,
        Braves the chill damps, and fells the pond'rous doors,
        Plucks from the flinty walls the clanking chains,
        Where many a dreadful tale of woe remains,
        Where many a sad memorial marks the hour,
        That gave the *rights of man*[120] to *rav'nous pow'r;*
        Now snatch'd from death, the wond'ring wretch shall prove
        The rapt'rous energies of social love;
        Whose limbs each faculty denied,- - -whose sight
260   Had long resign'd all intercourse with light;
        Whose wasted form the humid earth receiv'd,
        Who numb'd with anguish,- - -scarcely felt he *liv'd;*
        Who, when the midnight bell assail'd his ears,
        From fev'rish slumbers woke- - -to drink his tears:
        While slow-consuming grief each sense enthrall'd,
        'Till *Hope* expir'd, and *Valour* shrunk,- - -appall'd:
        Where veil'd suspicion lurk'd in shrewd disguise,
        While eager vengeance op'd her thousand eyes;
        While the hir'd slave, the fiend of wrath, design'd
270   To lash, with scorpion scourges, human-kind,- - -
        Dragg'd with ingenious pangs, the tardy hour,
        To feed the rancour of *insatiate Pow'r.*

        BLEST be the favor'd delegates of heav'n,
        To whose illustrious souls the task was giv'n
        To wrench the bolts of tyranny,- - -and dare
        The petrifying confines of despair;
        With heav'n's own breeze to chear the gasping breath,
        And spread broad sun-shine in the caves of death.

        WHAT is the charm that bids mankind disdain
280   The Tyrant's mandate and th' Oppressor's chain;
        What bids exulting Liberty impart
        Extatic raptures to the Human Heart;

120. Here and below, a reference to Thomas Paine's *Rights of Man* (1791), which defended the French Revolution by arguing a "natural" right of the people to rebel against governments that broke their "contract" to protect the people's well-being and rights. Paine was indicted as a traitor in Great Britain in 1792 and fled to France.

Calls forth each hidden spark of glorious fire,
Bids untaught minds to valiant feats aspire;
What gives to Freedom its supreme delight?
'Tis Emulation, Instinct, Nature, Right.

WHEN this revolving Orb's first course began,
Heav'n stamp'd divine pre-eminence on Man;
To him it gave the intellectual mind,
Persuasive Eloquence and Truth refin'd;   290
Humanity to harmonize his sway,
And calm Religion to direct his way;
Courage to tempt Ambition's lofty flight,
And Conscience to illume his erring sight.
Who shall the nat'ral Rights of Man deride,
When Freedom spreads her fost'ring banners wide?
Who shall contemn[121] the heav'n-taught zeal that throws
The balm of comfort on a Nation's woes?
That tears the veil from superstition's eye,
Bids despots tremble, scourg'd oppression die?   300
Wrests hidden treasure from the sordid hand,
And flings profusion o'er a famish'd land?- - -
Nor yet, to GALLIA are her smiles confin'd,
She opes her radiant gates to *all mankind*;
Sure on the peopled earth there cannot be
A foe to Liberty- - -that dares be free.
Who that has tasted bliss will e'er deny
The magic power of thrilling extacy?
Who that has breath'd Health's vivifying breeze,
Would tempt the dire contagion of Disease?   310
Or prodigal of joy, his birth-right give
In shackled slavery- - -a wretch to live?

YET let Ambition hold a temp'rate sway,
When Virtue rules- - -'tis Rapture to obey;
Man can but reign his transitory hour,
And *love* may bind————when *fear* has lost its pow'r.
Proud may he be who nobly acts his part,
Who boasts the empire of each subject's heart,

121. Condemn.

Whose worth, exulting millions shall approve,
320   Whose richest treasure———is a Nation's love.

FREEDOM——blithe Goddess of the rainbow vest,
In dimpled smiles and radiant beauties drest,
I court thee from thy azure-spangled bed
Where Ether[122] floats about thy winged head;
Where tip-toe pleasure swells the choral song,
While gales of odour waft the Cherub throng;
On every side the laughing loves prepare
Enamel'd[123] wreaths to bind thy flowing hair:
For thee the light-heel'd graces[124] fondly twine,
330   To clasp thy yielding waist, a zone divine!
Venus[125] for thee her crystal altar rears,
Deck'd with fresh myrtle[126]———gemm'd with lovers' tears;
Apollo[127] strikes his lyre's rebounding strings,
Responsive notes divine Cecilia sings,
The tuneful sisters prompt the heavenly choir,
Thy temple glitters with Promethean[128] fire.
The sacred Priestess in the centre stands,
She strews the sapphire floor with flow'ry bands.
See! from her shrine electric incense rise;
340   Hark! "Freedom" echoes thro' the vaulted skies.
Thy Goddess speaks! O mark the blest decree,———
TYRANTS SHALL FALL———TRIUMPHANT MAN BE FREE!

(1790)

---

122. The clear sky; the upper regions of space beyond the clouds.
123. Beautified with various colors.
124. The goddesses Euphrosyne, Aglaia, and Thalia, who presided over all social enjoyments and elegant arts.
125. Goddess of love.
126. Myrtle, a tree with dark, shiny green leaves. A garland of myrtle is regarded as a symbol of love and peace.
127. In Greek mythology, the god of music and poetry; he was frequently depicted with a lyre.
128. In Greek mythology, Prometheus was the Titan who lighted his torch on the chairs of the sun and brought fire down to man, having stolen it from the gods. As punishment for the crime, Jupiter chained him to a mountain peak and sent woman down to earth in the form of Pandora.

Sources

Wharton: *The Temple of Death; a Poem,* 2nd ed. (London, 1695), 242–44; Manley: *Agnes de Castro. A Tragedy, by Catharine Trotter [Cockburn]* (London, 1696), iii; Finch: *The Poems of Anne Countess of Winchilsea,* ed. Myra Reynolds (Chicago: University of Chicago Press, 1903), 92–94; Thomas: *Miscellany Poems on Several Subjects* (London, 1722), 145–50, 150–51; Darwall: *Original Poems on Several Occasions. By Miss Whateley* (London, 1764), 109–13; A. Williams: *Miscellanies in Prose and Verse* (London, 1766), 59–62; H. Williams: *Julia, a Novel; Interspersed with Some Poetical Pieces,* 2 vols. (London, 1790), 1:15–24; Robinson: *Ainsi va le monde, a poem. Inscribed to Robert Merry. By Laura Maria,* 2nd ed. (London, 1790), 1–16.

✥B✥

The Muses

Some of the most amusing poetry in the English language is addressed to the Muses, and research has demonstrated that poems and passages about the Muses are one of the sites of the most marked gender differences.[1] The Muses are, after all, *women,* and men treat them as such. They find them mysterious, frustrating, and subject to seduction but above all they find them sexual and Other. As Raymond Stephanson writes, male poets "constructed their notions of the poetic imagination and the poet's life-long output as masculine sexual dramas." They "mimicked and replicated in some predictable ways the heterosexual life-dramas of real men."[2] In contrast, women often treat them as sisters, friends, or potential advisers, and some of the poems in this section illustrate the truth of Anna Laetitia Barbauld's observation that "friendship, better than a Muse, inspires" (*To Mrs. P[riestley]*). Poets, male and female, converse and compete with them, cajole, berate, seduce, beg, and rail at them. Elusive, fickle, independent, and apparently unmoved by most appeals, the Muses hold the keys to inspiration and creativity. They symbolize aspiration and attainment of ideal knowledge and artistry.[3] Most often represented as a group, as though help from any and all quarters might be best, the most specific to poetry are occasionally named: Euterpe, lyric poetry; Calliope, epic poetry; Erato, love poetry; and Polyhymnia, sacred poetry (songs to the gods). Urania (astronomy), Terpsichore (choral dance), and Clio (history) are occasionally addressed, and if tone or mode is the subject, Thalia (comedy) and Melpomene (tragedy) may be invoked. Their lineage was formidable. They were the daughters of Jupiter and the Titan Mnemosyne (Memory), and Apollo was their guardian. Not only did they inherit the power of their parents but their mother's trait was crucial to poets, for it allowed them not only to be part of the great tradition but also to compose and perform their own poetry.

The myths and stories about the Muses explain some of the characteristics associated with them. The Thracian poet Thamyris challenged them to a competition and lost; they blinded him. The Sirens once tried to compete with the Muses and, when defeated, lost their wings. When the nine daughters of Peirus challenged the Muses to a singing contest, the Muses won and turned the daughters into crows. The most influential account is Hesiod's in *Theogony*, in which the Muses approach the poet on Helicon, their sacred mountain in the Parnassus range in Greece, and give him a scepter, a voice, and knowledge. Hesiod wrote: "They are all of one mind, their hearts are set upon song and their spirit is free from care. He is happy whom the Muses love. For though a man has sorrow and grief in his soul, yet when the servant of the Muses sings, at once he forgets his dark thoughts and remembers not his troubles. Such is the holy gift of the Muses to men."[4] The ideal of this life—"hearts . . . set upon song and their spirit . . . free"—expresses a dedication to their art and the relief and joy immersion in it brought to many women. Elizabeth Teft cleverly casts her poem in this section in the Muse's voice and writes, "I sooth'd thy Cares." The determined, often joyous declarations that, regardless of what happened, they would continue to write, sometimes draw upon this myth, as does Joanna Baillie's lyrical *Address to the Muses*.

Stephanson quotes George Sandys's frequently reprinted *Ovid's Metamorphosis Englished*: "*Jupiter* the divine mind inspires *Apollo*; *Apollo* the Muses; and they their legitimate issue."[5] Renaissance poetry often connected the writer to the Muses in this and other powerful tropes that gave additional authority to their poetry's content. As Isobel Grundy explains, "This was a potent myth, lending poetry a supernatural fiat."[6] From the classical conception of them as inspired, supreme practitioners of their arts who sang and danced at the festivities of Olympians and heroes, they came to be portrayed by men as either passive inspirers, rather like an Aladdin's lamp, or teasing jilts and jades.

It could be argued that Restoration and eighteenth-century women reinvigorated the topos of the Muses. Placing Dryden in the position of Apollo, Delarivière Manley produced *The Nine Muses*, a collection of elegies commemorating his death. The six women who contributed to the volume represented themselves as the Muses (Manley was both Melpomene and Thalia, and Sarah Fyge Egerton was Erato, Euterpe, and Terpsichore).[7] This new kind of identification allowed poems that represented the relationship between poet and the Muses in creative ways. All of the women claimed the ability to inspire and the right to elegize, a powerful authority that asserted a right of possession and succession, as well as the poetic authority of the Muses.[8] Anne Finch turned the sexualized identification of woman and Muse into an acute and witty observation in *A Song: Melinda to Alcander:* "No, we posesse alike that fire, / And all you boast of, we inspire. / Fancy does from beauty rise, / Beauty, teatches you to write, / . . . / Witt, and love, we give and claime" (not included).[9] This identification of women with the Muses laughs at male pretension and makes women equal to the Muses. Well into the eighteenth century, individual women poets were rather archly styled the "tenth muse." Although this designation was a compliment to the excellence of the woman's poetry, it portrayed her as an isolated example that was unexpected and violated the natural order. In the second half of the century, however, women poets became one of the glories of the nation, and they were often praised in periodicals. Richard Samuel's painting *The Nine Living Muses of Great Britain* was exhibited at the Royal Academy in 1779 and was frequently reproduced.[10] At various moments, women, including Anna Seward, were named "Britannia's Muse."

The poems in this section and others exhibit a delightful range of exchanges with the Muses. Jane Cave Winscom depicts them in *The Author's Plea* (3.E) as guests who drop in no matter how busy she is, and "They oft affect a deafness, draw more near, / Declare that they can no repulses bear"; or "they take offence, and fly away." All of the women speak intimately with the Muses, and their voices range from Sarah Fyge Egerton's poetic flyting, a series of insults and curses aimed at the uncooperative ladies, to Sarah Dixon's description of the contentment and joy the Muses have brought her. In *Satyr against the Muses,* Egerton's adaptation of Nicolas Boileau's *Satire II. To M. De Moliere,* the Muses "fire" her rage, but to Dixon they are "Friend to my *Peace,* thou Object of my Love," and "kind indulgent Muse" (*To the Muse*). Mary Whateley Darwall at different times describes a muse as "rural," "sprightly," "gentle," "liberal" (politically), or "pastoral"; and in one poem, *On the Author's Husband Desiring Her to Write Some Verses* (not included), she gains the special help of Erato, who will aid her in writing on "Connubial Love! enchanting theme."[11] In two of the poems in this section, the women decide that even without the help of the Muses their subject will inspire them. These poems, by Mary Masters and Joanna Baillie, are thought-provoking meditations on the identification of poet with Muse and on the highest aspirations for their art. Masters, for instance, brings in the qualities the Muses symbolize, including "tuneful," the characteristic the Muses were most thought to achieve in their own work and most sought to inspire: "Her Thoughts are beautiful, refin'd and new, / Polish'd her Language, and her Judgment true; / Each Word deliver'd with that soft address" *(The Female Triumph).* This careful preparation for the poem's conclusion, in which her friend takes the place of a Muse, is discerning in its uniting of sound and sense.

Four more poems take up the theme of "friendship, better than a Muse, inspires." Barbauld, Elizabeth Carter, and Ann Murry all begin with the good-natured, conventional pattern, "Eliza [or Amanda or Miss Coker] bids me boldly try / To pluck the Laurel Bough" (Carter, *From Miss [Wilbraham]*). The themes and images found in poems on friendship (2.A) and retirement (2.B) animate these poems and are especially strong in Elizabeth Hands's *Friendship. An Ode.* Hands shows that friendship not only inspires poetry but is a worthy subject for the high form of the ode. As this anthology makes clear, women wrote for many audiences and for many reasons, but they also wrote for each other, and their friendships and the mutual enjoyment of poetry are central to the poetic process for many of them. The support, interest, and "commands" are potent prompts to poetry, and in many of the poems, friends encourage greater poetic aspiration—for excellence, publication, and recognition as poets. Relationships persuade these women that they can do things beyond their ordinary capacities. Elizabeth Carter will obey the injunctions of a friend that motivate her otherwise "unambitious brow" (certainly these poems have some posturing as well): "Less prompted by Desire of Fame, / Than fond complying Love." Carter assigns the power previously given to the Muse to her friend: "With Steps by her Injunctions wing'd, / I seek th' immortal Grove" *(From Miss [Wilbraham]).* The urgings of a friend take the place of the wings of poesy that other poems imagistically use as motivation. Ann Murry's playful iambic tetrameter meets the challenge of a friend and offers the voice of the Muse who commands, "Nor ever more attempt to rhyme; / . . . / Enough has been already wrote, / For thee to copy or to quote" (*A Familiar Epistle to Miss Coker*). She rejects the Muse's mandate in order to satisfy her desire to praise Laura.

The poems illustrate how deeply imbricated the personal and professional communities of letters truly were for women. Some, although successful and competitive in the marketplace, created an alternative economy of praise and reward. The lack of competition in these poems is striking. Indeed, the one poem that directly addresses female literary competition, Anne Finch's *Circuit of Apollo* (3.A), resists making a final judgment. Instead, Apollo praises the work of all the women poets, claiming "that t'were injustice, one brow to adorn, / With a wreath, which so fittingly by each might be worn." While public, these poems are also private.

The image of inspiration links many of the poems, and it is useful to recall that the literal meaning of *inspire* is "to breathe life into." It most famously appears in the *Vulgate,* Genesis 2:7 ("et inspiravit in faciem eius spiraculum vitae"), when God breathes the spirit of life into the face of Adam. The variety of forms—odes, verse epistles, satires, and more—multiply the possibilities for poetic positioning. As the poets depict representations of relationships with the Muses and with real women, they create sites for the development of subjectivity and agency. Poems that portray interactions with the Muses testify to the fact that for many poets writing was as necessary as the air they breathed and the food they ate. They renewed their commitments in poems in which the Muses courted *them,* and they expressed their independence when the Muses seemed to neglect them. As a group, these poems extend our understanding of poetry as practice. Not only are they illuminating examples of life writing but, because identifying with the Muses elevates the poet, they are places where the women could avow their commitment to the highest standards of wisdom and poetry.

Notes

1. Isobel Grundy, "The Poet and Her Muse," in *The Timeless and the Temporal,* ed. Elizabeth Maslen (London: University of London, 1993), 173–93; Joanne F. Dieh, "'Come Slowly: Eden': An Exploration of Women Poets and Their Muse," *Signs* 3 (1978): 572–87.

2. Raymond Stephanson, "The Symbolic Structure of Eighteenth-Century Male Creativity: Pregnant Men, Brain-Wombs, and Female Muses," *Studies in Eighteenth-Century Culture* 27 (1998): 104–5.

3. On the Muses' symbolic value, see Elizabeth Eger, "Representing Culture: 'The Nine Living Muses of Great Britain' (1779)," in *Women, Writing, and the Public Sphere, 1700–1830,* ed. Eger, Charlotte Grant, Penny Warburton, and Clíona Gallchoir (Cambridge: Cambridge University Press, 2001), 104–32.

4. Quoted in Edith Hamilton, *Mythology* (1940; New York: Signet, 1969), 37. Although Hesiod named them, their association with different spheres developed later.

5. Stephanson, "Symbolic Structure," 108. Stephanson develops these ideas in *The Yard of Wit: Male Creativity and Sexuality, 1650–1750* (Philadelphia: University of Pennsylvania Press, 2004).

6. Grundy, "Poet and Her Muse," 174.

7. Susan Goulding provides an important interpretation of this collection in "'Mourn, Mourn, Ye Muses': Eighteenth-Century Women as Elegists," *1650–1850* 7 (2002): 156–61.

8. On the "right to mourn" and possession claims in the classical-elegy tradition, see Paula R. Backscheider, *Eighteenth-Century Women Poets and Their Poetry* (Baltimore: Johns Hopkins University Press, 2005), 292–94.

9. Anne Finch, *A Song: Melinda to Alcander,* in *The Poems of Anne Countess of Winchilsea,* ed. Myra Reynolds (Chicago: University of Chicago Press, 1903), 128.

10. On the cultural meaning of Samuel's painting, see Eger, "Representing Culture," 107–16.

11. See *Poems on Several Occasions. By Mrs. Darwall (Formerly Miss Whateley) in Two Volumes,* 2 vols. (Walsall, West Midlands, 1794), 2:55–57.

Satyr against the Muses
Sarah Fyge Egerton

By my abandon'd Muse, I'm not inspir'd,
Provok'd by Malice, and with Rage I'm fir'd.
Fly, fly, my Muse from my distracted Breast,
Who e'er has thee, must be with Plagues possest:
Fool that I was, e'er to sollicite you,
Who make not only Poor, but wretched too.
Happy I liv'd, for almost Eight years time,
Curss'd be your Skill, you taught me then to Rhime:
The Jingling noise, shed its dark Influence, ⎫
On my then pleased, unwary Innocence, ⎬ 10
I scarce have had one happy Moment since. ⎭
Here all the Spite and Rage of Womankind, ⎫
Cannot enough advance my threatning Mind, ⎬
Let Furies[1] too, be in the Consort[2] join'd. ⎭
Passion, that common Rage, I here refuse,
Call Hell itself, to curse my Torturing Muse;
Not the calm Author of blest Poetry,
But the black Succubus[3] of Misery:
There let her sit, with her Infernal Chyme,[4]
And put the Schreiks and Groans of Fiends in Rhime. 20
May their *Parnassus*,[5] like *Vesevius*[6] burn,
Their Laurels wither, or to Cypriss turn;[7]
May Stuff like *Hopkin*'s Rhyme,[8] degrade their Fame,
And none but Ballad-makers use their Name.
May they despis'd, sad and neglected sit,
Be never thought upon by Men of Wit.

---

1. Alecto, Megaera, and Tisiphone, the three daughters of Mother Earth, created from the blood of Uranus when Kronos castrated him. They are the avenging spirits of retributive justice, and because they punish crimes not within the reach of human justice, they often personify conscience. They are especially dedicated to crimes against kin.

2. Group of ships sailing together.

3. Demon in female form said to have sex with men while they slept.

4. The semi-fluid pulpy acid matter into which food is converted in the stomach by the action of the gastric secretion.

5. Mountain near Delphi, Greece, sacred to Apollo and the Muses, hence to poetry and the arts.

6. Vesuvius, the active volcano on the Bay of Naples, in Italy.

7. Were Egerton's curse to be fulfilled, the laurel wreath for poets and conquerors would wither or become a cypress, the tree sacred to the god of death, Dis.

8. Matthew Hopkins was a professional witch finder in the 1640s.

May all the Ills a fond Imperious Dame,
Wishes the Man that dare reject her Flame,
Light upon him, that does commit the Crime,
30   Of writing any thing, in jingling Rhime;
Nothing like that, to Dangers can expose,
May none be Happy, but what write in Prose.
Curse on the Whimsical, Romanick Fool,
That yielded first, to his Phantastick Rule;
That Wit like Morris-dancers[9] must advance,
With Bells at Feet, and in nice measures Dance.
Let pregnant Heads, but think of Poetry,
And just before the Brain-delivery;
Fancy shall make a Prodigy of Wit,
40   Which soon, as born, shall run upon its Feet:
Sure, 'tis some Necromantick Ordinance,[10]
That Sence, beyond the Circle mayn't advance;
Was all the learned Ancients Courage dead,
That Wit, in Fetters, is tame Captive led?
Had Some oppos'd, when Rhyme at first grew bold,
Then her Defeat, not Triumphs had been told?
But now the Plague is grown so populous,
'Tis hard to stop the universal Curse.
Doubtless, they are mistaken who have told
50   Spightful *Pandora*'s pregnant Box[11] did hold
Plurality of Plague, She only hurl'd
Out Verse alone, and that has damn'd the World.
Curses, in vain, on Poets I bestow;
I'm sure, the greatest is, that they are so;
Fate, send worse if thou can'st, but Rescue me
From trifling torturing wretched Poetry.

(1703)

9. The most widely known ceremonial dance in England, dating from the fifteenth century. The dancers, almost always male, are divided into teams, as well as characters such as a fool and Maid Marian, and waved scarves, ribbons, or cloth on sticks. They wore special costumes with bells on the legs and shoes.

10. A command or order from a sorcerer, especially one who communes with the dead.

11. Pandora is a mythical woman to whom each god gave a gift to ruin man. Jupiter gave her the box of gifts, which she was to present to the man who married her. Curious about its contents, she opened it, and Work, Conflict, Disease, and other evils were released. Only Hope remained in the box. A Pandora's box is an unpredictable gift that seems valuable but is often a curse.

The Female Triumph
Mary Masters

Swell'd with vain Learning, vainer Man conceives,
That 'tis with him the bright MINERVA[12] lives;
That she descends to dwell with him alone,
And in his Breast erects her starry Throne:
Pleas'd with his own, to Female Reason blind,
Fansys all Wisdom in his Sex confin'd.
Proudly they boast of Philosophick Rules, ⎫
Of Modes and Maxims taught in various Schools, ⎬
And look on Women as a Race of Fools. ⎭
But if CALISTA's[13] perfect Soul they knew,   10
They'd own their Error, and her Praise pursue.
Centred in her the brightest Graces meet,
Treasures of Knowledge and rich Mines of Wit.
Her Thoughts are beautiful, refin'd and new,
Polish'd her Language, and her Judgment true;
Each Word deliver'd with that soft address,
That as she speaks the melting Sounds we bless.
O! could I praise her without doing wrong,
Could to the Subject raise my daring Song;
Were I enrich'd with PRIOR's Golden Vein,[14]   20
Her would I sing in an exalted Strain;
Her Merit in the noblest Verse proclaim,
And raise my own upon CALISTA's Fame:
Her elevated Sense, her Voice, her Mien,
Her innate Goodness, and her Air serene,
Should in my Lays[15] to future Ages shine,
And some new Charm appear in ev'ry Line.

Fir'd with the Theme how great would be the Flight?
In what unbounded Numbers should I write!
Each Line, each Word, would more majestick grow,   30
And ev'ry Page with finish'd Beauty glow.

12. Roman goddess of wisdom and of the arts and trade.

13. Probably the playwright, novelist, philosopher, and poet Catharine Trotter Cockburn. Calista was the name of the heroine in Nicholas Rowe's tragedy *The Fair Penitent* (1703), which was a great favorite in the century.

14. Matthew Prior's poetic ability. Prior (1664–1721) was much admired by women poets for his wit, women characters, and accessible style. Elizabeth Tollet styled him Britain's Horace.

15. Ballads; lyric or narrative poems meant to be sung.

But me alas the *tuneful Nine*[16] disdain,
Scorn my rude Verse, and mock my feeble Strain:
No kind Poetick Pow'rs descend to fill
My humble Breast, and guide my trembling Quill:
My Thoughts, in rough and artless Terms exprest,
Are incorrect[17] and negligently drest.
Yet sure my just Ambition all must own
The well-chose Subject has my Judgment shown
40   And in the weak Attempt my great Design is known. }

(1733)

To the Muse

Sarah Dixon

Friend to my *Peace,* thou Object of my Love,
E're dawning Reason could the Choice approve,
Through every change of Life and Fortune, *Thou,*
My constant Solace, to this instant *Now.*
Can'st thou so soon forget my seeming Scorn,
Forgive my Weakness, and with Smiles return?
We, like fond Lovers when they're piqu'd, resent,
Then feel in Absence mutual Punishment.
By Friends and Foes, forewarn'd I'd often been,
10   To shun thy *Syren* Note[18] like deadly Sin,
Was told thy Strains, so *wond'rous* sweet to me,
To half the World at least want Harmòny;
That *Criticks* no Compassion had in Store,
And Fortune ever gives thy Votaries[19] o'er;
That Nature err'd, when tempting me to sing,
Who never tasted the *Parnassian* Spring.[20]
Too just Reproof,—then like the tim'rous Maid,

16. The Muses.
17. Metrically imperfect.
18. Monsters, half-woman and half-bird, the sirens sang such sweet songs that seamen forgot everything and starved.
19. Fervent believers, those sworn and devoted to a religion, cause, or activity.
20. One of the summits of Parnassus, a mountain near Delphi, Greece, was consecrated to Apollo and the Muses. The spring of Castalia, on the southern slope, is a symbol of poetic creativity and its source.

Who loves, and fears to be by Love betray'd,
I banish'd thee, which gave a greater Pain
Than all their spiteful Eloquence cou'd feign.   20
Frighted, provok'd, yet griev'd, I rashly swore
Thy Soul delighting Charms shou'd sooth no more;
No more advent'rous wou'd my Genius stretch,
To soar at empty Fame, beyond my Reach.
I then at once grew peevish, sullen, wise, ⎫
Cou'd even *Pope*[21] and *Addison*[22] despise, ⎬
And call'd their Inspirations—Fooleries. ⎭
'Midst the *polite*, the trifling, gigling Crowd,
I thrust my vacant self, and laugh'd aloud;
Rally'd th' absurd Impertinence of those   30
Who Books and stupid Solitude had chose.
But—e're the long, the irksome Day was done,
Oh! how I've sigh'd, and wish'd my self alone:
'Tis then the Soul her *Heaven* born Freedom finds,
Learns its own *Worth,* and this mad World resigns;
This Farce of Life the World! with some soon past,
Traverse the Stage, and to their Period haste.
Others in larger Characters appear,
With loud Applauses rend the Theatre;
Are blest or curst with all that they desire,   40
In Splendor enter,—triumph, and retire:
The shifting Scenes no Change of Fortune bring,
Constant to them, tho' ever on the Wing.
My Scene of Action is the tragick Part,
How e're perform'd,—I feel it at my Heart;
Taste every Drop of well digested Woe,
And quaff the bitter Fountains as they flow.
Honour, with all her Train of rigid Laws,
Which, like the Diamond, admits no Flaws,
Love, Fear and Pity, war within my Breast,   50
Active as Whirlwinds, never let me rest.
No Truce with *Fortune*[23]—nor so mean to stop
At every Toy, which *she* thinks fit to drop.

21. Alexander Pope (1688–1744), author of *The Rape of the Lock,* the *Dunciad,* and many other poems.

22. Joseph Addison (1672–1719), author of the patriotic poem *The Campaign* (1705); the *Tatler* and *Spectator* papers; and the play *Cato* (1713).

23. Goddess of luck. Her emblem is the wheel of fortune, symbolizing change or mutability.

But why, my MUSE, shou'd Thee and I complain,
In these still Shades, and Friendship met again?
These conscious Shades, sacred to Love and Thee,
Have tun'd my ruffl'd Soul; and set it free
From galling Spleen, and from corroding Care:
Be only Love and Hope, Attendants here.
60   O, gently sooth me with thy wonted Charm;
Let lambent Flames my tender Bosome warm:
Collect soft Sounds from each harmonious Thing;
The Soul of Musick, to my Refuge bring;
In Numbers melting as the *Mantuan* Swain,[24]
Tuneful as *Orpheus* on the *Thracian* Plain.[25]
I feel thy Influence, and sweet Peace comes on;
Care flies before thee;—so the rising Sun
Dispels the noxious Mists; what Joy to find
My lov'd Companion to my Wishes kind!
70   Nature resumes her Bloom, and my past Years
Are in Oblivion lost; a new gay World appears!
Serene the Air, How fresh the Evening Breeze?
Hush'd are the Waves, and murmuring roll the Seas:
Delightful all! Hark, how the Wood Larks sing!
The bubling Brooks with softer Cadence ring;
Obliging *Philomel*[26] her Note improves,
Forgets her Woe, and warbles through the Groves:
The rival Songsters flutter all around,
And Eccho[27] lengthens each melodious Sound.
80   Here fearless Innocence has fixt her Seat,
Queen of all chaste Desires, and calm Retreat;
Without Allay, her Pleasures does bestow,
And, grateful, I confess,—there's Bliss below:

24. Virgil (70–19 BC), here identified by the town, Mantua, near his birthplace.

25. Orpheus, in mythology the greatest of human musicians, was the son of King Oeagrus, of Thrace, and the muse of epic poetry, Calliope. Apollo gave him his lyre, and he was trained by the Muses. He refused the seductions of the women of Thrace, and several of them dismembered him. His head continued to sing.

26. Philomela was the sister of Procne, whose husband, Tereus, raped her and then cut out her tongue so that she could not tell, but she weaved the story into a tapestry and sent it to Procne. As Tereus pursued the sisters to kill them, the gods changed them into birds. Procne was turned into a nightingale and Philomela into a swallow, but English poetry casts Philomela as the nightingale. See section 3.F, "The Nightingale in Poetry."

27. Nymph deprived of speech by Hera in order to stop her chatter; she could do nothing but repeat what others said. She fell in love with Narcissus, who rejected her, and in her grief wasted away until nothing but her voice remained.

Thou kind indulgent Muse wer't ever sure
To ease, what *Æsculapius*[28] cannot cure.

(1740)

Orinthia reprov'd by her Muse
Elizabeth Teft

In what, *Orinthia*,[29] have I injur'd thee,
That thus thou shutt'st the Door of Thought on me?
Say, why am I prohibited thy Breast,
Assign'd by Heav'n my Asylum of Rest?
How err'd, that now I'm exil'd from my Home?
I sooth'd thy Cares, and gave Offence to none;
No Theme gave Joy like Praise of true Desert,
Nor Hate, nor Envy, made my Satire sharp:
Flew to admire, but slowly crept to blame,
Equally scorn'd to flatter and defame;   10
Nor to your Pen did e'er suggest a Thought,
But what your Soul's Choice darling *Virtue* taught;
Nor wish'd to tread the flow'ry Paths of Fame,
Obscure Amusement was my utmost Aim;
Nor tempt thee from the Sphere which Wisdom's King
Wisely adapted for thy acting in.
Nor urge thee to neglect thy just Employ.
Say why, unjust one, should'st thou me destroy?
I'd weed each sprouting Folly from thy Heart,
And with soft Counsel mend thy better Part;   20
From Storms impetuous guard thy tender Plant
Of growing Virtue, and supply each Want;
Prune the fair Tree, and, like the early Sun,
Nourish the Root from which the Flowers sprung;
Blossoms and Buds support with tender Care,⎫
Preserve the precious Fruits from blasting Air, ⎬
And kill the Vermin which destructive are, ⎭
Inrich the Soil, to make its Growth more strong,
Vast in Extent, and in Duration long.—
This I'd have done, and thought the Bus'ness sweet,   30

28. The god of healing.
29. Teft's pseudonym.

To give thy leaden Minutes downy Feet.
Ev'n Toil itself could not thy Peace destroy,
In servile Labour I had brought thee Joy.
Ungrateful Fool! to treat me as a Foe,
Who have the Will and Pow'r to sooth thy Woe;
Thy Will is free, say, must I be refus'd?
I'll stay thy Friend, but scorn to be abus'd.

(1747)

From Miss [Wilbraham]
Elizabeth Carter

Eliza bids me boldly try
    To pluck the Laurel Bough,[30]
And with unfading Garlands deck
    My unambitious Brow.

When Friendship's Voice thus soothing calls
    Thro' Vanity to stray,
Tho' conscious of the rash Attempt,
    I readily obey.

With Steps by her Injunctions wing'd,
10   I seek th' immortal Grove:
Less prompted by Desire of Fame,
    Than fond complying Love.

Th' offended Laurel seem'd to shrink,
    As trembling I drew near:
The vocal Leaves these Sounds convey'd
    To my attentive Ear:

"Rash Spoiler cease; nor let thy Hand
    My sacred Branch profane:
These Honours to the Wise belong,
20   Not to the Weak and Vain."

(1762)

30. The laurel is the symbol of poetic achievement; to "pluck the laurel bough" is to strive for poetic success.

To Mrs. P[riestley],
With some Drawings of Birds and Insects
Anna Laetitia Barbauld

The kindred arts to please thee shall conspire,
One dip the pencil, and one string the lyre.[31]
POPE.

Amanda[32] bids; at her command again
I seize the pencil, or resume the pen;
No other call my willing hand requires,
And friendship, better than a Muse inspires.

    Painting and poetry are near allied;
The kindred arts two sister Muses guide;[33]
This charms the eye, that steals upon the ear;
There sounds are tun'd; and colours blended here:
This with a silent touch enchants our eyes,
And bids a gayer brighter world arise: 10
That, less allied to sense, with deeper art
Can pierce the close recesses of the heart;
By well set syllables, and potent sound,
Can rouse, can chill the breast, can sooth, can wound;
To life adds motion, and to beauty soul,
And breathes a spirit through the finish'd whole:
Each perfects each, in friendly union join'd;
This gives Amanda's form, and that her mind.

    But humbler themes my artless hand requires,
Nor higher than the feather'd tribe aspires.   20
Yet who the various nations can declare
That plow with busy wing the peopled air?
These cleave the crumbling bark for insect food;

---

31. These lines are a modified version of lines 69–70 of *Epistle to Mr. Jervas, with Dryden's Translation of Fresnoy's Art of Painting*, by Alexander Pope (1688–1744): "The kindred Arts shall in their praise conspire, / One dip the pencil, and one string the lyre."

32. Identified as Mary Priestly (1744–96), Barbauld's "warmest attachment," by William McCarthy and Elizabeth Kraft in *The Poems of Anna Letitia Barbauld*, ed. McCarthy and Kraft (Athens: University of Georgia Press, 1994), 224, 219.

33. Painting and poetry were known as the "sister arts" as understood in the tradition of *ut pictura poesis* (as is painting, so is poetry), a relationship of fundamental similarity theorized by the Roman poet Horace in *Ars Poetica*, line 361.

Those dip their crooked beak in kindred blood:
Some haunt the rushy moor, the lonely woods;
Some bathe their silver plumage in the floods;
Some fly to man; his houshold gods implore,
And gather round his hospitable door;
Wait the known call, and find protection there
30   From all the lesser tyrants of the air.

The tawny EAGLE seats his callow brood
High on the cliff, and feasts his young with blood.
On Snowden's[34] rocks, or Orkney's[35] wide domain,
Whose beetling[36] cliffs o'erhang the western main,[37]
The royal bird his lonely kingdom forms
Amidst the gathering clouds, and sullen storms;
Thro' the wide waste of air he darts his sight,
And holds his sounding pinions[38] pois'd for flight;
With cruel eye premeditates the war,
40   And marks his destin'd victim from afar:
Descending in a whirlwind to the ground,
His pinions like the rush of waters sound;
The fairest of the fold he bears away,
And to his nest compels the struggling prey;
He scorns the game by meaner hunters tore,
And dips his talons in no vulgar gore.

With lovelier pomp along the grassy plain
The silver PHEASANT draws his shining train;
On India's painted shore, by Ganges' stream,
50   He spreads his plumage to the sunny gleam:
But when the wiry net his flight confines,
He lowers his purple crest, and inly[39] pines;
The beauteous captive hangs his ruffled wing
Oppress'd by bondage, and our chilly spring.
To claim the verse, unnumber'd tribes appear

34. Mount Snowden, in Wales, at 3,456 feet the highest point in England and Wales.

35. The Orkney Islands, an archipelago six miles north of Scotland and extending about fifty miles north and northeast.

36. Projecting, overhanging.

37. Open sea.

38. Wings.

39. Inwardly.

That swell the music of the vernal year:
Seiz'd with the spirit of the kindly spring
They tune the voice, and sleek the glossy wing:
With emulative strife the notes prolong,
And pour out all their little souls in song.   60
When winter bites upon the naked plain,
Nor food nor shelter in the groves remain;
By instinct led, a firm united band,
As marshall'd by some skilful general's hand,
The congregated nations wing their way
In dusky columns o'er the trackless sea;
In clouds unnumber'd annual hover o'er
The craggy Bass, or Kilda's utmost shore:[40]
Thence spread their sails to meet the southern wind,
And leave the gathering tempest far behind;   70
Pursue the circling sun's indulgent ray,
Course the swift seasons, and o'ertake the day.

    Not so the Insect race, ordain'd to keep
The lazy sabbath of a half-year's sleep.
Entomb'd, beneath the filmy web they lie,
And wait the influence of a kinder sky;
When vernal sun-beams pierce their dark retreat,
The heaving tomb distends with vital heat;
The full-form'd brood impatient of their cell
Start from their trance, and burst their silken shell;   80
Trembling a-while they stand, and scarcely dare
To launch at once upon the untried air:
At length assur'd, they catch the favouring gale,
And leave their sordid spoils, and high in Ether sail.
So when Rinaldo struck the conscious rind,
He found a nymph in every trunk confin'd;
The forest labours with convulsive throes,
The bursting trees the lovely births disclose,
And a gay troop of damsels round him stood,
Where late was rugged bark and lifeless wood.[41]   90

---

40. The Bass Isle lies in the Firth of Forth, Saint Kilda west of the Hebrides. Both islands have large bird populations. McCarthy and Kraft, *Poems of Anna Letitia Barbauld,* 225.

41. In *Jerusalem Delivered,* by Torquato Tasso, Rinaldo discovers a forest where trees give birth to women: "A lab'ring oak a sudden cleft disclos'd, / And from its bark a living birth expos'd; / Whence

Lo! the bright train their radiant wings unfold,
With silver fring'd and freckl'd o'er with gold:
On the gay bosom of some fragrant flower
They idly fluttering live their little hour;
Their life all pleasure, and their task all play,
All spring their age, and sunshine all their day.
Not so the child of sorrow, wretched man,
His course with toil concludes, with pain began;
Pleasure's the portion of the inferior kind;
100   But glory, virtue, Heaven for man design'd.

What atom forms of insect life appear![42]
And who can follow nature's pencil here?
Their wings with azure, green, and purple gloss'd,
Studded with colour'd eyes, with gems emboss'd,
Inlaid with pearl, and mark'd with various stains
Of lively crimson thro' their dusky veins.
Some shoot like living stars, athwart the night,
And scatter from their wings a vivid light,
To guide the Indian to his tawny loves,
110   As thro' the woods with cautious step he moves.

See the proud giant of the beetle race;
What shining arms his polish'd limbs enchase!
Like some stern warrior formidably bright,
His steely sides reflect a gleaming light;
On his large forehead spreading horns he wears,
And high in air the branching antlers bears;
O'er many an inch extends his wide domain,
And his rich treasury swells with hoarded grain.

(passing all belief!) in strange array, / A lovely damsel issu'd to the day. / A hundred diff'rent trees the knight beheld, / Whose fertile wombs a hundred nymphs reveal'd." *Jerusalem Delivered; An Heroic Poem: Translated from the Italian of Torquato Tasso*, trans. John Hoole, 2 vols. (London: 1763), bk. 18, lines 171–76, vol. 2, p. 210. McCarthy and Kraft note that Barbauld conflates this imagery with her own when Clorinda is trapped within a tree: "*Clorinda* once I was!—nor here confin'd, / My soul alone informs a rugged rind: / The like mysterious fate attends on all / . . . / By strange enchantment here (relentless doom!) / They find in Sylvan forms a living tomb." McCarthy and Kraft, *Poems of Anna Letitia Barbauld*, 225. Quoted from Tasso, *Jerusalem Delivered*, bk. 13, lines 310–15, vol. 2, pp. 80–81.
    42. The atom was thought to be one of the ultimate particles of matter by which the universe was formed.

Thy friend thus strives to cheat the lonely hour,
With song, or paint, an insect, or a flower: 120
Yet if Amanda praise the flowing line,
And bend delighted o'er the gay design,
I envy not, nor emulate the fame
Or of the painter's, or the poet's name:
Could I to both with equal claim pretend,
Yet far, far dearer were the name of FRIEND.

(1773)

Address to the Muse, and Her Answer
Mary Savage

I have ask'd thee my muse, and now ask thee again;
To grant me once more a poetical strain;
'Tis not to indulge, in the hopes of applause;
Nor to speak to the men, in defence of our cause;
But the season demands, that my friend should be clear,
That I wish her much mirth and a happy new year.

ANSWER

Away with thy folly, nor give thy self pain,
Thy friend doth not want, to be told it again:
For long has she known, how thy thoughts are arrang'd,
Nor would she believe, should you swear they were chang'd.   10
And often of late have I skimm'd o'er thy brain,
To tempt thee to write—but my offer was vain;
If serious I came—'twas too much for your mind;
In sentiment drest, I was thought too refin'd;
If satire I nam'd—in a fright you would say,
They surely with int'rest the debt will repay.
But I look'd thro' your heart, and found out the scheme,
That love, was your Ladyship's favourite theme.
And, (most strange to behold;) however express'd,
To your husband alone, that love was address'd: 20
But custom forbad you, to speak your mind plain,
Or him to applaud, such an old fashion'd strain:

Disgusted at this, now the pen you refuse;
Then; (true Poet like,) lay the blame on your muse;
But think not that I, for your faults will atone,
Either follow your genius or let me alone.

(1777)

A Familiar Epistle to Miss Coker[43]
Ann Murry

You challenge me to write in Rhyme,
Tho' I have neither sense or time:
Nor can I well the boon[44] refuse,
So thus invoke the sacred Muse.
Hail! gentle Clio![45] form the verse,
In numbers musical and terse;
Diffuse thy softness o'er each line,
Friendship and Love, with grace combine!
In vain I strive to bring things pat in,
And have recourse to French and Latin:
Yet fear that I at last must seek,
A firm ally in ancient Greek.
Or grown perhaps quite gay and airy,
Address bright Oberon the Fairy,[46]
To take me in his pigmy train,
Of his light shackles proud and vain;
Reclin'd on bank of Asphodel,[47]
Hearing thy note, sweet Philomel![48]

10

43. Miss Laura Coker subscribed to Murry's volume, as she did to Jane Cave Winscom's.
44. Request.
45. Muse of history and heroic poetry.
46. Oberon is king of the fairies in William Shakespeare's *A Midsummer Night's Dream.*
47. A perennial flower, also known as King's spear, with narrow leaves, elongated stem, and spiky flowers. In Greek mythology, also the name of the immortal flower said to cover the Elysian meadows. Elysium, a place on the west of the earth, is a happy land that is never cold and is always warmed by the soft breezes of Zephyrus, god of the west wind.
48. A nightingale. In the Roman legend, Philomela, sister to Procne, was forced into marriage by Procne's husband, Tereus, who tricked her into believing that Procne was dead. When she learned the truth, and he cut out her tongue so that she could not speak, she wove a tapestry recounting the events. Upon learning of his crime against Philomela, Procne killed her son by Tereus, cooked him in a stew, and served it to Tereus. He tried to kill Philomela and Procne, but the gods turned them all into birds: Tereus a hawk, Procne a swallow, and Philomela a nightingale.

With dulcet tones enrich my song,
For such alone to thee belong.   20
Or sipping of the midnight dew,
In Acorn cup, or Vi'let blue,
The magic orgies[49] nightly keep,
Whilst mortals are absorb'd in sleep.
When thus I paus'd——the Muse reply'd,
"All vain pretenders I deride:
'Tis not to take a Pen and Ink,
And sit thee down intent to think,
With fine gilt paper, silver standish,[50]
And lofty plume with grace to brandish,   30
That will express a thought complete,
Or raise it on heroic feet![51]
I should prefer a Garreteer,[52]
Who writes with Chalk or dregs of Beer;
Whose lines on scraps are badly writ,
The remnants of neglected wit.
Hear my decree, nor ever write,
Unless good-sense the lays[53] indite.[54]
In works of fancy spend thy time,
Nor ever more attempt to rhyme;   40
The needle thou canst wield with skill,
Which time and vapours sure will kill.
If thou this edict wilt not brook,
And still desire to read a Book,
Enough has been already wrote,
For thee to copy or to quote."
Thus ended her severe discourse,
Which struck my mind with poignant force:
Yet summon'd courage to reply,
Why dost thou spurn me? tell me why,   50
Most cruel Clio! or refuse,
To be my patronizing Muse?
Didst thou but know, as well as me,

49. Rites or ceremonies.
50. Inkstand.
51. Heroic couplets, rhymed couplets in iambic pentameter.
52. Impecunious author (one who lives in a garret).
53. Ballads; lyric or narrative poems meant to be sung.
54. Inspire or express.

My Laura's manners kind and free,
Thou would'st not then reject my suit,
Or doom me to be ever mute:
The mere narration of her worth,
May well supply my fancy's dearth;
The pleasing qualities I find
Implanted in her tender mind,
Ask not the foreign aid of verse,
Their various merits to rehearse;
But wrote in plain and simple prose,
Will clearly their own worth disclose.
Thus I thy mandate will obey,
Nor ever more attempt to lay
An off'ring at thy golden shrine,
But Willows[55] round my temples twine.

(1779)

Friendship. An Ode
Elizabeth Hands

Friendship inspires;
The sacred lay[56]
My bosom fires;
Let friendly virgins tune their lyres,
In concert join, angelic choirs,
Due rites to pay.

Let envy shrink away,
As darkness flies approaching day;
Her serpent crest in vain she rears,
And her curst sting prepares;
She counteracts herself; for see
Her blast,
Binds fast

55. Willows instead of a laurel. A willow is a tree characterized by very pliant branches and long narrow drooping leaves. A willow sprig is a symbol of grief for unrequited love or the loss of a mate.
56. Ballad; lyric or narrative poem meant to be sung.

The knot of friendship ty'd,
   In virtuous pride,
   And firm sincerity.

O friendship, first of blessings here below;
  The best gift Heaven can bestow!
    Thou secret balm,
    Serene and calm;   20
O stream of bliss, in gentlest currents flow!

  Calm, humble bliss of friendship rise,
  Superior to the splendid joys,
    That glitter round the world;
  Temptations so profusely spread,
    With dazzling glares mislead
    The feet that heedless tread,
And all those joys are in confusion hurl'd.

  But Oh! 'tis friendship's rite,
  To give and take delight,   30
    Dividing care:
    Fly hence, despair,
    Nor more annoy;
    Firm friendship's joy
  Shines undiminish'd in distress,
  The wretched and the blest to bless;
Its sweet and sovereign power let every tongue confess.

(1789)

An Address to the Muses

Joanna Baillie

Ye tuneful Sisters of the lyre,
Who dreams and fantasies inspire;
Who over poesy preside,
And on the lofty hill abide[57]

---

57. Parnassus, a mountain near Delphi, Greece, sacred to Apollo and the Muses, hence to poetry and the arts.

Above the ken[58] of mortal sight,
Fain would I sing of you, could I address ye right.

Thus known, your pow'r of old was sung,
And temples with your praises rung;
And when the song of battle rose,
10   Or kindling wine, or lovers' woes,
The poet's spirit inly burn'd,
And still to you his upcast eyes were turn'd.

The youth all wrapp'd in vision bright,
Beheld your robes of flowing white:
And knew your forms benignly grand,
An awful, but a lovely band;
And felt your inspiration strong,
And warmly pour'd his rapid lay[59] along.

The aged bard all heav'n-ward glow'd,
20   And hail'd you daughters of a god:
Tho' to his dimmer eyes were seen
Nor graceful form, nor heav'nly mien,
Full well he felt that ye were near,
And heard you in the blast that shook his hoary hair.

Ye lighten'd up the valley's bloom,
And deeper spread the forest's gloom:
The lofty hill sublimer stood,
And grander rose the mighty flood;
For then Religion lent her aid,
30   And o'er the mind of man your sacred empire spread.

Tho' rolling ages now are past,
And altars low, and temples waste;
Tho' rites and oracles[60] are o'er,
And gods and heros rule no more;
Your fading honours still remain,
And still your vot'ries[61] call, a long and motley train.

58. Understanding.

59. Ballad; lyric or narrative poem meant to be sung.

60. Shrines consecrated to a prophetic god, such as Apollo; the priests who convey the prophecies.

61. Fervent believers, those sworn and devoted to a religion, cause, or activity.

They seek you not on hill and plain,
Nor court you in the sacred sane;[62]
Nor meet you in the mid-day dream,
Upon the bank of hallowed stream;   40
Yet still for inspiration sue,
And still each lifts his fervent prayer to you.

He knows ye not in woodland gloom,
But wooes ye in the shelfed room;
And seeks you in the dusty nook,
And meets you in the letter'd book;
Full well he knows you by your names,
And still with poets faith your presence claims.

The youthful poet, pen in hand,
All by the side of blotted stand,   50
In rev'rie deep, which none may break,
Sits rubbing of his beardless cheek;
And well his inspiration knows,
E'en by the dewy drops that trickle o'er his nose.

The tuneful sage of riper fame,
Perceives you not in heated frame;
But at conclusion of his verse,
Which still his mutt'ring lips rehearse,
Oft' waves his hand in grateful pride,
And owns the heav'nly pow'r that did his fancy guide.   60

O lovely sisters! is it true,
That they are all inspir'd by you?
And while they write, with magic charm'd,
And high enthusiasm warm'd,
We may not question heav'nly lays,
For well I wot,[63] they give you all the praise.

O lovely sisters! well it shews
How wide and far your bounty flows:
Then why from me withhold your beams?
Unvisited of heav'nly dreams,   70

62. Temple.
63. Know.

Whene'er I aim at heights sublime,
Still downward am I call'd to seek some stubborn rhyme.

No hasty lightning breaks the gloom,
Nor flashing thoughts unsought for come,
Nor fancies wake in time of need;
I labour much with little speed;
And when my studied talk is done,
Too well, alas! I mark it for my own.

Yet should you never smile on me,
80   And rugged still my verses be;
Unpleasing to the tuneful train,
Who only prize a flowing strain;
And still the learned scorn my lays,
I'll lift my heart to you, and sing your praise.

Your varied ministry to trace,
Your honour'd names, and godlike race,
And lofty bow'rs where fountains flow,
They'll better sing who better know;
I praise ye not with Grecian lyre,
90   Nor will I hail ye daughters of a heathen fire.

Ye are the spirits who preside
In earth, and air, and ocean wide;
In hissing flood, and crackling fire;
In horror dread, and tumult dire;
In stilly calm, and stormy wind,
And rule the answ'ring changes in the human mind.

High on the tempest-beaten hill,
Your misty shapes ye shift at will;
The wild fantastic clouds ye form;
100   Your voice is in the midnight storm,
Whilst in the dark and lonely hour,
Oft' starts the boldest heart, and owns your secret pow'r.

From you, when growling storms are past,
And light'ning ceases on the waste,
And when the scene of blood is o'er,

And groans of death are heard no more,
Still holds the mind each parted form,
Like after echoing of th' o'erpassed storm.

When closing glooms o'erspread the day,
And what we love has pass'd away,   110
Ye kindly bid each pleasing scene
Within the bosom still remain,
Like moons who doth their watches run
With the reflected brightness of the parted sun.

The shining day, and nightly shade,
The cheerful plain and gloomy glade,
The homeward flocks, and shepherds play,
The busy hamlet's closing day,
Full many a breast with pleasures swell,
Who ne'er shall have the gift of words to tell.   120

Oft' when the moon looks from on high,
And black around the shadows lie;
And bright the sparkling waters gleam,
And rushes rustle by the stream,
Shrill sounds, and fairy forms are known
By simple 'nighted swains,[64] who wander late alone.

Ye kindle up the inward glow,
Ye strengthen ev'ry outward show;
Ye overleap the strongest bar,
And join what Nature sunders far: 130
And visit oft' in fancies wild,
The breast of learned sage, and simple child.

From him who wears a monarch's crown,
To the unletter'd artless clown,[65]
All in some strange and lonely hour
Have felt, unsought, your secret pow'r,
And lov'd your roving fancies well,
You add but to the bard the art to tell.

64. Benighted (unenlightened or ignorant) country men.
65. Countryman, peasant, uncouth man.

Ye mighty spirits of the song,
140   To whom the poets' pray'rs belong,
My lowly bosom to inspire,
And kindle with your sacred fire,
Your wild obscuring heights to brave,
Is boon,[66] alas! too great for me to crave.

But O, such sense of matter bring!
As they who feel and never sing
Wear on their hearts, it will avail
With simple words to tell my tale;
And still contented will I be,
150   Tho' greater inspirations never fall to me.

(1790)

Sources

Egerton: *Poems on Several Occasions, Together with a Pastoral* (London, 1703), 14–16; Masters: *Poems on Several Occasions* (London, 1733), 8–10; Dixon: *Poems on Several Occasions* (Canterbury, 1740), 121–25; Teft: *Orinthia's Miscellanies* (London, 1747), 18–19; Carter: *Poems on Several Occasions* (London, 1762), 141–42; Barbauld: *Poems* (London, 1773), 41–48; Savage: *Poems on Various Subjects and Occasions,* 2 vols. (London, 1777), 1:75–77; Murry: *Poems on Various Subjects* (London, 1779), 114–17; Hands: *The Death of Amnon. A Poem. With an Appendix: Containing Pastorals, and other Poetical Pieces* (Coventry, 1789), 109–10; Baillie: *Poems; Wherein It Is Attempted to Describe Certain Views of Nature and of Rustic Manners* (London, 1790), 73–81.

66. Blessing, favor.

✣C✣

The Experience of Writing

The experience of writing for women seems to be the same regardless of the century. Harriet Beecher Stowe compared it to rowing against wind and tide; Maya Angelou, to living in a golden palace. One day it is flowing and wonderful, and the next day it is frustrating and unproductive. One day there are countless interruptions and a power outage, and the next day glorious solitude. One day writing seems as necessary as the air we breathe, and the next day it is a troublesome commitment with an inconvenient deadline. The poems in this anthology capture every mood, and the ones in this section are distinguished by the openness of their authors' expressions of conviction. Mary Barber writes from the point of view of Apollo, the god of poetry, delivering an edict, and Anna Seward writes a complex Miltonic sonnet summarizing her claim for the nobility and primacy of the sonnet form (1.B).[1] The poems range from lighthearted satire to serious manifestoes. Jane Barker in *Resolved never to Versifie more* calls verse "th' tender'st *Plant* i'th' Field of Wit" and uses a series of Restoration-comedy wit statements to describe a poet's chances of success. Laetitia Pilkington's poem is both a joke and a clever reworking of the promise of immortality made by a writer to his beloved.

In these poems and others in the section, serious undertones turn apparently facetious statements into insightful, reflective moments. Mary Leapor's *Epistle to a Lady* and Anna Laetitia Barbauld's *Verses written in an Alcove* are quiet, beautiful, searching poems that return us to the themes of some of the friendship poems, in section 2.A, that claim that "friendship, better than a Muse, inspires" (Barbauld, *To Mrs. P[riestley]*, 3.B). The poems acknowledge confrontations with the expectations for women and for poetry all around them. Barbauld's beautifully controlled *On a Lady's Writing* is a powerfully compressed statement of hard-won wisdom *and* freedom. Both Jane Barker's *To My Friends against Poetry* and Mary Barber's *Apollo's Edict* collect the clichés of their time and mock poetic fads, yet the tones of their poems could hardly be more different as they consider the serious purposes of poetry. The poems collected in this section move surely and tellingly from the private, personal thoughts of writers to the milieu in which writing is done and back to the convictions that are born in this dynamic.

Note

1. On Seward's rather combative participation in controversies over the sonnet, see Stuart Curran, "The I Altered," in *Romanticism and Feminism,* ed. Anne K. Mellor (Bloomington: Indiana University Press, 1988), 185–207; and Paula R. Backscheider, *Eighteenth-Century Women Poets and Their Poetry* (Baltimore: Johns Hopkins University Press, 2005), 339–44.

Resolved never to Versifie more
Jane Barker

Fear not, my Friends, you ever more shall see
    The folly of a Verse from me;
For howsoe'er my inclinations drive,
    Yet in this Town they will not thrive;
At best but blasted, wither'd Rhimes they are,
    Such as appear in *Smithfield*[1] once a year.

    For,
No more than Beauty, without Wealth, can move
    A Gallants heart to strokes of Love;
Than fair perswasions, without stripes, reduce   10
    The Birds of *Bridewell,* or of Stews;[2]
Than *Gypsies* without Money can foreshow,
    No more can Verse in *London* grow.

    For,
Verse is th' tender'st *Plant* i'th' Field of Wit,
    No Storm must ever blow o'er it;
A very *Noli-me-tangere*[3] it is,
    It shrivels with the touch of business;
But, *Heliotropian* like,[4] it seeks the *gleams*
    Of *Quietudes* reviving Beams.   20
How shou'd it then endure this irksome shade,
    Which is by noise of Plots and Bus'ness made?

(1688)

---

1. Smithfield was a plain, grassy field outside the London city walls. Bartholomew Fair was held there once a year from 1123 until it was suppressed in 1855 because of rowdiness and debauchery.

2. Formerly a royal palace, Bridewell was given to the city of London by Edward VI for the punishment of petty offenders and disorderly women, including prostitutes, unmarried pregnant women, and keepers and occupants of "stews," or brothels. There those who violated the public's moral sense were beaten with switches or whips on their bare backs, leaving stripes.

3. Literally, "touch me not"; here a reference to the "sensitive plant," *Mimosa pudica,* whose seed capsules, or fruits, burst open at a touch.

4. The heliotrope, a flower, always turns toward the sun.

To my Friends against Poetry

Jane Barker

Dear Friends, if you'll be rul'd by me,
Beware o'th' Charms of *Poetry;*
And meddle with no fawning *Muse,*
They'll but your harmless Loves abuse.
Though to *Orinda*⁵ they were ty'd,
That nought their Friendship cou'd divide;
And *Cowley*'s Mistriss⁶ had a Flame
As pure and lasting as his *Fame:*
Yet now they're all grown *Prostitutes,*
And wantonly admit the Suits
Of any *Fop,*⁷ that will pretend
To be their Servant or their Friend.
Though they to *Wit* no *Homage* pay,
Nor yet the Laws of *Verse* obey,
But ride poor *Six-foot* out of breath,⁸
And wrack a *Metaphor* to death;
Who make their Verse *imbibe* the crimes,
And the lewd Follies too o'th' times;
Who think all Wit consists in Ranting,
And Vertuous Love in wise Gallanting:
And Thousand sorts of Fools, like these,
Make Love and Vertue what they please:
And yet as silly as they show,
Are Favourites o'th' *Muses* now.
Who then would honour such a *Shee,*
Where *Fools* their happier *Rivals* be?
We, surely, may conclude there's none,
Unless they're drunk with *Helicon,*⁹
Which is a Liquor that can make

10

20

---

5. Katherine Philips, known as "the Matchless Orinda."

6. Abraham Cowley (1618–67), like Barker, was a Royalist. *The Mistress,* a cycle of love poems by Cowley, was published in 1647 and reprinted in his 1656 *Poems.* It was extremely popular; individual poems were frequently published in miscellanies, and many were set to music by the most eminent composers of the period.

7. A pretender to wit, often foolishly attentive to his appearance.

8. Verse in hexameter feet, each line made up of six sets of syllables. Tetrameter (four) and pentameter (five) feet were more common in the century.

9. The fountains of Aganippe and Hippocrene rose on the Helicon, the mountain in Greece sacred to the Muses.

A *Dunce* set up for Rhiming Quack: 30
A Liquor of so strange a temper,
As can our Faculties all hamper;
That whoso drinks thereof is curs'd
Unto a constant Rhiming thirst;
I know not by what *spell* of *Witch*,
It strikes the Mind into an *itch;*
Which being scrub'd by praise, thereby
Becomes a spreading *Leprosie*;
As hard to cure as Dice[10] or Whore,
And makes the Patient too as poor;   40
For Poverty's the certain Fate
Which attends a *Poet*'s state.

(1688)

Apollo's Edict[11]
Mary Barber

Ierne's[12] now our royal Care:
We lately fix'd our Vice-roy[13] there.
How near was she to be undone,
Till pious Love inspir'd her Son!
What cannot our Vice-gerent[14] do,
As Poet, and as Patriot too?
Let his Success our Subjects sway,
Our Inspirations to obey:
Let beaten Paths no more be trac'd;
But study to correct your Taste,   10

10. Gambling, already recognized as addictive.

11. Oliver Ferguson and others argue that this poem is by Barber, although it was attributed to Jonathan Swift for many years. It was undoubtedly the product of Barber's participation in an active writing circle. Paula Backscheider, "Inverting the Image of Swift's 'Triumfeminate,'" *Journal for Early Modern Cultural Studies* 4 (2004): 49–52.

12. Ancient name for Ireland.

13. Dr. Swift. *Barber.* [Jonathan Swift (1667–1745), author of *Gulliver's Travels* (1726). *Eds.*]

14. A person appointed to represent a king or political or religious authority. Swift was the dean of St. Patrick's in Dublin, and he wrote a number of important poems, as well as *The Drapier's Letters*, in this period. Swift's courageous publication of the latter was a brilliant campaign against a coinage scheme much to the disadvantage of the Irish. It made him a national hero, and bonfires were lit on his birthday, 30 November, for the rest of his life.

No Simile shall be begun
With *rising,* or with *setting Sun;*
And let the secret Head of *Nile*
Be ever banish'd from your Isle.

WHEN wretched Lovers live on Air,
In Pity the *Chameleon*[15] spare:
And when you'd make a Hero grander,
Forget he's like a *Salamander.*[16]

No Son of mine shall dare to say,
20   Aurora[17] *usher'd in the Day.*

YOU all agree, I make no Doubt,
The *Prophet's Mantle's*[18] quite worn out.

THE *Bird of Jove*[19] shall toil no more,
To teach the humble *Wren* to soar.

YOUR tragic Heroes shall not rant,
Nor Shepherds use poetic Cant.
Simplicity alone can grace
The Manners of the rural Race.

WHEN *Damon's* Soul shall take its Flight,[20]
30   (Tho' Poets have the *second Sight*)

15. A small, slow-moving lizard with the ability to change colors. That it lives on air is, of course, a myth.

16. A lizard that was associated with the element fire (earth, air, and water were the other elements) and believed to be able to live in fire. It had a shiny, gaudy skin but was marked with "loathsome spots." According to Pliny's famous description, in a tempest it comes out of a hole and will "Become a general, poet, and beau," only to "shrink into its hole again" when the air clears. Some believed it caused leprosy and baldness. Barber may have had in mind Swift's satire of Lord Cutts, *The Description of a Salamander* (1705). Ricardo Quintana, *The Mind and Art of Jonathan Swift* (Gloucester: Peter Smith, 1965), 157–58.

17. Goddess of the dawn. According to legend, she sets out before the sun and is the sister of the moon.

18. Elijah designated Elisha as his successor as prophet of Israel by casting his mantle on Elisha's shoulders (2 Kings 2:13). The saying involving the passing on of the responsibility for prophecy by giving a mantle (a loose, sleeveless coat) became conventional and overused.

19. The eagle, which carried the arrows for the supreme Roman god, the great father god and protector of the state; also Jupiter, the Greek god Zeus.

20. Shepherd singer in Virgil's Eighth *Eclogue*. Milton uses the name for a friend, Charles Diodati, in his Elegy 6.

No *Trail of Light* shall upwards rise,
Nor a new Star adorn the Skies:
For who can hope to place one there,
So glorious as *Belinda*'s Hair?[21]
Yet, if his Name you eternize,
And *must* exalt him to the Skies;
Without a Star it may be done ——
So *Tickell* mourn'd his *Addison*.[22]

If *Anna*'s[23] happy Reign you praise,
Say not a Word of *Halcyon-Days:*[24]   40
Nor let my Vot'ries shew their Skill,
In apeing Lines from *Cooper's-Hill;*
For, know, I cannot bear to hear
The Mimickry of *deep, yet clear*.[25]

WHENE'ER my Viceroy is address'd,
Against the *Phœnix*[26] I protest.

WHEN *Kelly*'s[27] Beauties you survey,
Forget they're like the *Milky Way*.

WHEN Poets soar in youthful Strains,
No *Phaeton*,[28] to hold the Reins.   50

21. *Rape of the Lock. Barber.* [A mock epic by Alexander Pope. *Eds.*]

22. Thomas Tickell (1685–1740) was a poet, critic, and translator of part of Pope's *Iliad*. He published an elegy on Joseph Addison's death in his edition of Addison's *Works* (1721). Addison (1672–1719) is known for the *Tatler* and *Spectator* papers and for his play *Cato* (1713).

23. Queen Anne reigned from 1702 to 1714.

24. A time when the world was idyllically happy and peaceful.

25. In his much-imitated and much-quoted topographical poem *Cooper's-Hill*, John Denham ($16\frac{14}{15}$–1669) describes the Thames as follows: "Though deep, yet clear, though gentle, yet not dull / Strong without rage, without o're-flowing full." John Denham, *Cooper's-Hill: A Poem* (London, 1709), 11.

26. In classical mythology, the phoenix is a bird resembling an eagle but with sumptuous red and gold plumage. Said to live for five or six hundred years in the deserts of Arabia, it makes a nest of spices, sings a beautiful dirge, and burns itself to ashes on a funeral pyre ignited by the sun and fanned by its own wings, only to rise from its ashes with renewed youth and repeat the cycle.

27. *Mrs.* Frances-Arabella Kelly. *Barber.* [Kelly was a beautiful young woman in Swift's circle whose failing health troubled her friends; she died in 1733. *Eds.*]

28. Son of the Greek sun god, Helios. When Helios foolishly allowed Phaeton to drive his chariot across the sky for a day, Phaeton lost control of the chariot, which would have crashed into the earth and destroyed it had Zeus not killed Phaeton.

CUPID[29] shall ne'er mistake another,
Not ev'n *Eliza*,[30] for his *Mother;*
Nor shall his Darts at Random fly,
From Magazines in *Rochford*'s Eye.[31]

W H E N *Boyle*'s exalted Genius[32] shines,
Distinguish'd in your noblest Lines;
With his own Worth your Patron grace,
And let *Mæcenas*[33] sleep in Peace.

W H E N you describe a lovely Girl,
60   No *Coral Lips,* or *Teeth of Pearl.*

W I T H *Women Compounds* I am cloy'd,
Which only pleas'd in *Biddy Floyd.*[34]
For foreign Aid what need they roam,
Whom Fate hath amply bless'd at Home?
Unerring Heav'n, with bounteous Hand,
Has form'd a Model for your Land;
Whom *Jove* endow'd with ev'ry Grace,
The Glory of the *Granard* Race;[35]
Now destin'd by the Pow'rs divine,
70   The Blessing of another Line.
Then, would you paint a matchless Dame,
And raise her to immortal Fame;
Invoke not *Cytherea*'s[36] Aid,

29. God of love; usually depicted as a winged boy with a bow and a quiver of arrows.

30. *Mrs.* Elizabeth Penifeather. *Barber.* [The daughter of the comptroller and accountant general of Ireland; the correct spelling of her name is Pennefather. *Eds.*]

31. Deborah Staunton Rochfort, wife of John Rochfort. She and her husband lived near Swift and were part of his inner circle.

32. John *Earl* of Orrery. *Barber.* [He met Swift in 1732, socialized with the circle, and wrote *Remarks on the Life and Writings of Dr. Jonathan Swift* (1751), a biography praised today for its objectivity, research, and innovative form. *Eds.*]

33. A patron of letters, named after Gaius Cilnius Maecenas, the patron of Horace and Virgil, who kept an open house for all men of letters.

34. Reference to Swift's "compound" poem, *To Mrs. Biddy Floyd* (1708), which includes the lines, "Jove mix'd up all, and his best Clay imploy'd; / Then call'd the happy Composition, *Floyd.*"

35. Catherine, the only daughter of the first Earl of Granard; she married Arthur Chichester, third Earl of Donegal.

36. A name for Venus, from Cythera, a mountainous island noted for the worship of Aphrodite (Venus).

Nor borrow from the *Blue-ey'd Maid,*
Nor need you on the *Graces*[37] call;
Take Qualities from *Donegal.*[38]

(1734)

Carte Blanche[39]
Laetitia Pilkington

O spotless Paper, fair and white!
On whom, by Force, constrain'd I write,
How cruel am I to destroy
Thy Purity, to please a Boy?[40]
Ungrateful I, thus to abuse
The fairest Servant of the Muse.
Dear Friend, to whom I oft impart
The choicest Secrets of my Heart;
Ah, what Attonement can be made
For spotless Innocence betray'd?   10
How fair, how lovely didst thou show,
Like lilly'd Banks, or falling Snow!
But now, alas, become my Prey;
No Floods can wash thy Stains away.
Yet this small Comfort I can give,
That which destroy'd, shall make thee live.

(1748)

37. Algaia (brilliance), Thalia (bloom), and Euphrosyne (joy), the attendants of Aphrodite, enhanced the enjoyments of life for all they visited.

38. *Countess Dowager* Donegal, *Daughter to the late Earl of* Granard. *Barber.* [Her husband was killed near Barcelona in 1706 while fighting in the War of Spanish Succession. *Eds.*]

39. The title, which translates "Blank Paper," was given to the poem by George Colman and Bonnell Thornton, the editors of *Poems by Eminent Ladies* (1755), and plays on the meaning of the phrase: unrestricted authority and freedom of action.

40. In her *Memoirs*, where the poem was first published, Pilkington explains that she wrote the poem after being challenged by her brother to "write some Verse as a School Exercise for him." Upon her asking "what I should write upon; Why, said he pertly, what should you write upon but the Paper?" She remarks that "the Lines did not suit my Brother's Purpose." *The Memoirs of Mrs. Lætitia Pilkington*, 2 vols. (Dublin, 1748), 1:88–89.

An Epistle to a Lady[41]
Mary Leapor

In vain, dear Madam, yes in vain you strive;
Alas! to make your luckless *Mira*[42] thrive.
For *Tycho*[43] and *Copernicus*[44] agree,
No golden Planet bent its Rays on me.

'Tis twenty Winters, if it is no more;
To speak the Truth it may be Twenty four.
As many Springs their 'pointed Space have run,
Since *Mira*'s Eyes first open'd on the Sun.
'Twas when the Flocks on slabby Hillocks lye,
10   And the cold Fishes rule the watry Sky:
But tho' these Eyes the learned Page explore,
And turn the pond'rous Volumes o'er and o'er,
I find no Comfort from their Systems flow,
But am dejected more as more I know.
Hope shines a while, but like a Vapour flies,
(The Fate of all the Curious and the Wise)
For, Ah! cold *Saturn*[45] triumph'd on that Day,
And frowning *Sol*[46] deny'd his golden Ray.

You see I'm learned, and I shew't the more,
20   That none may wonder when they find me poor.
Yet *Mira* dreams, as slumbring Poets may,
And rolls in Treasures till the breaking Day:
While Books and Pictures in bright Order rise,
And painted Parlours swim before her Eyes:

41. This poem is probably addressed to Bridget Freemantle (1698–1779), Leapor's close friend and supporter. They met just fourteen months before Leapor's death in November 1746, but Freemantle had been acquainted with Leapor's poetry for some time. Leapor addresses Freemantle in many of her poems, usually referring to her by the pseudonym Artemisia. See Richard Greene, *Mary Leapor: A Study in Eighteenth-Century Women's Poetry* (Oxford: Clarendon, 1993), 17–19.

42. Leapor's pen name.

43. Tycho Brahe (1546–1601), Danish astronomer; he maintained that the earth was motionless but that the five planets revolved around the sun. He also discovered Cassiopeia.

44. Copernicus Nicolaus (1473–1543), Polish astronomer known for arguing that the earth and planets revolved around the sun.

45. According to astrologists, Saturn was an evil planet under which to be born since it was represented by lead.

46. Personification of the sun.

Till the shrill Clock impertinently rings,
And the soft Visions move their shining Wings:
Then *Mira* wakes,- - - -her Pictures are no more,
And through her Fingers slides the vanish'd Ore.
Convinc'd too soon, her Eye unwilling falls
On the blue Curtains and the dusty Walls: 30
She wakes, alas! to Business and to Woes,
To sweep her Kitchen, and to mend her Clothes.

    But see pale Sickness with her languid Eyes,
At whose Appearance all Delusion flies:
The World recedes, its Vanities decline,
Clorinda's Features seem as faint as mine:
Gay Robes no more the aking[47] Sight admires,
Wit grates the Ear, and melting Musick tires:
Its wonted Pleasures with each Sense decay,
Books please no more, and Paintings fade away: 40
The sliding Joys in misty Vapours end:
Yet let me still, Ah! let me grasp a Friend:
And when each Joy, when each lov'd Object flies,
Be you the last that leaves my closing Eyes.

    But how will this dismantl'd Soul appear,
When strip'd of all it lately held so dear,
Forc'd from its Prison of expiring Clay,
Afraid and shiv'ring at the doubtful Way.

    Yet did these Eyes a dying Parent see,
Loos'd from all Cares except a Thought for me,   50
Without a Tear resign her short'ning Breath,
And dauntless meet the ling'ring Stroke of Death.
Then at th' Almighty's Sentence shall I mourn:
"Of Dust thou art, to Dust shalt thou return."[48]
Or shall I wish to stretch the Line of Fate,
That the dull Years may bear a longer Date,
To share the Follies of succeeding Times
With more Vexations and with deeper Crimes:
Ah no- - - tho' Heav'n brings near the final Day,

47. Aching, painful.
48. Eccles. 3:20.

60   For such a Life I will not, dare not pray;
       But let the Tear for future Mercy flow,
       And fall resign'd beneath the mighty Blow.
       Nor I alone- - - -for through the spacious Ball,
       With me will Numbers of all Ages fall:
       And the same Day that *Mira* yields her Breath,
       Thousands may enter through the Gates of Death.

                                                        (1748)

On a Lady's Writing
Anna Laetitia Barbauld

Her even lines her steady temper show;
Neat as her dress, and polish'd as her brow;
Strong as her judgment, easy as her air;
Correct though free, and regular though fair:
And the same graces o'er her pen preside
That form her manners and her footsteps guide.

                                                        (1773)

Verses written in an Alcove
Anna Laetitia Barbauld

Jam Cytherea choros ducit Venus imminente Luna.
                                        Horat.[49]

Now the moon-beam's trembling lustre
    Silvers o'er the dewy green,
And in soft and shadowy colours
    Sweetly paints the checquer'd scene.

Here between the opening branches
    Streams a flood of soften'd light,

---

49. "Already Cytherean Venus leads her dancing bands beneath the o'erhanging moon." Horace, *Odes* 1.4.5, translated by William McCarthy and Elizabeth Kraft, *The Poems of Anna Letitia Barbauld,* ed. McCarthy and Kraft (Athens: University of Georgia Press, 1994), 259.

There the thick and twisted foliage
    Spreads the browner gloom of night.

This is sure the haunt of fairies,
    In yon cool Alcove they play;   10
Care can never cross the threshold,
    Care was only made for day.

Far from hence be noisy clamour,
    Sick disgust and anxious fear;
Pining grief and wasting anguish
    Never keep their vigils here.

Tell no tales of sheeted spectres,
    Rising from the quiet tomb;
Fairer forms this cell shall visit,
    Brighter visions gild the gloom.   20

Choral songs and sprightly voices
    Echo from her cell shall call;
Sweeter, sweeter than the murmur
    Of the distant water fall.

Every ruder gust of passion
    Lull'd with music dies away,
Till within the charmed bosom
    None but soft affections play:

Soft, as when the evening breezes
    Gently stir the poplar grove;   30
Brighter than the smile of summer,
    Sweeter than the breath of love.

Thee, th' inchanted Muse shall follow,
    LISSY![50] to the rustic cell,

---

50. Probably Elizabeth Rigby, daughter of John Rigby, provisioner to the Warrington Academy, and granddaughter of John Taylor, Hebraist and Warrington Academy tutor. See McCarthy and Kraft, *Poems of Anna Letitia Barbauld*, 231, 260. Barbauld's brother, John Aikin, had become a tutor at the academy in 1758, and her husband had become a student there in 1767.

And each careless note repeating
Tune them to her charming shell.

Not the Muse who wreath'd with laurel,[51]
Solemn stalks with tragic gait,
And in clear and lofty vision
40   Sees the future births of fate;

Not the maid who crown'd with cypress[52]
Sweeps along in scepter'd pall,[53]
And in sad and solemn accents
Mourns the crested heroe's fall;

But that other smiling sister,
With the blue and laughing eye,
Singing, in a lighter measure,
Strains of woodland harmony:

All unknown to fame or glory,
50   Easy, blithe and debonair,
Crown'd with flowers, her careless tresses
Loosely floating on the air.

Then, when next the star of evening
Softly sheds the silent dew,
Let me in this rustic temple,
LISSY! meet the Muse and you.

(1773)

Sources

Barker: *Poetical Recreations* (London, 1688), 108–9, 95–96; Barber: *Poems on Several Occasions* (London, 1734), 105–10; Pilkington: *The Memoirs of Mrs. Lætitia Pilkington*, 2 vols. (Dublin, 1748), 1:88–89; Leapor: *Poems upon Several Occasions* (London, 1748), 38–41; Barbauld: *Poems* (London, 1773), 52, 33–36.

51. In classical times, leaves from this tree were made into wreaths for poets and conquerors.
52. Cypress was sacred to the god of death, Dis. The Romans dedicated the cypress tree to Pluto because once cut, the tree never grows again.
53. Coffin on its way to the grave.

✤D✤

The Experience of Reception

These poems describe the reception women and their poetry received. Perhaps the most remarkable thing about the poems is how performative they are. They dramatize the cacophony of voices around them—the ignorant, the pretentious, the emboldening, the accusatory, the bracing, the dubious, the presuming, and the encouraging. Highly conscious of the variety of roles society assigns them as women and poets, they catch the tones of the moralists, gossips, and self-appointed connoisseurs. Their poems are full of accounts of the scrutiny that follows publication, either manuscript or print, and of insults aimed at their detractors. The poems in this section are divided into three groups. The first takes up a charge made against a number of women writers: plagiarism. The second portrays critics, both amateurs and the rising group of professionals, and the third extends portraits of reception into additional public and private settings where everyone, regardless of their qualifications, is a critic.

We open this section with one of the few well-known poems by a woman, Anne Killigrew's *Upon the Saying That My Verses Were Made by Another,* and follow it with three more poems in which women respond, in different tones, to accusations of plagiarism. Killigrew asserts her poetic ambitions and achievements, and Jane Cave Winscom states with dignity that "there are beauties of the mind, / Which are not to the great confin'd" and "As Wisdom does, the Muses do, / . . . / Sometimes they deign to call on me." Priscilla Poynton fires back, calling her accuser a coxcomb and an ape and concluding, "Ignoble Man! unworthy of my lays, / I scorn your satire. . . ." A critical commonplace is that women were often accused of plagiarism in order to silence them or devalue their work, and Aphra Behn is a much-studied example. In fact, it is hard to identify a long-eighteenth-century writer, canonical or not, who was not accused of plagiarism. John Dryden, the poet laureate, responded to accusations of theft in two ways: "He became careful to acknowledge his sources; and he provided extensive arguments to justify his appropriation of them," which was exactly what Charlotte Smith would do one hundred years later.[1] As Laura Rosenthal and Paulina Kewes make persuasive in two books on "appropriation," changing conceptions of authorship, intellectual property, and literary practices such as adaptation, imitation, and "borrowing" are the real sources of accusations of plagiarism and mark a century-long negotiation of what Kewes calls the "proprieties of appropriation." As she writes, "After 1660 the pressure on playwrights to acknowledge and justify their use of sources escalated sharply."[2] Both of these studies are about the theater, but some of the evidence Kewes and Rosenthal use, such as prefaces, dedications, critical essays, and poems, are adaptable to the study of poetry, and the wealth of reviews of books of poems in the second half of the century could be used to extend plagiarism studies to poetry—a much needed critical and social endeavor.

The second group of poems opens with two much-quoted responses to critics, Aphra Behn's *Epilogue to "Sir Patient Fancy"* and Anne Finch's *The Introduction*. Both know, as Behn says, that "We once were fam'd in Story, and cou'd write / Equall to men; cou'd Govern, nay cou'd Fight." Both find it unjust and narrow-minded that their work is devalued because, in Finch's words, "by a Woman writt. / ... / Such an intruder on the rights of men." Behn's verse was to be performed in the often rude exchanges of the public theater, where everyone in the audience was a judgmental critic, whereas Finch chose to preserve her poem carefully in two meticulously prepared manuscripts but to open her published book of poems with the more comical but defiant *Mercury and the Elephant: A Prefatory Fable*. Both of Finch's poems address a much narrower audience. Susanna Centlivre's *Prologue to "The Wonder"* also refers to the caustic, vociferous theater critics and addresses the women in the audience, who "must favour such a Cause," the encouragement of a woman writer. Insults fly; Mary Jones resents a literary marketplace "Where footmen in the seat of critics sit."

Taking the opposite approach, Clara Reeve pretends to demonstrate why male and female poets are not equal and in doing so proves herself a creative match for the best. At the end of the poem, she interpolates, "(You need not let the fellows know it, / They'll praise the wit, but damn the poet.)" Reeve's jab is at those who attack anything written by a woman, regardless of its point. Several of the poets also note that they are accused, as Mary Masters says, of invading men's "learn'd Authority" and becoming, in Reeve's image, "As owls are shown, but to be hooted." These statements are early heralds of the way the professionalization of many occupations used formal education, which women were largely denied, as the means to banish women from occupations. The poems in this group contemplate "professional" critics, whose occupation is new to the literary marketplace, as well as the amateurs that Behn, Centlivre, and Finch address. In *The Critick and the Writer of Fables* Finch creates a pedantic arbiter of taste and authority on influence in order to have her say on the hierarchy of genres; Mary Masters pits her judgment against that of the critics of a book of poems she enjoyed, and Mary Savage finds Lady Anne Miller superior to the critics. It is notable that these poems are in the most public forms of verse—fables, satire, prologues, and epilogues. That alone shows that the women were willing to challenge their detractors and, as the generation of women that included Sarah Fyge Egerton did, dispute opinion about the nature and capacity of women.

The final group of poems in this section ventriloquize a dazzling array of those who would beat them from the field of poetic achievement. Delarivière Manley's prologue ends with a witty shot: to assure success and approval, she will copy the pack of beaus who are so satisfied with themselves. Eliza Tuite is encouraged to write by one lady and advised against it by another, put in a position where she must displease and offend one of them. Mary Barber, Esther Lewis Clark, and Elizabeth Hands depict chattering women as detractors filled with opinions about the proper conduct of women and about the poetry they are likely to write. Mary Jones in *An Epistle to Lady Bowyer*, a poem that has come to be frequently anthologized, gives her slant on patrons and many other aspects of the literary marketplace. These poems are filled with remarkable moments. For instance, Esther Lewis Clark writes in *Slander delineated*, "All tongues are presently in motion, / About her person, mind, and portion." A woman is always a *body*, and this sequence not only reminds us of that but also sandwiches her mind between the two characteristics that the century usually used to market and price a woman—her person (her physical appearance) and her portion (her dowry).

Poems in other sections of the anthology show women deeply aware of the roles women writers can fashion and play and how they can "tell it slant" when necessary. Those in this section are remarkable for their unsparing depictions of what they faced and their direct answers to those who resisted their writing. Two lines of Barber's might summarize what they all felt about the sharks around them: "Whene'er *she thinks* a Fault she spies, / How Pleasure sparkles in her Eyes!" Whether the poems are set in crowded, gossip-filled rooms or, as in Elizabeth Thomas's *To Pulcheria*, only the speaker, intensely focused on an opinion she must resist, seems to exist, they give us immediate access to their experiences. Some are capacious poems celebrating a vision in which poetry will "like truth, love, and time must for evermore last" or sweeping back in history to a time when the biblical Deborah was poet and warrior and a model to Queen Elizabeth I. Thus, we gain diachronic and synchronic perspectives.

These poems are among the most indicative of cultural shifts. Patronage, subscription publishing, reviewing, and public opinion were part of the changing economics that women had to master. With the rise of the professional woman writer and the dominance of the politeness movement, resistance grew, and the resistance to writing women, as well as to their texts, shifted ground. While the earlier women wrote extensively about jealousy, the later women described attacks on their class and person, many delivered through denigrating code phrases.

Throughout this section, women allow revealing glimpses of writers' relationships to their work. Mary Masters writes, "But still the Poem, howsoe'er design'd, / Is a true Picture of the Author's Mind." Constantia Grierson finds Barber's poetry also a "transcript" of her mind and takes the occasion of the completion of her friend's book to write an eloquent statement of the highest purposes of poetry. Masters's sense of humor, Behn's outrage, Winscom's playfulness, Grierson's self-possession, and Killigrew's resignation are but a few of the moods these poems create as they work self-consciously within the milieu in which they publish. In many cases, collecting the poems of a lifetime, we find that the same woman writes all of these conclusions at one time or another. Indeed, reception and response differ from woman to woman, time to time, and even day to day, but none avoided encounters with detractors who wanted them to lay down their pens.

Notes

1. The quotation is from Paulina Kewes, *Authorship and Appropriation: Writing for the Stage in England, 1660–1710* (Oxford: Clarendon, 2004), 54–55. On Charlotte Smith and "plagiarism" in her poetry, see Susan Wolfson, "Charlotte Smith's *Emigrants:* Forging Connections at the Borders of a Female Tradition," *Huntington Library Quarterly* 63 (2000): 509–46; and Paula R. Backscheider, *Eighteenth-Century Women Poets and Their Poetry* (Baltimore: Johns Hopkins University Press, 2005), 335–38.

2. Laura J. Rosenthal, *Playwrights and Plagiarists in Early Modern England: Gender, Authorship, and Literary Property* (Ithaca, NY: Cornell University Press, 1996); Kewes, *Authorship and Appropriation,* quotation from 5; see esp. 32–95, 117–18. Unlike earlier studies, Kewes argues that critics were more lenient toward women than toward men, unless the men were aristocratic.

PLAGIARISM

Upon the saying that my verses were made by another
Anne Killigrew

Next Heaven my Vows to thee (O Sacred *Muse!*)
I offer'd up, nor didst thou them refuse.

O Queen of Verse, said I, if thou'lt inspire,
And warm my Soul with thy Poetique Fire,
No Love of Gold shall share with thee my Heart,
Or yet Ambition in my Brest have Part,
More Rich, more Noble I will ever hold
The *Muses* Laurel,[1] than a Crown of Gold.
An Undivided Sacrifice I'le lay
Upon thine Altar, Soul and Body pay;   10
Thou shalt my Pleasure, my Employment be,
My All I'le make a Holocaust[2] to thee.

The Deity that ever does attend
Prayers so sincere, to mine did condescend.
I writ, and the Judicious prais'd my Pen:
Could any doubt Insuing Glory then?
What pleasing Raptures fill'd my Ravisht Sense?
How strong, how Sweet, Fame, was thy Influence?
And thine, False Hope, that to my flatter'd sight
Didst Glories represent so Near, and Bright?   20
By thee deceiv'd, methought, each Verdant[3] Tree,
Apollos transform'd *Daphne*[4] seem'd to be;
And ev'ry fresher Branch, and ev'ry Bow[5]
Appear'd as Garlands to empale my Brow.
The Learn'd in Love say, Thus the Winged Boy[6]
Does first approach, drest up in welcome Joy;

1. In classical times, leaves from this tree were made into wreaths for poets and conquerors.
2. Sacrifice wholly consumed by fire; burnt offering.
3. Fresh green.
4. Apollo is the god of the sun and of music and poetry. Daphne is the daughter of a river god who escaped Apollo's amorous advances by being changed into a laurel tree.
5. Bough.
6. Cupid god of love; usually represented as a winged boy carrying a bow and a quiver of arrows.

At first he to the Cheated Lovers sight
Nought represents, but Rapture and Delight,
Alluring Hopes, Soft Fears, which stronger bind
30   Their Hearts, than when they more assurance find.

Embolden'd thus, to Fame I did commit,
(By some few hands) my most Unlucky Wit.
But, ah, the sad effects that from it came!
What ought t'have brought me Honour, brought me shame!
Like *Esops* Painted Jay[7] I seem'd to all,
Adorn'd in Plumes, I not my own could call:
Rifl'd like her, each one my Feathers tore,
And, as they thought, unto the Owner bore.
My Laurels thus an Others Brow adorn'd,
40   My Numbers they Admir'd, but Me they scorn'd:
An others Brow, that had so rich a store
Of Sacred Wreaths, that circled it before;
Where mine quite lost, (like a small stream that ran
Into a Vast and Boundless Ocean)
Was swallow'd up, with what it joyn'd and drown'd,
And that Abiss yet no Accession found.

Orinda,[8] (*Albions*[9] and her Sexes Grace)
Ow'd not her Glory to a Beauteous Face,
It was her Radiant Soul that shon With-in,
50   Which struk a Lustre through her Outward Skin;
That did her Lips and Cheeks with Roses dy,
Advanc't her Height, and Sparkled in her Eye.
Nor did her Sex at all obstruct her Fame,
But higher 'mong the Stars it fixt her Name;
What she did write, not only all allow'd,
But ev'ry Laurel, to her Laurel, bow'd!

Th'Envious Age, only to Me alone,
Will not allow, what I do write, my Own,
But let 'em Rage, and 'gainst a Maide Conspire,

7. In Aesop's fable, Zeus was going to appoint the most beautiful bird to be king over all the birds. The jackdaw, a crowlike bird, collected molted feathers from all the birds and fastened them all over his body. He was the brightest of them all, and Zeus was going to award him the throne when the other birds indignantly attacked him and took their feathers back.

8. Katherine Philips, known as "the Matchless Orinda."

9. Britain's.

So Deathless Numbers from my Tuneful Lyre   60
Do ever flow; so *Phebus*[10] I by thee
Divinely Inspired and possest may be;
I willingly accept *Cassandras* Fate,[11]
To speak the Truth, although believ'd too late.

(1686)

To a Gentleman who questioned my being the Author
of the foregoing Verses

Mary Masters

Sir, 'tis allow'd, as it has oft been said,
Poets are only *Born* and never *Made*.
Where Nature does her friendly Warmth exert,
A Genius may supply the Pedant's Art.
Hence 'tis, that I, unletter'd Maid, pretend
To paraphrase a Psalm, or praise a Friend;
Wholly unpractis'd in the learned Rules,
And arduous Precepts of the noisy Schools;
Nature's strong Impulse gives my Fancy[12] Wings:
Prompted by her, I sing of various Things,   10
A flow'ry Meadow, or a purling Stream,
And Notes that differ with the diff'ring Theme.
But still the Poem, howsoe'er design'd,
Is a true Picture of the Author's Mind.
Whate'er I write, whatever I impart,
Is simple Nature unimprov'd by Art.
Search but those Strains, you think so much excel,
Scan ev'ry Verse, and try the Numbers well:
You'll plainly see, in almost ev'ry Line,
Distinguishing Defects to prove them Mine.   20

(1733)

10. Apollo the sun god, here the personification of the sun.

11. Because Cassandra rejected his advances, Apollo cursed her gift of prophecy by decreeing that her prophecies would never be believed.

12. A creative faculty, usually treated as lighter and more whimsical and playful than imagination or as an assistant to it. Imagination, with the power to transform its material, was considered the higher power.

The AUTHOR, one evening, in company with some gentlemen, repeated a Poem of her own composition; when one of them was so cruel to tell her, her boasted Muse was borrowed, without being able to give the least account from whom or where: she being something chagrin'd at his unjust censure, in less than an hour sent him the following lines.

Priscilla Poynton

Be cautious, Sir, how next you do declare
That any borrow, when you can't tell where:
For me, I hold this practice much too mean;
For know, as yet, I ne'er did want a theme.
Stranger to sense and reason sure you be,
Or first you'd weigh'd; what tho' I cannot see,
Kind Heav'n might lend peculiar gifts to me.
MILTON[13] and HOMER,[14] like me, wanted sight,
Yet all must own, sublime they both did write;
10   With Attic fire[15] so nobly drest each line,
As if the Gods conspir'd to make 'em shine.
Their Muse you'll find adorn'd with ev'ry grace,
Divine their thoughts, and smooth each couplet plac'd;
So lovely they their similies have drew,
By none excell'd that e'er existence knew.
I own I nothing of URANIA[16] know,
From simple Nature all my thoughts do flow:
Her native innocence shall be my care,
Her modest sense does matchless beauty wear.
20   What tho' my Muse is not sublimely drest,
Yet oft this Fair does gently sooth to rest
My anxious soul, whene'er with care oppress'd.
Chearful my hours in humble verse I spend,
And to my fate without a sigh I bend:
Then surely wisdom guides the hapless Fair,
Who does teneb'rous[17] woe with patience bear:

13. John Milton (1608–74), author of *Paradise Lost.*

14. Name conventionally given to the ancient Greek poet or poets who composed the *Iliad* and the *Odyssey,* the first great epic poems. Poets at this time treated "Homer" as an actual individual.

15. Athenian creativity.

16. Muse of astronomy. Milton makes her the spirit of the greatest, most elevated poetry in *Paradise Lost.*

17. Dark and gloomy.

So I disdain all you can say of me,
No judge a Coxcomb[18] e'er was thought to be.
I'll not repine, tho' such an ape's my foe,
What good sense means, sure such a wretch can't know: 30
Grimace and nonsense is your chief delight,
To please the wise ('tis not for fools) I write.
Ignoble Man! unworthy of my lays,[19]
I scorn your satire, nor do wish your praise- - -
When you commend, you strait[20] contempt must raise.

(1770)

A Poem, occasioned by a Lady's doubting whether the Author composed an Elegy, to which her Name is affix'd

Jane Cave Winscom

If good Miss H- - - will condescend,
To read these lines which I have penn'd,
Perhaps it may her doubts confute,
And she'll no more my word dispute,
But own I may the Author be,
Of what she did on Sunday see.
    You'd hate a base perfidious youth,
Such *my* disgust to all untruth.
A gen'rous mind is never prone
To claim a merit not her own.   10
I wou'd disdain t' affix my name
To that, which is another's claim.
Of beauteous form Heav'n made me not,
(Nor has soft affluence been my lot,)
But fix'd me in an humble station,
Remote from those of rank and fashion;
But there are beauties of the mind,
Which are not to the great confin'd;
Wisdom does not erect her seat
Always in palaces of state;   20
This blessing Heav'n dispenses round,

18. Fop; conceited dandy; "ape of fashion."
19. Ballads; lyric or narrative poems meant to be sung.
20. Immediately.

She's sometimes in a cottage found,
And tho' she is a guest majestic,
May deign to dwell in a domestic.
    Yet, of this great celestial guest,
I dare not boast myself possest,
But this wou'd represent to you,
As Wisdom does, the Muses do,
No def'rence shew to wealth or ease,
30   But pay their visits as they please.
Sometimes they deign to call on me,
And tune my mind to poetry;
But ah! they're fled, I'll drop my pen,
Nor raise it till they call again.

(1783).

CRITICS

Epilogue to *Sir Patient Fancy*
Spoken by Mrs. Gwin[21]
Aphra Behn

I Here, and there, o'reheard a Coxcomb[22] Cry   [Looking about]
Ah, Rott it—'tis a Womans Comedy,
One, who because she lately chanc't to please us,
With her Damn'd stuff will never cease to teaze us.[23]
What has poor Woman done that she must be,
Debar'd from Sense and Sacred Poetrie?
Why in this Age has Heaven allow'd you more,

21. Anne Marshall Quin (or Quyn or Guin, fl. 1660–82), one of the first actresses to appear on the English public stage, played Lady Knowell in *Sir Patient Fancy*. An early member of the King's troupe, she was considered by the Lord Chamberlain to be one of the more important actresses in the company. After a ten-year absence from the stage, she joined the Duke's Company and acted in *Sir Patient Fancy* and several other plays. She is often confused with the notorious seventeenth-century actress Nell Gwyn (1651?–1687).

22. Foolish, conceited, garishly dressed fop.

23. Behn was one of the most successful playwrights of the Restoration. *Sir Patient Fancy* was her ninth play to be produced, and her recent plays, the bloody tragedy of lawless love, *Abdelazer* (1676), and *The Rover* (1677), had been solid hits.

And Women less of Wit than heretofore?
We once were fam'd in Story, and cou'd write
Equall to men; cou'd Govern, nay cou'd Fight.   10
We still have passive Valour, and can show
Wou'd Custom give us leave the Active too,
Since we no provocations want from you.
For who but we, cou'd your Dull Fopperies[24] bear,
Your Saucy Love, and your brisk Nonsense hear;
Indure your worse then womanish affectation,
Which renders you the Nusance of the Nation;
Scorn'd even by all the Misses of the Town,
A jest to Vizard Mask,[25] the *Pitt-Buffoone;*[26]
A Glass by which th' admiring Country Fool   20
May learn to dress himself en Ridicule:
Both striving who shall most Ingenious grow
In Lewdness, Foppery, Nonsense, Noise and Show.
And yet to these fine things we must submit
Our Reason, Arms, our Lawrells,[27] and our Wit.
Because we do not Laugh at you when Lewd,
And scorn and cudgell ye when you are Rude;
That we have Nobler Souls than you, we prove,
By how much more we're sensible of Love;
Quickest in finding all the subtlest waies   30
To make your Joys: why not to make you Plays?
We best can find your Feables,[28] know our own,
And Gilts[29] and Cuckolds[30] now best please the Town;
Your way of writing's out of Fashion grown.
Method, and Rule[31]—you only understand,

24. Foolish, imbecilic behavior calling attention to foppish dress or mannerism.

25. Prostitute. Although even modest women sometimes wore masks to protect their complexion, "vizard mask" signals an intent to conceal either the person or the person's intentions, and prostitutes working the theater audience wore them as a sign of their availability.

26. A fool who sits in the pit, the part of the theater directly in front of the stage, where, according to Henry Fielding, "sit the *Judges, Wits* and *Censurers,* or rather the *Censurers without either Wit or Judgment.*" *The Tricks of the Town Laid Open,* 2nd ed. (London, 1747), 28.

27. Laurels. In classical times, leaves from this tree were made into wreaths for poets and conquerors.

28. Foibles, follies.

29. Jilts; flirtatious, inconstant women.

30. Husbands of unfaithful wives.

31. Adherence to the unities of time, place, and action, a fashion in playwriting then going out of fashion. Aristotle in the *Poetics* demanded unity of action (no important subplots or extraneous scenes) and mentioned the unity of time (all action taking place in a single day). In the Renaissance,

Pursue that way of Fooling, and be Damn'd.
Your Learned Cant of Action, Time, and Place,
Must all give way to the unlabour'd farce.
To all the Men of Witt we will subscribe:
40   But for you half Wits, you unthinking Tribe,
We'll let you see, what e're besides we doe,
How Artfully we Copy some of you
And if you're drawn to th' life, pray tell me then
Why Women should not write as well as Men.

(1678)

The Introduction[32]
Anne Finch

Did I, my lines intend for publick view,
How many censures, wou'd their faults persue,
Some wou'd, because such words they do affect,
Cry they're insipid, empty, uncorrect.
And many, have attain'd, dull and untaught
The name of Witt, only by finding fault.
True judges, might condemn their want of witt,
And all might say, they're by a Woman writt.
Alas! a woman that attempts the pen,
10   Such an intruder on the rights of men,
Such a presumptuous Creature, is esteem'd,
The fault, can by no vertue be redeem'd.
They tell us, we mistake our sex and way;
Good breeding, fassion, dancing, dressing, play[33]
Are the accomplishments we shou'd desire;
To write, or read, or think, or to enquire
Wou'd cloud our beauty, and exaust our time,
And interrupt the Conquests of our prime;

---

unity of time became a fixed rule, and unity of place (one setting) was added. Ludovico Castelvetro (1505–71) first formally stated them as the rules for dramatic composition in 1570. The French respected them for two centuries, but the British playwrights, including Shakespeare and Christopher Marlowe (1564–93), began an English rebellion against them.

32. This poem appears both in the folio and octavo manuscripts of Finch's poetry, but she chose not to publish it during her lifetime.

33. Gambling.

Whilst the dull mannage,[34] of a servile house
Is held by some, our outmost art, and use.   20
    Sure 'twas not ever thus, nor are we told
Fables, of Women that excell'd of old;
To whom, by the diffusive hand of Heaven
Some share of witt, and poetry was given.
On that glad day, on which the Ark return'd,[35]
The holy pledge, for which the Land had mourn'd,
The joyfull Tribes, attend itt on the way,
The Levites[36] do the sacred Charge convey,
Whilst various Instruments, before itt play;
Here, holy Virgins in the Concert joyn,   30
The louder notes, to soften, and refine,
And with alternate verse, compleat the Hymn Devine.
Loe! the yong Poet, after Gods own heart,
By Him inspired, and taught the Muses Art,
Return'd from Conquest, a bright Chorus meets,
That sing his slayn ten thousand in the streets.[37]
In such loud numbers they his acts declare,
Proclaim the wonders, of his early war,
That Saul[38] upon the vast applause does frown,
And feels, itts mighty thunder shake the Crown.   40
What, can the threat'n'd Judgment now prolong?
Half of the Kingdom is already gone;
The fairest half, whose influence guides the rest,
Have David's Empire, o're their hearts confess't.
    A Woman here, leads fainting Israel on,
She fights, she wins, she tryumphs with a song,[39]

34. Management.

35. In early biblical narratives, the ark of the Covenant of Yahweh was a simple wooden chest, but even as its description changed, it was always identified with the presence of God. The ark was captured by the Philistines; David defeated them, and he and "all the chosen *men* of Israel, thirty thousand," brought it to Jerusalem (2 Sam. 6).

36. The hierarchy of cultic officials is as follows: high priest, priest, Levite. The Levites were one of the original tribes of Israel, and they came to be set apart for conducting the service of praise and for the lower duties of the sanctuary, such as caring for the courts and chambers of the sanctuary and serving as porters, gatekeepers, choristers, and treasurers. George A. Buttrick et al., eds., *Interpreter's Dictionary of the Bible*, 4 vols. (New York: Abingdon, 1962).

37. The song the women sang when David returned from defeating the Philistines: "Saul hath slain his thousands, / And David his ten thousands." 1 Sam. 17:6, s.v., "Levite."

38. The first king of Israel. Praise for David aroused his jealousy.

39. Deborah went to battle with Barak against Sisera and then celebrated the victory in a famous song; she is sometimes styled, "the judge and restorer of the house of Israel." Judg. 4, 5.

Devout, Majestick, for the subject fitt,
And far above her arms, exalts her witt,
Then, to the peacefull, shady Palm withdraws,
50   And rules the rescu'd Nation, with her Laws.
How are we fal'n, fal'n by mistaken rules?
And Education's, more then Nature's fools,
Debarr'd from all improve-ments of the mind,
And to be dull, expected and dessigned;
And if some one, wou'd Soar above the rest,
With warmer fancy, and ambition press't,
So strong, th' opposing faction still appears,
The hopes to thrive, can ne're outweigh the fears,
Be caution'd then my Muse, and still retir'd;
60   Nor be dispis'd, aiming to be admir'd;
Conscious of wants, still with contracted wing,
To some few freinds, and to thy sorrows sing;
For groves of Lawrell,[40] thou wert never meant;
Be dark enough thy shades, and be thou there content.

(before 1689; 1903)

The Critick and the Writer of Fables
Anne Finch

Weary, at last, of the *Pindarick* way,[41]
Thro' which advent'rously the Muse wou'd stray;
To *Fable* I descend with soft Delight,
Pleas'd to Translate, or easily Endite:
Whilst aery Fictions hastily repair
To fill my Page, and rid my Thoughts of Care,
As they to Birds and Beasts new Gifts impart,
And Teach, as Poets shou'd, whilst they Divert.

But here, the *Critick* bids me check this Vein. ⎫
10   *Fable*, he crys, tho' grown th' affected Strain, ⎬
But dies, as it was born, without Regard or Pain. ⎭

40. Leaves of the laurel tree were used to make wreaths for poets and conquerors.
41. People of this period admired Pindar's odes for their evocative, brilliant imagery; emotional, intense tone; complex metrical arrangement; and abrupt shifts of subject. He influenced a trend toward public poetry that contained deeply personal statements.

Whilst of his Aim the lazy Trifler fails,
Who seeks to purchase Fame by childish Tales.

Then, let my Verse, once more attempt the Skies, ⎤
The easily persuaded Poet cries,   ⎬
Since meaner Works you Men of Taste despise.   ⎦
The Walls of *Troy* shall be our loftier Stage,
Our mighty Theme the fierce *Achilles* Rage.
The Strength of *Hector,* and *Ulysses* Arts
Shall boast such Language, to adorn their Parts,[42]   20
As neither *Hobbes,*[43] nor *Chapman*[44] cou'd bestow,
Or did from *Congreve,*[45] or from *Dryden*[46] flow.
Amidst her Towers, the dedicated Horse
Shall be receiv'd, big with destructive Force;[47]
Till Men shall say, when Flames have brought her down.
"*Troy is no more, and* Illium *was a Town.*"[48]

Is this the way to please the Men of Taste,
The Interrupter cries, this old Bombast?
I'm sick of *Troy,* and in as great a Fright, ⎤
When some dull Pedant wou'd her Wars recite, ⎬   30
As was soft *Paris,*[49] when compell'd to Fight. ⎦

To Shades and Springs shall we awhile repair,
The Muse demands, and in that milder Air
Describe some gentle Swain's[50] unhappy Smart ⎤
Whose folded Arms still press upon his Heart, ⎬
And deeper drive the too far enter'd Dart? ⎦

42. The subjects of the *Iliad* and the *Odyssey.*

43. Thomas Hobbes (1588–1679), the philosopher who wrote *Leviathan* (1651), also published translations of Thucydides and Homer (the latter in quatrains, 1674–75).

44. George Chapman (1559?–1634), playwright and translator of Homer.

45. The playwright William Congreve (1670–1729) also wrote Pindaric and other public poetry that was much admired.

46. John Dryden (1631–1700), poet and playwright, composed a number of distinguished translations of classical authors.

47. The Greeks, who were besieging Troy, built an immense wooden horse, which they advertised as an offering to Minerva, goddess of wisdom, the arts, and martial prowess. Unknown to the Trojans, the horse was filled with armed men. After the rest of the Greek army appeared to sail away, the Trojans dragged the horse into the city. That night the soldiers were let out, opened the gates to the city to admit the rest of the Greeks, and took Troy.

48. Quotation from John Dryden's translation of the *Aeneid,* bk. 2, line 436. *The Works of Virgil in English,* 2 vols. (London, 1697).

49. Paris kidnapped Helen, the wife of Menelaus, beginning the Trojan War.

50. Country man's; lover's.

Whilst *Phillis*[51] with a careless pleasure reigns
The Joy, the Grief, the Envy of the Plains;
Heightens the Beauty of the verdant[52] Woods,
40   And softens all the Murmurs of the Floods.

Oh! stun me not with these insipid Dreams,
Th' Eternal Hush, the Lullaby of Streams.
Which still, he cries, their even Measures keep,
Till both the Writers, and the Readers sleep.
But urge thy Pen, if thou would'st move our Thoughts,
To shew us private, or the publick Faults.
Display the Times, *High-Church* or *Low* provoke;[53]
We'll praise the Weapon, as we like the Stroke,
And warmly sympathizing with the Spite
50   Apply to Thousands, what of One you write.

Then, must that single Stream the Town supply, ⎫
The harmless *Fable*-writer do's reply,   ⎬
And all the Rest of *Helicon*[54] be dry?   ⎭
And when so many choice Productions swarm,
Must only Satire keep your Fancies warm?
Whilst even there, you praise with such Reserve, ⎫
As if you'd in the midst of Plenty starve,   ⎬
Tho' ne'er so liberally we Authors carve.   ⎭

Happy the Men,[55] *whom we divert with Ease,*
60   *Whom* Opera's *and* Panegyricks[56] *please.*

(before 1689; 1713)

---

51. Conventional name for a rustic maiden, from a character in Virgil's third and fifth *Eclogues*.
52. Fresh, green.
53. Throughout this period the two factions of the Church of England caused considerable turmoil in the nation. They disagreed on doctrinal and political matters. The High Church was the stricter, more ceremonial of the two.
54. Home of the Muses, a mountain in the Parnassus range, in Greece. It contained the fountains of Aganippe and Hippocrene.
55. An echo of Virgil's *Georgics*, Book 2, and Horace's Ode 29, Book 3, poets used the conventional clause "Happy the man . . ." Especially popular were echoes of Dryden's translation: "Happy the Man, and happy he alone, / He, who can call today his own" (lines 65–66).
56. Speeches or poems of unmixed praise of persons or events.

Prologue to *The Wonder: A Woman Keeps a Secret*
Spoken by Mr. Mills[57]
Susanna Centlivre

Our *Author* fears the Criticks of the Stage,
Who like Barbarians, spare nor Sex, nor Age;
She trembles at those Censors in the Pit,
Who think good Nature shows a want of Wit:
Such Malice, Oh, what Muse can undergo it?
To save themselves, they always Damn the Poet.
Our Author flies from such a Partial Jury,
As wary Lovers from the Nymphs of *Drury:*[58]
To the few Candid Judges for a Smile,
She humbly sues to Recompence her Toil.   10
To the bright Circle of the Fair, she next,
Commits her Cause, with Anxious Doubts perplext.
Where can she with such hopes of Favour kneel,
As to those Judges, who her Frailties feel?
A few Mistakes, her Sex may well excuse,
And such a Plea, No *Woman* shou'd refuse:
If she succeeds, a *Woman* gains Applause,
What *Female* but must favour such a Cause.
Her Faults,—If such there be:—Then,—pass 'em by,
And only on her Beauties fix your Eye.   20
In Plays, like Vessels floating on the Sea,
There's none so Wise to know their Destiny.
In this, howe'er the Pilot's Skill appears,
While by the Stars his constant Course he steers;
In this our *Author* does her Judgment shew,
That for her Safety she relies on You.
Your Approbation Fair ones, can't but move,
Those stubborn Hearts, which first you taught to Love:

---

57. John Mills (d. 1736), a versatile actor with the Drury Lane Theatre for many years, played Colonel Britton in Centlivre's *The Wonder: A Woman Keeps a Secret* (1714). During his lifetime Mills was cast in hundreds of roles, both tragic and comic. In the 1721–22 season alone he acted in fifty out of seventy plays. Colley Cibber, the Drury Lane co-manager, wrote that Mills "was an honest, quiet, careful Man, of as few Faults, as Excellencies, and [lead actor and theater manager Robert] *Wilks* rather chose him for his second, in many Plays." *An Apology for the Life of Mr. Colley Cibber*, 2nd ed., 2 vols. (London, 1740), 1:213.

58. Prostitutes.

The Men must all Applaud this Play of ours,

30   For who dares See with other Eyes, than Yours?

(1714)

Defence of Myrtillo[59]

Mary Masters

Long hath it been the Critick's poor Delight,
To damn the Piece, they wanted Sense to write.
Where-e'er superior Qualities abound,
The snarling Crew too surely will be found:
MYRTILLO now provokes their venom'd Wit,
He has excell'd, and therefore merits it.
But the bright Youth above their Malice shines,
Secure in his unperishable Lines:
So barking Curs pursue the gen'rous Horse,

10   Who blest with nobler Parts and greater Force,
Disdains their little Fury to engage,
And is unmov'd at such enervate Rage.

  Here I should stop, lest I my self expose
To the Resentment of MYRTILLO's Foes.
For what am I, a poor illit'rate Maid,
That durst their learn'd Authority invade?
True; but my Safety is in being mean,
A foolish Thing, that's plac'd below their Spleen.[60]
Yet had I Merit to deserve their Hate,

20   I'd mock their Censure and provoke my Fate.
Judicious Heat my glowing Bosom fires,
And equitable Rage my Soul inspires.
I hate the carping Tribe, their Knowledge slight,
Nor would enjoy their Learning with their Spite.
Void of their Envy and its pointed Stings,
I taste Good-nature's more delightful Springs.

---

59. The Poems here vindicated make up a small Volume published by the Author at *18* Years of Age, under the Title of *Poems on several Occasions, by a young Gentleman,* and printed for *W. Mears,* at the *Lamb* without *Temple-Bar.* 1724. Price 1s. 6d. *Masters.*

60. Malice, irritation.

Where I see Merit, I admire it too,
A gen'rous Virtue which they never knew.

   With Pleasure I Myrtillo's Lines peruse,
The charming Products of a vig'rous Muse.   30
All that is soft, that's delicate and fine,
Does in his Verse in nameless Beauties join.
Such moving Language and the Sense so strong,
While ev'ry Grace adorns the pleasing Song:
Nature and Art, to give me Joys, unite,
And ev'ry Word administers Delight.
But, if there's ought defective or untrue,
Take it, ye Criticks, That belongs to you.

                        (1733)

To My Friend Mrs. ——,
On Her Holding an Argument in Favour of the Natural Equality of Both the Sexes
Written in the Year MDCCLVI

Clara Reeve

   Silence best serves to disapprove
False reasoning in those we love.
Tho' t'other day I held my tongue,
I thought you greatly in the wrong;
How could you so unfairly try'd
With no one present to decide,
Argue the best, that woman can
Pretend to triumph o'er a man?
I once was half of your opinion,
But now subscribe to their dominion.   10
The same unchanging law that fixes,
Eternal difference of sexes,
Has for the wisest ends assign'd
Due bounds to either sex's mind.
Your heart with argument elated,
Thinks both were equal when created,
And holds its own imagination,
That all depends on cultivation:

But to speak plainly, in reality
20   I don't believe in this equality,
But think that partial heav'n design'd,
To them the more capacious mind;
And that their brains, dame Nature's college,
Are best receptacles for knowledge.
Lend me my friend a while your hand,
I'll lead you over classic land,
To hear what sages fam'd of old
On this nice subject shall unfold.
Thus much may serve for introduction,
30   Leading to pleasure and instruction.

NOT every one can write that chuses,
But those invited by the Muses:
These are nine wit-inspiring lasses,
Who dwell about the hill Parnassus.
Their patron whom they serve and follow,
A beardless youth—the Greek Apollo—
Still lovely, active, young, and gay,
He drives the chariot of the day,[61]
Teaches these girls polite behaviours,
40   For which they grant him certain favours:
(But modest ones you may be sure,
For they are virgins chaste and pure.)
He leads their concerts, which they fill
With wond'rous harmony and skill;
For he's the prince of all musicians,
Beside the greatest of physicians.
He finds them music for their frolics,
And cures their head-achs, nerves, and cholics.

FROM out the side of this fam'd mountain,
50   Rises a wit-inspiring fountain;[62]

61. The nine Muses were the daughters of Jupiter and the Titan Mnemosyne (Memory). They lived on Parnassus, and Apollo was their guardian. As god of the sun he drove his chariot around the earth each day to control day and night, and as god of music and poetry, he instructed them. In some myths, he was also the god of healing, as the verse goes on to say. On the Muses, see the introduction to section 3.B.

62. The fountain of the Muses, Aganippe, was at the foot of Mount Helicon, one of the mountains in the Parnassus range. Reeve may be confusing it with the fountain Hippocrene, which was made by the hoof of Pegasus, the Muses' winged horse, and was the source of poetic inspiration.

Which murmurs music as it plays,
Laurels its banks produce and bays.[63]
Here all the scholars drink their fill,
And then attempt to climb the hill;
(But first from trees the boughs they take,
And garlands for their heads they make;
Whose strange effects, to us a wonder,
Secure them from the power of thunder:)
With pain and care they clamber up,
And very rarely gain the top: 60
But if they reach the Muses seat,
They have assign'd them a retreat.
Apollo's self records their name,
And gives it to the charge of Fame;
Who first displays to earth and sky,⎫
Then folds it up and lays it by,   ⎬
In her immortal library.   ⎭
Now comes our case.—The ancients tell us,
These nymphs were always fond of fellows;
For by their records it is clear,   70
Few women ever have been there.
Not that it contradicts their laws,
But they assign the following cause;
The sacred Heliconian spring,
Of which old poets sweetly sing:
(Tho' modern writers only flout it,
Alledging they can do without it)
Produces very strange effects,
On the weak brains of our soft sex;
Works worse vagaries in the fancy,[64]   80
Then Holland's gin,[65] or royal Nancy.[66]
In short, to what you will compare it,
Few women's heads have strength to bear it.
See some with strong and lively fancies,

63. Leaves of the laurel tree, used to make wreaths for conquerors or poets.

64. A creative faculty, usually treated as lighter and more whimsical and playful than imagination or as an assistant to it. Imagination, with the power to transform its material, was considered the higher power.

65. Gin, whose name is derived from *geneva*, the Dutch word for juniper berries that flavor it, was first made in Holland in the late sixteenth century; in the period 1690–1727 annual consumption soared to 5 million gallons. London gin is drier and less "assertively flavored." *An A–Z of Food and Drink*, ed. John Ayto (Oxford: Oxford University Press, 2002), s.v. "gin."

66. The Royal Navy distributed its daily issue of grog to the tune of the song "Nancy Dawson."

Write essays, novels, and romances.
Others by serious cares and pains,
With politics o'erset their brains.
Children, some call themselves of Phœbus,[67]
By virtue of a pun, or rebus.[68]
90   Some much affect the strain satyric,
And others all for panegyric.[69]
In all, and each of these you find,
Strong markings of the female mind,
Still superficial, light and various;
Loose, unconnected, and precarious:
Life and vivacity I grant,
But weight and energy they want;
That strength that fills the manly page,
And bids it live to future age.

100   Now as it oft hath been evinc'd,
We do not love to be convinc'd;
So if conviction give you grief,
Restriction may afford relief.
Exceptions to all gen'ral rules,
Are still'd allow'd of in the schools:
And Phœbus's favours to the fair
Are not impossible, tho' rare.
In Fame's great library, we're told,
Some female names there are enroll'd;
110   Matrons of Greece, others of Rome,
And some, to please you, nearer home:
Moderns there are, France brags of many,
And England shews as good as any.
See our Orinda[70] swell the page,
Carter,[71] and Lenox[72] grace this age;
But leaving these consign'd to Fame,

67. Apollo the sun god, here the personification of the sun.
68. A riddle composed of words or syllables depicted by pictures or symbols that suggest the sound of the syllables or words.
69. Speech or poem of unmixed praise of a person or event.
70. Katherine Philips, known as "the Matchless Orinda."
71. Elizabeth Carter.
72. Charlotte Lennox.

Lusus Naturæ[73] is their name.
As some among the men we find,
Effeminate in form and mind;
Some women masculine are seen   120
In mind, behaviour, and in mien:
For Nature seldom kindly mixes,
The qualities of both the sexes.
These instances are sometimes quoted,
As owls are shown, but to be hooted.
Dare now to ope your eyes and see,
These truths exemplified in me.
What tho' while yet an infant young,
The numbers trembled on my tongue;[74]
As youth advanc'd, I dar'd aspire,   130
And trembling struck the heavenly lyre.
What by my talents have I gained?
By those I lov'd to be disdain'd,
By some despis'd, by others fear'd,
Envy'd by fools, by witlings jeer'd.
See what success my labours crown'd,
By birds and beasts alike disown'd.
Those talents that were once my pride,
I find it requisite to hide;
For what in man is most respected,   140
In woman's form shall be rejected.
Thus have I prov'd to demonstration,
The fallacy of your oration.
(You need not let the fellows know it,
They'll praise the wit, but damn the poet.)
This point illustrated, my friend,
Brings my long story to its end.
When you have read it o'er at leisure,
Keep it—or burn it—at your pleasure.

(1756; 1769)

---

73. Freak of nature; the sport or joke of Nature.
74. Reworking of line 128 of Alexander Pope's *Epistle to Dr. Arbuthnot:* "I lisp'd in Numbers, for the Numbers came."

On the Use——Abuse of Poetry
The Critic, and the Sylph of the Vase,[75]
At Bath-Easton

Mary Savage

If I chose to write—says a Critic; in spleen,
I would quickly decide, this poetical theme;
And prove it as clear, as the light to your eyes,
That poetry, serves as a shelter for lies.
If a hero they paint, he is prais'd to the sky.
And a God or a Goddess his wants must supply;
If they beauty describe; I defy you to know,
The face; by the picture they set out to show.
And for Satire, (believe me,) they say that in rhime,
10   Which they dare not in prose attempt to define.
They would have you believe, that the muses inspire,
And fill all their works, with poetical fire;
But, from what I have said, (which is but a part)
You may see their abuse of the Lyrical Art.
Cease, cease then to rave, nor an art strive to blast,
Which like truth, love, and time must for evermore last.
Reply'd the Sylph—(who bending o'er the vase,
Upholds the mirtle wreath,[76] which crowns applause.)
While there's a heart that friendship's pow'r can feel;
20   While there's a heart, inspir'd by heavenly zeal;
While tender lovers, fear to speak their woe,
While blushing fair ones fear true love to show;
While truth sublime, shall o'er the mind prevail;
While wit shall flourish, and while beauty's frail;
While lays,[77] poetic, from this vase resound,
By genius prompted, and by MILLER crown'd;
So long shall every tender feeling breast,
That can by joy be rais'd, or grief opprest,

---

75. Lady Anne Miller hosted gatherings in Bath-Easton during which poets and would-be poets, including Mary Savage and Anna Seward, drew topics from an urn and composed poems. The poems were read, and prizes awarded. Lady Miller collected and published four volumes of them.

76. Myrtle was sacred to Aphrodite, goddess of love and beauty, and to Venus, adding the characteristic of marriage and fertility. A crown of myrtle given to generals commemorated the union of Sabine and Roman tribes at the foundation of Rome. Here it symbolizes friendship.

77. Ballads; lyric or narrative poems meant to be sung.

Confess the bliss, poetick lays inspire,
And sing the praises of APOLLO's lyre.[78]   30

(1777)

RESISTANCE

Prologue to *The Lost Lover*
Spoken by Mr. Horden[79]
Delarivière Manley

The first Adventurer for her fame I stand,
The Curtain's drawn now by a Lady's Hand,
The very Name you'l cry boads Impotence,
To Fringe and Tea they shou'd confine their Sense, }
And not outstrip the bounds of Providence.
I hope then Criticks, since the Case is so,
You'l scorn to Arm against a Worthless Foe,
But curb your spleen and gall, and trial make,
How our fair Warriour gives her first Attack.
 Now all ye chattering Insects straight[80] be dumb,   10
The Men of Wit and Sense are hither come,
Ask not this Mask[81] to Sup, nor that to show
Some Face more ugly than a Fifty Beau,
Who, if our Play succeeds, will surely say,
Some private Lover helpt her on her way,
As Female Wit were barren like the Moon,
That borrows all her influence from the Sun.

---

78. Apollo, god of music and poetry, was given the lyre, invented by Mercury.

79. Hildebrand Horden (1675–96), an actor with the Drury Lane Theatre from 1694 until his death, played Wildman in Manley's *The Lost Lover*. Horden died on 18 May, just two months after this performance, the victim of a quarrel at Rose Tavern, London. Horden and a group of players were drinking and being loud when some gentlemen drew swords on them; Horden was killed by Captain Elizius Burgess. After Horden's death, Colley Cibber, the Drury Lane co-manager, was moved to say, "This young Man had almost every natural Gift, that could promise an excellent Actor; he had besides, a good deal of Table-wit, and Humour, with a handsome Person, and was every Day rising into publick Favour." *Apology for the Life of Mr. Colley Cibber*, 1:246.

80. Immediately.

81. Woman wearing a mask. Even respectable women sometimes wore masks to protect their complexion, but those looking for assignations and hoping to go unrecognized wore them in the theater during performances.

The Sparks and Beaus[82] will surely prove our Friends,
For their good Breeding must make them commend
20   What Billet Deux[83] so e'er a Lady sends.
She knew old Thread-bare Topicks would not do, ⎫
But Beaus a Species thinks it self still new,   ⎬
And therefore she resolved to Coppy you.   ⎭

(1696)

Mercury and the Elephant[84]
A Prefatory Fable
Anne Finch

As *Merc'ry*[85] travell'd thro' a Wood,
(Whose Errands are more Fleet than Good)
An *Elephant* before him lay,
That much encumber'd had the Way:
The Messenger, who's still in haste,
Wou'd fain have bow'd, and so have past;
When up arose th' unweildy Brute,
And wou'd repeat a late Dispute,
In which (he said) he'd gain'd the Prize
10   From a wild Boar of monstrous Size:
But Fame (quoth he) with all her Tongues,
Who Lawyers, Ladies, Soldiers wrongs,
Has, to my Disadvantage, told
An Action throughly Bright and Bold;
Has said, that I foul Play had us'd,
And with my Weight th' Opposer bruis'd;
Had laid my Trunk about his Brawn,
Before his Tushes[86] cou'd be drawn;
Had stunn'd him with a hideous Roar,

82. Dandies, fops, and potential lovers.
83. Love letters.
84. Finch selected this poem to open her *Miscellany Poems, on Several Occasions* (1713).
85. Jupiter's messenger, Mercury was the god of science and commerce and the patron of travelers, rogues, vagabonds, and thieves. He is usually represented wearing a winged hat and winged sandals.
86. Tusks.

And twenty-thousand Scandals more: 20
But I defy the Talk of Men,
Or Voice of Brutes in ev'ry Den;
Th' impartial Skies are all my Care,
And how it stands Recorded there.
Amongst you Gods, pray, What is thought?
        Quoth *Mercury*—Then have you Fought!
    Solicitous thus shou'd I be
For what's said of my Verse and Me;
Or shou'd my Friends Excuses frame,⎫
And beg the Criticks not to blame   ⎬   30
(Since from a Female Hand it came) ⎭
Defects in Judgment, or in Wit;
They'd but reply———Then has she Writ!

    Our Vanity we more betray,
In asking what the World will say,
Than if, in trivial Things like these,
We wait on the Event with ease;
Nor make long *Prefaces,* to show
What men are not concern'd to know:
For still untouch'd how we succeed,   40
'Tis for themselves, not us, they *Read;*
Whilst that proceeding to requite,   ⎫
We own (who in the Muse delight)   ⎬
'Tis for our Selves, not them, we *Write.*⎭
Betray'd by Solitude to try
Amusements, which the Prosp'rous fly;
And only to the Press repair,
To fix our scatter'd Papers there;
Tho' whilst our Labours are preserv'd,
The Printers may, indeed, be starv'd.   50

                        (1713)

To Pulcheria,[87]
On Her saying behind My back, I made my self ridiculous,
by writing Verses

Elizabeth Thomas

Mistaken Nymph! in vain you strive
   To discompose my Breast;
Alas! these groundless Taunts you give,
   Can never break my Rest.

II.
Like Breath on Steel, your peevish Spight
   May for a Moment stain;
But as that quickly grows more bright,
   So will my injur'd Fame.

III.
With Patience I your Scoffs endure,
   Pleas'd with my Innocence:
In that alone, I rest secure;
   And seek no more Defence.

IV.
Go then, some other Trick invent
   My placid Soul to move;
For this can ne'er your *Shame* prevent;
   Your *Wit* or *Virtue* prove.

(1722)

To a Lady, who commanded me to send her an Account in Verse,
how I succeeded in my Subscription

Mary Barber

How I succeed, you kindly ask;
Yet set me on a grievous Task,

---

87. A playful name suggesting that the lady had physical beauty and appeal; from the Latin word *pulcher,* meaning "beautiful."

When you oblige me to rehearse
The Censures past upon my Verse.

THO' I with Pleasure may relate,
That many, truly good, and great,
With candid Eye my Lines survey,
And smile upon the artless Lay;[88]
To those with grateful Heart I bend—
But your Commands I must attend.   10

SERVILLA cries, *I hate a Wit*;
Women should to their Fate submit,
Should in the Needle take Delight;
'Tis out of *Character* to write:
She may succeed among the Men;
They tell me, SWIFT subscribes for *Ten*;[89]
And some say, DORSET[90] does the same;
But she shall never have my Name:
Her Poetry has cost me dear;
When Lady CARTERET[91] was here,   20
The Widow *Gordon*[92] got my Guinea;
For which I own myself a *Ninny*.

OLIVIA loses oft at Play;
So will not throw her Gold away.

THUS SYLVIA, of the haughty Tribe:
She never ask'd me to subscribe,
Nor ever wrote a Line on me,
I was no Theme for Poetry!

88. Ballad; lyric or narrative poem meant to be sung.

89. Jonathan Swift (1667–1745), author of *Gulliver's Travels* (1726). He helped Barber prepare the poems for the press and eagerly pressed his friends to subscribe.

90. Lionel Cranfield Sackville (1688–1765), first Duke of Dorset, was Lord Lieutenant of Ireland from 1730 to 1737 and from 1750 to 1755; he also subscribed for ten copies of Barber's poems.

91. Frances Worsley Carteret (1694–1743), wife of John, Lord Carteret (1690–1763), a Whig, a friend of Swift's and a member of his circle; he was Lord Lieutenant of Ireland (1724–30) when Barber sent the poem to his wife. Barber's poem addressed women directly: "Tremble, ye Daughters, who at Ease recline . . ."

92. Barber wrote two poems aimed at securing assistance for the widow Gordon; the first asked Frances Carteret to champion it, and the second addressed Thomas Tickell (1685–1740), then chief secretary in Ireland. Barber's poem *The Widow Gordon's Petition* is in section 2.F.

She rightly judg'd; I have no *Taste*—
30   For *Womens Poetry,* at least.

THEN FULVIA made this sage Reply;
(And look'd with self-sufficient Eye:)
I oft have said, and say again,
Verses are only writ by Men;
I know a Woman cannot write;
I do not say this out of Spite;
Nor shall be thought, by those who know me,
To envy one so much below me.

SABINA, fam'd in Wisdom's School,
40   Allows I write—but am a Fool:
"What!—must our Sons be form'd by Rhyme?
A fine Way to employ one's Time!"

ALBINO has no Gold to waste,
Far gone in the Italian *Taste:*
He vows he must subscribe this Year,
To keep dear CARESTINI[93] here;
Not from a narrow Party View;
He doats on SENESINO[94] too;
By Turns their Int'rest he'll espouse;
50   He's for the public Good, he vows;
A gen'rous Ardor fires his Breast.
Hail, *Britain,* in such Patriots blest!

SAYS BELVIDERA, Since a Wit
Or Friend or Foe alike will hit,
Deliver me from Wits, I say;
Grant Heav'n, they ne'er may cross my Way!
Besides, I oft have heard it hinted,
Her Poems never will be printed:

93. Two famous *Italian* Singers, zealously supported by different Parties. *Barber.* [Charles Burney described Giovanni Carestini, a castrato, as "the fullest, finest and deepest counter-tenor that has perhaps ever been heard." Burney, *A General History of Music, from the earliest ages to the present period,* 4 vols. (London, 1776–89), 4:369–70. George Frideric Handel engaged him from 1733 to 1735 to rival Senesino (Francesco Bernardi) and later Farinelli (Carlo Broschi), stars of Nicola Porpora's rival group. *Eds.*]

94. Senesino was an alto castrato. He sang for Handel's company and later with Porpora's rival one until 1736. See also n. 93.

Her Sickness is a Feint, no Doubt,
To keep her Book from coming out.   60

Of wit, says Celia, I'll acquit her;
Then archly fell into a *Titter.*

A Female Bard! Pulvillio[95] cries;
'Tis *possible* she may be wise;
But I could never find it yet,
Tho' oft in Company we met:
She talks just in the common Way:
Sure Wits their Talents should display;
Their Language surely should be bright,
Before they should pretend to write: 70
I'll ne'er subscribe for Books, says he;
'Fore Gad, it looks like *Pedantry.*

High-born Belinda loves to blame,
On Criticism founds her Fame:
Whene'er *she thinks* a Fault she spies,
How Pleasure sparkles in her Eyes!
Call it not *Poetry,* she says;
No— Call it *Rhyming,* if you Please:
Her Numbers might adorn a Ring,
Or serve along the Streets to sing: 80
Stella and *Flavia's* well enough;
What else I saw, was stupid Stuff;
Nor Love nor Satire in her Lays,
Insipid! neither pain nor please:
I promis'd once to patronize her;
But on Reflection, I was wiser:
Yet I subscrib'd among the rest;
I love to carry on a Jest.

BELINDA thus her Anger shows,
Nor tells the World, from whence it flows: 90
With more Success to wound my Lays,
She gilds the Dart with other Praise:

95. Character named after the perfumed cosmetic powder notoriously used by fops on their hair and wigs.

To her own Breast I leave the Fair,
Convinc'd I stand acquitted there.

AMANDA, your Commands, you see,
Tho' grievous, are obey'd by me.
What my Friends told me had been said,
Just as it came into my Head,
No matter for the Place or Time,
100   To shew your Pow'r, I tag with Rhyme.

Now let some News salute your Ear,
Tho' I have weary'd you, I fear:
Know, — has Vengeance vow'd,
And in the *Furies* Temple[96] bow'd:
He but suspends his Wrath, he says,
Till he can criticise my Lays.
Malice, thy Rancour I expect,
And shall return it——with Neglect:
Go on, display your treasur'd Rage:
110   Invectives shall not blot my Page:
What real Faults you note, I'll mend:
So now your Efforts I attend;
Taught early, DRYDEN, by thy Song,
They ne'er forgive, who do the Wrong.[97]

Now to the Muse I bid Adieu;
Nor rail at her, as Poets do:
Protected by the Good and Great,
I'll not repine, but bless my Fate.

YOU, Madam, who your Sex adorn,
120   Who Malice and Detraction scorn,

96. Alecto, Megaera, and Tisiphone, the three daughters of Mother Earth, created from the blood of Uranus when Kronos castrated him. They are the avenging spirits of retributive justice, and because they punish crimes not within the reach of human justice, they often personify conscience. They are especially dedicated to crimes against kin.

97. Reworking of a quotation from part 2 of John Dryden's play *The Conquest of Granada* (1671): "Forgiveness to the injur'd does Belong; / But they ne'er pardon who have done the Wrong," 1.2.5–6. The lines are spoken by Zulema, chief of the Zegrys. Dryden was poet laureate and author of plays, poems, and prestigious translations of the classics.

Who with superior Sense are bless'd,
Of ev'ry real Worth possess'd;[98]
With Eye indulgent view my Lays:
You know to blame, but love to praise:
You know my Faults, and know beside,
I want not to be mortify'd.
One Merit I presume to boast,
And dare to plead but one at most:
The Muse I never have debas'd;
My Lays are innocent at least;   130
Were ever ardently design'd
To mend and to enlarge the Mind.
This must be own'd a virtuous Aim.
The Praise of Wit—let others claim.

(1734)

To Mrs. Mary Barber,[99] under the Name of Sapphira: Occasion'd by the Encouragement She met with in England, to publish her Poems by Subscription

Constantia Grierson

Long has the Warrior's, and the Lover's Fire,
Employ'd the Poet, and ingross'd the Lyre;
And justly too the World might long approve
The Praise of HEROES and of virtuous LOVE;
Had Tyrants not usurp'd the HERO's Name,
Nor low Desires debas'd the LOVER's Flame;
If on those Themes, all Triflers had not writ,
Guiltless of Sense, or Elegance, or Wit.

FAR different Themes We in thy Verses view;
Themes, in themselves, alike sublime, and new: 10
Thy tuneful Labours all conspire to show
The highest Bliss the Mind can taste below;
To ease those Wants, with which the Wretched pine;
And imitate Beneficence divine:

---

98. In this verse, Barber writes the conventional conclusion to a satiric apologia, the tribute to an ideal, who is in contrast to the poem's satiric objects.

99. Barber and Constantia Grierson were friends and part of a literary circle in Ireland.

A Theme, alas! forgot by Bards too long;
And, but for Thee, almost unknown to Song.

SUCH wise Reflections in thy Lays are shown,
As FLACCUS' Muse,[100] in all her Pride, might own:
So Elegant, and so Refin'd, thy Praise,
20   As greatest Minds, at once, might mend and please:
No florid Toys, in pompous Numbers drest;
But justest Thoughts, in purest Stile, exprest:
Whene'er thy Muse designs the Heart to move,
The melting Reader must, with Tears, approve;
Or when, more gay, her spritely Satire bites,
'Tis not to wound, but to instruct, She writes.

COU'D * * *, or * * *, from the Tomb,
Which shades their Ashes till the final Doom,
The dire Effects of vitious Writings view,
30   How wou'd they mourn to think what might ensue!
Blush at their Works, for no one End design'd,
But to embellish Vice, and taint the Mind!
No more their dear-bought Fame wou'd raise their Pride;
But Terrors wait on Talents misapplied.

NOT SO SAPPHIRA: her unsullied Strain
Shall never give her Soul one conscious Pain;
To latest Times shall melt the harden'd Breast,
And raise her Joys, by making others blest.

THESE Works, which Modesty conceal'd in Night,
40   Your Candor, gen'rous BRITONS, brings to Light;
Born, by your Arms, for Liberty's Defence;
Born, by your Taste, the Arbiters of Sense:
Long may your Taste, and long your Empire stand,
To Honour, Wit, and Worth, from every Land.

OH! cou'd my conscious Muse but fully trace
The silent Virtues which SAPPHIRA grace;

---

100. Quintus Horatius Flaccus (65–8 BC), Roman poet and satirist, known as Horace. Grierson was a formidable classicist.

How much her Heart, from low Desires refin'd;
How much her Works, the Transcript of her Mind;
Her tender Care, and Grief for the Distrest;
Her Joy unfeign'd, to see true Merit blest;   50
Her Soul so form'd for every social Care;
A Friend so gen'rous, ardent, and sincere;
How wou'd you triumph in yourselves to find
Your Favours shewn to so complete a Mind;
To find her Breast with every Grace inspir'd,
Whom first You only for her Lays admir'd.
Thus the great Father of the *Hebrew* State,
Who watch'd for weary'd Strangers at his Gate;
The Good He thought conferr'd on Men unknown,
He found to more exalted Beings shown.[101]   60
Dublin, Jan. 5, 1732

(1734)

An Epistle to Lady Bowyer[102]
Mary Jones

How much of paper's spoil'd! what floods of ink!
And yet how few, how very few can think!
The knack of writing is an easy trade;
But to think well requires—at least a Head.
Once in an age, *one* Genius may arise,
With wit well-cultur'd, and with learning wise.
Like some tall oak, behold his branches shoot!
No tender scions springing at the root.
Whilst lofty *Pope* erects his laurell'd head,[103]
No lays,[104] like mine, can live beneath his shade.   10
Nothing but weeds, and moss, and shrubs are found.
Cut, cut them down, why cumber they the ground?

---

101. Abraham entertained three men who were messengers from God. Gen. 18; see also Heb. 13:2: "Be not forgetful to entertain strangers: for thereby some have entertained angels unawares."

102. Anne Stonehouse Bowyer, wife of Sir William, third Baronet. She was a relative of Martha Lovelace's, perhaps Jones's closest friend, and maid of honor to Queen Caroline.

103. Alexander Pope (1688–1744), the most admired poet of the century. Jones represents him as wearing the laurel crown, or wreath, symbol of poetic greatness.

104. Ballads; lyric or narrative poems meant to be sung.

And yet you'd have me write!——For what? for whom?[105]
To curl a Fav'rite in a dressing-room?
To mend a candle when the snuff's too short?
Or save rappee for chamber-maids at Court?[106]
Glorious ambition! noble thirst of fame!——
No, but you'd have me write——to get a name.
Alas! I'd live unknown, unenvy'd too;

20   'Tis more than *Pope,* with all his wit can do.
'Tis more than You, with wit and beauty join'd,
A pleasing form, and a discerning mind.
The world and I are no such cordial friends;
I have my purpose, they their various ends.
I say my pray'rs, and lead a sober life,
Nor laugh at *Cornus,*[107] or at *Cornus'* wife.
What's fame to me, who pray, and pay my rent?
If my friends know me honest, I'm content.

Well, but the joy to see my works in print;

30   My self too pictur'd in a Mezzo-Tint![108]
The Preface done, the Dedication fram'd,
With lies enough to make a Lord asham'd!
Thus I step forth; an Auth'ress in some sort.
My Patron's name? "O choose some Lord at Court.
One that has money which he does not use,
One you may flatter much, that is, abuse.
For if you're nice, and cannot change your note, ⎫
Regardless of the trimm'd, or untrimm'd coat; ⎬
Believe me, friend, you'll ne'er be worth a groat." ⎭

40   Well then, to cut this mighty matter short,
I've neither friend, nor interest at Court.

---

105. One of the conventional issues to be addressed in formal poetic apologias.

106. Jones is listing uses of scrap paper: to extend the wick of a candle; as hair rollers; to wrap cheap snuff.

107. A cuckold. Cornus is a character from Pope's satire *Epistle to Dr. Arbuthnot* (1735); line 25 reads: "Poor *Cornus* sees his frantic Wife elope." In his *Notes on Pope* (London, 1876) Horace Walpole says that Cornus was Robert, Lord Walpole, and therefore his "frantic Wife" was Margaret, Lady Walpole (43).

108. One of the most popular kinds of engraving. Mezzotint portraits of authors were often placed in published volumes of their work.

Quite from St. *James*'s to thy stairs, *Whitehall*,[109] ⎫
I hardly know a creature, great or small,   ⎬
Except one Maid of Honour,[110] worth 'em all.   ⎭
I have no bus'ness there. Let those attend   ⎫
The courtly Levee,[111] or the courtly Friend,   ⎬
Who more than fate allows them, dare to spend.⎭
Or those whose avarice, with much, craves more,
The pension'd Beggar, or the titled Poor.[112]
These are the thriving Breed, the tiny Great!   50
Slaves! wretched Slaves! the Journeymen of State!
Philosophers! who calmly bear disgrace,
Patriots! who sell their country for a place.[113]

  Shall I for these disturb my brains with rhyme?
For these, like *Bavius* creep,[114] or *Glencus* climb?[115]
Shall I go late to rest, and early rise,
To be the very creature I despise?
With face unmov'd, my poem in my hand,
Cringe to the porter, with the footman stand?
Perhaps my lady's maid, if not too proud,   60
Will stoop, you'll say, to wink me from the croud.
Will entertain me, till his lordship's drest,
With what my lady eats, and how she rests:

---

109. St. James Palace, built by Henry VIII, was the principal royal residence in London at the time. Whitehall is the thoroughfare between Holbein Gate and Charing Cross. Stairs descend to the river Thames. The path Jones describes is the one Charles I took to his execution.

110. Honourable Miss Lovelace. *Jones.*

111. Morning assembly at which people asked favors, often around the host's or hostess's dressing table.

112. Jones describes the situations of those with government pensions in a state of perpetual uncertainty, begging for payment and the continuance of their support, and of the nobility lacking financial resources, both frequent situations in the century.

113. Position, job.

114. Character in Pope's *Epistle to Dr. Arbuthnot:* "May some choice Patron bless each gray goose quill! / May ev'ry *Bavius* have his *Bufo* still!" (lines 249–50). Bavius and Maevius were two malicious critics notorious for their harsh reviews of Horace and Virgil during the reign of Augustus Caesar. Bufo is the Theophrastan character of a patron, and Pope's model for the patron is identified as Bubb Dodington, who was notorious for his bad judgment and pretenses to patronage.

115. Another character in Pope's *Epistle to Dr. Arbuthnot:* "A Knave's a Knave, to me, in ev'ry State, / Alike my scorn, if he succeed or fail, / *Glencus* at Court, or *Japhet* in a Jail" (lines 361–63). Glencus is believed to be modeled on James Johnston, a former secretary of state for Scotland before the Union of England and Scotland (1707); Pope satirizes him as "Scoto" in *Epistle to Cobham,* lines 158–61. In the second edition, Pope replaced the allusion to him with "Sporus," Lord Hervey, the object of the devastating satiric portrait in lines 305–33. Japhet Crook was a forger.

How much she gave for such a birth-day gown,
And how she trampt to ev'ry shop in town.

Sick at the news, impatient for my lord,
I'm forc'd to hear, nay smile at ev'ry word.
Tom[116] raps at last,—"His lordship begs to know
Your name? your bus'ness?"—Sir, I'm not a foe.

70   I come to charm his lordship's list'ning ears
With verses, soft as music of the spheres.
"Verses!—Alas! his lordship seldom reads:
Pedants indeed with learning stuff their heads;
But my good lord, as all the world can tell,
Reads not ev'n tradesmen's bills, and scorns to spell.
But trust your lays with me. Some things I've read,
Was born a poet, tho' no poet bred:
And if I find they'll bear my nicer view,
I'll recommend your poetry——and you."

80   Shock'd at his civil impudence, I start,
Pocket my poem, and in haste depart;
Resolv'd no more to offer up my wit,
Where footmen in the seat of critics sit.

Is there a Lord[117] whose great unspotted soul,
Not places, pensions, ribbons can control;
Unlac'd, unpowder'd, almost unobserv'd,
Eats not on silver, while his train are starv'd;
Who tho' to nobles, or to kings ally'd,
Dares walk on foot, while slaves in coaches ride;

90   With merit humble, and with greatness free,
Has bow'd to *Freeman*,[118] and has din'd with Me;
Who bred in foreign courts, and early known,
Has yet to learn the cunning of his own;
To titles born, yet heir to no estate,
And, harder still, too honest to be great;
If such an one there be, well-bred, polite?
To Him I'll dedicate, for Him I'll write.

116. Generic name for a footman.

117. Right Hon. Nevil Lord Lovelace, who dy'd soon after, in the 28th year of his age. *Jones.* [Martha Lovelace's brother; Jones wrote an elegy for him. *Eds.*]

118. Perhaps not a particular person but a name intended to signal an admirably independent and self-sufficient man.

Peace to the rest. I can be no man's slave;[119]
I ask for nothing, tho' I nothing have.
By Fortune humbled, yet not sunk so low   100
To shame a friend, or fear to meet a foe.
Meanness, in ribbons or in rags, I hate;
And have not learnt to flatter, ev'n the Great.
Few friends I ask, and those who love me well;
What more remains, these artless lines shall tell.

Of *honest* parents, not of *great,* I came;
Not known to fortune, quite unknown to fame.
Frugal and plain, at no man's cost they eat,
Nor knew a baker's, or a butcher's debt.
O be their precepts ever in my eye!   110
For one has learnt to live, and one to die.
Long may her widow'd age by heav'n be lent
Among my blessings! and I'm well content.
I ask no more, but in some calm retreat,
To sleep in quiet, and in quiet eat.
No noisy slaves attending round my room;
My viands[120] wholesome, and my waiters dumb.
No orphans cheated, and no widow's curse,
No houshold lord, for better or for worse.
No monstrous sums to tempt my soul to sin,   120
But just enough to keep me plain, and clean.
And if sometimes, to smooth the rugged way,
Charlot should smile,[121] or You approve my lay,
Enough for me. I cannot put my trust
In lords; smile lies, eat toads, or lick the dust.[122]
Fortune her favours much too dear may hold:
An honest heart is worth its weight in *gold.*

(1750)

---

119. These and several lines that follow echo the closing of Pope's *Epistle to Arbuthnot.*
120. Food, provisions.
121. Charlot Clayton, another relative of Martha Lovelace's and a close friend of Jones's.

122. A toad eater was a flatterer, often a woman forced into employment as a "humble companion." This verse has a number of echoes of *Epistle to Arbuthnot;* for instance, "lick the dust" comes from Pope's portrait of Sporus, whom Pope calls "familiar toad": "Pride that licks the dust" (lines 319, 333).

Slander delineated
Address'd to a Friend

Esther Lewis Clark

This wit was with experience bought,
(And that's the best of wit, 'tis thought)
That when a woman dares indite,
And seek in print the public sight,
All tongues are presently in motion,
About her person, mind, and portion;
And ev'ry blemish, ev'ry fault,
Unseen before, to light is brought.
Nay gen'rously they take the trouble,
10   Those blemishes and faults to double.

Whene'er you chance her name to hear,
Be sure, with a contemptuous sneer,
Some one exclaims, O, she's a wit!
And I've observ'd that epithet[123]
Means self-conceit, ill nature, pride,
And fifty hateful things beside.

The men are mighty apt to say,
This silly girl has lost her way,
Out of that sphere attempts to shine,
20   Which nature for her did design;
No doubt she thinks, we must admire
And such a rhyming wit desire;
But here her folly does appear,
We never choose a learned fair,
Nor like to see a woman try
With our superior parts to vie.
She ought to mind domestic cares,
The sex were made for such affairs.
She'd better take in hand the needle,
30   And not pretend to rhyme, and riddle.
Shall women thus usurp the pen?
That weapon nature made for men.
Presumptuous thing! how did she dare,
This implement from us to tear?

123. Descriptive, characterizing word or phrase.

In short, if women are allow'd,
(Women by nature vain, and proud)
Thus boldly on the press to seize,
And say in print whate'er they please,
They'll soon their lawful lords despise,
And think themselves, as Sybils,[124] wise.   40

Thus far the men their wit display,
Let's hear now what the women say.

Now we'll suppose a tattling set
Of females, o'er tea-table met,
While from its time-consuming streams,
Arise a hundred idle themes,
Of fans, of flounces, flies,[125] and faces,[126]
Of lap-dogs, lovers, lawns and laces.
At length this well-known foe to fame,
In luckless hour brings forth my name;   50
Then all exclaim with great good-nature,
O Lord! that witty rhyming creature!
Alternate all their parts sustain;
Pray, don't you think she's mighty vain,
Says one; no doubt, another cries:
Vain, Lord, of what? a third replies,
What tho' suppose the thing can rhyme,
And on the changing numbers chyme,[127]
No merit lies in that, 'tis plain,
And others if they were as vain,   60
I make no doubt, could write as well,
Would they but try, perhaps excel.

Then thus Philantha, in whose breast,
Good-nature is a constant guest,
I own, I've heard before, with pain,
Some people call her proud, and vain,

124. Prophetesses who sometimes interceded with the gods on behalf of mortals. The sibylline books were a collection of oracles consulted in times of emergency or disaster by the Roman senate.

125. Patches, small pieces of black silk cut into circles, stars, or other decorative shapes and worn on the face for adornment or to conceal a blemish.

126. Decorative buttons.

127. Chime.

I know her well, yet ne'er could see,
Either her pride, or vanity.

> You, madam, are, I find, her friend,⎫
70 But really I don't apprehend,   ⎬
> She ever yet a poem penn'd.   ⎭
They're all another's works, no doubt,
With which she makes this mighty rout.

That's very like, but, Miss, suppose,
She does the tedious stuff compose,
Yet for my part, tho' some may praise,
And stick the creature out with bays,[128]
I can see nothing in the scrawls,
That for such vast encomiums calls,
80 'Tis true, in length if merit lies,
From all she'll bear away the prize,
Of real wit 'twas still the way,
Much in not many words to say;
But she this happy method slights,
And little says, tho' much she writes.

This for her poems may be said,
They're mighty good to lull the head;
For nothing there peccant[129] you'll find,
To raise the laugh, or rouse the mind.
90 As smooth as oil the numbers[130] glide,
Like chaff upon a silver tide;
They neither please, nor pain the mind:
Then thus the friendly nymph rejoin'd:

It is to many so well known,
That all those poems are her own,
I wonder any one can doubt it,
Or have a single thought about it,
And oft I've heard the lines commended,
Then all allow, they're well intended.

128. Leaves of the laurel tree, used to make wreaths for conquerors or poets.
129. Faulty, violating any kind of rules.
130. Poetics; shorthand for rhyme, meter, and other poetic features.

That may perhaps be true enough;   100
But who's the better for her stuff.
I see no difference in the times,
The world's not mended by her rhymes.
She to the men, I apprehend,
Intends herself to recommend
By rhyming, but too late she'll find,
They don't so much regard the mind;
For tho' they're civil to her face,
'Tis all a farce, and mere grimace;
Her back once turn'd, I've heard 'em swear,   110
They hated wisdom in the fair.

Then she's so nice[131] and so refin'd
About the morals, and the mind,
That really, madam, I'm afraid,
This rhyming wit will die a maid;
And if she weds, it is high time,
I think she's almost past her prime.
Why, with the men, as I've been told,
She'll paper conversations hold.[132]

Madam, that's fact, I long have known it,   120
Without a blush I've heard her own it.

Good Lord! some women are so bold,
I vow, I blush to hear it told;
I hate censoriousness, but when
Girls freely correspond with men,
I can't forbear to speak my mind,
Altho' to scandal ne'er inclin'd.
Well, I protest I never yet
To any man a letter writ;
It may be innocent, 'tis true,   130
But 'tis a thing I ne'er could do.

131. Neat, clean.
132. Exchange letters. There were rigid opinions about when it was acceptable for women to write letters to men, and in many cases, should they receive a letter from a man, they were to return it un-read.

Well, cry'd Philantha, I protest,
I almost think you are in jest,
For really, Miss, I cannot see
In this the breach of modesty;
With men we chat away our time,
And none regard it as a crime;
And where's the difference, if we write,
'Tis but our words in black and white.
140   I think we may without offence,
Converse by pen with men of sense,
Improving correspondence hold,
And yet be neither free, nor bold.

Well, let us say no more about her,
But entertain ourselves without her;
No harm I meant, nor none I wish;
Miss, won't you drink another dish?
Not one drop more, I thank you, madam,
Here take away the tea-things, Adam.
150   And bring the cards, and since we're met,
Pray let us make at whist[133] a set.

Thus tea and scandal, cards and fashion,
Destroy the time of half the nation.

Now why must this, sir, be the case,
When women seek in print a place?
Why are the needle, and the pen,
Thought incompatible by men?
May not a woman touch the quill,
And yet be a good housewife still?
160   Why is it thought in us a crime,
To utter common sense in rhyme?
Why must each rhymer be a wit?
Why mark'd with that loath'd epithet?
For envy, hatred, scorn, or fear
To wit, you know, is often near.
Good-natur'd wit, polite, refin'd,
Which seeks to please, not pain the mind,

133. Card game played by two teams of two players each.

How rare to find! for O, how few
Have true and gen'rous wit like you!

Why must we certainly be vain,   170
If nature gives a rhyming brain?
This trifling talent 'bove the croud
Can only make vain folly proud.

But why to you thus should I write,
Whose soul's above such abject spite,
Your mind in different mould was cast,
To raise a character, not blast;
Yet don't mistake, nor think my muse
The world in general means t' accuse,
Since many still, in these degen'rate days,   180
Of either sex, like you, with pleasure praise.

(1789)

A Poem,
On the Supposition of an Advertisement appearing in a Morning Paper, of the Publication of a VOLUME of POEMS, by a SERVANT MAID
Elizabeth Hands

The tea-kettle bubbled, the tea things were set,
The candles were lighted, the ladies were met;
The how d'ye's were over, and entering bustle,
The company seated, and silks ceas'd to rustle:
The great Mrs. Consequence open'd her fan;
And thus the discourse in an instant began:
(All affected reserve, and formality scorning,)
I suppose you all saw in the paper this morning,
A Volume of Poems advertis'd—'tis said
They're produc'd by the pen of a poor Servant Maid.   10
A servant write verses! says Madam Du Bloom;
Pray what is the subject?—a Mop, or a Broom?
He,he,he,—says Miss Flounce; I suppose we shall see
An Ode on a Dishclout[134]—what else can it be?

---

134. Dishcloth; rag used for washing dishes.

Says Miss Coquettilla, why ladies so tart?
Perhaps Tom the Footman has fired her heart;
And she'll tell us how charming he looks in new clothes,
And how nimble his hand moves in brushing the shoes;
Or how the last time that he went to May-Fair,
20   He bought her some sweethearts of ginger-bread ware.
For my part I think, says old lady Marr-joy,
A servant might find herself other employ:
Was she mine I'd employ her as long as 'twas light,
And send her to bed without candle at night.
Why so? says Miss Rhymer, displeas'd; I protest
'Tis pity a genius should be so deprest!
What ideas can such low-bred creatures conceive,
Says Mrs. Noworthy, and laught in her sleeve.
Says old Miss Prudella, if servants can tell
30   How to write to their mothers, to say they are well,
And read of a Sunday the Duty of Man;[135]
Which is more I believe than one half of them can;
I think 'tis much *properer* they should rest there,
Than be reaching at things so much out of their sphere.
Says old Mrs. Candour, I've now got a maid
That's the plague of my life—a young gossipping jade;[136]
There's no end of the people that after her come,
And whenever I'm out, she is never at home;
I'd rather ten times she would sit down and write,
40   Than gossip all over the town ev'ry night.
Some whimsical trollop most like, says Miss Prim,
Has been scribbling of nonsense, just out of a whim,
And conscious it neither is witty or pretty,
Conceals her true name, and ascribes it to Betty.[137]
I once had a servant myself, says Miss Pines,
That wrote on a Wedding, some very good lines:
Says Mrs. Domestic, and when they were done,
I can't see for my part, what use they were *on;*
Had she wrote a receipt,[138] to've instructed you how

---

135. Richard Allestree's *The Whole Duty of Man Laid Down in a Plain and Familiar Way for the Use of All* (1713) was frequently reprinted throughout the century.

136. Willful, often flighty girl.

137. Generic name for a servant maid.

138. Recipe.

To warm a cold breast of veal, like a ragou,[139]   50
Or to make cowslip wine, that would pass for Champaign;
It might have been useful, again and again.
On the sofa was old lady Pedigree plac'd,
She own'd that for poetry she had no taste,
That the study of heraldry[140] was more in fashion,
And boasted she knew all the crests[141] in the nation.
Says Mrs. Routella,—Tom, take out the urn,
And stir up the fire, you see it don't burn.
The tea things remov'd, and the tea-table gone,
The card-tables brought, and the cards laid thereon,   60
The ladies ambitious for each others crown,[142]
Like courtiers contending for honours sat down.

(1789)

A Poem,
On the Supposition of the Book having been published and read
Elizabeth Hands

The dinner was over, the table-cloth gone,
The bottles of wine and the glasses brought on,
The gentlemen fill'd up the sparkling glasses,
To drink to their king, to their country and lasses:
The ladies a glass or two only requir'd,
To th' drawing-room then in due order retir'd;
The gentlemen likewise that chose to drink tea;
And, after discussing the news of the day,
What wife was suspected, what daughter elop'd,⎫
What thief was detected, that 'twas to be hop'd,⎬   10
The rascals would all be convicted, and rop'd;⎭
What chambermaid kiss'd when her lady was out;
Who won, and who lost, the last night at the rout;[143]
What lord gone to France, and what tradesman unpaid,
And who and who danc'd at the last masquerade;

139. Ragout, a meat and vegetable stew.
140. The study of pedigrees and the rules of precedence, armorial bearings, and insignia.
141. An ornament placed above the shield on a coat of arms and sometimes used by itself on seals and stationery.
142. Money.
143. A large evening party, assembly, or reception, very fashionable in the eighteenth century.

What banker stopt payment with evil intention,
And twenty more things much too tedious to mention.
Miss Rhymer says, Mrs. Routella, ma'am, pray
Have you seen the new book (that we talk'd of that day,
20   At your house you remember) of Poems, 'twas said
Produc'd by the pen of a poor Servant Maid?
The company silent, the answer expected;
Says Mrs. Routella, when she'd recollected;
Why, ma'am, I have bought it for Charlotte; the child
Is so fond of a book, I'm afraid it is spoil'd:
I thought to have read it myself, but forgat it;
In short, I have never had time to look at it.
Perhaps I may look it o'er some other day;
Is there any thing in it worth reading, I pray?
30   For your nice attention, there's nothing can 'scape.
She answer'd,—There's one piece, whose subject's a Rape.[144]
A Rape! interrupted the Captain Bonair,
A delicate theme for a female I swear;
Then smerk'd at the ladies, they simper'd all round,
Touch'd their lips with their fans,—Mrs. Consequence frown'd.
The simper subsided, for she with her nods,
Awes these lower assemblies,[145] as Jove[146] awes the gods.
She smil'd on Miss Rhymer, and bad her proceed—
Says she, there are various subjects indeed:
40   With some little pleasure I read all the rest,
But the Murder of Amnon's the longest and best.
Of Amnon, of Amnon, Miss Rhymer, who's he?
His name, says Miss Gaiety's quite new to me:—
'Tis a Scripture tale, ma'am,—he's the son of King David,[147]
Says a Reverend old Rector: quoth madam, I have it;
A Scripture tale?—ay—I remember it—true;
Pray is it i'th' old Testament or the new?
If I thought I could readily find it, I'd borrow

---

144. The full title of Hands's book of poetry is *The Death of Amnon. A Poem. With an Appendix: Containing Pastorals, and other Poetical Pieces. The Death of Amnon* is the biblical story of Amnon's rape of his sister, Tamar. Their brother Absalom has Amnon murdered (2 Sam. 13).

145. Evening gatherings, often with entertainment such as music or cards.

146. Supreme Roman god, the great father god and protector of the state; also Jupiter, the Greek god Zeus.

147. The alleged author of many of the Psalms. As a shepherd boy, David killed Goliath, and later he was anointed king by the prophet Samuel.

My house-keeper's Bible, and read it to-morrow.
'Tis in Samuel, ma'am, says the Rector:—Miss Gaiety   50
Bow'd, and the Reverend blush'd for the laity.
You've read it, I find, says Miss Harriot Anderson;
Pray, sir, is it any thing like Sir Charles Grandison?[148]
How you talk, says Miss Belle, how should such a girl write
A novel, or any thing else that's polite?
You'll know better in time, Miss:—She was but fifteen:
Her mamma was confus'd—with a little chagrin,
Says,—Where's your attention, child? did not you hear
Miss Rhymer say, that it was poems, my dear?
Says Sir Timothy Turtle, my daughters ne'er look   60
In any thing else but a cookery book:
The properest study for women design'd;
Says Mrs. Domestic, I'm quite of your mind.
Your haricoes,[149] ma'am, are the best I e'er eat,
Says the Knight, may I venture to beg a receipt.
'Tis much at your service, says madam, and bow'd,
Then flutter'd her fan, of the compliment proud.
Says Lady Jane Rational, the bill of fare
Is th' utmost extent of my cookery care:
Most servants can cook for the palate I find,   70
But very few of them can cook for the mind.
Who, says Lady Pedigree, can this girl be;
Perhaps she's descended of some family:—
Of family, doubtless, says Captain Bonair,
She's descended from Adam, I'd venture to swear.
Her Ladyship drew herself up in her chair,
And twitching her fan-sticks, affected a sneer.
I know something of her, says Mrs. Devoir,
She liv'd with my friend, Jacky Faddle, Esq.
'Tis sometime ago though; her mistress said then,   80
The girl was excessively fond of a pen;
I saw her, but never convers'd with her—*though*
One can't make acquaintance with servants, you know.
'Tis pity the girl was not bred in high life,
Says Mr. Fribbello:—yes,—then, says his wife,

148. *The History of Sir Charles Grandison* (1753–54), by Samuel Richardson. Grandison is an exemplary man.
149. Stew, usually made with lamb and vegetables.

She doubtless might have wrote something worth notice:
'Tis pity, says one,—says another, and so 'tis.
O law! says young Seagram, I've seen the book, now
I remember, there's something about a mad cow.[150]
90   A mad cow!—ha, ha, ha, ha, return'd half the room;
What can y' expect better, says Madam Du Bloom?
They look at each other,—a general pause—
And Miss Coquettella adjusted her gauze.
The Rector reclin'd himself back in his chair,
And open'd his snuff-box with indolent air;
This book, says he, (snift, snift) has in the beginning,
(The ladies give audience to hear his opinion)
Some pieces, I think, that are pretty correct;
A stile elevated you cannot expect:
100   To some of her equals they may be a treasure,
And country lasses may read 'em with pleasure.
That Amnon, you can't call it poetry neither,
There's no flights of fancy, or imagery either;
You may stile it prosaic, blank-verse at the best;
Some pointed reflections, indeed, are exprest;
The narrative lines are exceedingly poor:
Her Jonadab[151] is a —— the drawing-room door
Was open'd, the gentleman came from below,
And gave the discourse a definitive blow.

(1789)

The Excuse
On Being Desired to Write Verses by One Lady, After Having Been Advised against It by Another
Eliza Tuite

Oh, Jenny, to what an extreme
   Am I brought by your fatal desire;
To offend her I so much esteem,
   Or displease whom I justly admire.

---

150. Hands's book of poetry includes *Written, originally extempore, on seeing a Mad Heifer run through the Village where the Author lives* (1.C).
  151. A nephew of David, Amnon's ambitious friend who incited Amnon to rape Tamar.

To the Muses and Phœbus[152] I pray'd,
  To pronounce in a matter so nice;
But Apollo[153] denied me his aid,
  And the Muses refus'd their advice.

They declar'd they could never pretend,
  In this intricate case to decide;   10
For that you had been ever their friend,
  And with Anna they'd long been allied.

From Parnassus[154] obliged to depart,
  Without knowing what course to pursue,
Inclination (who gave you my heart)
  Would have giv'n you my promises too.

But Gratitude bid me delay,
  Till Reflection had time to be heard,
Who said "Is it thus you obey
  The advice, you once vow'd you prefer'd.   20

"Is it *thus* that you follow the rule,
  Your fair monitor earnestly set?
But I see, that you too can grow cool,
  Even you can in absence forget!"

Unable her words to withstand,
  And struck with the truths she had said,
My pen quickly fell from my hand,
  And my verses went out of my head.

(1796)

Sources

Plagiarism. Killigrew: *Poems* (London, 1686), 44–47; Masters: *Poems on Several Occasions* (London, 1733), 44–45; Poynton: *Poems on Several Occasions* (Birmingham, 1770), 26–27;

152. Apollo the sun god, here the personification of the sun.
153 God of the sun and of music and poetry.
154. A mountain near Delphi, Greece, sacred to Apollo and the Muses, hence to poetry and the arts.

Winscom: *Poems on Various Subjects, Entertaining, Elegiac, and Religious* (Winchester, 1783), 44–46.

Critics. Behn: *The Works of Aphra Behn*, ed. Janet Todd, 7 vols. (Columbus: Ohio State University Press, 1992–96), 6:79–80. Finch: *The Poems of Anne Countess of Winchilsea*, ed. Myra Reynolds (Chicago: University of Chicago Press, 1903), 4–6; *Miscellany Poems, on Several Occasions* (London, 1713), 162–66. Centlivre: *The Wonder: A Woman Keeps a Secret* (London, 1714), unpaginated. Masters: *Poems on Several Occasions* (London, 1733), 54–56. Reeve: *Original Poems on Several Occasions* (London, 1769), 4–11. Savage: *Poems on Various Subjects and Occasions*, 2 vols. (London, 1777), 1:98–100.

Resistance. Manley: *The Lost Lover* (London, 1696), unpaginated; Finch: *Miscellany Poems, on Several Occasions* (London, 1713), 1–4; Thomas: *Miscellany Poems on Several Subjects* (London, 1722), 85–86; Barber: *Poems on Several Occasions* (London, 1734), 275–83; Grierson: Mary Barber, *Poems on Several Occasions* (London, 1734), xlv–xlviii; Jones: *Miscellanies in Prose and Verse* (Oxford, 1750), 1–7; Clark: *Poems Moral and Entertaining* (Bath, 1789), 162–69; Hands: *The Death of Amnon. A Poem. With An Appendix: Containing Pastorals, and other Poetical Pieces* (Coventry, 1789), 47–50, 50–55; Tuite: *Poems by Lady Tuite* (London, 1796), 78–80.

✠E✠

The Determination to Write

Love Intrigues (1713), the first novel in Jane Barker's Galesia trilogy, includes a poem that details her heroine's decision to "cast off thy Chain," her romantic attachment to the faithless Bosvil, and devote herself to writing, "a Virgin to remain." She hears "the Muses sing, / . . . / And call upon me to take Wing." Offering to assist her "Flight, / Till thou reach fair ORINDA's Height," they urge her to "Write, write thy Vow upon this Tree, / By us it shall recorded be; / And thou enjoy Eternity" (*Methinks these Shades, strange Thoughts suggest*, not included).[1] Not every poet in this anthology recounts her determination to write so dramatically, although every poem included is evidence of a woman's perseverance, creativity, skill, and determination. The poems in this section deal directly with three shaping influences on women's ability to write: the inescapable force of their poetic ability, the domestic situation that impeded or advanced their art, and the social customs that urged their conformity. Read together, the poems illustrate women's articulation of their will to succeed and their hopes for the triumph of their verse.

Many poets describe the inescapable power of their poetic impulses—the experience Barker describes as "my rolling Thoughts turn'd themselves into . . . verses."[2] "My thoughts" writes Elizabeth Singer Rowe, "*burst out a chiming; / My active Genius* will by no means sleep" (*To one that Perswades me to leave the Muses*). The preface to Mary Jones's *Miscellanies in Prose and Verse* (1750) details her lifelong focus on poetry: "her thoughts ever rambled into rhyme." Mary Whateley Darwall claims to "write in Rhyme before I knew to think" (*The Power of Destiny*); she notes in the "Advertisement" to her second volume of poems that "some of the pieces have been written nearly thirty years."[3] Imitating Pope's apologia for his career in *Epistle to Arbuthnot* (1735), Darwall observes that had she been born a man she would have abandoned a career in the clergy, medicine, or the law "had an Itch for scribbling fill'd my Brain"; nothing, she says, can save "the Poet—from—the Poet's Curse." The "strong Propensity" to write, for anyone who possesses it, necessarily means yielding "to this darling *Sin*" (*The Power of Destiny*). The need to write is inescapable; "I cannot stop 'till paper fail," writes Esther Lewis Clark (*Woman's Frailty*). Charlotte Smith, who began composing verse when she was a child, famously wrote that she was "compelled to live only to write & to write only to live."[4] In a letter, Smith describes how "in the stillness of the night, verses occur to me, & I hasten to put them down in the morning."[5]

Smith's productivity, driven by her financial need, occurred in the face of what Judith Phillips Stanton describes as "every possible obstacle: isolation from both the London literary scene and from circles of writers in the provinces; ill health; the burden of many children ill, wounded, or dying; legal impediments to inheritance; expenses that drove her to move continually to cheaper and more humble lodgings."[6] Many other women poets recount personal or domestic challenges to their sustained activity. Mary Jones details "the many disadvantages, the almost perpetual interruptions that have attended it, and last of all, the death of the dearest and best of mothers, when it was near its publication."[7] Mary Barber laments the delay in publishing her volume, occasioned by her long confinement and "my Want of Health."[8] The detailing of the "numerous disadvantages" suffered by Priscilla Poynton, blind from the age of thirteen, in the preface to her 1770 collection frames her verse with evidence of her dedication although "frequently at the greatest loss for a amanuensis, held under the strictest subjection of an aged parent ... deprived of the advantages of a refin'd education."[9] Poynton, like the other poets in this volume, was undeterred.

The personal demands on individual poets differ greatly, as do the distinct cultural moments in which they wrote. Some, such as Anne Finch, lived comfortably and benefited from a husband's support, which enhanced both her productivity and the preservation of her work. Others were in very different circumstances. Elizabeth Thomas never married and spent most of the last three years of her life in prison for debt. Darwall describes her poems as "the effusions of a mind generally occupied in the domestic duties."[10] Jane Cave Winscom, a skilled poet, wife, and mother, details her relationship with the Muses as she successfully balances her domestic and poetic responsibilities, simultaneously trying to answer her "duty" to both. "Thus, what the Author to the World presents," concludes Winscom, "Appears through numberless impediments" (*The Author's Plea*). The phrase "numberless impediments" is particularly evocative. At first glance, it summons the stereotypical image of a woman writer hampered by children, husband, or daily household tasks—the impediments that can limit creativity. More suggestively, however, it acknowledges that the domestic realm offers a wealth of experiences, some of which become material for poetry (and are thus "numbered" in a metrical sense) and some of which remain unsung, or "numberless." While Winscom may represent the literary enterprise as at times contingent or often precarious, that situation is certainly not unique to women.

Elizabeth Thomas graphically describes the constricted cultural expectations for women whose fate "By Customs *Tyranny* confin'd / To foolish *Needle-work*, and *Chat,* / Or such like *Exercise* as that, / But still deny'd th' Improvement of our Mind!" (*On Sir J——S—— saying in a sarcastick Manner, My Books would make me Mad*). Thomas warns women who meet cultural expectations and marry that "Those, who to *Husbands* have their Pow'r resign'd, / Will in their House a full Employment find, / And little Time command to cultivate the Mind." Thomas's ode, the most metrically complex poem in this section, with its varying hexameter, tetrameter, and pentameter lines, skillfully explores the collision of the force of gender expectations and the work of poetry. While Rowe admits the "lovers cares," her "genius" remains "Unburden'd yet" with any others (*To one that Perswades me to leave the Muses*).

Writing poetry provides a voice and sense of agency, (limited) financial remuneration, and a sense of immortality; as Anne Killigrew writes, "for a Monument, I leave my VERSE" (*An Epitaph on her Self*). The passionate desire and need to write, the confrontation with the blank page, the ridicule of detractors, the carping of critics, and the need for money and the often scant compensation are shared by all who embark on a poetic career, if, perhaps, intensified for women. Yet "To heat with Poetry my colder Brain" (Anne Finch, *The Appology*) is a goal realized by every women poet in this anthology.

Notes

1. Jane Barker, *Love Intrigues: or, the History of the Amours of Bosvil and Galesia as related to Lucasia, in St. Germains Garden* (London, 1713), 14. In the 1719 edition of the novel the last line reads, "And thou fam'd to Eternity."

2. Barker, *Love Intrigues,* 13.

3. Mary Whateley Darwall, *Poems on Several Occasions. By Mrs. Darwall (Formerly Miss Whateley) in Two Volumes,* 2 vols. (Walsall, West Midlands, 1794), 1:i.

4. Charlotte Smith to Dr. Thomas Shirley, 22 August 1789, in *The Collected Letters of Charlotte Smith,* ed. Judith Phillips Stanton (Bloomington: Indiana University Press, 2003), 23.

5. Charlotte Smith to her publishers Thomas Cadell Jr. and William Davies, 20 October 1797, in Smith, *Collected Letters,* 295.

6. Judith Phillips Stanton, "Charlotte Smith's 'Literary Business'; Income, Patronage, and Indigence," *Age of Johnson* 1 (1987): 396.

7. Mary Jones, *Miscellanies in Prose and Verse* (Oxford, 1750), vi.

8. Mary Barber, *Poems on Several Occasions* (London, 1734), xxv.

9. Priscilla Poynton, *Poems on Several Occasions* (Birmingham, 1770), vi.

10. Darwall, *Poems on Several Occasions,* 2:i.

An Epitaph on her Self
Anne Killigrew

When I am Dead, few Friends attend my Hearse,
And for a Monument, I leave my VERSE.

(1686)

To one that Perswades me to leave the Muses
Elizabeth Singer Rowe

Forgo the *charming Muses*! No, in spight[1]
Of your ill-natur'd Prophecy I'll write,
And for the future *paint* my thoughts at large,
I waste no paper at the *Hunderds*[2] charge:
I rob no *Neighbouring Geese* of Quills, nor slink
For a collection to the Church for ink:
Besides my *Muse* is the most gentle thing
That ever yet made an attempt to *sing:*
I call no Lady *Punk,*[3] nor Gallants *Fops,*[4]
10   Nor set the *married world an edge for Ropes;*[5]
Yet I'm so scurvily inclin'd to Rhiming,
That undesign'd my thoughts *burst out a chiming;*
My *active Genius* will by no means sleep,
And let it then its proper channel keep.
I've told you, and you may believe me too,
That I must this, or greater mischiefe do;
And let the world think me *inspir'd, or mad,*
I'le surely write whilst paper's to be had;

---

1. Alternate spelling of *spite*.

2. Subdivision of a county or shire, having its own court; also formerly applied to the court itself.

3. Prostitute.

4. Pretender to wit; one who is foolishly vain about his appearance, dress, or manners.

5. To "set an edge for" is to incite someone to something. In this instance, to incite a married couple to "ropes" alludes to the practice of a wife sale. As detailed in *The Laws Respecting Women, as They Regard Their Natural Rights, or Their Connections and Conduct* (London, 1777), "When a husband and wife find themselves heartily tired of each other, and agree to part," the man "puts a halter" or a rope noose around the wife's neck "and thereby leads her to the next market place, and there puts her up to auction to be sold" (55). It is important to note, however, that such a "sale" would not have been legally valid.

Since Heaven to me has a *Retreat assign'd,*[6]
That would inspire a less *harmonious* mind.   20
All that a Poet loves I have in view,
Delightsome Hills, refreshing Shades, and pleasant Valleys too,
Fair spreading Valleys cloath'd with lasting green,
And Sunny Banks with gilded *streams between,*
Gay as Elisium,[7] in a Lovers Dream,
Or *Flora's* Mansion,[8] seated by a stream,
Where free from sullen cares I live at ease,
Indulge my Muse, and wishes, as I please,
Exempt from all that looks like want or strife,   30
I smoothly glide along the Plains of Life,
Thus Fate conspires, and what can I do to't?
Besides, I'm *veh'mently in love to boot,*
And that there's not a *Willow Sprig*[9] but knows,
In whose sad shade I breathe my direful woes.
But why for these dull Reasons do I pause,
When I've at hand my genuine *one, because*!
    And that my Muse may take no counter Spell,
I fairly bid the *Boarding Schools* farewel:
No *Young Impertinent,* shall here intrude,   40
And vex me from this blisful solitude.
Spite of her heart, *Old Puss*[10] shall damn no more
Great *Sedley's*[11] Plays, and never look 'em o're;
Affront my *Novels,* no, nor in a Rage,

---

6. After 1692 Rowe lived at Eggford Farm at Frome, Somerset, in the West Country.

7. In Greek mythology, and in this poem, Elysium is a happy land at the west end of the earth that is never cold and is always warmed by the soft breezes of Zephyrus, god of the west wind. The Roman poet Virgil changed the association of Elysium when he made it the residence in the underworld for the spirits of the blessed after death.

8. In Roman mythology, Flora was the goddess of flowers and fertility, beloved by Zephyrus, god of the west wind.

9. A sprig is a branch or twig. A willow is a tree characterized by very pliant branches and long, narrow drooping leaves. A willow sprig is a symbol of grief for unrequited love or the loss of a mate.

10. *Puss* can refer to a woman; here it refers to an imagined or remembered teacher at the boarding school. It can also describe a sour or ugly face, which would seem to be a secondary meaning here.

11. Sir Charles Sedley (bap. 1639, d. 1701) belonged to the court of Charles II and was a friend of John Wilmot, Earl of Rochester (1647–80). He wrote three plays for the stage: *The Mulberry Garden* (1668), *Antony and Cleopatra* (1677), and *Bellamira* (1687). In a poem entitled *To Sir Charles Sedley,* Rowe writes that "nothing but his own Cœlestial lays / Are fit the Author of such flights to praise." *Poems on Several Occasions. Written by Philomela* (London, 1696), 16.

Force *Drydens*[12] lofty Products from the Stage,
Whilst all the rest of the *melodious crew,*
With the *whole* System of *Athenians*[13] too, ⎫
For Study's sake out of the Window flew. ⎭
But I'to Church, shall fill her Train no more,
50   And walk as if I sojurn'd by the hour.
    To *Stepwel* and his Kit[14] I bid adieu,
Fall off, and on, be hang'd and *Coopee*[15] too
Thy self for me, my *dancing days* are o're;
I'le act th'inspired *Bachannels*[16] no more.
Eight Notes must for another Treble look,
In *Burlesque* to make Faces by the book.
Japan,[17] and my esteemed *Pencil* too,
And pretty Cupid, in the Glass adieu,
And since the dearest friends that be must part,
60   *Old Governess* farewell with all my heart.
Now welcome all ye *peaceful Shades* and *Springs,*
And welcome all the *inspiring* tender things;
That please my *genius,* suit my make and years,
Unburden'd yet with all but lovers cares.

(1696)

12. John Dryden (1631–1700), in addition to being a poet, was regarded as one of the premiere playwrights of the Restoration stage.

13. In May 1691, inspired by an idea for a new type of periodical, the bookseller John Dunton (1659–1732) began to publish his most successful project of all, the *Athenian Gazette, or, Casuistical Mercury.* Readers were invited to send their queries on any subject to an anonymous club of "learned men" who met at Smith's coffee house, the Athenian Society. The club actually consisted of Dunton, his brother-in-law Samuel Wesley (bap. 1662, d. 1735), and another brother-in-law, Richard Sault (d. 1702). Dunton first published Rowe's poems.

14. A proverbial dancing master (Stepwell) and the small violin, or "kit," that dancing masters carried with them to play dances for their pupils or other dancers. See Jeremy Montague, *The World of Baroque and Classical Musical Instruments* (London: David & Charles, 1979), 65.

15. A common dance step in which the dancer rests on one foot and passes the other forward or backward, making a sort of salutation. Sometimes used for a bow made while advancing.

16. Alternate spelling of *bacchanal,* indulging in an occasion of drunken revelry.

17. Varnish of exceptional hardness, usually black, introduced to England about 1688. It was very popular as a furniture finish.

The Appology
Anne Finch

'Tis true I write and tell me by what Rule
I am alone forbid to play the fool
To follow through the Groves a wand'ring Muse
And fain'd Idea's for my pleasures chuse
Why shou'd it in my Pen be held a fault
Whilst Mira paints her face, to paint a thought
Whilst Lamia to the manly Bumper[18] flys
And borrow'd Spiritts sparkle in her Eyes
Why shou'd itt be in me a thing so vain
To heat with Poetry my colder Brain   10
But I write ill and there-fore shou'd forbear
Does Flavia cease now at her fortieth year
In ev'ry Place to lett that face be seen
Which all the Town rejected at fifteen
Each Woman has her weaknesse; mine indeed
Is still to write tho' hoplesse to succeed
Nor to the Men is this so easy found
Ev'n in most Works with which the Witts abound
(So weak are all since our first breach with Heav'n)
Ther's lesse to be Applauded then forgiven.   20

(c. 1706–9; 1903)

On Sir J——S—— saying in a sarcastick Manner, My Books would make me Mad. An Ode
Elizabeth Thomas

Unhappy *Sex!* how hard's our Fate,
     By Customs *Tyranny* confin'd
To foolish *Needle-work,* and *Chat,*
     Or such like *Exercise* as that,
But still deny'd th' Improvement of our Mind!
     "*Women!* Men cry, alas, poor Fools!

---

18. Glass of wine filled to the brim, especially when drunk as a toast.

What are they but *domestick Tools?*
On purpose made our *Toils* to share,
And ease the Husband's *Oeconomick* Care.
10   To *dress*, to *sing*, to *work*, to *play*, ⎫
    To watch our *Looks*, our *Words* obey, ⎬
And with their little *Follies*, drive dull Thoughts away. ⎭
    Thus let them humbly in *Subjection* live;
But Learning leave to *Man*, our great Prerogative."

II.
    Most mighty *Sov'reigns* we submit,
And own ye Monarchs of the Realms of *Wit:*
    But might a *Slave* to her Superiours speak,
        And without *Treason* Silence break,
        She'd first implore your royal *Grace,*
20   Then humbly thus expostulate the Case.
Those, who to *Husbands* have their Pow'r resign'd, ⎫
    Will in their House a full Employment find, ⎬
    And little Time command to cultivate the Mind. ⎭
        Had we been made intuitively wise,
        Like Angels vast Capacities;
        I would allow we need not use,
        Those Rules Experience does infuse:
        But if born ignorant, tho' fit for more,
    Can you deny we should improve our Store?
30   Or won't you be so just to grant,
        That those Perfections which we want,
    And can't acquire when in a married State,
        Should be attain'd before.
    Believe me, 'tis a *Truth* long understood;
That those who know not why they're so, can ne'er be *wise* or *good.*

III.
    What surer Method can we take,
        Than this ye seem to chuse?
    'Tis *Books* ye write, and *Books* ye use;
    But yet we must a serious Judgment make,
40   What to elect, and what refuse.
    Is't not by *Books* we're taught to know
    The great *Creator* of this World below?
    The vast Dimensions of this Earth,

And to what minute Particles poor Mortals owe their Birth?
   By *Books,* th' *Almighty's* Works, we learn and prize,
   But those *Phænomena's,* which dazle vulgar Eyes,
      We can as much despise.
   And more than this, well chosen *Books* do show,
     What unto *God,* and what to *Man* we owe.
       Yet, if we enquire for a *Book,*   50
       Beyond a *Novel,* or a *Play,*
   Good Lord! how soon th' Alarms took,
   How soon your Eyes, your Souls betray,
      And with what Spite ye look!
   How nat'rally ye stare and scowl,
     Like wond'ring *Birds* about an *Owl,*
And with malicious Sneer, these dismal Accents howl.

IV.

     Alas, poor *Plato!*[19] all thy Glory's past:
   What, in a *Female* Hand[20] arriv'd at last!
   Sure, adds another, 'tis for something worse;   60
   This Itch of Reading's sent her as a Curse.
   No, no, cries good Sir *John,* but 'tis as bad,
For if she's not already *craz'd,* I'm sure she will be *mad.*
     'Tis thus ye rail to vent your Spleen,
     And think your wond'rous Wit is seen:
   But 'tis the Malice of your Sex appears,
     What suffer *Woman* to pretend to Sense!
     Oh! how this *Optick*[21] magnifies the Offence,
      And aggravates your Fears?
     But since the *French* in all ye ape,   70
   Why should not they your Morals shape?
     Their *Women* are as gay and fair,
   Yet *learned Ladies* are no Monsters there.
     What is it from our *Sex* ye fear,

19. Greek philosopher (428–348 BC) who helped lay the philosophical foundation of Western culture.

20. French classicist Anne Dacier (1654–1720), translator and scholar of classical figures such as Plautus, Anacreon, and Sappho. She was the daughter of the French humanist Tanneguy Lefèbvre, who educated her and launched her in the field of classical studies. Thomas misattributes to her *The Works of Plato Abridg'd* (London, 1701), which was actually translated by her husband, André. Anne Dacier was widely recognized for her translations of the *Iliad* (1699) and the *Odyssey* (1708).

21. Instrument or device constructed to assist vision.

That thus ye curb our Pow'rs?
D'ye apprehend a *bookish* War,
Or are your Judgments less, for raising ours?
Come, come, the real *Truth* confess,
(A Fault acknowledg'd is the less)
80   And own it was an *avaricious* Soul,
Which would, with greedy Eyes, *monopolize* the whole:
And bars us *Learning* on the selfish Score;
That conscious of our native Worth,
Ye dread to make it more.
Then thanks to *Heav'n,* we're *English* born and free,
And thank our gracious *Laws* that give such *Liberty.*

(1722)

The Question. Occasion'd by a serious Admonition
Mary Leapor

Is Mirth a Crime? Instruct me you that know;
Or shou'd these Eyes with Tears eternal flow:
No (let ye Powers) let this Bosom find,
Life's one grand Comfort, a contented Mind:
Preserve this Heart, and may it find no room
For pale Despondence or unpleasing Gloom:
Too well the Mischief and the Pangs we know
Of doubtful Musing and prophetick Woe.
But now these Evils for a Moment rest,
10   And brighter Visions please the quiet Breast,
Where sprightly Health its blessed Cordial pours,
And chearful Thought deceives the gliding Hours:
Then let me smile, and trifle while I may,
Yet not from Virtue nor from Reason stray:
From hated Slander I wou'd keep my Tongue;
My Heart from Envy, and from Guilt my Song:
Nature's large Volume with Attention read,
Its God acknowledge, and believe my Creed:
Through Weakness, not Impiety, offend;
20   But love my Parent, and esteem my Friend.

If (like the most) my undistinguish'd Days
Deserve not much of Censure or of Praise:

If my still Life, like subterraneous Streams,
Glides unobserv'd, nor tainted by Extremes,
Nor dreadful Crime has stain'd its early Page,
To hoard up Terrors for reflecting Age;
Let me enjoy the sweet Suspence of Woe,
When Heav'n strikes me, I shall own the Blow:
Till then let me indulge one simple Hour,
Like the pleas'd Infant o'er a painted Flow'r: 30
Idly 'tis true: But guiltlesly the Time
Is spent in trifling with a harmless Rhyme.

   Heroick Virtue asks a noble Mind,
A Judgment strong, and Passions well refin'd:
But if that Virtue's measur'd by the Will,
'Tis surely something to abstain from Ill.

                      (1748)

The Power of Destiny
Mary Whateley Darwall

Sure some malignant Star diffus'd its Ray,
When first my Eyes beheld the Beams of Day:
Whose baleful Influence made me dip in Ink,
And write in Rhyme before I knew to think.[22]
Had Fate, propitious to my Wish, assign'd
Me, wayward Girl, of Man's *superior* kind;
This strong Propensity had marr'd each Scheme,
And Prudence yielded to a golden Dream.
Perhaps I'd then been bred a learn'd Divine,
With *Greek* and *Hebrew* in this Head of mine;   10
With musty Classics stuff'd, dry Grammar Rules,
And all the specious Lumber of the Schools:
Yet had an Itch for scribbling fill'd my Brain,
This Care and Cost had been bestow'd in vain.
   Or had I, studious of the healing Art,

---

22. Throughout this poem, Darwall loosely imitates Alexander Pope's apologia, *Epistle to Dr. Arbuthnot* (1735), which begins with the image of the "Dog-star" (3), which brings out aspiring poets. He asks, "Why did I write? what sin to me unknown / Dipt me in Ink, my Parent's, or my own?" (lines 125–26).

Been taught with Care to act old *Galen*'s[23] Part,
Perus'd *Hippocrates*'s[24] labour'd Page,
And thumb'd with Rev'rence each time-honour'd Sage;
Yet when from College Rules and Orders free,

20   My Pen had once regain'd its Liberty;
Thoughtless of Gain, and warm with fancy'd Fire,
I certainly had quitted *Mead*[25] and *Floyer*,[26]
For *Milton, Shakespear, Dryden, Pope,* and *Young;*[27]
And left *Sanctorius*[28] for an idle Song:
Strother,[29] *Boerhaave,*[30] and *Celsus,*[31] had giv'n way
To a smart Satire or a Roundelay:[32]
For who bemus'd, and in a rhyming Strain,
Cou'd mark the various Fibres of the Brain?
Leave all the dear Ideas Fancy forms,

30   To learn the strange Effect of *Snails* and *Worms?*
Try with what Qualities each Drug is fraught,
And praise the Virtues of some nauseous Draught?
Had I been bred at *Gray*'s or *Lincoln*'s Inn,[33]

23. Galen (AD 129–216) was a Greek physician, writer, and philosopher who exercised a dominant influence on medical theory and practice in Europe from the Middle Ages until the mid-seventeenth century.

24. The Greek physician Hippocrates (460–375 BC) is traditionally regarded as the father of medicine.

25. Richard Mead (1673–1754) was a leading eighteenth-century British physician who contributed to the study of preventive medicine. He published more than sixteen central textbooks that went through multiple editions throughout the century.

26. Sir John Floyer (1649–1734), a physician, wrote *The Touchstone of Medicines*, 2 vols. (1687–90).

27. The five poets named in this line were considered central to the English tradition. They include: John Milton (1608–74), author of *Paradise Lost;* the Elizabethan dramatist and poet William Shakespeare (1564–1616); the dramatist and poet John Dryden (1631–1700); the poet Alexander Pope (1688–1744); and the poet Edward Young (1683–1756), author of *Night Thoughts* and *The Universal Passion,* which had gone through two dozen editions by 1765. Young, although less well known today than the others named here, was considered one of the premier poets of his period.

28. Sanctorius (1561–1636), an Italian physician, was the author of *De Statica Medicina* (1614), the first systematic study of basal metabolism.

29. Edward Strother (1675–1737), a physician, wrote numerous medical works, including *Criticon Febrium* (1716), *Dissertations upon the Ingraftment of the Small-Pox* (1722), and *An Essay on Sickness and Health* (1725).

30. Hermann Boerhaave (1668–1738) is often regarded as the greatest physician of the eighteenth century. His publications include *Institutiones Medicae* (1708), *Aphorismi de Cognoscendis et Curandis Morbis* (1709), and *Elementa Chemiæ* (1724).

31. Aulus Cornelius Celsus (first century AD), Roman medical writer, author of *De Medicina,* now considered one of the finest medical classics.

32. A short simple song with a refrain.

33. Two of the four Inns of Court, the legal societies and their physical location, which have the exclusive right of admitting persons to practice at the bar and offer instruction and examination in the law.

'Mid Law-suits, empty Quibbles, Doubts, and Din,
Attended duly at the wrangling Hall,
And learnt to *baffle, bluster, bounce*, and *bawl:*
Yet with Impatience in the long Vacation,
I shou'd have left this profitable Station;
Have quitted *Salkeld*[34] and the Lawyer's Gown,
And all the gay Amusements of the Town;   40
Have fled in Raptures to the peaceful *Grange*,[35]
And left *Coke*,[36] *Carthew*,[37] *Nelson*,[38] *Wood*,[39] and *Strange*,[40]
Hughes,[41] *Hale*,[42] and *Hawkins*,[43] *Bacon*,[44] *King*,[45] and *Cay*,[46]
For *Swift, Hill, Congreve, Cowley, Garth*, and *Gay*:[47]
And in some Cot,[48] retir'd from Crowd and Noise,
Have sought serene Delights and rural Joys;
Mus'd by a Fountain, slept beneath a Tree;

34. William Salkeld (1671–1715), sergeant-at-law and law reporter. He was well known for his legal reports, and his *Reports of Cases adjudg'd in the Court of King's Bench, 1689–1712* (1717–18) became the standard work for that period and was reprinted throughout the century.

35. Country house.

36. Sir Edward Coke (1552–1634), lawyer and legal writer. His four *Institutes of the Laws of England* (1628) went through at least ten editions in the eighteenth century.

37. Thomas Carthew (1657–1704), lawyer. His *Reports of Cases Adjudged in the Court of King's Bench from 3 Jac. II to 12 Will. III* was published by his son Thomas in 1728.

38. William Nelson (b. 1652/53), legal writer who published *Office and Authority of a Justice of Peace* (1704) and the three-volume *Abridgment of the Common Law* (1725–26).

39. Thomas Wood (1661–1722), a lawyer and jurist, published *A New Institute of the Imperial or Civil Law* (1704), *Some Thoughts Concerning the Study of the Laws of England* (1708), and *An Institute of the Laws of England* (1720).

40. Hamon L'Estrange (bap. 1674, d. 1767), legal and religious writer who published *The Justices' Law* (1720).

41. William Hughes (1587/88–c. 1663), translator and compiler of the three-volume collection *The Grand Abridgement of the Law Continued* (1660–63).

42. Sir Matthew Hale (1609–76), judge and author of *The History and Analysis of the Common Law of England* (1713), published posthumously throughout the eighteenth century.

43. William Hawkins (1681/82–1750) best known as the author of *A Treatise of the pleas of the Crown*, 2 vols. (1716–21).

44. Francis Bacon (1561–1626), though remembered now primarily as a philosopher, authored *Law Tracts* (1737), which was republished throughout the eighteenth century.

45. Peter King (1669–1734) was chief justice (1714–25) and Lord Chancellor (1725–33) of the Court of King's Bench.

46. John Cay (1700–1757), legal writer who published *The Statutes at Large, from Magna Charta, to the 30th Geo. II* (1758). His son, Henry Boult Cay, continued to publish supplements to his father's earlier work.

47. The poet and satirist Jonathan Swift (1667–1745), the poet and author Aaron Hill (1685–1750), the playwright William Congreve (1670–1729), the poet Abraham Cowley (1618–67), the physician and poet Sir Samuel Garth (1660/61–1719), and the playwright and poet John Gay (1685–1732). Swift, Pope, and Gay were members of the Scriblerus Club, which collaboratively produced works after 1714. Congreve and Garth were members of the Kit-Cat Club, founded by leading Whigs, including Addison and Steele.

48. Cottage.

And,'stead of Draughts,[49] compos'd—an Elegy.
Inspir'd by *Silvia*'s Eyes, or *Daphne*'s Air,
Or *Cynthia*'s[50] rosy Cheeks, and curling Hair;
My most exalted Wish, and only Aim,
Had been to eternize the fav'rite Dame:[51]
Her Charms in softest Numbers to express,
And paint my Passion in the liveliest Dress.
 In short, whatever my Employ had been,
It soon had yielded to this darling *Sin:*
And nought but *Russel*'s Land,[52] or *Gideon*'s Purse,[53]
Had sav'd the Poet—from—the Poet's Curse.

(1764)

The Author's Plea
Jane Cave Winscom

Who with a Critic's eye this book runs o'er,
Detects perhaps, a thousand faults, and more,
Impartially the Author's plea must hear,
And then perhaps will cease to be severe.

 When reason first adorn'd my infant mind,
To books and poetry my heart inclin'd,
And as my years advanc'd, the passion grew,
And fair ideas round my fancy flew.
The Muses seem'd to court me for their friend,
But Fortune would not to their suit[54] attend;
She understood who proper subjects were,
To hold a converse with these airy fair,
Must be possess'd at least of independence,
That to the Muses they may give attendance,

50

10

49. Formal legal order for the payment of money.
 50. The names Silvia, Daphne, and Cynthia are commonly used in pastoral poetry.
 51. Muse.
 52. John Russell (1710–71), fourth Duke of Bedford, though a career politician, devoted much of his energy to his estates and urban lands, both of which were considerable. Additionally, he was an advocate of street improvement near his home in London.
 53. Samson Gideon (1699–1762), financier with an unrivaled command of the financial market during the first half of the eighteenth century. At the time of his death his fortune was £350,000.
 54. Appeal; legal act of supplication or suing.

By books and study fructify the mind,
And lead the genius where it was inclin'd.
The inauspicious Dame deny'd that I,
Should thus, where Nature's self inclin'd, apply;
For she perceiv'd, I did the Muse befriend,
And could my days in contemplation spend,   20
Yet so contracted, circumscrib'd my line,
I paus'd—if to discard the tuneful Nine.

   Now duty calls my thoughts a different way;
Justice enjoins; I must her call obey.
So when the Muses come on anxious wing,
Some pleasing subject to my fancy[55] bring,
I bid them fly where peaceful leisure rests,
I have no time to entertain such guests.
They oft affect a deafness, draw more near,
Declare that they can no repulses bear,   30
Demand admittance, vow they are inclin'd,
To stay till they imprint it on my mind.

   Sometimes they are less bold, more shyly come,
And with indiff'rence ask if I'm at home.
If duty will admit, I ask them in,
When some engaging converse they begin;
But ere, perhaps, the conversation's o'er,
Duty commands that we converse no more.
Now Duty's call, I never must refuse,
I rise,—and with a blush myself excuse;   40
Tell them I must withdraw a while, and when
Duty admits, I will return again.
Sometimes till I return, they deign to stay,
Sometimes they take offence, and fly away,
And never on that subject visit more,
But bid me Fate's contracted hand deplore.

   Thus, what the Author to the World presents,
Appears through numberless impediments;

---

55. A creative faculty, usually treated as lighter and more whimsical and playful than imagination or as an assistant to it. Imagination, with the power to transform its material, was considered the higher power.

And what of praise, or of dispraise you view,
50   To Nature and the Muse is wholly due;
This, she presumes, will candid minds suffice,
And for her each defect apologize.

(1783)

Woman's Frailty

Esther Lewis Clark

I Lately quarrel'd with my pen,
And vow'd I'd never write agen,
But women's vows, alas! how frail,
I cannot stop 'till paper fail:
For 'till each scrip[56] of that be gone,
My pen's bewitch'd and will go on,
For tho' I'm stupid as that fowl,
Which is in English call'd an owl,
I cannot make my pen lie still,
10   Was ever such a stubborn quill.

(1789)

Sources

Killigrew: *Poems* (London, 1686), 82; Rowe: *Poems on Several Occasions. Written by Philomela* (London, 1696), 6–9; Finch: *The Poems of Anne Countess of Winchilsea*, ed. Myra Reynolds (Chicago: University of Chicago Press, 1903), 13; Thomas: *Miscellany Poems on Several Subjects* (London, 1722), 181–86; Leapor: *Poems upon Several Occasions* (London, 1748), 224–26; Darwall: *Original Poems on Several Occasions. By Miss Whateley* (London, 1764), 13–16; Winscom: *Poems on Various Subjects, Entertaining, Elegiac, and Religious* (Winchester, 1783), 1–5; Clark: *Poems Moral and Entertaining* (Bath, 1789), 152.

56. Small piece or scrap of paper, usually with writing on it.

⊀F⊁

The Nightingale in Poetry

Hans Christian Andersen creates an exquisite imperial garden surrounding a bejeweled porcelain castle in his fairy tale *The Nightingale* (1844). At the edge of the garden, a beautiful forest with delightful lakes stretches to the ocean. People come from all over the world to enjoy the castle and the gardens, and the most exquisite and unforgettable experience for them is hearing the song of the nightingale that lives in the forest. Even laborers and poor fishermen pause and listen when the nightingale sings. At the end of the fairy tale, the emperor is revived from near death by a visit from this bird, whose transcendent song banishes "the evil visions and Death himself" from the emperor's mind. Such is the power of this small, nondescript, "secretive" brown bird[1] to inspire.

Great poets have always written poems identifying the poet with the nightingale and celebrating the power of its song. We conclude this anthology with some women's contributions to this important tradition. Scores of allusions to the nightingale appear in this anthology, and the poems in this section affirm the bird's power to give rise to art and to the construction of the poetic identity. The nightingale's song is unlike that of any other bird; one of the group of "open-ended learners," a nightingale can develop more than 180 song types. It sings throughout the night, and with the coming of dawn its song becomes louder and more joyous. Rich and loud, its song, like poetry, has many phrases and repetitions; it is "exquisite in variety and tune, especially the deep, low sustained notes."[2] Poems about the nightingale try to capture its song; several are odes, the most musical of the poetic forms. The central section of Anne Finch's poem captures the bird's trills with sound effects such as alliteration and rising and falling emphases. Mary Robinson does the same in the part of her poem that begins, "The ling'ring cadence doth prolong? / Ah! tell me, tell me, why, / Thy dulcet Notes ascend the sky."

There were two well-known myths about the nightingale, but since one has been all but forgotten, allusions to it are often confusing to modern readers. The best-known today is the Greek one to which Sarah Dixon and Catherine Talbot refer, that of Philomela, sister to Procne. According to this myth, Procne married Tereus, and when Philomela came to visit, he tricked her into believing that Procne was dead and forced her into marriage. When she discovered the truth, he cut out her tongue so that she could not tell, but she wove a tapestry that revealed the crime. Procne found Philomela, and they wept together. While they were mourning, Tereus and Procne's son entered the room, and Procne said, "How like your father you are." In revenge for Tereus's act, Procne killed the son, made a stew from his flesh, and served it to Tereus. Enraged, Tereus prepared to kill the women, but the gods turned them all into birds: Tereus became a hawk or hoopoe; Procne a nightingale, whose song is the saddest because she never forgot the son she killed; and Philomela, since she had no tongue, a swallow, a bird that twitters and cannot sing. The Romans changed the fraudulent marriage into a rape and reversed the women. Philomela became the nightingale, who retreated to the deep woods and ceaselessly mourned her rape in song.[3]

A second, now less familiar source of allusions comes from Christian iconography and myths. Sarah Dixon's poem *The Nightingal* begins with a reference to the classical myth, then draws on the bird's natural characteristics and adds a hint of the Christian associations. Persecuted Christians in the subterranean sanctuaries of Rome painted the bird, and it was depicted in the medieval bestiaries singing its sweetest notes to herald the dawn and singing louder and sweeter at the moment when the "sun shoots forth its first rays."[4] Dixon writes, "every Glory of the *Spring* be thine," and the bird was a harbinger of spring associated with joy, the renewal of life, and Easter. In the late Middle Ages an image of the nightingale pressing her breast against a thorn became important in Christian allegories. Some were humble, as is the comparison between the nightingale singing to stay awake to warm and protect her young and an old woman grinding corn or washing late into the night for her children. An influential tale by Julius Spearatus has the bird teaching humankind "to stay awake to fulfill his duty cheerfully" and to remain vigilant against evil.[5] It became common to depict the bird building nests in thorny bushes or making nests out of thorn branches and pressing her breast against a thorn to stay awake to guard against serpents after her young. The serpent, of course, is a traditional symbol of the devil. From being the dutiful, watchful servant of God, the nightingale came to represent the Virgin Mary or Christ. The self-sacrifice, the crown of thorns, mourning for humankind, and Bible stories about watching through the night allowed the identification between the bird and Mary or Jesus. Through books by John Peckham and John of Hoveden, the name of this nightingale symbol became Philomena,[6] and readers of poetry of the period need to distinguish between Philomena and Philomela.

In ancient mythology the nightingale was also identified with the poet and the singer. For example, after the Thracian maidens ripped Orpheus into pieces, the Muses gathered the fragments and buried them at Libethra, and the nightingale was said "to sing over his grave more sweetly than in any other part of

Greece."[7] Today reference books often assign the identification of bird with poet to the Romantic and Victorian periods, but it is clear that women poets were making this identification throughout most of the eighteenth century and in a variety of ways that are found more often in later periods. Finch, Talbot, and Anne Bannerman refer to the freedom of the nightingale's song, with its unrestrained melodies, pitch, and volume. Neither Finch's nor Mary Robinson's poems refer to the myths, and they are interesting examples of changes in poetic taste. Finch begins with a joyous comparison between the bird's nature and her aspirations and concludes with a fable that contrasts the birds to poets. Robinson finds comfort in the bird's song and imagines herself joining it, but in the end her sorrow, like that of Goethe's *Werther*, is too impenetrable. Both she and Anne Bannerman use the trope to explore the sources of sorrow and melancholy. As melancholy became the great mood of poetic inspiration in the second half of the eighteenth century, allusions to the nightingale became more frequent, and the sonnets by Charlotte Smith, in which the bird is a central image for the poetic voice (1.B), are good illustrations of the ways the conceit could be deployed.

Notes

1. Michael Allaby, ed., *Dictionary of Zoology*, http://www.oxfordreference.com/views/ ENTRY.html?subview=main+entry=t8.e9178, s.v. "turdidae."

2. Percy Trett, "Nightingale," in *Birds of Britain* (March 2007), www.birdsofbritain .co.uk/bird-guide/nightingale.htm; Sarah Kiefer, Anne Spiess, Silke Kipper, et al., "First-Year Common Nightingales (Luscinia megarhynchos) Have Smaller Song-Type Repertoire Sizes than Older Males," *Ethology* 112 (2006): 1217.

3. See Edith Hamilton, *Mythology* (1940; New York: Signet, 1969), 270–71. This retelling is largely based on Ovid, *Metamorphoses* 6; see Appollodorus mythographus, *Bibliotheca*, pt. 3, 193ff.

4. Louis Charbonneau-Lassay, *The Bestiary of Christ*, trans. D. M. Dooling (New York: Penguin, 1940), 224; he is quoting Saint Bonaventure.

5. Carol Maddison, "'Brave Prick Song': An Answer to Sir Thomas Browne," *Modern Language Notes* 75 (1960): 470. Our information about this second source of imagery comes largely from this essay, 468–78.

6. Peckham allegorized the last day of a dying nightingale into a divine office for the day and the story of salvation from creation. Some editors have assumed that poets misspell *Philomela* when they write "Philomena." *Hoveden* is spelled "Howden," and *Peckham* is spelled "Pecham," in the *Oxford Dictionary of National Biography*. I have used Maddison's spellings. On these medieval books, see Maddison, "Brave Prick Song," 473–75. We are grateful to Lacy Marschalk for her research on this topic.

7. *Bulfinch's Mythology* (New York: Avenel Books, 1979), 187; this edition is a collection of three of Thomas Bulfinch's reference books.

To the Nightingale
Anne Finch

Exert thy Voice, sweet Harbinger of Spring!
  This Moment is thy Time to sing,
  This Moment I attend to Praise,
And set my Numbers[1] to thy Layes.[2]
  Free as thine shall be my Song;
  As thy Musick, short, or long.
Poets, wild as thee, were born,
  Pleasing best when unconfin'd,
  When to Please is least design'd,
Soothing but their Cares to rest;
  Cares do still their Thoughts molest,
  And still th' unhappy Poet's Breast,
Like thine, when best he sings, is plac'd against a Thorn.
She begins, Let all be still!
  Muse, thy Promise now fulfill!
Sweet, oh! sweet, still sweeter yet
Can thy Words such Accents fit,
Canst thou Syllables refine,
Melt a Sense that shall retain
Still some Spirit of the Brain,
Till with Sounds like these it join.
  'Twill not be! then change thy Note;
  Let division shake thy Throat.
Hark! Division now she tries;
Yet as far the Muse outflies.
  Cease then, prithee, cease thy Tune;
  Trifler, wilt thou sing till *June?*
Till thy Bus'ness all lies waste,
And the Time of Building's past!
  Thus we Poets that have Speech,
Unlike what thy Forests teach,
  If a fluent Vein be shown
  That's transcendent to our own,

10

20

30

---

1. Poetics; shorthand for rhyme, meter, and other poetic features.
2. Ballads; lyric or narrative poems meant to be sung.

Criticize, reform, or preach,
Or censure what we cannot reach.

(1713)

The Nightingal
Sarah Dixon

Forgive me, *Philomel,* if I no more
Can *Tereus* matchless Cruelty deplore;
I must believe thy Sense of Grief is past,
Who so melodiously the Night canst waste,
Nor can the pointed Thorn annoy thy Breast,
Was ever Sorrow in such Notes exprest?
O, no, the Gods, in Pity to thy Wrong,
Gave in Exchange, for a frail Woman's Tongue,   }
A lasting Power to please with thy inimitable Song.
Indulgent of thy Fate, they now assign,   10
That every Glory of the *Spring* be thine;
Where, undisturb'd, thou may'st its Joys possess,
And listening Ears, with me, thy tuneful Numbers[3] bless.

(1740)

Sonnet: In the Manner of Petrarch—
Catherine Talbot

The nightingale that sits on Yonder spray,
   Tho' all of night she plains her hapless Fate,
   Yet since she can in liberty relate
Her griefs, that freedom does those griefs allay.—
But I, aye me! must all the livelong day,
Conceal with sembled[4] cheer a cheerless state,
Nor for dark night does that restraint abate,

---

3. Poetics; shorthand for rhyme, meter, and other poetic features.
4. Pretended, seeming.

Since Reasons eye supplies a brighter ray,
Forbidding every fond delusive thought,
10   Sitting in rigid Judgment on my heart;
And against each gay dream by Fancy wrought,
Taking *Stern Wisdoms* harsh & angry part;
Respect thyself it cries, nor in thy mind,
Harbor one Image that it durst not show,
Restrain thy looks, thy Sighs, & every kind
Indulgence, of a Vain, Imagined Woe.

(1758)

Ode to the Nightingale
Mary Robinson

SWEET BIRD OF SORROW!—why complain
In such soft melody of Song,
That ECHO,[5] am'rous of thy Strain,
The ling'ring cadence doth prolong?
Ah! tell me, tell me, why,
Thy dulcet Notes ascend the sky.
Or on the filmy vapours glide
Along the misty mountain's side?
And wherefore dost Thou love to dwell,
10   In the dark wood and moss-grown cell,
Beside the willow-margin'd stream—
Why dost Thou court wan Cynthia's[6] beam?
Sweet Songstress—if thy wayward fate
Hath robb'd Thee of thy bosom's mate,
Oh, think not thy heart-piercing moan
Evap'rates on the breezy air,
Or that the plaintive Song of Care
Steals from THY Widow'd Breast alone.
Oft have I heard thy mournful Tale,
20   On the high Cliff, that o'er the Vale
Hangs its dark brow, whose awful shade

5. Nymph deprived of speech by Hera in order to stop her chatter; she could do nothing but repeat what others said. She fell in love with Narcissus, who rejected her, and in her grief wasted away until nothing but her voice remained.
6. The moon's.

Spreads a deep gloom along the glade:
Led by its sound, I've wander'd far,
Till crimson evening's flaming Star
On Heav'n's vast dome refulgent[7] hung,
And round ethereal vapours flung;
And oft I've sought th' HYGEIAN MAID,[8]
In rosy dimpling smiles array'd,
Till forc'd with every HOPE to part,
Resistless Pain subdued my Heart.   30

Oh then, far o'er the restless deep
    Forlorn my poignant pangs I bore,
Alone in foreign realms to weep,
    Where ENVY's voice could taunt no more.
I hop'd, by mingling with the gay,
To snatch the veil of Grief away;
I hop'd, amid the joyous train,
To break Affliction's pond'rous chain;
VAIN was the Hope—in vain I sought
The placid hour of careless thought,   40
Where Fashion wing'd her light career,
    And sportive Pleasure danc'd along,
    Oft have I shunn'd the blithsome throng,
To hide th' involuntary tear,
        For e'en where rapt'rous transports glow,
From the full Heart the conscious tear will flow,
When to my downy couch remov'd,
    FANCY recall'd my wearied mind
    To scenes of FRIENDSHIP left behind,
Scenes still regretted, still belov'd!   50
Ah, then I felt the pangs of Grief,
Grasp my warm Heart, and mock relief;
    My burning lids Sleep's balm defied,
And on my fev'rish lip imperfect murmurs died.

Restless and sad—I sought once more
A calm retreat on BRITAIN's shore;
Deceitful HOPE, e'en there I found

7. Shining brilliantly.
8. The goddess of health, Hygieia.

That soothing FRIENDSHIP's specious name
Was but a short-liv'd empty sound,
60   And LOVE a false delusive flame.

Then come, Sweet BIRD, and with thy strain,
Steal from my breast the thorn of pain;
Blest solace of my lonely hours,
In craggy caves and silent bow'rs,
When HAPPY Mortals seek repose,
By Night's pale lamp we'll chaunt our woes,
And, as her chilling tears diffuse
O'er the white thorn their silv'ry dews,
I'll with the lucid boughs entwine
70   A weeping Wreath, which round my Head
Shall by the waning Crescent shine,
    And light us to our leafy bed. —
But ah! nor leafy beds nor bow'rs
Fring'd with soft MAY's enamell'd flow'rs,
Nor pearly leaves, nor Cynthia's beams,
Nor smiling Pleasure's shad'wy dreams,
Sweet BIRD, not e'en THY melting Strains
Can calm the Heart, where TYRANT SORROW REIGNS.

(1791)

Ode V. To the Nightingale
Anne Bannerman

Translation of the 15th Ode of Rousseau.[9]

I.
Why, plaintive warbler! tell me why
    For ever sighs thy troubled heart?
Cannot these groves, that glowing sky,
    A solace to thy woes impart?
Shall spring his blooming wreaths entwine,
To circle every brow, but thine?

9. Jean-Jacques Rousseau (1712–78), Swiss-born French author and intellectual. This poem was first published in the *Edinburgh Magazine*, 11 (1798): 64–64, perhaps from a draft copy.

II.

See! nature, at thy wish'd return,
　　Renews her robe of gayest green;
And can thy wayward bosom mourn,
　　When nature wakes the vernal[10] scene;　　　　　10
When every dryad[11] lends her shade,
For thine and contemplation's aid.

III.

See! from thy haunts the stormy north
　　His surly blasts leads far away;
Each blossom of the teeming earth,
　　The glories of the op'ning day;
The promise of the coming year,
All, all, sweet bird, for thee appear

IV.

For thee, Aurora[12] steeps in dews
　　The new-born flow'rets of the dale;　　　　　20
For thee, with liberal hand, she strews
　　Her fragrance on the western gale;
And rifles all the sweets of morn,
To deck her fav'rite's mossy thorn.

V.

Hark! while thy sad strain seems to tell
　　Some mournful tale of luckless love;
On each soft note's ecstatic swell,
　　In silence hang the warbling grove;
And e'en the fowler loves to spare
The Poet of the midnight air.　　　　　30

VI.

O! if a friend's untimely tomb
　　Bids all that tide of sorrow flow;
Alas! ev'n there, thy wretched doom
　　Is mercy to my weight of woe;

10. Spring.
11. Tree nymph.
12. Goddess of the dawn.

For pain now past, thy bosom sighs;
Mine, present always,—never flies.

VII.
Thee, bounteous nature blooms to cheer,
    And beauty smiles, thy woes to still;
To nature, love, and pity dear,
40   Well may'st thou yield thy load of ill,
To beings, as forlorn as I,[13]
    Denied the freedom of a tear,
The rapture[14] of a single sigh.

(1800)

Sources

Finch: *Miscellany Poems, On Several Occasions* (London, 1713), 200–202; Dixon: *Poems on Several Occasions* (Canterbury, 1740), 59; Talbot: Rhoda Zuk, ed., *Catherine Talbot and Hester Chapone, Bluestocking Feminism: Writings of the Bluestocking Circle, 1738–1785,* vol. 3 (London: Pickering & Chatto, 1999), 158; Robinson: *Poems by Mrs. M. Robinson,* 2 vols. (London, 1791), 1:29–32; Bannerman: *Poems by Anne Bannerman* (Edinburgh, 1800), 71–73.

13. While only beings as forlorn as I. MRS. SMITH. *Bannerman.* [Bannerman is quoting a sonnet that first appeared in Charlotte Smith's *Montalbert. A Novel,* 3 vols. (London, 1795), 3:188, and then in *Elegiac Sonnets and Other Poems,* 8th ed., 2 vols. (London, 1797), 2:8. *Eds.*]

14. The rapture of a single tear. SCHILLER. *Bannerman.* [Johann Christoph Friedrich von Schiller (1759–1805) was a German poet, dramatist, historian, and philosopher. *Eds.*]

BIOGRAPHIES OF THE POETS

Information in these biographical sketches is from the *Oxford Dictionary of National Biography*; the *Dictionary of Literary Biography*; Philip H. Highfill Jr., Kalman A. Burnim, and Edward A. Langhans's *Biographical Dictionary of Actors, Actresses, Musicians, Dancers, Managers & Other Stage Personnel in London, 1660–1800*; Joanne Shattock's *Oxford Guide to British Women Writers*; Paula R. Backscheider's *Eighteenth-Century Women Poets and Their Poetry*; Roger Lonsdale's *Eighteenth-Century Women Poets*; Janet Todd's *Dictionary of British and American Women Writers, 1660–1800*; Paul Schlueter and June Schlueter's *Encyclopedia of British Women Writers*; Virginia Blain, Isobel Grundy, and Patricia Clements's *Feminist Companion to Literature in English*; Frederic Rowton's *Female Poets of Great Britain*; Joyce Fullard's *British Women Poets, 1660–1800*; Paula R. Feldman's *British Women Poets of the Romantic Era; Scottish Women Poets of the Romantic Period*, ed. Nancy Kushigian and Stephen Behrendt (http://asp6new.alexanderstreet .com/swrp); the Orlando Project; prefaces to the women's poetry; and sources cited here and throughout the anthology.

ALCOCK, MARY CUMBERLAND (c. 1741–1798). Alcock, the youngest of four children of Bishop Denison Cumberland and Joanna Bentley and sister to the novelist and playwright Richard Cumberland (1732–1811), lived with her family in Stanwick, Northamptonshire, and then Clonfert, Galway, Ireland, when her father was appointed to the Church of Ireland there. In Ireland, Alcock married, although her husband has been misidentified and his identity remains uncertain; her brother's letters suggest that the marriage was not happy. After caring for her father and mother until their deaths in 1774 and 1775, respectively, she moved to Bath. There she, like her brother, participated in the literary circle of Lady Anne Miller. This association may have encouraged her first publication, *The Air Balloon; or, Flying Mortal* (1784), a poem that displays, as does much of her work, a concern with political and social issues. Money earned from her poetry allowed Alcock to support her sister's seven orphans and various charities. Her niece Joanna Hughes published a posthumous collection of her poems and other work,

Poems &c. &c. by the Late Mrs Mary Alcock (1799), a collection to which Elizabeth Carter and Hannah More subscribed.

BAILLIE, JOANNA (1762–1851). Baillie moved from Glasgow, where she had been educated at a good boarding school, to London in 1784, after the death of her father, a professor of divinity at the University of Glasgow. In London her mother's famous brother, John Hunter, and his wife, the poet Anne, opened a distinguished intellectual society to her. A member of the Church of Scotland, she became part of Rochemont Barbauld's congregation in Hampstead. In 1790 she published *Poems* anonymously (identified by Roger Lonsdale in 1984 as different from *Fugitive Verses*) and became one of the best-known women writers of the day with her *Plays on the Passions*. John Philip Kemble and Sarah Siddons starred in the Drury Lane production of *De Monfort* (1800). Baillie continued to write poetry and became a popular composer of songs and ballads, many of them Scottish in derivation.

BANNERMAN, ANNE (1765–1829). An Edinburgh woman, Bannerman came to Robert Anderson's attention when she published two sonnets and a translation of Rousseau's fifteenth ode in the *Edinburgh Magazine*. Her poems include translations from Italian as well. An acquaintance, Sydney Smith, a founder of the *Edinburgh Review*, described her as a "crooked poetess" because of a physical deformity. Bannerman published *Poems By Anne Bannerman* in 1800 and, with the help of Anderson and his contacts, *Tales of Superstition and Chivalry* (1802), which is considered her most important work today. Impoverishment unrelieved by a revised, subscription edition of *Poems* (1807) led to her becoming a governess in Exeter and, as far as we know, ended her publishing career.

BARBAULD, ANNA LAETITIA AIKIN (1743–1825). The very well educated daughter of a Nonconformist minister in Warrington, Lancashire, Barbauld knew five languages, including Greek and Latin, and worked much of her life as a teacher. She published her first volume of poems in 1773 and, with her brother John, *Miscellaneous Pieces in Prose* in the same year. In 1774 she married Rochemont Barbauld, who later became unstable and finally committed suicide. She was one of the most prolific writers and editors of her time; in addition to poetry, she wrote political and pedagogical tracts and was an important author of children's literature. Among her projects were editing Samuel Richardson's correspondence and the fifty-volume *British Novelists*.

BARBER, MARY (1690?–1757). Barber was the wife of an English woolen draper in Dublin and the mother of four children. Jonathan Swift described her as "wholly turn'd to Poetry" and Ireland's "chief poetess." She had published several poems before she met Swift, including a progress of poetry and strongly worded appeals on behalf of a military officer's widow. Poverty drove her to England, and she lived in Bath intermittently. Her *Poems on Several Occasions* (1734) was published by subscription. Rheumatism and gout crippled her hands and feet, and she appears to have given up writing. She died in Ireland, to which she had returned in the early 1740s.

BARKER, JANE (bap. 1652; d. 1732). Baptized in Blatherwycke, Northamptonshire, Barker was largely self-educated, although her beloved brother Edward tutored her in Latin and even medicine. Her poems in *Poetical Recreations* (1688) may have been given to the bookseller by her circle of St. John's College, Cambridge, friends, with whom she had exchanged poetry for many years. She later corrected them for the Magdalen Manuscript, Oxford. She became a Catholic and by 1689 had followed the exiled Stuart court to St. Germain-en-Laye. Her political poetry, especially her verse history *Poems Refering to the Times,* is among the best surviving Jacobite poetry. Her father bequeathed the lease to his Wilsthorp estate to her; she became its manager in 1704 and by 1710 she was responsible for two young grandnieces. During this period she wrote the prose fictions that are now recognized as among the most innovative and significant of the early English novels; *Love Intrigues* (1713) is the best known. She returned to France in 1727 and died there.

BEHN, APHRA (1640?–1689). Often considered the first professional woman writer, Behn was one of the most prolific, well known, and versatile authors of her period. Whether writing drama, prose fiction, or poetry, Behn consistently interrogated dominant constructions of gender, power relationships within marriage, and the nature of human sexuality. Likely from Kent, she appears to have acted as a spy for King Charles II during the latter years of the Interregnum and the early years of the Restoration. During this period she also spent some time in the English colony of Surinam and married a merchant of German extraction. Her first play was produced in 1670, and for the next dozen years roughly one new play a year appeared on the London stage. The 1680s, Behn's greatest period of productivity, saw the publication of her first collection of poems, *Poems upon Several Occasions* (1684); her most notable fiction, such as *Oroonoko* (1688); and her continuation of *Lycidus* (1686), which included some of her most significant poems. Despite her prolific production, Behn consistently faced financial difficulties, and she was plagued by ill health in the 1680s and died in 1689.

BLAMIRE, SUSANNA (1747–1794). "The Muse of Cumberland" was reared and educated after her mother's death by her wealthy, widowed aunt in Thackwood. She was an accomplished musician, and some of her songs were printed as single sheets in the 1780s and included in collections such as *Calliope, or the Musical Miscellany* (1788). After her death, Patrick Maxwell and Henry Lonsdale devoted considerable effort to collecting her poems, and some, written on backs of recipes, came from relatives. The assembled poems were not published until 1842.

BOYD, ELIZABETH (fl. 1727–1745). Little is known of Boyd beyond what can be gleaned from her published work. The proposal for the subscription to her 1732 novel, *The Happy-Unfortunate,* describes her efforts to "settle" herself "in a Way of Trade; that may enable me to master those Exigencies of Fortune, which my long Illness hath for some Time past reduc'd me to suffer: That I may be capable of providing for my now ancient, indulgent Mother." Similarly, *The Snail* (1745), the sole printed issue of her monthly magazine, mentions that her "deceased Father" had "long and zealously serv'd the *Stuart* Family, in a credible Employ." Little else is known. Her first published poem, *Variety: a poem,* in 1727, was followed by a decade of activity that included a series of occasional poems; a miscellany of riddles and poems, *The Humorous Miscellany* (1733); an unproduced ballad opera, *Don Sancho* (1739); and her novel, which attracted 353 subscribers and was reissued in 1737 as *The Female Page.*

BRERETON, CHARLOTTE (b. 1720?). The younger daughter of Thomas and Jane Brereton, Charlotte Brereton collected and published a subscription edition of her mother's poems with a few of her own. Her father died in a swimming accident in February 1722, and her mother, who shortly thereafter moved the family to Wrexham, as Charlotte says, "for the benefit of the children's education," died in August 1740. Like her mother, she published poetry in the *Gentleman's Magazine,* and a few are reprinted in the volume of her mother's poetry, *Poems on Several Occasions. By Mrs. Jane Brereton* (1744). After her mother's death, she became a governess in the home of a Scottish family, probably that of Alexander Stewart, of Galloway House. Nothing is known of her later life.

BRERETON, JANE HUGHES (1685–1740). The well-educated daughter of a Bryn-Griffith, Wales, family married Thomas Brereton in 1711. They separated in 1721 because of his violent, intemperate personality; he drowned the next year. She began publishing individual poems in 1716 and was "Melissa" in a series of poems published in the *Gentleman's Magazine.* Her collected poems were published posthumously by subscription, perhaps for her daughters' benefit.

CARTER, ELIZABETH (1717–1806). Educated in classical languages and modern subjects with her brothers by her father, the perpetual curate of Deal Chapel, Carter published her first volume of poetry, *Poems upon Particular Occasions,* in 1738, and except for an edition of the works of Talbot (1780), the last publication of her lifetime was the third edition of the augmented 1762 *Poems on Several Occasions* in 1789. After her mother's death, she kept her father's house for forty-seven years. Inheritances and annuities from friends allowed her to maintain her independence. She was a respected translator and essayist and a patron of other women's writing. Her translation of Epictetus's *Works* remained the standard English translation at least until 1966.

CENTLIVRE, SUSANNA FREEMAN CARROLL (1669?–1723). Centlivre left her home in Lincolnshire while still young; her education has been described as owing to "her own Industry and Application." She was well read and probably knew French. A reasonably credible story describes her living at Cambridge with Anthony Hammond (later editor of *New Miscellany of Original Poems*, 1720, and a minor politician) as his cousin Jack and attending lectures at the university for a while. Her first publication was a poem in *The Nine Muses* (1700), the woman-authored tribute to mark John Dryden's death. She was one of the most successful dramatists of the period, having eighteen plays produced. Some, notably *The Basset-Table*, *The Busy Body*, and *The Wonder: A Woman Keeps a Secret*, held the stage well into the nineteenth century. She was an ardent Whig, which occasionally caused her legal problems, and most of her surviving poetry is political.

CHANDLER, MARY (1687–1745). A Nonconformist born in Wiltshire, Chandler opened a milliner's shop in Bath when she was about twenty years old. She cultivated her mind and knew both Elizabeth Singer Rowe and Mary Barber. She refers occasionally to her crooked spine, which she believed ruled out any hope of marriage. Her *My Own Epitaph* (1736), for instance, begins, "Here lies a true Maid, deformed and old." Her *Description of Bath* (1733) was immediately popular; beginning with its third edition, she added other poems.

CHAPONE, HESTER MULSO (1727–1801). Chapone managed her father's home from an early age and became a member of the Bluestocking circle of Elizabeth Carter and Elizabeth Montagu. Her first publication was in Samuel Johnson's *Rambler* (1750). In 1760 she married John Chapone, who died within nine months. From that point on because of economic straits she moved between friends' homes and that of her uncle, the bishop of Winchester. A plan for educating girls written for her niece, *Letters on the Improvement of the Mind. Addressed to a Young Lady* (1773), made Chapone famous. After her death, her relatives collected her writings and published a two-volume and a four-volume *Works and Life* (both 1807), which included her correspondence with Samuel Richardson.

CHUDLEIGH, LADY MARY LEE (1656–1710). Chudleigh was born and married in Devon, and her first publication was the provocative *Ladies Defence* (1700).

She was married at age seventeen and described her life as "solitary." She corresponded with learned women, including Mary Astell, and wrote throughout her life but published only in her last ten years. *Poems on Several Occasions* (1703) included poems such as *The Resolve* that were frequently anthologized throughout the century. She moved to Exeter for her health about 1703, suffered severely from rheumatism, and died an invalid.

CLARK, ESTHER LEWIS (c. 1716–1794). Little is known about the childhood and education of Clark, the only child of the Reverend John Lewis, of the parish church at Holt, and his wife, Esther. Her father, an antiquarian, may have encouraged her studies in the classics. She was inoculated for smallpox in the 1740s by the physician and poet Samuel Bowden who published a poem about the event. He also promoted her work, and they published poems together in various London periodicals about 1749, the same time that her works appeared in the *Bath Journal* under the name "Sylvia." Bowden's *Poems on Various Subjects* (1754) contains a number of pieces by Clark. During the 1750s and 1760s, she formed relationships with literary persons, including novelist Sarah Fielding. When her father died in November 1761, Clark may have been left without a home, but in October 1762, she married Robert Clark, of Tetbury, where she lived when she published the only collection of her poetry, *Poems Moral and Entertaining* (1789), for the benefit of charitable and religious institutions in Bath, Gloucester, and Tetbury.

COCKBURN, CATHARINE TROTTER (1674?–1749). Born of Scottish parents in London, Cockburn was the first woman since Aphra Behn to have a play produced at a royal theater (1695). By age fourteen she had already published a poem and *Olinda's Adventures,* a short novel. She married Patrick Cockburn in 1708, and they moved to Northumberland in 1726. In addition to plays and poems, she published philosophical essays and defenses of women's education and intellect as well. After her death, Thomas Birch published her *Works* in 1751.

COWPER, MARIA FRANCES CECILIA MADAN (1726–1797). Daughter of the poet Judith Madan (1702–81) and cousin to William Cowper (1731–1800), one of the best-known English poets of the eighteenth century, Cowper was born into a literary family that supported her interest in foreign languages and literature. In 1749 she married another cousin also named William Cowper (1721?–1769), a major in the Hertfordshire militia. The marriage produced seven children. Janet Todd notes that like her mother, a Methodist convert of John Wesley, Cowper became deeply religious and "fervently evangelical" and corresponded extensively with her cousin the poet William on spiritual subjects. After her husband's death in 1769, she moved to London, where her cousin William revised and helped her sell *Original Poems, on Various Occasions* (1792). The advertisement to the collection describes her poems as "the genuine fruits of retirement and leisure; . . . occasioned by such a series of adverse events, as led the Author to a peculiar habit of contemplating the ways of an all-wise, over-ruling Providence." She died in London on 15 October 1797.

DARWALL, MARY WHATELEY (1738–1825). Born in Beoley, Worcestershire, Darwall published her first poems in the *Gentleman's Magazine* (beginning in 1759). Her *Original Poems on Several Occasions by Miss Whateley* (1764) came out by well-organized subscription. In it, she described her poems as "the Amusements of Youth, Leisure, and Solitude." She married the vicar of Walsall in 1766, reared twelve children, and after his death in 1789 lived a fairly insecure life in the Midlands and Wales. In 1774 she was recognized as one of "the British Nine," and her modern biography argues that she is such a good subject for study because she was an ordinary woman coping with "being both a woman and a poet." *Poems on Several Occasions* (1794) was also published by subscription.

DIXON, SARAH (1672–1765). Dixon was born in Kent, and her *Poems on Several Occasions* was published by subscription in Canterbury in 1740. She was encouraged to publish by her niece, Elizabeth, and Elizabeth's husband, the vicar of St. Stephen's, near Canterbury. She described herself as beginning to write poetry when she was "a Youth of much Leisure." According to a manuscript note, she was still writing in her seventies.

EGERTON, SARAH FYGE FIELD (1670–1723). Egerton was born in London, and her first publication was the notorious *Female Advocate* (1686). *Poems on Several Occasions* was published in 1703. In spite of her critiques of marriage, she married twice, once to an attorney named Field and later to the Reverend Thomas Egerton. The Reverend Egerton took a young attorney's clerk to Chancery to recover a gift she had made him from her substantial legacy from Field. Sarah and Thomas sued each other unsuccessfully for divorce. When he died in 1720, she enjoyed a brief, economically secure widowhood. In spite of her tumultuous and somewhat scandalous life, she wrote in most of the verse forms of her time and made some of the strongest contributions to the "fair-sex debate." She was a respected poet in her time and contributed to a volume of memorial poems when Dryden died, *The Nine Muses* (1700).

FALCONAR, HARRIET (b. 1774?). Falconar's first publications were three poems in the February 1787 *European Magazine and London Review*. She was probably the daughter of Jane Hicks Falconar and the daughter or niece of the Scottish poet William Falconar. She and her sister Maria published three books of poetry:

Poems; Poems on Slavery: by Maria Falconar, aged 17, and Harriet Falconar, aged 14 (both 1788); and *Poetic Laurels for characters of distinguished merit: interspersed with poems, moral and entertaining* (1791). The sisters were something of a sensation, and their books were widely reviewed. *Poems on Slavery* is dedicated to William Dolben, author of the sensational 1788 report on conditions on slave ships and the mortality rates of slaves and British sailors and proposer of the 1799 Slave Limitation Bill, intended to regulate the number of slaves ships could carry.

FALCONAR, MARIA (b. 1771?). Maria Falconer was probably the daughter of Jane Hicks Falconar and the daughter or niece of the Scottish poet William Falconar. At some point the family lived in London, where they knew Richard Cosway, the principal painter to the Prince of Wales and engraver of his drawing of the sisters for the frontispiece for *Poetic Laurels* (1791). Although Falconar published a few poems in periodicals, most of her poetry came out in books with poetry by her younger sister Harriet. *Poems* (with more than four hundred prominent subscribers) and *Poems on Slavery: by Maria Falconar, aged 17, and Harriet Falconar, aged 14* appeared in 1788, when, according to the latter title, she was still a teenager. As Roger Lonsdale's introduction to an excerpt of their poetry suggests, they were part of a fad for poetry by precocious teenagers. *Poetic Laurels*, a nationalistic project celebrating the Prince of Wales, Richard Sheridan, the actor John Palmer, Queen Charlotte, and other prominent people, seems to have been their last book.

FINCH, ANNE KINGSMILL, COUNTESS OF WINCHILSEA (1661–1720). A member of an aristocratic family that had served the monarch since the twelfth century, Finch was orphaned at age three and became a maid of honor to Mary of Modena. She married Heneage Finch in 1684 and followed him into retirement after the demise of King James II. She circulated poems in manuscript, published a few poems in miscellanies, including Charles Gildon's and Delarivière Manley's, and *Miscellany Poems on Several Occasions* in 1713. Her poems are now routinely included in textbooks, and she is widely accepted as one of the two best women poets of the century. At her death she left many unpublished poems; the continued lack of a complete edition is remarkable.

GREVILLE, FRANCES MACARTNEY (1727?–1789). The daughter of Catherine Coote and the MP in Ireland for Longford and Granard, James Macartney, Greville grew up in London in the circle of the Prince of Wales. Frances married the socialite Fulke Greville, and they had seven children, five of whom survived into adulthood. Her husband, who aspired to the achievements of his sixteenth-century relative for whom he had been named, became abusive and repressive as Frances's poetry won praise. Betty Rizzo, her biographer, concludes that she no longer dared anything but secretive *vers de société*. Rizzo describes her as "a woman preeminently talented, clever, witty, beautiful, entertaining, deemed brilliant and, when she chose charming, . . . famous . . . for her verses . . . but scarcely less famous for the wit of her conversation and letters" (Rizzo, "The Frances Greville Letters: An Edition, Part 1," *Eighteenth-Century Women* 4 [2006]: 313). Fulke gambled the family fortune away, and Frances moved to Ireland under the protection of the Lennox daughters. She gained a legal separation in 1788 and rented a house on Sackville Street, in London, where she died in 1789.

GRIERSON, CONSTANTIA CRAWLEY (1706–1732). Although born to a poor, illiterate Irish country family, Grierson was given books by her father, and she became a poet and was responsible for editions of Terence and Tacitus. She was apprenticed to Laetitia Pilkington's father, the obstetrician John Van Lewen, and married George Grierson, a Scot who was the King's Printer in Dublin in 1725. Her poems are still being discovered (A. C. Elias announced finding a manuscript volume with ten of her poems in 1987), but most are probably lost.

HALE, MARTHA RIGBY (d. 1803). Hale was the daughter of Richard Rigby, of Mistley Hall, Essex, and married an army officer, Bernard Hale. She lived at Chelsea Hospital from 1773, where her husband was Lieutenant Governor. The preface to her *Poetical Attempts* describes the poems as "written in the thoughtless years of youth" and brought out for a benevolent purpose, to rescue "an amiable and worthy family from their present difficulties." The *Monthly Review* identified Hale as "a lady of fashion and fortune" whose charity was for a clergyman. The poems give some hint of the circles in which she moved; among them is a poem congratulating Catherine Eden Moore on bearing the first baby born in Lambeth Palace, the official residence of the archbishop of Canterbury, then John Moore. Two hundred thirty people, including dukes, earls, countesses, archbishops, and poets, subscribed to the volume.

HAMILTON, ELIZABETH (c. 1756–1816). Hamilton was primarily a novelist and essayist, although her verse capturing the dialect and romanticized attitudes of Scotland was tremendously popular. Born in Belfast, after 1762 Hamilton lived with her paternal aunt near Stirling when her widowed mother could no longer care for her children. Her early education was traditional, but she read widely and deeply. Hamilton was close to her brother Charles, who traveled with the East India Company, and in 1788 she moved with him to London, where he introduced her into literary society. Her first two works, *Translations of the Letters of a Hindoo Rajah* (1796), inspired by her brother's stories about India, and *Memoirs of Modern Philosophers* (1800) both satirized British society. Hamilton's *Letters on Education* (1801) is a series of essays promoting gender equality and morality as the basis of education. Her most popular and most widely reprinted work was *The Cottagers of Glenburnie* (1808), a satiric novel about the Scots. In 1804 Hamilton moved to Edinburgh and developed friendships with Sir Walter Scott, Maria Edgeworth, and Joanna Baillie.

HANDS, ELIZABETH HERBERT (1746–1815). For many years a servant, Hands had married a blacksmith by 1784. She described herself as "never emerging beyond the lower stations in life" in the dedication to her collection of poems, *The Death of Amnon: A Poem. With An Appendix: Containing Pastorals, and other Poetical Pieces,* which was published by subscription in Coventry in 1789. A few of her poems had appeared earlier in *Jopson's Coventry Mercury* and in a Birmingham newspaper. Donna Landry says of some of Hands's verse that "not since Swift have we seen comical satirical verse of the order" of hers. She was buried in Bourton-on-Dunsmore.

HARRISON, SUSANNAH (1752–1784). A domestic servant from age sixteen who taught herself to read and write, Harrison suffered a debilitating illness at age twenty from which she never recovered. Expecting to die, she gave her manuscripts to the Congregational minister John Condor, who edited the poems and published them for her as *Songs in the Night* (1780). There were at least twenty-one editions in Britain and America by 1823. The semi-invalid left 133 hymns, as well as other kinds of poems, some of which are still included in hymnals.

HOLT, JANE WISEMAN (d. 1717). Holt's origins are obscure until she became a servant to William Wright, recorder of Oxford, to whose large library she seems to have had access. She began *Antiochus the Great* there, and it was acted at Lincoln's Inn Fields in 1701. She married a vintner, and they opened a tavern in Westminster. As Mrs. Holt she published *A Fairy Tale inscrib'd, to the Honourable Mrs. W—— With other poems, by Mrs. Holt* (1717). In *To a Lady from the Country in 1709* she writes, "Cheerful and Healthy here I dwell, / In a little homely Cell / . . . / If gaudy Opera's still thrive, / Or if the Tragick Muse revive, / If *Rich* and *Bracegirdle* agree, / Or part, 'tis much the same to me." This kind of lively, knowledgeable verse commentary on the theater links her writing careers. Nothing is known of her burial.

HUNTER, ANNE HOME (1742–1821). The eldest daughter of Robert Boyne Home and Mary Hutchinson, of Greenlaw, Berwickshire, Anne married John Hunter, the famous London surgeon, in 1771. Beginning in 1765, she published poetry throughout her life, and she wrote the lyrics for Franz Joseph Haydn's *Six Original Canzonettas* (1794), which he dedicated to her. In 1802 she published *Poems,* and in 1804 *The Sports of the Genii,* which she had written in 1797 partly to illustrate the drawings of Susan Macdonald. She was a close friend of the Bluestockings, Elizabeth Carter, Mary Delany, Elizabeth Montagu, and Hester Thrale Piozzi, and encouraged the writing career of her niece by marriage, Joanna Baillie. Her husband's death in 1793 left her in financial need, and she found employment as the companion to the wards of her husband's friend Dr. Maxwell Garthshore for seven difficult years. After a series of government grants and Parliament's purchase of the Hunterian Museum in 1799, she moved to Lower Grosvenor Street, near her nephew Dr. Matthew Baillie, where she died after a long illness.

JONES, MARY (1707–1778). Born in Oxford, Jones lived her entire life there, most of the time with her brother, the chanter of Christ Church Cathedral. She said that "her thoughts ever rambled into rhyme," and her *Lass of the Hill* was a popular broadside ballad in 1742. Her *Miscellanies in Prose and Verse* (1750) had about fourteen hundred subscribers; she claimed that its proceeds assisted "a relation, grown old and helpless." Admired for her intellect, poetry, and wit, she was invited to be one of Ralph Griffiths's reviewers, and at the invitation of the family, she wrote the prose inscription for Lord Aubrey Beauclerk's tomb in Westminster Abbey. At the time of her death she was postmistress of Oxford.

KILLIGREW, ANNE (1660–1685). Killigrew was the daughter of Judith and Henry Killigrew, chaplain to the Duke of York and a prebendary of Westminster, and her uncles, Thomas and William Killigrew, were major figures in the Restoration theater. She was carefully educated, and her painting and poetry writing were encouraged. Few of her paintings survive, although they were praised by those who saw them; Horace Walpole, for instance, said she worked "in the manner of Sir Peter Lely," and Dryden and others praised her portraits of King James II and the queen. She was a maid of honor to Mary of Modena at the same time that Anne Finch was. Her father collected and published her *Poems by Mrs. Anne Killigrew* (1686) with the famous poem by Dryden, then poet laureate, *To the Pious Memory of the Accomplist Young Lady, Mrs. Anne Killigrew.* She died of smallpox and was buried in the chancel of St. John the Baptist's Chapel, in the Savoy, with a long Latin epitaph on her monument (destroyed by fire in 1864).

LEAPOR, MARY (1722–1746). The daughter of a gardener, Leapor was educated by her mother, who at least for a while encouraged her poetic talent. After her mother's death, Leapor's father moved from St. Lawrence, Northants, to Brackley, where he managed a nursery, and Mary, who had been a cookmaid, kept house for him. She is said to have built up a library of seventeen books. A subscription collection of her poetry was under way at the time of her death, but both volumes were published posthumously.

LEIGH, HELEN (fl. 1788, d. before 1795). The only information known about this poet comes from her 1788 collection *Miscellaneous Poems*. She lived in Middlewich, a small town southwest of Manchester, and declared herself "the Wife of a Country Curate, and Mother of seven Children." Her husband was most likely George Leigh, curate of Middlewich, Cheshire. The 659 names on the lengthy subscribers' list are mostly of families from Manchester, where the volume was published, and the surrounding towns. One subscriber, Thomas Willis of Swettenham, is also the man to whom the volume is dedicated. Willis was sheriff of Swettenham in 1784 and lived at the county seat, Swettenham Hall, from at least 1787 to 1796. Her collection covers a wide range of poetic types and topics. She writes about the perils of diversion and of spoiled children and the fleeting nature of earthly pleasure. Leigh must have died before 1795, the year her husband remarried.

LENNOX, (BARBARA) CHARLOTTE RAMSAY (1730?–1804). Little is known about Lennox's early life, but the daughter of Captain James Ramsay and Catherine Tisdall was probably born in Gibraltar, reared in New York, and sent to Essex at fifteen, where she became the companion to Lady Isabella Finch and published her first book, *Poems on Several Occasions* (1747). Shortly afterward she married Alexander Lennox, a lieutenant in the Surrey militia. After a failed attempt at acting, Lennox published two novels, *The Life of Harriot Stuart, Written by Herself* (1750) and *The Female Quixote, or, The Adventures of Arabella* (1752), the former drawing the early admiration of Samuel Johnson and the latter becoming a classic, reprinted in German, French, and Spanish. While she continued to write novels and even composed the three-volume *Shakespear Illustrated* (1753–54), the first comprehensive study of Shakespeare's sources, she struggled financially. Her tumultuous marriage ended in 1793, when the couple permanently separated, and Lennox spent the rest of her life alone and destitute. She died on 4 January 1804 in London.

LITTLE, JANET (bap. 1759, d. 1813). Little was born in Nether Bogside, Dumfriesshire, and became a servant at an early age. Her parents had given her "a common education," according to James Paterson in *The Contemporaries of Burns*, and various employers had encouraged her reading and poetic interests. One of them, Frances Dunlop, a friend of Robert Burns's, became her patron. She was put in charge of the dairy at Loudoun Castle. Her *Poetical Works of Janet Little, the Scotch Milkmaid* appeared in 1792 with 650 subscribers, including Robert Burns. In that year she married John Richmond, a laborer on the estate and a widower with five children. Like many Scottish poets, she wrote in both standard English and the Scots dialect. As Donna Landry notes in *Muses of Resistance,* Little expresses "the cultural specificity of English imperialism . . . against an emergent Scottish nationalism." "Doctor Johnson," Little writes in *Given to a Lady Who Asked me to Write a Poem*, "Unto posterity did shew / Their blunders great, their beauties few. / But now he's dead, we weel may ken; / For ilka dunce maun hae a pen, / To write in hamely, uncouth rhymes."

MADAN, JUDITH COWPER (1702–1781). Madan's father was the judge and MP Spencer Cowper, her uncle was a Lord Chancellor, and her nephew was the poet William Cowper. She began publishing in 1720, but only five of her approximately fifty poems appeared before her death. *The Progress of Poetry* and *Verses Written in her Brother's Coke upon Littleton* are her best-known poems. She married Martin Madan, equerry to Frederick, Prince of Wales, in 1723, and they had nine children. She became a Methodist about 1756 and then wrote more religious than secular verse.

MANLEY, DELARIVIÈRE (c. 1670–1742). Known for her "secret histories" and political tracts, Manley also wrote plays and poems; she was an important early professional woman writer. The daughter of Sir Roger Manley, a historian and lieutenant governor of Jersey, she became the ward of her cousin John Manley after the successive deaths of her parents. He led her into a bigamous marriage with him that produced a son in 1694. The couple separated that year. Subsequently Manley lived with Barbara Villiers, Duchess of Cleveland and mistress to Charles II, a six-month experience that provided her an insight into the world of the Whig aristocracy that she used in her scandal fiction. Sixteen ninety-six saw the unauthorized publication of her letters detailing her travel in southwestern England as well as the production of her first plays. She produced a collection of poems by women in memory of John Dryden called *The Nine Muses* (1700), which initiated fifteen years of celebrated work: *The Secret History of Queen Zarah* (1705), a scandal history of John and Anne Churchill; *The New Atalantis* (1709), a two-volume *roman à clef* of the Whig aristocracy; and *The Adventures of Rivella* (1714), an autobiographical narrative.

MANNERS, LADY CATHERINE REBECCA GREY (1766?–1852). *On Leaving Lehena, In October 1788* begins, "Dear fields, where oft in infancy I strayed." From Cork, Ireland, Catherine married William Manners, later Lord Huntingtower of Leicester. *Poems by Lady Manners* appeared in 1793 and required a second edition that year. *Review of Poetry, Ancient and Modern, A Poem, by Lady M****** was published in 1799; the title poem was a progress of poetry from Homer and Pindar through Akenside and Churchill.

MASTERS, MARY (1694?–1755). Daughter of parents who discouraged her writing poetry or even learning beyond "common Household Affairs," Masters grew up in Norwich. She published *Poems on Several Occasions* (1733) by subscription. She wrote often about women's lack of educational and work opportunities, and *Familiar Letters and Poems on Several Occasions* (1755), also published by subscription, recommends Mary Astell's ideas. In the 1750s she sometimes stayed in London with Elizabeth Carter, Edward Cave, or Catharine Macaulay.

MOLESWORTH, ELIZABETH WELWOOD (1690?–1725). The probable author of the poem usually considered Mary Monck's best, *Verses from a Lady at Bath, Dying with a Consumption, to Her Husband,* was born in London, the youngest of three daughters of Barbara Armor and James Welwood. Her mother died about 1700. Her family moved in 1687 to Newcastle-upon-Tyne and in 1689 to London, where her father rapidly rose to influential medical positions in London. Elizabeth married Captain Walter "Watty" Molesworth, fifth son of Viscount Robert Molesworth. According to her friend Henrietta Howard, theirs was a "stolen" love match, but both the Molesworths and James Welwood embraced them. Elizabeth's family was a literary one. Her father was a friend of many literary figures; her brothers-in-law John and Richard Molesworth, as well as her sister-in-law Mary Molesworth Monck, wrote poetry, and her husband's letters comment on writers and express opinions about the poets of the time. Molesworth never fully recovered after the birth of her son; she died of consumption in 1725, and a few of Walter's agonized letters survive. Their marriage, unlike the Moncks', contextualizes *Verses,* and it is possible that searches of the Molesworth archives would yield additional poems by Elizabeth. We are indebted to Elizabeth Furdell's *James Welwood* and her entry in the *Oxford Dictionary of National Biography* and to Suzanne Previte, who made this attribution while a graduate student at Auburn University.

MONCK, MARY MOLESWORTH (1677?–1715). The daughter of Robert, Viscount Molesworth, of Dublin, Monck taught herself Latin, Italian, and Spanish. She married George Monck, who may have had periods of mental illness but was an MP in the Irish Parliament from 1703 to 1713. Her father published sixty-three of her poems in the year after her death as *Marinda. Poems and Translations upon Several Occasions.* She died in Bath after a lengthy illness.

MONTAGU, LADY MARY PIERREPONT WORTLEY (1689–1762). Montagu's mother died when she was four, and her father was Earl of Kingston. Her grandmother educated her until her death, and then Lady Mary "set herself to 'stealing' an education" in her father's library. She eloped with Edward Wortley in 1712 and accompanied him on his unsuccessful embassy to Constantinople. Her *Embassy Letters* (1763) may be her best-known work today. Some of her poetry was published in 1716 without her permission. She published periodical essays anonymously and wrote *The Nonsense of Commonsense*, a political journal, but the first collection of her poetry did not appear until 1768. In spite of a fine edition of her poems and a magisterial biography, the complexity and variety of her poetry are still unrecognized.

MORE, HANNAH (1745–1833). Born north of Bristol in Fishponds, More was the carefully educated daughter of a schoolmaster who was preparing her and her four sisters to run a boarding school for girls. She began teaching in her father's school before she was twenty years old, and the success of the sisters' school gave her a lasting reputation as an educator. She became engaged to William Turner, a wealthy country gentleman, in 1767, but he postponed the wedding three times, and her family insisted that she break it off, which she did in 1773. In recompense, Turner set up an annuity of £200 per year for her, which gave her security and independence. Her first publication was a play for her schoolgirls, *The Search after Happiness* (1773), and *Percy* was the hit of the 1777–78 theatrical season. William Wilberforce cultivated her friendship, and More contributed to his abolitionist cause in a variety of ways. She wrote many didactic works, including 49 of 114 enormously successful *Cheap Repository Tracts*. She started schools for working-class children in the face of hostile resistance to teaching the lower classes to read. She was painted by Richard Samuel as one of *The Nine Living Muses of Great Britain* in 1779, and by the time she died in 1833 she was one of the best-known writers in Great Britain. She is buried next to her sisters in Wrington.

MURRY, ANN (c. 1755–after 1816). Murry's most popular work was *Mentoria: Or, The Young Ladies Instructor* (1776), and there were numerous editions and several sequels; many of the lessons ended with a poem. *Poems on Various Subjects* (1779) was published by subscription. The carefully educated daughter of a London wine merchant, Murry was preceptress in the royal nursery by 1791.

NAIRNE, CAROLINA OLIPHANT (1766–1845). Nairne's mother, Margaret Robinson Oliphant, was the oldest daughter of the chief of Clan Donnachie and a poet who died when Nairne was eight. Her Jacobite parents named her in honor of the exiled Prince Charles Edward Stuart, and Nairne has been described as standing with James Hogg, although "in several she stands first and alone," as a writer of Jacobite songs. Her songs, sometimes enhanced by collaboration with the gifted fiddlers Niel Gow and his son Nathaniel, were sung in public long before their author was known. After a long engagement, she married her cousin Major William Murray Nairne in 1806; they moved to Edinburgh, and his attainted barony was restored in 1824. Popular art song was the dominant literary form in her time, and she studied the innovations and success of contemporaries like Burns joined in the movement to make ballads suitable for drawing-room enjoyment. She published as "Mrs Bogan of Bogan" in a collection of poems entitled *The Scottish Minstrel* (6 vols., 1821–24) and signed other published poems "S.M.," for "Scottish Minstrel." Not until the *Lays from Strathearn* (1846) was she named as author. She was widowed in 1830, lived in Ireland and Europe, but died at her birthplace, the Auld Hoose of Gask, and was buried in the family chapel.

OPIE, AMELIA ALDERSON (1769–1853). Opie was the daughter of a politically radical Norwich physician and became a member of the Godwin-Inchbald circle. She married the Cornish painter John Opie in 1798, and they lived a fashionable life in London. After his death in 1807 she returned to Norwich and became a Quaker. She published novels, poems, tales, and moral texts. Probably her best-known work is *Adeline Mowbray*, a novel that dramatizes some of Godwin's and Wollstonecraft's theories.

PHILIPS, KATHERINE FOWLER (1632–1664). The daughter of Katherine Oxenbridge and John Fowler, a cloth merchant, Philips was educated at home and then at Mrs. Salmon's respected Presbyterian boarding school in Hackney. When she was about fourteen, she moved to Wales with her widowed mother, and at sixteen she married Colonel James Philips, who, like her own family, was a supporter of Parliament and a Puritan. In 1662 she accompanied a newly married friend to Dublin and became a member of the literary circle of James Butler, Duke of Ormond. She was one of the first English women, if not *the* first, to have a play produced on the British stage, her translation of Corneille's *Pompée* (in Dublin in 1663 and London in 1664). At the time of her death from smallpox, she was preparing a second translated play, Corneille's *Horace,* and an edition of her poems to displace *Poems. By the Incomparable Mrs. K.P.,* an unauthorized edition she described as "my imagination rifled." After her death, Charles Cotterell, master of ceremonies to the court, published her poems and also her letters to him, *Letters from Orinda to Poliarchus* (1705). She died at her brother-in-law's house and was buried in London beside her infant son, Hector.

PILKINGTON, LAETITIA VAN LEWEN (c. 1708–1750). Daughter of a Dutch physician emigrant to Dublin, Pilkington married Matthew Pilkington in 1725. Although he was unfaithful, he divorced her, and she lived a financially precarious life in London and spent time in the Marshalsea prison for debt. She is still notorious because of her *Memoirs,* which include many of her poems and anecdotes about Swift.

PIOZZI, HESTER LYNCH SALUSBURY THRALE (1741–1821). The only child of the cousins Hester Maria and John Salusbury, Piozzi was descended from Catrin of Berain, "Mother of Wales." Her parents encouraged her extensive learning. Poverty forced her into marriage with the London brewer Henry Thrale; she was pregnant thirteen times, but only four children lived into adulthood. She became one of the most celebrated hostesses in London, and among the Thrales' friends were Frances Burney, Edmund Burke, and Samuel Johnson. Johnson lived with them for extended periods after 1766 and toured Wales with them. Thrale is best known today for her *Anecdotes of the Late Samuel Johnson* (1786) and her diary, *Thraliana,* which includes more than 150 poems. After her husband died in 1781, Thrale scandalized London by marrying the Italian Catholic musician Gabriel Mario Piozzi in 1784. After traveling in Europe for several years, in 1795 the couple built a villa in her beloved Wales, where Gabriel died in 1809. As a widow she lived primarily in Bath; she died of complications from a fall in Bristol in 1821.

POYNTON, PRISCILLA (c. 1740–1801). Poynton was born in Lichfield about 1740, and what little is known of her life comes primarily from the prefaces to her poems and referential material in them. She lost her sight at age twelve after "a violent head-ach." The preface to her volume *Poems on Several Occasions* (1770) describes how Poynton was "deprived of the advantages of a refin'd education" and "held under the strictest subjection by an aged parent." Having only the "most illiterate amanuensis" and barred from "the most distinguished modern Authors," she was largely an autodidact. Her first published volume, *Poems on Several Occasions* (1770), attracted nearly thirteen hundred subscribers, including Lucy Porter, Samuel Johnson's stepdaughter. In 1788 Poynton married Mr. I. Pickering, who died in 1794. To support herself, Poynton published a second edition of her poems in 1794, *Poems by Mrs. Pickering,* edited by Joseph Weston. Her death was noted in the *Birmingham Gazette* on 15 June 1801.

REEVE, CLARA (1729–1807). Educated by her father, an Ipswich clergyman, Reeve had wide-ranging literary interests and made a major contribution to Gothic fiction. Her first book was *Original Poems on Several Occasions* (1769). In its "Address to the Reader" she noted that "popular taste runs strongly toward music," and she included an essay on musical composition and *Ruth. An Oratorio.* She wrote six romances, her earliest published in 1772, and *The Progress of Romance* (1785) is an important contribution to early literary criticism of the novel. She also wrote a book on the education of women, *Plans of Education* (1792), and was an excellent translator of works that included John Barclay's *Argenis* (1621), a political historical romance in Latin.

ROBINSON, MARY DARBY (1758–1800). Educated by her genteel Bristol mother and in the school run by the sisters of Hannah More, Robinson taught for a while in her mother's school. Her father was a sea captain of Irish descent, probably born in Newfoundland, who lost the family money speculating on cod-, salmon-, and seal-trading posts in Labrador. Her husband, Thomas Robinson, was profligate, and her publishing career began with *Verses* (1775) while she was in debtors' prison with him. She began acting at Drury Lane in 1776, entranced the Prince of Wales, the future George IV, as Perdita in *The Winter's Tale*, and became his mistress; later she was Banastre ("Bloody") Tarleton's companion for ten years. From 1788 to 1791 she was a part of the Della Cruscan movement, and then she was a member of a radical circle that included William Godwin, Mary Wollstonecraft, Mary Hays, and Helen Maria Williams. Her literary output was prodigious, and because she often published poetry in periodicals, recovering all of it is difficult.

Rowe, Elizabeth Singer (1674–1737). A Nonconformist from Ilchester, Rowe first published as Philomela in the *Athenian Mercury*, the groundbreaking periodical by the eccentric John Dunton, who also brought out her first collection of poems in 1696. Her poems also appeared in popular miscellanies. In 1710 she married Thomas Rowe, who died only five years later. She retired to Frome, received a substantial legacy, and was an active philanthropist and correspondent. Her *Friendship in Death, or Letters from the Dead to the Living* (1728) and her poetry remained popular for more than a century.

Sansom, Martha Fowke (1689–1736). The daughter of Major Thomas Fowke and his third wife, Mary Chandler, Sansom was educated by private tutors and then at a boarding school. She moved to London in 1705, after her mother's death and her father's return to active duty in the army. There she lived an unconventional life, one made scandalous by her enemies, especially the novelist and playwright Eliza Haywood. She began publishing poetry with *Delights for the Ingenious* (1711) and became a member of the Hillarian circle, the group clustered around the entrepreneurial and intellectual Aaron Hill. It was a talented and racy crowd that included Richard Savage, David Mallet, and Haywood. According to Christine Gerrard, Fowke drifted through relationships with a number of men, and her *Clio*, written in 1723 but not published until 1752, is an autobiographical love letter to Hill. Pushed into marriage with one of her lovers, Arnold Sansom, a wealthy lawyer and violent drunk, in 1720, she moved with him in 1730 to East Anglia, where he died of alcoholism. She then joined her brother in Leicestershire.

Savage, Mary (fl. 1763–1777). Nothing is known of this engaging poet beyond what is offered in the prefatory letter to her two-volume *Poems on Various Subjects and Occasions* (1777), although some scholars offer speculations about her based on a George Savage who attended King's College, Cambridge. This letter to an unidentified "Miss E.B." may in fact be a parody of dedicatory apologeias for writing, as she calls attention to such stock phrases as "at the desire of several Persons of Quality" and concludes by saying that "the Approbation of the World will be best shown by buying up my first Edition, and calling for a second." Although obviously well read in the poetry of her time and earlier, Savage claims to be uneducated "even to the Grammar of her native Language" and to have the care of a large family. She also describes herself as having "a Disposition rather inclined to gaiety" and "the Spirit of Contradiction," both of which are apparent in her poetry.

SAWYER, ANNA (fl. 1794–1801). The prefatory and poetic material in Sawyer's *Poems on Various Subjects* (1801), "the first production of her unpracticed Muse," provides what information can be gathered about her life. At some point prior to the publication of that work, she lived near Somerset, where she came to know of the poet Hannah More, who built a cottage there in 1784 and, along with Anna Seward, subscribed to her volume. An unspecified misfortune associated with her husband, whom Lonsdale tentatively identifies as William Sawyer, "formerly a resident at Bristol," necessitated their subsequent move to Birmingham. This incident informed her poetry, which was written "partly for the amusement of a private circle, but chiefly to dissipate unavoidable sorrow." Indeed, many of Sawyer's poems are melancholy in mood, but they suggest a steadfast dedication to her husband, despite their situation. Another advocates religious education as a means to escape the hardships of life.

SEWARD, ANNA (1742–1809). Seward lived in the Bishop's Palace in Lichfield from 1754, even after her father, canon of the Lichfield Cathedral, died. She was well educated and a prodigious reader. Her poems published in the 1780s on Captain Cook, Major André, General Eliott, and others made her "Our British Muse," recorder and celebrant of British men and events. Her verse novel *Louisa* (1784) required five editions. She became something of a literary arbiter and monument. In venues such as the *Gentleman's Magazine* she fearlessly pitted her opinions against those of Samuel Johnson and joined arguments over the relative merits of Dryden and Pope.

SEYMOUR, FRANCES THYNNE (1699–1754). From her youth Seymour was exposed to noteworthy poets—her great-aunt was Anne Finch, and her childhood at Longleat enabled her to befriend the poet Elizabeth Singer Rowe, who lived in nearby Frome—and early on she developed an affinity for literature. In July 1715 she married Algernon Seymour, Earl of Hertford, and they had two children. In 1723 she was appointed lady of the bedchamber to Caroline, Princess of Wales, later the queen. Many of her poems appear embedded in letters she wrote to friends and family, including Rowe, Catherine Talbot, and Elizabeth Carter. She published six poems anonymously and pseudonymously during her lifetime; two posthumous collections of her correspondence were published in 1778 and 1805.

SMITH, CHARLOTTE TURNER (1749–1806). Smith's mother died when she was three, and her father, a Sussex, Surrey, and London property owner and poet, educated her at elite boarding schools and encouraged her writing. One of her childhood classmates described her as "continually composing verses." Married at age fifteen to Benjamin Smith, a Cheapside merchant, she went from a life of privilege to living over a shop. She was in debtors' prison when the first edition of *Elegiac Sonnets* appeared in 1784. Better known as a novelist than as a poet, she published ten novels between 1788 and 1798. These novels trace international political movements and wars. One of her translations, *Les causes célèbres et interessantes* (1735–45), includes what we now know as *The Return of Martin Guerre*, which Natalie Zemon Davis has described as a primary document about the status of woman within early bourgeois culture. A lengthy Chancery suit over the inheritance that had made her marriage desirable to her family lasted for more than thirty years, and the funds were not disbursed until after her death. In her last years she moved frequently; she is buried in the churchyard of Stoke Church, Guildford, Surrey.

STOCKDALE, MARY R. (b. 1769). Daughter of the publisher and bookseller John Stockdale and Mary Ridgway, Stockdale spent a sickly childhood in London that prevented her from attending school. However, she was well educated at home and began writing poetry at an early age; her first poem was on the death of a servant whom she attended in poor health. This focus on the poor, disenfranchised, or needy continued throughout her work. Stockdale's father obtained her permission to publish her poems, and in 1798 he produced *The Effusions of the Heart*, dedicated to Queen Charlotte. The collection includes a variety of poetic genres, including songs, pastoral poems, elegies, hymns, sonnets, and a gothic poem, *Henry and Mary*. In her prefatory address, "To the Reader," Stockdale refers to herself as "the Child of Solitude" and notes that her work is meant for sufferers and for those who "weep over one who, shrouded for ever in the cold, the silent tomb, has now paid the debt, the awful, the certain debt of mortality." Stockdale published only poems and translations in her lifetime, although she may have planned a prose work consisting of moral guidance for young people. Her 1810 two-volume collection of poems, *The Mirror of the Mind*, which includes an autobiographical note, addresses social issues such as slavery and poverty; poverty is also addressed in two poems published separately, *The*

Widow and Her Orphan Family (1812) and *The Mother and Child* (1818). Stockdale operated a bookshop on Piccadilly from 1816 to 1833.

TALBOT, CATHERINE (1721–1770). A member of a family of Church of England clerics, Talbot and her widowed mother lived with Thomas and Catherine Secker, who educated her; Thomas became dean of St. Paul's and the archbishop of Canterbury. She circulated manuscripts from the time she was very young but published little. Upon her death, her mother gave her manuscripts to Elizabeth Carter, who published Talbot's *Reflections on the Seven Days of the Week* (1770), *Essays on Various Subjects* (1771), and in 1772 a volume of essays, dialogues, pastorals, allegories, imitations of Ossian, and poems. Carter's nephew Montagu Pennington edited Talbot's *Works* (1809). *A Series of Letters between Mrs. Elizabeth Carter and Miss Catherine Talbot* (1809) displays Talbot's mind and her importance to Elizabeth Carter's career, and manuscript poems and the poetry and commentary Eliza Berkeley released to the *Gentleman's Magazine* gloss the attachment sacrificed by Talbot and George Berkeley.

TEFT, ELIZABETH (b. c. 1723). Teft, an Anglican from the middling ranks, wrote interesting, topical poetry; her first published poem signed as "Orinthia" appeared in the *Gentleman's Magazine* in September 1741. *Orinthia's Request to the Gentleman of Fortune* details that, "fortuneless," she is beset with "present cares" and "gloomy thoughts" but solicits a share in the year's lottery to help alleviate her money problems. She published again as "Orinthia" in June and July 1742, detailing the responses to her initial poem. She published her first volume, *Orinthia's Miscellanies, or, A Compleat Collection of Poems* (1747), apparently funded by herself or a political benefactor. The poems reveal her knowledge of contemporary authors, discuss military actions such as the Jacobite Rebellion and the War of Austrian Succession, and explore the status of women in society, especially in terms of their inequality with men in marriage and in education. She also frankly discussed her own physical appearance, asking, "Was Nature angry when she form'd my Clay?" Nothing is known of her later life.

THICKNESSE, ANN FORD (1737–1824). Thicknesse was born in London and broadly educated. A talented singer, she also played the English guitar, musical glasses, and the viola da gamba. In her early twenties, determined to be independent, she left home and attempted to support herself by performing publicly. Outraged, her father had her arrested and brought home, but Thicknesse left again and continued her public performances. Her publication *A Letter from Miss F——d, Addressed to a Person of Distinction* (1761) defended her right to perform in public and sold five hundred copies in five days. In September 1762 she married Philip Thicknesse, and the couple had two children. They traveled frequently, both writing books about the people and places they encountered. Philip died while they were traveling through France, and Thicknesse was placed in a convent until she proved that she could provide for herself. She moved back to England, where she died.

Thomas, Ann (fl. 1782–1795). Almost nothing is known about Ann Thomas except what we learn from the title page of her subscription volume of poetry, *Poems on Various Subjects, by Mrs. Ann Thomas, of Millbrook, Cornwall, an officer's widow of the Royal Navy* (1784), which was published in Plymouth, Cornwall. In 1795 she published a novel by subscription; she was still living in Millbrook, near Plymouth, at that time.

Thomas, Elizabeth (1675–1731). Thomas's father, a member of the Inner Temple, died when she was two, and she educated herself. She showed a few poems to John Dryden, who complimented them as "too good to be a Woman's." She was engaged to Richard Gwinnet for seventeen years, but he died in 1717, before they married. During this time she was reputed to be the mistress of Henry Cromwell, a dandy, social butterfly, and occasional contributor to poetic miscellanies. Gwinnet left her £600, of which she received only about £213, and by 1727 she was in Fleet Prison for debt, remaining there until 1729. In that year she sold letters from Cromwell, Dryden, Chudleigh, Pope, and John Norris to Edmund Curll. Her *Miscellany Poems* (1722) was reissued as *Poems on Several Occasions* in 1726 and 1727. In Pope's *Dunciad* she is "Curll's Corinna." At the time of her death she was writing an autobiography to accompany an edition of her correspondence with Gwinnet; it is included in the posthumously published *Honourable Lovers* (2 vols., 1731–32). Ironically, after her release from prison she rented lodgings on Fleet Street, where she died in February 1731.

Tollet, Elizabeth (1694–1754). Tollet grew up in the Tower of London, where her father resided as commissioner of the Royal Navy. With the encouragement of Isaac Newton, her father educated her carefully in subjects such as mathematics and history, and she was fluent in French, Italian, and Latin. Tollet was described as a "little, crooked woman." *Poems on Several Occasions* was published in 1724, and a larger collection appeared the year after she died. *Hypatia*, which begins, "What cruel laws depress the female kind," deserves to be studied with the best of the feminist protest poems. Tower lore appears in some of her poems, including *Anne Boleyn to King Henry VIII* and *Written by Lady Jane Grey, when Prisoner in the Tower*. Some of her poems, including many paraphrases of the Psalms, were admired by her contemporaries, and her poems praising such public figures as Newton, Handel, Lady Mary Wortley Montagu, and Anne Finch display her wide interests and acute judgment.

TUITE, ELIZA DOROTHEA COBBE (1764–1850). Irish by birth, Tuite published *Poems by Lady Tuite* (1796), which enjoyed a second edition in 1799. Some of its sixteen songs were popular; among them was the timely *Come drink with me a social glass,* which includes the line, "When we have sunk the Frenchman's pride." *Miscellaneous Poetry,* actually an augmented edition of *Poems,* appeared in 1841. Like so many of the poets of her generation, she also wrote a children's book, *Edwina and Mary* (1838). She may have been living in Bath at the time of her death.

WALSH, OCTAVIA (bap. 1677, d. 1706). Daughter of Joseph and Elizabeth Walsh, of Abberley, Worcestershire, Octavia never married and died of smallpox at age twenty-nine. Her brother William, who was about fifteen years her senior, was a publishing poet and a friend of John Dryden by the time she began writing poetry. Her poetry, described as "The Private Entertainment of Mrs. Octavia Walsh In her Vacant Hours," was discovered by her family after her death. Some of it was submitted for publication and admired, as seven religious poems were printed in *Poems upon Divine and Moral Subjects* (1719) and reprinted later in the century. She was buried in Worcester Cathedral, where an impressive monument in the north aisle of the nave survives (Valentine Green, *The History and Antiquities of the City . . . of Worcester* [1796], 148).

WEST, JANE ILIFFE (1758–1852). Born in London, West moved with her parents to Northamptonshire when she was eleven. She began writing poetry at age thirteen and published poems throughout her life. She married Thomas West, a yeoman farmer, and spent the rest of her life in Little Bowden, Leicestershire, his home. Thomas was related to clergymen, and there was a useful library. West was a prolific writer known for her didacticism, which extended into anti-Jacobin and other public-sphere themes. She was quoted as saying, "My needle always claims the preeminence of my pen," and sometimes published as "Prudentia Homespun," who, for all her conservatism, was a delightfully gossipy character. Poems such as her *Elegy on the Death of the Right Honourable Edmund Burke* (1797) demonstrate her active engagement with the larger world. She went blind in her old age and described herself as unjustly forgotten.

WHARTON, ANNE LEE (1659–1685). Wharton's father died of plague four months before she was born, and her mother, Anne Danvers, daughter of Sir John Danvers, died a few days after her birth. She and her sister were raised by their paternal grandmother, Anne, Countess of Rochester, mother of the poet Rochester, to whom Wharton was close. She was well versed in the ways of court, but no records indicate that she received any formal education. In 1673 she married the reputed rake Thomas Wharton, and the marriage was apparently unhappy. Her 1680 poem on the death of her uncle, *An Elegy on the Earl of Rochester,* was noticed by the literary community; after that, many of her poems circulated in manuscript, although they were never collected in her lifetime. She exchanged verses with Aphra Behn and received praise from Edmund Waller and John Dryden. Despite her small literary output (just twenty-four poems and one play), Wharton became one of the most eminent poets of the Restoration period. After a lifetime of frequent illness, she died in October 1685.

WILLIAMS, ANNA (1706–1783). The daughter of the medical practitioner and experimenter Zachariah Williams, Anna Williams received a comprehensive education in the arts, sciences, and foreign languages. Although cataracts caused her eyesight to deteriorate in the 1740s, Williams worked with her father in the laboratory and supported their livelihood by sewing. In 1746 she published her first work, *The Life of the Emperor Julian,* a translation from the French. In 1748 she and her father were evicted from the Charterhouse; Samuel Johnson then invited them to live with him. The cataract surgery Johnson arranged for Williams blinded her, and subsequently she was a lifelong member of his household. In 1766, sixteen years after the initial subscription proposal, Williams published *Miscellanies in Prose and Verse,* which included contributions from Johnson and Hester Thrale Piozzi. Upon Williams's death in September 1783, Johnson wrote, "Her curiosity was universal, her knowledge was very extensive, and she sustained forty years of misery with steady fortitude. Thirty years and more she has been my companion, and her death has left me very desolate."

WILLIAMS, HELEN MARIA (1761–1827). Williams, a Nonconformist, was born in London to a Welsh army officer and a Scottish mother. Her father died in 1762, and the family moved to Berwick-upon-Tweed, where her mother carefully educated her and her sister. In 1781 she moved to London, where she quickly became a star in the literary sky and was hailed as a poetic genius. At age twenty-one she published *Edwin and Eltruda* (1782), a metrical tale about the Wars of the Roses, and then made all the papers with *An Ode on the Peace* (1783), a post–American War reflection on the benefits of peace, and with *Peru* (1784), a condemnation of Pizarro's conquest of the Indians. The 1786 collection of her poems listed more than one thousand five hundred subscribers, and William Wordsworth's first published poem is a tribute to her. *Julia: A Novel, Interspersed with some Poetical Pieces* (1790) is an important Wertheriad. She visited France in 1790 and settled there in 1792. She is best known today for her *Letters Written in France,* eight eye-witness books that gave her the reputation with modern literary historians as "a foreign correspondent, interpreting French history to readers in England." She became a naturalized citizen of France in 1817 and is buried in Paris.

WINSCOM, JANE CAVE (1754/55–c. 1813). Winscom was most likely born in Wales, where her father, like her husband, Thomas Winscom, whom she married in 1783, was an exciseman. In 1783 at Winchester she printed under her birth name *Poems on Various Subjects, Entertaining, Elegiac, and Religious.* To her two thousand subscribers she modestly confides that they should "Seward, Steele, or Moore, hope not to see" in her collection. She was, however, an affecting, powerful poet who often used the carefully observed details of her life with her husband and two sons in her poetry. During the last two decades of her life she suffered intense, incapacitating headaches, which she made the subject of her poem *The Head-ach, or, An Ode to Health;* it appeared in a May 1793 Bristol newspaper as well as in her final collection (1794). The poem addresses failed headache remedies, including sea-bathing, to which her obituary in the January 1813 *Gentleman's Magazine* alludes, noting that two years before her death she experienced a "miraculous escape from a watery grave." The obituary also celebrates her poetry and her "extraordinary genius and vigour of intellect."

WRIGHT, MEHETABEL WESLEY (1697–1750). One of five children born to Samuel and Susanna Wesley, Wright received the same extensive classical and biblical education as did her brothers John and Charles, founders of the Methodist movement. Her intellect, vivacity, and engaging nature conflicted with the moralistic inclinations of her parents. In 1725 Wright eloped with a man disfavored by her family and returned pregnant, whereupon her parents forced her to marry William Wright, a plumber and glazier, who was "utterly unsuited to her in mind, education, manners." Wright blamed her husband's profession and the leadworks in their home for the infant deaths of all of her children, a loss she records in many of her poems. She published poems in the *Gentleman's Magazine,* but her work was never collected into a single volume in her lifetime. Her brothers' fame and the inclusion of her poetry in their published correspondence helped preserve her work. Her poetry contains powerfully affecting representations of overwhelming loss, dissatisfaction with both her own marriage and the institution, and, at times, a sense of despair and desperation.

YEARSLEY, ANN CROMARTIE (1752–1806). Yearsley was the daughter of working-class parents in Clifton and followed her mother's trade as a milkwoman. Her mother taught her to read and write. She married a yeoman at age twenty-two and had seven children. Hannah More offered the nearly destitute family charity in 1784, and when she saw Yearsley's poems, she edited them and arranged their subscription publication. *Poems on Several Occasions* (1785) and its subsequent editions earned six hundred pounds, and acrimonious disputes over money and the editing of the poems resulted. In addition to poetry, Yearsley wrote a novel and a play, but her reputation is based on her poetry, perhaps especially *Poems on Various Subjects* (1787) and *The Rural Lyre* (1796). Anna Seward called her "a proud and jealous spirit," and Yearsley once wrote a poem attacking a powerful man for punishing her children for playing on his property. In 1793 she opened a circulating library at Bristol Hotwells, and in 1803 she retired to Melksham, Wiltshire, where she died.

ALTERNATE TABLE OF CONTENTS
The Poets and Their Poems